W9-AJO-869

The MEDICAL and HEALTH ENCYCLOPEDIA

The MEDICAL and HEALTH ENCYCLOPEDIA

Volume Two

EDITED BY
RICHARD J. WAGMAN, M.D., F.A.C.P.
Associate Clinical Professor of Medicine
Downstate Medical Center
New York, New York

THE SOUTHWESTERN COMPANY • NASHVILLE, TENNESSEE

Portions of *The Medical and Health Encyclopedia* have been previously published under the titles of *The Complete Illustrated Book of Better Health, The Illustrated Encyclopedia of Better Health,* and *The New Complete Medical and Health Encyclopedia,* all edited by Richard J. Wagman, M.D.

International Standard Book Number 0-89434-081-6
Library of Congress Catalog Card Number 77-81669
Printed in the United States of America
K-4

Contents

The MEDICAL and HEALTH ENCYCLOPEDIA

21

Skin and Hair

Not many people have perfectly proportioned faces and bodies, but practically anyone, at any age, can present an attractive appearance if skin is healthy-looking and glowing and hair is clean and shining. Healthy skin and hair can be achieved through good health habits, cleanliness, and personal grooming. Expensive skin-and-hair products may boost self-confidence, but they are a poor substitute for proper diet, exercise, enough sleep, and soap and water or cleansing creams.

The condition of skin and hair reflects a person's physical and emotional health. Of course, general appearance is determined not only by what is going on inside the body but also by outward circumstances, such as extremes of temperature or the use of harsh soaps. Appearance can also be altered temporarily by cosmetics and permanently by surgery.

The Skin

The skin is one of the most important organs of the body. It serves as protection against infection by germs and shields delicate underlying tissue against injury. Approximately one-third of the bloodstream flows through the skin, and as the blood vessels contract or relax in response to heat and cold, the skin acts as a thermostat that helps control body temperature. The two million sweat glands in the skin also regulate body temperature through the evaporation of perspiration. The many delicate nerve endings in the skin make it a sense organ responsive not only to heat and cold but also to pleasure, pain, and pressure.

Certain cells in the skin produce a protective pigmentation that determines its color and guards against overexposure to the ultraviolet rays of the sun. By absorption and elimination, the skin helps regulate the body's chemical and fluid balance. One of the miracles of the skin is that it constantly renews itself.

Structure of the Skin

The skin is made up of two layers. The outer later, or *epidermis,* has a surface of horny, nonliving cells that form the body's protective envelope. These cells are constantly being shed and replaced by new ones, which are made in the lower or inner layer of the epidermis.

Underneath the epidermis is the *dermis,* the thicker part of the skin. It contains blood vessels, nerves, and connective tissue. The sweat glands are located in the dermis, and they collect fluid containing water, salt, and waste products from the blood. This fluid is sent through tiny canals that end in pores on the skin's surface.

The oil, or *sebaceous,* glands that secrete the oil that lubricates the surface of the skin and hair are also located in the dermis. They are most often associated with hair *follicles.* Hair follicles and oil glands are found over most of the body, with the exception of the palms of the hands and the soles of the feet.

The layer of fatty tissue below the dermis, called *subcutaneous* tissue, acts as an insulator against heat and cold and as a shock absorber against injury.

Skin Color

The basic skin color of each person is determined at birth, and is a part of his heritage that cannot be changed.

Anatomy of the Skin

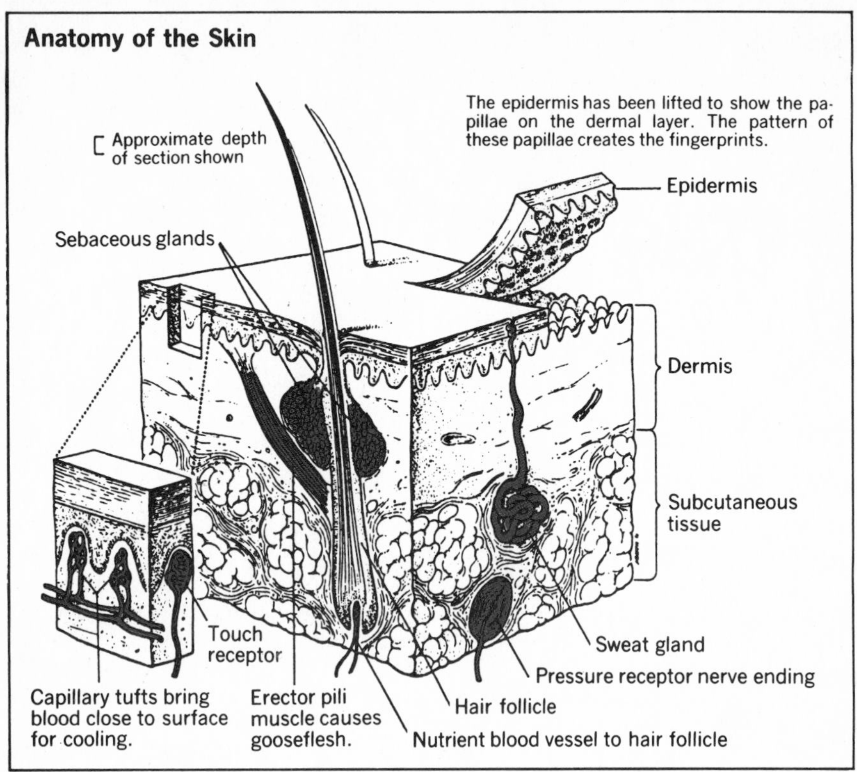

Melanin

There are four pigments in the normal skin that affect its color: melanin, oxygenated hemoglobin, reduced hemoglobin, and various carotenes. Of these, *melanin* is the most powerful. The cells that produce it are the same in all races, but there is wide variation in the amount produced, and wide variation in its color, which ranges from black to light tan. Every adult has about 60,000 melanin-producing cells in each square inch of skin.

Melanin cells also affect eye color. When the cells are deep in the eye, the color produced is blue or green. When they are close to the surface, the eye is brown. An *albino,* a person with no melanin, has eyes that appear pink, because the stronger pigment that ordinarily masks the blood vessels is lacking.

Hemoglobin

The pigment that gives blood its color, called *hemoglobin,* has the next greatest effect on skin color. When it is combined with oxygen, a bright red is the result, and this in turn produces the rosy complexion associated with good health in light-skinned people. When such people suffer from reduced hemoglobin because of anemia, they appear to be excessively pale. A concentration of reduced hemoglobin gives the skin a bluish appearance. Because hemoglobin has a weaker coloring effect than the melanin that determines basic skin color, these variations are more visible in lighter-skinned individuals.

Carotenes

The weakest pigments in the skin are the *carotenes.* These produce a yellowish tone that is increased by eating excessive amounts of carrots and oranges. In people with black or brown skin, excess carotene is usually masked by the melanin pigment.

Aging Skin

Skin appearance is affected by both internal and external factors. A baby's skin has a silken quality because it has not yet begun to show the effects of continued exposure to sun and wind. The skin problems associated with adolescence reflect the many glandular changes that occur during the transition to adulthood. As the years pass, the skin becomes the most obvious indicator of aging.

Heredity, general health, and exposure to the elements are some of the factors that contribute to aging skin. Because people with darker skin have built-in protection against the ravages of the sun, their skin usually has a younger appearance than that of lighter-skinned people of comparable age.

In general, the skin of an older person is characterized by wrinkles and shininess. It feels thinner when pinched because it has lost its elasticity and part of the underlying fat that gives firmness to a younger skin.

Constant exposure to sunlight is now thought to play a more important role in the visible aging of skin than the aging process itself. Such exposure also appears to be directly related to the greater frequency of skin cancer among farmers, sailors, and others who spend most of their working hours out of doors.

Care of the Skin

Healthy, normal skin should be washed regularly with mild soap and warm water to remove grease, perspiration, and accumulated dirt. For those with a limited water supply or inadequate bath and shower facilities, sponge baths are a good substitute if the sponge or washcloth is thoroughly rinsed as various parts of the body are washed. Many people feel that a shower is a much more efficient way of getting clean than a bath, since the bath water becomes the receptacle for the dirt washed from the body, instead of its being rinsed away.

No matter what method is used, all soap should be thoroughly rinsed off the skin after washing. Unless specifically prescribed by a physician, medicated or germicidal soaps should not be used, since they may be an irritant. Skin should be dried with a fluffy towel, and bath towels should never be shared. Hands should be washed several times a day, and fingernails kept clean.

Facial skin requires special care because of its constant exposure. The face should be cleaned in the morning and before bedtime. Some women may prefer to use a cleansing cream rather than soap and water. Everyone should avoid massaging soap into the skin, because this may cause drying.

Dry and Oily Skin

Both heredity and environment account for the wide variation in the amount of oil and perspiration secreted by the glands of different people. Also, the same person's skin may be oily in one part of the body and dry in another.

Dry Skin

This condition is the result of loss of water from the outer surface of the epidermis and its insufficient replacement from the tissues below. Some causes of the moisture loss are too frequent use of soap and detergents, and constant exposure to dry air. Anyone spending a great deal of time in air-conditioned surroundings in which the humidity has been greatly lowered is likely to suffer from dry skin.

To correct the condition, the use of soap and water should be kept to a minimum for those parts of the body where the skin is dry. Cleansing creams or lotions containing lanolin should be used on the face, hands, elbows, and wherever else necessary. If tub baths are taken, a bath oil can be used in the water or applied to the skin after drying. Baby oil is just as effective and much cheaper than glamorously packaged and overadvertised products. Baby oil or a protective lotion should also be used on any parts of the body exposed to direct sunlight for any extended length of time. Applying oil to the skin will not, however, prevent wrinkles.

Oily Skin

The amount of oil that comes to the surface of the skin through the sebaceous glands is the result not only of heredity but also of temperature and emotional state. In warm weather, when the skin perspires more freely, the oil spreads like a film on the surface moisture. Nonoily foundation lotions can be helpful in keeping the oil spread to a minimum, and so can frequent washing with soap and water. When washing is inconvenient during the day, cleansing pads packaged to fit in pocket or purse are a quick and efficient solution for both men and women.

Too much friction from complexion brushes, rough washcloths, or harsh soaps may irritate rather than improve an oily skin condition.

Deodorants and Antiperspirants

Sweat glands are present almost everywhere in the skin except for the lips and a few other areas. Most of them give off the extremely dilute salt water known as sweat, or perspiration. Their purpose is to cool the body by evaporation of water. Body odors are not produced by perspiration itself but by the bacterial activity that takes place in the perspiration. The activity is most intense in warm, moist parts of the body from which perspiration cannot evaporate quickly, such as the underarm area.

Deodorants

The basic means of keeping this type of bacterial growth under control is through personal cleanliness of both skin and clothing. Deodorant soaps containing antiseptic chemicals are now available. Though they do not kill bacteria, they do reduce the speed with which they multiply.

Underarm deodorants also help to eliminate the odor. They are not meant to stop the flow of perspiration but rather to slow down bacterial growth and mask body odors with their own scent. Such deodorants should be applied immediately after bathing. They are usually more effective if the underarm area is shaved, since the hair in this unexposed area collects perspiration and encourages bacterial growth.

Antiperspirants

Antiperspirants differ from deodorants in that they not only affect the rate of bacterial growth but also reduce the amount of perspiration that reaches the skin surface. Because the action of the chemical salts they contain is cumulative, they seem to be more effective with repeated use. Antiperspirants come under the category of drugs, and their contents must be printed on the container. Deodorants are considered cosmetics, and may or may not name their contents on the package.

No matter what the nature of the advertising claim, neither type of product completely stops the flow of perspiration, nor would it be desirable to do so. Effectiveness of the various brands differs from one person to another. Some may produce a mild allergic reaction; others might be too weak to do a good job. It is practical to experiment with a few different brands, using them under similar conditions, to find the type that works best for you.

Creams and Cosmetics

The bewildering number of creams and cosmetics on the market and the exaggerated claims of some of their advertising can be reduced to a few simple facts. In most cases, the higher price of such products is an indication of the amount of money spent on advertising and packaging rather than on the ingredients themselves. Beauty preparations should be judged by the user on their merits rather than on their claims.

Cold Creams and Cleansing Creams

These two products are essentially the same. They are designed to remove accumulated skin secretions, dirt, and grime, and should be promptly removed from the skin with a soft towel or tissue.

Lubricating Creams and Lotions

Also called night creams, moisturizing creams, and conditioning creams, these products are supposed to prevent the loss of moisture from the skin and promote its smoothness. They are usually left on overnight or for an extended length of time. Anyone with dry skin will find it helpful to apply a moisturizer under foundation cream. This will help keep the skin from drying out even further, and protect it against the effects of air-conditioning.

Vanishing Creams and Foundation Creams

These products also serve the purpose of providing the skin with moisture, but are meant to be applied immediately before putting on makeup.

Rejuvenating Creams

There is no scientific proof that any of the "royal jelly," "secret formula," or "hormone" creams produce a marked improvement on aging skin. They cannot eliminate wrinkles, nor can they regenerate skin tissue.

Medicated Creams and Lotions

These products should not be used except on the advice of a physician, since they may cause or aggravate skin disorders of various kinds.

Lipsticks

Lipsticks contain lanolin, a mixture of oil and wax, a coloring dye, and pigment, as well as perfume. Any of these substances can cause an allergic reaction in individual cases, but such reactions are uncommon. Sometimes the reaction is caused by the staining dye, in which case a "nonpermanent" lipstick should be used.

Cosmetics and the Sensitive Skin

Anyone with a cosmetic problem resulting from sensitive skin should consult a *dermatologist,* a physician specializing in the skin and its diseases. Cosmetic companies will inform a physician of the ingredients in their products, and he or she can then recommend a brand that will agree with the patient's specific skin problems. The physician may also recommend a special nonallergenic preparation.

Eye Makeup

Eye-liner and mascara brushes and pencils—and lipsticks, for that matter—can carry infection and should never be borrowed or lent. *Hypoallergenic* makeup, which is specially made for those who get allergic reactions to regular eye makeup, is available and should be used by anyone so affected.

Suntanning Creams and Lotions

Growing awareness that exposure to the sun may cause skin cancer (see "Skin Cancer" in Ch. 18, *Cancer*) has led to a demand for a variety of skin creams and lotions. The preparations protect the skin or speed the tanning process. Many of the "sunblocks" and "sunscreens" keep the ultraviolet radiation in sunlight from reaching the skin. They are adapted to six basic skin types, ranging from type 1, which burns easily and never tans, to types 5 and 6, which never burn and usually tan well.

Skin lotions and creams are rated according to a "sun protection factor" (SPF). Basic rating levels for lotions and creams include SPF 2, giving minimal protection; SPF 4, providing "moderate" protection; SPF 6, for "extra" protection; SPF 8, a "maximal" sunscreen; and SPF 15, with "ultra" protection. Other ratings range up to SPF 23. The latter are called "complete sunblocks." Food and Drug Administration ratings go only to SPF 15, but the stronger applications are generally available. Among the most effective creams is zinc oxide, purchasable in a number of bright colors.

Sunscreen ratings indicate, in theory, how long the user can stay in the sun without burning. A lotion or cream with a rating of SPF 2 should allow users to remain exposed twice as long as they could with no protection at all. But the Skin Cancer Foundation and many dermatologists believe that persons who burn in the sun should uniformly wear an SPF 15 protective preparation.

Persons who want suntans have many products from which to choose. "Tanning accelerators" in lotion form speed up the tanning process. A pocket-sized "sun exposure meter" operated electronically alerts the user when overexposure may be taking place. The meter is programmed with the individual's skin type and SPF. Tanning pills containing such chemicals as beta-carotene help to brown the skin more rapidly. But some of the latter turn the skin an orange color rather than brown or tan.

Hair

Hair originates in tiny sacs or follicles deep in the dermis layer of skin tissue. The part of the hair below the skin surface is the root; the part above is the shaft. Hair follicles are closely connected to the sebaceous glands, which secrete oil to the scalp and give hair its natural sheen.

Hair grows from the root outward, pushing the shaft farther from the scalp. Depending on its color, there may be as many as 125,000 hairs on an adult's head. The palms of the hands, the soles of the feet, and the lips are the only completely hairless parts of the surface of the body.

Texture

Each individual hair is made up of nonliving cells that contain a tough protein called *keratin.* Hair texture differs from one part of the body to another. In some areas, it may be soft and downy; in others, tough and bristly. Hair texture also differs between the sexes, among individuals, and among the different races.

If an individual hair is oval in cross-section, it is curly along its length. If the cross-section is round, the hair is straight. Thick, wiry hair is usually triangular or kidney-shaped. The fineness or coarseness of hair texture is related to its natural color.

Curling

Anyone using a home permanent preparation should read and follow instructions with great care. If a new brand is tried, the instructions should be read all over again, since they may be quite different from the accustomed ones.

Electric curling irons are not safe, because they may cause pinpoint burns in the scalp that are hardly noticeable at the time but may lead to permanent small areas of baldness. The danger can be minimized, however, if instructions for use are followed exactly and the recommended moisturizing lotions are used. It is especially important that the iron not be hot enough to singe the hair. The results, even if there is no damage, are not long-lasting and are adversely affected by dampness. Setting lotions used with rollers or clips have a tendency to dull the hair unless they are completely brushed out.

Straightening

The least harmful as well as the least effective way of straightening the hair temporarily is the use of pomades. They are usually considered unsatisfactory by women because they are too greasy, but are often used by men with short, unruly hair. Heat-pressing the hair with a metal comb is longer-lasting but can cause substantial damage by burning the scalp. When this method is used, humidity or scalp perspiration will cause the hair to revert to its natural curl. The practice of ironing the hair should be discouraged, since it causes dryness and brittleness, with resultant breakage. Chemical straighteners should be used with great care, since they may cause serious burns. Special efforts must be made to protect the eyes from contact with these products.

Hair Color

In the same way that melanin colors the skin, it also determines hair color. The less melanin, the lighter the hair. As each hair loses its melanin pigment, it gradually turns gray, then white. It is assumed that the age at which hair begins to gray is an inherited characteristic and therefore can't be postponed or prevented by eating special foods, by taking vitamins, or by the external application of creams. The only way to recolor gray hair is by the use of a chemical dye.

Dyes and Tints

Anyone wishing to make a radical change in hair color should consult a trained and reliable hairdresser. Trying to turn black hair bright red or dark red hair to blond with a home preparation can sometimes end up with unwanted purplish or greenish results. When tints or dyes are used at home to lighten or darken the hair color by one or two shades, instructions accompanying the product must be followed carefully. Anyone with a tendency to contract contact dermatitis should make a patch test on the skin to check on possible allergic reactions. Hair should be tinted or dyed no more often than once a month.

Dye Stripping

The only safe way to get rid of an unwanted dye color that has been used on the hair is to let it grow out. The technique known as stripping takes all color from the hair and reduces it to a dangerously weak mass. It is then redyed its natural color. Such a procedure should never be undertaken by anyone except a trained beautician, if at all.

Bleaching

Hydrogen peroxide is mixed with a hair lightener to prebleach hair before applying blond tints. Bleaching with peroxide alone can cause more damage to the hair than dyeing or tinting it with a reliable commercial preparation, because it causes dryness, brittleness, and breakage.

General Hair Care

Properly cared for hair usually looks clean, shiny, and alive. Unfortunately, too many people mask the natural good looks of their hair with unnecessary sprays and "beauty" preparations.

Washing the Hair

Hair should be washed about once a week—more often if it tends to be oily. The claims made by shampoo manufacturers need not always be taken too seriously, since most shampoos contain nothing more than soap or detergent and a perfuming agent. No shampoo can restore the natural oils to the hair at the same time that it washes it. A castile shampoo is good for dry hair, and one containing tincture of green soap is good for oily hair.

Thorough rinsing is essential to eliminate any soap deposit. If the local water is hard, a detergent shampoo can be rinsed off more easily than one containing soap.

Drying the Hair

Drying the hair in sunlight or under a heat-controlled dryer is more satisfactory than trying to rub it dry with a towel. Gentle brushing during drying reactivates the natural oils that give hair its shine. Brushing in general is excellent for the appearance of the hair. Be sure to wash both brush and comb as often as the hair is washed.

Hair pomades should be avoided or used sparingly, since they are sometimes so heavy that they clog the pores of the scalp. A little bit of olive oil or baby oil can be rubbed into dry hair after shampooing. This is also good for babies' hair.

There is no scientific evidence that creme rinses, protein rinses, or beer rinses accomplish anything for the hair other than making it somewhat more manageable if it is naturally fine and flyaway.

Dandruff

Simple dandruff is a condition in which the scalp begins to itch and flake a few days after the hair has been washed. There is no evidence that the problem is related to germ infection.

Oiliness and persistent dandruff may appear not only on the scalp but also on the sides of the nose or the chest. In such cases, a dermatologist should be consulted. Both light and serious cases often respond well to prescription medicines containing tars. These preparations control the dandruff, but there is no known cure for it.

Nits

Head lice sometimes infect adults as well as children. These tiny parasites usually live on the part of the scalp near the nape of the neck, and when they bite, they cause itching. They attach their eggs, which are called *nits,* to the shaft of the hair, and when they are plentiful, they can be seen by a trained eye as tiny, silvery-white ovals. This condition is highly contagious and can be passed from one head to another by way of combs, brushes, hats, head scarfs, and towels. A physician can be consulted for information on effective ways of eliminating nits—usually by the application of chemicals and the use of a fine-tooth comb.

Baldness

Under the normal circumstances of combing, brushing, and shampooing, a person loses anywhere from 25 to 100 hairs a day. Because new hairs start growing each day, the loss and replacement usually balance each other. When the loss rate is greater than the replacement rate, thinning and baldness are the result.

Alopecia

The medical name for baldness is *alopecia,* the most common form of which is *male pattern baldness.* Dr. Eugene Van Scott, Professor of Dermatology of Temple University's Health Sciences Center, sums up the opinion of medical authorities on the three factors responsible for this type of baldness: sex, age, and heredity. Unfortunately, these are three factors over which medical science has no control.

Other Causes of Baldness

Other forms of baldness may be the result of bacterial or fungal infections, allergic reactions to particular medicines, radiation, or continual friction. It has also been suggested that constant stress from hair curlers or tightly pulled ponytails can cause loss

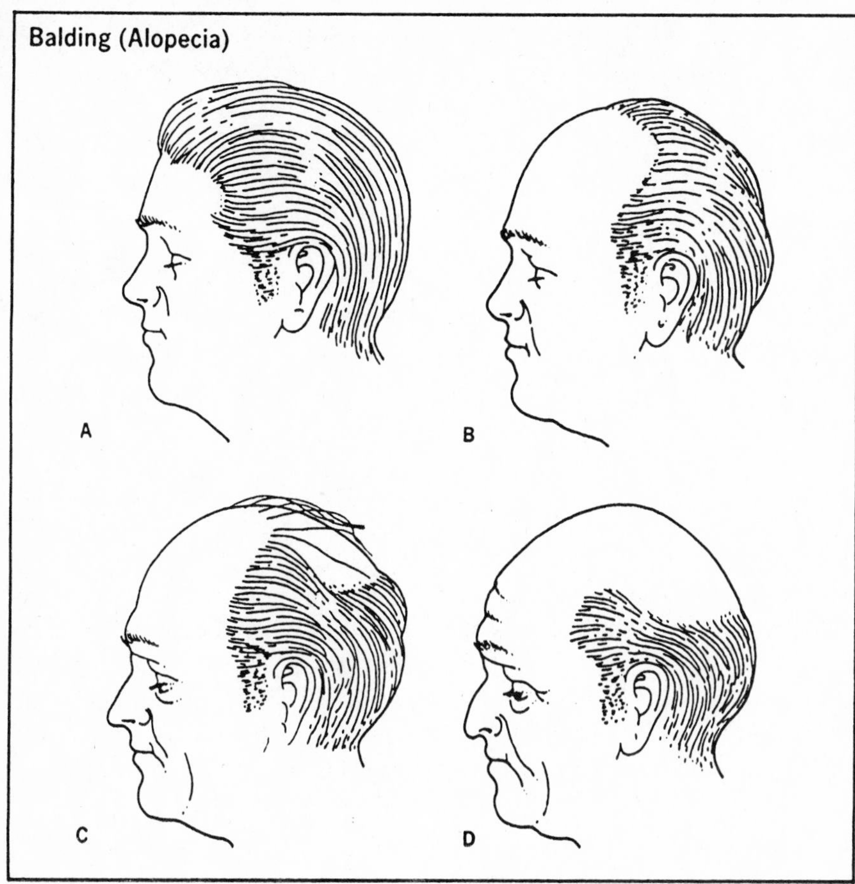

Balding (Alopecia)

of hair. These forms of baldness usually disappear when the cause is eliminated.

Although diet has very little to do with baldness, poor nutrition can result in hair that is dry, dull, and brittle enough to break easily. Any serious illness can lead to hair loss as well. It is thought that vitamin A taken in grossly excessive amounts can contribute to hair loss.

Women ordinarily lose some of their hair at the end of pregnancy, after delivery, and during the menopause, but regrowth can be expected in a few months.

It is now possible for anyone suffering from temporary baldness or from male pattern baldness to choose from a wide variety of attractively styled wigs and hairpieces.

A surgical procedure for treating male pattern baldness and baldness in women is called hair transplantation; it is discussed in Ch. 20, *Surgery*.

Hair Removal

Over the centuries and around the world, fashions in whiskers and beards come and go, but the average American male still subjects at least part of his face to daily shaving. Although feminine shaving practices are a more recent phenomenon, most American women now consider it part of good grooming to remove underarm and leg hair with a razor as often as twice a week. Shaving removes not only the dead skin cells that make up the protective layer of the body's surface but also some of the living skin underneath. Instead of being harmful, this appears to stimulate rather than damage new skin growth.

Male Shaving

The average beard grows about two-tenths of an inch a day. However, the density of male face hair varies a great deal depending on skin and hair color. In all races, the concentration is usually greatest on the chin and in the area between the nose and upper lip.

There is no proof that an electric razor is safer or better for all types of skin than a safety razor. Both types result in nicks and cuts of the living skin tissue, depending on the closeness of the shave.

Twice as many men prefer wet shaving to dry because the use of soap and hot water softens the hair stubble and makes it easier to remove. Shaving authorities point out that thorough soaking is one of the essentials of easy and safe shaving. Leaving the shaving lather on the face for at least two minutes will also soften whiskers a good deal.

The razor should be moistened with hot water throughout the process, and the chin and upper lip left for last so that the heavier hair concentration in these areas has the longest contact with moisture and lather.

Oily Skin

Men with oily skin should use an aerosol shaving preparation or a lather type applied with a brush. These are really soaps and are more effective in eliminating the oils that coat the face hair, thus making it easier to shave.

Dry Skin

A brushless cream is advisable for dry skin, since it lubricates the skin rather than further deprives it of oil.

Ingrown Hairs

One of the chief problems connected with shaving is that it often causes ingrown hairs, which can lead to pore-clogging and infection. Hair is more likely to turn back into the skin if it is shaved against the grain, or if the cutting edge of the blade is dull and rough rather than smooth. Men with coarse, wiry, curly, rather than fine, hair may find that whisker ends are more likely to become ingrown than men with fine hair. The problem is best handled by shaving with the grain, using a sharp blade, and avoiding too close a shave, particularly in the area around the neck.

Shaving and Skin Problems

For men with acne or a tendency to skin problems, the following advice is offered by Dr. Howard T. Behrman, Director of Dermatological Research, New York Medical College:

- Shave as seldom as possible, perhaps only once or twice a week, and always with the grain.
- If wet shaving is preferred, use a new blade each time, and shave as lightly as possible to avoid nicking pimples.
- Wash face carefully with plenty of hot water to make the beard easy to manage, and after shaving, rinse with hot water followed by cold.
- Use an antiseptic astringent face lotion.
- Instead of plucking out ingrown hairs, loosen them gently so that the ends do not grow back into the skin.
- Although some people with skin problems find an electric shaver less irritating, in most cases, a wet shave seems best.

Female Shaving

Millions of American women regularly shave underarm and leg hair, and most of them do so with a blade razor. In recent years, various types of shavers have been designed with blade exposure more suited to women's needs than the standard type used by men. To make shaving easier and safer, the following procedures are recommended.

- Since wet hair is much easier to cut, the most effective time to shave is during or immediately following a bath or shower.
- Shaving cream or soap lather keeps the water from evaporating, and is preferred to dry shaving.
- Underarm shaving is easier with a contoured razor designed for this purpose. If a deodorant or antiperspirant causes stinging or irritation after shaving, allow a short time to elapse before applying it.
- Light bleeding from nicks or scrapes can be stopped by applying pressure to a sterile pad placed on the injured area.

Unwanted Hair

The technical word for excess or unwanted hair on the face, chest, arms, and legs is *hirsutism.* The condition varies greatly among different ethnic strains, and so does the attitude toward it. Women of southern European ancestry are generally hairier than those with Nordic or Anglo-Saxon ancestors. Caucasoid peoples are hairier than Negroid peoples. The sparsest amount of body hair is found among the Mongolian races and American Indians. Although heredity is the chief factor of hirsutism, hormones also influence hair growth. If there is a sudden appearance of coarse hair on the body of a young boy or girl or a woman with no such former tendency, a glandular disturbance should be suspected and investigated by a physician.

A normal amount of unwanted hair on the legs and under the arms is usually removed by shaving. When the problem involves the arms, face, chest, and abdomen, other methods of removal are available.

Temporary Methods of Hair Removal

Bleaching

Unwanted dark fuzz on the upper lip and arms can be lightened almost to invisibility with a commercially prepared bleach or with a homemade paste consisting of baking soda, hydrogen peroxide (bleaching strength), and a few drops of ammonia. Soap chips can be used instead of baking soda. The paste should be left on the skin for a few minutes and then washed off. It is harmless to the skin, and if applied repeatedly, the hair will tend to break off as a result of constant bleaching.

Chemical Depilatories

These products contain alkaline agents that cause the hair to detach easily at the skin surface. They can be used on and under the arms, and on the legs and chest. However, they should not be used on the face unless the label says it is safe to do so. Timing instructions should be followed carefully. If skin irritation results, this type of depilatory should be discontinued in favor of some other method.

Abrasives

Devices that remove hair from the skin surface by rubbing are cheap but time-consuming. However, if an abrasive such as pumice is used regularly, the offending hairs will be shorter with each application. A cream or lotion should be applied to the skin after using an abrasive.

Waxing

The technique of applying melted wax to the skin for removal of excess facial hair is best handled by an experienced cosmetician. The process involves pouring hot wax onto the skin and allowing it to cool. The hairs become embedded in the wax, and are plucked out from below the skin surface when the wax is stripped off. Because this method is painful and often causes irritation, it is not very popular, although the results are comparatively long-lasting.

Plucking

The use of tweezers for removing scattered hairs from the eyebrows, face, and chest is slightly painful but otherwise harmless. It is not a practical method for getting rid of dense hair growth, however, because it takes too much time.

Permanent Hair Removal by Electrolysis

The only permanent and safe method of removing unwanted hair is by *electrolysis.* This technique destroys each individual hair root by transmitting electric current through fine wire needles into the opening of the hair follicle. The hair thus loosened is then plucked out with a tweezer. The older type of electrolysis machine uses galvanic current. The newer type, sometimes called an *electrocoagulation machine,* uses modified high-frequency current. In either case, the efficiency and safety of the technique depends less on the machine than on the care and skill of the operator.

Because the process of treating each hair root is expensive, time-consuming, and uncomfortable, it is not recommended for areas of dense hair growth, such as the arms or legs. Before undertaking electrolysis either at a beauty salon or at home, it would be wise to consult a dermatologist about individual skin reaction.

Nails

Fingernails and toenails are an extension of the epidermis, or outer layer of the skin. They are made of elastic tissue formed from keratin, the substance that gives hair its strength and flexibility.

Some of the problems associated with fingernails are the result of too much manicuring. White spots, for example, are often caused by too much pressure at the base of the nail when trying to expose the "moon"—the white portion that contains tissue not yet as tough as the rest of the nail.

To ensure the health of toenails, feet should be bathed once a day and the nails cleaned with a brush dipped in soapy water. Shoes should fit properly so that the toenails are not subjected to pressure and distortion. To avoid ingrown toenails, trimming should be done straight across rather than by rounding or tapering the corners.

Splitting

Infection or injury of the tissue at the base of a fingernail may cause its surface to be rigid or split. Inflammation of the finger joints connected with arthritis will also cause nail deformity. For ordinary problems of splitting and peeling, the nails should be kept short enough so that they don't catch and tear easily. For practical purposes, the top of the nail should not be visible when the palm is held about six inches from the eye. As the nails grow stronger, they can be grown longer without splitting.

Brittleness

This condition seems to be caused by such external factors as the chemicals in polish removers, soaps, and detergents. It is also a natural consequence of aging. Commercial nail-hardening preparations that contain formaldehyde are not recommended, because they are known to cause discoloration, loosening, or even loss of nails in some cases.

Nail damage can be reduced by wearing rubber gloves while doing household chores. Hand cream mas-

Nail Anatomy

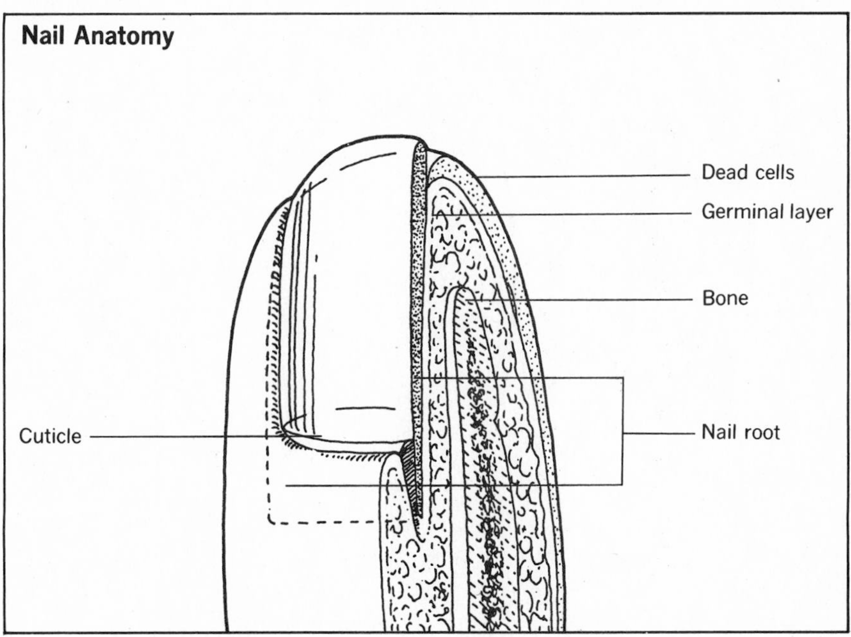

saged into the skin around the nails will counteract dryness and lessen the possibility of hangnails. Although nail polish provides a shield against damage, it should not be worn all the time, particularly if the nail is polished right down to the base; this prevents live tissue from "breathing."

Disorders of the Skin

The skin is subject to a large number of disorders, most of which are not serious even though they may be temporarily uncomfortable. A disorder may be caused by one or another type of allergy; by excessive heat or cold; or by infection from fungi, bacteria, viruses, or parasites. Many skin ailments are caused or aggravated by emotional disturbances.

The symptoms and treatment of the more common disorders are discussed in the following pages. Any persistent change in skin condition should be brought to the attention of a physician.

Allergies and Itching

Itching and inflammation of the skin may be caused by an allergic reaction, by exposure to poisonous plants, or by a generalized infection.

Dermatitis

Dermatitis is the term used for an inflammation of the skin. The term for allergic reactions of the skin resulting from surface contact with outside agents is *contact dermatitis*. This condition is characterized by a rash and may be brought out by sensitivity to cosmetics, plants, cleaning materials, metal, wool, and so on. Other forms of dermatitis can be caused by excesses of heat or cold, by friction, or by sensitivity to various medicines. Dermatitis is usually accompanied by itching at the site of the rash.

Poison Ivy

This common plant, unknown in Europe but widespread everywhere in the United States except in California and Nevada, produces an allergic reaction on the skin accompanied by a painful rash and blisters. Some people are so sensitive to it that they are affected by contact not only with the plant itself but with animal fur or clothing that might have picked up the sap weeks before.

A mild attack of poison ivy produces a rash and small, watery blisters that get progressively larger. The affected area of the skin becomes crusty and dry, and after a few weeks, all symptoms vanish. If the exposed area is thoroughly washed with laundry soap immediately after contact, the poison may not penetrate the skin.

If the symptoms do develop, they can be relieved with Burow's solution—one part solution to fifteen parts of cool water—or with the application of calamine lotion. If the symptoms are severe, and especially if the area around the eyes is involved, a physician should be consulted. He may prescribe an application or an injection of cortisone.

The best way to avoid the unpleasantness of a poison ivy attack is to learn to recognize the plant and stay away from it. Children especially should be warned against putting the leaves and berries in their mouths.

Poison oak and poison sumac produce somewhat the same symptoms and should also be avoided.

Under no circumstances should these plants be burned to eliminate them, because the inhaling of the contaminated smoke even from a distance can cause a serious case of poisoning. The application of special sprays, if the instructions are followed carefully, will get rid of the plants without affecting people or the neighborhood greenery.

Hives

These are large, irregularly shaped swellings on the skin that burn and itch. The cause is unknown, but allergic reactions to certain foods and medicine or to insect bites have been suggested as possible causes. The swellings of hives usually disappear within a day or so, but they can be very uncomfortable while they last. The itching and burning can often be relieved by applying cold water and a calamine solution. However, some people are sensitive to cold and develop wheals when subjected to intense cold. Commercial preparations containing surface anesthetics are seldom effective and may cause allergic reactions.

If the outbreak of hives can be traced to a specific food, such as shellfish or strawberries, the food should be eliminated from the diet. If a medicine such as penicillin or a sulfa drug is the cause, a physician should be told about the reaction.

Eczema

This condition is an allergic reaction that produces itching, swelling, blistering, oozing, and scaling of the skin. It is more common among children than among adults and may sometimes cover the entire body, although the rash is usually limited to the face, neck, and folds of the knees and elbows. Unlike contact dermatitis, it is likely to be caused by an allergy to a food or a pollen or dust. Advertised cures for eczema cannot control the cause and sometimes make the condition worse. A physician should be consulted if the symptoms are severe, particularly if the patient is an infant or very young child.

Itching

The technical name for the localized or general sensation on the skin that can be relieved by scratching is *pruritus*. Itching may be caused by many skin disorders, by infections, by serious diseases such as nephritis or leukemia, by medicines, or by psychological factors such as tension. A physician should always be consulted to find the cause of persistent itching, because it may be the symptom of a basic disorder. Repeated scratching may provide some relief, but it can also lead to infection.

Anal Pruritus

If itching in the anal area is so severe that only painful scratching will relieve it, the condition is probably *anal pruritus*. It is often accompanied by excessive rectal mucus that keeps the skin irritated and moist. This disorder is most commonly associated with hemorrhoids, but many other conditions, such as reactions to drugs, can cause it. Anxiety or tension can also contribute to it. Sitz baths with warm water are usually recommended. Every effort should be made to reduce scratching and to keep the anal skin clean and dry. Cortisone cream may be prescribed in persistent cases.

Skin Irritations and Weather

Extremes of weather produce local inflammations and other skin problems for many people.

Chapping

In cold weather, the sebaceous glands slow down the secretions that lubricate the skin, causing it to become dry. When dry skin is exposed to wintry weather, it becomes irritated and is likely to crack, particularly around the lips. Chapped skin is especially sensitive to harsh soaps. During such periods of exposure, the skin can be protected with a mild cream or lotion. A lubricating ointment should be used on the lips to prevent them from cracking. Children who lick their lips continually no matter what the weather can benefit from this extra protection. Chapped hands caused by daily use of strong soaps and detergents can be helped by the use of a lubricating cream and rubber gloves during housework.

Frostbite

Exposure to extreme cold for a prolonged period may cause freezing of the nose, fingers, toes, or ears, thus cutting off the circulation to the affected areas. Frostbitten areas are of a paler color than normal and are numb. They should not be rubbed with snow or exposed to intense heat. Areas should be thawed gradually, and a physician should be consulted for aftercare in extreme cases.

Chilblain

A localized inflammation of the skin called *chilblain* is common among people who are particularly sensitive to cold because of poor circulation. Chilblain may occur in the ears, hands, feet, and face, causing itching, swelling, and discoloration of the skin. Anyone prone to chilblain should dress protectively during the cold weather and use an electric pad or blanket at night. Affected parts should not be rubbed or massaged, nor should ice or extreme heat be applied directly, since these measures may cause additional damage. Persistent or extreme attacks of chilblain should be discussed with a physician.

Chafing

This condition is an inflammation of two opposing skin surfaces caused by the warmth, moisture, and friction of their rubbing together. Diabetics, overweight people, and those who perspire heavily are particularly prone to chafing. Chafing is accompanied by itching and burning, and sometimes infection can set in if the superficial skin is broken. Parts of the body subject to chafing are the inner surfaces of the thighs, the anal region, the area under the breasts, and the inner surfaces between fingers and toes.

To reduce the possibility of chafing, lightweight clothing should be worn and strenuous exercise avoided during hot weather. Vaseline or a vitamin A and D ointment may be applied to reduce friction. In general, the treatment is the same as that for diaper rash in infants. If the condition becomes acute, a physician can prescribe more effective remedies.

Prickly Heat

This skin rash is usually accompanied by itching and burning. It is caused by an obstruction of the sweat ducts such that perspiration does not reach the surface of the skin but backs up and causes pimples the size of a pinhead. If the obstruction is superficial, the pimples are white; if it is deeper, they are red. The condition can be brought on by other minor skin irritations, by continued exposure to moist heat, such as a compress, or by exercise in humid weather. Infants and people who are overweight are especially prone to prickly heat.

The discomfort can be eased by wearing lightweight, loose-fitting clothing, especially at night, and keeping room temperature low. Alcoholic beverages, which tend to dehydrate the body, should be avoided. Tepid baths and the application of cornstarch to the affected skin areas will usually relieve itching. If the rash remains for several days, a physician should be consulted to make sure it does not arise from some other cause.

Calluses and Corns

As a result of continued friction or pressure in a particular area, the skin forms a tough, hard, self-protecting layer known as a *callus.* Calluses are common on the soles of the feet, the palms of the hands, and, among guitarists and string players, on the tips of the fingers. A heavy callus that presses against a bone in the foot because of poorly fitted shoes can be very painful. The hard surface can be reduced somewhat by the use of pumice, or by gently paring it with a razor blade that has been washed in alcohol.

Corns are a form of callus that appear on or between the toes. They usually have a hard inner core that causes pain when pressed against underlying tissue by badly fitted shoes. A hard corn that appears on the surface of the little toe can be removed by soaking for about ten minutes and applying a few drops of ten percent salicylic acid in collodion. The surface should be covered with a corn pad to reduce pressure, and the corn lifted off when it is loose enough to be released from the skin. Anyone suffering from a circulatory disease and particularly from diabetes should avoid home treatment of foot disturbances. Those with a tendency to callus and corn formations should be especially careful about the proper fit of shoes and hose. A *chiropodist* or *podiatrist* is a trained specialist in foot care who can be visited on a regular basis to provide greater foot comfort.

Fungus Infections

Fungi are plantlike parasitic growths found in the air, in water, and in the soil. They comprise a large family that includes mushrooms, and are responsible for mildew and mold. Only a small number cause disease.

Ringworm

This condition is caused not by a worm but by a group of fungi that live on the body's dead skin cells in those areas that are warm and damp because of accumulated perspiration. One form of ringworm attacks the scalp, arms, and legs, especially of children, and is often spread by similarly affected pets. It appears as reddish patches that scale and blister and frequently feel sore and itchy. Ringworm is highly contagious and can be passed from person to person by contaminated objects such as combs and towels. It should therefore be treated promptly by a physician. Ringworm can best be prevented by strict attention to personal cleanliness.

Athlete's Foot

Another form of ringworm, *athlete's foot,* usually attacks the skin between the toes and under the toenails. If not treated promptly, it can cause an itching rash on other parts of the body. Athlete's foot causes the skin to itch, blister, and crack, and as a result, leaves it vulnerable to more serious infection from other organisms. The disorder can be treated at home by gently removing the damaged skin, and, after soaking the feet, thoroughly drying and dusting between the toes with a medicated foot powder. Some of the powder should be sprinkled into shoes. If the condition continues, a fungicidal ointment can be applied in the morning and at night. Persistent cases require the attention of a physician.

Scabies

An insectlike parasite causes the skin irritation called *scabies,* otherwise known as "the itch." The female itch mite burrows a hole in the skin, usually in the groin or between the fingers or toes, and stays hidden long enough to build a tunnel in which to deposit her eggs. The newly hatched mites then work their way to the skin surface and begin the cycle all over again. There is little discomfort in the early period of infestation, but in about a week, a rash appears, accompanied by extreme itching, which is usually most severe at night. Constant scratching during sleep can lead to skin lesions that invite bacterial infection.

Scabies is very contagious and can spread rapidly through a family or through a community, such as a summer camp or army barracks. It can also be communicated by sexual contact.

Treatment by a physician involves the identification of the characteristic tunnels from which sample mites can be removed for examination. Hot baths and thorough scrubbing will expose the burrows, and medical applications as directed by the physician usually clear up the condition in about a week.

Bacterial Infections

The skin is susceptible to infection from a variety of bacteria. Poor diet and careless hygiene can lower the body's resistance to these infectious agents.

Boils

These abscesses of the skin are caused by bacterial infection of a hair follicle or a sebaceous gland. The pus that accumulates in a boil is the result of the encounter between the bacteria and the white blood cells that fight them. Sometimes a boil subsides by itself and disappears. Sometimes the pressure of pus against the skin surface may bring the boil to a head; it will then break, drain, and heal if washed with an antiseptic and covered with a sterile pad. Warm-water compresses can be applied for ten minutes every hour to relieve the pain and to encourage the boil to break and drain. A fresh, dry pad should be applied after each period of soaking.

Anyone with a serious or chronic illness who develops a boil should consult a physician. Since the bacteria can enter the bloodstream and cause a general infection with fever, a physician should also be consulted for a boil on the nose, scalp, upper lip, or in the ear, groin, or armpit.

Carbuncles

This infection is a group of connected boils and is likely to be more painful and less responsive to home treatment. Carbuncles may occur as the result of poor skin care. They tend to occur in the back of the neck where the skin is thick, and the abscess tends to burrow into deeper tissues. A physician usually lances and drains a deep-seated carbuncle, or he may prescribe an antibiotic remedy.

Impetigo

This skin infection is caused by staphylococcal or streptococcal bacteria, and is characterized by blisters that break and form yellow crusted areas. It is spread from one person to another and from one part of the body to another by the discharge from the sores. Impetigo occurs most frequently on the scalp, face, and arms and legs. The infection often is picked up in barber shops, swimming pools, or from body contact with infected people or household pets.

Special care must be taken, especially with children, to control the spread of the infection by keeping the fingers away from infected parts. Bed linens should be changed daily, and disposable paper towels, as well as paper plates and cups, should be used during treatment. A physician should be consulted for proper medication and procedures to deal with the infection.

Barber's Itch

Sycosis, commonly called *barber's itch,* is a bacterial infection of the hair follicles of the beard, accompanied by inflammation, itching, and the formation of pus-filled pimples. People with stiff, curly hair are prone to this type of chronic infection, because their hair is more likely to curve back and reenter the skin. The infection should be treated promptly to prevent scarring and the destruction of the hair root. In some cases, physicians recommend antibiotics. If these are not effective, it may be necessary to drain the abscesses and remove the hairs from the inflamed follicles. During treatment, it is best to avoid shaving, if possible. If one must shave, the sterilization of all shaving equipment and the use of a brushless shaving cream are recommended.

Erysipelas

An acute streptococcal infection of the skin, *erysipelas* can be fatal, particularly to the very young or very old, if not treated promptly. One of its symptoms is the bright redness of the affected areas of the skin. These red patches enlarge and spread, making the skin tender and painful. Blisters may appear nearby. The patient usually has a headache, fever, chills, and nausea. Erysipelas responds well to promptly administered antibiotics, particularly penicillin. The patient is usually advised to drink large amounts of fluid and to eat a nourishing, easily digested diet.

Viral Infections

The most common skin conditions caused by viruses are cold sores, shingles, and warts, discussed below.

Cold Sores

Also called fever blisters, *cold sores* are technically known as *herpes simplex.* They are small blisters that appear most frequently in the corners of the mouth, and sometimes around the eyes and on the genitals. The presumed cause is a virus that lies dormant in the skin until it is activated by infection or by excessive exposure to sun or wind. There is no specific cure for cold sores, but the irritation can be eased by applying drying or cooling agents such as camphor ice or cold-water compresses. Recurrent cold sores, especially in infants, should be called to a physician's attention.

Recent studies have shown that a variety of the herpes simplex virus called HSV-II (for herpes simplex virus-Type II) can be a serious danger to the fetus of a pregnant woman. For a discussion of this condition, see Ch. 25, *Women's Health.* The variety that causes cold sores is called Type I.

Shingles

The virus infection of a sensory nerve, accompanied by small, painful blisters that appear on the skin along the path of the nerve—usually on one side of the chest or abdomen—is called *shingles.* The medical name for the disorder, which is caused by the chicken pox virus, is *herpes zoster,* Latin for "girdle of blisters." When a cranial nerve is involved, the blisters appear on the face near the eye. The preliminary symptom is neuritis with severe pain and, sometimes, fever. The blisters may take from two to four weeks to dry up and disappear. Although there is no specific cure, the pain can be alleviated by aspirin. In severe cases, or if the area near the eye is involved, a physician should be seen.

Warts

These growths are caused by a virus infection of the epidermis. They never become cancerous, but can be painful when found on the soles of the feet. In this location, they are known as *plantar warts,* and they cause discomfort because constant pressure makes them grow inward. Plantar warts are most likely to be picked up by children because they are barefooted so much of the time, and by adults when their feet are moist and they are walking around in showers, near swimming pools, and in locker rooms. Warts can be spread by scratching, by shaving, and by brushing the hair. They are often transmitted from one member of the family to another. Because warts can spread to painful areas, such as the area around or under the fingernails, and because they may become disfiguring, it is best to consult a physician whenever they appear.

In many ways, warts behave rather mysteriously. About half of them go away without any treatment at all. Sometimes, when warts on one part of the body are being treated, those in another area will disappear. The folklore about "witching" and "charming" warts away has its foundation in fact, because apparently having faith in the cure, no matter how ridiculous it sounds, sometimes brings success. This form of suggestion therapy is especially successful with children.

There are several more conventional ways of treating warts. Depending on their size and the area involved, electric current, dry ice, or various chemicals may be employed. A physician should be consulted promptly when warts develop in the area of the beard or on the scalp, because they spread quickly in these parts of the body and thus become more difficult to eliminate.

Sebaceous Cysts

When a sebaceous gland duct is blocked, the oil that the gland secretes cannot get to the surface of the skin. Instead, it accumulates into a hard, round, movable mass contained in a sac. This mass is known as a *sebaceous cyst.* Such cysts may appear on the face, back, ears, or in the genital area. A sebaceous cyst that forms on the scalp is called a *wen,* and may become as large as a billiard ball. The skin in this area will become bald, because the cyst interferes with the blood supply to the hair roots.

Some sebaceous cysts just disappear without treatment. However, those that do not are a likely focus for secondary infection by bacteria, and they may become abscessed and inflamed. It is therefore advisable to have cysts examined by a physician for possible removal. If such a cyst is superficial, it can be punctured and drained. One that is deeper is usually removed by simple surgical procedure in the physician's office.

Acne

About 80 percent of all teenagers suffer from the skin disturbance called *acne.* It is also fairly common among women in their twenties. Acne is a condition in which the skin of the face, and often of the neck, shoulders, chest, and back, is covered to a greater or lesser extent with pimples, blackheads, whiteheads, and boils.

The typical onset of acne in adolescence is related to the increased activity of the glands, including the sebaceous glands. Most of the oil that they secrete gets to the surface of the skin through ducts that lead into the pores. When the surface pores are clogged with sebaceous gland secretions and keratin, or when so much extra oil is being secreted that it backs up into the ducts, the result is the formation of the skin blemishes characteristic of acne. Dirt or makeup does not cause acne.

The blackheads are dark not because they are dirty but because the fatty material in the clogged pore is oxidized and discolored by the air that reaches it. When this substance is infected by bacteria, it turns into a pimple. Under no circumstances should such pimples be picked at or squeezed, because the pressure can rupture the surrounding membrane and spread the infection further.

Although a mild case of acne usually clears up by itself, it is often helpful to get the advice of a physician so that it does not get any worse.

Cleanliness

Although surface dirt does not cause acne, it can contribute to its spread. Therefore, the affected areas should be cleansed with a medicated soap and hot water twice a day. Hair should be shampooed frequently and brushed away from the face. Boys who are shaving should soften the beard with soap and hot water. The blade should be sharp and should skim the skin as lightly as possible to avoid nicking pimples.

Creams and Cosmetics

Nonprescription medicated creams and lotions may be effective in reducing some blemishes, but if used too often, they make the skin dry. They should be applied according to the manufacturer's instructions and should be discontinued if they cause additional irritation. If makeup is used, it should have a nonoily base and be completely removed before going to bed.

Forbidden Foods

Although acne is not caused by any particular food, it can be made worse by a diet overloaded with candy, rich pastries, and fats. Chocolate and cola drinks must be eliminated entirely in some cases.

Professional Treatment

A serious case of acne, or even a mild one that is causing serious emotional problems, should receive the attention of a physician. He or she may prescribe antibiotics, usually considered the most effective treatment, or recommend sunlamp treatments. A physician can also be helpful in dealing with the psychological aspects of acne that are so disturbing to teenagers.

Psoriasis

Psoriasis is a noncontagious chronic condition in which the skin on various parts of the body is marked by bright red patches covered with silvery scales. The areas most often affected are the knees, elbows, scalp, and trunk, and less frequently, the areas under the arms and around the genitals.

The specific cause of psoriasis has not yet been discovered, but it is thought to be an inherited abnormality in which the formation of new skin cells is too rapid and disorderly. In its mild form, psoriasis responds well to a variety of long-term treatments. When it is acute, the entire skin surface may be painfully red, and large sections of it may scale off. In such cases, prompt hospitalization and intensive care are recommended.

Conditions That Can Bring On an Outbreak

The onset or aggravation of psoriasis can be triggered by some of the following factors:

- bruises, burns, scratches, and overexposure to the sun
- sudden drops in temperature—a mild, stable climate is most beneficial
- sudden illness from another source, or unusual physical or emotional stress
- infections of the upper respiratory tract, especially bacterial throat infections and the medicines used to cure them

Treatment

Although there is no specific cure for psoriasis, these are some of the recommended treatments:

- controlled exposure to sunlight or an ultraviolet lamp
- creams or lotions of crude coal tar or tar distillates, used alone or in combination with ultraviolet light
- psoralen and ultraviolet light (PUVA), a combined systemic-external therapy in which a psoralen drug is taken orally before exposure to ultraviolet light
- systemic drugs, such as methotrexate, which can be taken orally
- steroid hormone medications applied to the skin surface under dressings

Pigment Disorders and Birthmarks

The mechanism that controls skin coloration is described above under "Skin Color." Abnormalities in the creation and distribution of melanin result in the following disorders, some of which are negligible.

Freckles

These are small spots of brown pigment that frequently occur when fair-skinned people are exposed to the sun or to ultraviolet light. For those whose skin gets red rather than tan during such exposure, freckles are a protective device. In most cases, they recede in cold weather. A heavy freckle formation that is permanent can be covered somewhat by cosmetic preparations. No attempt should be made to remove freckles with commercial creams or solutions unless supervised by a physician.

Liver Spots

Flat, smooth, irregularly placed markings on the skin, called *liver spots,* often appear among older people, and result from an increase in pigmentation. They have nothing to do with the liver and are completely harmless. Brownish markings of similar appearance sometimes show up during pregnancy or as a result of irritation or infection. They usually disappear when the underlying cause is eliminated.

Liver spots are permanent, and the principal cause is not aging but the accumulated years of exposure to sun and wind. They can be disguised and treated in the same way as freckles. A liver spot that becomes hard and thick should be called to a physician's attention.

Moles

Clusters of melanin cells, called *moles,* may appear singly or in groups at any place on the body. They range in color from light tan to dark brown; they may be raised and hairy or flat and smooth. Many moles are present at birth, and most make their appearance before the age of 20. They rarely turn into malignancies, and require medical attention only if they become painful, if they itch, or if they suddenly change in size, shape, or color.

There are several ways of removing moles if they are annoying or particularly unattractive. They can be destroyed by the application of an electric needle, by cauterizing, and by surgery. A mole that has been removed is not likely to reappear. The hairs sometimes found in moles can be clipped close to the surface of the skin, or they can be permanently removed. Hair removal often causes the mole to get smaller.

Vitiligo

The condition called *vitiligo* stems from a loss of pigment in sharply defined areas of the skin. There is no known cause for this abnormality of melanin distribution. It may affect any part of the body and may appear any time up to middle age. It is particularly conspicuous when it occurs among blacks, or when a lighter skinned person becomes tanned except around the paler patches. There is no cure for vitiligo, but cosmetic treatment with pastes and lotions can diminish the contrast between affected areas and the rest of the skin.

Birthmarks

About one-third of all infants are born with the type of birthmark called a *hemangioma,* also known as a vascular birthmark. These are caused by a clustering of small blood vessels near the surface of the skin. The mark, which is flat, irregularly shaped, and either pink, red, or purplish, is usually referred to as "port wine stain." There is no known way to remove it, but with cosmetic covering creams, it can usually be successfully masked.

The type of hemangioma that is raised and bright red—called a strawberry mark—spontaneously disappears with no treatment in most cases during early childhood. If a strawberry mark begins to grow rather than fade, or if it begins to ulcerate, a physician should be promptly consulted.

See Ch. 18, *Cancer,* for a discussion of skin cancer; see Ch. 3, *The Teens,* for a discussion of adolescent skin problems; see Ch. 23, *Aches, Pains, Nuisances, Worries,* for further discussion of minor skin problems.

22

The Teeth and Gums

Although a human baby is born without teeth, a complete set of 20 *deciduous,* or baby, teeth (also called *primary teeth*) already has formed within the gums of the offspring while it still is within the mother's womb. The buds of the permanent or secondary teeth are developing even before the first baby tooth appears at around the age of six months. The baby teeth obviously are formed from foods eaten by the mother. Generally, if the mother follows a good diet during pregnancy, no special food items are required to ensure an adequate set of deciduous teeth in the baby.

It takes about two years for the full set of deciduous teeth to appear in the baby's mouth. The first, usually a central incisor at the front of the lower jaw, may erupt any time between the ages of three and nine months. The last probably will be a second molar at the back of the upper jaw. As with walking, talking, and other characteristics of infants, there is no set timetable for the eruption of baby teeth. One child may get his first tooth at three months while another must wait until nine months, but both would be considered within a normal range of tooth development.

The permanent teeth are never far behind the deciduous set. The first permanent tooth usually appears around the age of six years, about four years after the last of the baby teeth has erupted. But the last of the permanent molars, the third molars or *wisdom teeth,* may not break through the gum line until the offspring is an adult.

Types of Teeth

The permanent teeth number 32. In advancing from deciduous to permanent teeth, the human gains six teeth in the lower jaw, or *mandible,* and six in the upper jaw, or *maxilla,* of the mouth. The primary set of teeth includes the following:

UPPER JAW	LOWER JAW
2 central incisors	2 central incisors
2 lateral incisors	2 lateral incisors
2 cuspids	2 cuspids
2 first molars	2 first molars
2 second molars	2 second molars

The permanent set of teeth has an equivalent combination of incisors, cuspids, and first and second molars. But it also includes:

2 first bicuspids	2 first bicuspids
2 second bicuspids	2 second bicuspids
2 third molars	2 third molars

An *incisor* is designed to cut off particles of food, which is then pushed by muscles of the tongue and cheeks to teeth farther back in the mouth for grinding. The front teeth, one on each side, upper and lower, are central incisors. Next to each central incisor is a lateral incisor.

A *cuspid* is so named because it has a spear-shaped crown, or *cusp.* It is designed for tearing as well as cutting. Cuspids sometimes are called *canine teeth* or *eyeteeth; canine teeth* owe their name to the use of these teeth by carnivorous animals, such as dogs, for tearing pieces of meat. There are four cuspids in the mouth, one on the outer side of each lateral incisor in the upper and lower jaws.

Bicuspids sometimes are identified

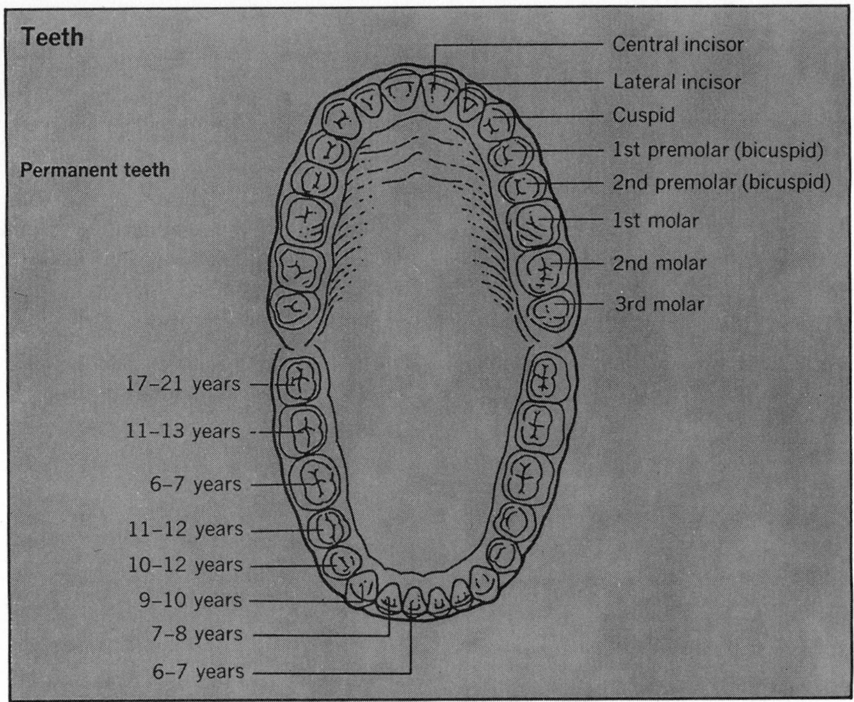

as *premolars.* The term "bicuspid" suggests two cusps, but a bicuspid may in fact have three cusps. The function of the bicuspids is to crush food passed back from the incisors and cuspids. The permanent set of teeth includes a total of eight bicuspids.

The *molars,* which also number eight and are the last teeth at the back of the mouth, are the largest and strongest teeth, with the job of grinding food. The third molars, or wisdom teeth, are smaller, weaker, and less functional than the first and second molars.

Structure of the Tooth

The variety of shapes of teeth make them specialized for the various functions in preparing food for digestion—biting, chewing, and grinding. All varieties, however, have the same basic structure.

Enamel

The outer covering of the part of the tooth that is exposed above the gum line is *enamel,* the hardest substance in the human body. Enamel is about 97 percent mineral and is as tough as some gemstones. It varies in thickness, with the greatest thickness on the surfaces that are likely to get the most wear and tear.

Enamel begins to form on the first tooth buds of an embryo at the age of about 15 weeks, depending upon substances in the food eaten by the mother for proper development. Once the tooth has formed and erupted through the gum line, there is nothing further that can be done by natural means to improve the condition of the enamel. The enamel has no blood supply, and any changes in the tooth surface will be the result of wearing, decay, or injury.

While the health and diet of the mother can affect the development of tooth enamel in the deciduous teeth, certain health factors in the early life of a child can result in defective enamel formation of teeth that have not yet erupted. Some infectious or metabolic disorders, for example, may result in enamel pitting.

Dentin

Beneath the enamel surface of a tooth is a layer of hard material—though not as hard as enamel—called *dentin,* which forms the bulk of a tooth. The dentin forms at the same time that enamel is laid down on the surface of a developing tooth, and the portion beneath the crown of the tooth probably is completed at the same time as the enamel. However, the dentin, which is composed of calcified material, is not as dense as the enamel; it is formed as myriad tubules that extend downward into the pulp at the center of the tooth. There is some evidence that dentin formation may continue slowly during the life of the tooth.

Cementum

The *cementum* is a bonelike substance that covers the root of the tooth. Though harder than regular bone, it is softer than dentin. It contains attachments for fibers of a periodontal ligament that holds the tooth in its socket. The periodontal ligament serves as a kind of hammock of fibers that surround and support the tooth at the cementum surface, radiating outward to the jawbone. This arrangement allows the tooth to move a little while still attached to the jaw. For example, when the teeth of the upper and lower jaws are brought together in chewing, the periodontal ligament allows the teeth to sink into their sockets. When the teeth of the two jaws are separated, the hammocklike ligament permits the teeth to float outward again.

Pulp

The cavity within the dentin contains the *pulp.* There is a wide pulp chamber under the crown of the tooth and a pulp canal that extends from the chamber down through the root or roots. Some teeth, such as the molars, may contain as many as three roots, and each of the roots contains a pulp canal.

The pulp of a tooth contains the blood vessels supplying the tooth and the lymphatic system. Although the blood supply arrangement is not the same for every tooth, a typical pattern includes a dental artery entering through each passageway, or *foramen,* leading into the root of a tooth. The artery branches into numerous capillaries within the root canal. A similar system of veins drains the blood from the tooth through each foramen. A lymphatic network and nerve system also enter the tooth through a foramen and spread through the pulp, as branches from a central distribution link within the jawbone. The nerve fibers have free endings in the tooth, making them sensitive to pain stimuli.

Supporting Structures

The soft, pink gum tissue that surrounds the tooth is called the *gingiva,* and the bone of the jaw that forms the tooth socket is known as *alveolar bone.* The gingiva, alveolar bone, and periodontal ligaments sometimes are grouped into a structural category identified as the *periodontium.* Thus, when a dentist speaks of periodontal disease, he is referring to a disorder of these supporting tissues of the teeth. The ailment known as *gingivitis* is an inflammation of the gingiva, or gum tissue around the teeth.

Care of the Teeth and Gums

Years ago, loss of teeth really was unavoidable. Today, thanks to modern practices of preventive dentistry, it is possible for nearly everyone to enjoy the benefits of natural teeth for a lifetime. But natural teeth can be preserved only by daily oral-hygiene habits and regular dental checkups.

The Dental Examination

During the teen years, careful supervision by the dentist and cooperation from the teenager are especially necessary. The poor eating habits of many youngsters are reflected in high cavity rates, which may be greater during adolescence than in later life. Neglect of proper dental care also occurs in the middle years when an often used excuse is that eventual loss of teeth is inevitable. After the permanent teeth are established, the dentist should be visited every six months, or at whatever intervals he recommends for an individual patient who may need more or less care than the typical patient.

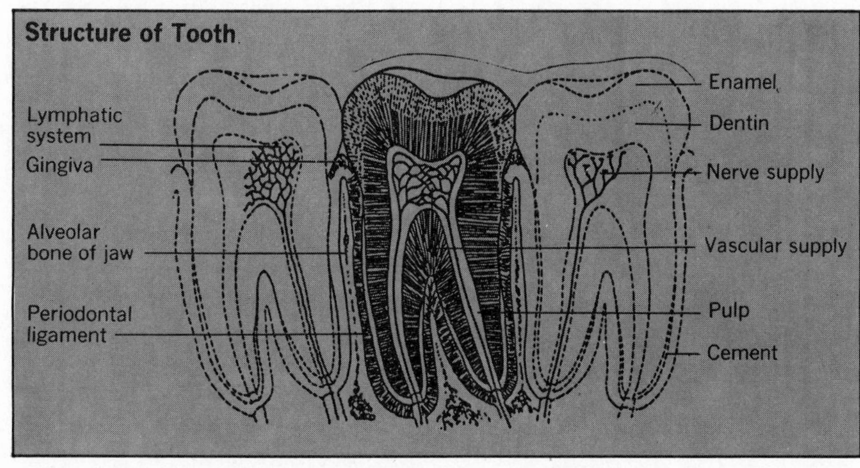

The dentist, like the family physician, usually maintains a general health history of each patient, in addition to a dental health history. He examines each tooth, the gums and other oral tissues, and the *occlusion,* or bite. A complete set of X-ray pictures may be taken on the first visit and again at intervals of perhaps five to seven years. During routine visits, the dentist may take only a couple of X-ray pictures of teeth on either side of the mouth; a complete set of X rays may result in a file of 18 or 20 pictures covering every tooth in the mouth.

X rays constitute a vital part of the dental examination. Without them the dentist cannot examine the surfaces between the teeth or the portion of the tooth beneath the gum, a part that represents about 60 percent of the total length of the tooth. The X rays will reveal the condition of the enamel, dentin, and pulp, as well as any impacted wisdom teeth and the alveolar bone, or tooth sockets. Caps, fillings, abscessed roots, and bone loss resulting from gum disease also are clearly visible on a set of X rays.

Other diagnostic tests may be made, such as a test of nerve response. Sometimes the dentist will make an impression of the teeth, an accurate and detailed reverse reproduction, in plaster of paris, plastic impression compound, or other material. Models made from these impressions are used to study the way the teeth meet. Such knowledge is often crucial in deciding the selection of treatment and materials.

After the examination, the dentist will present and explain any proposed treatment. After oral restoration is completed, he will ask the patient to return at regular intervals for a checkup and *prophylaxis,* which includes cleaning and polishing the teeth. Regular checkups and prophylaxis help prevent periodontal diseases affecting the gum tissue and underlying bone. Professional cleaning removes hard deposits that trap bacteria, especially at the gum line, and polishing removes stains and soft deposits.

Dental Care in Middle Age

Although periodontal (gum) disease and cavities—called *dental caries* by dentists—continue to threaten oral health, two other problems may assume prominence for people of middle age: replacing worn-out restorations, or fillings, and replacing missing teeth. No filling material will last forever. The whitish restorations in front teeth eventually wear away. Silver restorations tend to crack and chip with age because they contract and expand slightly when cold or hot food and drinks come in contact with them. Even gold restorations, the most permanent kind, are subject to decay around the edges, and the decay may spread underneath.

If a needed restoration is not made or a worn-out restoration is not replaced, a deep cavity may result. When the decay reaches the inner layer of the tooth—the dentin—temporary warning twinges of pain may occur. If the tooth still is not restored, the decay will spread into the pulp that fills the inner chamber of the tooth. A toothache can result from inflammation of the pulp, and although the pain may eventually subside, the pulp tissue dies and an abscess can form at the root of the tooth.

Dental Care during Pregnancy

It may be advisable for a pregnant woman to arrange for extra dental checkups. Many changes take place during pregnancy, among them increased hormone production. Some pregnant women develop gingivitis (inflammation of the gums) as an indirect consequence of hormonal changes. A checkup by the dentist during the first three months of pregnancy is needed to assess the oral effects of such changes, and to make sure all dental problems are examined and corrected. Pregnant women should take special care to brush and floss their teeth to minimize these problems.

Infection

To avoid the problem of toxic substances or poisons circulating in the mother's bloodstream, all sources of infection must be removed. Some of these sources can be in the mouth. An abscessed tooth, for example, may not be severe enough to signal its presence with pain, but because it is directly connected to the bloodstream it can send toxic substances and bacteria through the mother's body with possible harmful effects to the embryo.

It is during pregnancy that tooth buds for both the deciduous and permanent teeth begin to form in the unborn child. If the mother neglects her diet or general health care during this period, the effects may be seen in the teeth of her child.

Maintaining Good Oral Hygiene

Fluoridation

Among general rules to follow between dental checkups are using fluorides, maintaining a proper diet, and removing debris from the teeth by brushing and by the use of dental floss. Fluorides are particularly important for strengthening the enamel of teeth in persons under the age of 15. Many communities add fluorides to the water supply, but if the substance is not available in the drinking water, the dentist can advise the patient about other ways of adding fluoride to water or other fluids consumed each day. Studies show that children who drink fluoridated water from birth have up to 65 percent fewer cavities than those who do not drink fluoridated water. However, using excessive amounts of fluoride in the drinking water can result in mottled enamel.

Diet

Although a good diet for total health should provide all of the elements needed for dental health, several precautions on sugars and starches should be added. Hard or sticky sweets should be avoided. Such highly refined sweets as soft drinks, candies, cakes, cookies, pies, syrups, jams, jellies, and pastries should be limited, especially between meals. One's intake of starchy foods, such as bread, potatoes, and pastas, should also be controlled. Natural sugars contained in fresh fruits can provide sweet flavors with less risk of contributing to decay if the teeth are brushed regularly after eating such foods. Regular chewing gum may help remove food particles after eating, but it deposits sugar; if you chew gum, use sugarless gum.

Because decay is promoted each time sugars and other refined carbohydrates are eaten, between-meals snacks of sweets should be curtailed to lessen the chances of new or additional caries. Snack foods can be raw vegetables, such as carrots or celery, apples, cheese, peanuts, or other items that are not likely to introduce refined carbohydrates into the mouth between meals.

Brushing

Brushing the teeth is an essential of personal oral hygiene. Such brushing rids the mouth of most of the food

Brushing

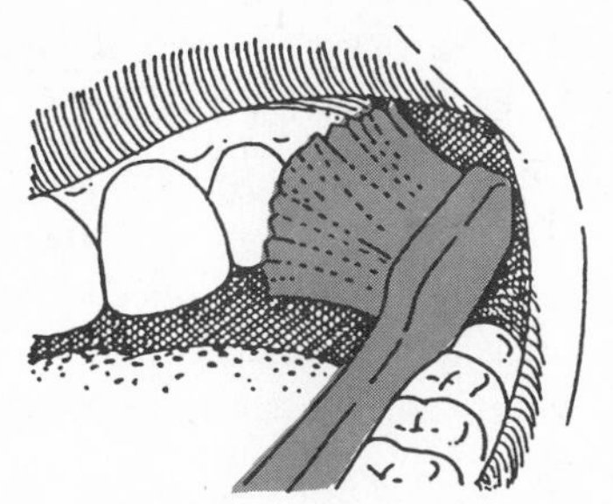

Begin by brushing the tops of the upper and lower molars, using a scrubbing motion without much pressure. A soft toothbrush with a straight handle is most recommended.

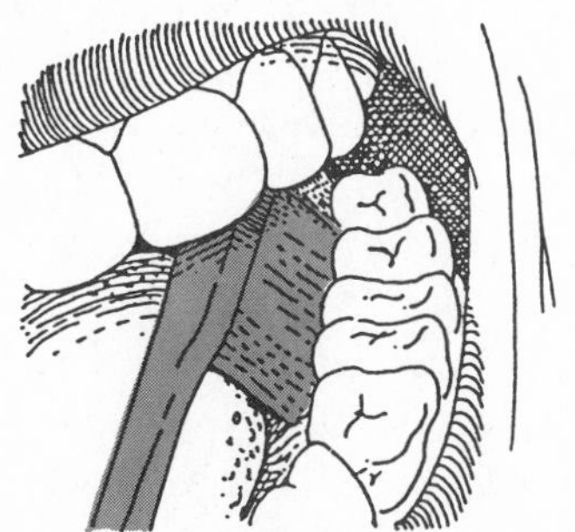

Next, keeping the brush parallel to the teeth, angle the bristles against the lower gums and brush back and forth with short strokes against both sides of every tooth. Use the same technique for the upper teeth.

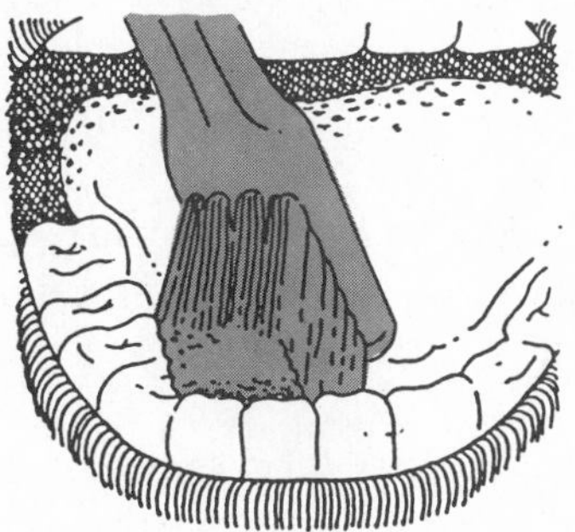

Apply the tip of the brush to the backs of upper and lower front teeth. Scrub in an up-and-down motion holding the brush handle directly out in front.

debris that encourages bacterial growth, which is most intense 20 minutes after eating. Therefore, the teeth should be cleaned as soon as possible after a meal.

There is no one kind of toothbrush that is best for every person. Most dentists, however, recommend a soft toothbrush with a straight handle and flat brushing surface that can clean the gums without irritating them. As for claims about whether toothbrushes should have bristles with square corners or rounded shapes, a dentist may point out that there are both curved and straight surfaces in the mouth, so what one design offers in advantages may be offset by equivalent disadvantages. There also are special brushes for reaching surfaces of crooked teeth or cleaning missing-tooth areas of the mouth.

Although several different methods may be used effectively, the following is the technique most often recommended. Brush the biting surfaces, or tops, of the back upper and lower teeth. The lines and grooves on these surfaces make them prone to decay. They should be brushed first, before moisture has softened the brush. The cheek and tongue surfaces of the lower teeth are brushed next. Hold the brush parallel to the teeth with the bristle edges angled against and touching the gums. Using short strokes, move the brush back and forth several times before proceeding to the next one or two teeth. Use the same technique on all the inner surfaces of your teeth as well. For the hard-to-brush inner surfaces of the front teeth, hold the handle of the brush out in front of the mouth and apply the tip in an up-and-down motion. For all brushing, a scrubbing motion—but without too much pressure—should be used.

Some people prefer electric toothbrushes, which require less effort to use than ordinary toothbrushes. These are available with two basic motions—up and down and back and forth. Your dentist may advise which kind best serves an individual's needs and proper use of equipment. Some dentists point out that back-and-forth brushing applied with too much pressure can have an abrasive effect on tooth enamel because it works against the grain of the mineral deposits. The American Dental Association also evaluates electric toothbrushes and issues reports on the safety and effectiveness of various types.

Removing Debris with Dental Floss

Brushing often does not clean debris from between the teeth. But plaque and food particles that stick between the teeth usually can be removed with dental floss. A generous length of floss, about 18 inches, is needed to do an effective job. The ends can be wrapped several times around the

Flossing

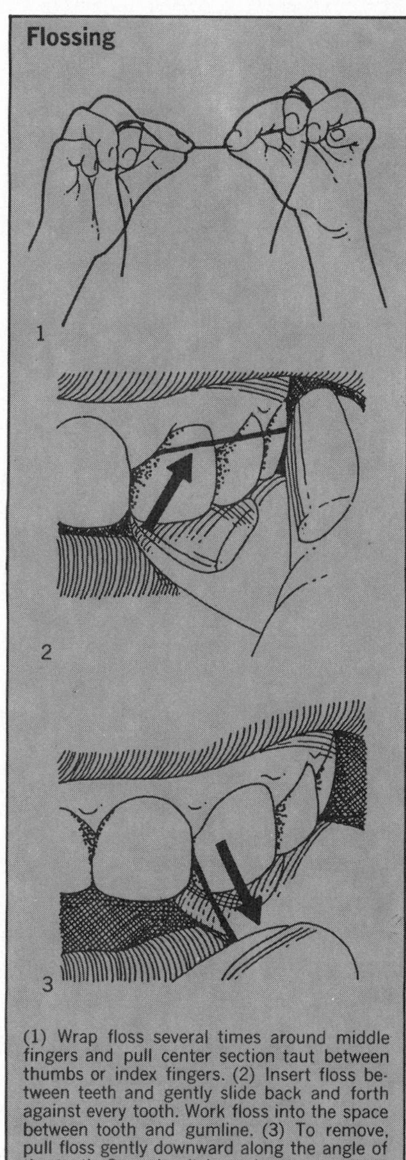

(1) Wrap floss several times around middle fingers and pull center section taut between thumbs or index fingers. (2) Insert floss between teeth and gently slide back and forth against every tooth. Work floss into the space between tooth and gumline. (3) To remove, pull floss gently downward along the angle of the tooth. Snapping it in and out may cause gum irritation.

first joint of the middle finger of each hand. Using the thumbs or index fingers, the floss is inserted between the teeth with a gentle, sawing, back-and-forth motion. Then it is slid gently around part of a tooth in the space at the gum line and gently pulled out; snapping the floss in and out may irritate the gums. After brushing and flossing, the mouth should be rinsed with water. A mouthwash is unnecessary, but it may be used for the good taste it leaves in the mouth.

The dentist may recommend the use of an oral irrigating device as part of dental home care. These units produce a pulsating stream of water that flushes food debris from between teeth. They are particularly useful for patients wearing orthodontic braces or for those who have had recession of the gums, creating larger spaces between the teeth.

The person who wants to see the areas of plaque on his teeth can chew a *disclosing tablet,* available at most pharmacies, which leaves a harmless temporary stain on plaque surfaces. Some dentists recommend the use of disclosing tablets about once a week so that patients can check on the effectiveness of their tooth-cleaning techniques.

Tooth Decay

In addition to wear, tear, and injury, the major threat to the health of a tooth is bacteria. Bacteria can cause tooth decay, and the human mouth is a tremendous reservoir of bacteria because the mouth is warm, dark, moist, and usually contains tiny particles of food that help nourish the organisms. The bacteria found in the mouth are of two kinds, *aerobic* and *anaerobic.* Aerobic bacteria need oxygen to survive; anaerobic bacteria do not. Anaerobic bacteria can find their way through cracks and crevices into areas of the mouth or teeth where there is little or no oxygen and continue their *cariogenic,* or decay, activity.

Saliva

Saliva offers some protection against the decay germs, for reasons not well understood, but there are crevices and deep pockets around the teeth and gums where saliva does not penetrate. Paradoxically, saliva itself contains millions of different bacterial organisms. Dental scientists have calculated that one ounce of saliva may contain as many as 22 billion bacteria. Even a presumably healthy mouth may contain more than ten varieties of bacteria, plus protozoa and yeast cells. The yeast cells and at least three of the different kinds of bacteria are capable of producing acids that erode the tough enamel surface of a tooth.

Bacterial Acids and Plaque

The acids produced by decay bacteria actually are waste products of the organisms' digestive processes; bacteria, like other living creatures, eventually excrete waste products after a meal. As unpleasant as the thought may be, tooth decay can be the result of feeding a colony of germs in the mouth. Bacterial growth—hence the production of harmful acids—is encouraged by the consumption of too many foods composed of refined sugars. The sugars of candies, cakes, soft drinks, and the like are easier for the bacteria to eat and digest than those of fruits, vegetables, and other less thoroughly processed foods. Even a tiny bit of food remaining in the mouth after a meal may be enough to support many millions of bacteria for 24 hours or more.

An additional contributing factor to tooth decay is *plaque* formation. Plaque is a sticky, transparent substance that forms a film over the surface of the teeth. Plaque forms every day, which is the reason that the teeth must be brushed every day. Plaque frequently begins with deposits of soft food debris along the gum line after a meal; it consists mainly of bacteria and its products. When mixed with mucus, molds, tissue cells from the membranes lining the mouth, and mineral salts, it takes the form of a white, cheesy substance called *materia alba.* If not removed regularly by brushing and the use of dental floss, this substance becomes a thick, sticky mass that has been compared to epoxy cement. Then it becomes a rough-surfaced hard substance with the texture of stone, otherwise known as *dental calculus,* or *tartar.*

Other Causes of Decay

Bacterial acid is not the only way in which the tooth enamel may be damaged to permit the entry of decay bacteria. Certain high-acid foods and improper dental care can erode the molecules of enamel. Temperature extremes also can produce cracks and other damage to the enamel; some dental scientists have suggested that repeated exposure to rapid temperature fluctuations of 50° F., as in eating alternately hot and cold foods or beverages, can cause the enamel to develop cracks.

Complications of Tooth Decay

Once decay activity breaks through the hard enamel surface, the bacteria can attack the dentin. Because the dentin is about 30 percent organic material, compared to 5 percent in the enamel layer, the decay process can advance more rapidly there. If the tooth decay is not stopped at the dentin layer, the disease organisms can enter the pulp chamber, where they will multiply quickly, producing an acute inflammation and, if unchecked, spread through the blood vessels to other parts of the body. Osteomyelitis, an infection of the membrane covering the skeletal bones, and endocarditis, an extremely dangerous heart ailment, are among diseases in other parts of the body that can begin with untreated tooth decay.

Periodontal disease, described below, is another possible complication of tooth decay.

Tooth Restoration

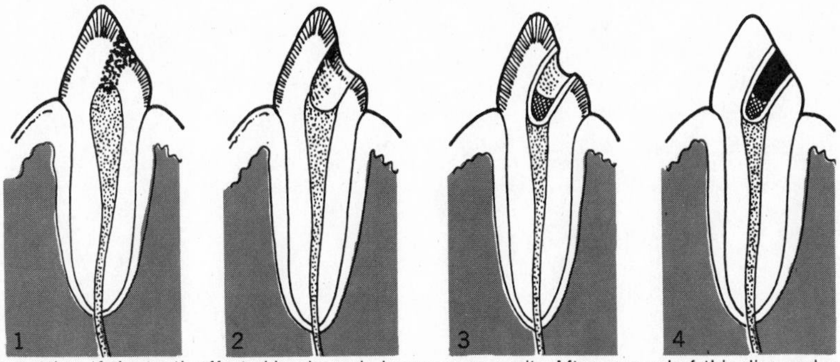

1 2 3 4

The portion of the tooth affected by decay is known as a *cavity*. After removal of this diseased area (2), using drill, hand instrument, or other method, the dentist fills the cleaned cavity with a base or liner material (3). Finally, the tooth is filled with a restorative substance such as an amalgam, inlay, or ceramic material.

Treatment of Tooth Decay

The portion of a tooth invaded by decay is called a *cavity;* it may be compared to an ulcer that develops because of disease in soft tissues. In treating the decay process, the dentist tries to prevent further destruction of the tooth tissue. The dentist also tries to restore as much as possible the original shape and function of the diseased tooth. The procedure used depends on many factors, including the surfaces affected (enamel, dentin, etc.) and the tooth face and angle involved, as well as whether the cavity is on a smooth area or in a pit or fissure of the tooth surface.

The decayed portions of the tooth are removed with various kinds of carbide burrs and other drill tips, as well as with hand instruments. The dentist may also use a caries removal system that reduces or eliminates drilling. In this system two solutions are combined in one liquid and squirted in a pulsating stream onto the decayed area. The stream does not harm gums or healthy teeth; rather, it softens the caries so that it can easily be scraped away. Used, generally, in conjunction with rotary or hand instruments, the "squirt" system may make anesthesia unnecessary.

In other cases an anesthetic may be injected for the comfort of the patient. The dentist usually asks whether the patient prefers to have an anesthetic before work commences. In the cleaning process, an effort is made to remove all traces of diseased enamel or dentin, but no more of the tooth material than is necessary.

The cleaned cavity is generally filled in a layering procedure. The layers of liners and bases used before insertion of the filling are determined by the depth of the cavity and other factors. If pulp is exposed, special materials may be applied to help the pulp recover from the irritation of the procedure and to form a firm base for the amalgam, inlay, or other restorative substance that becomes the filling.

In the 1980s, new ceramic materials came into use for fillings. Many dentists believed that ceramics could provide more natural-looking restorations. With ceramics, also, teeth would be less sensitive to changes of temperature—a problem with some more traditional materials.

Tooth Extraction

When it becomes necessary to remove a diseased, damaged, or malpositioned tooth, the procedure is handled as a form of minor surgery, usually with administration of a local anesthetic to the nerves supplying the tooth area. However, there is no standard routine for extraction of a tooth, because of the numerous individual variations associated with each case. The dentist usually has a medical history of the patient available, showing such information as allergies to drugs, and medications used by the patient that might react with those employed in oral surgery. Because the mouth contains many millions of bacteria, all possible precautions are taken to prevent entry of the germs into the tooth socket.

The condition of the patient is checked during and immediately after tooth extraction, in the event that some complication develops. The patient is provided with analgesic (pain-killing) and other needed medications, along with instructions regarding control of any postoperative pain or bleeding. The dentist also may offer special diet information with suggested meals for the recovery period, which usually is quite brief.

Dry Socket

Severe pain may develop several days after a tooth has been extracted if a blood clot that forms in the socket becomes dislodged. The condition, commonly called *dry socket,* can involve infection of the alveolar bone that normally surrounds the roots of the tooth; loss of the clot can expose the bone tissue to the environment and organisms that produce *osteitis,* or inflammation of the bone tissue. Dry socket may be treated by irrigating the socket with warm salt water and packing it with strips of medicated gauze. The patient also is given analgesics, sedatives, and other medications as needed to control the pain and infection.

General anesthetics are sometimes necessary for complicated oral surgery. In such cases, there are available dental offices or clinics that are as well equipped and staffed as hospital operating rooms.

Root Canal Therapy

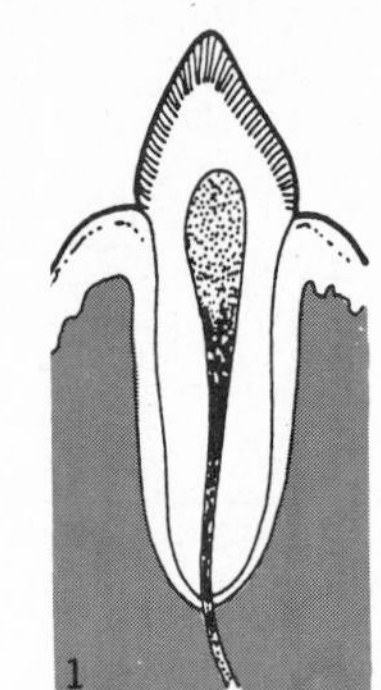

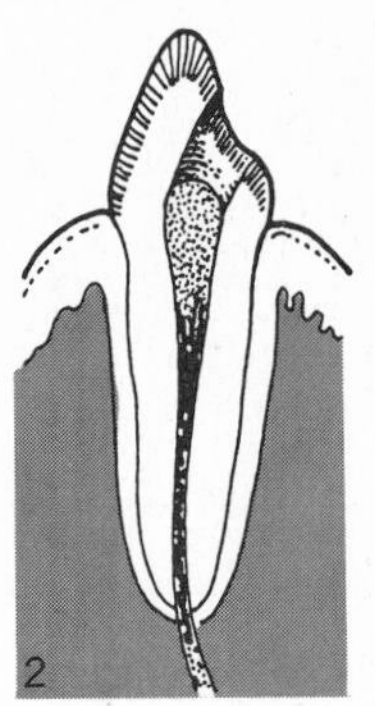

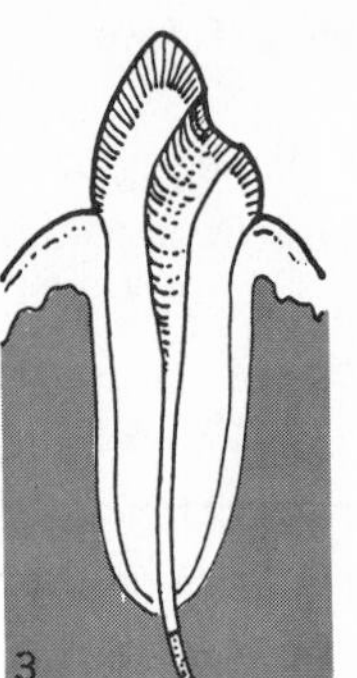

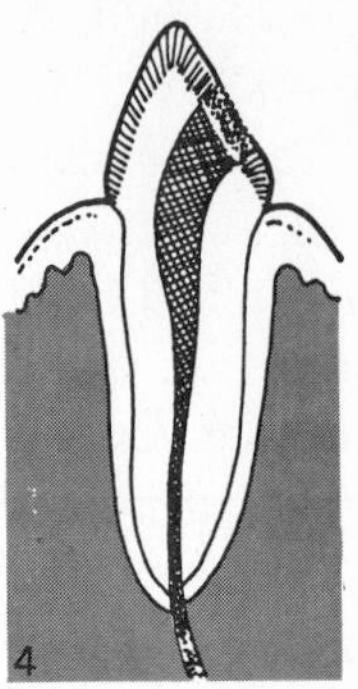

(1) The first step of root canal, or removal of the nerve of a tooth, begins with examining the infected pulp to determine its vitality. (2) The depth of the root is measured by X ray and, after administering local anesthetic, the dentist extracts the pulp with drill or hand instrument marked to indicate when the end of the root has been reached. (3) When the entire pulp and nerve have been removed the canal is sterilized to prevent infection. (4) After filling the tooth with silver or a tough plastic substance known as *gutta-percha,* or sometimes a combination of both, the dentist then caps the tooth.

Endodontic Therapy

Tooth extraction because of caries is less common today than in previous years, although an estimated 25 million Americans have had all of their teeth removed. Modern preventive dentistry techniques of *endodontics* now make it possible to save many teeth that would have been extracted in past decades after the spread of decay into the pulp canal. The procedures include *root canal therapy, pulp capping,* and *pulpotomy.*

Root Canal Therapy

Once the tooth has fully developed in the jaw, the nerve is not needed, so if the pulp is infected the nerve as well as the pulp can be removed. Only minor effects are noticeable in the tooth structure after the pulp is removed, and the dentist compensates for these in filling the tooth after root canal therapy.

Briefly, the procedure of root canal work begins by examination and testing of the pulp viability. The pulp may be tested by heat, cold, or an electrical device called a *vitalometer,* which measure the degree of sensation the patient feels in a tooth. If the pulp is dead, the patient will feel no sensation, even at the highest output of current.

After the degree of vitality in the pulp has been determined, a local anesthetic is injected and the dentist begins removing the pulp, using rotary drills and hand instruments. By means of X-ray pictures, the dentist measures the length of the root, which may be about one and a half times the length of the crown. Stops or other markers are placed on the root excavation tools to show the dentist when the instrument has reached the end of the root. The canal is then sterilized and filled with gutta-percha—a tough plastic substance—silver, or a combination of the two, and a cap is added.

Pulp Capping

Pulp capping consists of building a cap over the exposed pulp with layers of calcium hydroxide paste, which is covered by zinc oxide and topped with a firm cement.

Pulpotomy

A pulpotomy procedure involves removal of the pulp in the pulp chamber within the crown of the tooth, while leaving the root canal pulp in place. The amputated pulp ends are treated and a pulp-capping procedure is used to restore the crown of the tooth.

Periodontal Disease

It is important in the middle years of life and later to continue good oral-hygiene habits and the practice of having regular dental checkups. Studies have found that after the age of 50 more than half the people in America have periodontal disease. At the age of 65, nearly everybody has this disease.

The Course of the Disease

The combination of bacterial action described above and the roughness of the resulting calculus injures the surrounding gum tissue and makes it susceptible to infection and recession. The irritation causes swelling, inflammation, and bleeding into the crevices between the teeth and gums, which is one of the early signs of impaired tissue health.

The inflammation of the gums, known as *gingivitis,* can spread to the roots of the teeth if not treated. The gums separate from the teeth, forming pockets that fill up with more food particles and colonies of bacteria. As the disease progresses, the bone support for the teeth is weakened and the affected teeth begin to loosen and drift from their normal position. Finally, unless the disease is treated in time, the teeth may be lost.

Periodontal disease is sometimes called *pyorrhea,* a Greek word meaning a discharge of pus. But "pyorrhea" is a somewhat misleading term, because it identifies only one manifestation of the disease, an abscess that usually forms along the side of an affected tooth. In some cases, a membrane forms around the abscess, creating a pus-filled cyst in the tooth socket.

Other Signs and Complications

Another manifestation of periodontal disease is periodontal atrophy, or recession of the gingiva, or gum tissue, and the underlying bone away from the outer layer of the tooth that joins it to its socket. Recession tends to expose the dentin below the gum line, which is not protected by a layer of enamel. The exposed dentin may be hypersensitive to hot or cold foods or beverages, air, and sweet or sour food flavors.

Inflammation of the gingival tissue in periodontal disease may be increased in intensity by toxic chemicals from tobacco smoke, bacterial infections, vitamin deficiencies, and defective dental restorations. The normal pink color of the gingival tissue may be altered by periodontal disease to a bright red or a darker coloration ranging to bluish purple.

The inflamed gingival tissue may lead to a complication called *periodontitis* in which the bone under the gum tissue is gradually destroyed, widening the crevice between the tooth and surrounding tissues. Pregnant women seem particularly vulnerable to periodontitis and gingivitis if they have been experiencing periodontal disorders, because the temporary hormonal imbalance of the pregnancy tends to exaggerate the effects of this condition.

One kind of gingivitis that involves projections of gum tissue between the teeth is sometimes referred to as *trench mouth,* because it was not an uncommon form of periodontal disease affecting soldiers during World War I. The infection is associated with poor oral hygiene, along with nutritional deficiencies and general depressed condition of health.

Periodontal Disease

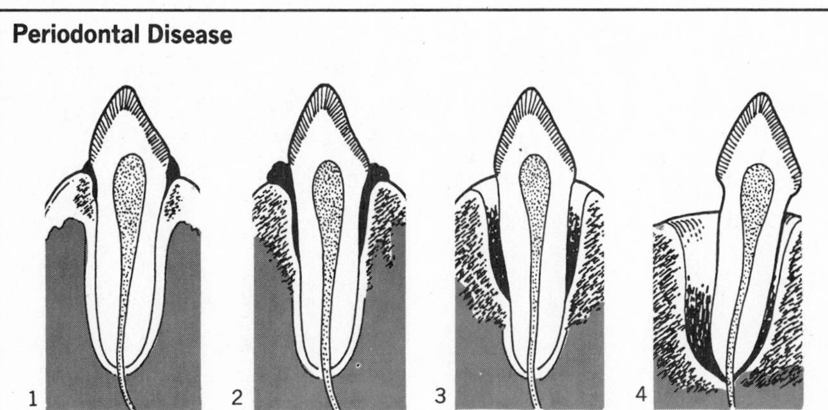

(1) If allowed to build up at the gumline, deposits of plaque and calculus result in damage to the gum tissues (periodontal disease). (2) As gums become increasingly irritated and inflamed, they may bleed easily and begin to recede from the tooth itself. (3) Untreated, the inflammation spreads to the roots of the teeth. Bacteria and particles of food lodge in the pockets between tooth and gums, aggravating the condition. (4) A tooth held by the diseased gum loses most of its bony support structure, causing it to loosen and move out of position. Eventually, such teeth may need to be extracted.

Causes

At one time it was assumed that periodontal diseases were associated with the life styles of persons living in more technologically advanced societies, where soft, rich foods are eaten regularly, providing materials toward the formation of plaque and support of bacteria in the plaque. But recent investigations show that people living in the less developed nations, who are relatively free of tooth decay, eventually develop periodontal disease. However, this does not alter the fact that the accumulation of plaque and harmful bacteria are the chief causes of periodontal disease, as well as of tooth decay.

Although periodontal disease generally becomes troublesome in middle age, there is some evidence that early symptoms of gingival disorders occur during childhood or adolescence. Also, because more people live longer today, periodontal disease has become more common than in the past.

Bruxism

Bruxism—the nervous habit, often unconsciously done, of clenching and grinding the teeth—can contribute to the development of periodontal disease. Bruxism frequently occurs during sleep.

Malocclusion

Another contributing cause to periodontal disease is repeated shock or undue pressure on a tooth because of *malocclusion,* or an improper bite. This effect accelerates damage to the tooth and gum structure during such simple activities as biting and chewing.

Treatment

Periodontal treatment may include a variety of techniques ranging from plaque removal to oral surgery to form new contours on the alveolar bone surrounding the tooth. If treatment is not begun until periodontal disease is well advanced, it may be difficult to fit replacement teeth, or *dentures,* as substitutes for lost teeth. Dentures fit over the ridges of the jaws, and if the top edge of the ridge has been destroyed by periodontal disease, the procedure for holding the denture firmly in place will be complicated.

Dentures

If it becomes necessary to have some teeth removed, they should be replaced as soon as possible with a *bridge*—a mounting for false teeth anchored to natural teeth on either side—or a partial or full denture.

Why Missing Teeth Must Be Replaced

Chewing ability and clarity of speech may be impaired if missing teeth are not replaced. Also, each tooth functions to hold the teeth on either side and opposite it in place. If a tooth is lost, the tooth opposite may erupt further and the teeth on either side shift in their positions because there is no counterforce to keep them in place. Food particles lodge in the spaces created by the shifting teeth, plaque forms, and periodontal disease develops, causing the loss of additional teeth. This loss may take years if the movement of intact teeth is slow, but if they tilt and shift rapidly into the empty spaces, the remaining teeth may be lost in a much shorter time.

The loss of a few teeth can also alter a person's appearance. The cheeks may become puckered and the lips drawn together, making the individual look older.

Fitting of Dentures

Modern techniques and materials of construction and the skill of modern dentists should assure well-fitting, natural-looking dentures. The dentist selects the tooth shade and shape that are best for an individual's face size, contours, and coloring. No one, however, has perfectly arranged, perfectly white natural teeth. Tooth coloring depends upon genetic factors and changes as one grows older. These factors must be considered in designing dentures.

Bridges and Partial Dentures

Several different types of dental appliances may be constructed to fill empty spaces. Some, such as dental bridges, may be attached to the remaining natural teeth by cementing them. Others, such as complete sets of dentures, are removable.

A bridge may be made entirely of gold, a combination of gold and porcelain, or combinations of gold and porcelain and other materials. If there is a sound natural tooth on either side of the space, a *pontic,* or suitable substitute for the missing tooth, may be fused to the metal bridge. The crown retainer on either side of the pontic may then be cemented to the crowns of the neighboring natural teeth.

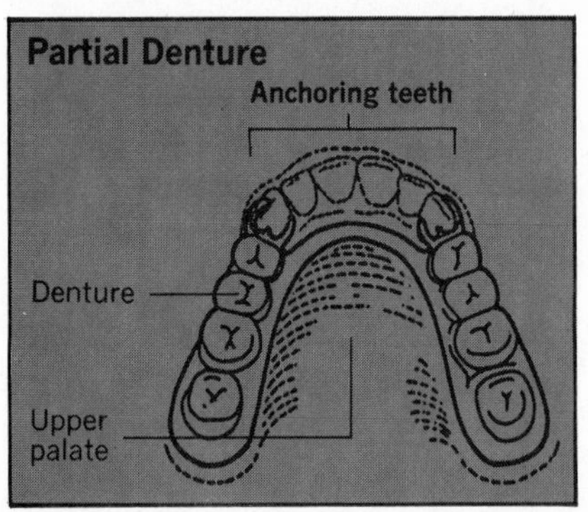

If there are no natural teeth near the space created by an extracted tooth, a partial denture may be constructed to replace the missing teeth. This appliance usually fastens by a clasp onto the last tooth on each side of the space. A bar on the inside of the front teeth provides stability for the partial denture.

A "Maryland bridge," a fixed partial denture developed by the University of Maryland's Baltimore College of Dental Surgery, eliminates the need for crowns to anchor false teeth. With the Maryland bridge, hidden metal "wings" are used to anchor the partial denture. The wings are bonded to the backs of neighboring teeth. Because it eliminates the need for drilling, the Maryland bridge saves healthy teeth, makes anesthesia unnecessary, and reduces costs considerably.

New materials have brought bonding into more common use as an alternative to crowning and for cosmetically restoring chipped, malformed, stained, or widely spaced teeth. In the bonding process the dentist isolates a tooth with a rubber dam, cleans and dries the tooth, and applies a phosphoric acid solution that produces microscopic pores in the enamel. The etched area is then filled in with a liquid plastic. To that base the dentist applies thin layers of tooth-colored plastics known as composite resins. The layers can be sculpted, hardened with a beam of light or by some other method, contoured, and polished.

A removable partial denture should

be taken out and cleaned whenever the natural teeth are brushed. A special brush, usually cone-shaped to fit into the clasp, is available as a cleaning tool. The pontic, or tooth substitute of a bridge, remains in place permanently and is brushed like a natural tooth.

A bridge or partial denture helps prevent further deterioration of the mouth if it is kept clean and in good condition. But a dentist should check bridges and partial dentures periodically to make sure they have not become loosened. A loose clasp of a partial denture can rock the teeth to which the device is attached, causing damage and possible loss.

Complete Dentures

Before a full set of removable dentures is constructed, the dentist will take X rays to determine whether there are any abnormalities in the gum ridges, such as cysts or tooth root tips that may have to be removed. If the gums are in poor condition, treatments may be needed to improve the surfaces of the ridges on which the dentures will be fitted. The dentist may also have to reconstruct the bone underlying the gums—the alveolar ridge. Human bone "harvested" from another part of the patient's body has for decades been used in such reconstruction, but is today giving way to ceramic materials.

Two ceramic materials used in such surgery are hydroxylapatite and beta tricalcium phosphate. Oral surgeons have reported good results with both. The new materials are said to be safer and simpler to use and less expensive than human bone. They also eliminate the need for preliminary surgery to obtain transplants of the patient's bone.

With preliminary work done, the dentist makes an impression of the patient's mouth. Tooth and shade choices are discussed. Several other appointments may be arranged before the new dentures are delivered to the patient. Appointments may be needed for "try-ins" of dentures as they are being constructed and for adjustments after completion of the set.

Although dentures do not change with age, the mouth does. Therefore, it is necessary for the denture-wearer to have occasional dental checkups. At denture checkup appointments, the dentist examines oral tissues for irritation and determines how the dentures fit with respect to possible changing conditions of the mouth. If the dentures no longer fit properly, a replacement may be recommended. The dentist also seeks to correct any irritations of the oral tissues of the mouth and polishes the dentures, making them smooth and easier to keep clean between checkups. If any of the teeth in the dentures has become damaged, the dentist can repair or replace the denture tooth.

Care of Dentures

Dentures should be cleaned daily with a denture brush and toothpaste; once a week they should be soaked for seven or eight hours in a denture cleaner. To avoid breaking them during the brushing process, fill a wash basin with water and place it under the dentures while they are being cleaned; if they are dropped, the dentures will be cushioned by the water. A harsh abrasive that could scratch the denture surface should not be used. Scratches allow stains to penetrate the surface of the dentures, creating permanent discoloration.

The use of adhesives and powders is only a temporary solution to ill-fitting dentures. In time, the dentist may rebuild the gum side of the denture to conform with the shape of the patient's gum ridge. The patient should never try to make his own changes in the fit of dentures. Rebuilding the gum side of the dentures, or *relining,* as it is called, usually begins with a soft temporary material if the patient's gums are in poor condition, and requires several appointments over a period of two or three weeks while the gum tissues are being restored to good health.

Most patients show some concern over the replacement of natural teeth with dentures, even when a set of complete dentures is needed to replace an earlier set. Some people associate the loss of teeth with old age in the same way that others resist the advice that they should wear eyeglasses or a hearing aid. The fact is that many millions of persons of all ages have found they can improve their eating, speaking, and physical appearance by obtaining attractive and well-fitted dentures.

Orthodontics

Orthodontics is a term derived from the Greek words for straight, or normal, teeth. Straight teeth are easier to keep clean and they make chewing food more efficient. There also is a cosmetic benefit in being able to display a smile with a set of straight teeth, although many dentists consider the cosmetic aspect of orthodontics as secondary to achieving proper occlusion, or bite.

Causes of Improper Bite

Orthodontic problems can be caused by hereditary factors, by an infectious or other kind of disease, by the premature loss of primary teeth, by the medications used in treatment, or by individual factors such as injury or loss of permanent teeth. A person may have congenitally missing teeth resulting in spaces that permit drifting

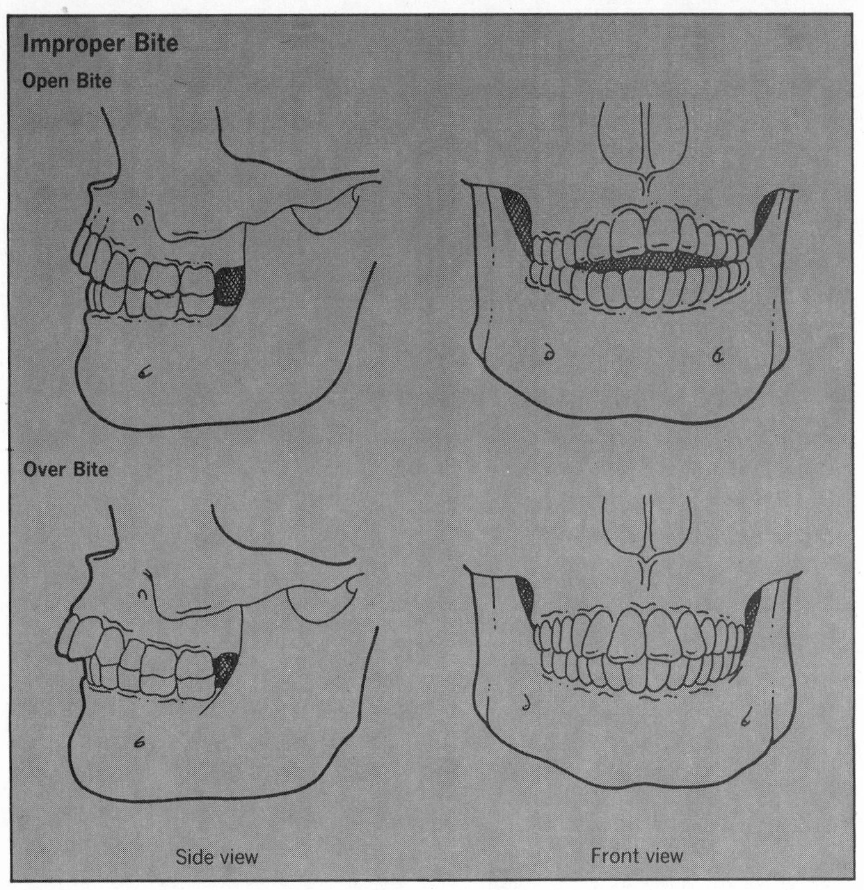

of neighboring teeth or collapse of the dental arch. Or he may develop extra (supernumerary) teeth resulting from an inherited factor. The supernumerary teeth may develop during the early years of life while the deciduous teeth are in use. A supernumerary tooth may force permanent teeth into unnatural positions.

Nutritional disorders can also affect the development of jaws and teeth, while certain medications can cause abnormal growth of gingival, or gum, tissues, resulting in increased spaces between the teeth.

Teeth that erupt too early or too late, primary teeth that are too late in falling out when permanent teeth have developed, and habits such as grinding of the teeth, thumb-sucking, or pushing the tongue against the teeth are among other factors that can result in *malocclusion,* or improper bite, and the need for orthodontic treatment.

Diagnosis of Orthodontic Problems

Each child should visit a dentist before the eruption of his permanent teeth for an examination that may determine the need for orthodontic treatment. Because there are many genetic and other influences that help shape the facial contours and occlusion of each individual, there are no standard orthodontic procedures that apply to any or all children. The dentist may recommend what treatment, if any, would be needed to produce normal occlusion and when it should begin; some dentists advise only that necessary procedures for correcting malocclusion be started before the permanent set of teeth (excluding wisdom teeth) has become established, or around the age of 12 or 13. However, there are few age limits for orthodontic care, and an increasing number of adults are receiving treatment today for malocclusion problems that were neglected during childhood.

In the normal or ideal occlusion positions of the teeth, the first and second permanent upper molars fit just slightly behind the same molars of the lower jaw; all of the teeth of the upper jaw are in contact with their counterparts of the lower jaw. In this pattern of occlusion, all of the biting surfaces are aligned for optimum use of their intended functions of cutting, tearing, or grinding.

There are numerous variations of malocclusion, but generally, in simple deformities, the teeth of the upper jaw are in contact with lower jaw teeth once removed from normal positions. Other variations include an *open bite,* in which the upper and lower incisors do not contact each other, or *closed bite,* in which there is an abnormal degree of overlapping (*overbite*) of the front teeth.

Diagnosis is made with the help of X-ray pictures, photographs of the face and mouth, medical histories, and plaster models of the patient's teeth and jaws. The plaster models are particularly important because the dentist can use them to make experimental reconstructions without touching an actual tooth of a patient. For example, the dentist can remove one or more teeth from the plaster model and reorganize neighboring teeth in the jawbones to get an accurate representation of the effects of extracting teeth or forcing teeth into different developmental situations.

Orthodontic Appliances

Once a plan of orthodontic treatment has been determined by the dentist, he may choose from a dozen or more types of bands, braces, or other orthodontic appliances, some removable and some nonremovable, for shaping the teeth and jaws of the patient. A typical orthodontic appliance may include small curved strips or loops of metal cemented to the surfaces of the

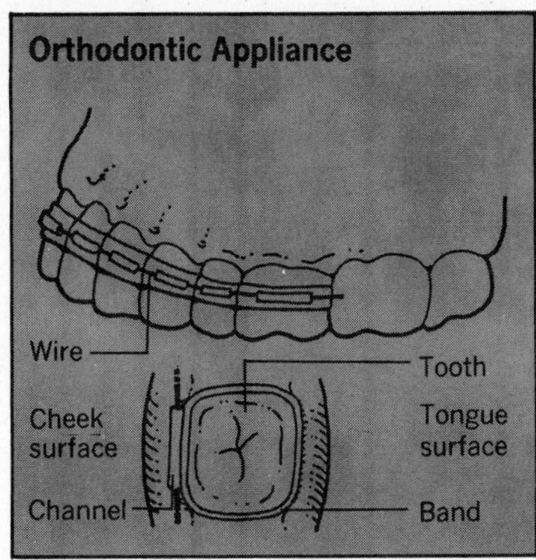

Orthodontic Appliance

teeth as anchors for arch wires that pass around the dental arch. Springs and specially designed rubber bands, called elastics, are sometimes used to bring about alignment of the two jaws, or to align teeth within a dental arch.

In addition to the appliances that are attached to and between the upper and lower dental arches, the dentist may prescribe the use of an elastic tape device with a strap that fits around the back of the patient's neck and is attached also to the arch wire inside the mouth, thus providing a force from outside the mouth to bring teeth into alignment.

Orthodontic appliances are custom-designed and built for the individual patient. This requires several rather long sessions or one all-day session in the dental chair while the appliance is being organized and properly anchored. Thereafter, the patient must return at regular intervals spaced a few weeks to a month apart so the dentist can make adjustments in the appliance, determine if any of the bands have pulled away from tooth surfaces, and prevent plaque from building up in places that the braces may make impervious to brushing.

The patient, meanwhile, must follow a diet that prohibits sticky foods or items that may damage the appliance or any of its parts. A conscientious program of oral hygiene, including regular cleaning by the dentist or hygienist, also is necessary because, as indicated above, it is more difficult to do a thorough job of cleaning the teeth when orthodontic appliances are in the mouth.

Orthodontics for Adults

Although orthodontic treatment originally was applied only to children, the technique has been requested with increasing frequency for the correction of a variety of facial and dental disorders. Receding chins, buck teeth, sunken cheeks, sunken mouths, and other abnormalities have been treated successfully in adults beyond the age of 40. Orthodontists have observed that adult patients usually are more patient and cooperative during the long periods of treatment than youngsters.

The upper age limit for orthodontic work has not really been established, but doctors at the National Institute of Dental Research believe it is possible to treat adult patients with protrusion of the upper jaw and related disfigurements until the age of 70. This is possible because the upper jaw does not completely unite with the frontal bone of the skull, according to the experts, until after the age of 70 in most people.

Orthodontic treatments can be relatively expensive and involve many visits to a dentist's office over a long period of time. Any parent of a prospective patient or a responsible older patient seeking orthodontic work for himself should have a frank discussion with the dentist regarding the time and money to be invested in the corrective procedures before making an agreement to begin the work. In nearly every case some arrangement can be made for covering the costs of dental work that is vital to the health and welfare of a patient.

23

Aches, Pains, Nuisances, Worries

And Other Things You Can Live With But Could Get Along Very Well Without

None of the variety of discomforts discussed in this chapter is a laughing matter. The best thing about most of them is that they will pass, given your commonsense attention, or will disappear if you follow your physician's advice. This includes taking the medications prescribed by your physician exactly as directed. In a few cases, such as allergies or gout, long-term drug therapy may be necessary on a self-supervised basis, once treatment has been established by a physician. Of course, when symptoms of any kind persist or get worse, you should waste no time in seeking a professional diagnosis.

There may be somebody, somewhere, who has never felt rotten a day in his life. But most of us are not so fortunate. Among the most common nuisance ailments are:

- upper respiratory infections
- allergies
- occasional headaches
- backaches
- weight problems
- weather discomforts
- disturbances of normal sleep patterns
- aching feet
- indigestion

The unpleasant feeling associated with any of these common disorders can almost always be banished with a modicum of care and thought. For example, allergic reactions to particular foods can be curtailed by identifying the offending food and avoiding it. Self-diagnosis and self-discipline can often enable one to cope with weight problems. A backache may be cured by attention to posture, or adjusting your office chair. A sensible approach to clothing and exposure can often do away with weather discomforts.

For many minor disorders and discomforts, particularly those caused by stress, massage may be the answer. Massage is a process that is at least 3,000 years old and has been used to help relieve tension, increase muscle tone, improve blood and oxygen circulation, and aid major body functions. Massage has also helped alleviate aches and pains resulting from exercise, improve posture, and increase joint flexibility. Among the disorders for which massage should not be used are osteoporosis, varicose veins, inflamed joints, herniated discs, tumors, and some cardiovascular problems.

Massage invariably involves kneading, manipulation, and methodical pressure on various body parts. The process should never be painful. The three kinds of massage in most common use are Swedish, a pleasant, muscle-kneading procedure; Shiatsu, or "acupressure," which depends on finger and hand pressure on so-called energy meridians in the body; and reflexology, a system that calls for pressure on various points of the foot.

When symptoms do not respond to

self-help—as when sporadic difficulty in sleeping burgeons into a string of near-sleepless nights, or when abdominal pain you interpret as indigestion is intense or frequent in spite of avoiding rich or heavy foods, it's time to see a physician.

The Common Cold and Upper Respiratory Infections

Common cold is the label attached to a group of symptoms that can be caused by one or more of some 20 different viruses. Colds are considered highly contagious, but some physicians think that people don't entirely catch others' colds—in a sense they catch their own. While the viruses that carry the infection are airborne and practically omnipresent, somebody in good health is usually less susceptible to a cold than someone who is run down. Both environmental factors (such as air pollution) and emotional ones (such as anxiety or depression) seem to increase susceptibility.

Symptoms

Symptoms differ from person to person and from cold to cold with the same person. Generally, a cold starts with sneezes, a running nose, teary eyes, and a stuffed head. Sometimes the nasal membranes become so swollen that a person can breathe only through the mouth; sometimes the senses of smell and taste simply disappear. The throat may be sore; a postnasal drip may cause a constant cough when the person is lying down at night.

When these symptoms are acute and are accompanied by fever and aching joints, the illness is usually referred to as influenza or "the flu." There are many different viruses that cause influenza, and new ones are always turning up. Unfortunately, there is as yet no medicine that can cure either a cold or a flu attack, although many people do get relief from symptoms by taking various cold remedies. Antibiotics are sometimes prescribed by doctors to prevent more serious bacterial diseases, such as pneumonia, from developing, but antibiotics are not effective against the cold viruses.

Treatment

Some people can get away with treating a cold with contempt and an occasional aspirin, and go about their business. Others are laid low for a few days. If you are the type who is really hit hard by a cold, it isn't coddling yourself to stay home for a couple of days. In any event, a simple cold usually runs its course, lasting anywhere from a few days to two weeks.

Discomfort can be minimized and recovery speeded by a few simple steps: extra rest and sleep, drinking more liquids than usual, and taking one or two aspirin tablets every four hours. Antihistamine preparations or nose drops should be avoided unless specifically prescribed by a physician.

A painful sore throat accompanied by fever, earache, a dry, hacking cough, or pains in the chest are symptoms that should be brought to the attention of a physician.

Prevention

Although taking massive doses of vitamin C at the first sign of a cold is said by some authorities to prevent the infection from developing, there is not yet general agreement on the effectiveness of this treatment.

Actually, there are several commonsense ways of reducing the risk of infection, particularly for those people who are especially susceptible to catching a cold. For most people, getting a proper amount of sleep, eating sensibly, avoiding exposure to sudden chill, trying to stay out of crowds, and trying to keep emotional tensions under control can increase resistance to colds and other minor respiratory infections.

Inoculation against particular types of viruses is recommended by many physicians in special cases: for pregnant women, for the elderly, and for those people who have certain chronic heart and lung diseases. Flu shots are effective against a particular virus or viruses for a limited period.

Allergies

Discomforts of various kinds are considered allergies when they are brought on by substances or conditions that ordinarily are harmless. Not too long ago, perturbed allergy sufferers would say things like:

"I can't use that soap because it gives me hives."

"Smelling roses makes me sneeze."

"Eating almonds gives me diarrhea."

Nowadays, such complaints are commonly recognized as indications of allergies.

Symptoms

Allergic symptoms can range from itching eyes, running nose, coughing, difficulty in breathing, welts on the skin, nausea, cramps, and even going into a state of shock, depending upon the severity of the allergic individual's response. Almost any part or system of the body may be affected, and almost anything can pose an allergic threat to somebody.

Allergens

Substances that trigger an allergic reaction are called *allergens.* The system of an allergic individual reacts to such substances as if they were germs, producing *antibodies* whose job it is to neutralize the allergens. But the body's defense mechanism overreacts: in the process of fighting off the effects of the allergens, various chemicals, particularly *histamines,* are dumped indiscriminately into the bloodstream. It is the overabundance of these "good" chemicals that causes the discomforts associated with allergies.

Allergens are usually placed in the following categories:

- Those that affect the respiratory tract, or *inhalants,* such as pollens, dust, smoke, perfumes, and various airborne, malodorous chemicals. These bring on sneezing, coughing, and breathing impairment.
- Food substances that affect the digestive system, typically eggs, seafood, nuts, berries, chocolate, and pork. These may cause not only nausea and diarrhea but also hives and other skin rashes.
- Medicines and drugs, such as penicillin, or a particular serum used in inoculations.
- Agents that act on the skin and mucous membranes, such as insecticides, poison oak, and poison ivy, particular chemical dyes, cosmetics, soaps, metals, leathers, and furs.
- Environmental agents, such as sunlight or excessive cold.
- Microbes, such as particular bacteria, viruses, and parasites.

Treatment

In general, approaches to treatment for allergies fall into three categories: removing or avoiding as many allergens from the environment as possible; using creams, inhalers, pills, and other medications to control the symptoms; and undergoing immunotherapy (allergy shots) to reduce the allergic response. The type of treatment selected often depends on test findings that indicate what is causing the allergic reaction; the tests may produce such identification quickly or they may have to be continued for weeks or months before the allergen is finally tracked down.

As soon as the source of the allergen is identified, the obvious course is to avoid it, if possible. Avoidance may not, however, be possible. Few persons can avoid breathing pollen in the spring and fall. Giving up a house pet may be almost as difficult, but may be necessary as a health or comfort measure.

New medications that control the symptoms of allergies have been marketed in recent years. Newer antihistamines, for example, relieve allergic reactions but do not cause the drowsiness associated with earlier medications. Other medicines that have been used to treat allergies include adrenaline, ephedrine, and cortisone. Aerosol drugs may be used to attack specific symptoms. Some, for example, may be inhaled to treat the linings of the nose and throat.

In addition to histamines, other body chemicals are released during an allergy "attack." Researchers have found that these chemicals include leukotrienes. Consequently, antileukotrienes have tested as medications.

Direct or specific immunotherapy constitutes the third approach to treatment of allergy. The shots are effective in reducing allergic responses. A person with a substance allergy receives increasing amounts of the substance over a period of years. For example, a person who is allergic to insect stings receives injections of the particular insect's venom.

A life-threatening allergic reaction calls for emergency treatment, usually with adrenalin. Physicians suggest that persons with very intense food allergies or who are allergic to insect stings should carry special kits that include an adrenalin-filled syringe. The allergy victims administer the medication to themselves in case of *anaphylaxis*— an acute, life-threatening response (see "Allergic Shock" in Ch. 31, *Medical Emergencies*).

Persons subject to severe, disabling allergy attacks by a known allergen should also carry a card describing both the allergen and the allergic reactions. Detailed information on the latest developments in allergy treatment is available from the Asthma and Allergy Foundation of America, 1302 18th St., NW, Suite 800, Washington, DC 20036. See also Ch. 24, *Allergies and Hypersensitivities.*

Headaches

The common headache is probably as ancient as primitive man. The headache, a pain or ache across the forehead or within the head, may be severe or mild in character, and can last anywhere from under half an hour to three or four days. It may be accompanied by dizziness, nausea, nasal stuffiness, or difficulty in seeing or hearing. It is not a disease or illness but a symptom.

Causes

Headaches in today's modern world can arise from any of a number of underlying causes. These include excessive drinking or smoking, lack of sleep, hunger, drug abuse, and eyestrain. Eyestrain commonly results from overuse of the eyes, particularly

Pokeweed. Poke or Pokeweed is a bush of the eastern United States. Eating uncooked leaves, the roots, or using the cooking water in a soup, causes abdominal cramps and vomiting.

Wisteria. All parts of the vine—leaves, flowers, or the seeds in the pod—may cause a prolonged nausea, abdominal pain, and vomiting.

Daffodil or Narcissus. Mistaking the bulb of this plant for an onion is the cause of most poisonings. These are characterized by repeated vomiting for several hours.

Rhododendron and Azalea. Some, but not all, of these bushes are poisonous. The one pictured from the state flower of California is toxic. Poisoning is characterized by a dangerous slowing of the heart and fall in blood pressure.

Jimson Weed. This weed is the cause of the first recorded plant poisoning in the United States, in the Jamestown Settlement. Eating the seeds or leaves causes the mouth to become dry, the pupils to dilate and reading becomes impossible.

Yellow Jessamine or Carolina Yellow Jasmine. Children have been poisoned sucking the nectar from the trumpet shaped flowers. The muscles become weak.

Dieffenbachia or Dumbcane. Biting into the leaf causes an immediate intense, painful burning in the mouth. This houseplant is the one most frequently involved in injury to young children.

Philodendron or Heart-Leaf Ivy. This produces a response similar to Dieffenbachia, but not usually as intense.

Tree Tobacco. Primarily a plant of the southwest, it has been responsible for a number of deaths, usually from eating the leaves prepared in a salad.

Golden Chain or Laburnum. All parts of the plant, but particularly the seeds in the flat pods, are poisonous. Intoxications rarely are serious.

Rosary Pea. This vine grows as a weed in Florida, the Virgin Islands and Puerto Rico, Mexico, and Hawaii. The toxic seeds are strung as jewelry and rosaries, or are used in novelty toys and, hence, may be found throughout the United States.

Oleander. All parts of this attractive bush contain a toxin similar to digitalis. Most poisonings have involved ingestion of the leaves. There may be some burning in the mouth and usually there is vomiting. The heart slows.

Poison Oak *Tom Stack and Associates*

Poison Sumac *James P. Rowan*

Poison Sumac in Autumn *Tom Stack and Associates*

Poison Ivy *Tom Stack and Associates*

Poison Ivy in Autumn *James P. Rowan*

Tom Stack and Associates

Tom Stack and Associates

Tom Stack and Associates

Tom Stack and Associates

James P. Rowan (Shedd Aquarium)

The poisonous mushroom Amanita Muscaria shows many different shapes, forms, and colors and grows in many parts of the United States.

Poisonous Fish

Scorpion Fish
Tom Stack and Associates

Lion Fish
James P. Rowan

Fire Coral
Tom Stack and Associates

Man-O-War
Tom Stack and Associates

Warty Stone Fish
Tom Stack and Associates

Venomous snakes and lizard

Gila Monster
Tom Stack and Associates

Mojave Rattlesnake
Tom Stack and Associates

Banded Rock Rattlesnake
James P. Rowan

Prairie Rattlesnake
Tom Stack and Associates

Copperhead Snake
Tom Stack and Associates

Black and Yellow Mud Dauber
Tom Stack and Associates

Giant Desert Hairy Scorpion
Tom Stack and Associates

Spiny Oak Slug Caterpillar
Tom Stack and Associates

Black Widow Spider
Tom Stack and Associates

Centipede
James P. Rowan (Lincoln Park Zoo)

Myopia

Hyperopia

Normal vision

(All photographs © R. Flanagan—Image Finders)

(Photos on the following four pages demonstrate normal and abnormal eyesight.)

Glaucoma

Retinal detachment

Astigmatism

Diabetic retinopathy

(All photographs © R. Flanagan—Image Finders)

Normal vision

Cataract

James P. Rowan

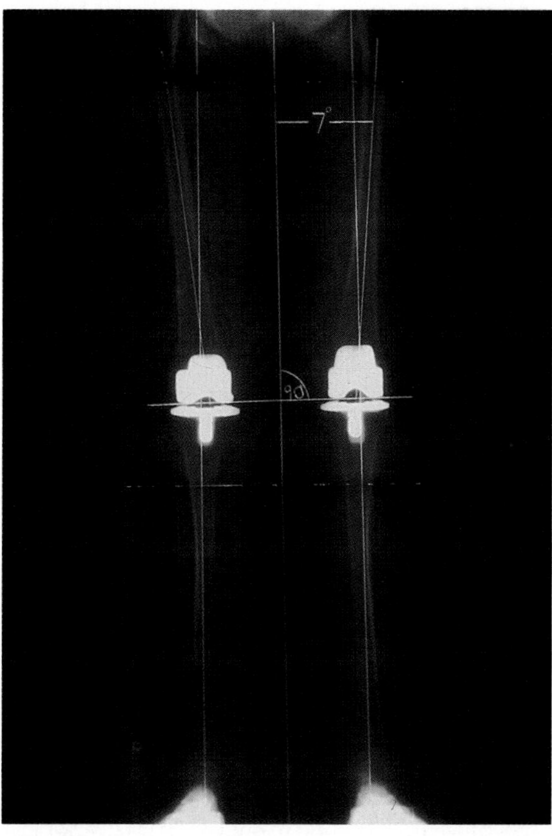

Total knee system
(Courtesy Dow Corning Wright)

Total knee system implanted
(Courtesy Dow Corning Wright)

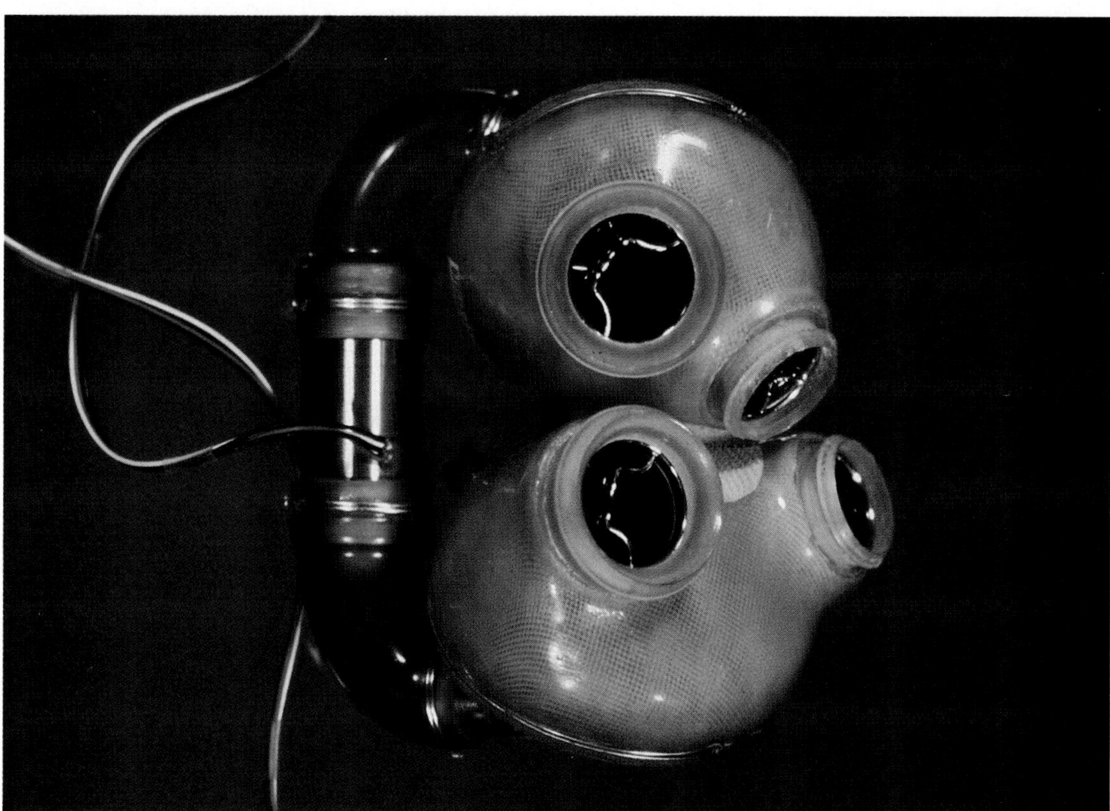

Jarvik-7 artificial heart
(© Hank Morgan, Photo Researchers, Inc.)

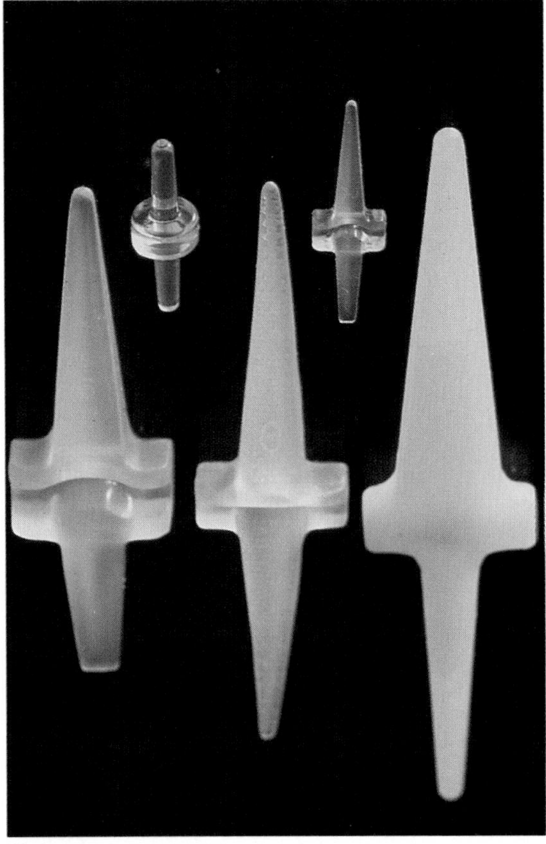
Various hand implants

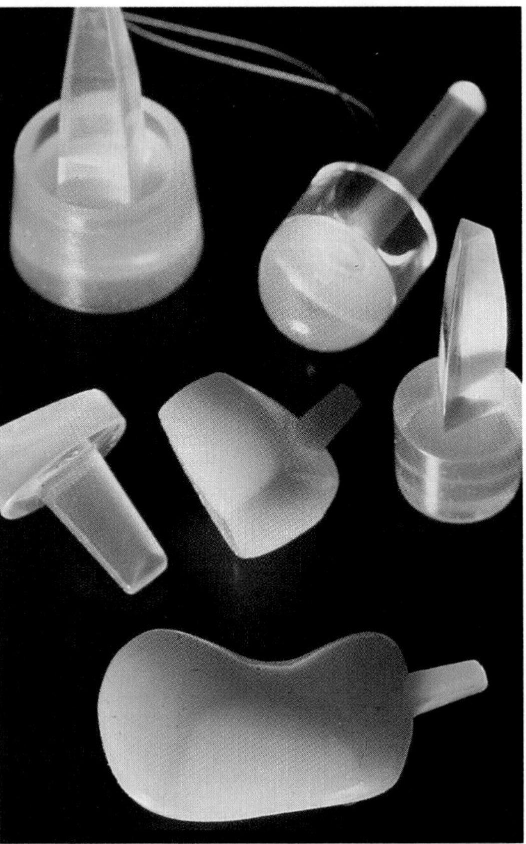
Toe, finger, wrist implants

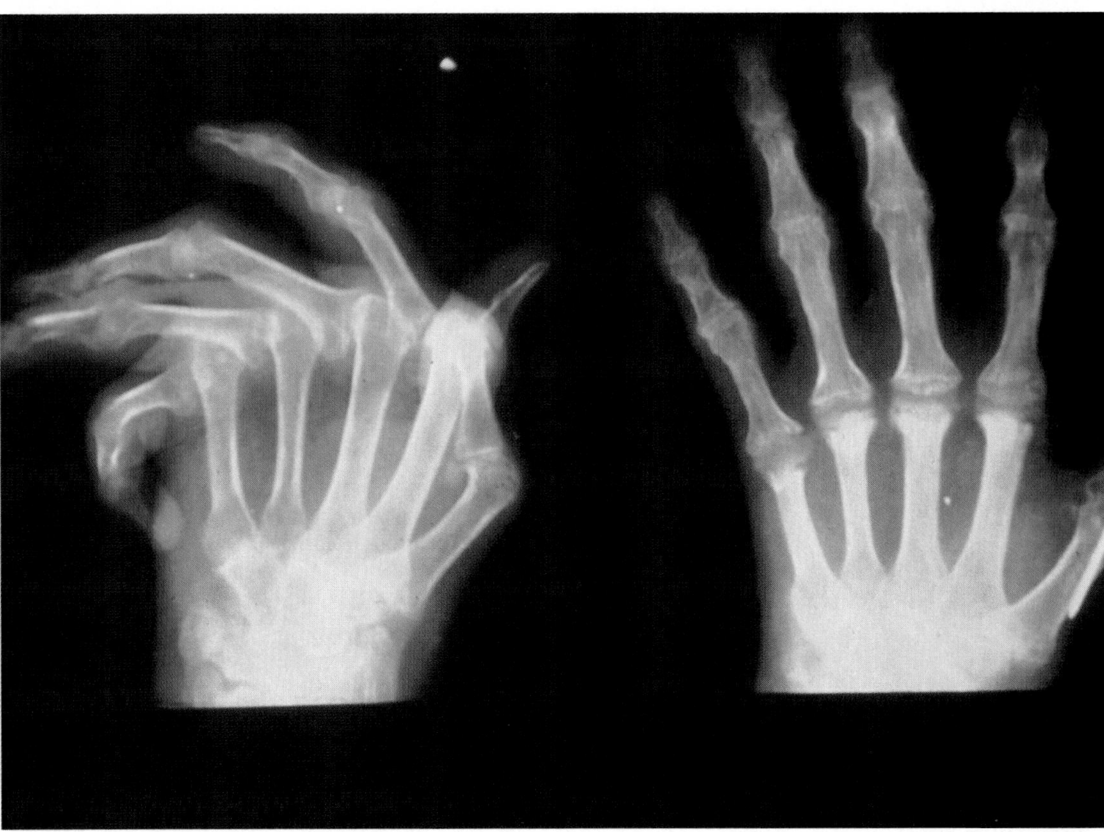
Deformed hand (left) and same hand after flexible implant resection arthroplasty

(All photographs courtesy Dow Corning Wright)

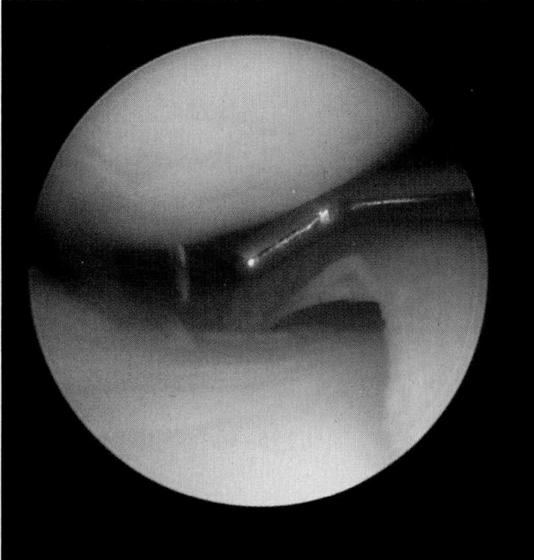

Arthroscopic knee surgery on torn ligaments

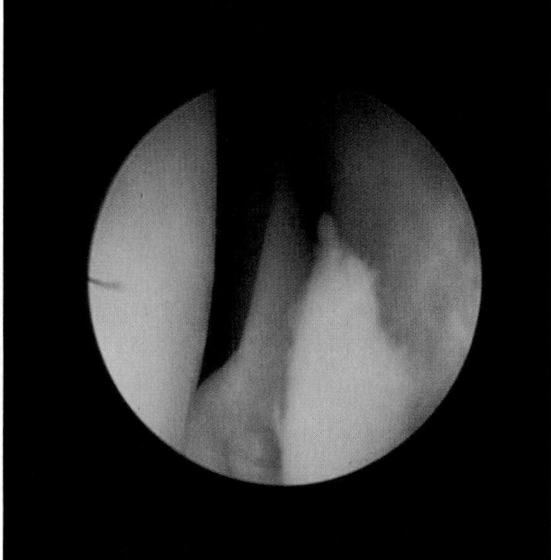

Arthroscopic photograph of knee joint

Intraocular lens implant in human eye

(All photographs © Photo Researchers, Inc.)

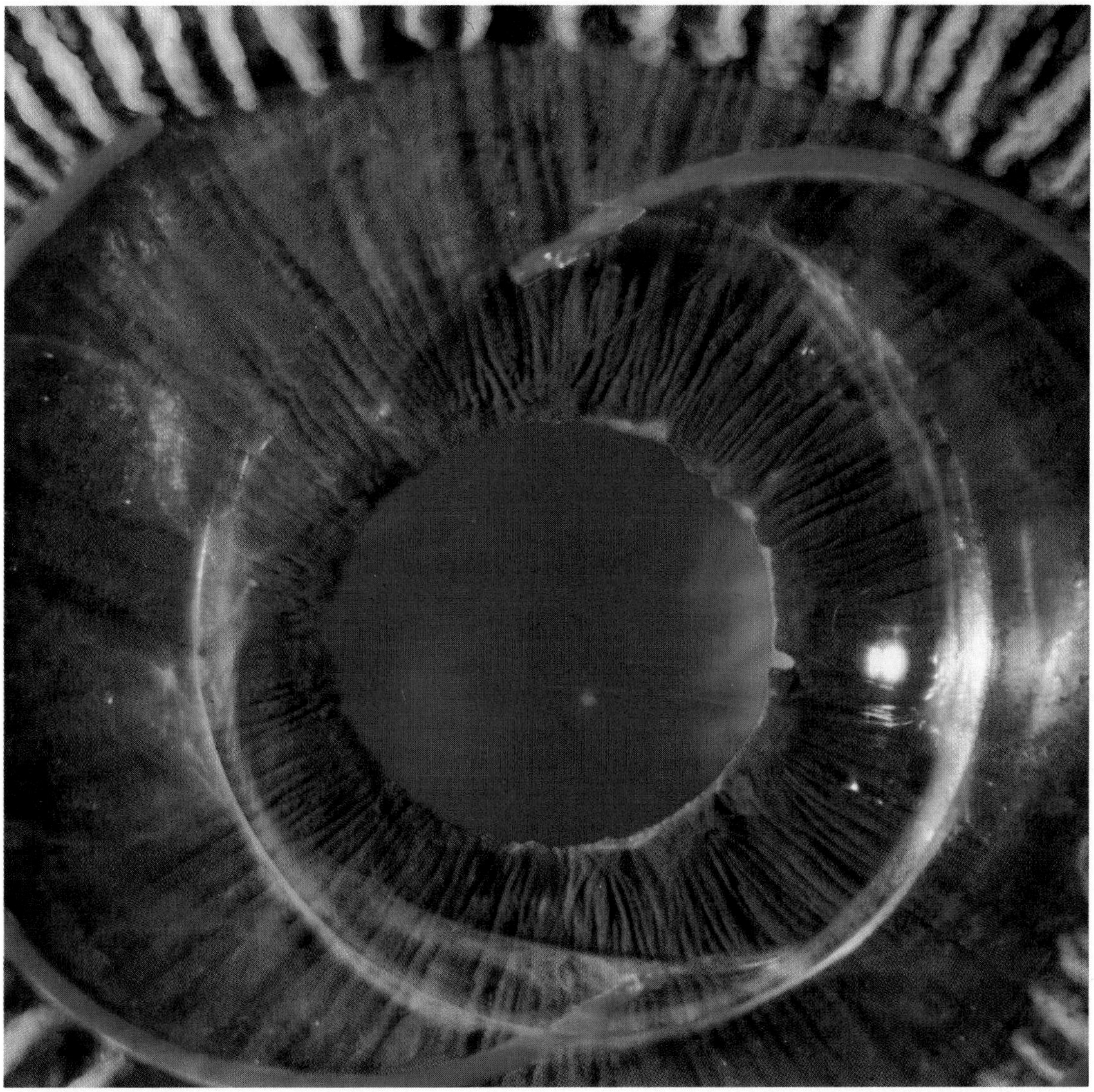

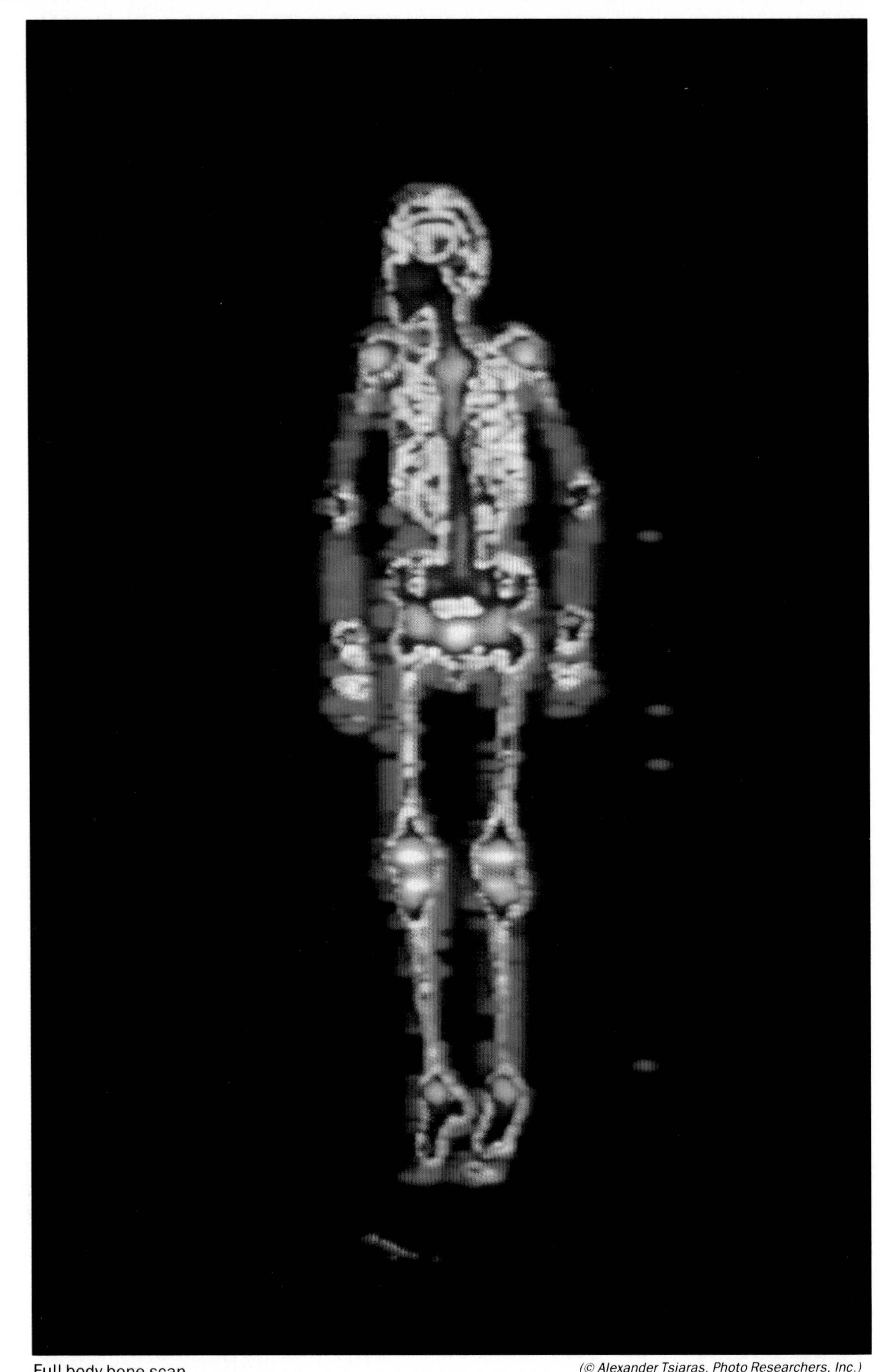

Full body bone scan

under glaring light, or from failure to correct defective vision.

Headaches can also be caused by exposure to toxic gases, such as carbon monoxide and sulfur dioxide, which are common components in polluted air. Some headaches are symptoms of illness or disease, including pneumonia, constipation, allergy, high blood pressure, and brain tumor. Finally, emotional strain or tension can cause headache by muscle constriction in the head and neck. Many of these causes give rise to the common physiological cause of headache—dilation of the blood vessels in the head.

Headaches may be suffered on an occasional basis, or they may be chronic. Chronic headaches are usually *tension* or *migraine headaches.*

Migraine

Migraine, also called *sick headache,* is a particularly severe, intense kind of headache. An attack may last several days and necessitate bed rest. Dizziness, sensitivity to light, and chills may accompany a migraine headache.

The exact cause of migraine is unknown, but researchers suspect a hereditary link, since the majority of migraine patients have one or more close relatives with migraine.

Migraine headaches can be precipitated by changes in body hormone balance (as from oral contraceptives), sudden changes in temperature, exposure to bright light or noise, shifts in barometric pressure, or by the intake of alcoholic beverages or the abuse of drugs. An attack can also be triggered by allergic responses to certain foods or beverages, such as chocolate or milk, and by emotional stress. Women, who outnumber men by a 2 to 1 ratio in the incidence of migraine, may have an attack brought on by premenstrual tension. Many migraine sufferers have been found to conform to a personality type characterized as compulsive; their standards of achievement are exacting, their manner of work meticulous, and they tend to avoid expression of their anxieties.

Anyone suffering from very severe or chronic headaches should see a physician and get a complete physical checkup.

Tension Headaches

Tension headaches can be avoided by getting adequate amounts of sleep and exercise and by learning to cope with frustrations and anxieties. Find time to relax each day, and resist the temptation to be a perfectionist or overachiever in all things. Tension headaches can be helped by neck massage, use of a heating pad, or a long, hot bath.

Headache Relief

Aspirin is often effective against headaches, but should be taken according to directions. A double dose is dangerous, and is not doubly effective. A cup of coffee or other caffeine beverage may prove helpful, because caffeine helps constrict blood vessels. In some cases headaches can be helped by nothing more than a few deep breaths of fresh air. Excess use of alcohol and tobacco should be avoided. If you must skip a meal, have a candy bar, piece of fruit, or some soup to prevent or relieve a hunger headache.

Take care of your eyes. Do not read in dim or glaring light. Have your eyes checked regularly, and if you have glasses, wear them when you need them.

Backaches

"Oh, my aching back" is probably the most common complaint among people past the age of 40. Most of the time, the discomfort—wherever it occurs, up or down the backbone—can be traced to some simple cause. However, there are continuous backaches that have their origin in some internal disorder that needs the attention of a physician. Among the more serious causes are kidney or pancreas disease, spinal arthritis, and peptic ulcer.

Some Common Causes

Generally a backache is the result of strain on the muscles, nerves, or ligaments of the spine. It can occur because of poor posture, carelessness in lifting or carrying heavy packages, sitting in one position for a long time in the wrong kind of chair, or sleeping on a mattress that is too soft. Backache often accompanies menstruation, and is common in the later stages of pregnancy. Emotional tension can also bring on back pain.

Prevention

In general, maintaining good posture during the waking hours and sleeping on a hard mattress at night—if necessary, inserting a bed board between the mattress and bedsprings—are the first line of defense against backaches. Anyone habitually carrying heavy loads of books or groceries, or even an overloaded attaché case, should make a habit of shifting the weight from arm to arm so that the spine doesn't always get pulled in one direction. Workers who are sedentary for most of the day at a desk or factory table should be sure that the chair they sit in provides firm support for back muscles and is the right height for the working surface.

Treatment

Most cases of simple backache respond to rest, aspirin, and the application of heat, applied by a hot water bottle or heating pad. In cases where the pain persists or becomes more acute, a physician should be consulted. He may find that the trouble is caused by the malfunctioning of an internal organ, or by pressure on the sciatic nerve (*sciatica*). With X rays he may also locate a slipped disk or other abnormality in the alignment of the vertebrae of the spine. See "Back Pain and Its Causes" in Ch. 7, *Diseases of the Skeletal System.*

Weight Problems

A few people can maintain the weight that is right for their body build without ever having to think about it. However, most experts believe that just about half the people in the United States may be risking shorter lives because they are too heavy. By one estimate, approximately one out of five American men and one out of four American women are 10 percent or more overweight, a group that may be called the borderline obese.

There is no longer any reasonable doubt that, if you are overweight, you have statistically a greater chance of high blood pressure, diabetes, and *atherosclerosis* (lumpy deposits in the arteries). And because atherosclerotic heart disease alone accounts for 20 percent of deaths among adults in the United States, it is understandable why physicians consider weight truly a national problem.

Causes

In practically all cases, weighing too much is the result of eating too much and exercising too little. In many cases, the food eaten is of the wrong kind and leisure time is used for riding around in a car rather than walking, or for watching television rather than playing tennis.

Many people like to think that they weigh too much only because they happen to like good food; but the real explanations may be considerably more complicated. In some cases, overeating has been found to have emotional sources: feelings of inadequacy; the need to compensate for a lack of affection or approval, or an unconscious desire to ward off the attention of the opposite sex. Psychological weight problems of this kind can be helped by consulting a psychiatrist or psychologist.

Treatment

There are many overweight people who merely need the support and encouragement that come from participating in a group effort, and for them, joining one of the various weight-control organizations can be extremely beneficial in taking off extra pounds and keeping them off.

Permanent results are rarely achieved by crash diets, faddish food combinations, or reducing pills. Not only are such solutions usually temporary; they may actually be harmful. See "Weight" in Ch. 27, *Nutrition and Weight Control,* for further information about weight problems.

Weather Discomforts

Using good sense about clothing, exercise, and proper diet is probably our best protection against the discomforts caused by extremes of temperature. Sometimes circumstances make this exercise of good sense impossible, with unpleasant but rarely serious results, if treatment is promptly administered. Following are some of the more common disorders resulting from prolonged exposure to excessive heat or cold, and what you can do to alleviate them.

Heat Cramps

In a very hot environment, a person may drink great quantities of water while "sweating buckets" of salty perspiration. Thus, the body's water is replaced, but its salt is not. This salt–water imbalance results in a feeling of faintness and dizziness accompanied by acute stomach cramps and muscle pains in the legs. When the symptoms are comparatively mild, they can be relieved by taking coated salt tablets in five-to-ten-grain doses with a full glass of tepid or cool—not iced—water. Salt tablets along with plenty of fluids should be taken regularly as a preventive measure by people who sweat a great deal during hot weather.

Sunburn

If you have not yet been exposed to much sun, as at the beginning of summer, limit your exposure at first to a period of 15 to 20 minutes, and avoid the sun at the hours around midday even if the sky is overcast. Remember, too, that the reflection of the sun's rays from water and beach sand intensifies their effect. Some suntan lotions give effective protection against burning, and some creams even prevent tanning; but remember to cover all areas of exposed skin and to reapply the lotion when it's been washed away after a swim.

Treatment

A sunburn is treated like any other burn, depending upon its severity. See "Burns" in Ch. 31, *Medical Emergencies.* If there is blistering, take care to avoid infection. Extensive blistering requires a physician's attention.

Heat Exhaustion

This condition is different from heatstroke or sunstroke, discussed below. Heat exhaustion sets in when large quantities of blood accumulate in the skin as the body's way of increasing its cooling mechanism during exposure to high temperatures. This in turn lowers the amount of blood circulating through the heart and decreases the blood supply to the brain. If severe enough, fainting may result. Other symptoms of heat exhaustion include unusual pallor and profuse cold perspiration. The pulse may be weak, and breathing shallow.

Treatment

A person suspected of having heat exhaustion should be placed in a reclining position, his clothing loosened or removed, and his body cooled with moist cloths applied to his forehead and wrists. If he doesn't recover promptly from a fainting spell, smelling salts can be held under his nose to revive him. As soon as he is conscious, he can be given salt tablets and a cool sugary drink—either tea or coffee—to act as a stimulant. Don't give the patient any alcoholic beverages.

Sunstroke or Heatstroke

Sunstroke is much more of an emergency than heat exhaustion and requires immediate attention. The characteristic symptom is extremely high body temperature brought on by cessation of perspiration. If hot, dry, flushed skin turns ashen gray, a physician must be called immediately. Too much physical activity during periods of high temperature and high humidity is a direct contributing cause.

Treatment

See "Heatstroke" in Ch. 31, *Medical Emergencies,* for a description of the emergency treatment recommended for this condition.

Chapped Skin

One of the most widespread discomforts of cold weather is *chapped skin.* In low temperatures, the skin's sebaceous glands produce fewer oils that lubricate and protect the skin, causing it to become dry. Continued exposure results in reddening and cracking. In this condition, the skin is especially sensitive to strong soaps.

Treatment

During cold, dry weather, less soap should be used when washing, a bath oil should be used when bathing, and a mild lotion or creme should be applied to protect the skin from the damaging effects of wind and cold. A night cream or lotion containing lanolin is also helpful, and the use of cleansing cream or oil instead of soap can reduce additional discomfort when cleansing chapped areas. The use of a colorless lip pomade is especially recommended for children when they play out of doors in cold, dry weather for any length of time.

Chilblain

A *chilblain* is a local inflammation of the skin brought on by exposure to cold. The condition commonly affects people overly sensitive to cold because of poor circulation. When the hands, feet, face, and ears are affected, the skin in these areas itches and burns, and may swell and turn reddish blue.

Treatment

The best way to avoid chilblains is to wear appropriate clothing during cold weather, especially warm socks, gloves, and ear coverings. The use of bed socks and a heating pad at night is also advisable. Once indoors, cold, wet feet should be dried promptly, gently, and thoroughly. Rubbing or massaging should be avoided, because these can cause further irritation. People who suffer from repeated attacks of chilblains should consult a physician for diagnosis of circulatory problems.

Frostbite

Frostbite is a considerably more serious condition than chilblains, because it means that a part or parts of the body have actually been frozen. The fingers or toes, the nose, and the ears are most vulnerable. If frostbitten, these areas turn numb and pale and feel cold when touched. The dangerous thing about frostbite is that pain may not be a warning. If the condition is not treated promptly, the temperature inside the tissues keeps going down and eventually cuts off blood circulation to the overexposed parts of the body. In such extreme cases, there is a possible danger of gangrene.

Treatment

In mild cases, prompt treatment can slowly restore blood circulation. The frozen parts should be rewarmed *slowly* by covering them with warm clothing or by soaking them in lukewarm water. Nothing hot should be applied—neither hot water nor a heating pad. Nor should the patient be placed too close to a fireplace or radiator. Because the affected tissues can be easily bruised, they should not be massaged or rubbed. If you are in doubt about restoring circulation, a physician should be called promptly or the patient taken to a hospital for emergency treatment.

Sleep and the Lack of It

Until rather recently, it was assumed that sleep was the time when the body rested and recovered from the activities of wakefulness. Although there is still a great deal to learn about why we sleep and what happens when we are sleeping, medical researchers have now identified several different phases of sleep, all of them necessary over the long run, but some more crucial than others.

How much sleep a person needs varies a great deal from individual to individual; and the same individual may need more or less at different times. Children need long periods of unbroken sleep; the elderly seem to get along on very little. No matter what a person's age, too little sleep over too long a time leads to irritability, exhaustion, and giddiness.

Insomnia

Almost everybody has gone through periods when it is difficult or impossible to fall asleep. Excitement before bedtime, temporary worries about a pressing problem, spending a night in an unfamiliar place, changing to a different bed, illness, physical discomfort because of extremes of temperature—any of these circumstances can interfere with normal sleep patterns.

But this is quite different from *chronic insomnia,* when a person consistently has trouble falling asleep for no apparent reason. If despite all your commonsense approaches insomnia persists, a physician should be consulted about the advisability of taking a tranquilizer or a sleeping pill. Barbiturates should not be taken unless prescribed by a physician.

The Vulnerable Extremities

Aches and pains in the legs and feet occur for a wide variety of reasons, some trivial and easily corrected, others serious enough to require medical attention. Those that originate in such conditions as arthritis and rheumatism can often be alleviated by aspirin or some of the newer prescription medications.

Gout

Gout, which is usually a metabolic disorder, is a condition that especially affects the joint of the big toe, and sometimes the ankle joint, causing the area to become swollen, hot, and acutely painful. Although the specific cause of gout is not yet clearly understood, the symptoms can be alleviated by special medication prescribed by a physician. An attack of gout can be triggered by a wide variety of causes: wearing the wrong shoes, eating a diet too rich in fats, getting a bad chill, surgery in some other part of the body, or chronic emotional anxiety, as well as the use of certain medicines, such as diuretics ("waterpills"). See also "Gout" in Ch. 7, *Diseases of the Skeletal System.*

Fallen Arches

Fallen arches can cause considerable discomfort because the body's weight is carried on the ligaments of the inside of the foot rather than on the sole. When the abnormality is corrected by orthopedic shoes with built-in arches for proper support, the pressure on the ligaments is relieved. A physician rather than a shoe salesman should be consulted for a reliable diagnosis. In some cases, the physician may also recommend special exercises to strengthen the arch.

Flat Feet

Flat feet can usually be revealed by a simple test—making a footprint on level earth or hard-packed sand. If the print is solid rather than indented by a curve along the big-toe side of the foot, the foot is flat. Aching ligaments in the area of the instep are often a result, but can be relieved by proper arch supports inside the shoes. Corrective arch supports are particularly important for young children, for anyone who is overweight, and for anyone who has to stand a great deal of the time.

Blisters

Although blisters are sometimes a sign of allergy, fungus infection, or sunburn, they most commonly appear on the feet because of the friction of a shoe or of hosiery that does not fit properly. A *water blister* is a collection of lymph that forms inside the upper level of the skin; a *blood blister* goes down deeper and contains some blood released from broken capillaries. A normal amount of walking in shoes and hosiery that fit comfortably—neither too loose nor too tight—rarely results in blisters. When blisters do appear, it is best to protect them from further friction by the use of a sterile bandage strip.

Treatment

A blister that causes acute pain when one is walking can be treated as follows: after cleaning the area with soap and water, pat it dry and swab it with rubbing alcohol. Sterilize the tip of a needle in a flame, let it cool a little, and then puncture the edge of the blister, absorbing the liquid with a sterile gauze. The loose skin can be removed with manicure scissors that have been sterilized by boiling for ten minutes. The surface of raw skin should then be covered with an adhesive bandage. This procedure is best done before bedtime so that healing can begin before shoes are worn again.

If redness appears around the area of any blister and inflammation appears to be spreading, a physician should be consulted promptly.

Bunions

A *bunion* is a deformation in the part of the foot that is joined by the big toe. The swelling and pain at the joint is caused by inflammation of the *bursa* (a fluid-filled sac) that lubricates the joint. Although bunions often develop because of wearing shoes that don't fit correctly, they most frequently accompany flat feet. Pain that is not too severe can be relieved by the application of heat; the condition may eventually be cured by doing foot exercises recommended by a physician, who will also help in the choice of correct footwear. A bunion that causes acute pain and difficulty in walking can be treated by a simple surgical procedure.

Calluses

A *callus* is an area of the skin that has become hard and thick as a result of constant friction or pressure against it. Pain results when the callus is pressed against a nerve by poorly fitting shoes. A painful callus can be partially removed by rubbing it—very cautiously—with a sandpaper file or a pumice stone sold for that purpose. The offending shoes should then be discarded for correctly fitted ones. Foot care by a podiatrist is recommended for anyone with recurring calluses and corns (see below), and especially for those people who have diabetes or any disorder of the arteries.

Corns

A *corn* is a form of callus that occurs on or between the toes. When the thickening occurs on the outside of the toe, it is called a *hard corn;* when it is located between the toes, it is called a *soft corn.* The pain in the affected area is caused by pressure of the hard inside core of the corn against the tissue beneath it. The most effective treatment for corns is to wear shoes that are the right size and fit. Corns can be removed by a podiatrist, but unless footwear fits properly, they are likely to return.

Treatment

To remove a corn at home, the toes should be soaked in warm water for about ten minutes and dried. The corn can be rubbed away with an emery file, or it can be treated with a few drops of 10 percent salicylic acid in collodion, available from any druggist. Care should be exercised in applying the solution so that it doesn't reach surrounding tissue, because it is highly irritating to normal skin. The area can then be covered with a corn pad to relieve pressure. This treatment may have to be repeated several times before the corn becomes soft enough to lift out. Diabetics or those suffering from any circulatory disorder should never treat their own corns.

Housemaid's Knee

Housemaid's knee is actually a form of *bursitis,* in which the fluid-filled bursa in front of the kneecap becomes inflamed by injury or excessive pressure, as because of constant kneeling. When the inflammation is mild, it can usually be corrected by rest. In the acute stage, the knee becomes swollen and painful, particularly when bent. It is especially prone to infection if scratched, bruised, or cut. Acute housemaid's knee is usually treated by anti-inflammatory-type drugs, injections of cortisone, or surgery under local anesthesia in a physician's office. Anyone whose daily activities involve a great deal of kneeling should make a habit of using a thick rubber mat.

Tennis Elbow

This disorder can affect not only tennis players but also people who have injured their elbow joint or subjected it to various stresses and strains. It may be a form of bursitis similar in nature to housemaid's knee, but it is more correctly called *tendinitis,* that is, an inflammation of the tendons that can affect any joint in the arms and legs. Rest and the application of heat usually relieve the painful symptoms. If the pain becomes acute, a physician should be consulted.

Tenosynovitis

Tenosynovitis is an inflammation of a tendon sheath. One of the commoner sites of trouble is that of the wrist muscles. It can be caused by injury, infection, or constant use of the wrist muscles in piano playing, typing, or some form of labor involving the wrist. The condition is usually treated by splinting the wrist and resting it for a while. Pain can be relieved with aspirin.

Writer's Cramp

Writer's cramp is a muscular pain caused by constant use of a set of muscles for a particular activity. The same set of muscles will function with no difficulty when the activity is changed. The best way to treat the discomfort is to give the muscles a rest from the habitual activity and to relieve the pain with heat and aspirin.

Other Muscle Cramps

A sharp cramp or pain in the leg muscles, and sometimes in the arm, can occur because blood circulation has been impaired, either by hardening of the arteries or because of undue pressure, such as habitually sitting with one leg tucked under the upper thigh. The cramp is usually relieved either by changing the activity involved or by shifting the position of the affected limb. Constant or acute muscle cramps should be brought to the attention of a physician.

The Exposed Integument

Common skin and scalp annoyances such as rashes, itches, dandruff, excessive perspiration, and infections of various kinds (such as athlete's foot and ringworm), as well as acne, wrinkles, and baldness, are discussed in Ch. 21, *Skin and Hair.*

Splinters

If lodged superficially in the hand, a splinter will usually work its own way out, but a splinter of no matter what size in the sole of the foot must be removed promptly to avoid its becoming further embedded by pressure and causing infection. The simplest method of removal is to pass a needle through a flame; let the needle cool; then, after the skin surface has been washed with soap and water or swabbed with alcohol, press the point of the needle against the skin, scraping slightly until the tail of the splinter is visible and loosened. It can then be pulled out with tweezers that have been sterilized in boiling water or alcohol.

Hangnails

Hangnails are pieces of partly living skin torn from the base or side of the fingernail, thus opening a portion of the underskin to infection. A hangnail can cause considerable discomfort. It should not be pulled or bitten off; but the major part of it can be cut away with manicuring scissors. The painful and exposed area should then be washed with soap and water and covered with a sterile adhesive bandage. Hangnails are likely to occur when the skin is dry. They can therefore be prevented by the regular use of a hand cream or lotion containing lanolin.

"Normal" Disorders of the Blood and Circulation

Almost everybody is bothered occasionally by minor disturbances of the circulatory system. Most of the time these disturbances are temporary, and in many cases where they are chronic they may be so mild as not to interfere with good health. Among the more common disturbances of this type are the following.

Anemia

Anemia is a condition in which there is a decrease in the number of red blood cells or in the hemoglobin content of the red blood cells. *Hemoglobin* is the compound that carries oxygen to the body tissues from the lungs. Anemia in itself is not a disease but rather a symptom of some other disorder, such as a deficiency of iron in the diet; excessive loss of blood resulting from an injury or heavy menstrual flow; infection by industrial poisons; or kidney or bone marrow disease. A person may also develop anemia as a result of hypersensitivity (allergy) to various medicines.

In the simple form of anemia, caused by a deficiency of iron in the diet, the symptoms are rarely severe. There may be feelings of fatigue, a loss of energy, and a general lack of vitality. Deficiency anemia is especially common among children and pregnant women, and can be corrected by adding foods high in iron to the diet, such as liver, lean meat, leafy green vegetables, whole wheat bread, and dried peas and beans.

If the symptoms persist, a physician should be consulted for diagnosis and treatment. For more information on anemia, see "Diseases of the Blood" in Ch. 9, *Diseases of the Circulatory System.*

Varicose Veins

Varicose veins are veins that have become ropy and swollen, and are therefore visible in the leg, sometimes bulging on the surface of the skin. They are the result of a sluggish blood flow (poor circulation), often combined with weakened walls of the veins themselves. The condition is common in pregnancy and occurs frequently among people who find it necessary to sit or stand in the same position for extended periods of time. A tendency to develop varicose veins may be inherited.

Even before the veins begin to be visible, there may be such warning symptoms as leg cramps, feelings of fatigue, or a general achiness. Unless the symptoms are treated promptly, the condition may worsen, and if the blood flow becomes increasingly impeded, ulcers may develop on the lower area of the leg.

Treatment

Mild cases of varicose veins can be kept under control, or even corrected, by giving some help to circulation, as follows:

- Several times during the day, lie flat on your back for a few minutes, with the legs slightly raised.
- Soak the legs in warm water.
- Exercise regularly.

- Wear lightly reinforced stockings or elastic stockings to support veins in the legs.

If varicose veins have become severe, a physician should be consulted. He or she may advise injection treatment or surgery. See also "The Inflammatory Disorders" in Ch. 9, *Diseases of the Circulatory System.*

Chronic Hypertension

Hypertension, commonly known as *high blood pressure,* is a condition that may be a warning of some other disease. In many cases, it is not in itself a serious problem and has no one underlying specific cause: this is called *functional, essential,* or *chronic hypertension.* The symptoms of breathing difficulty, headache, weakness, or dizziness that accompany high blood pressure can often be controlled by medicines that bring the pressure down, by sedatives or tranquilizers, and in cases where overweight is a contributing factor, by a change in diet, or by a combination of these.

More serious types of high blood pressure can be the result of kidney disease, glandular disturbances, or diseases of the circulatory system. Acute symptoms include chronic dizziness or blurred vision. Any symptoms of high blood pressure call for professional advice and treatment. See "Hypertensive Heart Disease" in Ch. 10, *Heart Disease.*

Tachycardia

Tachycardia is the medical name for a condition that most of us have felt at one time or another—abnormally rapid heartbeat, or a feeling that the heart is fluttering, or pounding too quickly. The condition can be brought on by strong feelings of fear, excitement, or anxiety, or by overtaxing the heart with sudden exertion or too much exercise. It may also be a sign of heart disease, but in such cases, it is usually accompanied by other symptoms.

The most typical form of occasional rapid heartbeat is called *paroxysmal tachycardia,* during which the beat suddenly becomes twice or three times as fast as it is normally, and then just as suddenly returns to its usual tempo. When the paroxysms are frequent enough to be disturbing and can be traced to no specific source, they can be prevented by medicines prescribed by a physician.

Nosebleed

Nosebleeds are usually the result of a ruptured blood vessel. They are especially common among children, and among adults with high blood pressure. If the nosebleed doesn't taper off by itself, the following measures should be taken: the patient should be seated—but not lying down—clothing loosened, and a cold compress placed on the back of the neck and the nose. The soft portion of the nostril may be pressed gently against the bony cartilage of the nose for at least six minutes, or rolled wads of absorbent cotton may be placed inside each nostril, with part of the cotton sticking out to make its removal easier. The inserted cotton should be left in place for several hours and then gently withdrawn.

Fainting

Fainting is a sudden loss of consciousness, usually caused by an insufficient supply of blood and oxygen to the brain. Among the most common causes of fainting are fear, acute hunger, the sight of blood, and prolonged standing in a room with too little fresh air. Fainting should not be confused with a loss of consciousness resulting from excessive alcohol intake or insulin shock. A person about to faint usually feels dizzy, turns pale, and feels weak in the knees.

Treatment

If possible, the person should be made to lie down, or to sit with his head between his knees for several minutes. Should he lose consciousness, place him so that his legs are slightly higher than his head, loosen his clothing, and see that he gets plenty of fresh air. If smelling salts or aromatic spirits of ammonia are available, they can be held under his nose. With these procedures, he should revive in a few minutes. If he doesn't, a physician should be called.

Troubles Along the Digestive Tract

From childhood on, most people are occasionally bothered by minor and temporary disturbances connected with digestion. Most of the disturbances listed below can be treated successfully with common sense and, if need be, a change in habits.

The Mouth

The digestive processes begin in the mouth, where the saliva begins chemically to break down some foods into simpler components, and the teeth and the tongue start the mechanical breakdown. Disorders of the teeth such as a malocclusion or poorly fitted dentures that interfere with proper chewing, should promptly be brought to the attention of a dentist.

Inflammation of the Gums

Also known as *gingivitis,* inflammation of the gums is caused by the bacteria that breed in food trapped in the spaces between the gums and the teeth. The gums become increasingly swollen, may bleed easily, and be sore enough to interfere with proper chewing. The condition can be prevented by cleaning the teeth thoroughly and frequently, which includes the use of dental floss or the rubber tip on the toothbrush to remove any food particles lodged in the teeth after eating. Because gingivitis can develop into the more serious condition of *pyorrhea,* persistent gum bleeding or soreness should receive prompt professional treatment. See Ch. 22, *The Teeth and Gums.*

Canker Sores

Canker sores are small ulcers inside the lips, mouth, and cheeks. Their specific cause is unknown, but they seem to accompany or follow a virus infection, vitamin deficiency, or emotional stress. They may be additionally irritated by citrus fruit, chocolate, or nuts. A canker sore usually clears up in about a week without special treatment. A bland mouth rinse will relieve pain and, in some cases, speed the healing process.

Coated Tongue

Although a coated tongue is commonly supposed to be a sure sign of illness, this is not the case. The condition may occur because of a temporary lack of saliva.

Glossitis

Glossitis, an inflammation of the tongue causing the tongue's surface to become bright red or, in some cases, glazed in appearance, may be a symptom of an infection elsewhere in the body. It may also be a symptom of anemia or a nutritional deficiency, or it may be an adverse reaction to certain forms of medication. If the inflammation persists and is accompanied by acute soreness, it should be called to a physician's attention.

Halitosis or Bad Breath

Contrary to the millions of commercial messages on television and in print, bad breath cannot be cured by any mouthwash, lozenge, spray, or antiseptic gargle now on the market. These products can do no more than mask the odor until the basic cause is diagnosed and cured. Among the many conditions that may result in bad breath (leaving out such fleeting causes as garlic and onions) are the following: an infection of the throat, nose, or mouth; a stomach or kidney disorder; pyorrhea; respiratory infection; tooth decay; improper mouth hygiene; and excessive drinking and smoking. Anyone who has been made self-conscious about the problem of bad breath should ask his physician or dentist whether his breath is truly offensive and if it is, what to do about it.

Gastritis

Gastritis, one of the most common disorders of the digestive system, is an inflammation of the lining of the stomach that may occur in acute, chronic, or toxic form. Among the causes of *acute gastritis* are various bacterial or viral infections; overeating, especially heavy or rich foods; excessive drinking of alcoholic beverages; or food poisoning. An attack of acute gastritis may be severely painful, but the discomfort usually subsides with proper treatment. The first symptom is typically sharp stomach cramps, followed by a bloated feeling, loss of appetite, headache, and nausea. When vomiting occurs, it rids the stomach of the substance causing the attack but usually leaves the patient temporarily weak. If painful cramps persist and are accompanied by fever, a physician should be consulted about the possibility of medication for bacterial infection. For a few days after an attack of acute gastritis, the patient should stay on a bland diet of easily digested foods, taken in small quantities.

Toxic Gastritis

Toxic gastritis is usually the result of swallowing a poisonous substance, causing vomiting and possible collapse. It is an emergency condition requiring prompt first aid treatment and the attention of a physician. See "Poisoning" in Ch. 31, *Medical Emergencies.*

Chronic Gastritis

Chronic gastritis is a recurrent or persisting inflammation of the stomach lining over a lengthy period. The condition has the symptoms associated with indigestion, especially pain after eating. It can be caused by excessive drinking of alcoholic beverages, constant tension or anxiety, or deficiencies in the diet. The most effective treatment for chronic gastritis is a bland diet from which caffeine and alcohol have been eliminated. Heavy meals should be avoided in favor of eating small amounts at frequent intervals. A tranquilizer or a mild sedative prescribed by a physician may reduce the tensions that contribute to the condition. If the discomfort continues, a physician should be consulted about the possibility of ulcers. See Ch. 11, *Diseases of the Digestive System.*

Gastroenteritis

Gastroenteritis is an inflammation of the lining of both the stomach and the intestines. Like gastritis, it can occur in acute or toxic forms as a result of food poisoning, excessive alcohol intake, viral or bacterial infections, or food allergies. Vomiting, diarrhea, and fever may be more pronounced and of longer duration. As long as nausea and vomiting persist, no food or fluid should be taken; when these symptoms cease, a bland, mainly fluid diet consisting of strained broth, thin cereals, boiled eggs, and tea is best. If fever continues and diarrhea doesn't taper off, a physician should be called.

Diarrhea

Diarrhea is a condition in which bowel movements are abnormally frequent and liquid. It may be accompanied by cramps, vomiting, thirst, and a feeling of tenderness in the abdominal region. Diarrhea is always a symptom of some irritant in the intestinal tract; among possible causes are allergy, infection by virus or bacteria, accidentally swallowed poisonous substances, or excessive alcohol. Brief attacks are sometimes caused by emotions, such as overexcitement or anxiety.

Diarrhea that lasts for more than two days should be diagnosed by a physician to rule out a more serious infection, a glandular disturbance, or a tumor. Mild attacks can be treated at home by giving the patient a light, bland diet, plenty of fluids, and the prescribed dosage of a kaolin-pectin compound available at any drugstore.

Constipation

Many people have the mistaken notion that if they don't have a bowel movement every day, they must be constipated. This is not necessarily so. From a physician's viewpoint, constipation is determined not by an arbitrary schedule of when the bowel should be evacuated but by the individual's discomfort and other unpleasant symptoms. In too many instances, overconcern and anxiety about bowel movements may be the chief cause of constipation.

The watery waste that results from the digestion of food in the stomach and small intestine passes into the large intestine, or colon, where water is absorbed from the waste. If the waste stays in the large intestine for too long a time, so much water is removed that it becomes too solid and compressed to evacuate easily. The efficient removal of waste material from the large intestine depends on wavelike muscular contractions. When these waves are too weak to do their job properly, as often happens in the elderly or the excessively sedentary, a physician may recommend a mild laxative or mineral oil.

Treatment

Constipation is rarely the result of an organic disorder. In most cases, it is caused by poor health habits; when these are corrected, the disorder corrects itself. Often, faulty diet is a major factor. Make sure that meals contain plenty of roughage in the form of whole-grain cereals, fruit, and leafy green vegetables. Figs, prunes, and dates should be included from time to time. Plenty of liquid intake is important, whether in the form of juices, soups, or large quantities of water. Scheduling a certain amount of exercise each day strengthens the abdominal muscles and stimulates muscle activity in the large intestine. Confronting the sources of worries and anxieties, if necessary with a trained therapist, may also be helpful.

An enema or a laxative should be considered only once in a while rather than as regular treatment. The colon should be given a chance to function properly without relying on artificial stimulation. If constipation resists these commonsense approaches, the problem should be talked over with a physician.

Hemorrhoids

Hemorrhoids, commonly called *piles,* are swollen veins in the mucous membrane inside or just outside the rectum. When the enlargement is slight, the only discomfort may be an itching sensation in the area. Acute cases are accompanied by pain and bleeding. Hemorrhoids are a very common complaint and occur in people of all ages. They are usually the result of straining to eliminate hard, dry stools. The extra pressure causes a fold of the membranous rectal lining to slip down, thus pinching the veins and irritating them.

Because hemorrhoids may be a symptom of a disorder other than constipation, they should be treated by a physician. If neglected, they may bleed frequently and profusely enough to cause anemia. Should a blood clot develop in an irritated vein, surgery may be necessary.

Treatment

Advertised cures should be avoided because they are not only ineffective but can cause additional irritation. Laxatives and cathartics, which may temporarily solve the problem of constipation, are likely to aggravate hemorrhoids.

If pain or bleeding becomes acute, a physician should be consulted promptly. Treatment can be begun at home. Sitting for several minutes in a hot bath in the morning and again in the evening (more frequently if necessary) will provide temporary relief. Preventing constipation is of the utmost importance.

Anal Fissure

This is a condition in which a crack or

split or ulcerated place develops in the area of the two anal sphincters, or muscle rings, that control the release of feces. Such breaks in the skin are generally caused by something sharp in the stool, or by the passage of an unusually hard and large stool. Although discomfort often accompanies a bowel movement when there is a fissure, the acute pain typically comes afterward. Healing is difficult because the injured tissue is constantly open to irritation. If the condition persists, it usually has to be treated by a minor surgical procedure. Intense itching in this area is called *anal pruritis*.

Minor Ailments in the Air Pipes

In addition to all the respiratory discomforts that go along with the common cold, there are various other ailments that affect breathing and normal voice production.

Bronchitis

Usually referred to as a chest cold, *bronchitis* is an inflammation of the bronchial tubes that connect the windpipe and the lungs. If bronchitis progresses down into the lungs, it can develop into pneumonia. Old people and children are especially susceptible to acute bronchitis. The symptoms include pain in the chest, a feeling of fatigue, and a nagging cough. If the infection is bacterial, it will respond to antibiotics. If it is viral, there are no specific medicines. The attack usually lasts for about ten days, although recovery may be speeded up with bed rest and large fluid intake.

Chronic Bronchitis

Chronic bronchitis is a condition that may recur each winter, or may be present throughout the year in the form of a constant cough. The condition is aggravated by smoking and by irritants such as airborne dust and smog. The swollen tissues and abnormally heavy discharge of mucus interfere with the flow of air from the lungs and cause shortness of breath. Medicines are available that lessen the bronchial phlegm and make breathing easier. People with chronic bronchitis often sleep better if they use more than one pillow and have a vaporizer going at night.

Coughing

Coughing is usually a reflex reaction to an obstruction or irritation in the trachea (windpipe), pharynx (back of mouth and throat), or bronchial tubes. It can also be the symptom of a disease or a nervous habit. For a simple cough brought on by smoking too much or breathing bad air, medicines can be taken that act as sedatives to inhibit the reflex reaction. Inhaling steam can loosen the congestion (a combination of swollen membranes and thickened mucus) that causes some types of coughs, and hot drinks such as tea or lemonade help to soothe and relax the irritated area. Constant coughing, especially when accompanied by chest pains, should be brought to a physician's attention. For a discussion of whooping cough and croup, see the respective articles under the "Alphabetic Guide to Child Care" in Ch. 2, *The First Dozen Years*.

Laryngitis

Laryngitis is an inflammation of the mucous membrane of the larynx (voice box) that interferes with breathing and causes the voice to become hoarse or disappear altogether. This condition may accompany a sore throat, measles, or whooping cough, or it may result from an allergy. Prolonged overuse of the voice, a common occupational hazard of singers and teachers, is also a cause. The best treatment for laryngitis is to go to bed, keep the room cool, and put moisture into the air from a vaporizer, humidifier, or boiling kettle. Don't attempt to talk, even in a whisper. Keep a writing pad within arm's reach and use it to spare your voice. Drinking warm liquids may help to relieve some of the discomfort. If you must go out, keep the throat warmly protected.

Chronic laryngitis may result from too many acute laryngitis attacks, which can cause the mucous membrane to become so thick and tough that the voice remains permanently hoarse. The sudden onset of hoarseness that lasts for more than two weeks calls for a physician's diagnosis.

Hiccups

Hiccups (also spelled *hiccoughs*) are contractions of the diaphragm, the great muscle responsible for forcing air in and out of our lungs. They may be brought on by an irritation of the diaphragm itself, of the respiratory or digestive system, or by eating or drinking too rapidly. Common remedies for hiccups include sipping water slowly, holding the breath, and putting something cold on the back of the neck. Breathing into a paper bag is usually effective because after a few breaths, the high carbon dioxide content in the bag will serve to make the diaphragm contractions more regular, rather than spasmodic. If none of these measures helps, it may be necessary to have a physician prescribe a sedative or tranquilizer.

The Sensitive Eyes and Ears

Air pollution affects not only the lungs but the eyes as well. In addition to all the other hazards to which the eyes are exposed, airborne smoke, chemicals, and dust cause the eyes to burn, itch, and shed tears. Other common eye troubles are discussed below.

Sty

This pimplelike inflammation of the eyelid is caused by infection, which may be linked to the blocking of an eyelash root or an oil gland, or to general poor health. A sty can be treated at home by applying clean compresses of hot water to the area for about 15 minutes at a time every two hours. This procedure should cause the sty to open, drain, and heal. If sties are recurrent, a health checkup may be indicated.

Pinkeye

Pinkeye, an acute form of *conjunctivitis,* is an inflammation of the membrane that lines the eyelid and covers the eyeball, causing the eyes to become red and the lids to swell and stick together while one is sleeping. The condition may result from bacterial or viral infection—in which case it is extremely contagious—or from allergy or chemical irritation. A physician should be consulted.

Conjunctivitis can be treated by washing the eyes with warm water, drying them with a disposable tissue to prevent the spread of infection, and applying a medicated yellow oxide of mercury ophthalmic ointment (as recommended by your physician) on the inner edges of the lids. This should be done upon rising in the morning and upon retiring at night. The eyes should then be closed until the ointment has spread. Apply compresses of hot water three or four times a day for five-minute periods.

Eyestrain

Eyestrain—with symptoms of fatigue, tearing, redness, and a scratchy feeling in the eyelids—can be caused by a need for corrective glasses, by a disorder of the eye, or by overuse of the eyes. One of the most common causes of eyestrain, however, is improper lighting. Anyone engaged in close work, such as sewing or miniature model building, and at all times when reading, should have light come from behind and from the side so that no shadow falls on the book or object being scrutinized. The light should be strong enough for comfort—not dazzling. Efforts should be made to avoid a shiny or highly polished work surface that produces a glare. To avoid eyestrain when watching television, be sure the picture is in sharp focus; the viewer should sit at least six feet from the screen; and see that the room is not in total darkness.

Ear Infections

Ear infections related to colds, sore throats, or tonsillitis can now be kept from spreading and entering the mastoid bone by the use of sulfa drugs and antibiotics. Any acute earache should therefore be called to a physician's attention promptly. Aspirin can be taken for temporary relief from pain; holding a heating pad or a hot-water bottle to the affected side of the face may also be helpful until proper medication can be prescribed.

Earwax

An excessive accumulation of earwax can sometimes cause pain as well as interfere with hearing. When the ear canal is blocked in this way, gently rotating a small wad of cotton may clean it. The ears should never be cleaned with sharp objects such as hairpins or matchsticks. If earwax has hardened too much to be removed with cotton, it can be softened by a few drops of hydrogen peroxide. When the wax is so deeply and firmly imbedded that it can't be removed at home, a physician may have to flush it out with a syringe.

Ear Blockage

A stopped-up feeling in the ear can be caused by a cold, and also by the change in air pressure experienced when a plane makes a rapid descent. The obstruction of the Eustachian tube can usually be opened by swallowing hard or yawning.

Ringing in the Ear

The general word for a large variety of noises in the ear is *tinnitus.* People who experience such noises describe the sounds in many ways: hissing, ringing, buzzing, roaring, whistling. When they are heard only occasionally for brief periods, without any other symptoms, they can be ignored. However, when they are constant, they should be considered a symptom of some disorder, such as an infection, high blood pressure, allergy, or an improper bite (malocclusion). Sounds in the ears may also be caused be excessive smoking or drinking, or by large doses of aspirin or other medicines. In cases where the source of the ear disturbance can't be diagnosed and the noises become an unsettling nuisance, the physician may recommend a sedative or tranquilizer.

The Path from the Kidneys

Cystitis

Cystitis is the general term for inflammation of the bladder caused by various types of infection. It is more common in women than in men. Infecting microbes may come from outside the body by way of the urethra, or from some other infected organ, such as the kidney. When the bladder becomes inflamed, frequent and painful urination results.

Cystitis may also occur as a consequence of other disorders, such as enlargement of the prostate gland, a structural defect of the male urethra, or stones or a tumor in the bladder. Although there is no completely reliable way to prevent cystitis, some types of infection can be prevented by cleansing the genital region regularly so that the entrance of the urethra is protected against bacterial invasion. Cystitis is usually cured by medicines prescribed by a physician. For a detailed discussion of cystitis and related conditions affecting women, see "Disorders of the Urinary System" in Ch. 25, *Women's Health.*

Prostatitis

Prostatitis is an inflammation of the prostate gland (present in males only), caused by an infection of the urinary tract or some other part of the body. It may occur as a result of venereal infection. The symptoms of painful and excessive urination generally respond favorably to antibiotics. *Acute prostatitis* is less common: the patient is likely to have a high fever, as well as a discharge of pus from the penis. These symptoms should be brought to a physician's attention without delay.

Excessive Urination

A need to empty the bladder with excessive frequency can be merely a nuisance caused by overexcitement or tension, or it can be the sign of a disorder of the urinogenital system. A physician should be consulted if the problem persists.

The All-Important Feet

The *podiatrist* is the specialist who treats foot problems. Causes of foot ailments range from lack of cleanliness to ill-fitting shoes and overindulgence in athletic activities (see "Care of the Feet" in Ch. 5, *The Middle Years,* "The Vulnerable Extremities" in Ch. 23, *Aches, Pains, Nuisances, Worries*).

An ache, pain, or other disorder of the foot can be particularly annoying because it usually hampers mobility. A severe problem can keep a person bedridden, sometimes in the hospital, for substantial periods of time. As humans, we move about on our feet. They deserve the best of care from us, as their owners, and from the podiatrist in case a serious problem arises.

Podiatry, the science of foot care, has become more and more important as Americans have taken to athletics and exercises of various kinds. Most of these activities require the use of the feet. Increasing numbers of persons in the adult years are also taking up walking, jogging, or running as diversions or exercises.

Podiatrists believe that some persons "walk old"—they give the appearance, by the way they walk, of greater age than their chronological years. Others "walk young," or walk normally. Those who walk old may be inviting foot problems, and a fact of podiatric science is that every foot problem has its reflection in another part, or other parts, of the body.

By contrast, good foot and body posture often suggests that the owner of the feet enjoys good health in other parts of the body. Foot care may in effect help other body parts to function better. Because many problems with parts of the body remote from the feet make good foot posture and normal walking difficult or impossible, individuals with diverse problems, such as back pains, sometimes go to a podiatrist for treatment. The back pain may disappear when the feet have been brought into good working order.

Diabetes and the Feet

"Care" for the feet of diabetics means prevention. The diabetic tries to keep his feet so healthy that he avoids major problems. He knows that diabetes affects blood circulation, and that the leg and foot are extremely vulnerable to circulatory problems. Where blood cannot reach a limb or member, gangrene becomes a possibility.

Foot Care

What kind of care serves the diabetic best? Effective care means that the diabetic takes steps quickly to treat such problems as abrasions or ulcers that refuse to heal. Other conditions that warn of possible future problems are dry skin, numbness, and dry or brittle nails. Ulcers that appear in the skin of the foot and that appear to have roots in deeper layers of tissue serve as danger signals. Such ulcers may appear on the site of an injury, cut, or scratch. A physician will usually prescribe medication, dietary adjustments, or other measures.

Ulcers may result from neglect of a corn or callus. But such neglect itself indicates the risks that diabetics incur: they may neglect to have a foot problem such as a corn treated because their disease has, over time, reduced the sensitivity of their feet. They may lose much of their ability to feel pain, heat or cold, or stress in the foot. Because of such problems, diabetics generally follow certain rules of foot care, including the following:

- Give the feet a daily examination for cuts, bruises, or other abnormalities

- Use only prescribed medications in caring for the feet—and avoid over-the-counter preparations
- Visit a podiatrist regularly, as often as once a month, and avoid medical "treatment" of one's own feet or even cutting one's own toenails
- Wash the feet daily in warm, not hot, water and dry them carefully, including the area between the toes
- Use a gentle lubricant on the feet after washing and drying—and never go barefoot
- Avoid the use of items of clothing that may interfere with circulation, including wraparound garters and support hosiery
- Avoid "holey" socks, darned socks, or anything else that may irritate the soles of the feet and
- Avoid constrictive boots or shoes

Jogging and Running

The podiatrist usually tries to learn about a patient's work, his hobbies and sports, and other facts before undertaking treatment. In particular, the podiatrist asks whether the patient runs or jogs or takes part in other strenuous exercises. With such background information, he or she can suggest appropriate treatment.

A podiatrist will advise runners or joggers on the kind of footwear that would be best—especially if problems have been encountered or may be expected. Shoe inserts may be custom-designed if needed. The podiatrist may also advise runners and joggers to run on softer surfaces rather than cement. Jogging or running "in place," without forward movement, is to be avoided if possible; even when jogging inside the home or apartment, the jogger should move from room to room.

Podiatrists point out that even the more serious knee and ankle problems incurred in running and jogging can be treated. "Jogger's ankle," pain resulting from too much jogging and the attendant strain, can be controlled if the jogger will use moderation. Beginning joggers in particular should start slowly and gradually increase their level of participation. Runners' knee problems may be cured in many cases by treatment that enables the feet to carry the weight of the body properly. In part, the treatment requires practice in throwing the body weight onto the balls of the feet, not on the inner sides of the feet. The remainder of the body, including the knees, can be kept in proper alignment with the feet if the weight falls where it should.

Podiatrists also advise runners, joggers, and others taking part in sports to make certain *all* their clothing and equipment are appropriate. That applies especially in skiing, ice-skating, and other sports requiring extensive foot use. Proper equipment helps runners and joggers avoid colds and similar respiratory problems.

With proper equipment, including good shoes, and a moderate approach, runners and joggers can avoid many other potentially troublesome physical difficulties that could require podiatric care. These others include fallen arches; corns, calluses, and bunions; and "aging feet" that grow weaker from lack of proper foot attention.

24

Allergies and Hypersensitivities

Allergy is a broad term used to describe an unusual reaction of the body's tissues to a substance that has no noticeable effect on other persons. About 17 out of every 100 persons in America are allergic, or hypersensitive, to one or more substances that are known to precipitate an unusual reaction. Such substances, known as *allergens,* include a variety of irritants, among them mold spores, pollens, animal dander, insect venoms, and house dust. Some individuals are allergic to substances in soap, which produce a skin irritation. Others react to the smell of a rose by sneezing. Still others react with an outbreak of hives, diarrhea, or other symptoms to allergens in foods.

How Allergens Affect the Body

Allergic symptoms can range from itching eyes, running nose, coughing, difficulty in breathing, and welts on the skin to nausea, cramps, and even going into a state of shock, depending upon the severity of the particular individual's sensitivity and response. Almost any part or system of the body can be affected, and almost anything can pose an allergic threat to somebody.

The Role of Antibodies

The system of an allergic individual reacts to such substances in the way it would react to an invading disease organism: by producing *antibodies* whose job it is to neutralize the allergen. In the process of fighting off the effects of the allergen, the body's defense mechanism may overreact by dumping a chemical mediator, *histamine,* indiscriminately into the individual's bloodstream. It is the overabundance of this protective chemical that causes the discomforts associated with allergies.

At the same time, the antibodies can sensitize the individual to the allergen. Then, with each new exposure to the allergen, more antibodies are produced. Eventually the symptoms of allergy are produced whenever the allergen is encountered. Most allergic reactions, including hay fever, asthma, gastrointestinal upsets, and skin rashes, are of the type just described; their effect is more or less immediate. A second type, known as the delayed type, seems to function without the production of antibodies; contact dermatitis is an example of the delayed type.

Eosinophils

Some individuals seem to be sensitive to only one known allergen, but others are sensitive to a variety of substances. Persons who suffer acute allergic reactions have abnormally high levels of a type of white blood cell called *eosinophil.* The eosinophil contains an enzyme that may have some control over the allergic reaction, and varying degrees of the enzyme's efficiency appear to account for individual differences in the severity of allergic reactions.

Allergic Symptoms in Children

Many of the common allergies appear during the early years of life. It has been estimated that nearly 80 percent of the major allergic problems begin to appear between the ages of 4 and 9. Allergic youngsters may have nasal speech habits, breathe through the mouth, have coughing and wheezing spells, or rub their eyes, nose, and ears because of itching. A not uncommon sign of allergic reaction in a child may be dark circles under the eyes caused by swelling of the mucous membranes to such an extent that blood does not drain properly from the veins under the lower eyelids. Nose twitching and mouth wrinkling also are signs that a youngster has allergic symptoms.

Common Allergens

The allergens responsible for so many unpleasant and uncomfortable symptoms take a variety of forms too numerous and sometimes too obscure for any book to enumerate. Discussed below are some of the more common types of allergens.

Foods

Foods are among the most common causes of allergic reactions. While nearly any food substance is a potential allergen to certain sensitive individuals, those most frequently implicated are cow's milk, orange juice, and eggs, all considered essential in a child's diet. However, substitute foods are almost always available. Many natural foods contain vitamin C, or ascorbic acid, found in orange juice. Ascorbic acid also is available in vitamin tablets. All of the essential amino acids and other nutrients in cow's milk and eggs also can be obtained from other food sources, although perhaps not as conveniently packaged for immediate use. Other common food offenders are chocolate, pork, seafoods, nuts, and berries. An individual may be allergic to the gluten in wheat, rye, and oats, and products made from those grains.

Inhaled Allergens

Allergens also may affect the respiratory tract, bringing on sneezing, coughing, and breathing impairment. The substances involved can be pollens, dust, smoke, perfumes, and various airborne chemicals.

Mold Spores

A person also can become allergic to a certain mold by inhaling the spores, or reproductive particles, of fungus. In the nose, the mold spores trigger a reaction in cells of the tissues beneath the mucous membranes that line the nasal passages. This in turn leads to the symptoms of allergy. Because they are small, mold spores can evade the natural protective mechanisms of the nose and upper respiratory tract to reach the lungs and bring on an allergic reaction in that site. Usually, this leads to the buildup of mucus, wheezing, and difficulty in breathing associated with asthma.

Less frequently, inhaling mold spores can result in skin lesions similar to those of eczema or chronic hives. In all but the very warmest areas of the United States, molds are seasonal allergens, occurring from spring into late fall. But unlike pollens, molds do not disappear with the killing frosts of autumn. Actually, frost may help increase the activity of molds, which thrive on dying vegetation produced by cold temperatures.

Dust and Animal Hair

House dust and animal hair (especially cat and dog hair) are also responsible for respiratory allergies in many people. Asthma attacks are often triggered by contact with these substances. Symptoms of dust allergy are usually most severe in the spring and fall, and tend to subside in the summer.

Man-Made Allergens

An example of respiratory allergy caused by man-made allergens is the complaint known as "meat wrappers' asthma," which results from fumes of the price-label adhesive on the polyvinyl chloride film used to package foods. The fumes are produced when the price label is cut on a hot wire. When the fumes are inhaled, the result is burning eyes, sore throat, wheezing and shortness of breath, upset stomach, and other complaints. Studies show that exposure to the fumes from the heat-activated label adhesive for as little as five minutes could produce airway obstruction in food packagers.

Another source of respiratory allergy is the photochemical smog produced by motor vehicle exhaust in large city areas. The smog is composed of hydrocarbons, oxides of nitrogen, and other chemicals activated by the energy of sunlight. When inhaled in the amounts present along the nation's expressways, the smog has been found to impair the normal function of membranes in the lungs.

Drugs

Medicines and drugs, such as penicillin, or serums used in inoculations, can cause allergic reactions. Estimates of the incidence of allergy among those receiving penicillin range from one to ten percent. The National Institutes of Health has calculated that just three common drugs—penicillin, sulfonamides, and aspirin—account for as much as 90 percent of all allergic drug reactions. The allergic reactions include asthmatic symptoms, skin rash, shock, and other symptoms similar to tissue reactions to other allergens. Medical scientists theorize that chemicals in certain drugs probably combine with protein molecules in the patient's body to form a new substance that is the true allergen. However, it also has been noted that some persons show allergic reactions to placebo drugs, which may contain sugar or inert substances rather than real drugs.

Insect Venom

Insect stings cause serious allergic reactions in about four of every 1,000 persons stung by bees, fire ants, yellow jackets, wasps, or hornets. A single sting to a sensitive person may lead to a serious drop in blood pressure, shock, and possibly death. There are more than 50 reported fatalities a year, and experts suspect that other deaths occur as a result of insect stings but are listed as heart attacks, stroke, or convulsions.

Sensitivity tests of persons who might be acutely allergic to insect stings have been difficult to develop, because allergic individuals reacted in the same way as nonallergic persons to skin tests performed with extracts from insect bodies. More recently, physicians have found that using pure insect venom produces a reaction that determines whether a person is allergic to the sting. Medical scientists also have isolated the major allergen in an insect venom for use in diagnosing and treating patients who are particularly sensitive to stings.

Skin Allergies

Allergies affecting the skin take many forms, the most common being eczema, urticaria (hives), angioedema (swelling of the subcutaneous tissues), and contact dermatitis. Among the most common causes are foods, cosmetics, fabrics, metals, plants and flowers, plastics, insecticides, furs and leather, jewelry, and many industrial chemicals. Studies of patients who seem to be especially sensitive to skin allergies show that they have higher than average amounts of a body protein called *immunoglobulin E* in their systems.

In certain instances, a person who is sensitive to an allergen in a plant food also may be allergic to the pollen of the plant. The fava bean, for example, produces severe reactions when eaten by individuals who are allergic to the food; inhaling the pollen of the growing plant can cause similar reactions.

Poisonous Plants

Poison ivy, poison oak, and poison sumac contain an extremely irritating oily resin that sensitizes the body; repeated contact seems to increase the severity of the allergic reactions. About 50 percent of the population who come in contact with the resin will experience a severe form of dermatitis, and up to 10 percent will be temporarily disabled by the effects. Exposure to the resin may come from direct contact with the plant, from contact with other objects or animals that have touched the plant, or from inhaling smoke from the burning plant.

Cosmetics and Jewelry

A wide variety of cosmetics and jewelry can cause allergic reactions through skin contact. Even jewelry that is presumably pure gold can contain a certain amount of nickel that will produce a mild reaction that causes a skin discoloration, sometimes aided by chemical activity resulting from perspiration in the area of jewelry contact. Among cosmetics that may be involved in allergic reactions are certain permanent-wave lotions, eyelash dyes, face powders, permanent hair dyes, hair-spray lacquers, and skin-tanning agents. Of course, not all persons are equally sensitive to the ingredients known to be allergens, and in most cases a similar product with different ingredients can be substituted for the cosmetic causing allergic reactions. For more information on skin allergies, see "Disorders of the Skin" in Ch. 21, *Skin and Hair.*

Environmental Allergies

Environmental agents such as sunlight, excessive cold, and pressure are known to produce allergic reactions in certain individuals. Cold allergy, for example, can result in hives and may even lead to a drop in blood pressure, fainting, severe shock, and sometimes death. Research into the causes of cold allergy has shown that cold urticaria, or hives, results from a histamine released from body tissues as they begin to warm up after a cold stimulus. Extremely high histamine levels coincide with episodes of very low blood pressure, the cause of fainting.

Although reaction of the body tissues to the invasion of microbes, such as bacteria, viruses, and other microorganisms, generally is not thought of as an allergic situation, the manner in which the body musters its defenses against the foreign materials is essentially the same as the way the antibodies are mobilized to neutralize other allergens. Thus, there is a similarity between infectious diseases and allergies.

Temporary Allergies

Occasionally, a change in the body's hormonal balance may trigger a hypersensitivity to a substance that previously had no effect on the individual. Pregnant women are especially susceptible to these temporary allergies, which almost always disappear after childbirth. Some women during pregnancy, on the other hand, experience complete relief from allergies that have plagued them since childhood.

People who suffer from seasonal allergies, such as hay fever, often have heightened allergic reactions to dust, animal dander, and even certain foods, such as chocolate and pineapple, during the season when ragweed pollen or other airborne allergens are plentiful.

Diagnosis of Allergies

Some allergic reactions are outgrown; some don't develop until adulthood; some become increasingly severe over the years because each repeated exposure makes the body more sensitive to the allergen. In many instances, the irritating substance is easily identified, after which it can be avoided. In other cases, it may take a long series of tests before the offending allergen is tracked down.

Medical History

If a person suspects he may have an allergy, the first thing he should do is consult a physician to see if the help of an allergy specialist should be sought. The physician or allergist will first take a complete medical history and check the patient's general health. Not infrequently the source of an allergy can be found by general questioning about the patient's life style. For example, the reaction may occur only on or immediately after the patient eats seafood. Or a patient may have an apparently chronic allergy but be unaware that it may be related to daily meals that include milk and eggs. A patient who keeps several cats or sleeps every night with a dog in the bedroom may not realize that an asthmatic condition actually is an allergic reaction to dander from the fur of a pet animal.

The history taken by the physician will include questions about other known allergies, allergies suffered by other members of the family, variations in symptoms according to the weather, time of day, and season of the year. The symptoms may be related to a change in working conditions or the fact that the symptoms, if perhaps a result of house dust, diminish during periods of outdoor exercise. A person sensitive to cold may unwittingly exacerbate the symptoms with cold drinks, while another person who is sensitive to heat may not realize that symptoms can be triggered by hot drinks but relieved by cold drinks, and so on.

Skin Testing

If the patient is referred to an allergy specialist, the allergist will continue the detective story by conducting skin tests.

Scratch Test

Based on information in the medical history of the patient and the allergist's knowledge of molds, pollens, and other airborne allergens in the geographical area, "the allergist" will conduct what is called a *scratch test.*

A diluted amount of a suspected allergen is applied to a small scratch on the patient's arm or back. If the results of the scratch test are inconclusive, a more sensitive test may be tried.

Intracutaneous Test

In the *intracutaneous* test, a solution of the suspected allergen is injected into the underlayer of skin called the *dermis.* The intracutaneous test also may be used to verify the results of a positive scratch test. With either test, a positive reaction usually consists of a raised reddish welt, or *wheal.* The welt should develop within 15 or 20 minutes if that particular allergen is the cause of the symptoms.

Culture Plates

If the allergen has been identified, or if the allergist still suspects a substance in the environment of the patient despite negative or inconclusive tests, the patient may be given a set of culture plates to place around his home and office or work area. If the allergen has been identified, the culture plates can help the physician and patient learn where his exposure to the substance takes place. If the allergen is not known, the cultures may pick up samples of less common allergens that the specialist can test.

Mucosal Test

Another kind of approach sometimes is used by allergists when skin tests fail to show positive results despite good evidence that a particular allergen is the cause of symptoms. It is called the *mucosal test.* The allergist using the mucosal test applies a diluted solution of the suspected allergen directly to the mucous membranes of the patient, usually on the inner surface of a nostril or by aerosol spray into the bronchial passages. In some cases, the allergic reaction occurs immediately and medication is administered quickly to counter the effects. Because of the possibility of a severe reaction in a hypersensitive patient, the mucosal test is not employed if other techniques seem to be effective.

Relief from Allergies

Other Tests

Allergists have other ways to test for allergies. They can, for example, use the *prick test,* a kind of skin test in which a physician or nurse pricks the skin as many as 30 or 40 times. On each pricked spot a drop of a watery solution is dropped; the solution contains a small amount of one allergen. A red welt appears on the spot within 15 to 30 minutes if the patient is allergic. Using another approach, an *elimination diet,* an allergist may specify a diet that omits certain foods for stated periods. Improvement in the patient's condition while avoiding certain foods usually indicates that the individual has an allergy to that food.

A variation of the prick test involves injection of small amounts of food in solution under the skin or application of the solution under the tongue. If the injection or drops provoke reactions, an allergy is indicated.

Avoidance

For a patient sensitive to a particular type of allergen, such as molds, complete avoidance of the substance can be difficult, but some steps can be taken to avoid undue exposure. For example, the mold allergy sufferer should avoid areas of his home, business, or recreational areas that are likely spots for mold spores to be produced. These would include areas of deep shade or heavy vegetation, basements, refrigerator drip trays, garbage pails, air conditioners, bathrooms, humidifiers, dead leaves or wood logs, barns or silos, breweries, dairies, any place where food is stored, and old foam, rubber pillows and mattresses.

Medication

To supplement avoidance measures, the allergist may prescribe medications that will significantly reduce or relieve the irritating symptoms of the allergic reaction. Antihistamines, corticosteroids, and a drug called cromolyn sodium are among medications that may be prescribed, depending upon the nature and severity of the patient's reactions to the allergen.

Immunotherapy

If avoidance measures and medications do not control the symptoms effectively, the allergist may suggest *immunotherapy.* Immunotherapy consists of injections of a diluted amount of the allergen, a technique similar to that used in the skin tests. A small amount of a very weak extract is injected once or twice a week at first. The strength of the extract is gradually increased, and the injections are given less frequently as relief from the symptoms is realized. The injections are continued until the patient has experienced complete relief of the symptoms for a period of two or three years. However, some people may have to continue the injections for longer time spans. Even though the treatments may relieve the symptoms, they may not cure the allergy.

Identification Cards

Any person subject to severe disabling allergy attacks by a known allergen should carry a card describing both the allergic reaction and the allergen. Detailed information can be obtained from the Asthma and Allergy Foundation of America, 1302 18th St., NW, Washington, DC 20036. See also "Allergic Respiratory Diseases" in Ch. 12, *Diseases of the Respiratory System,* and "Asthma Attack" in Ch. 31, *Medical Emergencies.*

25

Women's Health

The special health matters that are related to a woman's reproductive system belong to the branch of medicine known as *gynecology. Obstetrics* is a closely related specialty associated with pregnancy and childbirth. The distinction is something of a technicality for most patients, since obstetricians usually are quite capable of handling gynecological cases and vice versa. The practice of obstetrics and gynecology is commonly combined in a medical service identified by the contraction *Ob-Gyn*. However, there are medical matters that are specifically concerned with female reproductive organs and related tissues but have little to do with obstetrics. For a discussion of obstetrics, see "Infertility, Pregnancy, and Childbirth" in Ch. 4, *The Beginning of a Family.*

The Gynecological Examination

What should a woman expect on her first visit to a gynecologist? First, the gynecologist will interview her, asking about her family, her medical history, and any fears or apprehensions she may have about her personal health. The woman's answers and comments are written into her medical records for future reference. The information can contain important clues that may help in diagnosing any present or future disorders.

A sample of urine and a sample of blood are usually obtained for laboratory tests. During the ensuing physical examination, the woman lies on a special examination table with her feet in metal stirrups and her knees apart. A nurse will be present to assist the doctor. While she is in the *lithotomy position*, the woman's abdomen will be palpated for lumps or other abnormalities. The breasts also will be palpated for possible lumps. Then an external inspection of the vulva and surrounding areas is made by the physician, followed by internal inspection, in which a speculum is used to spread apart the sides of the vagina so that the cervix is exposed. A digital examination (using the fingers) is made of the walls of the vagina and rectum and the neighboring tissue areas, in a search for possible growths or other abnormal conditions. And a sample of cells and secretions from the cervix is taken for a Pap-smear test.

In addition to the examination of the breasts and reproductive system, the gynecologist usually conducts a general physical examination, recording information about height, weight, blood pressure, heart and lung condition, and so on. The routine physical examination, like the medical history, provides additional clues that, when added to the results of the examination of the breasts and reproductive system, will give a complete picture of the patient's gynecological health.

Following the examination, the gynecologist discusses his appraisal of the woman's condition and answers questions. He will discuss whatever treatment she needs. Medications can be explained at this time, including reasons why certain drugs can or should not be taken. If any surgery or further testing is recommended, those aspects of the health picture also should be discussed in some detail. Any important information that might be misunderstood or forgotten should be jotted down for future reference.

Results of some laboratory tests and the Pap smear are not usually available for several days. But the physician or nurse will contact the patient when the results are available and advise if she should return in the near future for follow-up testing. The

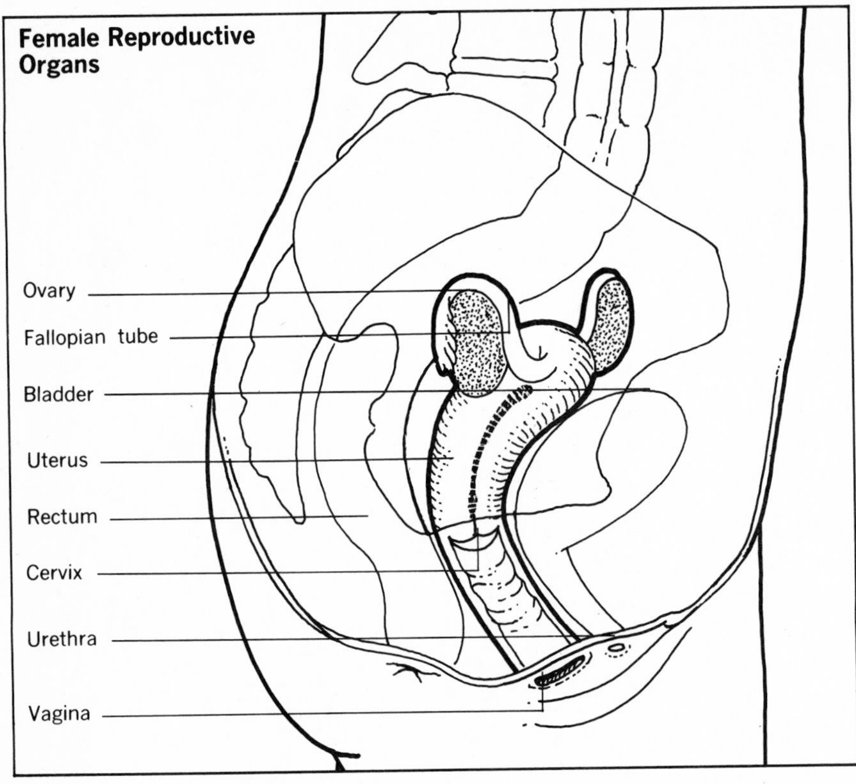

woman also should discuss arrangements for future checkups or Pap smear tests rather than wait until signs or symptoms of a serious disorder warrant an immediate visit. In the event of some possible future physical complaint, the fact that the woman has established some basic medical records with her gynecologist will be of help in making a proper diagnosis and establishing the best course of treatment.

Menstrual Disorders

Among the health concerns of women that specifically belong to gynecology are menstrual disorders. Normally, the first menstrual period (menarche) occurs about age 12 or 13, or sometimes earlier or later. Periods are generally irregular for the first year or two, and then they tend to recur at intervals of 24 to 32 days. Each period begins about two weeks after ovulation, or the release of an egg cell (ovum) from the ovary—unless, of course, the ovum happens to be fertilized in the interval and pregnancy interrupts the whole process.

The menstrual flow, which lasts from three to seven days, is composed mainly of serum, mucus, and dead cells shed from the lining (endometrium) of the uterus. The loss of blood is minimal, usually from two to four ounces. The volume of flow, as well as the time schedule, tends to be fairly regular for most women. When one's menstrual pattern varies noticeably from the expected pattern, and in the absence of pregnancy, it may be a sign of a physical or emotional disorder.

Amenorrhea

Failure to menstruate is called *amenorrhea.* Amenorrhea is a natural effect of pregnancy and of nursing a baby. In an older woman, it may be a sign of menopause. But if a nonpregnant or nonnursing woman after menarche and before menopause (say between the ages of 17 or 18 and 52) fails to menstruate for two or more periods, she should bring it to the attention of a doctor—unless, of course, she has undergone a hysterectomy or other surgical or medical treatment that eliminates menstruation.

Primary Amenorrhea

When menarche has not occurred by the age of 16 or 17, the absence of menstruation is called *primary amenorrhea.* In such a case, a physical examination may show that an imperforate hymen or a closed cervix is obstructing the flow of menses, or a congenital defect may be interfering with menstruation. In almost all cases, menarche can be started with a bit of minor surgery, by treatment of any existing systemic disease, or by the injection of sex hormones; or it will start spontaneously later.

Secondary Amenorrhea

When menstrual periods cease after menarche, the condition is known as *secondary,* or *acquired, amenorrhea.* Secondary amenorrhea may involve missing a single menstrual period or many periods in consecutive months. Among possible causes of interrupted menstruation are certain medications, drugs of abuse, emotional stress, normal fluctuations in ovarian activity in the first few years after menarche, and a number of organic diseases. Medicines that can disrupt normal menstrual activity include tranquilizers and other psychotropic (mind-affecting) drugs that apparently influence hormonal activity in the brain centers, amphetamines, and oral contraceptives. When a particular medication is found to be the cause of amenorrhea, the medical treatment may be judged to be more important than maintaining normal menstrual cycles. When the use of oral contraceptives is followed by amenorrhea for six or more months, normal menstrual activity may resume eventually, but it can often be started sooner by a prescribed medication. Among drugs of abuse known to cause amenorrhea are alcohol and opium-based drugs.

Just as the mind-altering effects of psychotropic drugs involve the hypothalamus and pituitary glands in the brain, which control the hormones that regulate menstrual functions, emotional stress seems to have a parallel influence on the incidence of amenorrhea. *Anorexia nervosa,* a disorder associated with emaciation resulting from an emotional disturbance, also can result in an interruption of menstruation.

Other factors contributing to secondary amenorrhea are measles, mumps, and other infections; cysts and tumors of the ovaries; changes in the tissues lining the vagina or uterus; premature aging of the ovaries; diabetes; obesity; anemia; leukemia; and Hodgkin's disease. In many cases, normal or near-normal menstrual function can be restored by medical treatment, such as administration of hormones, or by surgery, or both. In one type of amenorrhea, marked by adhesion of the walls of the uterus, curettage (scraping of the uterus) is followed by insertion of an intrauterine contraceptive device (IUD) to help hold the uterine walls apart.

Menorrhagia

Almost the opposite of amenorrhea is *menorrhagia,* an excessive menstrual flow. The causes of menorrhagia are as varied as those associated with amenorrhea. They include influenza and other infectious diseases, emotional stress, polyps of the cervical or uterine tissues, hypertension, congestive heart failure, leukemia, and blood coagulation disorders. Menorrhagia may occur during the early stages of a young woman's reproductive life soon after reaching puberty, and medical treatment may be necessary to control the excessive loss of blood. In some cases, dilation and curettage is recommended in addition to the administration of hormones and other medications, such as iron tablets to correct anemia resulting from the loss of red blood cells.

Dilation and Curettage

Dilation and curettage, generally referred to as *D and C,* is a procedure in which the cervix is dilated and the cavity of the uterus is cleaned out by a scooplike instrument, a curette. The same procedure is sometimes used to abort an embryo or to remove a tumor or a polyp.

Although it takes only a few minutes to perform a D and C, the procedure is done in a hospital while the patient is anesthetized. There is no afterpain, only a dull discomfort in the lower pelvic region similar to menstrual awareness.

A physical examination is usually made to determine if there are tumors anywhere in the reproductive organs. Except where tumors are found to be a causative factor, most women will resume normal menstrual cycles after treatment of menorrhagia with medications and D and C. For women beyond the age of 40, the physician may recommend a hysterectomy to prevent recurrence of excessive menstrual blood loss.

Polymenorrhea and Metrorrhagia

These medical terms refer to two other ways in which menstrual periods may depart from typical patterns. *Polymenorrhea* is abnormally frequent menstruation, so that menstrual periods occur at intervals of less than 21 days. This short interval may be the natural established pattern for some women. If it is not, the cause may be physical or emotional stress. *Metrorrhagia* is marked by menstrual bleeding that occurs erratically at unpredictable times. It may be the result of a cyst in the lining of the uterus, a tumor in the reproductive tract, polyps, or some hormonal imbalance, including a disorder of the thyroid gland.

Dysmenorrhea

Abdominal or pelvic pain occurring just before or along with the onset of menstruation is known as *dysmenorrhea.* The symptoms include severe colicky abdominal cramps, backache, headache, and, in some cases, nausea and vomiting. As with amenorrhea, there are two general types of dysmenorrhea, primary and secondary.

Primary Dysmenorrhea

This type includes all cases in which no organic disorder is associated with the symptoms, which are presumed to be a result of uterine contractions and emotional factors. More than 75 percent of all cases are of this type. Primary dysmenorrhea generally begins before age 25, but it may appear at any time from menarche to menopause. It frequently ends with the birth of the first child.

Since primary dysmenorrhea by definition occurs in the absence of organic disease, the diagnosis can be made only after a careful medical history is compiled and a special study of the reproductive organs is made to ensure that no disorder has been overlooked. In some cases, oral contraceptives may be prescribed because of the effect such drugs have in suppressing ovulation; the contraceptives prevent the natural production of the hormone progesterone, which is responsible for certain tissue changes associated with the discomfort of dysmenorrhea. Analgesic drugs to relieve pain and medications that help to relax muscles may be prescribed. Medication is often less beneficial, however, than emotional support—including the easing of any stress at home, school, or work, and reassurance about the worries sometimes associated with menstruation.

Secondary Dysmenorrhea

This condition comprises all menstrual pain that is a result of or associated with an organic disease of the reproductive organs, such as endometriosis, to cite just one example. Secondary dysmenorrhea can occur at any age.

Premenstrual Syndrome

Premenstrual syndrome (PMS) has emerged in recent years as a major challenge to the medical profession. PMS clinics have begun to offer specialized counseling, physical examinations, and treatment for women unable to cope with the disorder. Treatment regimens or therapies range from aspirin to large doses of sex hormones, diet programs, and exercise.

A group of related symptoms, PMS involves both psychological and physical changes. Among the psychological are lethargy, tension, irritability, depression, and feelings of aggression. The physical signs may include headache, bloating, asthma, and more exotic problems, such as recurrent herpes or hives. In all, more than 300 different symptoms have been attributed to PMS.

The symptoms, gynecologists warn, should become "disturbing" before they are labeled PMS. Restlessness, minor cramps, and other premenstrual problems may indicate that menstruation is about to start but do not necessarily point to PMS. Such minor problems are called *menstrual molimina.* Cramping and other painful conditions occurring during menstruation are referred to as *dysmenorrhea* (see above).

Of the many treatments for PMS, none has proved uniformly effective. This is because the cause or causes of PMS are not totally understood. Most commonly, physicians believe the disorder represents some basic imbalance in the major female hormones, estrogen and progesterone. Thus one treatment calls for administration of "natural" progesterone to correct the supposed imbalance.

Another common treatment suggested for PMS is vitamin B_6, although the treatment remains partly experimental. Some researchers and physicians, however, have reported disturbing neurological side-effects.

Other theories and treatments exist. Some physicians who have studied PMS and its symptoms believe *prolactin,* a pituitary hormone that stimulates milk secretion, and PMS are associated. A diet and nutrition theory has evolved out of findings that some women report improvement after going on a hypoglycemic diet.

Treated over a substantial period, PMS victims often find that diagnostic tests combined with diet and exercise regimens and vitamin therapy bring good results. If such initial attempts fail, the physician may prescribe medications. In all cases of PMS, according to researchers, psychological support for the sufferer may be important to treatment effectiveness.

Minor Menstrual Problems

Blood Clots

There is not usually any cause for alarm if blood clots are expelled during menstruation. Ordinarily, the menstrual flow is completely liquefied, but a few clots tend to appear

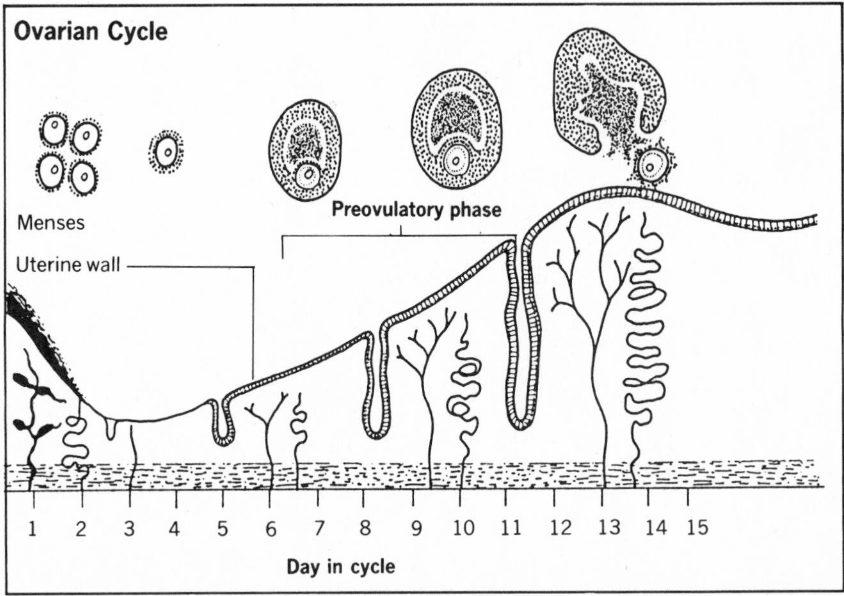

when the flow is profuse. However, if many clots appear and the flow seems excessive, medical advice is recommended, since these conditions may be a sign of fibroid tumors in the uterus.

Oral Contraceptives

Women on combination birth-control pills can expect to see a changed menstrual pattern. The flow becomes slighter than before and very regular. For a discussion of oral contraceptives, see "Birth Control" in Ch. 4, *The Beginning of a Family.*

Odor

The menstrual flow of a healthy woman generally has a mild odor that develops when it is exposed to the air or to the vulva. Some women are concerned about this odor, although it usually is not offensive. When it is, it tends to be associated with inadequate bathing. Detergents are added to some commercial tampons and pad products, and special deodorants have been developed to mask the odor. However, such materials produce allergic reactions in some women, and they can have the unfortunate effect of masking an odor that may be the sign of an abnormal condition.

Onset of Menopause

Menstrual irregularities almost always precede the natural cessation of menstrual function. For a full discussion of menopause, see Ch. 5, *The Middle Years.*

Postmenopausal Bleeding

Bleeding that occurs after the final cessation of menstrual activity should be seen as an urgent signal to seek medical advice. The bleeding may be painless or painful and may range from occasional spotting that is brownish or bright red to rather profuse bleeding that continues for several days or more. The various signs and symptoms should be noted carefully because they can help suggest to a physician the possible cause of bleeding. Bleeding after the menopause is often a sign of cancer of the cervix or the lining of the uterus, but there is a wide variety of other possible causes, including polyps, ulcers, hypertensive heart disease, an ovarian tumor, or infection. In many cases, the problem can be treated by dilation and curettage or withdrawal of any hormone medications, such as estrogens prescribed for menopausal symptoms, or both. In these cases, if D and C and treatment and discontinuance of hormone therapy fail, the physician may advise a hysterectomy.

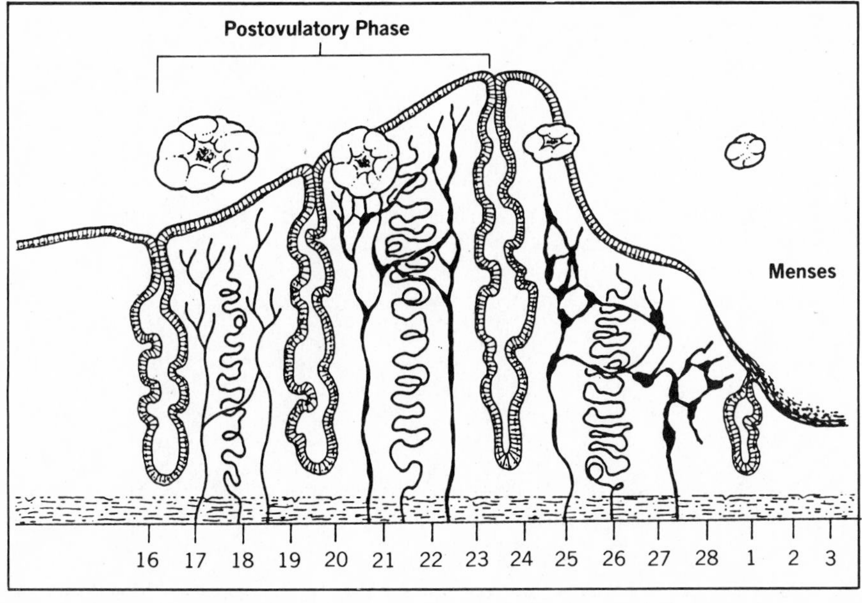

Infections of the Reproductive Tract

Vaginal and other reproductive tract infections are among the most common gynecological problems, and among the most stubborn to treat successfully.

Leukorrhea

A whitish, somewhat viscid discharge from the vagina, which is known medically as *leukorrhea,* may be quite normal, especially if it is not continual but occurs only intermittently—prior to menstruation, for example, or associated with sexual excitation. It may also be increased when oral contraceptives are used.

Constant leukorrhea, on the other hand, often is a symptom of an abnormality. Leukorrhea resulting from disease can occur at any age. It is generally associated with an infection of the lower reproductive tract. The discharge may occur without any discomfort, but in some cases there is itching, irritation, and *dyspareunia*—the medical term for painful intercourse.

Laboratory tests of vaginal secretions may be needed to help identify the precise cause of the discharge. Leukorrhea can result from vaginal ulcers; a tumor of the vagina, uterus, or Fallopian tubes; gonorrhea; or infection by any of various disease organisms of the vulva, vagina, cervix, uterus, or tubes. It may also result from an abnormality of menstrual function, or even emotional stress.

Treatment, of course, depends on the cause. If the discharge is because of an infection, care must be taken to avoid being reinfected or transmitting the disease organism through sexual contact or possibly contaminated underclothing, etc. The condition may be particularly difficult to control if the woman is pregnant or suffers from some chronic disorder, such as diabetes.

Moniliasis

Moniliasis, also known as *candidiasis,* is an infection by a yeastlike fungus that is capable of invading mucous membrane and sometimes skin in various parts of the body. Inside the mouth, the organism causes thrush, most commonly in babies. When the organism invades the vaginal area, it causes a scant white discharge of a thick consistency resembling that of cottage cheese. There is itching, burning, and swelling of the labial and vulvar areas. The symptoms tend to worsen just before the menstrual period. The occurrence of the disease is thought by some researchers to be fostered by oral contraceptives. Antibiotic therapy, too, generally favors the moniliasis organism, which is unaffected by the antibiotics that destroy many of the benign organisms that regularly share the same environment.

Moniliasis is treated with suppositories, creams, and other medications. The woman's partner should be treated at the same time to prevent a cycle of infection and reinfection of both partners, because the fungus will otherwise spread to the genital tissues of the man.

Trichomoniasis

A type of leukorrhea that consists of a copious yellow to green frothy and fetid discharge is caused by infection by the *Trichomonas* organism. The organism causes an irritating itching condition that tends to set in or worsen just after a menstrual period. The condition is diagnosed by a test similar to a Pap smear, made with a specimen taken from the vagina. Trichomonas organisms, if present, are easy to identify under a microscope; they are pear-shaped protozoa with three to five whiplike tails.

The organism favors warm, moist areas, such as genital tissues, but it can also survive in damp towels and washcloths, around toilet seats, and on beaches and the perimeters of swimming pools. Thus it can spread from one member of a family to other members and from one woman to other women. *Trichomoniasis* is not technically a venereal disease, but it can be transmitted by sexual contact. When one partner is infected with trichomoniasis, both must be treated at the same time and a condom must be worn during intercourse.

Several drugs are available for treating trichomoniasis, including tablets taken orally and suppositories inserted in the vagina. The tablets usually are taken three times daily for ten days, after which an examination is made to determine if any *Trichomonas* organisms are still present. The oral medication may be continued for several months if the infection resists the drug—some studies show that the organism appears to survive in about 10 percent of treated cases. There are douches available in drugstores for removing the discharge, but women are advised to consult their physicians before experimenting with home remedies or over-the-counter products that may be offered as douche treatments for trichomoniasis. The substances contained in some douches can aggravate the condition or irritate the vaginal tissues.

Herpes Simplex Virus Type 2

In recent years, physicians have become aware of a viral infection that is acquired by contact with the mucous membranes of an infected person. The mucous membrane of the mouth and lips, the genitals, or the rectum may be affected. The causative agent is known as *herpes simplex virus Type II,* or *HSV-II.* It is similar to but not the same as the virus that causes fever blisters, or cold sores, which is Type 1 (HSV-I). Information about the incidence of Type II is not well documented. The virus is associated with some spontaneous abortions, stillbirths, and deaths of newborn babies. If the mother is infected at the time of delivery, the virus can be transmitted to the baby as he or she passes through the vagina. The central nervous system, including the brain, may be damaged by the virus if the baby becomes infected. To avoid exposure to the virus, a caesarian delivery is recommended when the mother is infected.

Symptoms

Patients with their first HSV-II infection usually complain of intense itching, painful blisterlike eruptions, and ulcerated patches with a discharge. Other symptoms may include genital pain and vaginal bleeding. Fever, swelling, difficult urination, and a general feeling of ill health and lack of appetite may accompany the infection. Diagnosis of HSV-II is verified through biopsies and smears examined microscopically, cultures, and the presence of HSV-II antibodies.

Symptoms may subside after a few weeks, but recurrences are common, though they are less painful and of shorter duration. There is no known cure for the viral infection.

Treatment

Treatment was once limited to applications of anesthetic creams, steroid ointments, and other medications to relieve symptoms. No drug has been found to attack the viruses while they are "hibernating" in cells at the base of the spine. But one antiviral drug, *acyclovir,* has been found to reduce recurrent outbreaks and to block flare-ups for up to several months.

Taken orally in pill form, acyclovir in tests has brought relief, but not cures, to hundreds of subjects. The drug is ingested daily. Researchers have discovered that the capsules kill or neutralize the herpes viruses only when they are active. Because of evidence that the virus may be related to the subsequent development of cervical cancer, women sufferers should have Pap-smear tests at intervals of six months instead of the usual twelve.

Disorders of the Urinary System

Both men and women are subject to disorders of the urinary system, but there are a few disorders that affect women chiefly or women only, for reasons related to anatomical structure. See also Ch. 17, *Diseases of the Urinogenital System.*

Inflammation of the Bladder

Any inflammation of the bladder is known medically as *cystitis*. Factors such as urinary tract stones, injury, and obstructions to the normal flow of urine can aggravate or cause cystitis in either sex. Cystitis resulting from infectious organisms, however, is much more common in women than in men. This is understandable in view of the relative shortness of the female urethra—the tube through which urine is discharged from the bladder and through which infectious organisms can reach the bladder from the outside. In addition, the anus and the vagina, both of which may frequently be sources of infection, are situated relatively close to the external opening of the female urethra.

In women generally, the symptoms of cystitis may include a burning sensation around the edges of the vulva. There is usually a frequent urge to urinate and difficulty or pain (*dysuria*) associated with urination. Urinary retention and dehydration, which are generally under the control of the individual, can contribute to the spread of infection once it begins. The lining of the urinary bladder is relatively resistant to infection by most microorganisms as long as the normal flow of liquids through the urinary tract is maintained. In cases that do not yield quickly to copious fluid intake, there are medications that may be prescribed to cure the infection. Where urinary frequency or difficulty is accompanied by the appearance of blood in the urine, a physician should be consulted immediately.

Honeymoon Cystitis

One type of cystitis tends to occur mostly in young women during the first few weeks of frequent sexual activity, to which it is attributed. This so-called honeymoon cystitis may result in swelling of the urethra and the neck of the bladder, making urination difficult. The inflammation of these tissues can in turn make them more susceptible to infection. A treatment recommended specifically for honeymoon cystitis is to drink large quantities of water or other fluids and to empty the bladder before and after engaging in sexual intercourse. Adequate lubrication, such as petroleum jelly, is also important. Medical care should be sought if the condition persists.

Urethral Disorders

The urethra is perforce involved in the inflammation of cystitis because it is the route by which infectious organisms reach the bladder. In addition, there are disorders that are essentially confined to the urethra.

Urethral Caruncle

Urethral caruncle is a rather uncommon urinary tract disorder that tends to be confined to women after the menopause. A *caruncle* (not to be confused with *carbuncle*) is a small, red, fleshy outgrowth. It may be visible near the opening of the urethra. A caruncle growing from the cells of the urethra may be a sign of a bacterial infection, a tumor, or any of several other possible conditions. Symptoms may include vaginal bleeding, pain, tenderness, painful sexual intercourse (dyspareunia), a whitish, viscid discharge, and difficulty in urinating. A physician should be consulted when such symptoms are present. A tissue biopsy and Pap smear may be taken to diagnose the condition. Caruncles are easily treated and of no long-term consequence.

Urethral Diverticulum

Another disorder of the urethra is a *urethral diverticulum,* or outpocket-

The Female Urinary System

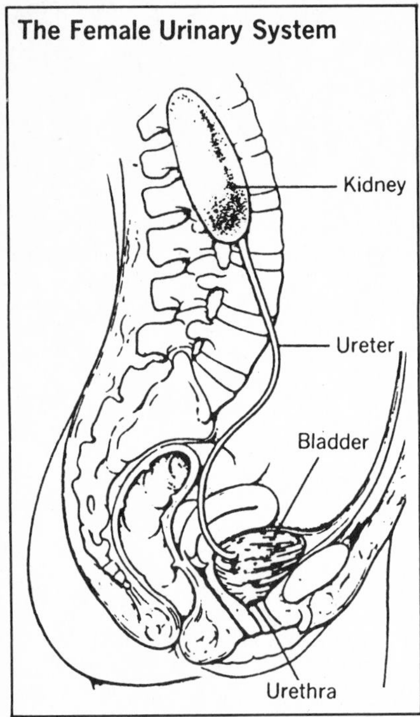

ing of the urethra. The problem can be caused by a developmental malformation, an injury, inflammation, a cyst, a urinary stone, or a venereal disease. Stones are a common cause, and in some patients there may be more than one diverticulum. The symptoms may include discomfort and urinary difficulty, as well as dyspareunia. The disorder can be diagnosed with the help of X-ray photographs of the region of the urethra and bladder after they have been filled with a radiopaque substance that flows into any diverticula that may be present.

Treatment of a urethral diverticulum includes antibiotics to stop infection, medications to relieve pain and discomfort, and douches. In some cases, surgery is needed to eliminate the diverticula.

Structural Anomalies

Various kinds of injury may be sustained by the female reproductive system and other abdominal organs, chiefly as a result of childbearing. The structural damage can generally be repaired by surgical measures.

Fistula

An abnormal opening between two organs or from an organ to the outside of the body is known as a *fistula.* Fistulas may involve the urinary and reproductive systems of a woman. Damage to the organs during pregnancy or surgery, for example, can result in a fistula between the urethra and the vagina, causing urinary incontinence. A similar kind of fistula can develop between the rectum and the vagina as a result of injury, complications of pregnancy, or surgery. Disorders of this sort must be repaired surgically.

Prolapsed Uterus

The uterus normally rests on the floor of the pelvis, held in position by numerous ligaments. Damage to the ligaments and other supporting tissues causes the uterus to descend, or *prolapse,* into the vagina. There are various degrees of prolapse, ranging from a slight intrusion of the uterus into the vagina to a severe condition in which the cervix of the uterus protrudes out of the vaginal orifice. Prolapse of the uterus resembles a hernia but is not a true hernia, because the opening through which the uterus protrudes is a normal one.

Backache and a feeling of heaviness in the pelvic region may accompany the condition. Many women complain of a "dragging" sensation. An assortment of complications may involve neighboring organ systems; bleeding and ulceration of the uterus are not uncommon. Coughing and straining can aggravate the symptoms.

Like the various types of hernia, a prolapsed uterus does not improve without treatment but tends instead to worsen gradually. The only permanent treatment is surgical repair. In mild cases, a woman may get relief from symptoms through exercises intended to strengthen the muscles of the pelvic region. Supporting devices, such as an inflatable, doughnut-shaped pessary, are available as temporary methods of correcting a prolapse. Preventive exercises may be recommended for childbearing women who want to avoid weakened muscles and ligaments leading to prolapse.

Prolapsed Uterus

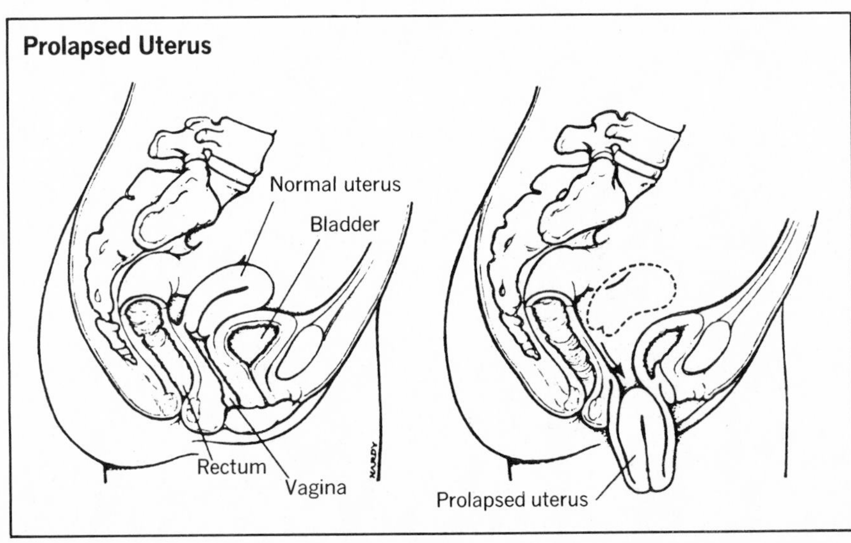

Tipped Uterus

The uterus may be out of its normal position without being prolapsed. A malpositioned uterus may be "tipped" forward, backward, or otherwise be out of alignment with neighboring organs. A malpositioned uterus may cause no symptoms, or it may be associated with dysmenorrhea or infertility. If a malpositioned uterus causes pain, bleeding, or other problems, the condition can be corrected surgically, or a pessary support may relieve the symptoms. Displacement of the uterus occasionally is the result of a separate pelvic disease that requires treatment.

Hernias of the Vaginal Wall

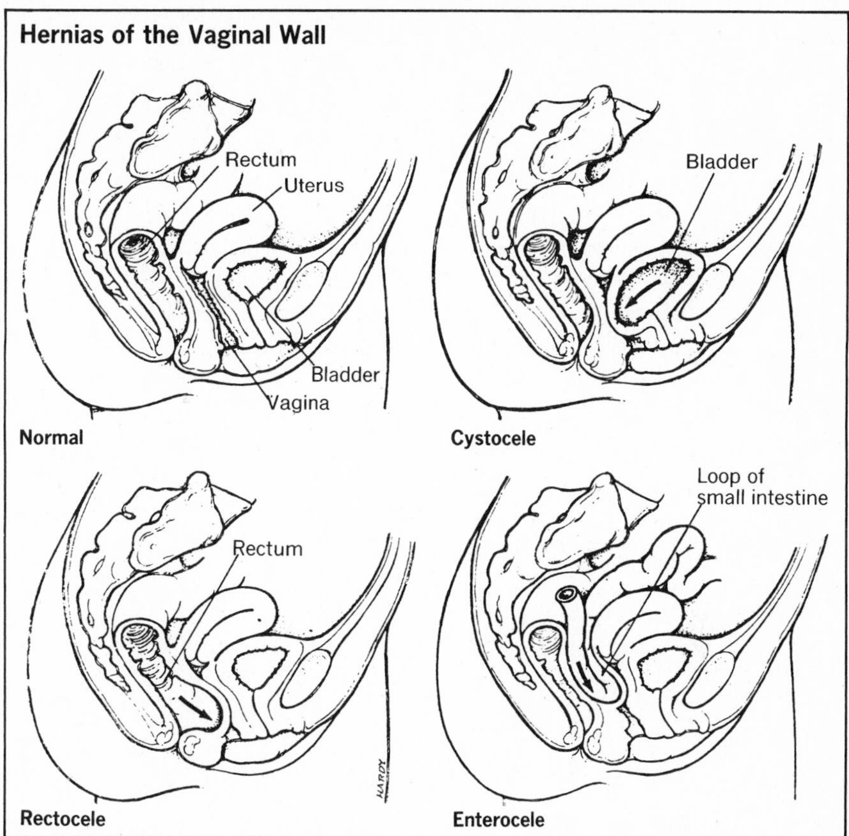

Hernias of the Vaginal Wall

The wall of the vagina may be ruptured in childbirth, especially in a multiple delivery or birth of a larger-than-average baby. The kind of hernia depends on the exact site of the rupture and what organ happens to lie against the vaginal wall at that point. The condition may be further complicated by a prolapsed uterus. Careful examination of the patient and X-ray pictures may be necessary to determine whether just one or several of the urinary, reproductive, and gastrointestinal organs in the pelvic cavity are involved.

Cystocele

Cystocele is a hernia involving the bladder and the vagina. Structurally, part of the bladder protrudes through the wall of the vagina. The symptoms, in addition to a feeling of pressure deep in the vagina, may be urinary difficulties, such as incontinence, a frequent urge to urinate, and inability to completely empty the bladder. Residual urine in the bladder may contribute to infection and inflammation of the bladder. Treatment includes surgery to correct the condition, pessaries if needed to support the structures, and medications to control infection.

Rectocele

A hernia involving the tissues separating the vagina and the rectum, behind the vagina, is called a *rectocele.* The symptoms are a feeling of fullness in the vagina and difficulty in defecating. Enemas or laxatives may be needed to relieve constipation because straining, or even coughing, can aggravate the condition. Surgery is the only permanently effective treatment. Special diets, laxatives, and rectal suppositories may be prescribed pending surgery.

Enterocele

A herniation of the small intestine into the vagina is called an *enterocele.* Some of the symptoms are similar to those of other hernias involving the vaginal wall, and in addition, a patient with an enterocele may experience abdominal cramps shortly after eating. An enterocele can be dangerous, as well as uncomfortable, because a segment of the small bowel can become trapped and obstructed, requiring emergency surgery.

Varicose Veins

Varicose veins of the vulva, vagina, and neighboring areas are another possible effect of pregnancy, although the legs are more often affected. Obesity, reduced physical activity during pregnancy, and circulatory changes associated with pregnancy can contribute to the development of varicose veins. The symptoms generally are limited to discomfort, although there can be bleeding, particularly at the time of childbirth.

Varicose veins that occur in the vulva and vagina during pregnancy and cause discomfort can be treated surgically during the early months of pregnancy. Some drugs and supportive therapy can be used to help relieve symptoms. But many physicians recommend that surgical stripping of veins be delayed until after the pregnancy has been terminated. A complication of untreated varicose veins can be development of blood clots in the abnormal blood vessels. For a discussion of varicose veins of the legs during pregnancy, see "Leg Cramps and Varicose Veins" in Ch. 4, *The Beginning of a Family.*

Benign Neoplasms

The word *neoplasm* refers to any abnormal proliferation of tissue that serves no useful function. There are numerous kinds of neoplasms but just two main groups—cancerous, or *malignant;* or noncancerous, or *benign.* In ordinary speech the word *benign* suggests some positive benefit, but a benign neoplasm, though noncancerous, may in fact be harmful to health or at least worrisome. Benign neoplasms that are of particular concern to women are discussed below.

Cysts

A *cyst* is a sac containing a gaseous, fluid, or semisolid material. (Certain normal anatomical structures, like the urinary bladder, are technically known as cysts—hence the term *cystitis* for inflammation of the bladder.) Abnormal, or neoplastic, cysts can develop at several sites within the urinary and reproductive systems.

Vaginal Cysts

A cyst may develop in a gland at the opening of the vagina as a result of infection with a venereal or other disease. Such a cyst can block the flow of secretions from the gland and produce swelling and pain. Dyspareunia, or painful intercourse, is sometimes a symptom. A vaginal-gland cyst usually is treated with antibiotics and hot packs. In some cases, it may be necessary for a physician to make an incision to drain the cyst.

Ovarian Cysts

Cysts in the ovaries may be caused by a malfunction of physiological process or by a pathological condition. Some pathological cysts are malignant. The cysts in the ovaries generally are filled with fluid that may range in color from pale and clear to reddish brown, depending upon the source of the fluid. Some cysts are too small to be seen with the naked eye, whereas others may be four or five inches in diameter when symptoms begin to cause discomfort. There are several different kinds of ovarian cysts.

Follicular Cyst

A *follicular,* or *retention,* cyst is a physiological cyst and is one of the most common types. It develops in an old follicle in which an ovum for some reason has failed to break out of its capsule during the ovulation process. Ordinarily, the contents of such a follicle are resorbed, but sometimes a cyst develops. It rarely grows larger than about two inches in diameter. It may rupture but usually disappears after a few months. The symptoms may include pain with some uterine bleeding and dyspareunia. Treatment consists of warm douches, analgesics, and hormone therapy designed to restore normal ovarian activity. If the symptoms persist or the cyst continues to increase in size, or if serious complications occur, the physician may recommend exploratory surgery.

Occasionally such cysts, whether or not they rupture, produce symptoms that mimic those of appendicitis, with severe abdominal pain. The abdomen may become so tender that a physician cannot palpate the organs in order to distinguish between an ovarian cyst and appendicitis, particularly if the right ovary is involved. The symptoms occur at the time that ovulation would be expected. If the physician cannot be certain that the cause of the abdominal pain is indeed a cyst, for which surgery is not needed, he may recommend surgery anyway—just to be on the safe side.

Multiple follicular cysts, involving the ovaries on both sides (*bilateral polycystic ovaries*) can result in a syndrome (or group of symptoms) that includes infertility, obesity, and abnormal growth of body hair. All of these effects are related to a disruption of normal sex-hormone activity; they generally occur in young women, from teenagers to those in their 20s. The therapy includes both medical and surgical efforts to restore normal menstrual function, a diet to control obesity, and the use of various depilatory techniques to remove unwanted body hair.

Corpus Luteum Cyst

This kind of cyst may develop in the ovary following ovulation or during the early part of a pregnancy. The corpus luteum is a small, temporary gland that forms in the empty follicle after the ovum has been released from the ovary. Its function is to produce the hormone progesterone, which is important in preparing the endometrium, the lining of the uterus, to receive a fertilized ovum. The corpus luteum, however, also can be overproductive of a brownish fluid that fills the former follicular space, causing it to swell to a diameter of two or three inches. The cyst causes symptoms of pain and tenderness and may also result in a disruption of normal menstrual cycles in a woman who is not pregnant.

Most corpus luteum cysts gradually decrease in size without special treatment, except to relieve the symptoms. There may, however, be complications, such as torsion, or painful twisting of the ovary, or a rupture of the cyst. A ruptured corpus luteum cyst can result in hemorrhage and peritonitis, requiring immediate surgery.

Chocolate Cyst

So called because of their brownish-red color, chocolate cysts consist of misplaced endometrial tissue growing on the ovary instead of in its normal position lining the uterus. Chocolate cysts are among the largest of the ovarian cysts, ranging up to five or six inches in diameter. They cause symptoms associated with a variety of disorders of the reproductive system, including infertility, dyspareunia, and dysmenorrhea. Surgery usually is a favored method of therapy, the precise procedure depending upon the amount of ovarian tissue involved. A small chocolate cyst can be cauterized, but a large cyst may require removal of a portion of the ovary. See also "Cancer of the Ovary" later in this chapter.

Cysts of the Breast

Cysts may form in the milk glands or the ducts leading from the glands. They are caused by imbalances in ovarian hormones and they tend to develop in mature women approaching the menopause. The cysts tend to fluctuate in size, often enlarging just before or during menstruation, and there may be a discharge from the nipple. Pain and tenderness are usually present, although painless cysts are sometimes discovered only when a woman examines her breasts for possible lumps. Cysts may be almost microscopic in size or as large as an inch or more in diameter. It is not uncommon for more than one cyst to occur at the same time in one breast or both.

A medical examination is recommended when any kind of lump can be felt in the breast tissue. This is particularly important for women who have passed menopause. The physician frequently can determine whether a lump is a result of a cyst or cancer by the patient's history and by physical examination, especially when repeated at intervals of several weeks. Mammography and biopsy study of a small bit of tissue are used to confirm the diagnosis.

Women who are troubled by breast cysts may be helped by wearing a good brassiere at all times, even during sleep, to protect tender areas. The only medications available are those that relieve pain and discomfort—symptoms that usually subside when the menopause is reached.

Other Noncancerous Masses

A benign lump in the breast can be caused by either a fat deposit or an abscess. A fatty mass frequently forms if an injury to the breast damages adipose tissue. Because of a similarity of the symptoms to those of breast cancer, a biopsy is usually required to distinguish the lesion from a cancer. The involved tissue may in any case be removed surgically.

An abscess of the breast as a result of an infection, although a rare problem, may produce a lump that requires treatment with antibiotic medications or by an incision to drain the pus. Breast infections leading to abscesses are most likely to occur in nursing mothers but can also develop in women who are not lactating. When an infection develops in a breast being used to nurse a baby, nursing has to be discontinued temporarily while the infection is treated. See also "Cancer of the Breast" later in this chapter.

Polyps

A *polyp* is a strange-looking growth, even for an abnormal growth of tissue. It has been described as having the appearance of a tennis racket or a small mushroom. Polyps are found in many parts of the body, from the nose to the rectum. Usually they are harmless. But a polyp can result in discomfort or bleeding and require surgical excision. A polyp on the breast, for example, can become irritated by rubbing against the fabric of a brassiere. Although polyps generally are not cancerous, it is standard procedure to have the polyp tissue, like any excised tissue, tested in the laboratory. If malignant cells accompany a polyp, they are usually found at the base of the growth, which means that some of the tissue around the polyp must be excised along with the growth itself. Once a polyp is removed it does not grow again, although other polyps can occur in the same region.

Cervical Polyp

Polyps in the cervix are not uncommon, occurring most frequently in the years between menarche and menopause. A cervical polyp may be associated with vaginal bleeding or leukorrhea; the bleeding may occur after douching or sexual intercourse. In some cases, the bleeding is severe. Cervical polyps can usually be located visually by an examining physician and removed by minor surgery.

Endometrial Polyp

Endometrial polyps, which develop in the lining of the uterus, usually occur in women who are over 40, although they can develop at any age after menarche. They are frequently the cause of nonmenstrual bleeding. They tend to be much larger than polyps that grow in other organs of the body: an endometrial polyp may be rooted high in the uterus with a stem reaching all the way to the cervix. Such a polyp is usually located and removed during a D- and C- procedure. As in the case of a cervical polyp, the growth and a bit of surrounding tissue are studied for traces of cancer cells.

Benign Tumors

Tumors are rather firm growths that may be either benign or malignant. In practice, any tumor is regarded with suspicion unless malignancy is ruled out by actual laboratory tests. Even a benign tumor represents a tissue abnormality, and if untreated can produce symptoms that interfere with normal health and activity.

Fibromas

Among the more common of the benign tumors is the *fibroma,* commonly known as a *fibroid tumor,* composed of fibrous connective tissue. About one of every 20 ovarian tumors is a fibroma, and a similar growth in the uterus is the most common type of tumor found in that organ. Fibromas also occur in the vulva.

Ovarian Fibroma

Ovarian fibromas are usually small, but there are instances in which they have grown to weigh as much as five pounds. A large fibroma can be very painful and produce symptoms such as a feeling of heaviness in the pelvic area, nausea, and vomiting. The growth may crowd other organs of the body, causing enlargement of the abdomen and cardiac and respiratory symptoms. The only treatment is surgical removal of the tumor, after which there is usually a quick and full recovery.

Uterine Fibroma

Fibroid tumors of the uterus can also grow to a very large size, some weighing many pounds. Like ovarian fibromas, they can press against neighboring organs such as the intestine or the urinary bladder, producing constipation or urinary difficulty. More commonly, there is pain and vaginal bleeding, along with pelvic pressure and enlargement of the abdomen. It is possible in some cases for a fibroid tumor to grow slowly in the uterus for several years without causing serious discomfort to the patient. If the tumor obstructs or distorts the reproductive tract, it may be a cause of infertility.

Treatment of fibroid tumors varies according to their size, the age of the patient and her expectations about having children, and other factors. If the tumor is small and does not appear to be growing at a rapid rate, the physician may recommend that surgery be postponed as long as the tumor poses no threat to health. For an older woman, or for a woman who does not want to bear children, a hysterectomy may be advised, especially if symptoms are troublesome. If the patient is a young woman who wants to have children, the physician is likely to advise a *myomectomy,* a surgical excision of the tumor, since a fibroid tumor of the uterus can cause serious complications during pregnancy and labor. It can result in abortion or premature labor, malpresentation of the fetus, difficult labor, and severe loss of blood during childbirth. While fibroid tumors of the uterus are not malignant, special tests are made of the endometrial tissue as part of any myomectomy or hysterectomy to rule out the possibility that cancer cells may be involved in the disorder.

Endometriosis

Endometriosis is the medical term for a condition in which endometrial tissue, the special kind of tissue that lines the uterus, grows in various areas of the pelvic cavity outside the uterus. Endometrial cells may invade such unlikely places as the ovaries (the most common site), the bladder, appendix, Fallopian tubes, intestinal tract, or the supporting structure of the uterus. The external endometrial tissue may appear as small blisters of endometrial cells, as solid nodules, or as cysts, usually of the ovary, which may be four inches or more in diameter, like the chocolate cysts of the ovaries. Such a mass of sometimes tumorlike endometrial cells is called an *endometrioma.*

The misplaced endometrial tissue causes problems because it goes through menstrual cycles just as the endometrium does within the cavity of the uterus. The endometrial tissue proliferates after ovulation and may cause almost constant pain, wherever it is located, for a few days before the start of menstruation. The symptoms subside after the menstrual flow begins. The effects may include dyspareunia, rectal bleeding, backache, and generalized pain in the pelvic region as sensitive tissues throughout the pelvic cavity are irritated by monthly cycles of swelling and bleeding.

Because infertility is associated with endometriosis, which can become progressively worse, young women who want to bear children are sometimes encouraged to begin efforts to become pregnant as early as possible if they show signs or symptoms of the disorder. Treatment includes hormone medication and surgery to remove the lesions of endometriosis or the organ involved. For patients with extensive spread of endometrial tissue outside the uterus, the physician may recommend removal of one or both ovaries. Destruction of the ovaries surgically or by radiation therapy may be employed to eliminate the menstrual cycle activity that aggravates the symptoms of endometriosis. These procedures cause sterility and premature menopause, but some women prefer this to the discomfort of endometriosis. The hormone therapy inhibits the ovulation phase of the menstrual cycle. Without ovulation, the endometrial tissue does not proliferate. For this reason, pregnancy often eliminates or eases the symptoms of endometriosis during parturition and for a period of time thereafter.

Dyspareunia

Dyspareunia, or painful intercourse, is often associated with endometriosis and is attributed to irritation of nerve fibers in the area of the cervix from the pressure of sexual activity. There are many other possible causes of painful intercourse, some functional and some organic in nature. In addition to endometriosis, the problem may be owing to a vaginal contracture, a disorder involving the muscles of the pelvic region, inflammation of the vagina or urethra, prolapsed or malpositioned uterus, *cervicitis* (inflammation of the cervix), or a disorder of the bladder or rectum. A cause of dyspareunia in older women may be a degeneration of the tissues lining the vagina, which become thin and dry. Temporary therapy for dyspareunia may include water-soluble lubricants, anesthetic ointments, steroid hormones, analgesics, and sedatives. In appropriate cases, surgery is effective in correcting an organic cause of painful sexual intercourse. Functional or psychogenic (of psychological origin) causes of dyspareunia usually require psychological counseling for the patient and her sexual partner.

Backache

Still another effect of endometriosis that can suggest other disorders is backache. When endometrial tissue invades the pelvic region, there may be a fairly constant pain in the back near the tailbone or the rectum. Usually the backache subsides only after the cause has been eliminated. Temporary measures include those advised for other kinds of backache: sleeping on a firm mattress, preferably reinforced with a sheet of plywood between springs and mattress; application of dry heat or warm baths; sedatives to relieve tension, and analgesics to relieve the pain.

A backache that radiates down the back and into a leg, following the path of a sciatic nerve, can be the result of a disorder of the ovaries or uterus. An ovarian cyst or infection of the Fallopian tubes can produce a backache that seems to be centered in the lumbosacral area of the spinal column. Such backaches, sometimes called gynecologic backaches, tend to occur most frequently during a woman's childbearing years and more often affect women who have had several children than women who have not been pregnant. Tumors also can produce backache symptoms. X-ray pictures, myelograms, and laboratory studies may be required in order to rule out the possibilities that the back pain may be caused by a tumor, a herniated or "slipped" disk, or a deformity of the spinal column that might have been aggravated by one or more pregnancies. Most backaches, however, relate to poor posture or muscle tension. Anxiety or other kinds of emotional stress can aggravate the symptoms. See also "Backaches" in Ch. 23, *Aches, Pains, Nuisances, Worries,* and "Back Pain and Its Causes" in Ch. 25, *Women's Health.*

Cancers of the Reproductive System

Cancer of the Cervix

The cervix of the uterus is the second most common site of cancers affecting the reproductive system of women. As compared with all cancers affecting women, it rates third, after breast cancer and colon and rectum cancer. It has been estimated that about 20,000 cases of cervical cancer are found among American women each year, and approximately 7,500 deaths every year are a result of this disease.

Though it is not considered a venereal disease, cancer of the cervix seems to be closely related to past sexual activity. Statistically, women who began sexual intercourse at an early age or who have had many partners are much more likely to have cervical cancer than women who have never engaged in sexual activity or who have had one or very few sexual partners. The actual causes of cervical cancer are still unknown. Current medical thinking suggests that there is no causal relationship between cervical cancer and the use of oral contraceptives.

Preinvasive Stage

The earliest signs of cervical cancer tend to appear between the ages of

25 and 45. At this early, *preinvasive* stage, the cancer is described as *in situ*—confined to its original site. If the cancer is not treated at this stage, the disease spreads and becomes a typical invasive cancer within five to ten years. Signs of bleeding and ulceration usually do not appear until this has occurred. However, because of the relatively slow growth of cervical cancer in the early stage, the disease usually can be detected by a Pap smear test before it becomes invasive.

Diagnostic Methods

Pap Smear Test

The *Pap smear* test (named for Dr. George Papanicolaou, who developed the technique in 1928) is a quick and simple method of detecting cancerous cells in secretions and scrapings from mucous membrane. It requires the collection of small samples of cells from the surface of the cervix and from the cervical canal. Such samples are obtained by inserting a plastic spatula or a cut wooden tongue depressor into the vagina, into which a speculum has been placed previously. The device is scraped gently over the areas of the cervix in which a cancer is most likely to develop, or from any other surface of the cervix that appears abnormal during visual inspection. The physician may collect also a sample of vaginal secretions, which may contain possibly cancerous cells not only from the cervix but from the ovaries and uterus as well. (This is the only way a Pap smear test can be done if a woman has had a complete hysterectomy and has no cervix.) All cell samples are placed (smeared) on microscope slides and treated with a chemical preservative. The slides are sent to a laboratory for study and a report is made to the examining physician, usually within a few days, on the findings.

The laboratory report may classify the cell samples as negative (normal), suspicious, or positive. If the findings are negative, the woman will be advised to return in one year for another Pap smear test. If the findings are suspicious, the woman usually will be asked to return for a second test either immediately or within six months. A report of suspicious findings generally indicates the presence of unusual or abnormal cells, which may be a result of an infection or inflammation, as well as of a cancerous condition. If a specific disease organism is found in a sample—such as a *Trichomonas* organism, for example—the laboratory report includes that information.

Other Diagnostic Tests

A positive Pap smear is one containing cells that are probably or definitely cancerous. When a report of positive findings is returned by the laboratory, the physician immediately arranges for further studies. These involve examination of the cervix visually by a special microscopic technique known as *colposcopy,* and the removal of small tissue samples. These studies are usually done in a physician's office. In some cases a biopsy is necessary. This requires that the woman enter a hospital, where she can receive an anesthetic. The biopsy sample is taken when possible from the same location on the cervix as the Pap smear that resulted in positive findings. Other tests, including X-ray films of the chest and bones, can be made during the hospital stay to determine whether the cancer, if verified by biopsy, has extended to nearby areas or spread to other areas of the body by metastasis. Treatment ordinarily is not started until all of the studies have verified that there is cancer in the tissues of the cervix; other disorders, such as cervicitis, venereal infection, and polyps, can mimic symptoms of cervical cancer.

Therapy

The kind of treatment recommended for a case of cervical cancer generally depends upon several factors, such as the stage of cancer development and the age and general health of the patient. For a young woman who wishes to have children despite cancer *in situ,* which is limited to the cervix, surgeons may excise a portion of the cervix and continue watching for further developments with frequent Pap smears and other tests. The treatment of choice for cervical cancer in the early stage, however, is surgical removal of the body of the uterus, as well as of the cervix—a procedure called a *total hysterectomy.* This is the usual treatment for women over the age of 40 or for those who do not wish to have children. Sometimes more extensive surgery is necessary.

Radiation treatment may be advised for women who are not considered to be good surgical risks because of other health problems. Radiation may be recommended along with surgery for women with advanced cervical cancer in order to help destroy cancer cells that may have spread by metastasis to other tissues.

The five-year cure rate for cervical cancer is about 99 percent when treatment is started in the early, preinvasive stage. The chances of a cure drop sharply in later stages, but the five-year cure rate is still as high as 65 percent if treatment is started when the cancer has just begun to spread to the vagina or other nearby tissues.

Cancer of the Body of the Uterus

Cancer of the body of the uterus, or *endometrial cancer,* is less common than cancer of the cervix. Cervical cancer primarily affects women before middle age; endometrial cancer occurs more frequently among women beyond the menopause, with its highest rate occurring among women between the ages of 60 and 70. A statistical correlation has been found between the increased use of estrogen hormones and the growing rate of cancer of the uterus among middle-aged women since the 1960s. It has been suggested that the uterine lining (endometrium) in some women is particularly sensitive to the effects of estrogens.

Diagnostic Methods

Early symptoms usually include bleeding between menstrual periods or after menopause, and occasionally a watery or blood-stained vaginal discharge. Most patients experience no pain in the early stages, although pain is a symptom in advanced uterine cancer or when the disease is complicated by an infection. Unfortunately, there is no simple test, like the Pap smear for cervical cancer, that provides a good diagnostic clue to the presence of endometrial cancer. The Pap smear does occasionally pick up cells sloughed off by the endometrium, and laboratory tests can tell if they might be malignant. But a physician who is suspicious of symptoms of endometrial cancer must depend upon more direct methods to confirm or rule out the disease. The usual method is a D and C, during which a small sample of uterine lining will be removed for biopsy, or a sample may be withdrawn by suction (aspirated) from the uterine cavity. Aspiration can be done in the physician's office with local anesthesia of the cervix or with no anesthesia. There is little or no discomfort following aspiration.

Therapy

If the diagnostic D and C is done when the abnormal bleeding associated with uterine cancer first begins, the chances of a cure are very good. The first step, if the general health of the patient permits surgery, is complete removal of the uterus, ovaries, and Fallopian tubes—a procedure called a *radical hysterectomy.* Radiation may also be administered to control the spread of cancer cells in the pelvic region.

Because 90 percent of the women affected by endometrial cancer are past childbearing age, removal of the reproductive organs is usually less traumatic for them than it would be if they were young women with hopes of raising families. For premenopausal women, the natural ovarian hormones that are lost with the ovaries may be artificially replaced by prescription drugs in order to ease the sudden transition to a menopausal condition.

A hysterectomy should not affect a woman's normal sexual activity. Sexual relations usually can be resumed about six to eight weeks after the operation, or when the incision has healed. If the incision is made through the pubic region or vagina, there should be little or no visible scar.

A number of possible causes of uterine cancer have been suggested. High blood pressure, diabetes, and obesity are believed to increase the risk of developing endometrial cancer. There is some evidence that the disease tends to occur in families, particularly among women who experience a greater-than-average degree of menstrual difficulty.

Estrogen and Cancer

There is a higher incidence of cancer of the uterus among women who have tumors of the ovary that produce estrogen, as well as among women whose menopause begins later than the usual age (and hence who have produced estrogen naturally for a longer-than-usual period). Because of the statistical associations between uterine cancer and estrogen-producing tumors, as well as other factors, the American Cancer Society has cautioned that physicians should exert "close supervision of women on estrogen, with an awareness that sustained use [of estrogens] may stimulate dormant factors in the body and lead to development of endometrial cancer."

Among the conditions for which estrogen has been prescribed for women of middle age and beyond are uncomfortable effects of menopause, such as itching and irritation caused by dryness of the vagina and what is commonly referred to as "hot flashes." However, there are available hormone creams that help relieve dryness of the vaginal tissues; the creams may contain estrogen, but not enough to cause concern about their possible carcinogenic properties.

Diethylstilbestrol

An estrogenlike synthetic compound has definitely been implicated in the development of a type of cancer, *adenocarcinoma,* which primarily affects epithelial tissue. The synthetic hormone known chemically as *diethylstilbestrol* (DES) or stilbestrol was taken for the most part in the late 1940s and through the 1950s by pregnant women for the treatment of such complications as bleeding and threatened miscarriage. Around 1971, physicians became aware that some of the daughters whose mothers had taken DES during their pregnancy had developed an unusual cell formation in vaginal tissue, vaginal and cervical cancers, and some anatomical abnormalities. Cancers have been discovered in daughters as young as seven years of age. An unknown but substantial number of women in the United States alone received DES while pregnant, but only about 200 of their daughters have been found to be afflicted with cervical or vaginal cancers. The National Cancer Institute has urged that all mothers and daughters who may have been exposed to DES during the mother's pregnancy arrange to be examined by a physician for possible effects of the drug.

The use of DES for pregnant women has been discontinued, although the compound is still available for treating certain cases of breast cancer and menopausal symptoms in nonpregnant women.

Cancer of the Ovary

Cancer of the ovary is not as common as cervical and endometrial cancers, but ovarian cancer does account for nearly one out of every six malignant tumors of the female reproductive system. The disease is responsible for a greater number of deaths, because an ovarian cancer can remain symptomless until it has spread. There are several different kinds of malignant tumors of the ovary; some originate in the ovaries and others are caused by cells that have metastasized from a cancer at some other site, such as the uterus.

There are no age limits for cancer of the ovary, although most cases are detected in women between 50 and 70. A physician at a routine pelvic examination may notice a lump or other abnormal growth in the abdominal region. The symptoms reported by patients usually include abdominal discomfort or digestive problems, possibly because ovarian cancers often grow large enough to press on neighboring organs and cause urinary difficulties, constipation, or other digestive disorders. A clue is given in some cases by endometrial bleeding as a result of abnormal hormone production by the affected ovary. However, the more common kinds of ovarian cancers do not produce hormones. Occasionally, cancer cells from an ovarian tumor will be found in a Pap smear sample. But there are no direct, simple tests for cancer of the ovary.

Treatment for ovarian cancer varies with the individual case. As with cancer at other sites, surgery is generally necessary. The extent of the surgery depends upon the type of lesion and other factors. In an advanced case of an older woman, total hysterectomy along with removal of the ovaries and Fallopian tubes would be the treatment of choice. But if the patient is a young woman and the cancer is not extensive, the surgeon may excise the affected ovary and leave the remainder of the reproductive system intact. Radiation and chemotherapy are commonly applied in addition to surgery. The cure rate for ovarian cancers depends upon the type of tumor and the stage at which treatment started; the five-year survival chances range upward to about 65 percent.

Cancer of the Breast

Cancer of the breast is one of the oldest and best-known types of cancer. It is described in an ancient Egyptian papyrus of 5,000 years ago. The hormonal factors involved in the physiology of breast cancer have been studied by physicians for more than 100 years. But it remains the most common of cancers affecting woman. It kills more women than any other kind of cancer, and more people of both sexes (a minuscule number are men) than only two other cancers—lung cancer and cancer of the colon and rectum. About 90,000 women in the United States develop breast cancer each year, and more than a third die of the disease. Nearly everyone knows a friend or relative who has been stricken by breast cancer. Yet the cause of breast cancer is still unknown.

Breast cancer is less common in the Orient than in America and Western Europe, but Asian women who move to America seem to increase their risk of developing breast cancer—indicating that there may be a dietary factor or some other environmental influence. Women whose female relatives have had breast cancer are more likely to be victims than women from families in which breast cancer is not present. The disease appears to be linked statistically also to women who do not have children before their 30s or who do not have any children; to mothers who do not nurse their babies; to women who reach the menopause later than normal; and to women who began menstruation earlier in life than normal. There is increasing evidence also that ovarian activity may play an important role in the development of breast cancer. Women with ovarian tumors and women who use supplementary estrogen have been shown by some studies to be at increased risk, while the process of having many children and nursing them, which suppresses estrogen hormone activity, is associated with a decreased risk of developing breast cancer.

Cancer of the breast may occur as early as the teens, but this is rare. It is generally not found before the age of 30, and the incidence peaks around the time of menopause. Then there is a second period after the age of about

65 when the incidence of breast cancer rises again.

Breast cancer usually begins in the ducts of the milk glands; the first noticeable sign is a lump in the breast. The lump may appear anywhere in the breast, but the most common site is the upper, outer quadrant. Such lumps are not necessarily or even usually cancerous, but a biopsy (described below) must be performed to check the tissue involved.

In a typical case of breast cancer, a small tumor half an inch in diameter, large enough to be detected during careful self-examination, can grow to a cancer two inches in diameter in six months to a year. The lump generally causes no pain; pain is rarely associated with early breast cancer. If the tumor is allowed to grow unchecked, it may cause pulling of the skin from within. This effect may appear as a flattening of the breast or a dimpling of the skin, or a sinking, tilting, or flattening of the nipple. Less frequently, the tumor begins in a duct near the nipple, causing irritation of the skin of the nipple and a moist discharge. In such cases a scab eventually forms at that site. In time, cancer cells spread to the nearby lymph nodes and the danger becomes very serious of metastasis to any part of the body.

Detection of Breast Cancer

Fortunately, breast cancer can be treated effectively if it is detected early enough. Some 95 percent of breast cancers are discovered by the patient herself when she notices a lump. In all too many cases the discovery is made by chance and the lump may be quite large. The cure rate for breast cancer could be greatly improved if all women made a routine of monthly self-examination and then consulted a physician immediately if they found the least indication of a thickening or lump. Most such lumps are benign, but it is most important that the ones that are malignant be identified without delay.

The American Cancer Society and the National Cancer Institute recommend that every woman follow a prescribed method of self-examination just after the menstrual period, continuing every month after the menopause. The procedure consists of carefully looking at and feeling the breasts, and takes only a few minutes. A detailed description of the proper procedure is available in pamphlet form from the Superintendent of Documents, U.S. Government Printing Office, Washington, D.C. 20402. Ask for Public Health Service Publication No. 1730. A film entitled *Breast Self-Examination,* produced by the American Cancer Society and the National Cancer Institute, is also available.

If a tumor can be detected as even a small lump, it must have been developing for some time. There is a truism about breast cancer to the effect that a cancer that is undetectable is curable—leaving unspoken the implication that a cancer that is detectable may not be curable. In recent

Self-examination of the Breasts

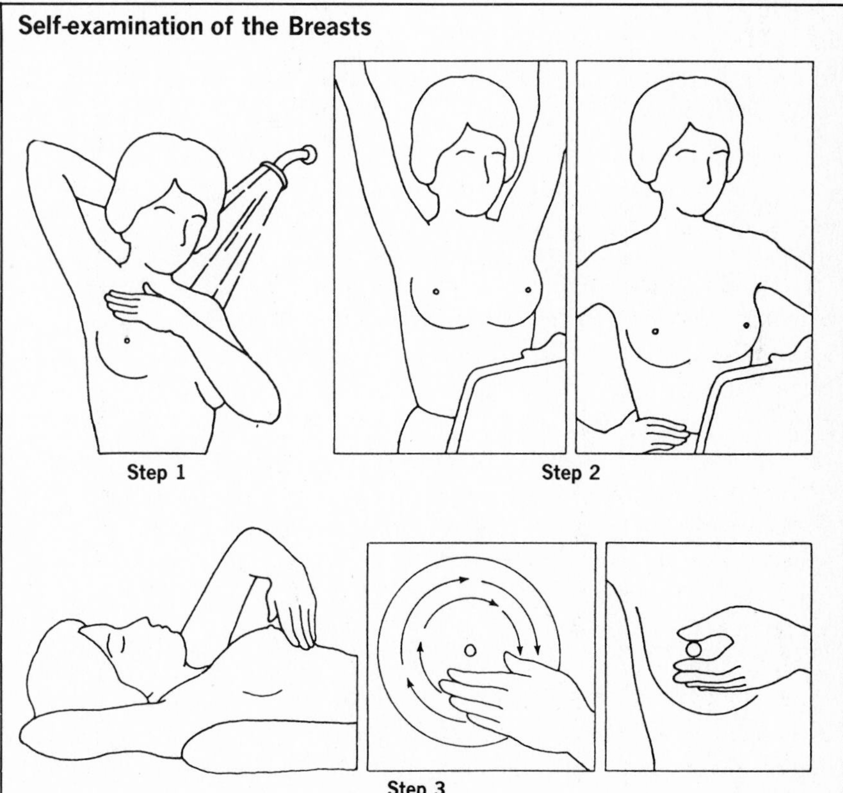

Self-examination of the breasts as recommended by the American Cancer Society. *(Step 1)* Examine breasts during a shower or bath; hands glide easier over wet skin. With fingers flat, move the left hand gently over every part of the right breast, then the right hand over the left breast. Check for any lump, hard knot, or thickening. *(Step 2)* Before a mirror, inspect the breasts with arms at the sides, then with arms raised. Look for any changes in the contour of each breast, a swelling, dimple of skin, or changes in the nipple. Then rest palms on hips and press down firmly to flex the chest muscles. Left and right breasts will not match exactly—few women's breasts do. But regular inspection will show what is normal for you. *(Step 3)* While lying down with a pillow or folded towel under the right shoulder and with the right hand behind the head, examine the right breast with the left hand. With fingers flat, press gently in small circular motions around an imaginary clock face. Begin at 12 o'clock, then move to 1 o'clock, and so on around back to 12. A ridge of firm tissue in the lower curve of each breast is normal. Next, move in an inch toward the nipple and keep circling to examine every part of the breast, including the nipple. This requires at least three more circles. Then repeat the procedure slowly on the left breast with the pillow under the left shoulder and left hand behind the head. Notice how the breast structure feels. Finally, squeeze the nipple of each breast gently between thumb and index finger. Any discharge, clear or bloody, should be reported to a physician immediately.

years, methods of early detection have been refined to the point that tumors once undetectable can now be detected before any lump becomes palpable.

Thermography

One early warning detection technique involves the use of *thermography,* which is based on the fact that tumor cells produce slightly more heat than normal tissue. Hence a device that is sufficiently heat sensitive can detect and pinpoint the location of an incipient tumor. A harmless tumor, too, would have a higher-than-normal temperature. Further tests would be needed to determine the true cause of the "hot" tissue-reading.

Mammography

Mammography is an X-ray technique developed specifically for examination of breast tissue. A tumor shows up on a mammogram as an opaque spot because of mineral concentrations associated with the growth. However, like thermography, mammography cannot determine whether a tumor is benign or malignant or if the opaque spot on the film is because of some other mineral-rich tissue rather than a tumor. The examining physician uses mammography only as one among other diagnostic tools.

Mammography has been widely used by cancer detection centers throughout America in past years. Since 1976, the National Cancer Institute and the American Cancer Society have cautioned physicians and patients about the routine use of mammography, particularly for women under 50 years of age and if older types of X-ray equipment are used. Studies have shown that exposure of the breasts to X rays, especially at the dosages produced by the older equipment, and perhaps even by the newer low-intensity equipment, increases the chances of breast cancer by about one percentage point. This means that a woman at low risk who has, say, a six percent chance of developing breast cancer would increase her risk to seven—by a factor of almost 17 percent—by exposure to X-ray mammography. A woman originally at higher risk would suffer a smaller percentage increment. Hence cancer experts continue to approve the use of X-ray mammography only for high-risk groups—women who have a history of breast cancer or who have had lumps in their breasts, women above the age of 50, and younger women in the high-risk categories outlined above.

Xeroradiography

Xeroradiography is a method that, like mammography, uses X rays, but it entails only about half the exposure to radiation. The pictures are developed by xerography, the process made familiar by Xerox copying machines. The picture consists of dots in varying shades of blue. The process produces a sharp picture, making interpretation simpler and more accurate than is possible with X-ray photographs. When performed by experienced medical technicians, xeroradiography can detect from 85 to 95 percent of all breast cancer, including those too small to be located by palpation. The xeroradiography examination and the physician's examination of the breast usually take only about 20 minutes.

Other Methods

Other diagnostic tools have come into use. *Ultrasound* and *diaphanography,* for example, have reportedly proved their value, especially when combined with other techniques, including mammography. Ultrasound depends on sound waves that vibrate at frequencies beyond the range of human hearing; transmitted into the breast, ultrasound can distinguish between lumps that are cystic and fluid-filled—and therefore benign—and those that are solid. Other tests, however, may be needed to differentiate between benign solid and malignant solid lumps. In diaphanography, or transillumination, a technician or physician shines an ordinary white light through the breast in the dark. An overhead camera takes pictures with infrared film. Diaphanography can determine whether breast lumps are fibrous, benign, or malignant.

Fine needle aspiration has also proved useful in diagnosing breast cancer. The surgeon uses a needle to draw out a sample approximately 0.5 cm in size. Microscopic examination of the sample follows.

Biopsy

When a physician believes there is good evidence of a cancer in a breast as a result of thermography, xeroradiography, mammography, palpation of lumps, and other factors, the next step is a biopsy study. The suspected lesion is located for the biopsy procedure and the exact position and extent of the planned incision is marked on the skin. The patient is then wheeled into the operating room and the tissue sample is excised while the patient is anesthetized. An entire nodule of breast tissue is removed for microscopic examination of the tissue cells. It is sent to the pathology department, which usually reports within 90 minutes whether the tissue is noncancerous or malignant. Provisional preparations are made for a mastectomy. If the lesion is not cancerous—and between 60 and 80 percent of biopsies of breast lumps are not—the patient is taken back to the recovery room and, as soon as possible, reassured that the tumor was benign. The incision made for the biopsy leaves an almost indiscernible scar.

The Two-Step Procedure

Because of the psychological and physical problems associated with breast cancer, approaches to surgery have changed drastically in recent years. The patient today has a choice: if she desires, she can request that the test and operation take place in two separate stages. To make that choice, the woman simply does not sign a form granting permission to perform both the biopsy and the *mastectomy,* or breast removal, on the same day.

In many cases, it may be necessary to perform both operations on the same day. In such cases, experts say, the woman should insist that her surgeon refer her for presurgical *staging.*

Staging involves administration of various tests that are carried out before a mastectomy. The tests show whether the cancer has already spread, or metastasized, to parts of the body other than the breast and local lymph node regions. Staging is widely regarded as a necessary procedure in all cases of breast cancer. A mastectomy has the single purpose of preventing the spread of cancer; the patient has to know, for her own peace of mind, whether it has already spread.

A two-step procedure involves other choices. Where the biopsy is to be carried out separately, the patient may ask to have it done under local anesthesia, as an outpatient. That possibility can be explored with the surgeon. If a general anesthetic appears preferable, the patient may have to spend a night in the hospital. But the *diagnostic biopsy*—involving surgical removal of the entire tumor—and mastectomy can still be performed separately. After a biopsy specimen is removed, the specimen may be subjected to an estrogen-receptor assay. The assay tells the surgeon whether or not the cancer depends on the female hormone estrogen for its growth. That information provides a clue to possible future treatment.

The two-step procedure offers some advantages insofar as diagnosis is concerned. In particular, it makes possible a "permanent section" in which excised tissue is chemically treated to produce a high-quality slide for microscopic examination. Such an examination is far more complete and accurate than the "frozen section" that is necessary in the one-step procedure. The freezing process may distort the cells, leading sometimes to inaccurate results. For many women, the one- to two-day wait for the results of a permanent-section biopsy is worth the time involved, especially because it may be possible to perform the biopsy under local anesthesia on an outpatient basis.

Following the biopsy, the patient receives the pathologist's report on whether the finding is positive or negative. If positive, precise information will usually be given on the type of cancer and where it is located in the breast. Then the patient may want to obtain a second opinion on the permanent-section pathology report and slides. The second opinion is also given by a pathologist. It helps materially in making decisions on appropriate surgery.

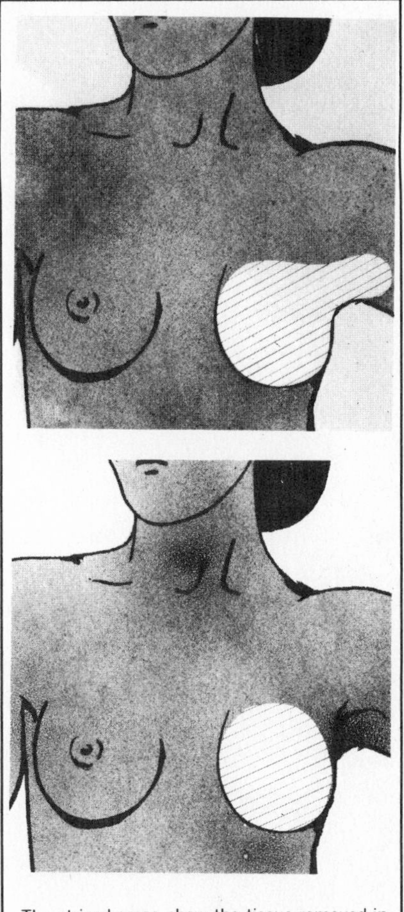

The striped areas show the tissue removed in a radical *(above)* and a simple *(below)* mastectomy, including the axillary lymph nodes in the former case.

Mastectomy

If the lesion is malignant, the surgeon proceeds with the mastectomy. Depending upon the seriousness of the case and the procedure recommended by the surgeon and the pathologist, the operation may be a *simple mastectomy,* a *radical mastectomy,* a *modified radical mastectomy,* or any of a number of other forms of breast operation. In the United States until recently, radical mastectomy was the usual procedure for breast cancer treatment. Today, at least seven different types of mastectomy, some more widely accepted than others, may be performed. All may be recommended in different cases depending upon the type of cancer, its invasive potential, or ability to spread, and other factors. The seven:

- *Wedge excision, lumpectomy,* or *segmental resection:* the tumor is removed along with some surrounding tissue

- *Simple mastectomy:* the breast alone is removed
- *Simple mastectomy* accompanied by *low axillary dissection:* the breast is removed along with some of the underarm nodes or glands
- *Modified-radical mastectomy* accompanied by *full axillary dissection:* the breast is removed along with all the lymph glands under the arm
- *Halsted-type radical mastectomy:* the breast is removed along with the underarm lymph glands and the chest muscles
- *Radical mastectomy* with *internal mammary node biopsy:* the same procedure as the Halsted-type radical mastectomy, except that the lymph nodes that lie under the ribs, next to the breastbone, are also sampled for biopsy and
- *Super-radical mastectomy:* the same as the above, but all of the internal mammary nodes are removed

Most patients have deep concern about many aspects of breast surgery, including the cosmetic effects. For that reason, it is important to select the appropriate type of surgery. The rates of survival appear to depend as much on timely use of pre- and postoperative radiotherapy and postoperative chemotherapy as on the type of operation. But the kind of operation may determine whether the patient will be able to function normally in a relatively short period of time.

Postoperative Therapies

The type of surgery recommended in any given case of breast cancer has significance for postoperative therapy. Breast surgery may be less extensive or radical where the cancer has spread to the lymph nodes or to other parts of the body; the use of chemotherapy and radiation therapy may then be more aggressive.

More commonly, the cancer is localized. The patient's options may, in consequence, include:

- surgery only;
- surgery with radiation;
- surgery with chemotherapy;
- surgery with a combination of these treatments; or
- radiation or chemotherapy without surgery.

The choices of alternative therapies should be made with an eye to still other factors.

Radiation

A lumpectomy, or segmental mastectomy, is usually followed by radiation therapy. Treatments are typically given five days a week for five weeks. A "booster" treatment may follow completion of the initial series of treatments. Side effects from radiation therapy include fatigue; reddened, moist, or dry skin at the site of the radiation; decreased or heightened sensitivity; enlarged pores; and sometimes changes in breast size.

Chemotherapy

Adjuvant chemotherapy, which follows surgery, is the usual treatment of choice where breast cancer has spread to the lymph nodes and where the patient has not entered menopause. Postmenopausal women may be given tamoxifen, an antiestrogen drug, or may undergo chemotherapy. Except for some high-risk patients, adjuvant chemotherapy is not recommended for women with noncancerous nodes.

Hormone Therapy

Less toxic than chemotherapy, hormone treatments are normally given to women whose cancer has not spread to the underarm nodes and whose tumors were hormone-dependent. This is especially the case if a patient is postmenopausal. For these women tamoxifen would also be a standard treatment if the cancers had spread to the lymph nodes.

Other Alternatives

Some other alternatives are open to the woman who has been diagnosed as having breast cancer. For example, radiation alone may be recommended where the disease is so far advanced that surgery is not feasible, or where the patient's health is too poor to risk surgery. In addition, radiation treatment may be effective in reducing the pain in bones or areas of the central nervous system where cancer cells may have metastasized. Radiation also may be used in addition to chemotherapy in certain cases because X rays, or similar radiation, can reach areas where chemical medications cannot penetrate.

The Rape Victim

The woman who has been raped faces special problems. Authorities agree that long-term health threats can be minimized if the victim takes certain precautions. Complications arising from sexual assault include contracting sexually transmitted disease (STD) or other diseases; becoming pregnant; and experiencing the aftereffects of contusions and abrasions. In general, the experts suggest that women take steps to protect themselves against rape and follow certain procedures in the event that a rape occurs.

Precautions

Because rapists generally attack without warning, the woman who feels that she is at risk can sometimes do little more than exercise vigilance in protecting herself. There are precautions, however, that women may take. Self-defense or martial-arts courses may be the answer for some. Although weapons may impart a sense of security, authorities are divided on the issue of their value. Additionally, the weapons themselves may be illegal in some cities or states. Noisemakers, including whistles and siren devices, may or may not be either available or effective, depending upon the circumstances.

Among the possible nonviolent methods of self-protection are the following:

- If you are being followed by a man who is more than 20 or so feet away, you can scream or use a noisemaker.
- Where possible, if followed, you should go into a store and tell the proprietor or clerk that you want to use a telephone.
- Again where possible, bring third parties into the situation—a chance pedestrian, perhaps another woman, or a passing group.
- Remain out of doors if your choice lies between entering a hallway or lobby or staying outside.
- Never go home if you know there is no one home. Instead ring all the door bells on apartment doors or go to a neighbor you know will be home.
- If you find it necessary to walk alone at night, walk in the street—again if possible and safe.
- Take a taxicab home if you have to travel late at night, and ask the driver to wait until you get indoors.
- Even when entering your own building, check the entrance and both sides before going inside.
- If you live alone, pretend you don't.

If a Rape Occurs

The rape victim may face a long period in which recovery and normal living seem impossible. The ability to enjoy life, sex, love, and work may appear to be elusive, even nonexistent. Six months or a year may pass without bringing relief from bad dreams, feelings of guilt, insomnia, and many other physical and psychological aftereffects. But authorities say that what a victim does after experiencing rape may make the transition to normal living easier while also protecting her against recurring health problems.

The Sympathetic Ear

Preferably before, but certainly after reporting to the police, the victim should confide in another person—whether husband, lover, close woman friend, counselor, pastor, hotline volunteer, or someone else trustworthy. The person confided in should go to the police station with the victim—if not the first time, then on any later occasions. The person confided in should be able to provide support, to make sure the victim's rights are protected, and to listen sympathetically to the victim's story.

Going to the Hospital

The rape victim should go as soon as possible to a hospital and undergo the pelvic and other examinations that physicians administer in such cases. If the woman goes to the hospital immediately, she should not wash herself or change clothes. A shower can remove valuable medical evidence. The pelvic examination is designed to find evidence of abrasions or internal damage, and for collection of any semen left by the rapist. Physicians will also examine for any of the rapist's hair, blood, skin, or semen. Any such evidence may be important in court later.

The hospital visit has other purposes. A physician can also administer preventive injections for sexually transmitted diseases and, if desired, an antipregnancy medication. The latter medication must be taken within three days if it is to be effective.

Importantly, the hospital visit may or may not bring the rape case automatically to the attention of the police. That would be true in some areas but not in all. Ultimately, the victim has to report the crime.

Reporting to the Police

Failure to report a rape immediately or after a few days probably means the rapist will not be apprehended. Even so, as many as nine out of ten rapes go unreported simply because most victims cannot face the added trauma of being questioned in detail and, possibly, rude treatment. The woman who does report to the police should, however, do so as soon as possible; each passing day increases the possibility that the police will want to know the reasons for the delay. But reporting late, experts stress, is better than not reporting at all. Reporting a rape does not mean that the victim has to press charges later.

Rape Crisis Centers

Rape crisis centers operate in most communities of any size. The staffs of these centers include many rape victims who have decided to devote time to helping other victims. To find help or advice, or an experienced person to accompany you to the police station with, you can:

- Check the front of your telephone directory for the number of a rape hotline.
- Call Women Against Rape (WAR) if the group has an office in your area. WAR should be listed in the telephone book under "Women."
- Failing the other alternatives, the local YWCA or women's center should have a rape crisis number.

26

Physicians and Diagnostic Procedures

Medicine is the umbrella term for the entire profession dealing with the maintenance of health and treatment of disease. In a narrower sense, however, it is often used in distinction to *surgery,* which deals with the correction of disorders or other physical change by operation or by manual manipulation. Thus the term *medical* is often used in distinction to *surgical,* and a *physician,* who treats his patients by medical means, may likewise be distinguished from a *surgeon.* The term *physician,* however, is also used broadly to apply to any authorized practitioner of medicine, including surgeons.

The two kinds of physicians most likely to be encountered when we have an undefined symptom or ailment that requires professional diagnosis and treatment are general or family practitioners and internists. These are the generalists of the medical profession, physicians who treat a wide variety of disorders and illnesses. Unlike other specialists, they usually do not require a referral from another physician and are the first to interview a person about his condition and any complaints he may have.

Diagnosing diseases and disorders requires highly developed skill on the part of the physician or other medical professional. Usually, the diagnosis calls for systematic use of instruments and diagnostic aids, various tests, and, often, extremely sophisticated machines. Questions that the physician asks are designed to provide additional information on which to base the diagnosis.

Using new diagnostic tests, physicians can determine during pregnancy whether a woman will bear a child with a genetic disorder. Tests make it possible to detect prenatally more than 200 diseases, among them sickle-cell anemia, normally fatal blood disorders called *thalassemias,* and hemophilia.

New and growing understanding of the genetic code, the pattern of genes that determines each person's makeup, has made these revolutionary diagnostic tests possible. Scientists cataloging the more than 100,000 human genes can both identify individual genes and work out their structures. Such information is stored in "gene libraries" for the use of physicians and others seeking to identify diseases and health problems long in advance of their actual occurrence.

The General Practitioner

The *general practitioner,* or GP, is about the closest thing we have to the old country doctor who hung out his shingle in front of his small-town house and made midnight carriage rides to deliver babies. The GP not only delivers babies but also listens to our problems, treats skin rashes, sets broken bones, sees children through difficult diseases, dispenses antibiotics and painkillers, and does all the other things we expect a physician to do. He may also perform appendectomies.

Internal Medicine

The *internist* is really a specialist in the branch of medicine called *internal medicine.* He usually refers surgery, and may also refer special problems affecting specific body systems, to physicians specializing in such areas. The internist's training is longer and

Medical Specialties and Subspecialties

Allergy and Immunology
Anesthesiology
Colon and Rectal Surgery
Dermatology
Emergency Medicine
Family Practice
Internal Medicine
  Cardiology
  Endocrinology and Metabolism
  Gastroenterology
  Hematology
  Infectious Diseases
  Medical Oncology
  Nephrology
  Pulmonary Disease
  Rheumatology
Neurological Surgery
Nuclear Medicine
Obstetrics and Gynecology
Ophthalmology
Orthopedic Surgery
Otolaryngology
Pathology
  Blood Banking
Pediatrics
  Pediatric Cardiology
  Pediatric Endocrinology
  Pediatric Hematology-Oncology
  Neonatal-Perinatal Medicine
  Nephrology
Physical Medicine and Rehabilitation
Plastic Surgery
Preventive Medicine
Psychiatry and Neurology
  Psychiatry
  Neurology/Special Competence in Child Neurology
  Psychiatry and Neurology
  Child Psychiatry
Radiology
Surgery
Thoracic Surgery
Urology

more intensified than that of the GP. In addition, most internists spend one or two years of study in a subspecialty, such as cardiology (heart), hematology (blood), etc. An internist is usually associated with at least one major hospital, its specialists, and its operating and laboratory facilities.

The field of an internist has been defined as "medical diagnosis and treatment"—obviously a very broad definition, to which must be added the observation that one of the responsibilities of the internist is to know when his knowledge is insufficient and when he should refer a patient to another specialist.

An internist should not be confused with an *intern* (or *interne*), who is a medical school graduate serving a year in residence at a hospital. The intern is, in a sense, an apprentice physician, putting the finishing practical touches on the knowledge he has accumulated in medical school by first-hand diagnosis and treatment of patients under the supervision of an experienced physician.

The American Medical Association officially recognizes and licenses physicians and surgeons as specialists in 23 fields (listed below). Before becoming a certified specialist in any of these fields, a physician must qualify in training and pass examinations supervised by a board made up of physicians already practicing that specialty. This training is known as residency training.

Subspecialties of Internal Medicine

An internist may develop a special interest in any of a number of subspecialties, including *cardiology* (the study of the diseases of the heart) or *gastroenterology* (the study of disorders of the digestive tract). Both cardiology and gastroenterology are unusual subspecialties in that the internist must pass an examination for certification as a *cardiologist* or *gastroenterologist.*

A number of other subspecialties of internal medicine probably sound familiar. *Hematology,* the scientific study of blood and blood-forming tissues, is the interest of the *hematologist. Endocrinology* is the study of the endocrine system, the network of ductless glands and other structures that secrete hormones directly into the bloodstream; the specialist is an *endocrinologist,* and may also specialize in metabolism, the chemical processes that take place to bring about growth, generation of energy, elimination of wastes, and other functions. The study of the connecting and supporting tissues of the body is called *rheumatology,* and the specialist is a *rheumatologist.*

Other specialties of internal medicine include infectious diseases; *medical oncology,* the study of tumors; *nephrology,* the study of the anatomy, physiology, and pathology of the kidneys; and pulmonary disease, disorders of the lungs or respiratory system.

Internists may also, of course, have satisfied the requirements of boards for both internal medicine and one of the other special branches of medicine.

Medical Specialties

The following major specialties are recognized by the American Medical Association:

Allergy and Immunology: The *allergist/immunologist* both diagnoses and treats allergies and specializes in the reactions of tissues of the immune system of the body to stimulation by antibodies (immunology).

Anesthesiology: The *anesthesiologist,* especially during major surgery, administers a patient's state of anesthesia (loss of the sensation of pain) either in parts of or all of the body.

Colon and Rectal Surgery: *Proctology* is the field dealing with diseases of the rectum and colon.

Dermatology: The *dermatologist* is a specialist in the diagnosis and treatment of skin diseases.

Emergency Medicine: The physician specializing in *emergency medicine* studies particularly those conditions that result from trauma or sudden illness.

Family Practice: The *family practice physician* specializes in family medicine, which is concerned with the diagnosis and treatment of health problems of people of either sex and any age. This specialist was once called a *general practitioner.*

Internal Medicine: The role of the *internist,* a kind of general specialist, is discussed above.

Neurological Surgery: The *neurological surgeon* deals with the diagnosis, treatment, and surgical management of disorders and diseases of the brain, spinal cord, and nervous systems.

Nuclear Medicine: The physician specializing in *nuclear medicine* is concerned with the use of radioactive material in the diagnosis and treatment of disease.

Obstetrics and Gynecology: A physician can be an *obstetrician,* a *gynecologist,* or both. The obstetrician's specialty is pregnancy and childbirth; the gynecologist specializes in the care and treatment of women and their diseases, especially of the reproductive system. In practice, he usually treats women who are not pregnant.

Ophthalmology: The *ophthalmologist* is a specialist in medical and surgical treatment of the eye.

Orthopedic Surgery: The *orthopedist,* or *orthopod,* specializes in diagnosing, treating, and surgically correcting, where possible, disorders and injuries associated with the bones, joints, muscles, cartilage, and ligaments.

Otolaryngology: The *otolaryngologist* is a specialist, with surgical competence, in practically all the cavities of the head except those holding the eyes and brain. He is the physician of the ear, nose, and throat, often abbreviated to ENT.

Pathology: The *pathologist* investigates the course and causes of diseases, using both laboratory devises and various established techniques.

Pediatrics: The *pediatrician* specializes in all medical aspects of child care. Subspecialties of pediatrics include *pediatric cardiology, pediatric endocrinology, pediatric hematology/oncology, neonatal/perinatal medicine,* and *nephrology.*

Physical Medicine and Rehabilitation: This specialist deals with the full or partial restoration of use and function to body parts that have been affected by disease or injury, or have been defective at birth.

Plastic Surgery: The *plastic surgeon* specializes in operations designed to give a more normal appearance to parts of the body that are disfigured or that the owner feels are unsightly.

Psychiatry and Neurology: Broadly speaking, the *psychiatrist* deals with the subjective feelings of his patients; the *neurologist* deals with the facts of the nervous system.

Radiology: The *radiologist* is an expert in using electromagnetic radiations (e.g., X rays) for the diagnosis and treatment of diseases.

Surgery: The *general surgeon* has been trained to perform surgery anywhere on the body, but he usually specializes in a particular area.

Thoracic Surgery: A *thoracic surgeon* specializes in operations involving the organs of the chest, or thoracic cavity.

Urology: The *urologist* specializes in the diagnosis, treatment, and surgical management of diseases affecting the male urinogenital tract and female urinary tract.

The Physical Examination

The use of physical examinations to determine the health of people is not new. Medical literature reveals that periodic health examinations were required of the Spartans of ancient Greece. American physicians have encouraged periodic examinations of children and adults as a preventive health measure since the beginning of the Civil War. But only in the last few decades has the general public accepted the idea that many physical disorders can be detected in the earliest stages by an examining physician, and corrective measures prescribed to ensure the maximum number of productive years for the patient. Heart disease, cancer, diabetes, hypertension, and glaucoma are just a few examples of diseases that a physician can detect during a routine physical examination long before disabling symptoms begin to be noticeable to the patient. The Pap test for women is a specific example of an examination technique that can predict the development of cervical cancer several years before the woman might notice signs and symptoms of the insidious disease.

On the other hand, physical examinations may determine that bothersome symptoms do not herald a dangerous disease. A man who suffers from abdominal pains and fears he has stomach cancer would be relieved to learn after an examination that the problem is only nervous tension, which can be corrected by other means. Heart palpitations and breathlessness similarly might be found through a physician's examination to be symptoms of anxiety rather than of heart disease.

The Importance of Periodic Physicals

Health examinations for most Americans unfortunately tend to be sporadic. During infancy and upon entering school, there may be detailed physical examinations, possibly followed by additional checkups during later childhood when required by the local educational system, and finally, a thorough examination for persons entering the military service or applying for a job or an insurance policy. But there may follow a period of 30 to 40 "lost years" for many persons before they feel the need for a checkup because of the symptoms of one of the degenerative diseases that may appear when they have reached their 50s or 60s. Unfortunately, statistics show that nearly 30 percent of chronic and disabling diseases begin before the age of 35 and about 40 percent between the ages of 35 and 55, with evidence that many chronic disabilities actually developed more or less unnoticed by the patients during the "lost years" when periodic physical examinations were considered by them unnecessary.

Periodic physical examinations are now encouraged for persons of all age groups, with four objectives:

- To detect abnormalities so that early diagnosis and treatment can prevent disability and premature death, especially from chronic diseases
- To improve the individual's understanding of health and disease
- To establish good relations between patient and physician as a basis for continuing health maintenance
- To provide specific preventive health measures, such as immunizations and advice about such life-style matters as cigarette smoking and weight control

General Diagnostic Procedures

A typical physical examination will include a careful health appraisal by an examining physician, including a detailed health history of the patient and study of the patient's body appearance and functions, an X ray of the chest area, and electrocardiogram of the heart in some cases, and laboratory analysis of blood and urine samples. Other appropriate procedures, such as a Pap smear test, may be added to the routine. Because no two persons are exactly alike and the differences among patients are likely to increase with advancing years, the examining physician's interest in a set of signs and symptoms may vary with different patients as he pieces evidence together to come up with a complete evaluation of a particular patient.

Medical History

The examination almost invariably begins with the *medical history* and includes details that may seem trivial or unimportant to the patient. But the information sometimes can provide important clues to a physician compiling data about a patient. This information usually includes the age, sex, race, marital status, occupation, and birthplace of the patient. The examiner also may want to know about any previous contacts with the physician's medical group, clinic, hospital, or other medical facility, in the event that previous medical records of the individual are on file.

Symptoms

The physician may ask a simple, obvious question, like "What is bothering you?" or "Why did you want to see a doctor?" The answer given may become for examining purposes the chief complaint and usually will involve any current or recent illness. If there is a current or recent illness to discuss, the physician will want to know more about it: when did it begin, how did it begin, and how has it affected you? If the physician asks about *symptoms,* he usually is probing for information about what the patient feels, and where. A symptom may be a pain, ache, bloated feeling, and so on. A *sign* is, in medical terminology, what somebody else, such as the physician, observes; signs and symptoms usually go together in solving a medical problem.

The physician's view of the importance of some symptoms may not be the same as the patient's. The physician may try to pursue complaints that may not seem important to the patient but actually can be more significant than the chief complaint. The physician's training and experience give him some advantages in concluding, for example, that a 45-year-old woman who has had a chronic cough for several years probably does not have lung cancer, even though that may be her chief concern.

Past Illnesses

Other details included in the medical history would be a list of childhood diseases, adult diseases such as pneumonia or tuberculosis, broken bones suffered, burns or gunshot wounds, unconsciousness as a result of an injury, a description of past operations, information about immunizations, medicines taken and side effects experienced from medications, and, for women, information about pregnancies, if any. Family history questions would cover information about the parents and blood relatives, including a variety of diseases they may have suffered.

Life-Style and Attitude

Next, the physician may review the

body systems, asking questions about any difficulties experienced with the head, eyes, ears, mouth, nose, lungs, heart, etc. Changes in body weight, hair texture, appetite, and other factors will be recorded, along with information about occupation, military service, and travel in foreign countries. Life-style questions could cover sleeping habits, sex life, use of coffee, tea, alcoholic beverages, vitamin tablets, sleeping pills, tobacco, exercise, and social activities. In addition to the answers given, the physician may record how the answers to questions are presented by a patient, since the patient's attitude can offer additional insight into the person's mental and physical health. For example, a patient who tries to dominate the examination interview or who answers the physician's questions with a response like "What do you mean by that?" may reveal more by the quality than the content of the answers.

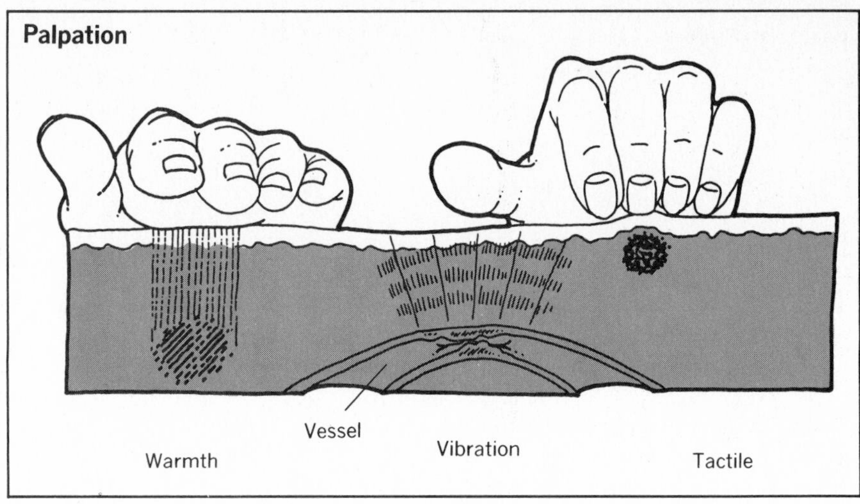

Observation

After the medical history has been recorded or updated, the physician may begin a general inspection of the patient's body, beginning with the head and neck and working down to the feet. The physician looks for possible deformities, scars or wounds, including insect bites, or pulsations or throbbing areas. Bruises, areas of skin peeling or flaking, areas of heavy skin pigmentation or loss of pigmentation, hair distribution, perspiration or goose bumps, firmness or slackness of the skin, warts, calluses, and other features are noted.

Palpation

The physician usually checks the exterior of the body by a method known as *palpation,* which means feeling with the fingers and hands. Because some parts of the hand are more sensitive to warmth and others are more sensitive to vibrations, the physician may shift from finger tips to palms at various times in his search for health clues. Rough vibrations from a disorder in the respiratory system, the trembling sensation of blood encountering an obstruction, or the grating feeling of a bone deformity can be detected during palpation. The physician also can tell from palpation where areas are tender or abnormally warm to the touch. If he finds a raised area of the skin, he can tell by palpation whether there is a growth within or beneath the skin.

Percussion and Auscultation

In addition to palpation, the examining physician may apply *percussion,* or tapping, of certain body areas. Tapping the chest, for example, gives the physician some information, from the sounds produced, about the condition of the lungs. He also uses a related technique of *auscultation,* or listening to sounds within the body, either with his ear against the body or through a stethoscope, the familiar Y-shaped instrument used to amplify internal sounds.

In percussion, the physician usually places one hand on the surface of the patient's body with the fingers slightly spread apart and taps on one of the fingers with the middle finger of the other hand. By moving the lower hand around on various areas of the chest surface while tapping one finger on the other, the physician can get a fairly accurate "sound picture" of the condition of organs within the chest. He can outline the heart, and the distance moved by the diaphragm in filling and emptying the lungs, by listening for changes in percussion sounds that range from resonance

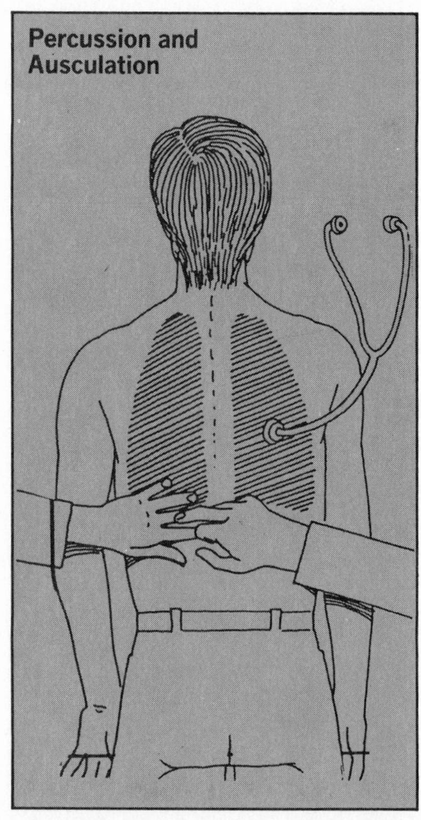

over hollow spaces to dullness over solid or muscular areas. Lack of resonance over a normally resonant area of the lung might indicate fluid, pneumonia, or perhaps an abnormal mass. Percussion may also give the first sign of enlargement of organs, such as the liver, heart, or spleen.

During auscultation, the physician listens for normal or abnormal breathing sounds. He can usually detect specific aberrations in lung function by noises made as the air rushes in and out of the lungs through the bronchi. A sound of frictional rubbing can suggest a rough surface on the lining of the pleura, a membrane surrounding the lung tissue; a splashing or slapping sound would indicate the presence of fluid in the lungs. In auscultation of the heart, the physician listens for extra heartbeats, rubbing sounds, the rumbling noises of a heart murmur, or the sounds of normally functioning heart valves opening and closing.

An experienced physician may use his stethoscope for listening to sounds beyond the chest area. He may listen to the sounds of blood flowing through vessels of the neck, bowel sounds through the wall of the abdomen, and the subtle noises made by joints, muscles, and tendons as various limbs are moved.

During examination of the chest, the physician usually asks the patient to perform certain breathing functions: take a deep breath, hold your breath, inhale, exhale, etc. On one or more of the exhalation commands, the physician may make a quick check of the air exhaled from the lungs to determine if there is any odor suggesting a disease that might be unnoticed by the patient. Just as the physician learns to recognize the meaning of percussion and auscultation sounds, he learns the meaning of certain odors of bacterial activity or other disorders.

Body Structure and Gait

Weight and height are checked as part of any routine examination. These factors are important in a health examination for children to determine the rate of growth, even though youngsters of the same age can vary considerably in height and weight and still be within the so-called normal range. Sudden changes in the rate of growth or abnormal growth may be signs that special attention should be given to possible problems. Adults also can vary greatly in weight and height, but special concern may be indicated by the physician if the individual is exceptionally tall, short, fat, or skinny. In addition to a possible disease associated with unusual stature, the facts and figures obtained about body build can be important because certain disorders tend to develop in individuals of a particular body structure. Posture also provides clues to the true condition of a patient; a person who has a slouch or who holds one shoulder higher than the other may have an abnormal spinal curvature. The physician may watch the patient's manner of walking, because a person's gait can suggest muscle, bone, or nervous-system disorders; a person who seems to lean forward and take short steps, for example, may have muscles that do not relax normally during movement of the legs.

Blood Pressure

Blood pressure is measured with the help of a device called a *sphygmomanometer* and the stethoscope. The sphygmomanometer has either a dial with a face that shows the blood pressure reading in millimeters of mercury, or a column of mercury in a glass tube with numbers alongside it. Either kind of device also has attached to it an inflatable cuff, which is wrapped around the upper arm; a rubber bulb is used to inflate the cuff and increase pressure in it so that it can control the blood flow in the arm. The physician or nurse places the bell-shaped end of the stethoscope on a point on the inside of the elbow where the pulse can be felt. The bulb is squeezed to increase the cuff pressure until the heartbeat, in the form of the pulse, can no longer be heard through the stethoscope. The reading on the sphygmomanometer at that stage may be well over 200. Then the physician slowly deflates the cuff and lets the reading on the gauge fall gradually until he hears the first beat of the heart. The reading on the gauge at that point is recorded as the *systolic pressure.* The physician continues to relax the pressure in the cuff and watches for the reading at the point where the thumping of the heart disappears. That number is recorded as the *diastolic pressure.*

If the systolic pressure is, for example, 130 and the diastolic pressure is 72, the physician may make a notation of "BP 130/72," which is the patient's blood pressure at the time of the examination. The records also may indicate whether the patient was sitting or lying down at the time and whether the pressure was taken on the right arm or the left arm. Sometimes the pressure is checked on both arms. If the patient appears tense or anxious, which could produce a higher than normal blood pressure reading, the physician may encourage the patient to relax for a few minutes and try again for a more meaningful reading.

Pulse Rate

The pulse itself usually is studied for rate and quality, or character, which means the force of the pulse beat and the tension between beats. The pulse beat for small children may be well over 100 per minute and still be con-

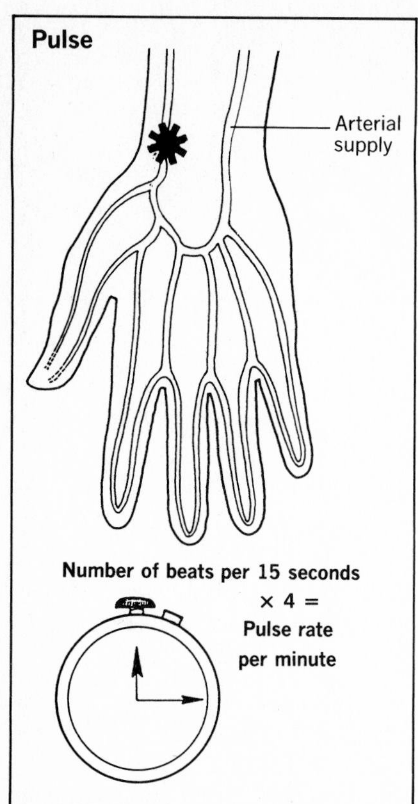

sidered normal. But in an adult who is relaxed and resting, any pulse rate over 100 suggests that something is wrong. An adult pulse rate of less than 60 also might indicate an abnormal condition.

Eyes

Inspection of the eyes is usually done with the aid of an *ophthalmoscope,* by means of which the physician can visualize the retina on the back inner surface of each eye, and its associated arteries, veins, and nerve fibers. Distended retinal veins may be a sign of a variety of disorders, including diabetes or heart disease; signs of hardening of the arteries also may be observed in the eyes before other indications are found elsewhere in the body. The condition of retinal blood vessels may, in addition, signal the development of hypertension.

Mouth, Nose, and Ears

The mouth, nose, and ears are inspected for signs of abnormalities. A device called an *otoscope* is inserted in the outer ear to examine the external auditory canal and eardrum. If the patient wears dentures, the physician may ask that they be removed during examination of the mouth so that the health of the gums can be checked. The condition of the tongue, teeth, and gums can reveal much about the health habits of the individual. An inadequate set of teeth, for example, can indicate that certain important food items that require chewing are being avoided. Tobacco stains obviously are a sign of tobacco use.

X Rays

A chest X ray is usually a routine part of the examination; the X ray usually covers the chest area, showing the condition of the heart and lungs. The finished X-ray picture looks something like a large photographic negative, but the film is designed so that areas filled with gas, such as the lungs or fatty tissues, appear almost transparent, and bone or solid metal objects appear sharply opaque. Muscle, blood, and other objects, including gallbladder stones, can be identified through a hazy kind of contrast between opaque and translucent. A number of special kinds of X rays may be ordered if the physician wants to make a more detailed check of some possible disorder involving a specific body cavity, such as a peptic ulcer in the stomach wall.

Electrocardiogram

An increasing number of health examinations today include an electrocardiographic study of the heart. An *electrocardiogram,* or *EKG,* is made as a kind of "picture" traced by a pen on a moving sheet of paper, with the movements of the pen controlled by electrical impulses produced by the heart. All muscle activity produces tiny electrical discharges, and the rhythmic contractions of heart muscle result in a distinctive pattern of electrical pulsations that forms the elec-

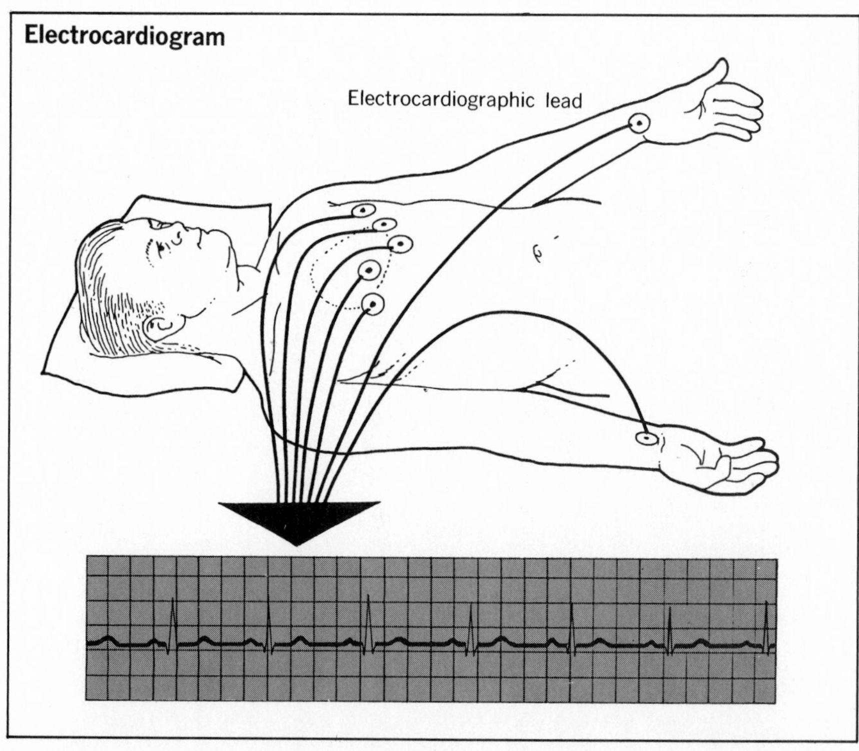

trocardiogram picture. The tracing appears to the patient as simply a long, wavy line, but the physician can identify each of the wave crests and dips in terms of different parts of the heart muscle contracting or relaxing in proper sequence, or—if the heart is not functioning normally—not in proper sequence.

The electrocardiogram is recorded by attaching electrodes, or leads, to the chest, arms, and legs, in a series of differing arrangements depending upon the kind of heart picture the physician wants to record. The wires from the electrodes are connected to the machine that translates the heartbeat rhythms into the electrocardiogram. There is no danger of electrical shock, because the only electricity flowing through the wires is the current produced continuously by the human body as part of its natural functions.

It is always an advantage for the patient to have an electrocardiogram taken early in adult life and when in a good state of health, because that record can serve as a benchmark for comparing electrocardiograms made later in life when the condition of the heart may have changed. This rule applies to all other health examination records as well.

Urinalysis

No patient health evaluation is complete without the findings of laboratory tests of blood and urine. The physician or his assistant may give special instructions about food and water intake well in advance of the time for delivering a urine specimen, because those factors can influence the chemical makeup of the sample. The time of day of the collection also can affect the composition of the urine sample; urine voided early in the morning is likely to be more acid in content, while urine collected after a meal may be more alkaline. Thus, for a routine physical, the physician may advise that a urine sample be taken at his office at 9:00 A.M. but that nothing be eaten since the previous evening meal. The physician also may want not the first but the second specimen of the day. In some cases, depending upon the patient's complaint, the physician may request a collection of all the urine voided during a period of 12 or 24 hours.

Chemical Content of the Urine

A typical urine sample is, of course, mostly water. But it also may contain about two dozen identifiable minerals and other chemicals, including sodium potassium, calcium, sulfur, ammonia, urea, and several different acids. A urine sample can range in color from pale straw to dark amber, depending upon the concentration. It also can be other colors, including orange or blue, or even colorless, depending upon foods eaten, medications taken, diseases, or exposure to toxic substances.

Appearance and Acidity

The urine sample's general appearance, including color, is noted by the laboratory technician. The sample also is tested for acidity or alkalinity, normal urine being just slightly on the acid side of neutral. Urine that is definitely acidic can be a sign of a variety of disorders, including certain metabolic problems. Urine that is markedly on the alkaline side of neutral also can suggest a number of possible disorders, including an infection of the urinary tract. Alkalinity could also be caused by certain medications, or even by the patient's use of large doses of bicarbonate of soda. Foods rich in protein can make the urine more acidic, while citrus fruits and some vegetables may tend to make a patient's urine more alkaline.

What the Urine Shows

A thorough analysis of a person's urine can turn up some clues to the condition of almost every part of the body and verify or rule out the presence of any of a number of physical disorders. The specific gravity of the urine, for example, can indicate the general health of the urinary tract; protein (albumin) tests may tell something about the condition of the kidneys and prostate and, in a pregnant women, indicate toxemia; glucose (sugar) in the urine could suggest diabetes; the presence of ketone bodies could be a sign of metabolic disorders; bilirubin (bile) in the urine could be a sign of liver disease, and so on. Various urine tests check for the presence of red blood cells or white blood cells, tissue cells from the lining of organs, various hormones, traces of drugs taken, fat bodies, parasites, indications of renal calculi (kidney stones), and a variety of bits of tissue, often microscopic, called *casts*. One kind of cast might be a sign of heart failure or shock, another might be a warning of heavy-metal poisoning, a third might indicate a kidney infection.

Blood Tests

Laboratory blood studies also can reveal bits of information about organ systems throughout the body. For a simple blood test, a few drops may be drawn from a capillary through a finger prick; more detailed blood tests can require the equivalent of a couple of teaspoonfuls of blood drawn from a vein in the arm. The amount of blood taken for a laboratory test is not harmful; a normal body manufactures a couple of ounces of new blood every day, several times the amount used for a laboratory test.

Red Cells

For a count of red blood cells (RBC),

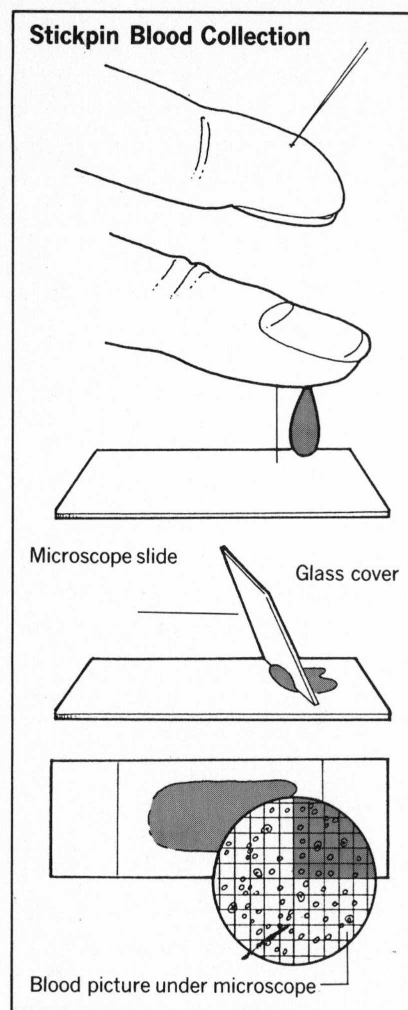

or *erythrocytes,* a small part of the original blood sample may be diluted and a bit of the solution placed on a special microscope slide that enables the technician to estimate the average number of red blood cells per cubic millimeter of blood. The normal RBC range for a man is in the neighborhood of 4.8 to 5.8 million red blood cells per cubic millimeter of blood; for a woman, the RBC count is about 4.4 to 5.4 million. For a child, the normal figure is slightly less than that of a woman.

The blood sample also may be checked for the level of hemoglobin, an iron-protein substance that gives the blood its red color and makes it possible for blood to carry oxygen to all parts of the body. A below-normal level of hemoglobin could be a sign of anemia resulting from a number of possible causes, including actual loss of blood from hemorrhage, vitamin deficiencies, lack of iron in the diet, or a disease.

White Cells

White blood cell (WBC), or *leukocyte,* counts are made the same way as RBC counts. The total normal WBC count for both men and women ranges from 5,000 to 10,000 per cubic millimeter. A higher count would indicate the presence of an infection or other disease problem.

Other Factors

Other blood studies may be performed for information about the coagulation characteristics of a patient's blood sample, levels of calcium, sodium, potassium, and other chemicals present, presence of certain enzymes, acidity of the blood, levels of sugar, bilirubin, urea nitrogen, cholesterol and other fatty substances, alcohol and other drugs, and proteins, including albumin.

Not all of these tests are performed during a routine physical examination, but they could be used if needed to track down the cause of an otherwise elusive set of symptoms. By comparing the results of two blood enzyme tests, for example, it would be possible to sort out symptoms of six different kinds of liver disease, as well as a heart attack and infectious mononucleosis. The results might not be the final answer to a medical problem, but the laboratory test data could be important pieces of the jigsaw puzzle that the physician needs to complete the health picture that begins to take form when the patient enters the physician's office for a physical examination.

Specialties and Their Diagnostic Procedures

If a definite diagnosis cannot be made on the basis of the medical history and preliminary physical examination, more specialized tests are employed. These are usually made under the direction of a specialist. These specialists and some of the most important of their diagnostic procedures—there are literally hundreds of them—are described below, arranged according to the major body systems.

The Skeleton and the Muscles

The *orthopedic surgeon,* or *orthopedist,* is the major specialist in the diagnosis, treatment, and surgical correction of diseases and injuries of the bones, joints, and musculature. Because the healthy functioning of muscles is closely involved with the nervous system, the *neurologist* is frequently consulted. The branch of internal medicine called *rheumatology* is specially concerned with the joints.

The teeth and their supporting structures are, of course, the concern of *dentistry* and the *dentist.* The *orthodontist* is a dentist specializing in the alignment of teeth and their proper positioning in the mouth. A *pediatric dentist* specializes in teeth problems of young people up to the time that the second set of teeth erupt. An *oral surgeon* (dental surgeon) performs surgery within the oral cavity, including tooth extraction. He and the orthodontist have had additional training after receiving the dental degree, and the oral surgeon may have a medical degree (MD) as well. The *periodontist* treats gum disorders.

Diagnostic Procedures

X rays are probably relied upon more than any other technique for special investigations of the bones, joints,

The Human Skeleton

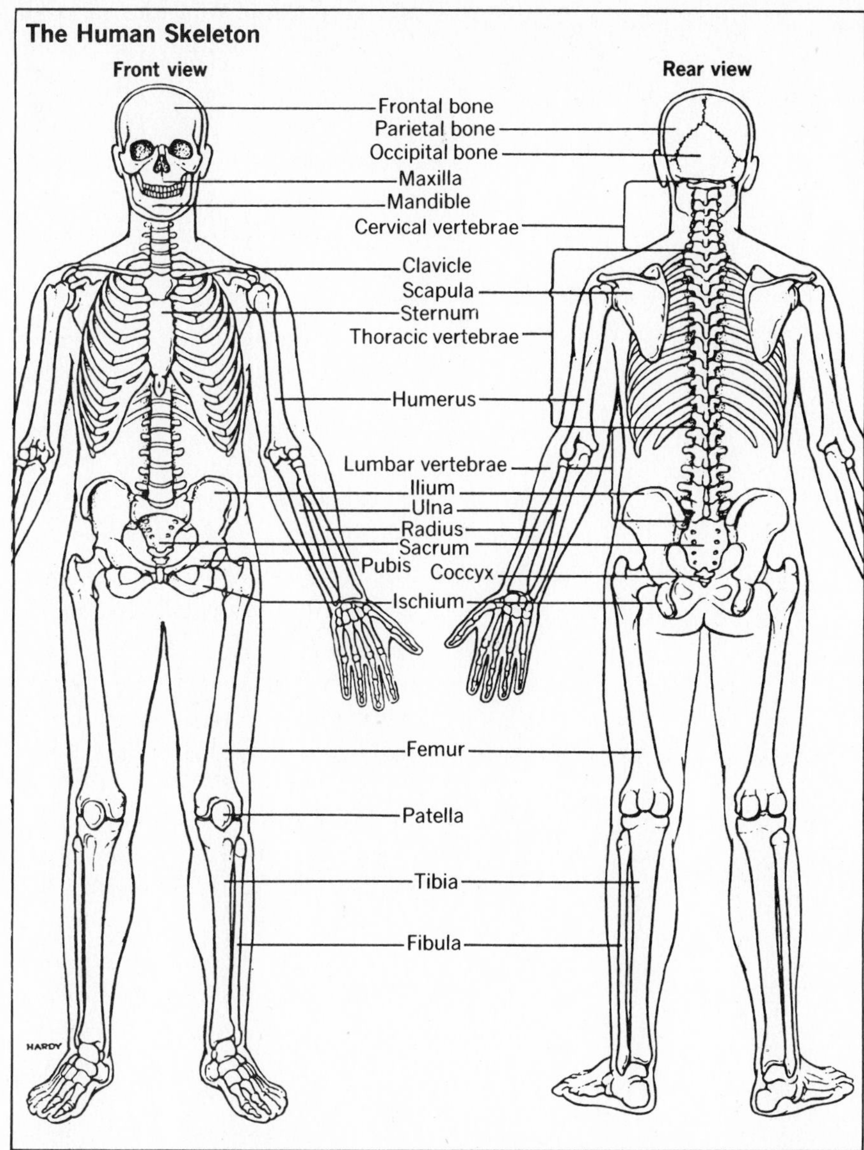

and teeth. They can reveal a tiny tooth cavity, a hairline fracture of a major bone, a bony deposit, or an eroded surface around a joint. *Serum analysis*—laboratory investigation of the clear portion separated from a person's blood sample—can also reveal underlying chemical irregularities that accompany or precede bone and joint diseases.

Synovial aspiration (also called *synovial fluid exam*) involves the withdrawal of a tiny amount of fluid (synovial fluid) with a needle inserted into a joint. The laboratory analysis of the fluid can diagnose gout and some forms of arthritis.

Electromyography can give an electrical tracing of muscle nerve function and reveal the presence of disorders.

Muscle biopsy is the surgical excision of a small piece of muscle tissue for laboratory examination and tests.

Skin, Hair, and Nails

The *dermatologist* is the principal specialist. *Skin biopsy,* the removal of a piece of skin tissue for laboratory testing and microscopic study, is used for difficult diagnoses.

The Nervous System and the Brain

The *neurosurgeon,* sometimes popularly referred to as a brain surgeon, is qualified for diagnosis, treatment, and surgery of the brain and nervous system. The term *neurologist* is generally restricted to a physician who does not perform surgery. The neurologist may be an internist having neurology as a subspecialty.

Diagnostic Procedures

A *spinal fluid exam,* or spinal tap, involves the withdrawal by special needle under sterile conditions, and subsequent laboratory examination, of a small amount of cerebrospinal fluid for the diagnosis of polio, meningitis, brain tumors, and other conditions. The *electroencephalogram* (EEG) gives a picture of, and shows irregularities in, a person's "brain waves." The *echoencephalogram* uses ultrasonic waves, rather than the electric currents of the EEG, to investigate the functioning of the brain. A *brain scan* calls for the injection of a radioactive element into the brain tissue or fluid and records its movements on a photographic plate.

Recently, an X-ray technique utilizing a computer and known as *CT scanning* (for *computed tomography*) has proved to be most effective for visualizing "slices" of the brain that would otherwise be inaccessible, and no injection is necessary. Sometimes called a *brain scanner,* the device takes a series of pictures as it is rotated around the patient. From data fed into a computer, the computer generates composite pictures of the brain.

An even later development, *nuclear magnetic resonance* (NMR), or *magnetic resonance imaging,* utilizes two simple elements, a magnet and radio waves, to make sophisticated analyses. Like CT, NMR provides

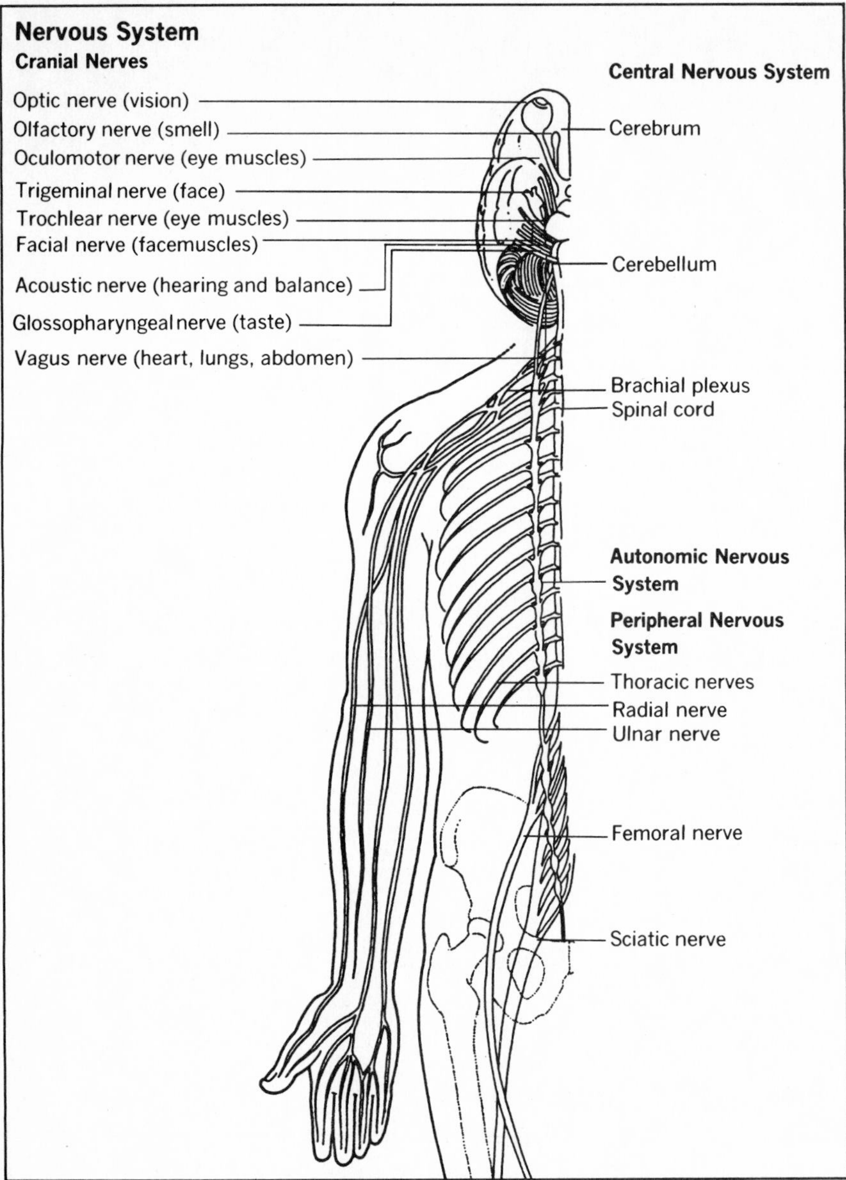

high-resolution pictures of the structures of various body parts and organs. But NMR does not utilize X rays and it can be used to examine the biochemistry of living cells.

The *cerebral arteriogram* is a method of visualizing and assaying brain damage by injecting a dye into the blood vessels serving the brain and then X-raying them. It is especially useful in judging the severity and location of hemorrhages and strokes. A *pneumoencephalogram* is an X-ray picture of the brain taken after air or gas has been injected into the ventricles of the brain.

The Circulatory System, the Heart, and Blood

The *cardiologist* is an internist who has special knowledge in the diagnosis and medical treatment of heart disease. The *hematologist* is an internist who has special training in the techniques of diagnosing and treating diseases of the blood (including lymph) and bone marrow.

The *thoracic surgeon* is a surgeon who has satisfied the requirements of licensing boards for both general surgery and thoracic (chest cavity) surgery. He has special training in the surgical treatment of defects and diseases of the heart and large blood vessels. The *vascular surgeon* is a general surgeon specializing in the surgical treatment of diseases of blood vessels.

Diagnostic Procedures

The *electrocardiogram* graphically records the electrical activity of the heart associated with contraction of the cardiac muscle. It can provide valuable information regarding disorders of or damage to the heart muscle (i.e., heart attack), disturbances in rhythm, or enlargement of any of the four chambers of the heart. A *vectorcardiogram* is similar to the electrocardiogram but more specifically attuned to the magnitude and direction of the electrical currents of the heart. Abnormalities not apparent on the electrocardiogram may often be revealed by a vectorcardiogram.

The *phonocardiogram* is a recording on paper of the heart sounds, which enables the physician to evaluate murmurs and abnormal heart sounds with more accuracy than by listening with the stethoscope. The timing of the murmur with relation to the specific events of heart muscle contraction may also be precisely evaluated. The *echocardiogram* provides a paper tracing of sound waves that are directed toward, and subsequently bounced back from, various internal heart structures. The technique is useful in diagnosing abnormalities of the heart valves, as well as abnormal collections of fluid in the sac (pericardium) enveloping the heart.

The *fluoroscope* visualizes the heart in action by use of X rays. It is useful in the evaluation of heart and vessel pulsation, as well as of valve or vessel calcification. Plain *chest X rays* may reveal enlargement of the heart, abnormal calcification of vessels or heart valves, and signs of a congestive heart valve. These are only three examples of the great number of abnormalities that can be revealed by a routine chest X ray.

The *cardiac X-ray series* are a number of X rays of the chest taken in several positions as the patient swallows a liquid, for example, barium sulfate, which makes the esophagus stand out on the X ray. This is usually called a barium swallow. Indentation of the esophagus by abnormally enlarged heart chambers may be revealed by this technique. "Barium meals" are also important in the radiologic diagnosis of disorders of the esophagus, stomach, and small intestine.

Cardiac catheterization is the insertion of a small tubular surgical instrument via a vein in the arm or artery of the leg, through the blood vessels, directly into the right or left side of the heart. This procedure is employed to confirm suspected intracardiac (within the heart) anomalies, determine intracardiac pressures, and take blood samples. Catheterization enables the physician to confirm suspected defects in the walls dividing the heart chambers or to estimate the severity of a lesion and the need for corrective surgery.

Angiocardiography (or simply *angiography*), if warranted, is performed at the same time as cardiac catheterization. Its principle involves the injection of a contrast material (e.g., a substance visible on a fluoroscopy screen or X-ray film) by means of the catheter, with consequent visualization of the heart and major blood vessels. Angiography is not limited to investigation of the heart chambers but can reveal abnormalities of large vessels such as the aorta, coronary arteries, and renal arteries.

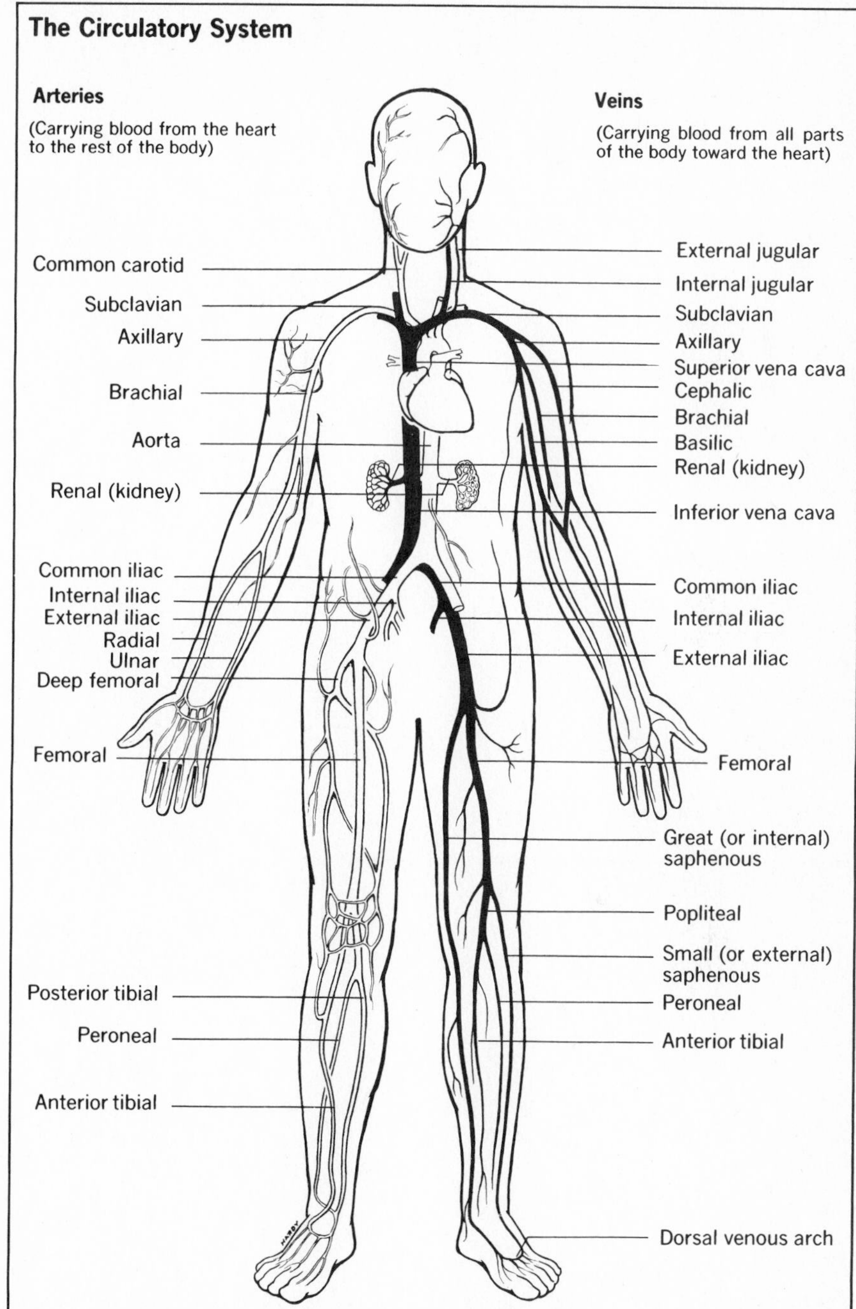

CT scanning, mentioned above, is becoming an increasingly important diagnostic tool and may in many cases make angiocardiography unnecessary. Sometimes called a *body scanner,* the CT scanner takes a series of computer-assisted X-ray pictures as it slowly rotates around the patient, thus providing cross-sectional pictures of the target organ. It is a painless and safe procedure, and is capable of providing pictures of areas of the body that would be very difficult to visualize by any other means.

Hematological (Blood Sampling) Diagnostic Techniques

Routine laboratory tests performed in all hospital admissions are the *peripheral smear* and *complete blood count.* Approximately 5 milliliters (ml) of blood are *aspirated* (withdrawn by suction) from a vein, typically in the crease of the elbow. From this sample, a determination of the patient's hemoglobin and percentage of red

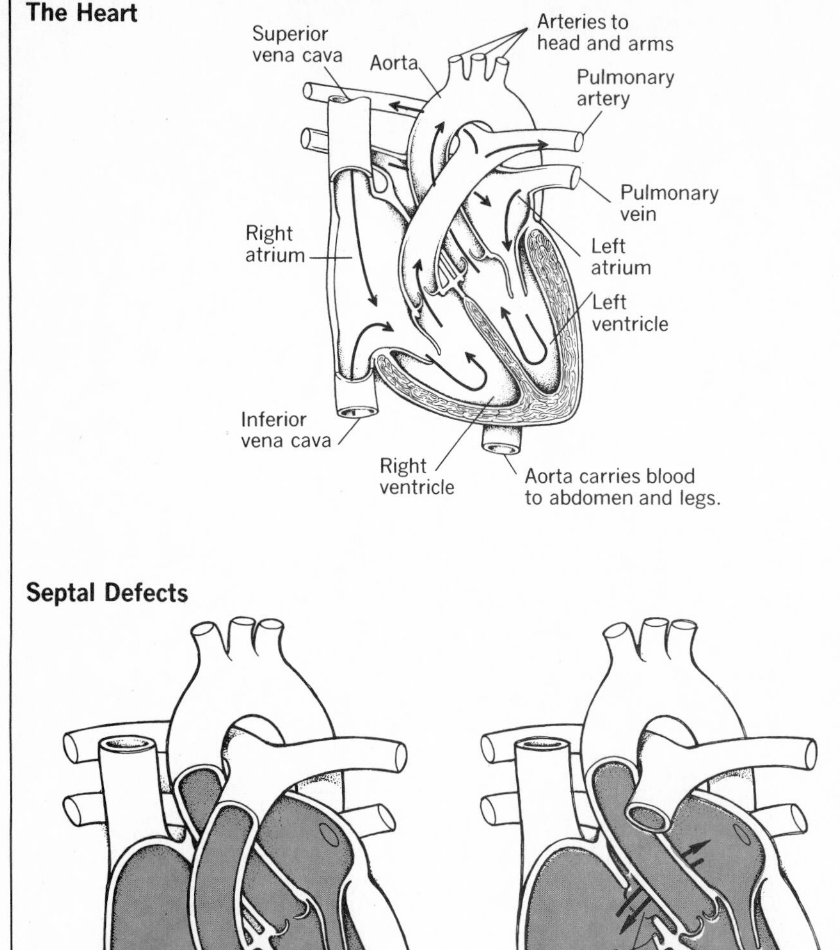

A normal heart in cross section *(top)*, shows the circulation of the blood. An interventricular defect *(bottom left)* allows blood to pass directly between the left and right ventricles. An interatrial defect *(bottom right)*, with the aorta seen in cross section over the left atrium, allows blood to pass freely between the two atria. Any septal defect interferes with the effectiveness of the pumping action of the heart.

corpuscles per milliliter of plasma may be calculated. Microscopic analysis of the number and character of the red cells, white cells, and platelets provides additional essential information.

If an abnormality such as decreased hemoglobin or overpopulation of white cells is noted on complete blood count and peripheral smear, the physician might request that a sample of the patient's bone marrow be obtained for evaluation—a procedure called *bone marrow biopsy.* Following local anesthesia of the operative site, typically the hipbone, a biopsy needle is inserted into the marrow of the bone and a small sample of marrow is withdrawn. If performed by an experienced physician, the patient feels only some pressure and very slight pain as the marrow sample is aspirated.

In suspected cases of *neoplastic* diseases—diseases involving abnormal growths that may be or may become malignant—a *lymph node biopsy* (surgical excision and microscopic examination of lymph node tissue) is performed. A *lymphangiogram* is used when tumors of the lymphatic system are suspected. A dye or contrast material visible on an X ray is injected into a lymphatic vessel, usually one on the top of the foot. X rays of the abdomen taken over the next several days are studied for abnormalities in the size and structure of internal lymph nodes.

There are numerous other hematological tests, including radioactive (radioisotope) tests, which are used in special situations when diagnosis by other means is inadequate.

The Digestive System and the Liver

The internist is generally able to treat most gastrointestinal disorders. The *gastroenterologist* is an internist who has special knowledge of disorders of the digestive tract. *Colon* and *rectal surgeons* operate on the large intestine, rectum, and anus; *proctology* deals with the diagnosis and treatment of disorders in this area. Surgeons and internists specializing in this region are called *proctologists.*

Diagnostic Procedures

Examination can be made of the esophagus, stomach, and duodenum, and sometimes of the entire length of the small intestine, by using a sequence of many fluoroscope, motion-picture, and X-ray pictures. This is called the *gastrointestinal series,* or simply the *GI series.* So that the internal walls of the digestive organs will stand out clearly in the pictures, the patient eats nothing for eight hours before, and when the exami-

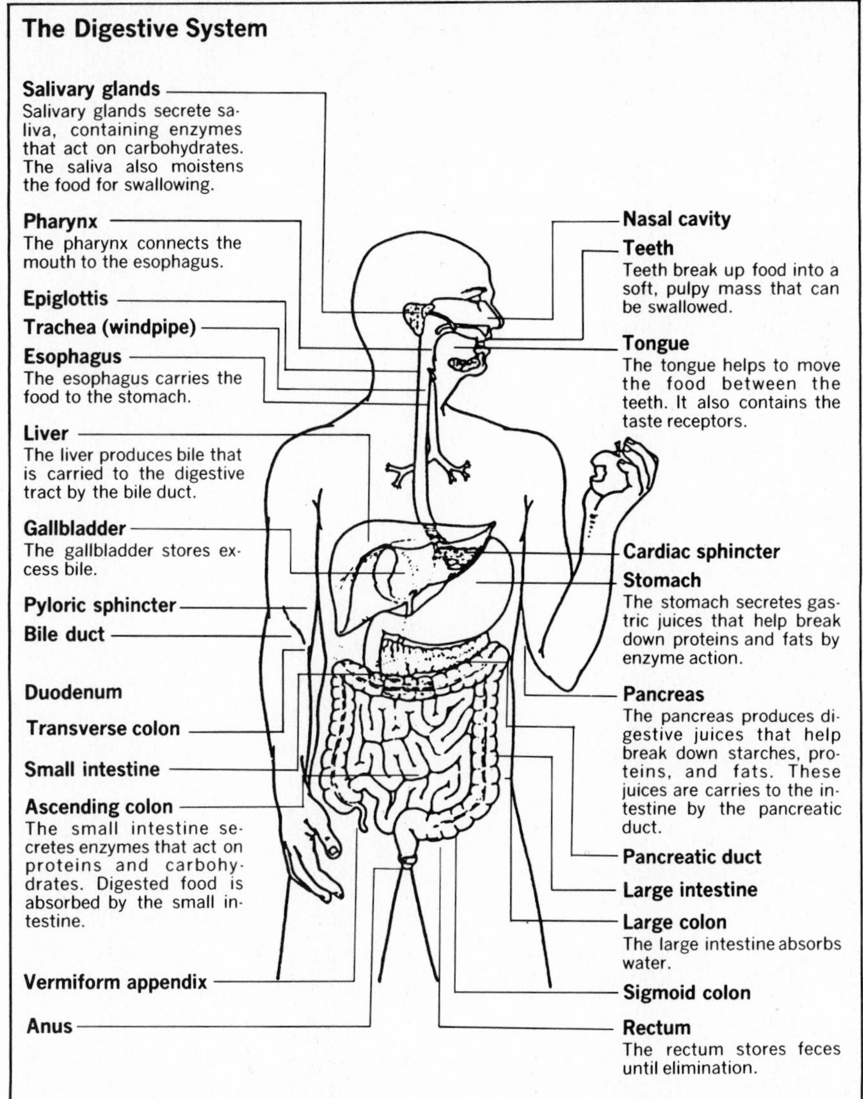

nation begins, he is asked to swallow a glassful of chalky, sticky barium sulfate. The GI series is one of the first tests administered when an ulcer or cancer is suspected in the stomach or duodenum.

Gastric analysis is the extraction and study of stomach juices for clues to intestinal disorders.

A *barium enema* is the injection via the anus of a barium solution; it usually precedes X-ray examination of the large intestine for signs of cancer or other diseases. *Stool exams,* laboratory studies of the feces, may also reveal cancer, as well as the presence of parasitic worms and amebas.

There are a wide variety of slender, hollow, tubular instruments equipped with a light and a lens to enable the physician to see into the GI tract: the *esophagoscope* for insertion by way of the mouth into the esophagus; the *gastroscope* for inspection of the stomach; the *gastroduodenal fiberscope* for inspection of the stomach and duodenum. "Scopes" inserted via the anus include the *proctosigmoidoscope* for visual examination of the rectum and lower colon, and the *colonoscope* for investigating farther up the large intestine. These are called *fiberoptic* instruments because they transmit light by means of a bundle of fibers of glass or plastic that permit observation of curved interior spaces of the body that would otherwise be inaccessible.

Special tests for the liver's health and function include the removal of a tiny piece of liver tissue, by means of a long needle inserted through the skin, and the tissue's subsequent laboratory examination; this procedure is called *needle biopsy of liver* and often is used to confirm diagnosis of cirrhosis. An injection of a chemical called *BSP,* followed later by analysis of a blood specimen, is used to investigate liver function. A *liver scan,* like a brain scan, employs a radioactive substance to visualize the function of the organ.

X-ray examination of the gallbladder, resulting in a *cholecystogram*—*cholecyst* is a medical name for "gallbladder"—is used to diagnose gallbladder disease and to locate gallstones. A dye is swallowed before the test.

The Respiratory System and the Lungs

The internist handles most nonsurgical disorders, and the thoracic surgeon specializes in surgical procedures involving the respiratory organs.

Diagnostic Procedures

In the *sputum exam* a number of bacteriological, chemical, and microscopic tests are peformed on the sputum (saliva, often mixed with mucus or other substances); these tests can detect a hidden abscess in the respiratory tract, pneumonia, tuberculosis, and other lung diseases.

Practically everybody is aware of the value of *chest X rays* in the diagnosis of diseases and disorders of the lungs, heart, and ribs. Many diseases of the lungs and respiratory system are also revealed by tests administered on the skin. For example, the skin's reaction to a substance called

The Respiratory System

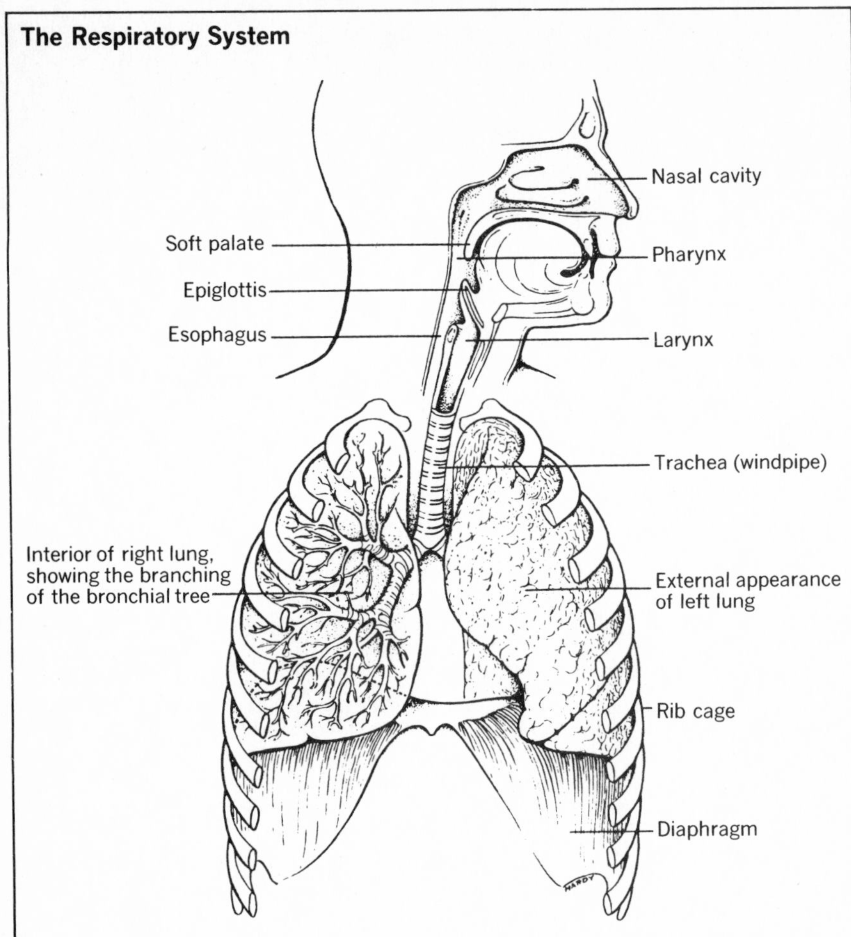

PPD (*p*urified *p*rotein *d*erivative) is used in diagnosing tuberculosis. *Bronchoscopy* is inspection of the bronchial tubes with the tube and scope instrument called the *bronchoscope.*

Special tests that measure lung volume, capacity, and function have become more common as physicians have become conscious of the adverse effects of air pollution and the growing incidence of irreversible diseases, such as emphysema.

The Endocrine Glands

There is no AMA/licensed specialty, but the internist/endocrinologist is the expert.

Diagnostic Procedures

There are a great many tests, using both blood and urine samples, that suggest or confirm the excess or insufficiency of a specific hormone in the body. In turn, these tests point to the overactivity or underactivity of one of the hormone-secreting endocrine glands.

The Sense Organs—Eye, Ear, Nose

The two specialists in this area are both licensed to peform surgery in their special areas of competence. The *ophthalmologist* is the eye doctor. The *otolaryngologist* is the ear, nose, and throat specialist.

Diagnostic Procedures

We are all familiar with the lettered test charts that determine whether we are nearsighted or farsighted or have some other defect in our eyes' focusing apparatus, such as an astigmatism. Color charts to test for color blindness are also commonly used.

With the *ophthalmoscope* and the *slit-lamp microscope,* which magnifies a beam of concentrated light, the ophthalmologist can examine the structures within the eye in great detail. The *retinoscope* reveals the actual structural abnormalities that account for nearsightedness or farsightedness. The *gonioscope* enables the ophthalmologist to inspect the angle between the cornea and the iris, which is of importance in diagnosing glaucoma. The fluid pressure itself within the anterior chamber can be measured by an extremely delicate spring-balance gauge called a *tonometer.* Finally, *perimeter* can be used to map boundaries of the visual field; the narrowing of these boundaries ("tunnel vision" is the extreme example) is a symptom of glaucoma and other eye disorders.

Hearing and hearing loss are measured by a device called the *audiometer,* with which a physician can measure accurately the whole range of vibrations heard as sound by the human ear. The *otoscope* is an instrument for examining the external auditory canal and eardrum.

The Urinogenital System and the Kidneys

The *urologist* is the acknowledged specialist. He does not deal, however, with the female reproductive organs, which are the specialty of the obstetrician and gynecologist.

Diagnostic Procedures

The collective name for a number of tests that analyze the contents of urine is *urinalysis.* These include tests of the urine's physical properties, as well as chemical and microscopic analysis. Telltale signs of diseases of the kidneys and bladder often show up in urine, and sugar in the urine may be an indication of diabetes. *Urine culture* is a test for microbial infections of the urinary tract.

Pyelograms are X-ray examinations of the interior of the kidney (kidney pelvis) and of the tube (ureter) carrying urine away from the kidney to the bladder. Pyelograms may involve the injection of a substance into the patient's bloodstream to facilitate viewing of the kidney area.

The special hollow tube, lens, and light instrument called a *cystoscope* is used to view the inside of the bladder after being inserted up the urethra. *Voiding cystometrics* test the condition and capacity of the bladder by pumping water into it, measuring the resulting pressures, and timing the onset of the desire to void.

The technique of *needle biopsy,* discussed in respect to the liver under "The Digestive System and the Liver" in this chapter, is also used to examine kidneys and prostate tissue.

For a discussion of diagnostic procedures for the female reproductive system, see "The Gynecological Examination" in Ch. 25, *Women's Health.*

Patients' Rights

Diagnostic procedures have raised many questions centering on patients' rights. The questions concern both physicians and hospitals and relate to the general right of a patient to know what is happening to him or her and why.

Efforts to develop lists of specific rights that the patient enjoys have gone far beyond the specific area of diagnosis and treatment. The lists touch on such matters as the patient's need to maintain privacy, his or her right to be informed of any surgical or other procedures to be peformed, and the right to refuse treatment to the extent permitted by law. One such "Bill of Rights" was issued by the American Hospital Association in 1973. It noted in part:

> Equitable and humane treatment at all times and under all circumstances is a right. This principle entails an obligation on the part of all those involved in the care of the patient to recognize and to respect his individuality and his dignity. This means creating and fostering relationships founded on mutual acceptance and trust.

Like other statements on patients' rights, the AHA list stressed *informed consent.* That meant the need on the part of the patient to be able to agree to medical and surgical treatment on the basis of complete, accurate information. Informed consent as a principle provided the foundation for many other specific or general rights. These include:

- The right to considerate and respectful care
- The right to take part in planning for one's own care
- The right to have records kept confidential
- The right to full explanation of the hospital bill

Questions to Ask the Physician

The various rights suggest some of the questions the patient may want to ask his physician—either at the time of the first visit or later. For example, most patients want to know the results of diagnostic tests and procedures. Patients may also ask about planned treatments, the risks and chances of success or failure with particular types of treatment, and the period of time for which the patient may be hospitalized.

Many other factors become important. Where one patient may want to know about alternative forms of care or treatment, another may ask about the surgeons who may perform an operation, the specialists who may be called in, and so on. Typically, most questions relate to the patient's situation: how far it has progressed, whether danger to life or health is involved, the physician's estimate of the chances of recovery, and other points. Physicians themselves suggest that patients ask questions to find out:

- Whether hospitalization, if it has been recommended, is really necessary
- Whether consultation with another physician or other physicians may be called for
- Whether—if necessary—medical terms or wordings can be clarified
- Whether, in case the patient is in doubt, the physician understood what the patient reported about symptoms, history, prescriptions already taken, and similar data

Common sense usually indicates what other questions the patient should ask the physician. The patient may have to make allowances for medical procedures. For instance, a thorough physical examination always requires that the patient undress—but no invasion of privacy is intended. Most important, the patient's right to free communication should be respected, and the patient should understand that it is.

Diagnostic Tests and Patients' Rights

Many diagnostic tests and procedures have been discussed. Many others could be listed.

One reason is that as medical costs have risen in recent years, some persons have questioned the necessity of various diagnostic tests. Consumer advocates have insisted that patients in some hospitals have been charged for tests that only increased their hospital bills. In some cases the tests were given in *batteries,* or sets. The question that has come up: Did the patients actually understand all those tests and what they involved?

Another reason why questions about patients' rights have been raised centers on the nature of test batteries and the time available to physicians. The batteries can be complex, and the physician may often be short of time. He may find it difficult or impossible to explain every test he has ordered—and to do so in enough detail so that the patient knows what each test requires and what it means in terms of discomfort, risk, and cost.

Hospital admission tests may be simple or complex. They may involve only "vital signs" tests of temperature, pulse rate, respiratory rate, and blood pressure. But they can include the *admission labs*—screening tests done by automated machines. These tests may include a urinalysis (UA), a complete blood count (CBC), and serum chemistries—Simultaneous Multiple Analyzer tests of 12 (SMA-12) or 24 (SMA-24) factors. The SMA-12 would typically call for chemical analyses for calcium, inorganic phosphorous, glucose, and nine other body elements.

Admission labs usually also include a test for syphilis, a chest X ray, and an EKG. The latter is often considered essential for patients over 40. Together, the admission labs tell the physician a number of important facts about the state of the patient's health.

Literally dozens of other tests could be noted. All involve some degree of risk and discomfort for the patient. But for most admission tests, both risk and discomfort are minimal. When the patient agrees to undergo them in batteries, is his or her right of informed consent being violated?

The Physician's Challenge

That question cannot be answered in a single word. The physician faces a dilemma in nearly all cases. He or she has to ask how much information can and should be transmitted—and how much the patient can absorb without becoming confused. He or she has also to ask what degree of risk is involved in any test or series of tests. Then the physician has to weigh the advantages of having test readings against the disadvantage involved in not having those test results. For a woman under 35, a test for cancer such as a mammogram may entail some risk if administered regularly (annually). For an older woman the risk is considered minimal.

With some tests, the risk for the patient is slight to virtually nonexistent. But all tests given in batteries involve some risk, however minor. Does that mean that administration of tests in batteries increases the risk element significantly? It may, say those who argue against administration of tests by sets or groups.

The protocols or understandings on patients' rights establish fairly loose standards. That applies particularly in the area of information to be given to the patient. Thus the physician has to make a judgment decision in many cases. He or she tries to find out what the patient wants to know and whether all the needed information is readily available. The physician may even have to do some "homework" to answer the patient's questions.

Authorities agree that physicians

A Guide to Some Home Medical Tests

Kind	Function	How It Works	Time Required
Blood glucose monitoring	Measures the level of glucose (a kind of sugar) in blood	Wash your hands thoroughly. Prick a finger or earlobe to obtain a drop of blood, then follow instructions.	1 to 2 minutes
Ovulation monitoring	Measures the quantity of luteinizing hormone (LH) in urine	A chemically treated strip is dipped in urine specimen and compared with a color guide.	20 minutes to 1 hour
Pregnancy	Detects human chorionic gonadotropin, produced by a developing placenta, in urine	Chemicals are mixed with a urine specimen in a small test tube. A ring formation or color change indicates pregnancy.	20 minutes to 2 hours
Urinary tract infections	Detects nitrite in urine	Chemically treated test strip is dipped in urine specimen on three consecutive mornings.	30 to 40 seconds
Occult fecal blood	Detects hidden blood in stools	A color change, appearing when stool specimen is brought into contact with peroxide and guaiac, indicates hidden blood.	30 seconds to 16 minutes
Gonorrhea	Detects the bacteria causing gonorrhea in the specimen of pus from the penis	Specimen, collected on a slide, is allowed to air-dry. Then follow directions.	Several days
Blood pressure	Measures the pressure of blood on the walls of the arteries	The center of a cuff is placed on the pulse point of the upper arm. With or without a microphone, the user listens for artery sounds.	2 to 5 minutes
Impotence	Detects, measures the rigidity of erections during sleep	Soft fabric band or stamps are placed around the penis before the subject goes to bed at night. The strips break at different degrees of pressure.	Overnight
Vision	Screens for visual acuity problems	Using three different tests, you read special eye charts.	2 to 3 minutes

should spend time with patients and their families to the extent necessary to clarify procedures, risks, and prognoses. Physicians are also advised to talk to patients in a direct and honest manner, and in layman's terms. By such means the patient's rights are protected. The physician also finds out what he or she needs to know to make an accurate diagnosis.

Home Testing

Various kinds of medical tests may be self-administered. In increasingly common use are tests designed to provide clues to vision problems, gastrointestinal diseases, ovulation, pregnancy, infections, diabetes, and other conditions. Generally the self-testing products fall into three categories. The first helps to diagnose a specific condition, such as pregnancy (for use after a missed menstrual period). A second type, for persons with obvious symptoms, is designed to identify such indications of disease as hidden blood in stools. A third class includes monitoring devices, used most often on the advice of a physician. Blood glucose test kits for diabetics are examples of the last.

Self-tests, while relatively cheap and effective, should be used cautiously. The tests may have the positive benefit of motivating a person to see a physician; but users should remember that test results are not uniformly reliable. For that reason, no single positive test should be taken as a "diagnosis." Nor should a subsequent negative test result be accepted as evidence of a "cure."

Exceptions to such general rules may be made where specific products help a person maintain testing regimens either at home or while traveling—as in the case of glucose monitoring. Fecal occult (hidden) blood tests have also proved so useful that the American Cancer Society has distributed free test kits.

27

Nutrition and Weight Control

Food and meals are man's best friends. His health and his social life are tied intimately and everlastingly to what he eats and how he eats it. Of all the physiological functions which maintain his life, eating and all that it entails is the one in which he most expresses his personal preferences and the cultural traditions of his ancestors.

Most people develop eating habits early in life that accord with family patterns and modify them only slightly over the years. Sometimes these habits conform to ideal food recommendations from the viewpoint of maintaining and fostering good health. More often, however, they do not.

Knowledge about food, eating, and their relationship to health is the best way to change inappropriate eating patterns of adults and to introduce youngsters to good eating habits that should last a lifetime.

Basic Nutritional Requirements

In a somewhat oversimplified way, a person can be compared with a working mechanism such as a car. The material of which each is made—tissue cells for the person, metal for the car—has to come from somewhere: the human's, from conception to birth, comes from the food eaten by his mother; after birth, from what he himself eats.

During growth and thereafter, the person's cells must be repaired and replaced just as a car must have new tires, parts, and paint from time to time. And like the car, the human has an engine—his muscular activity—which requires fuel. This fuel is provided by food in the form of calories.

In humans, the process by which food is used by the body is called *metabolism.* It begins with chemical processes in the gastrointestinal tract which change plant and animal food into less complex components so that they can be absorbed to fulfill their various functions in the body.

Protein

Of the several essential components of food, *protein* is in many ways the most important. This is so because much of the body's structure is made up of proteins. For example, the typical 160-pound man is composed of about 100 pounds of water, 29 pounds of protein, 25 pounds of fat, 5 pounds of minerals, 1 pound of carbohydrate, and less than an ounce of vitamins. Because the muscles, heart, brain, lungs, and gastrointestinal organs are made up largely of protein, and since the protein in these organs is in constant need of replacement, its importance is obvious.

Chemically, proteins are mixtures of amino acids that contain various elements, including nitrogen. There are 20 different amino acids that are essential for the body's protein needs. Eight of these must be provided in the diet; the rest can be synthesized by the body itself.

Meat, fish, eggs, and milk or milk products are the primary protein foods and contain all of the necessary amino acids. Grains and vegetables are partly made up of protein, but more often than not, they do not provide the whole range of amino acids required for proper nourishment.

Carbohydrates

Carbohydrates are another essential food component. They are also called *starches* or *sugars* and are present in large quantities in grains, fruits, and vegetables. They serve as the primary source of calories for muscle contraction and must be available in the body constantly for this purpose.

It takes one pound of carbohydrates to provide a 160-pound man with fuel for about half a day. Therefore, if he isn't getting new carbohydrate supplies during the day from his food, he will begin to convert his body fat or protein into sugar. This isn't desirable unless he has an excess of body fat, and in any event, could not go on indefinitely.

Fats

Fats are a chemically complex food component composed of *glycerol* (a sweet, oily alcohol) and fatty acids. Fats exist in several forms and come from a variety of sources. One way to think of them is to group them as visible fats, such as butter, salad oil, or the fat seen in meat, and as invisible fats, which are mingled, blended, or absorbed into food, either naturally, as in nuts, meat, or fish, or during cooking. Another way is to think of them as solid at room temperature (fats), or as liquid at room temperature (oils).

Saturated and Unsaturated

Fats are also classified as *saturated* or *unsaturated.* This is a chemical distinction based on the differences in molecular structure of different kinds of fat. If the carbon atoms in a fat molecule are surrounded or boxed in by hydrogen atoms, they are said to be saturated. This type of fat seems to increase the cholesterol content of the blood. *Polyunsaturated* fats, such as those found in fish and vegetable oils, contain the least number of hydrogen atoms and do not add to the blood cholesterol content. In general, fats in foods of plant origin are more unsaturated than in those of animal origin.

Fats play several essential roles in the metabolic process. First of all, they provide more than twice the number of calories on a comparative weight basis than do proteins and carbohydrates. They also can be stored in the body in large quantities and used as a later energy source. They serve as carriers of the fat-soluble vitamins A, D, E, and K, and—of no little importance—they add to the tastiness of food.

Vitamins

Vitamins, which are present in minute quantities in foods in their natural state, are essential for normal metabolism and for the development and maintenance of tissue structure and function. In addition to the fat-soluble vitamins noted above, there are a number of B vitamins, as well as vitamin C, also called *ascorbic acid.* If any particular vitamin is missing from the diet over a sufficiently long time, a specific disease will result.

The understanding of the subtle and complicated role of vitamins in maintaining life and health has come about during this century with the development of highly refined research methods. It is likely that continuing research will shed more light on their importance.

Minerals

Minerals are another component of basic nutritional needs. All living things extract them from the soil, which is their ultimate source. Like vitamins, they are needed for normal metabolism and must be present in the diet in sufficient amounts for the maintenance of good health. The essential minerals are copper, iodine, iron, manganese, zinc, molybdenum, fluorine, and cobalt.

When the normal diet is deficient in certain minerals, these minerals need to be specially added to the diet: iodine for thyroid function, and fluorine for protection against dental cavities. Additional iron for hemoglobin formation may be indicated when the diet is deficient in it, or when there has been an excessive loss of red blood cells, as some women experience with their menstrual periods.

Water

Water is not really a food in the fuel or calorie-producing sense, but it is in many ways a crucial component of nutrition. It makes up from 55 to 65 percent of the body's weight, and is constantly being eliminated in the form of urine, perspiration, and expired breath. It must therefore be replaced regularly, for while a person can live for weeks without food, he can live for only a few days without water.

Normally, the best guide to how much water a person needs is his sense of thirst. The regulating mechanism of excretion sees to it that an excessive intake of water will be eliminated as urine. The usual water requirement is on the order of two quarts a day in addition to whatever amount is contained in the solids which make up the daily diet. Information on the protein, fat, and carbohydrate content in specific foods, as well as the number of calories, may be obtained by consulting the table "Nutrients in Common Foods." The Metric Equivalents table converts spoon and cup measures into metric measures.

Basic Daily Diets

Everyone should have at least the minimal amount of basic nutrients for resting or basal metabolism. The specific needs of each individual are de-

Average Daily Calorie Consumption

Men	Calories
Sedentary	2,500
Moderately active	3,000
Active	3,500
Very active	4,250
Women	**Calories**
Sedentary	2,100
Moderately active	2,500
Active	3,000
Very active	3,750

Guidelines for average daily calorie consumption by men and women. With increasing use of labor-saving devices, most Americans fall into the sedentary category.

Calorie Consumption for Some Activities

Type of Activity	Calories Per Hour
Sedentary: reading, sewing, typing, etc.	30–100
Light: cooking, slow walking, dressing, etc.	100–170
Moderate: sweeping, light gardening, making beds, etc.	170–250
Vigorous: fast walking, hanging out clothes, golfing, etc.	250–350
Strenuous: swimming, bicycling, dancing, etc.	350 and more

Low Calorie Diet

Sample Menus

	800 calories		1,200 calories		1,600 calories	
	Weight (grams)	Household measure	Weight (grams)	Household measure	Weight (grams)	Household measure
Breakfast						
Orange, sliced	125	1 medium	125	1 medium	125	1 medium
Soft cooked egg	50	One	50	One	50	One
Toast	25	1 slice	25	1 slice	25	1 slice
Butter	5	1 teaspoon	5	1 teaspoon	5	1 teaspoon
Coffee or tea	—	As desired	—	As desired	—	As desired
Milk	240	1 cup skim	240	1 cup skim	240	1 cup whole
Luncheon						
Clear broth	—	As desired	—	As desired	—	As desired
Salad (cottage cheese, tomato, plain lettuce leaf)	90	½ cup	90	½ cup	90	½ cup
Egg			50	One	50	One
Green peas					100	½ cup
Baked apple, unsweetened	80	1 small	80	1 small	80	1 small
Bread			25	1 slice	25	1 slice
Butter			5	1 teaspoon	5	1 teaspoon
Milk	240	1 cup skim	240	1 cup skim	240	1 cup whole
Coffee or tea	—	As desired	—	As desired	—	As desired
Dinner						
Roast beef, lean	60	2 ounces	90	3 ounces	120	4 ounces
Carrots, plain	100	½ cup	100	½ cup	100	½ cup
Tossed vegetable salad with vinegar	50	¾ cup	50	¾ cup	50	¾ cup
Pineapple, unsweetened	80	½ cup	80	½ cup	80	½ cup
Bread			25	1 slice	25	1 slice
Butter			5	1 teaspoon	10	2 teaspoons
Coffee or tea	—	As desired	—	As desired	—	As desired
Nourishment						
Peach					100	1 medium

These diets contain approximately 800, 1,200, and 1,600 calories. The 800 calorie diet, even with variations in selections of food, will not meet the recommended daily allowances in iron and thiamine. The approximate composition is as follows:

	800 calories	1,200 calories	1,600 calories
Protein	60 gm.	75 gm.	85 gm.
Fat	30 gm.	50 gm.	80 gm.
Carbohydrate	75 gm.	110 gm.	130 gm.

From the *Clinical Center Diet Manual*, revised edition, prepared by the Nutrition Department. The Clinical Center, National Institutes of Health, Public Health Service, U.S. Department of Health, Education, and Welfare (Public Health Service Publication No. 989), pp. 67–68.

termined by whether he is still growing, and by how much energy is required for his normal activities. All those who are still growing—and growth continues up to about 20 years of age—have relatively high food needs.

For Infants

That food needs of an infant are especially acute should surprise no one. The newborn baby normally triples his birth weight during his first year and is very active in terms of calorie expenditure.

For his first six months, breast milk or formula, or a combination of both, fills his nutritional needs. The amount of milk he should get each day is about two and a half ounces per pound of his body weight. This provides 50 calories per pound, and in the early months is usually given in six feedings a day at four-hour intervals.

If his weight gain is adequate and he appears healthy, and if his stomach is not distended by swallowed air, his appetite is normally a satisfactory guide to how much he needs. The formula-fed baby should get a supplement of 35 milligrams of ascorbic acid each day and 400 international units of vitamin D if the latter has not been added to the milk during its processing.

Solid Foods

Between two and six months of age, the baby should begin to eat solid foods such as cooked cereals, strained fruits and vegetables, egg yolk, and homogenized meat. With the introduction of these foods, it is not really necessary to calculate the baby's caloric intake. Satisfaction of appetite, proper weight gain, and a healthy appearance serve as the guides to a proper diet.

By one year of age, a baby should be getting three regular meals a day, and as his teeth appear, his food no longer needs to be strained. By 18 to 24 months, he should no longer need baby foods. For further information on the care and feeding of infants, see under "Birth, Infancy, and Maturation" in Ch. 2, *The First Dozen Years*.

Basic Food Groups

The recommended daily amounts of food for people over the age of two have been established with reasonable accuracy. They are called minimal daily amounts, but they always contain a fairly generous safety factor.

The Four Group Division

In general, foods are divided into four major groups:

- Meat, fish, eggs
- Dairy products
- Fruits and vegetables
- Breads and cereals

The Seven Group Division

For purposes of planning daily requirements, a more detailed way of considering food groupings is the following:

- Leafy green and yellow vegetables
- Citrus fruits, tomatoes, and raw cabbage
- Potatoes and other vegetables and fruits
- Milk, cheese, and ice cream
- Meat, poultry, fish, eggs, dried peas, and beans
- Bread, flour, and cereals
- Butter and fortified margarine

Table 1

Desirable Weights for Men and Women Aged 25 and Over[1]
(in pounds by height and frame, in indoor clothing)

MEN (in shoes, 1-inch heels)				WOMEN (in shoes, 2-inch heels)			
Height	Small Frame	Medium Frame	Large Frame	Height	Small Frame	Medium Frame	Large Frame
5′ 2″	112–120	118–129	126–141	4′ 10″	92– 98	96–107	104–119
5′ 3″	115–123	121–133	129–144	4′ 11″	94–101	98–110	106–122
5′ 4″	118–126	124–136	132–148	5′ 0″	96–104	101–113	109–125
5′ 5″	121–129	127–139	135–152	5′ 1″	99–107	104–116	112–128
5′ 6″	124–133	130–143	138–156	5′ 2″	102–110	107–119	115–131
5′ 7″	128–137	134–147	142–161	5′ 3″	105–113	110–122	118–134
5′ 8″	132–141	138–152	147–166	5′ 4″	108–116	113–126	121–138
5′ 9″	136–145	142–156	151–170	5′ 5″	111–119	116–130	125–142
5′ 10″	140–150	146–160	155–174	5′ 6″	114–123	120–135	129–146
5′ 11″	144–154	150–165	159–179	5′ 7″	118–127	124–139	133–150
6′ 0″	148–158	154–170	164–184	5′ 8″	122–131	128–143	137–154
6′ 1″	152–162	158–175	168–189	5′ 9″	126–135	132–147	141–158
6′ 2″	156–167	162–180	173–194	5′ 10″	130–140	136–151	145–163
6′ 3″	160–171	167–185	178–199	5′ 11″	134–144	140–155	149–168
6′ 4″	164–175	172–190	182–204	6′ 0″	138–148	144–159	153–173

[1]Adapted from Metropolitan Life Insurance Co., New York. New weight standards for men and women. *Statistical Bulletin* 40:3.

Table 2

Average Weights for Men and Women[1]
(in pounds by age and height, in paper gown and slippers)

Height	18–24 Years	25–34 Years	35–44 Years	45–54 Years	55–64 Years	65–74 Years	75–79 Years
MEN							
5′ 2″	137	141	149	148	148	144	133
5′ 3″	140	145	152	152	151	148	138
5′ 4″	144	150	156	156	155	151	143
5′ 5″	147	154	160	160	158	154	148
5′ 6″	151	159	164	164	162	158	154
5′ 7″	154	163	168	168	166	161	159
5′ 8″	158	168	171	173	169	165	164
5′ 9″	161	172	175	177	173	168	169
5′ 10″	165	177	179	181	176	171	174
5′ 11″	168	181	182	185	180	175	179
6′ 0″	172	186	186	189	184	178	184
6′ 1″	175	190	190	193	187	182	189
6′ 2″	179	194	194	197	191	185	194
WOMEN							
4′ 9″	116	112	131	129	138	132	125
4′ 10″	118	116	134	132	141	135	129
4′ 11″	120	120	136	136	144	138	132
5′ 0″	122	124	138	140	149	142	136
5′ 1″	125	128	140	143	150	145	139
5′ 2″	127	132	143	147	152	149	143
5′ 3″	129	136	145	150	155	152	146
5′ 4″	131	140	147	154	158	156	150
5′ 5″	134	144	149	158	161	159	153
5′ 6″	136	148	152	161	164	163	157
5′ 7″	138	152	154	165	167	166	160
5′ 8″	140	156	156	168	170	170	164

[1]Adapted from National Center for Health Statistics: Weight by Height and Age of Adults, United States. *Vital Health Statistics*. PHS Publication No. 1000—Series 11, No. 14.

The "Daily Food Guide" is a general guide to planning nutritionally balanced meals for preteens, teens, and adults of any age.

The Years of Growth

Even though a child will never again triple his weight in a single year as he did during his first, a proper diet is crucial during the years from 2 to 18, since this is a period of tremendous growth.

Other food goals that should be realized during the childhood and adolescent years are an awareness of what a balanced diet is, a reasonable tolerance for a variety of foods, decent manners at the table, and a sense of timing about when to eat and when not to eat.

These are also the years that a young person should begin to learn something about how to buy and prepare food, how to serve it attractively, and how to clean up after a meal.

Creating a Pleasant Atmosphere at Mealtime

Although a child's attitudes about food and eating can often be exasperating, it is up to the parent to make mealtime as pleasant as possible, and above all, to avoid any battles of will.

If a young child is too tired, too excited, or too hungry to cope with a meal without ending up in tears or a tantrum, he should not be forced to eat. There are several ways to help children develop a wholesome attitude toward food and eating; here are a few suggestions:

- Children should never be bribed with candy, money, or the promise of special surprises as a way of getting them to eat properly.
- They should not be given the idea that dessert is a reward for finishing the earlier part of the meal.
- Relatively small portions should be served and completely finished before anything else is offered.
- Between-meal snacks should be discouraged if they cut down on the appetite at mealtime.
- From time to time, the child should be allowed to choose the foods that he will eat at a meal.

Parents should keep in mind that the atmosphere in which a child eats and the attitudes instilled in him toward food can be altogether as basic as the nourishment for his body.

Teenage Diet

From the start of a child's growth spurt, which begins at age 10 or 11 for girls and between 13 and 15 for boys, and for several years thereafter, adolescent appetites are likely to be unbelievably large and somewhat outlandish. Parents should try to exercise some control over the youngster who is putting on too much weight as well as over the one who is attracted by a bizarre starvation diet.

Adult Nutrition

Adult nutrition is concerned with more than 50 years of an individual's life span. In typical cases, there is a slow but steady weight gain that may go unnoticed at first; for some, there is an obesity problem that begins at about age 40.

Because it is never easy to lose weight, it is especially important for adults to eat sensibly and avoid excess calories. See under "Weight," for a discussion of weight control and obesity.

For Older People

People over 60 tend to have changes in their digestive system that are related to less efficient and slower absorption. Incomplete chewing of food because of carelessness or impaired teeth can intensify this problem. Avoiding haste at mealtimes ought to be the rule.

In cases where a dental disorder makes proper chewing impossible, food should be chopped or pureed. Older people occasionally have difficulty swallowing and may choke on a large piece of unchewed meat.

Food for older people should be cooked simply, preferably baked, boiled, or broiled rather than fried, and menus excessively rich in fats should be avoided. A daily multivitamin capsule is strongly recommended for those over 60. A poor appetite can be stimulated by an ounce or two of sherry before a meal unless there are medical reasons for avoiding alcoholic beverages of any kind. See under "Aging and What To Do About It" in Ch. 6, *The Later Years,* for a discussion of diet and eating habits in the later years.

Metric Equivalents of Traditional Food Measures

1 teaspoon	=	5 milliliters
1 tablespoon	=	15 milliliters
1/4 cup	=	60 milliliters
1/3 cup	=	80 milliliters
1/2 cup	=	120 milliliters
2/3 cup	=	160 milliliters
3/4 cup	=	180 milliliters
1 cup	=	240 milliliters or 0.24 liter

During Pregnancy

A pregnant woman needs special foods to maintain her own health as well as to safeguard the health of her baby. She should have additional vitamin D and iron, usually recommended as dietary supplements. More important for most women is the provision of adequate protein in the diet to prevent toxemia of pregnancy or underweight babies. Between 70 and 85 grams of protein a day should be eaten during pregnancy, even if this results in a weight gain of as much as 25 pounds. Adequate nutrition is more important than restricting weight gain to 20 pounds or less.

Nursing Mothers

A nursing mother has special dietary needs in addition to those satisfied by the normal adult diet. She should drink an extra quart of milk and eat two more servings of citrus fruit or tomatoes, one more serving of lean meat, fish, poultry, eggs, beans, or cheese, and one more serving of leafy green or yellow vegetables.

Malnutrition

The classic diseases of nutritional deficiency, or malnutrition, such as scurvy and pellagra, are now rare, at least in the United States. The chief reason for their disappearance is the application of scientific knowledge gained in this century of the importance of vitamins and minerals in the diet. Thus most bread is fortified with vitamins and minerals, and in addition, commercial food processing has made it possible for balanced diets of an appealing variety to be eaten all year round.

Many people do not get an adequate diet, either through ignorance or because they simply cannot afford it. A number of food programs have been created to assist them, but unfortunately, the programs don't reach everyone who needs help.

Causes of Malnutrition

Some people, either because of ignorance or food faddism, do not eat a balanced diet even though they can afford to. There are also large numbers of people with nutritional defi-

Nutrients in Common Foods

Food	Food energy	Protein	Fat	Carbohydrate
	Calories	Grams	Grams	Grams
Milk and Milk Products				
Milk; 1 cup:				
Fluid, whole	165	9	10	12
Fluid, nonfat (skim)	90	9	trace	13
Buttermilk, cultured (from skim milk)	90	9	trace	13
Evaporated (undiluted)	345	18	20	24
Dry, nonfat (regular)	435	43	1	63
Yogurt (from partially skimmed milk); 1 cup	120	8	4	13
Cheese; 1 ounce:				
Cheddar or American	115	7	9	1
Cottage:				
From skim milk	25	5	trace	1
Creamed	30	4	1	1
Cream cheese	105	2	11	1
Swiss	105	7	8	1
Desserts (largely milk):				
Custard, baked; 1 cup, 8 fluid ounces	305	14	15	29
Ice cream, plain, factory packed:				
1 slice or individual brick, ⅛ quart	130	3	7	14
1 container, 8 fluid ounces	255	6	14	28
Ice milk; 1 cup, 8 fluid ounces	200	6	7	29
Eggs				
Egg, raw, large:				
1 whole	80	6	6	trace
1 white	15	4	trace	trace
1 yolk	60	3	5	trace
Egg, cooked; 1 large:				
Boiled	80	6	6	trace
Scrambled (with milk and fat)	110	7	8	1
Meat, Poultry, Fish, Shellfish				
Bacon, broiled or fried, drained, 2 medium thick slices	85	4	8	trace
Beef, cooked without bone:				
Braised, simmered, or pot-roasted; 3 ounce portion:				
Entire portion, lean and fat	365	19	31	0
Lean only, approx. 2 ounces	140	17	4	0
Hamburger patties, made with				
Regular ground beef; 3-ounce patty	235	21	17	0
Lean ground round; 3-ounce patty	185	23	10	0
Roast; 3-ounce slice from cut having relatively small amount of fat:				
Entire portion, lean and fat	255	22	18	0
Lean only, approx. 2.3 ounces	115	19	4	0
Steak, broiled; 3-ounce portion:				
Entire portion, lean and fat	375	19	32	0
Lean only, approx. 1.8 ounces	105	17	4	0
Beef, canned: corned beef hash: 3 ounces	155	8	10	9
Beef and vegetable stew: 1 cup	220	16	11	15
Chicken, without bone: broiled; 3 ounces	115	20	3	0
Lamb, cooked:				
Chops; 1 thick chop, with bone, 4.8 ounces:				
Lean and fat, approx. 3.4 ounces	340	21	28	0
Lean only, 2.3 ounces	120	18	5	0

Nutrients in Common Foods

Food	Food energy	Protein	Fat	Carbohydrate
	Calories	Grams	Grams	Grams
Roast, without bone:				
Leg; 3-ounce slice:				
Entire slice, lean and fat	265	20	20	0
Lean only, approx. 2.3 ounces	120	19	5	0
Shoulder; 3-ounce portion, without bone:				
Entire portion, lean and fat	300	18	25	0
Lean only, approx. 2.2 ounces	125	16	6	0
Liver, beef, fried; 2 ounces	120	13	4	6
Pork, cured, cooked:				
Ham, smoked; 3-ounce portion, without bone	245	18	19	0
Luncheon meat:				
Boiled ham; 2 ounces	130	11	10	0
Canned, spiced; 2 ounces	165	8	14	1
Pork, fresh, cooked:				
Chops; 1 chop, with bone, 3.5 ounces:				
Lean and fat, approx. 2.4 ounces	295	15	25	0
Lean only, approx. 1.6 ounces	120	14	7	0
Roast; 3-ounce slice, without bone:				
Entire slice, lean and fat	340	19	29	0
Lean only, approx. 2.2 ounces	160	19	9	0
Sausage:				
Bologna; 8 slices (4.1 by 0.1 inches each), 8 ounces	690	27	62	2
Frankfurter; 1 cooked, 1.8 ounces	155	6	14	1
Tongue, beef, boiled; 3 ounces	205	18	14	trace
Veal, cutlet, broiled; 3-ounce portion, without bone	185	23	9	0
Fish and shellfish:				
Bluefish, baked or broiled; 3 ounces	135	22	4	0
Clams: raw, meat only; 3 ounces	70	11	1	3
Crabmeat, canned or cooked; 3 ounces	90	14	2	1
Fishsticks, breaded, cooked, frozen; 10 sticks (3.8 by 1.0 by 0.5 inches each), 8 ounces	400	38	20	15
Haddock, fried; 3 ounces	135	16	5	6
Mackerel: broiled; 3 ounces	200	19	13	0
Oysters, raw, meat only; 1 cup (13–19 medium-size oysters, selects)	160	20	4	8
Oyster stew: 1 cup (6–8 oysters)	200	11	12	11
Salmon, canned (pink); 3 ounces	120	17	5	0
Sardines, canned in oil, drained solids; 3 ounces	180	22	9	1
Shrimp, canned, meat only; 3 ounces	110	23	1	–
Tuna, canned in oil, drained solids; 3 ounces	170	25	7	0
Mature Beans and Peas, Nuts				
Beans, dry seed:				
Common varieties, as Great Northern, navy, and others, canned; 1 cup:				
Red	230	15	1	42
White, with tomato or molasses:				
With pork	330	16	7	54
Without pork	315	16	1	60

ciency diseases who can be described as abnormal, at least in regard to eating. Some are alcoholics; others live alone and are so depressed that they lack sufficient drive to feed themselves properly. Combination of any of these factors increase the likelihood of poor nutrition and often lead to health-damaging consequences.

Disease

People can also develop nutritional deficiencies because they have some disease that interferes with food absorption, storage, and utilization, or that causes an increased excretion, usually in the urine, of substances needed for nutrition. These are generally chronic diseases of the gastrointestinal tract including the liver, or of the kidneys or the endocrine glands.

Medications

Nutritional deficiencies can also result from loss of appetite caused by medications, especially when a number of different medications are taken simultaneously. This adverse affect on the appetite is a strong reason for not taking medicines unless told to do so by a physician for a specific purpose.

Most people are not aware of inadequacies in their diet until there are some dramatic consequences. Nor is it easy to recognize the presence of a disorder that might be causing malnutrition. A physician should be consulted promptly when there is a persistent weight loss, especially when the diet is normal. He should also be informed of any changes in the skin, mucous membranes of the mouth or tongue, or nervous system function, because such symptoms can be a warning of dietary deficiency.

The famliy or friends of a person with a nutritional deficiency can often detect his condition because they become aware of changes in his eating patterns. They can also note early signs of a deficiency of some of the B vitamins, such as cracks in the mucous membranes at the corners of the mouth, or some slowing of intellectual function.

Correction of Nutritional Deficiencies

Nutritional deficiences are among the most easily preventable causes of disease. It is important to realize that even mild deficiencies can cause irreparable damage, particularly protein deprivation in young children, which can result in some degree of mental retardation. Periodic medical checkups for everyone in the family are the best way to make sure that such deficiencies are corrected before they snowball into a chronic disease. In most cases, all that is required is a change of eating habits.

Weight

Probably the most important dietary problem in the United States today is obesity. It is certainly the problem most talked about and written about, not only in terms of good looks, but more important, in terms of good health.

All studies indicate that people who are obese have a higher rate of disease and a shorter life expectancy than those of average weight. From a medical point of view, people who are too fat may actually suffer from a form of malnutrition, even though they look overnourished.

Being too fat and being overweight are not necessarily the same. Heavy bones and muscles can make a person overweight in terms of the charts, but only an excess amount of fat tissue can make someone obese. However, height and weight tables are generally used to determine obesity.

Nutrients in Common Foods

Food	Food energy	Protein	Fat	Carbohydrate
	Calories	Grams	Grams	Grams
Beans, dry seed:				
Lima, cooked; 1 cup	260	16	1	48
Cowpeas or black-eyed peas, dry, cooked; 1 cup	190	13	1	34
Peanuts, roasted, shelled; 1 cup	840	39	71	28
Peanut butter; 1 tablespoon	90	4	8	3
Peas, split, dry, cooked; 1 cup	290	20	1	52
Vegetables				
Asparagus:				
Cooked; 1 cup	35	4	trace	6
Canned; 6 medium-size spears	20	2	trace	3
Beans:				
Lima, immature, cooked; 1 cup	150	8	1	29
Snap, green:				
Cooked; 1 cup	25	2	trace	6
Canned; solids and liquid; 1 cup	45	2	trace	10
Beets, cooked, diced; 1 cup	70	2	trace	16
Broccoli, cooked, flower stalks; 1 cup	45	5	trace	8
Brussels sprouts, cooked; 1 cup	60	6	1	12
Cabbage; 1 cup:				
Raw, coleslaw	100	2	7	9
Cooked	40	2	trace	9
Carrots:				
Raw: 1 carrot (5½ by 1 inch) or 25 thin strips	20	1	trace	5
Cooked, diced; 1 cup	45	1	1	9
Canned, strained or chopped; 1 ounce	5	trace	0	2
Cauliflower, cooked, flower buds; 1 cup	30	3	trace	6
Celery, raw: large stalk, 8 inches long	5	1	trace	1
Collards, cooked; 1 cup	75	7	1	14
Corn, sweet:				
Cooked; 1 ear 5 inches long	65	2	1	16
Canned, solids and liquid; 1 cup	170	5	1	41
Cucumbers, raw, pared; 6 slices (⅛-inch thick, center section)	5	trace	trace	1
Lettuce, head, raw:				
2 large or 4 small leaves	5	1	trace	1
1 compact head (4¾-inch diameter)	70	5	1	13
Mushrooms, canned, solids and liquid; 1 cup	30	3	trace	9
Okra, cooked; 8 pods (3 inches long, ⅝-inch diameter)	30	2	trace	6
Onions: mature raw; 1 onion (2½-inch diameter)	50	2	trace	11
Peas, green; 1 cup:				
Cooked	110	8	1	19
Canned, solids and liquid	170	8	1	32
Peppers, sweet:				
Green, raw; 1 medium	15	1	trace	3
Red, raw; 1 medium	20	1	trace	4
Potatoes:				
Baked or boiled; 1 medium, 2½-inch diameter (weight raw, about 5 ounces):				
Baked in jacket	90	3	trace	21
Boiled; peeled before boiling	90	3	trace	21
Chips; 10 medium (2-inch diameter)	110	1	7	10
French fried:				
Frozen, ready to be heated for serving; 10 pieces (2 by ½ by ½ inch)	95	2	4	15

Nutrients in Common Foods

Food	Food energy	Protein	Fat	Carbohydrate
	Calories	Grams	Grams	Grams
Ready-to-eat, deep fat for entire process; 10 pieces (2 by ½ by ½ inch)	155	2	7	20
Mashed; 1 cup:				
Milk added	145	4	1	30
Milk and butter added	230	4	12	28
Radishes, raw; 4 small	10	trace	trace	2
Spinach:				
Cooked; 1 cup	45	6	1	6
Canned, creamed, strained; 1 ounce	10	1	trace	2
Squash:				
Cooked, 1 cup:				
Summer, diced	35	1	trace	8
Winter, baked, mashed	95	4	1	23
Canned, strained or chopped; 1 ounce	10	trace	trace	2
Sweet potatoes:				
Baked or boiled; 1 medium, 5 by 2 inches (weight raw, about 6 ounces):				
Baked in jacket	155	2	1	36
Boiled in jacket	170	2	1	39
Candied; 1 small, 3½ by 2 inches	295	2	6	60
Canned, vacuum or solid pack; 1 cup	235	4	trace	54
Tomatoes:				
Raw; 1 medium (2 by 2½ inches), about ⅓ pound	30	2	trace	6
Canned or cooked; 1 cup	45	2	trace	9
Tomato juice, canned; 1 cup	50	2	trace	10
Tomato catsup; 1 tablespoon	15	trace	trace	4
Turnips, cooked, diced; 1 cup	40	1	trace	9
Turnip greens, cooked; 1 cup	45	4	1	8
Fruits				
Apples, raw; 1 medium (2½ inch diameter), about ⅓ pound	70	trace	trace	18
Apple juice, fresh or canned; 1 cup	125	trace	0	34
Apple sauce, canned:				
Sweetened; 1 cup	185	trace	trace	50
Unsweetened; 1 cup	100	trace	trace	26
Apricots, raw; 3 apricots (about ¼ pound)	55	1	trace	14
Apricots, canned in heavy syrup; 1 cup	200	1	trace	54
Apricots, dried: uncooked; 1 cup (40 halves, small)	390	8	1	100
Avocados, raw, California varieties: ½ of a 10-ounce avocado (3½ by 3¼ inches)	185	2	18	6
Avocados, raw, Florida varieties: ½ of a 13-ounce avocado (4 by 3 inches)	160	2	14	11
Bananas, raw; 1 medium (6 by 1½ inches), about ⅓ pound	85	1	trace	23
Blueberries, raw; 1 cup	85	1	1	21
Cantaloupes, raw, ½ melon (5-inch diameter)	40	1	trace	9
Cherries, sour, sweet, and hybrid, raw; 1cup	65	1	1	15
Cranberry sauce, sweetened; 1 cup	550	trace	1	142
Dates, "fresh" and dried, pitted and cut; 1 cup	505	4	1	134
Figs:				
Raw; 3 small (1½-inch diameter), about ¼ pound	90	2	trace	22
Dried; 1 large (2 by 1 inch)	60	1	trace	15

Table 1 lists standard desirable weights for people of various heights, calculated with indoor clothing and shoes on. Frame sizes are estimated in a general way. This table applies to anyone over the age of 25, indicating that weight gain for the rest of the life span is unnecessary for biological normalcy.

Table 2 gives average weights of American men and women, according to height and age. These measurements are made without clothing or shoes. Note that the weights are considerably higher than the corresponding ones of Table 1. There is a modest weight gain until the middle years and then a gradual loss.

To determine whether a person is obese according to the tables, the percent that he is overweight has to be calculated. An individual is usually considered obese in the clinical sense if he weighs 20 percent more than the standard tables indicate for his size and age.

The Pinch Test

Another method of determining obesity is to use the "pinch" test. In most adults under 50 years of age, about half of the body fat is located directly under the skin. There are various parts of the body, such as the side of the lower torso, the back of the upper arm, or directly under the shoulder blade, where the thumb and forefinger can pinch a fold of skin and fat away from the underlying bone structure.

If the fold between the fingers—which is, of course, double thickness when it is pinched—is thicker than one inch in any of these areas, the likelihood is that the person is obese.

The Problem of Overweight

The percentage of overweight people in this country has been increasing steadily, chiefly because people eat more and use less physical energy than they used to. Americans do very little walking because of the availability of cars; they do very little manual labor because of the increasing use of machines. They may eat good wholesome meals, but they have the time for nibbling at all hours, especially when sitting in front of the television screen.

These patterns usually begin in childhood. Youngsters rarely walk to school any more; they get there by bus or car. They often have extra money for snacks and soft drinks, and frequently parents encourage them to overeat without realizing that such habits do them more harm than good.

Most overweight children remain overweight as adults. They also have greater difficulty losing fat, and if they do lose it, tend to regain it more easily than overweight adults who were thin as children. Many adults become overweight between the ages of 20 and 30. Thus, by age 30, about 12 percent of American men and women are 20 percent or more overweight, and by age 60, about 30 percent of the male population and 50 percent of the female are at least 20 percent overweight. As indicated above, the phenomenon of weight gain while aging does not represent biological normalcy.

Why People Put On Weight

Why does weight gain happen? Excess weight is the result of the imbalance between caloric intake as food and caloric expenditure as energy, either in maintaining the basic metabolic processes necessary to sustain life or in performing physical activity. Calories not spent in either of these ways become converted to fat and accumulate in the body as fat, or *adipose* tissue.

A *calorie* is the unit of measure-

Nutrients in Common Foods

Food	Food energy	Protein	Fat	Carbohydrate
	Calories	Grams	Grams	Grams
Fruit cocktail, canned in heavy syrup, solids and liquid; 1 cup	175	1	trace	47
Grapefruit:				
Raw; ½ medium (4¼-inch diameter, No. 64's)	50	1	trace	14
Canned in syrup; 1 cup	165	1	trace	44
Grapefruit juice:				
Raw; 1 cup	85	1	trace	23
Canned:				
Unsweetened; 1 cup	95	1	trace	24
Sweetened; 1 cup	120	1	trace	32
Frozen concentrate, unsweetened:				
Undiluted; 1 can (6 fluid ounces)	280	4	1	72
Diluted, ready-to-serve; 1 cup	95	1	trace	24
Frozen concentrate, sweetened:				
Undiluted; 1 can (6 fluid ounces)	320	3	1	85
Diluted, ready-to-serve; 1 cup	105	1	trace	28
Grapes, raw; 1 cup:				
American type (slip skin)	70	1	1	16
European type (adherent skin)	100	1	trace	26
Grape juice, bottled; 1 cup	165	1	1	42
Lemonade concentrate, frozen, sweetened:				
Undiluted; 1 can (6 fluid ounces)	305	1	trace	113
Diluted, ready-to-serve; 1 cup	75	trace	trace	28
Oranges, raw; 1 large orange (3-inch diameter)	70	1	trace	18
Orange juice:				
Raw; 1 cup:				
California (Valencias)	105	2	trace	26
Florida varieties:				
Early and midseason	90	1	trace	23
Late season (Valencias)	105	1	trace	26
Canned, unsweetened; 1 cup	110	2	trace	28
Frozen concentrate:				
Undiluted; 1 can (6 fluid ounces)	305	5	trace	80
Diluted, ready-to-serve; 1 cup	105	2	trace	27
Peaches:				
Raw:				
1 medium (2½-inch diameter), about ¼ pound	35	1	trace	10
1 cup, sliced	65	1	trace	16
Canned (yellow-fleshed) in heavy syrup; 1 cup	185	1	trace	49
Dried: uncooked; 1 cup	420	5	1	109
Pears:				
Raw; 1 pear (3 by 2½-inch diameter)	100	1	1	25
Canned in heavy syrup; 1 cup	175	1	trace	47
Pineapple juice; canned; 1 cup	120	1	trace	32
Plums:				
Raw; 1 plum (2-inch diameter), about 2 ounces	30	trace	trace	7
Canned (Italian prunes), in syrup; 1 cup	185	1	trace	50
Prunes, dried:				
Uncooked; 4 medium prunes	70	1	trace	19
Cooked, unsweetened; 1 cup (17–18 prunes and ⅓ cup liquid)	295	3	1	78
Prune juice, canned; 1 cup	170	1	trace	45
Raisins, dried; 1 cup	460	4	trace	124
Raspberries, red:				
Raw; 1 cup	70	1	trace	17

Nutrients in Common Foods

Food	Food energy	Protein	Fat	Carbohydrate
	Calories	Grams	Grams	Grams
Frozen; 10-ounce carton	280	2	1	70
Strawberries:				
Raw; 1 cup	55	1	1	12
Frozen; 10-ounce carton	300	2	1	75
Tangerines; 1 medium (2½-inch diameter), about ¼ pound	40	1	trace	10
Watermelon: 1 wedge (4 by 8 inches), about 2 pounds (weighed with rind)	120	2	1	29
Grain Products				
Biscuits, baking powder, enriched flour; 1 biscuit (2½-inch diameter)	130	3	4	20
Bran flakes (40 percent bran) with added thiamine; 1 ounce	85	3	1	22
Breads:				
Cracked wheat:				
1 pound (20 slices)	1,190	39	10	236
1 slice (½ inch thick)	60	2	1	12
Italian; 1 pound	1,250	41	4	256
Rye:				
American (light):				
1 pound (20 slices)	1,100	41	5	236
1 slice (½ inch thick)	55	2	trace	12
Pumpernickel; 1 pound	1,115	41	5	241
White:				
1–2 percent nonfat dry milk:				
1 pound (20 slices)	1,225	39	15	229
1 slice (½ inch thick)	60	2	1	12
3–4 percent nonfat dry milk:				
1 pound (20 slices)	1,225	39	15	229
1 slice (½ inch thick)	60	2	1	12
5–6 percent nonfat dry milk:				
1 pound (20 slices)	1,245	41	17	228
1 slice (½ inch thick)	65	2	1	12
Whole wheat, graham, or entire wheat:				
1 pound (20 slices)	1,105	48	14	216
1 slice (½ inch thick)	55	2	1	11
Cakes:				
Angel food: 2-inch sector (1/12 of cake, 8-inch diameter)	160	4	trace	36
Butter cakes:				
Plain cake and cupcakes without icing:				
1 square (3 by 3 by 2 inches)	315	4	12	48
1 cupcake (2¾-inch diameter)	120	2	5	18
Plain cake with icing:				
2-inch sector of iced layer cake (1/16 of cake, 10-inch diameter)	320	5	6	62
Rich cake:				
2-inch sector layer cake, iced (1/16 of cake, 10-inch diameter)	490	6	19	76
Fruit cake, dark; 1 piece (2 by 1½ by ¼ inches)	60	1	2	9
Sponge; 2-inch sector (1/12 of cake, 8-inch diameter)	115	3	2	22
Cookies, plain and assorted; 1 cookie (3-inch diameter)	110	2	3	19
Cornbread or muffins made with enriched, degermed cornmeal; 1 muffin 2¾-inch diameter)	105	3	2	18
Cornflakes: 1 ounce	110	2	trace	24
Corn grits, degermed, cooked: 1 cup	120	3	trace	27

ment that describes the amount of energy potentially available in a given food. It is also used to describe the amount of energy the body must use up to perform a given function.

An ounce of protein contains 130 calories, as does an ounce of carbohydrate. An ounce of fat, by contrast, contains 270 calories. This biochemical information isn't too helpful in calculating the calories in a particular piece of meat, slice of bread, or pat of butter. For such practical figures, there are useful pocket guides, such as *Calories and Weight,* a U.S. Government publication that can be obtained by sending $1.00 to the Superintendent of Documents, U.S. Government Printing Office, Washington, D.C. 20401, and asking for the Agriculture Information Bulletin No. 364.

Counting Calories

If an adult gets the average 3,000 calories a day in his food from the age of 20 to 70, he will have consumed about 55 million calories. About 60 percent of these calories will have been used for his basic metabolic processes. The rest—22 million calories—might have resulted in a gain of about 6,000 pounds of fat, since each group of 3,500 extra calories could have produced one pound of fat.

In some ways, it's a miracle that people don't become more obese than they do. The reason, of course, is that most or all of these extra calories are normally used to provide energy for physical activity. Elsewhere in this chapter are some examples of calorie expenditure during various activities.

A reasonably good way for an adult to figure his daily caloric needs for moderate activities is to multiply his desirable weight (as noted in Table 1) by 18 for men and 16 for women. If the typical day includes vigorous or strenuous activities, extra calories will, of course, be required.

Parental Influences and Hereditary Factors

Although there are exceptions, almost all obese people consume more calories than they expend. The reasons for this imbalance are complex. One has to do with parental weight. If the weight of both parents is normal, there is only a 10 percent likelihood that the children will be obese. If one parent is obese, there is a 50 percent probability that the children will be too, and if both are, the probability of obese offspring is 80 percent.

No one knows for certain why this is so. It is probably a combination of diet habits acquired in youth, conditioning during early years to react to emotional stress by eating, the absence of appropriate exercise patterns, and genetic inheritance.

Some obese people seem to have an impairment in the regulatory mechanism of the area of the central nervous system that governs food intake. Simply put, they do not know when to stop eating. Others, particularly girls, may eat less than their nonobese counterparts, but they are considerably less active. Some researchers think that obese people have an inherent muscle rhythm deficiency. A few people appear to have an abnormality in the metabolic process which results in the accumulation of fat even when the balance between calories taken in and expended is negative and should lead to weight loss.

Obesity and Health

There are many reasons why obesity is a health hazard. The annual death rate for obese people between the ages of 20 and 64 is half again as high as that for people whose weight is close to normal. This statistical difference is due primarily to the increased likelihood that the obese per-

Nutrients in Common Foods

Food	Food energy	Protein	Fat	Carbohydrate
	Calories	Grams	Grams	Grams
Crackers:				
Graham; 4 small or 2 medium	55	1	1	10
Saltines; 2 crackers (2-inch square)	35	1	1	6
Soda, plain: 2 crackers (2½-inch square)	45	1	1	8
Doughnuts, cake type; 1 doughnut	135	2	7	17
Farina, cooked; 1 cup	105	3	trace	22
Macaroni, cooked; 1 cup:				
Cooked 8–10 minutets (undergoes additional cooking as ingredient of a food mixture)	190	6	1	39
Cooked until tender	155	5	1	32
Noodles (egg noodles), cooked; 1 cup	200	7	2	37
Oat cereal (mixture, mainly oat flour), ready-to-eat; 1 ounce	115	4	2	21
Oatmeal or rolled oats, regular or quick cooking, cooked; 1 cup	150	5	3	26
Pancakes, baked; 1 cake (4-inch diameter):				
Wheat (home recipe)	60	2	2	7
Buckwheat (with buckwheat pancake mix)	45	2	2	6
Pies; 3½-inch sector (⅛ of 9-inch diameter pie):				
Apple	300	3	13	45
Cherry	310	3	13	45
Custard	250	7	13	27
Lemon meringue	270	4	11	40
Mince	320	3	14	49
Pumpkin	240	5	13	28
Pretzels; 5 small sticks	20	trace	trace	4
Rice, cooked; 1 cup:				
Converted	205	4	trace	45
White	200	4	trace	44
Rice, puffed or flakes; 1 ounce	110	2	trace	25
Rolls:				
Plain, pan (16 ounces per dozen); 1 roll	115	3	2	20
Hard, round (22 ounces per dozen); 1 roll	160	5	2	31
Sweet, pan (18 ounces per dozen); 1 roll	135	4	4	21
Spaghetti, cooked until tender; 1 cup	155	5	1	32
Waffles, baked, with enriched flour: 1 waffle (4½ by 5½ by ½ inches)	215	7	8	28
Wheat, puffed: 1 ounce	100	4	trace	22
Wheat, rolled, cooked; 1 cup	175	5	1	40
Wheat flakes; 1 ounce	100	3	trace	23
Wheat flours:				
Whole wheat; 1 cup, sifted	400	16	2	85
All purpose or family flour: 1 cup, sifted	400	12	1	84
Wheat germ; 1 cup, stirred	245	17	7	34
Fats, Oils, Related Products				
Butter; 1 tablespoon	100	trace	11	trace
Fats, cooking:				
Vegetable fats:				
1 cup	1,770	0	200	0
1 tablespoon	110	0	12	0
Lard:				
1 cup	1,985	0	220	0
1 tablespoon	125	0	14	0
Margarine; 1 tablespoon	100	trace	11	trace
Oils, salad or cooking; 1 tablespoon	125	0	14	0

Nutrients in Common Foods

Food	Food energy	Protein	Fat	Carbohydrate
	Calories	Grams	Grams	Grams
Salad dressings; 1 tablespoon:				
Blue cheese	90	1	10	1
Commercial, plain (mayonnaise type)	60	trace	6	2
French	60	trace	6	2
Mayonnaise	110	trace	12	trace
Thousand Island	75	trace	8	1
Sugars, Sweets				
Candy; 1 ounce:				
Caramels	120	1	3	22
Chocolate, sweetened, milk	145	2	9	16
Fudge, plain	115	trace	3	23
Hard	110	0	0	28
Marshmallow	90	1	0	23
Jams, marmalades, preserves; 1 tablespoon	55	trace	trace	14
Jellies; 1 tablespoon	50	0	0	13
Sugar; 1 tablespoon	50	0	0	12
Syrup, table blends; 1 tablespoon	55	0	0	15
Miscellaneous				
Beverages, carbonated, cola types; 1 cup	105	–	–	28
Bouillon cubes; 1 cube	2	trace	trace	0
Chocolate, unsweetened; 1 ounce	145	2	15	8
Gelatin dessert, plain, ready-to-serve; 1 cup	155	4	0	36
Sherbet, factory packed; 1 cup (8-fluid-ounce container)	235	3	trace	58
Soups, canned, prepared with equal amount of water; 1 cup:				
Bean with pork	168	8	6	22
Beef noodle	140	8	5	14
Bouillon, broth, and consomme	30	5	0	3
Chicken consomme	44	7	trace	4
Clam chowder, Manhattan style	80	2	3	12
Tomato	90	2	3	16
Vegetable beef	80	5	2	10
Vinegar; 1 tablespoon	2	0	–	1

Adapted from *Nutritive Value of American Foods* by Catherine F. Adams, Agriculture Handbook No. 456, U.S. Department of Agriculture, issued November 1975. The cup measure used in the following table refers to the standard 8-ounce measuring cup of 8 fluid ounces or one-half liquid pint. When a measure is indicated by ounce, it is understood to be by weight—1/16 of a pound avoirdupois—unless a fluid ounce is indicated. All weights and measures in the table are in U.S. System units.

son will suffer from diabetes mellitus and from diseases of the digestive and circulatory systems, especially of the heart.

One possible reason for the increased possibility of heart disease is that there are about two-thirds of a mile of blood vessels in each pound of adipose tissue. Thus 20 or more pounds of excess weight are likely to impose a great additional work load on the heart.

Obese people are also poorer surgical risks than the nonobese, and it is often more difficult to diagnose and therefore to treat their illnesses correctly.

Permanent loss of excess weight makes the formerly obese person come closer to matching the life expectancy of the nonobese. However, losing and regaining weight as a repeated pattern is even more hazardous in terms of health than consistent obesity.

Psychological Consequences of Obesity

In ways that are both obvious and subtle, obesity often has damaging psychological consequences. This is particularly true for obese children, who tend to feel isolated and rejected by their peers. They may consider themselves victims of prejudice and blame their obesity for everything that goes wrong in their lives. In many cases, the destructive relationship between obesity and self-pity keeps perpetuating itself.

Obese adults are likely to experience the same feelings, but to a somewhat lesser degree. For some, obesity is an escape which consciously or unconsciously helps them to avoid situations in which they feel uncomfortable—those that involve active competition or relationships with the opposite sex.

Avoiding Excess Weight

Clearly, obesity is a condition that most people would like to avoid. Not putting on extra pounds does seem to be easier, in theory at least, then taking them off. One possible explanation for this is that additional adipose tissue consists of a proliferation of fat cells. Shrinking these cells is one thing, eliminating them is another. Our present lack of fundamental knowledge about the regulatory and metabolic mechanisms relating to obesity limits the technique of preventing overweight to recommending a balance between caloric intake and expenditure.

The real responsibility for preventing the onset of obesity in childhood rests with parents. All of the fundamentals of good nutrition and healthy eating habits are of the utmost importance in this connection. Caloric expenditure in the form of regular exercise is equally important.

Exercising by Habit

This does not necessarily mean that

exercise should be encouraged for its own sake. What it does mean is making a habit of choosing an active way of approaching a situation rather than a lazy way: walking upstairs rather than taking the elevator; walking to school rather than riding; walking while playing golf rather than riding in a cart; running to get the ball that has rolled away rather than ambling toward it. These choices should be made consistently and not just occasionally if obesity is to be avoided. Those people who naturally enjoy the more active way of doing things are lucky. Those who don't should make an effort to develop new patterns, especially if obesity is a family problem.

Anyone with the type of physical handicap that makes a normal amount of exercise impossible should be especially careful about caloric intake.

Losing Weight Must Be Self-Motivated

Unless there are compelling medical reasons for not doing so, anyone weighing 20 percent or more over the normal limit for his age and body build should be helped to slim down. It is extremely important, however, for the motivation to come from the person himself rather than from outside pressure.

Unless an overweight person really wants to reduce, he will not succeed in doing so, certainly not permanently, even though he appears to be trying. He must have convinced himself—intellectually and emotionally—that the goal of weight loss is truly worth the effort.

It is very difficult not only for his friends and family but for the person himself to be absolutely sure about the depth of his motivation. A physician treating an overweight patient has to assume that the desire to reduce is genuine and will try to reinforce it whenever he can. However, if a patient has made a number of attempts to lose weight over a period of years and has either been unable to reduce to any significant degree, or has become overweight again after reducing, it is probably safe to assume that the emotional desire is absent, or that there are emotional conflicts that stand in the way.

It is very possible that such a person could be harmed psychologically by losing weight, since he might need to be overweight for some deep-seated reason. This can be true for both children and adults. Occasionally it is possible for a psychiatrist or psychologist to help the patient remove a psychological block, and then weight reduction can occur if the caloric balance is straightened out.

Weight Reduction

The treatment of obesity is a complicated problem. In the first place, there is the question of who wants or needs to be treated and how much weight should be lost. Except in unusual situations, anyone who wants to lose weight should be encouraged to do so. Possible exceptions are teenagers who are not overweight but who want to be as thin as they can possibly be—the boy who is involved in an athletic event such as wrestling, or the girl who has decided she wants to look like a fashion model.

Crash dieting is usually unwise if the goal is to lose too much weight too rapidly and should be undertaken only after consulting a doctor about its advisability. As for adolescents who have become slightly overweight during puberty, they may be ill-advised to try to take off the extra pounds that probably relate to a temporary growth pattern.

Effect of Fat Accumulation in Abdomen

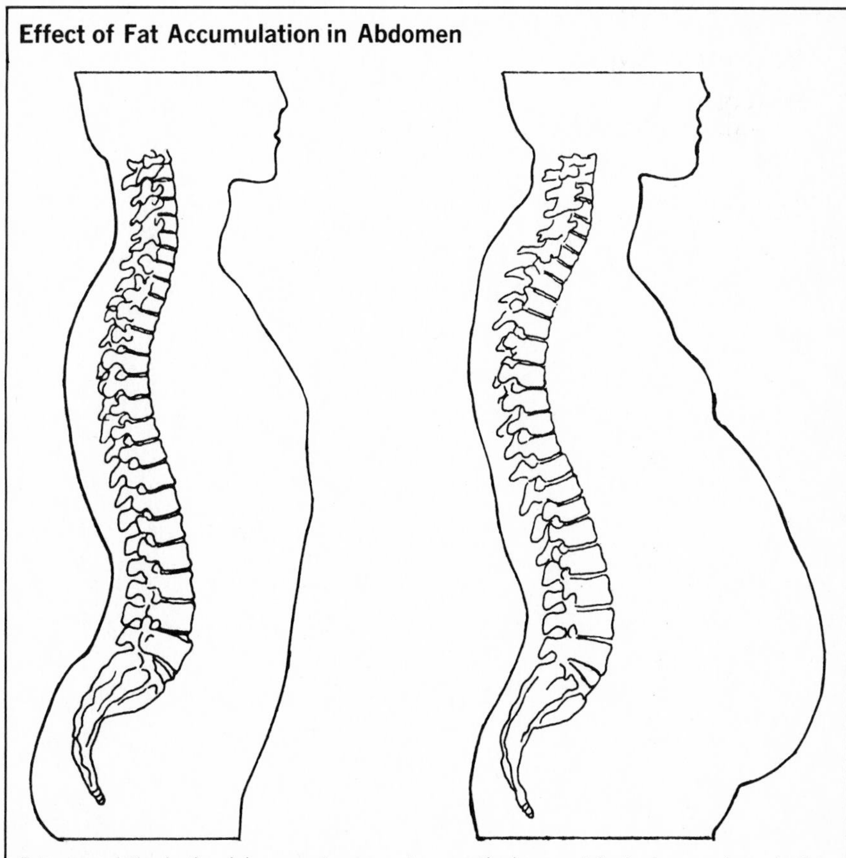

Fat accumulating in the abdomen puts severe stress on the lower vertebral column and can lead to many back problems.

Daily Food Guide

	Child	Preteen and Teen	Adult	Aging Adult
Milk or milk products (*cups*)	2–3	3–4 or more	2 or more	2 or more
Meat, fish, poultry, and eggs (*servings*)	1–2	3 or more	2 or more	2 or more
Green and yellow vegetables (*servings*)	1–2	2	2	at least 1
Citrus fruits and tomatoes (*servings*)	1	1–2	1	1–2
Potatoes, other fruits, vegetables (*servings*)	1	1	1	0–1
Bread, flour, and cereal (*servings*)	3–4	4 or more	3–4	2–3
Butter or margarine (*tablespoons*)	2	2–4	2–3	1–2

1. The need for the nutrients in 1 or 2 cups of milk daily can be satisfied by cheeses or ice cream. (1 cup of milk is approximately equivalent to 1½ cups of cottage cheese or 2–3 large scoops of ice cream.)
2. It is important to drink enough fluid. The equivalent of 3–5 cups daily is recommended.
3. The recommended daily serving of meat, fish, and poultry (3 oz.) may be alternated with eggs or cheese, dried peas, beans, or lentils.
4. Iron-rich foods should be selected as frequently as possible by teenage and adult females to help meet their high requirement for this mineral (liver, heart, lean meats, shellfish, egg yolks, legumes, green leafy vegetables, and whole grain and enriched cereal products).

From *Your Age and Your Diet* (1971), reprinted with permission from the American Medical Association.

Effective Planning for Weight Loss

The ultimate key to successful weight reduction is proper eating combined with proper physical activity. This balance is extremely difficult for many people to achieve because it involves a marked change in attitudes and behavior patterns that are generally solidly established and of long duration. Furthermore, once the changes are made, they will have to endure for a lifetime if the weight that has been lost is not to be regained.

It is therefore important that the reducing diet should be somewhat similar to the person's usual eating pattern in terms of style and quality. Ideally, only the caloric content should be changed, and probably the word "dieting" should not be used to describe the process, since most people don't find the idea of permanent dieting congenial.

Similarly, the increased physical activity that must accompany the new eating style should be of a type that the person enjoys. It is virtually impossible for an overeating person to reduce merely by restricting his caloric intake, or merely by increasing his caloric expenditure. The two must go together.

Cutting Down Step by Step

The first thing to determine when planning to lose weight is the number of pounds that have to go. A realistic goal to set is the loss of about one pound a week. This may seem too slow, but remember that at this rate, fifty pounds can be lost in a year.

Getting Started

Start by weighing yourself on arising, and then for two weeks try to eat in your customary manner, but keep a careful record of everything that you eat, the time it is eaten, and the number of calories it contains. During this period, continue to do your usual amount of physical activity.

When the two weeks are over, weigh yourself again at the same time of day as before. If you haven't gained any weight, you are in a basal caloric state. Then check over your food list to see what might be eliminated each day without causing discomfort.

Try to think in terms of eliminating fats and carbohydrates first, because it is essential that you continue to get sufficient vitamins and minerals which are largely found in proteins. The foods described in the "Daily Food Guide" chart should all continue to be included in your daily food consumption. If you are in the habit of having an occasional drink, remember that there are calories in alcohol but no nutrients, and that most alcoholic beverages stimulate the appetite. See *Low Calorie Diet* sample menus and *Nutrients in Common Foods* for estimating calories in particular foods.

Planning Meals

When you replan your meals, keep in mind that the items you cut down on must add up to between 300 and 400 calories a day if you are going to lose one pound a week.

Your total daily food intake should be divided among at least three meals a day, more if you wish. If you need to eat more food or to eat more often, try snacking on low calorie foods such as cabbage, carrots, celery, cucumber, and cauliflower. All of these can be eaten raw between meals.

There is definitely something to be said in favor of having breakfast every morning, or at least most mornings. This may be psychologically difficult, but try to do it, because it will be easier to control your urge to eat too much later in the day.

Increasing Exercise

At the same time that you begin to cut down on your food intake, start to increase your daily exercise in whatever way you find congenial so that the number of calories expended in increased exercise plus the number of calories eliminated from your diet comes to 500 or more. This is your daily caloric loss compared with your so-called basal caloric state.

Achieving Your Goal

You may wish to double your daily caloric loss so that you lose two pounds a week. Do not try to lose any more than that unless you are under close medical supervision.

If you gained weight during your two-week experimental period, you will have to increase your daily caloric loss by 500 for every pound gained per week. Thus, if you gained one pound during the two weeks, you will have to step up your daily caloric loss to 750 to lose a pound a week.

You'll have to keep plugging away to achieve your goal. It will be trying and difficult in many ways. You may get moody and discouraged and be tempted to quit. Don't. You'll probably go on periodic food binges. All this is natural and understandable, so try not to brood about it. Just do the best you can each day. Don't worry about yesterday, and let tomorrow take care of itself.

In many ways it can help, and in some cases it's essential, to have the support and encouragement of family and friends, particularly of those with whom you share meals. You may find it helpful to join a group that has been formed to help its members lose weight and maintain their weight loss. This is a good psychological support.

Maintaining Your Weight Loss

Once you have achieved your desired weight, you can test yourself to see what happens if you increase your caloric intake. Clearly, anyone who can lose weight in the manner described can't stay in a state of negative caloric imbalance indefinitely. But you will have to be careful, or you'll become overweight again. It's a challenge, but people who stick to a disciplined program can be rewarded by success.

Special Problems

If you do not succeed in losing weight in spite of carrying out the program

Soft and Bland Soft Diets

Soft Diet

Foods allowed on this diet are left whole. The fiber content is modified by using only cooked or canned fruits and vegetables (with skins and seeds removed); refined or finely ground cereals and breads are included. Some restrictions have been placed on highly seasoned and rich foods because of the specific needs for which the soft diet is usually ordered.

Bland Soft Diet

If further restrictions on seasonings and food items are necessary, a bland soft diet may be ordered. This diet follows the same pattern as the soft diet outlined below but is modified to eliminate all stimulants, such as meat extractives, spices, condiments (except salt), strongly flavored foods, and beverages that contain caffeine, such as coffee, tea, or cola drinks. The following foods are also omitted: all whole grain breads, rolls, muffins, and cereals; all gravies and salad dressings; pork; broth and soups with a meat base (use only strained cream soups); lettuce. Limit quantities of jelly, sugar, and hard candies. Extremely hot or cold foods are avoided. The foods allowed may be divided into five or six small meals with each feeding containing a good source of protein.

Soft Diet

Type of food	Foods included	Foods excluded
Beverages	Coffee, decaffeinated coffee, tea, carbonated beverages, cereal beverages, cocoa, milk.	None
Breads	White; whole wheat, finely ground; rye (without seeds), finely ground; white or whole wheat rolls or muffins, finely ground; plain crackers.	Coarse whole wheat breads; breads, rolls, and muffins with seeds, nuts, raisins, etc.
Cereals	Cooked or prepared cereals, such as cornflakes, strained oatmeal, cream of rice or wheat, farina, hominy grits, cornmeal, puffed rice, other rice cereals.	Cooked or prepared coarse cereals, such as bran, shredded wheat.
Desserts	Plain cake and cookies, sponge cake; custards, plain puddings, rennet desserts; gelatin desserts with allowed fruits; plain ice cream, sherbets (except pineapple), fruit ices.	Pies; pastries; desserts made with coconut, nuts, pineapple, raisins, etc.
Fats	Butter, cream, fortified fats, plain gravies, mayonnaise, cream sauces.	Fried foods; rich highly seasoned sauces and gravies with mushrooms, pimento, etc.
Fruits	Raw ripe bananas; canned or cooked fruits without skins or small seeds, such as applesauce, baked apple without skin, apricots, sweet cherries, peaches, pears; fruit juices as desired.	Raw fruits except bananas; canned or cooked fruits with skins, coarse fibers, or seeds, such as figs, raisins, berries, pineapple, etc.
Meat, poultry fish	Bacon, beef, ham, lamb, pork, veal, poultry, and fish that has been baked, boiled, braised, broiled, or roasted.	Fried meat, poultry, or fish; highly seasoned meats; stews containing celery, onions, etc.; cold cuts, sausages.
Cheese	All except strongly flavored cheeses.	Cheeses with pimento, caraway seeds, etc.; strongly flavored cheeses.
Eggs	Any raw, soft cooked, hard cooked, soft scrambled, poached; omelets made with allowed foods.	Fried eggs, omelets containing mushrooms, etc.

Soft Diet *(continued)*

Type of food	Foods included	Foods excluded
Potato or substitute	Hominy, macaroni, noodles, rice, spaghetti; white or sweet potatoes without skins.	Fried potatoes; potato chips; high seasoned sauces for spaghetti, macaroni, etc.
Soups	Broth, strained soups; cream soups made with allowed vegetables.	All others
Sweets	Hard candies, simple chocolate candies without nuts or fruit; strained honey, jelly, sugar, syrup.	Candies with whole fruit, coconut, or nuts; jam, marmalade.
Vegetables	Cooked or canned asparagus tips, string beans, wax beans, beets, carrots, chopped spinach, winter squash; tomato puree, tomato juice; raw lettuce leaf as garnish.	Cooked broccoli, brussels sprouts, cabbage, cauliflower, celery, corn, mustard greens, turnip greens, mushrooms, onions, fresh and dried peas, summer squash, whole tomatoes; dried beans, lima beans, lentils. All raw vegetables except lettuce as a garnish.
Miscellaneous	Salt; small amounts of white or black pepper used in cooking; creamy peanut butter.	Hot seasonings, such as chili sauce, red pepper, etc.; coconut, nuts, olives, pickles; spiced fruit.

From the *Clinical Center Diet Manual*, revised edition, prepared by the Nutrition Department, The Clinical Center, National Institutes of Health, Public Health Service, U.S. Department of Health, Education, and Welfare (Public Health Service Publication No. 989), pp. 45–52.

Soft Diet

Sample Menu

Breakfast	
Orange juice	½ cup
Cornflakes	½ cup
Poached egg	One
Whole wheat toast	1 slice
Butter or fortified fat	1 teaspoon
Milk, whole	1 cup
Coffee or tea	As desired
Cream	As desired
Sugar	As desired
Luncheon	
Creamed chicken on toast	½ to ¾ cup
Mashed potato	½ cup
Buttered carrots	½ cup
Bread, enriched	1 slice
Butter or fortified fat	1 teaspoon
Canned pear halves	2 halves
Milk, whole	1 cup
Coffee or tea	As desired
Cream	As desired
Sugar	As desired
Dinner	
Roast beef, gravy	2 to 3 ounces
Baked potato	1 medium
Buttered asparagus spears	1 serving
Bread, enriched	1 slice
Butter or fortified fat	1 teaspoon
Vanilla ice cream	½ cup
Coffee or tea	As desired
Cream	As disired
Sugar	As desired

described above, you may need professional help because of some special problem. A qualified physician may try some special diets, or he may even suggest putting you into a hospital so that he can see to it that you have no caloric food at all for as long as three weeks.

Perhaps the situation is complicated by a metabolic abnormality that can be corrected or helped by medication. Although such conditions are rare, they are not unheard of.

Obesity is almost never caused by a "glandular" problem—which usually means an underactive thyroid. Do not take thyroid pills to reduce unless your thyroid has been found to be underactive on the basis of a specific laboratory test.

The indiscriminate use of pills to reduce, even when prescribed, is never helpful in the long run, although it may appear to be at first. The unsupervised use of amphetamines, for example, can be extremely dangerous. See Ch. 29, *Substance Abuse*, for further information about the dangers of amphetamine abuse.

Because so many people are eager to reduce, and because losing weight isn't easy, there are many unethical professionals who specialize in the problem. Avoid them. All they are likely to do for you is take your money and make your situation no better—and often worse—than it was to begin with.

Underweight

Weighing too little is a problem that is considerably less common than weighing too much. In fact, in many cases, it isn't accurate to call it a problem at all, at least not a medical one.

There are some times, however, when underweight may indicate the presence of a disease, especially when a person rather suddenly begins and continues to lose weight, even though there has been no change in his eating habits. This is a situation that calls for prompt medical evaluation. Such a person may already be under a physician's care at the time the weight loss is first noticed.

More often, however, underweight is a chronic condition that is of concern to the person who feels his looks would improve if he could only add some extra pounds. This is especially true in the case of adolescent girls and young women.

What To Do about Weighing Too Little

Chronic underweight is rarely a reflection of underlying disease. It is rather an expression of individual heredity or eating patterns, or a combination of both. Treatment for the condition is the opposite of the treatment for overweight. The achievement of a positive caloric balance comes first; more calories have to be consumed each day than are expended. An underweight person should record his food history over a two-week period in the manner described for an overweight one. Once this has been done, various adjustments can be made.

First of all, he should see that he eats at least three meals a day and that they are eaten in a leisurely way and in a relaxed frame of mind. All of the basic foods should be represented in the daily food intake, with special emphasis on protein. The daily caloric intake should then be gradually increased at each meal and snacks added, so long as the snacks don't reduce the appetite at mealtimes.

Carbohydrate foods are the best ones to emphasize in adding calories. Since the extra food intake may cause a certain amount of discomfort, encouragement and support from family

Bland Soft Diet

Sample Menu (*six small meals*)

Breakfast	
Egg, poached	One
White toast, enriched	1 slice
Butter or fortified fat	1 teaspoon
Hot cocoa	1 cup
10:00 a.m.	
Orange juice	½ cup
Cornflakes	½ cup
Cream	¼ cup
Sugar	2 teaspoons
Luncheon	
Creamed chicken on toast	½ cup
Mashed potato	½ cup
Buttered carrots	½ cup
Milk	1 cup
Canned pears	1 half
2:30 p.m.	
Milkshake	1 cup
Soda crackers	Three
Dinner	
Roast beef	2 ounces
Baked potato	1 medium
Buttered asparagus	1 serving
Butter or fortified fat	1 teaspoon
Milk	1 cup
Vanilla ice cream	½ cup
8:30 p.m.	
Baked custard	½ cup
Vanilla wafers	Two

Sodium Restricted Diets

Diets Moderately Restricted in Sodium

If only a moderate sodium restriction is necessary, a normal diet *without added salt* may be ordered. Such an order is interpreted to mean that the patient will be offered the regular salted food on the general selective menu with the following exceptions:

1. No salt will be served on the tray.
2. Soups that are salted will be omitted.
3. Cured meats (ham, bacon, sausage, corned beef) and all salted cheeses will be omitted.
4. Catsup, chili sauce, mustard, and other salted sauces will be omitted.
5. Salt-free gravies, sauces, and salad dressings will be substituted for the regular salted items.
6. Salted crackers, potato chips, nuts, pickles, olives, popcorn, and pretzels will be omitted.

This diet contains approximately 3 grams of sodium or 7.5 grams of sodium chloride, depending on the type and quantity of the food chosen.

Low Sodium Diets[1] (*1,000 mg. Sodium and 800 mg. Sodium Diets*)

Type of food	Foods included	Foods excluded
Beverages	Coffee, tea, carbonated beverages, cereal beverages; milk, cream, or cocoa within stated milk limitations.	All others.
Breads	Any unsalted yeast bread or rolls; quick breads made with "sodium-free" baking powder; unsalted matzoth.	All bread and rolls containing salt, baking powder or baking soda; salted or soda crackers; pretzels.

Low Sodium Diets[1] *(1,000 mg. Sodium and 800 mg. Sodium Diets) (continued)*

Type of food	Foods included	Foods excluded
Cereals	Any cereal that is cooked without salt; puffed rice, puffed wheat; shredded wheat; specially prepared "sodium-free" cornflakes and rice flakes; unsalted popcorn.	All prepared cereals containing salt; hominy grits.
Desserts	Any unsalted dessert; custards and puddings made with allowed milk; puddings made without milk; unflavored gelatin desserts; fruit ices; unsalted fruit pie and fruit whips.	Desserts made with salt, baking powder, or baking soda; flavored gelatin desserts.
Fats	Any unsalted fat or oil, vegetable or animal; unsalted salad dressings.	Salted butter, salted margarine; commercial salad dressings; bacon drippings.
Fruits	Any fresh, canned, or frozen fruit or juice.	Dried fruits prepared with sodium preservatives.
Meat, poultry, fish	Prepared without salt: beef, lamb, fresh pork, veal; poultry; freshwater fish;[2] liver (limit to one serving per week).	Salted meats; bacon; smoked or canned meats or fish; shellfish; all glandular meats except liver as allowed.
Cheese	Unsalted cottage cheese; specially prepared "sodium-free" yellow cheese.	All other.
Eggs	Limit to one daily, prepared without salt.	Any prepared with salt.
Potato or substitute	Dried beans (navy, pea), macaroni, noodles, potato, rice, spaghetti, sweet potato, all prepared without salt.	Salted potato chips, hominy.
Soups	Unsalted meat broth; cream soups prepared with allowed milk and allowed vegetables.	Bouillon; all soups prepared with salt.
Sweets	Hard candies, honey, jam, jelly, white sugar, syrup.	Commercial candy prepared with sodium salts; brown sugar.
Vegetables, cooked and raw	Two servings (½ cup) of vegetables listed below, fresh, frozen, or canned without salt: asparagus, lima beans,[3] navy beans, snap beens (green or yellow wax), broccoli, brussels sprouts, cabbage, carrots, cauliflower, corn, cucumbers, eggplant, dried lentils, lettuce, mushrooms, okra, onions, parsley, parsnips, black-eyed peas, green peas,[3] green peppers, radishes, rutabaga, squash, tomatoes, turnips, turnip greens.	Beets, beet greens, celery, dandelion greens, kale, frozen lima beans, mustard greens, frozen peas, sauerkraut, spinach, frozen succotash, Swiss chard.

and friends can be extremely helpful. Just as there may be psychological blocks against losing weight, there may well be a complicated underlying resistance to adding it.

Anyone trying to gain weight should remain or become reasonably active physically. Adding a pound or two a month for an adult—and a little more than that for a growing youngster—is an achievable goal until the desired weight is reached. When this happens, there will probably have to be some adjustments in eating and exercise patterns so that a state of caloric balance is achieved.

How Food Relates to Disease

Just as proper food is essential in the prevention of some diseases, it is helpful in the treatment of others. It also plays an important role in protecting and fortifying the general health of a patient while a specific illness is being treated.

The components of therapeutic diets are usually prescribed by the physician in charge, but some general principles will be presented here. Remember that diets designed to treat a given disease must supply the patient's basic nutritional requirements.

Ulcers

Special diet is a major treatment consideration in the case of peptic ulcer, whether located in the stomach (gastric) or in the small intestine (duodenal). A major aim of such a diet is the neutralizing of the acidity of gastric juices by the frequent intake of high protein foods such as milk and eggs. Foods which irritate an ulcer chemically, such as excessive sweets, spices, or salt, or mechanically, such as foods with sharp seeds or tough skins, and foods that are too hot or too cold, should be avoided. It is also advisable to eliminate gravies, coffee, strong tea, carbonated beverages, and alcohol, since all of these stimulate gastric secretion. Such a diet is called a *bland* diet. See "Soft and Bland Soft Diets" in this chapter. A soft diet is recommended for some forms of gastrointestinal distress and for those people who have difficulty chewing. It is often combined with the bland diet recommended for peptic ulcer patients to reduce the likelihood of irritation. See Ch. 11, *Diseases of the Digestive System,* for further information about ulcers.

Low Sodium Diets[1] *(1,000 mg. Sodium and 800 mg. Sodium Diets) (continued)*

Type of food	Foods included	Foods excluded
Miscellaneous	Herbs and spices, except salt. Unsalted peanut butter.	Salt, celery salt, garlic salt; celery seed, parsley flakes; sauces containing salt, such as catsup, chili sauce, mustard, steak sauces; salted nuts and popcorn; olives, pickles; monosodium glutamate.

[1]Approximate composition is indicated in the following table. 1,000 milligrams (abbreviated *mg.*) equals 1 gram. The 500, 800, and 1,000 milligram sodium diets meet the recommended nutrient levels of the normal diet.

Nutrient	Unit	500 mg. sodium	800 mg. sodium	1,000 mg. sodium
Sodium	Milligrams	485	775	970
Protein	Grams	70	95	95
Fat	Grams	90	90	90
Carbohydrate	Grams	185	250	250
Calories*		1,830	2,190	2,190

*Calories can be augmented by using additional salt-free fats and oils, white sugar, and pure jellies.

[2]Unsalted saltwater fish is usually avoided because of the difficulty of obtaining a consistently unsalted supply.

[3]Use only fresh or canned without salt.

From the *Clinical Center Diet Manual*, revised edition, prepared by the Nutrition Department, The Clinical Center, National Institutes of Health, Public Health Service, U.S. Department of Health, Education, and Welfare (Public Health Service Publication No. 989), pp. 77–86.

Diabetes

As the section on diabetes mellitus indicates (see Ch. 15), the major objectives of the special diet are weight control, control of the abnormal carbohydrate metabolism, and as far as possible, psychological adjustment by the patient to his individual circumstances. To some extent, he must calculate his diet mathematically. First, his daily caloric needs have to be determined in terms of his activities:

If he is overweight or underweight, the total calories per pound of body weight will have to be adjusted downward or upward by about five calories per pound.

After his total daily caloric needs have been figured out, he can calculate the number of grams of carbohydrate he should have each day by dividing his total calories by 10. The number of grams of protein per day as well as the number of grams of fat should be half the number of grams of carbohydrate.

This will mean that 40 percent of his daily calories will come from carbohydrate, 40 percent from fat, and 20 percent from protein. One-fifth of the total should be obtained at breakfast and the rest split between lunch and dinner. Snacks that are taken during the day should be subtracted equally from lunch and dinner.

It is important that meals and planned snacks be eaten regularly and that no food servings be added or omitted. Growing children from 1 to 20 years of age who have diabetes will require considerably more daily calories. A rough estimate is 1,000 calories for a one-year-old child and 100 additional calories for each year of age.

Salt-Free Diets

There are a number of chronic diseases which are treated in part by restricting the amount of sodium in the diet. These diseases, which are associated with fluid retention in the body, include congestive heart failure, certain types of kidney and liver diseases, and hypertension or high blood pressure.

The restriction of sodium intake helps to reduce or avoid the problem of fluid retention. The normal daily diet contains about seven or more grams of sodium, most of it in the form of sodium chloride or table salt. This amount is either inherent in the food or added during processing, cooking, or at mealtime. Half the weight of salt is sodium.

For people whose physical condition requires only a small restriction of the normal sodium intake, simply not salting food at the table is a sufficient reduction. They may decide to use a salt substitute, but before doing so should discuss the question with their physician.

A greater sodium restriction, for example, to no more than 5 grams a day, requires the avoidance of such high salt content foods as ham, bacon, crackers, catsup, and potato chips, as well as almost entirely eliminating salt in the preparation and serving of meals. Severe restriction—1 gram or less a day—involves special food selection and cooking procedures, as well as the use of distilled water if the local water has more than 20 milligrams of sodium per quart. In restricting sodium to this extent, it is important to make sure that protein and vitamins are not reduced below the minimum daily requirements. See "Sodium Restricted Diets."

Other Diseases Requiring Special Diets

There are several other disorders in which diet is an important consideration: all chronic gastrointestinal disorders, such as ulcerative colitis, enteritis, gallbladder stones, and diverticulitis; a variety of hereditary disorders such as phenylketonuria

Low Sodium Diets[1] *(1,000 mg. Sodium and 800 mg. Sodium Diets)*

Sample Menus

	500 mg. Sodium		800 mg. Sodium	
	Weight grams	Household measure	Weight grams	Household measure
Breakfast				
Orange, sliced	125	1 medium	125	1 medium
Soft cooked egg	50	One	50	One
Unsalted oatmeal	100	½ cup	100	½ cup
Unsalted toast	25	1 slice	25	1 slice
Unsalted butter	10	2 teaspoons	10	2 teaspoons
Jelly	—	As desired	—	As desired
Milk, low sodium	None		None	
Milk (or cream)	240	1 cup	240	1 cup
Coffee or tea	—	As desired	—	As desired
Sugar	—	As desired	—	As desired
Luncheon				
Unsalted beef patty	60	2 ounces	60	2 ounces
Unsalted fried potatoes	100	½ cup	100	½ cup
Unsalted asparagus	100	½ cup	100	½ cup
Lettuce and tomato salad	100	1 small	100	1 small
Unsalted French dressing	15	1 tablespoon	15	1 tablespoon
Unsalted chocolate cookies	None			1 serving
Canned peaches	100	1 serving	—	As desired
Unsalted bread	25	1 slice	25	1 slice
Unsalted butter	10	2 teaspoons	10	2 teaspoons
Jelly	—	As desired	—	As desired
Milk, low sodium	None		None	
Milk	240	1 cup	240	1 cup
Coffee or tea	—	As desired	—	As desired
Sugar	—	As desired	—	As desired
Dinner				
Unsalted roast chicken	60	2 ounces	90	3 ounces
Unsalted gravy	30	2 tablespoons	30	2 tablespoons
Unsalted mashed potatoes	100	½ cup	100	½ cup
Unsalted green beans	100	½ cup	100	½ cup
Banana salad	100	One	100	One
Unsalted mayonnaise	15	1 tablespoon	15	1 tablespoon
Fresh fruit cup	100	½ cup	100	½ cup
Unsalted bread	25	1 slice	25	1 slice
Unsalted butter	10	2 teaspoons	10	2 teaspoons
Jelly	—	As desired	—	As desired
Milk, low sodium	—	As desired	None	
Milk	None		240	1 cup
Coffee or tea	—	As desired	—	As desired
Sugar	—	As desired	—	As desired
Nourishment				
Orange juice	240	1 cup	—	As desired
Milk	None		240	1 cup

Modified Fat Diet

Type of Food	Foods included	Foods excluded
Beverages	Coffee, tea, carbonated beverages, cereal beverages; skimmed milk, nonfat dried milk and buttermilk (made from skimmed milk).	Cream, evaporated milk, whole milk, whole milk beverages.
Breads	Whole wheat, rye, or enriched white bread; plain yeast rolls.	All others, including biscuits, cornbread, French toast, muffins, sweet rolls.
Cereals	Any; whole grain or enriched preferred.	None.
Desserts	Angel food cake; plain puddings made with skimmed milk; gelatin desserts; fruit ices, sherbets; fruit whips; meringues.	Cakes except angel food; cookies; ice cream; pastries; rich desserts.

and galactosemia; atherosclerosis, especially when it is associated with elevated blood levels of cholesterol or triglycerides or both; liver disease such as cirrhosis; many of the endocrine diseases; kidney stones; and sometimes certain neurological diseases such as epilepsy. Diet also plays a special role in convalescence from most illnesses and in post-surgical care. The "Modified Fat Diet" and "Low Fat Diet" are recommended for some diseases of the liver and gallbladder. The "Minimal Residue Diet" is recommended for some digestive troubles and before and after gastrointestinal surgery.

Diet and Individual Differences

Most discussions about food and eating tend to suggest that all normal people have identical gastrointestinal and metabolic systems. This is simply not true. There are many individual differences that explain why one man's meat is another man's poison. A person's intolerance for a given food may be caused by a disorder, such as an allergy or an ulcer, and it is possible that many of these intolerances will ultimately be related to enzyme deficiencies or some other biochemical factor.

More subtle are the negative physical reactions to particular foods as a result of psychological conditioning. In most such cases, the choice is between avoiding the food that causes the discomfort or eating it and suffering the consequences. Of course, compulsive overeating can also cause or contribute to discomfort. Practically no one can eat unlimited quantities of anything without having gastrointestinal discomfort or *dyspepsia.*

The establishment of so-called daily minimum food requirements suggests that every day's intake should be carefully balanced. Although this is beneficial, it is by no means necessary. Freedom from such regimentation can certainly be enjoyed during a holiday, or a trip to another country, or on a prolonged visit to relatives with casual food habits.

Sometimes a change in diet is dictated by a cold or an upset stomach or diarrhea. Liquids containing carbohydrates, such as tea with sugar and light soups, should be emphasized in treating a cold, while at the same time solid food intake should be somewhat reduced. In the case of an upset stomach or diarrhea, the discomfort may be eased by not eating or drinking anything at all for a whole day. This form of treatment may be helpful for an adult, but since children with diarrhea can become dehydrated in a day or so, professional advice is indicated when cutting down liquid intake.

Diet and Disease Prevention

Whether or not diet can be helpful in preventing various diseases other than those caused by nutritional deficiency is an unsettled question. Some specialists think that a diet low in cholesterol and saturated fats can help prevent cardiovascular disease caused by atherosclerosis, but the evidence for this point of view is not yet definitive. It has been said for years that vitamin C is helpful in preventing the common cold, and this point of view has recently received a great deal of publicity, but the evidence is not conclusive.

Food-Borne Diseases

There are several ways in which food can be the *cause* of disease, most commonly when it becomes contaminated with a sufficient amount of harmful bacteria, bacterial toxin, viruses, or other poisonous substances. The gastrointestinal diseases typically accompanied by nausea, vomiting, diarrhea, or stomach cramps that are produced in this

Modified Fat Diet *(continued)*

Type of food	Foods included	Foods excluded
Fats	Oils: corn, cottonseed, olive, peanut, safflower, soy bean. (If calories permit, 1½ to 3 ounces will be included daily.) Specially prepared margarines.	Bacon drippings, butter, coconut oil, regular fortified fats, salt pork, vegetable shortenings, commerical salad dressings.
Fruits	Any fresh (except avocado), canned, frozen, or dried fruit or juice (one citrus fruit to be included daily).	Avocado.
Meat, fish, poultry, cheese	Limit to 4 ounces daily from Group I or the equivalent from Groups II or III (below). Lean meat trimmed of all visible fat.	Fried meats; fat meats, such as bacon, cold cuts, duck, goose, pork, sausage; fish canned in oil; all other fish except those allowed. All cheese except dry cottage cheese.
Eggs	Egg whites as desired; whole eggs (a maximum of one per day or about 3 per week) poached, soft or hard cooked, fried in allowed oil.	Eggs or egg whites cooked with fat, except those fats allowed.
Potato or substitute	Hominy, macaroni, noodles, popcorn (prepared with allowed oil), potato, rice, spaghetti.	Potato chips; any of these items fried or creamed unless prepared with allowed fats.
Soups	Bouillon, clear broth, vegetable soup; cream soups made with skimmed milk.	All others.
Sweets	Hard candies, jam, jelly, sugar, syrup; chocolate syrup made only with cocoa, sugar, and water.	All other candies; chocolate.
Vegetables	Any fresh, frozen, or cooked without added fat (one green or yellow vegetable should be included daily).	Buttered, creamed, or fried vegetables unless prepared with allowed fats.
Miscellaneous	Condiments, pickles, salt, spices, vinegar.	Gravies, nuts, olives, peanut butter.

Group I	7 gms. fat per 30 gms. (1 ounce).	Lean beef, ham, lamb, and pork; tongue; veal; trout.
Group II	3 gms. fat per 30 gms. (1 ounce).	Beef liver, heart, kidney, dried or chipped beef; chicken, turkey; lean fish, such as codfish, haddock, halibut, mackerel, shad, salmon, tuna, whitefish.
Group III	Less than 1 gm. fat per 90 gms. (3 ounces).	Crab, clams, flounder, lobster, oysters, perch, scallops, shrimp.

This diet is planned to reduce the intake of fats containing a high degree of either saturated or short-chain fatty acids and to avoid the excessive carbohydrate intake associated with a very low fat diet. This is done through replacement of saturated fat sources with those containing higher quantities of polyunsaturated fatty acids. The fats ordinarily used are corn oil, cottonseed oil, safflower oil, olive oil, peanut oil, and soybean oil. Fats containing large amounts of saturated fatty acids are restricted to approximately 30 grams daily. Carbohydrate and protein are planned to conform to normal levels, with approximately 300–350 grams carbohydrate and approximately 70–80 grams protein. The modified fat diet is planned to meet normal dietary allowances. Calories can be adjusted to fit the needs of the individual. If normal or higher than normal calories are required, fats containing a high percentage of unsaturated fatty acids, such as corn oil, cottonseed oil, etc., may be added.

From the *Clinical Center Diet Manual*, revised edition, prepared by the Nutrition Department, The Clinical Center, National Institutes of Health, Public Health Service, U.S. Department of Health, Education, and Welfare (Public Health Service Publication No. 989), pp. 69–72.

Modified Fat Diet

Sample Menu

	Household measure[1]
Breakfast	
Orange juice	½ cup
Oatmeal	½ cup
Nonfat milk[2]	1 cup
Sugar	2 teaspoons
Poached egg	One
Toast, enriched or whole grain	2 slices
Jelly	1 tablespoon
Coffee or tea	As desired
Lucheon	
Clear broth, fat free	As desired
Lean roast beef	2 ounces
Baked potato	1 medium
Green beans	½ cup
Lettuce and tomato salad, oil dressing	1 serving
Bread, enriched or whole grain	1 slice
Jelly	1 tablespoon
Canned peach halves	2 halves
Nonfat milk[2]	1 cup
Coffee or tea	As desired
Sugar	1 teaspoon
Dinner	
Roast chicken (no skin)	4 ounces
Diced potato	½ cup
Green peas	½ cup
Head lettuce salad, oil dressing	1 serving
Bread, enriched or whole grain	1 slice
Jelly	1 tablespoon
Nonfat milk[2]	1 cup
Fruited gelatin	½ cup
Coffee or tea	As desired
Sugar	1 teaspoon

[1]Household measure is given to indicate the quantity of food necessary to supply 2,200 calories.

[2]As an example of the manner in which oil can be incorporated into the modified fat diet, a recipe for nonfat milk with oil follows:

For one quart of nonfat milk including one and one-half ounces of oil:

Dried powdered skim milk*	3¼ ounces (1⅓ cup)
Corn oil	1½ ounces
Water	to make 1 quart

Blend water with powdered skimmed milk in food blender until thoroughly mixed. Add corn oil and blend at a high speed until fully blended. Fresh skimmed milk may be substituted in the recipe for the powdered skimmed milk and water. The skimmed milk should be served cold, and the addition of flavoring is not recommended.

*Dried skimmed milk powders vary in weight. They may be reliquefied according to the directions on each package.

way are not, strictly speaking, caused by the foods themselves, and are therefore called food-borne diseases.

Most food-borne illnesses are caused by a toxin in food contaminated by staphylococcal or salmonella bacteria. In general, milk, milk products, raw shellfish, and meats are the foods most apt to be contaminated. This is most likely to happen when such foods are left standing at room temperature for too long between the time they are prepared and the time they are eaten. However, food can also become contaminated at many different points in time and at various stages of processing. Standards enforced by federal and local government agencies provide protection for the consumer for foods bought for the home as well as for use in restaurants, although whether the protection is adequate is a matter of dispute.

Food Storage

Food is best protected from contamination when it is stored below 40 degrees Fahrenheit or heated to 145 degrees or more. Cold slows bacterial growth; cooking kills it. Bacteria present in food can double in number every 15 minutes at room temperature.

All food stored in the refrigerator should be covered except ripe fruits and vegetables. Leftover foods cannot be kept indefinitely, nor can frozen foods be stored beyond a certain length of time. Specific information about these time periods for individual items is available from the Agricultural Extension Service in each state.

Commercially processed foods sold in the United States are under government control and generally are safe. However, any food can spoil or become contaminated at any point in time, and the consumer should not buy or serve food whose container (package or can) has been broken, cracked, or appears unusual.

Food Additives

From time to time, concern is expressed about one or another food additive as a hazard to health. Most of these additives are put into foods during processing in order to increase their nutritional value, or to improve their chemical or physical characteristics, such as taste and color. Perhaps as many as 2,000 different substances are used in this way in the United States. Some are natural products such as vanilla, others are chemicals derived from other foods, and a few, like artificial sweeteners, are synthetic. Other additives are referred to as indirect, since they are residues in the food from some stage of growing, processing, or packaging. Although additives are controlled and approved by agencies such as the federal Food and Drug Administration, they continue to be a cause of concern to many people.

Low Fat Diet *(continued)*

The low fat diet contains approximately 40 grams of fat. To maintain normal calorie intake with fat restricted, it has a high carbohydrate content. The low fat diet is adequate in all nutrients. Calories can be adjusted to fit the needs of the individual patient. Approximate composition is as follows:

Protein	85 gm.
Fat	40 gm.
Carbohydrate	325 gm.
Calories	2,000

Type of food	Foods included	Foods excluded
Beverages	Coffee, tea, carbonated beverages, cereal beverages, skimmed milk or nonfat buttermilk.	Cream, whole milk, whole milk beverages.
Breads	Whole wheat, rye, or enriched white bread; plain yeast rolls.	Mufflins, biscuits, sweet rolls, cornbread, pancakes, waffles, french toast.
Cereals	Any, whole grain or enriched preferred.	None.
Desserts	Plain angel food cake; custards and puddings made with skimmed milk and egg allowances; fruit puddings; gelatin desserts; ices; fruit whips made with egg white.	Rich desserts, pastries; sherbets, ice cream; cakes, except angel food.
Fats	None	All fats and oils; salad dressings
Fruits	Any fresh (except avocado), canned, frozen, or dried fruit or juice (one citrus fruit to be included daily).	Avocado.
Meat, poultry, fish, cheese	Limit to 5 ounces daily: lean meat, such as lean beef, lamb, liver, veal; chicken, turkey, canned salmon or tuna (canned without oil); shellfish, lean whitefish; dry cottage cheese.	Fried meats; fat meats, such as bacon, cold cuts, duck, goose, pork, sausage; fish canned in oil. All cheese except dry cottage cheese.
Eggs	Any poached, soft or hard cooked; limit to one egg daily.	Fried eggs; eggs scrambled with fat.
Potato or substitute	Hominy, macaroni, noodles, potatoes, rice, spaghetti.	Any of these items fried or creamed; potato chips.
Soups	Bouillon, clear broth, vegetable soup; cream soups made with milk.	All others.
Sweets	Hard candies, jam, jelly, sugar, syrup; chocolate syrup made only with cocoa, sugar, and water.	All other candies or chocolate.
Vegetables	Any fresh, frozen or cooked without added fat (one green or yellow vegetable should be included daily).	Buttered, creamed or fried vegetables.
Miscella-neous	Condiments, pickles, salt, spices, vinegar.	Gravies, nuts, olives, peanut butter.

From the *Clinical Center Diet Manual*, revised edition, prepared by the Nutrition Department, The Clinical Center, National Institutes of Health, Public Health Service, U.S. Department of Health, Education, and Welfare (Public Health Service Publication No. 989), pp. 73–75.

Organic Foods

Some people feel that industrial methods of food farming and processing introduced during the past century, and more particularly in the last four or five decades, have resulted in foods that are deficient in nutritional value. They have recommended a return to the techniques of food production of an earlier era, in which only organic fertilizers were used. Foods so produced are called *organic foods*. Standard, commercially prepared foods, they feel, lack the health benefits and better tastes of organic foods and may even be damaging to health.

The damage, they believe, is caused because chemical fertilizers, pesticides, and food additives make foods toxic in some way or other. These toxins include female hormones, antibiotics, and an inordinate number of organic and inorganic chemicals. They are thought to cause or contribute to the development of some cancers, arteriosclerosis, and other degenerative diseases, the causes of which really are unknown.

Organic foods are also said to make people less susceptible to viral infections such as common colds, and to tooth decay. All of these claimed health benefits could also be the result of having preserved in organically prepared foods various substances that are eliminated in normal commercial processing.

The organic food philosophy calls for growing your own foods, using only organic fertilizers such as compost or animal (not human) manure, and without using pesticides or herbicides. For those unable to grow their own foods, commercial sources of organic foods are becoming more and more readily available.

Low Fat Diet

Sample Menu

	Household measure[1]
Breakfast	
Orange juice	½ cup
Oatmeal	½ cup
Skimmed milk	1 cup
Sugar	1 tablespoon
Poached egg	One (limit to one daily)
Toast, enriched or whole grain	2 slices
Jelly	1 tablespoon
Coffee or tea	As desired
Luncheon	
Beef broth, fat free	As desired
Sliced chicken	2 ounces
Baked potato	1 small
Peas	½ cup
Lettuce and tomato salad	1 serving
Lemon ice	½ cup
Bread, enriched or whole grain	1 slice
Jelly	1 tablespoon
Skimmed milk	1 cup
Coffee or tea	As desired
Sugar	1 tablespoon
Nourishment	
Pineapple juice	1 cup
Dinner	
Lean roast beef	3 ounces
Steamed potato	1 small
Carrots	½ cup
Mixed fruit salad	1 serving
Angel food cake	1 serving
Bread, enriched or whole grain	1 slice
Jelly	1 tablespoon
Coffee or tea	As desired
Sugar	1 tablespoon
Nourishment	
Tomato juice	1 cup
Crackers	Five

[1]Household measures are given to indicate the quantity of food necessary to supply 2,000 calories.

Typical Organic Foods

Whole grain cereals such as brown rice, and wheat, beans, vegetables, and fruits are the major sources of organic foods. Unsulfured molasses and natural honey are the primary sweeteners. Sea salt and herbs are used for flavoring. Organic meat is available, but many organic food people are vegetarians. Fertile eggs, cheeses, especially those from raw goat or cow milk, and yogurt also are basic parts of an organic diet. Cold pressed vegetable oils, filtered in a special way, and made from sesame, corn germ, or soy are used regularly; they are not only unsaturated fats and therefore have low cholesterol contents but also contain many natural vitamins. Herb teas, fruit juices, and raw milk are among the preferred liquids. Ideally, all organic foods should be eaten when fresh or in season, because canning or freezing requires the addition of chemicals.

Natural Foods

Several other food styles are associated with organic foods. *Natural foods* are not necessarily grown organically, but are not processed very much. *Macrobiotics* is a special natural food concept, oriental in origin, and based upon the idea of maintaining an equilibrium between foods that make one active (*Yang*) and foods that make one relax (*Yin*). A proper mixture of grain and vegetables contains an excellent balance of Yin and Yang. Yoga diets center around such natural foods as fruits and nuts.

Psychological Aspects of Food and Meals

Food and meals play an important role in emotional well-being and interpersonal relationships as well as in physical health and appearance.

During Infancy

The infant whose needs are attended to by a loving family develops a general sense of trust and security. The major contribution to his emotional contentment is probably made at mealtimes, and perhaps in a special way if he is breast-fed.

For most infants, food comes to be identified with love, pleasure, protection, and the satisfaction of basic needs. If there is an atmosphere of tension accompanying his feeding times, his digestion can be impaired in such a way as to cause vomiting, fretting, or signs of colic. If the tension and the baby's reaction to it—and inevitably the mother's increasing tension as a consequence—become a chronic condition, the result may be a failure to gain weight normally, and in extreme cases, some degree of mental retardation. Throughout life, good nutrition depends not only on eating properly balanced meals that satisfy the body's physiological requirements, but also on a reasonable degree of contentment and relaxation while eating.

Everybody develops individual emotional reactions and attitudes about food and its role as a result of conditioning during the years of infancy and childhood. These attitudes relate not only to food itself and to mealtimes in general, but also to other aspects of eating, including the muscle activities of sucking, chewing, and swallowing.

If food symbolized contentment during the early years, it probably will have the same role later on. If it was associated with conflict, then it may be associated throughout life with strife and neurotic eating patterns.

Minimal Residue Diet

Type of food	Foods included	Foods excluded
Beverages	Black coffee, tea, carbonated beverages, cereal beverages.	Milk, milk drinks.
Breads	Salted and soda crackers.	All breads.
Cereals	Cooked rice cereals or refined wheat cereals, made with water.	Whole grain cereals.
Desserts	White angel food cake, arrowroot cookies; ices; clear gelatin dessert.	Custards, puddings; desserts made with milk; ice cream.
Fats	Bacon, butter, fortified fats.	Cream.
Fruits	Strained fruit juices only.	All fruits.
Meat, eggs, poultry, fish, cheese	Beef, lamb, veal; chicken, turkey; whitefish; eggs.	Fried meats, poultry, or fish; all cheese.
Potato or substitute	Macraroni, noodles, rice, spaghetti.	Potatoes, hominy.
Soups	Bouillon, broth.	Cream soups.
Sweets	Hard candies without nuts or fruit; honey, jelly, sugar, syrup.	Candies with fruit or nuts; jam, marmalade.
Vegetables	Tomato juice only.	All other vegetables.
Miscella-neous	Salt, small amounts of pepper used in cooking.	All other spices; condiments; nuts, olives, pickles, etc.

The foods included on the minimal residue diet are selected on the basis of the small amount of residue left in the intestines after digestion. Since milk, milk products, fruits, and vegetables are thought to leave a large residue, these foods (except fruit and vegetable juices) have been omitted from the diet. The minimal residue diet is adequate in protein and calories. All other nutrients are below the recommended allowances.

From the *Clinical Center Diet Manual*, revised edition, prepared by the Nutrition Department. The Clinical Center, National Institutes of Health, Public Health Service, U.S. Department of Health, Education, and Welfare (Public Health Service Publication No. 989), pp. 45, 56–57.

During Childhood

For the preschool child, mealtimes should provide the occasion for the development of interpersonal relationships, because they are a daily opportunity for both verbal and nonverbal self-expression. The child who eats with enthusiasm and obvious enjoyment is conveying one message; the one who dawdles, picks at food, and challenges his mother with every mouthful is conveying quite a different one.

Meals can become either positive or negative experiences depending in large part on how the adults in the family set the stage. Communication can be encouraged by relaxed conversation and a reasonably leisurely schedule. It can be discouraged by watching television or reading while eating, by not eating together, or by eating and running.

Reasonably firm attitudes about eating a variety of foods in proper quantities at proper times and avoiding excessive catering to individual whims can also help in the development of wholesome eating patterns.

Those who select and prepare the food can transmit special messages of love and affection by serving favorite dishes, by setting the table attractively, and by creating an atmosphere of grace and good humor. Or they can show displeasure and generate hostility by complaining about all the work involved in feeding everyone, or by constant criticism of table manners, or by bringing up touchy subjects likely to cause arguments at the table.

How Food Can Relieve Tension

Food can be instrumental in relieving individual tension as well as in smoothing over minor family conflicts. Most people are familiar with the type of individual who is grumpy before a meal and who visibly brightens when he begins to eat. Sometimes this is because of the condition of *hypoglycemia* in which the blood sugar is too low for comfort. More often, the good spirits come from the psychological uplift brought about by the comradeship of eating.

People often turn to food as a way of relieving tension, thus reverting to a pattern established in childhood. Milk, for example, is often sought in times of stress. The relationship between food and anxiety is a complex one, and if it becomes so distorted that neurosis results, the physical consequences can be extremely unpleasant. Gastrointestinal disorders such as ulcers, bloating, belching,

Minimal Residue Diet

Sample Menu

Breakfast	
Orange juice	½ cup
Cream of wheat (cooked in water with butter)	½ cup; 1 teaspoon butter
Poached egg	One
Salted crackers	4 to 5
Butter	2 teaspoons
Jelly	1 tablespoon
Coffee or tea	As desired
Sugar	As desired
Luncheon	
Roast beef	3 ounces
Buttered noodles	½ cup
Tomato juice	½ cup
Salted crackers	4 to 5
Butter	2 teaspoons
Jelly	1 tablespoon
Plain gelatin dessert	½ cup
Coffee or tea	As desired
Sugar	As desired
Dinner	
Grapefruit juice	½ cup
Clear broth	As desired
Baked chicken	4 ounces
Buttered rice	½ cup
Salted crackers	4 to 5
Butter	2 teaspoons
Fruit ice	½ cup
Coffee or tea	As desired
Sugar	As desired
Nourishment	
Strained fruit juices	As desired
Plain gelatin desserts	As desired
Fruit ices	As desired

passing gas, diarrhea, and constipation are more often than not emotional rather than purely physical in origin.

The Symbol of Food

Food has many symbolic aspects: it can transmit and reinforce ethnic traditions either regularly or on special holidays. It can be used at lavish dinner parties as an expression of economic success; it can denote worldliness and sophistication in the form of complicated gourmet dishes of obscure origin.

A great deal can be learned about a person by knowing something about his attitudes toward food—not only what, how, when, and where he eats, but also how the groceries are bought, how the refrigerator and pantry shelves are stocked, how the cooking is organized, and how the dishes are cleaned up. In many significant ways, all of us are not only *what* we eat; we truly express who we are by *how* we eat.

28

Mental and Emotional Disorders

The ability to adapt is central to being emotionally fit, healthy, and mature. An emotionally fit person is one who can adapt to changing circumstances with constructive reactions and who can enjoy living, loving others, and working productively. In everyone's life there are bound to be experiences that are anxious or deeply disturbing, such as the sadness of losing a loved one or the disappointment of failure. The emotionally fit person is stable enough not to be overwhelmed by the anxiety, grief, or guilt that such experiences frequently produce. His sense of his own worth is not lost easily by a setback in life; rather, he can learn from his own mistakes.

Communication and Tolerance

Even the most unpleasant experiences can add to one's understanding of life. Emerging from a crisis with new wisdom can give a sense of pride and mastery. The emotionally fit person can listen attentively to the opinions of others, yet if his decision differs from that being urged by friends and relatives, he will abide by it and can stand alone if necessary, without guilt and anger at those who disagree.

Communicating well with others is an important part of emotional fitness. Sharing experiences, both good and bad, is one of the joys of living. Although the capacity to enjoy is often increased by such sharing, independence is also essential, for one person's pleasure may leave others indifferent. It is just as important to appreciate and respect the individuality of others as it is to value our own individual preferences, as long as these are reasonable and do not give pain to others.

Ways of Expressing Disagreement

Communication should be kept open at all times. Anger toward those who disagree may be an immediate response, but it should not lead to cutting off communication, as it so frequently does, particularly between husbands and wives, parents and children.

Emotional maturity enables us to disagree with what another says, feels, or does, yet make the distinction between that person and how we feel about his thoughts and actions. To tell someone, "I don't like what you are doing," is more likely to keep the lines of communication open than telling him "I don't like you." This is particularly important between parents and children.

It is unfortunately common for parents to launch personal attacks when children do something that displeases them. The child, or any person to whom this is done, then feels unworthy or rejected, which often makes him angry and defiant. Revenge becomes uppermost, and communication is lost; each party feels misunderstood and lonely, perhaps even wounded, and is not likely to want to reopen communication. The joy in a human relationship is gone, and one's pleasure in living is by that much diminished.

Function of Guilt

The same principles used in dealing with others can be applied to ourselves. Everyone makes mistakes, has angry or even murderous thoughts that can produce excessive guilt. Sometimes there is a realistic reason for feeling guilty, which should be a spur to take corrective action. Differentiate clearly between thoughts, feelings, and actions. Only actions need cause guilt. In the privacy of one's own mind, anything may be thought as long as it is not acted out; an emotionally fit person can accept this difference.

Role of the Subconscious

Emotional disorders are similar to other medical diseases and can be treated by physicians or other professionals just as any other disease can be treated. Fortunately, this truth is widely accepted today, but as recently as 200 years ago it was believed that the emotionally ill were evil, possessed by the devil. Their illness was punished rather than treated. The strange and sometimes bizarre actions of the mentally ill were feared and misunderstood.

Freud and Psychoanalysis

Although we have penetrated many of the mysteries of the mind, much remains to be discovered. Significant steps toward understanding mental functioning came about through the work of Sigmund Freud. Building upon the work of others before him and making his own detailed observations, Freud demonstrated that there is a subconscious part of the mind which functions without our awareness.

He taught that mental illness resulting from subconscious memories could be cured by *psychoanalysis,* which brings the memories out into consciousness. He believed that dreams are a major key to the subconscious mind and that thoughts, dreams, fantasies, and abnormal fears follow the rules of cause and effect and are not random. This is called *psychic determinism,* meaning that emotional disorders can be understood by exploring the subconscious. *Psychiatrists* help the patient understand how his mind works and why it works that way—often the first step toward a cure.

Does psychic determinism rule out will power as a function of the mind? No, because the subconscious is only one part of the mind. Although it has an important influence, there are other forces influencing behavior and thought: the *id,* or instinctive force, the *superego,* or conscience, and the *ego,* or decision-maker. The more we know about how our minds work, what underlies our wishes and thoughts, the more control we can exercise in choosing how to behave in order to achieve our goals.

Role of Sexuality

Freud discovered that young children and even babies are aware of the sensations, pleasurable and painful, that can be experienced from all parts of the body. The sexual organs have a rich supply of nerves; the baby receives pleasure when these organs are touched, for example, during a bath or a diaper change. The child learns that when he touches these organs he obtains a pleasant feeling; therefore he repeatedly touches and rubs them (*infantile masturbation*).

This concept, that the child derives pleasure from his body and sex organs, is called *infantile sexuality.* It does not mean that the baby has adult sexual ideas or wishes. These do not develop until puberty. It does mean that parents have the responsibility to see to it that children learn early that sex is associated with tenderness and love between man and woman. Even young children are aware of what their parents do and how they treat each other.

Types of Mental Illness

Although there is considerable disagreement about the classification of mental disorders, a convenient system used by many doctors divides mental illnesses into two general categories, organic and functional.

Some types of mental illness show little or no evidence of changes in brain tissue: these are called *functional* disorders. Another group of mental illnesses does involve some definable impairment of brain tissue resulting from disease, injury, the introduction of poisonous substances, malfunction of the body's metabolic processes, nutritional problems, or inherited defects. These are *organic* disorders. Organic brain damage may be *congenital*—that is, existing at or prior to birth—or *acquired.* Examples of congenital defects are *hydrocephalus,* an accumulation of fluid within the skull of a newborn infant that destroys brain tissue; *phenylketonuria* (PKU), a type of mental retardation associated with an inability of the child's body to metabolize a protein substance; and *Down's syndrome* (also called *Mongolism*), a form of retardation that occurs more frequently in children of older mothers and which is marked by certain physical features such as eyes that resemble those of Oriental people. Some examples of acquired defects are cerebrovascular accidents such as stroke; injuries to the brain, as from a fall or from the introduction of poisonous substances such as lead, arsenic, or mercury; and arteriosclerosis, resulting in senile psychosis in aged people.

This chapter will deal only with functional illness. Organic disorders are treated in the chapters on diseases of particular systems of the body and often in other sections as well. If you are in doubt about where to find information about a particular disorder, consult the index.

Who Is Mentally Ill?

Most people occasionally experience spells of anxiety, blue moods, or temper tantrums, but unless the psychological suffering they endure or inflict upon others begins to interfere with their job or marriage, they seldom seek professional guidance. There is no exacting scientific standard for determining when an eccentric pattern of behavior becomes a mental illness. Norms vary from culture to culture and within each culture, and, as every student of history and every parent know, norms also change from generation to generation.

Just how can a determination be made as to who is mentally ill? No temperature reading, no acute pain, no abnormal growth can be looked for as evidence of a serious problem. Yet there are warning signs, and among the common ones are these:

- Anxiety that is severe, prolonged, and unrelated to any identifiable reason or cause
- Depression, especially when it is followed by withdrawal from loved ones, from friends, or from the usual occupations or hobbies that ordinarily afford one pleasure
- Loss of confidence in oneself
- Undue pessimism
- A feeling of constant helplessness
- Uncalled for or unexplainable mood changes—for example, an abrupt switch from happiness to unhappiness when nothing has happened to warrant it
- Rudeness or aggression that is without apparent cause or which is occasioned by some trivial incident
- An unreasonable demand for perfectionism, not only in oneself but in one's loved ones, friends, business associates, and even from things or situations
- Habitual underachievement, especially if one is adequately equipped to do the work one is called upon to perform
- The inability to accept responsibility, often manifested by a recurrent loss of employment
- Phobias
- Unreasonable feelings of persecution
- Self-destructive acts
- Sexual deviation
- A sudden and dramatic change in sleeping habits
- Physical ailments and complaints for which there are no organic causes

If one or more of these warning signs occur frequently or in severe form, a mental illness may be present, and professional help should be sought to evaluate the underlying problem.

Types of Functional Mental Illness

Functional mental disorders may be broken down into four general categories: neuroses; psychophysiological (or psychosomatic) disorders; personality or character disorders; and psychoses.

Neurosis

A *neurosis* (or *psychoneurosis*) is characterized primarily by emotional rather than physical symptoms—although physical symptoms may be present. The neuroses are usually categorized according to the type of reaction that the patient exhibits in his attempt to resolve the underlying emotional conflict. All of them involve anxiety as a prominent symptom.

Anxiety Reaction

The *anxiety reaction* is probably the most widespread of all the neurotic response patterns. Although, as noted above, all the neuroses share anxiety as a symptom, the most common and outstanding characteristic of the anxiety reaction is a feeling of dread or apprehension that is not related to any apparent cause. The anxiety is caused by conflicts of which the patient himself is unaware but which may be stimulated by thoughts or events in his present life. For example, the junior executive who is constantly apprehensive that his employer will ridicule his work and dismiss his ideas may be expressing an anxiety reaction to a childhood fear that equated ridicule with abandonment or mutilation.

While anxiety reaction symptoms are primarily mental or emotional—the patient feels inadequate or ineffectual, or behaves irrationally—anxiety is always accompanied by physiological changes such as sweating and heart palpitations. Fatigue and feelings of panic are also common symptoms.

Conversion Reaction

The *conversion reaction* (or *conversion hysteria*) describes a type of neurotic behavior in which the patient, instead of coming to grips with his underlying psychic conflict, manages to convert it into physical symptoms involving functions over which he ordinarily exerts complete control. Sometimes the physical symptoms are unimportant, but often they are markedly dramatic. For example, the soldier who becomes deaf to the sound of explosions even though there is no organic defect that would account for a loss of hearing has effectively obliterated a sensation that evokes associations too painful to acknowledge.

Obsessive-Compulsive Reaction

A person beset by persistent, unwanted ideas or feelings (*obsessions*), who is impelled to carry out certain acts (*compulsions*) ritualistically, no matter how irrational they are, is reacting to a psychic conflict in an *obsessive-compulsive* manner. The obsession may involve a feeling of violence or sexuality directed toward a member of his own family. Usually the feeling will never lead to any overt action of the type imagined, but the idea is nevertheless persistent and painful.

Obsessive-compulsive patients are typically exceptionally meticulous and conscientious, often intelligent and gifted in their work. But they expend an enormous amount of energy and time in observing compulsive acts. For example, they may take a dozen or more showers every day because they are obsessed with the idea that they are dirty or carrying a contagious disease. By performing an apparently harmless compulsive act, the patient is temporarily relieved of the obsession.

Depressive Reaction

Most people have blue moods from time to time in their lives. Indeed, when faced with a personal tragedy like the death of a loved one, a normal healthy individual may well undergo a period of depression. A person suffering from the *depressive reaction*, however, has persistent feelings of worthlessness and pessimism unrelated to events that might depress a normal person. An inability to cope with problem situations is gradually magnified into an inability to cope with anything at all. Attempts to mask the crisis by putting on a "front"—feigning cheerfulness and optimism—give way to episodes of total hopelessness. Suicide is often considered and sometimes attempted. Threats of suicide from a depressed person should always be regarded seriously.

Common physical symptoms accompanying depression are fatigue, loss of appetite, and insomnia.

Phobic Reaction

A *phobic reaction* is the result of an individual's attempt to deal with an anxiety-producing conflict, not by facing up to the actual source of that conflict but by avoiding something else. The substitute—whether it be an animal, closed places, or whatever—is responded to with the intense anxiety that is really felt for the true source of anxiety. This process is known as *displacement*, and the irrational fears or dreads are known as *phobias*.

Thus, a person who had been regularly punished as a child by having been forcibly confined in a closet might be unable to deal with the anxiety of the experience consciously. The anxiety might be displaced and emerge later in life in the form of terror of crowded or confined places—*claustrophobia*.

Phobias can involve almost anything one encounters in life—including things that go on in one's body and one's mind. Some of the most common phobias have to do with disease—*bacteriophobia*, for example, the fear of germs.

Scores of phobias exist, ranging alphabetically from *acrophobia*, the fear of heights, to *xenophobia*, the fear of strangers. Other well-known examples are *ailurophobia*, the fear of cats; *cynophobia*, the fear of dogs; *algophobia*, the fear of pain; *agoraphobia*, the fear of open spaces; *erythrophobia*, the fear of blushing; *mysophobia*, the fear of dirt and contamination; *nyctophobia*, the fear of the dark; and *lyssophobia*, the fear of rabies.

Dissociative Reaction

The *dissociative reaction* involves a basic disruption of the patient's personality. The dissociative reaction permits a person to escape from a part of his personality associated with intolerable anxiety. The escape is made in various ways: by forgetfulness or absent-mindedness, dream states (including sleepwalking), amnesia, and—most seriously—the adoption of multiple personalities, in which the patient behaves like one person at certain times and like an altogether different person at other times.

Psychophysiological Disorders

It has been estimated that one-half or more of the patients of a general practitioner either do not have any organic illness or do not have any organic disease that could account for the severity or extent of the symptoms described. These patients are obviously not inventing their symptoms. The symptoms—whether they be itching, constipation, asthma, or heart palpitations—are real enough. But in many cases they are either wholly or partly of psychological origin—*psychogenic* is the medical term.

The psychological and physiological aspects of humans are so closely interwoven that the problem of *psychophysiological* (or *psychosomatic*) disorders must be considered with attention to both aspects. Consider how many physiological changes in normal people can be induced by psychological states: sweating, blushing, gooseflesh, sexual arousal, weeping, the feeling of "a lump in the throat," etc. It should hardly be surprising, then, that when someone has a physical illness there are profound concomitant psychological factors that can materially affect the physiological disease.

In many cases, however, as noted above, there is no detectable organic disease. Anxiety and other disturbing emotions such as rage are sometimes dealt with by the individual by constructing a pattern of defense that involves physiological reactions. Confronted with an emotional conflict that cannot be handled consciously, the individual may channel his feelings inward and deal with it by the formation of troublesome physical symptoms. It must be stressed that this strategy is not consciously engineered by the patient and that the symptoms are genuinely experienced.

Psychophysiological disorders affect many parts of the body, but certain organs and tissues seem more vulnerable than others. The digestive tract, for example, is frequently beset by disorders that are psychophysiological, including diarrhea, constipation, regional enteritis (inflammation of the intestine), ulcerative colitis (ulcers and inflammation of the colon), and peptic ulcers. Hypertension is frequently associated with psychogenic causes. Muscle cramps, recurrent stiff necks, arthritis, backaches, and tension headaches are other common complaints. Many skin conditions such as hives and eczema can be triggered by or are aggravated by psychological factors.

The symptoms of a psychophysiological illness appear to have no logical relation to the conflict that is responsible for them, nor do they relieve the underlying anxiety.

Personality or Character Disorders

Another group of mental illnesses is the *personality* or *character disorders,* so called because they appear to stem from a kind of defect in or arrested development of the personality. Unlike neurotic patients, individuals with personality disorders do not especially suffer from anxiety, nor is their behavior markedly eccentric. But when observed over a period of time, the personality problem becomes evident.

Personality disorders fall into various categories including:

- The *passive-dependent* individual, needs excessive emotional support and reassurance from an authority figure.
- The *schizoid* individual is withdrawn from and indifferent to other people.
- The *paranoid* individual is exquisitely sensitive to praise or criticism and often suspicious of expressed or implied attitudes toward him, and who often is subject to feelings of persecution.
- The *cyclothymic* (or *cycloid*) individual is subject to sharply defined moods of elation or depression, seemingly without relation to external circumstances.
- The *sociopathic* individual is characteristically lacking in a sense of personal responsibility or of morality. Formerly called the *psychopathic* personality, the sociopath may be disposed to aggressive, hostile, sometimes violent behavior and frequently engages in self-destructive behavior such as alcoholism or addiction to drugs. Sociopathic behavior also includes sexual deviation.

Psychosis

The chief distinction between *psychosis* and neurosis is that a psychosis represents a more complete disintegration of personality and a loss of contact with the outside world. The psychotic is therefore unable to form relationships with people. Most people who suffer from nonpsychotic mental disorders are seldom, if ever, hospitalized, and then usually for very brief periods. But many psychotics are so crippled by their illness that they are hospitalized repeatedly or for protracted periods of time.

Schizophrenic Reaction

Schizophrenia, the most common and destructive of the psychotic reactions, is characterized by withdrawal from external reality, inability to think clearly, disturbances in affective reaction (capacity to feel and express emotion), and a retreat into a fantasy life—all of these resulting in a progressive deterioration of the patient's ordinary behavioral patterns.

Simple Schizophrenia

The patient with *simple schizophrenia* experiences a gradual loss of concern and contact with other people, and a lessening of the motivation needed to perform the routine activities of everyday life. There may be some personality deterioration, but the presence of hallucinations and delusions is rare.

Hebephrenic Schizophrenia

This form of schizophrenia is marked by delusions, hallucinations, and regressed behavior. Hebephrenics babble and giggle, and often react in inappropriately childish ways. Their silly manner can make them seem happier than other schizophrenics, but this disorder often results in severe personality disintegration—more severe, in fact, than in other types of schizophrenia.

Catatonic Schizophrenia

In *catatonic schizophrenia* there are dramatic disturbances of the motor functions. Patients may remain in a fixed position for hours, days, or even weeks. During this time their muscles may be rigid, their limbs held in awkward positions. They may have to be fed, and their urinary and bowel functions may be abnormal. This stuporous state may be varied by an occasional period of frenzied but purposeless excitement.

Paranoid Schizophrenia

The *paranoid schizophrenic* is preoccupied with variable delusions of persecution or grandeur. Men working with pneumatic drills on the street, for example, are really sending out supersonic beams designed to destroy his brain cells; the water supply is being poisoned by visitors from other planets; any mechanical malfunction, as of a telephone or an elevator, is part of a deliberate plot of harassment or intimidation.

Paranoid schizophrenia is often marked by the presence of hallucinations, by disturbances in mental processes, and by behavioral deterioration. The disorder is regarded as particularly serious—hard to deal with and likely to become permanent.

Paranoid Reaction

The patient with this disorder suffers from delusions, usually of persecution, sometimes of grandeur. In this respect, *paranoia* is very similar to paranoid schizophrenia. However, in paranoid schizophrenia the delusions are often variable, and usually there is a breakdown of the patient's behavioral patterns.

A case of true paranoia, by contrast, is characterized by an invariable delusion around which the patient constructs and adheres to a highly systematized pattern of behavior. When the delusion is of such a nature that its persistence does not engender a conflict between the patient and his surrounding social structure, the patient may never be suspected of mental illness, perhaps merely of eccentricity. If, however, the delusion does provoke conflict, the patient may react with destructive hostility, and hospitalization or some other kind of professional treatment will be necessary.

Manic-Depressive Reaction

This disorder, also called an *affective reaction,* is characterized by two phases—*mania* and *depression.* Patients are governed by one phase or another or by the alternation of both.

The manic phase may be mild and bring elation and a general stepping up of all kinds of activity. The patient tends to talk endlessly and in an associative rather than a logical way. If the disorder is more severe, he may act or dress bizarrely; he may be a whirlwind of activity and become so excited and agitated that he foregoes food and sleep and ends in a state of total collapse.

In a mild depressive phase, the individual feels dull and melancholy, his confidence begins to drain away, and he becomes easily fatigued by daily routines. When the depressive phase is more severe, the patient starts to retreat from reality, gradually entering into a state of withdrawal that is very much like a stupor. At this point he hardly moves or speaks. He may be unable to sleep. Eventually he begins to question his value as a human being and is crushed by feelings of guilt. He may refuse to eat. Symptoms may progress to the point where an attempt at suicide is a real possibility.

Although the manic-depressive psychosis may alternate from one of its phases to the other, one or the other phase is usually dominant for a prolonged period of time. Depression is more often dominant than mania. Manic-depressive patients often recover spontaneously for periods of time, but relapses are fairly common.

Depressive Reaction

The *depressive reaction* is a disorder connected with aging and its attendant changes in sexual functioning; it usually occurs at the time of the menopause in women, in the middle or late 40s, and somewhat later in men. Formerly called *involutional melancholia,* it is characterized, as that name suggests, by a sense of hopeless melancholy and despair.

Patients begin to feel that life has passed them by. They experience real physical symptoms such as loss of vigor, and develop various hypochondriacal complaints. Their interests become narrower, and they begin to retreat from the world.

As the melancholy deepens, there are periods of senseless weeping, bouts of intense anxiety, feelings of worthlessness, and growing concern—coupled with delusions—about dying and death. The depth of the depression is overwhelming, and the danger of suicide greater than in any other psychosis.

Treatment of Emotional Problems and Mental Disorders

When should help be sought for an emotional problem? Sometimes individuals themselves realize that they need help and seek it without urging. They may have symptoms such as anxiety, depression, or troublesome thoughts that they cannot put out of their mind. But many others who need help do not know it or do not want to know that they need it. They usually have symptoms that disturb others rather than themselves, such as irritability, impulsive behavior, or excessive use of drugs or alcohol that interferes with their family relationships and work responsibilities.

Other people in need of psychological guidance are those who have a physical disease that is based on psychological factors. They react to stress internally rather than externally. Instead of displaying anger, they feel it inside. We are all familiar with headaches or heartburn caused by tension; more serious diseases clearly associated with emotional factors are asthma, certain skin disorders, ulcerative colitis, essential hypertension, hyperthyroidism, and peptic ulcer. Other physical symptoms that may be related to psychological factors are some types of paralysis, blindness, and loss of memory.

In all these situations the patient's enjoyment of life is curtailed. He has no feeling of control over what he does and little or no tolerance for himself and others. Such an existence is completely unnecessary today, with the many agencies and specialists, capable of effectively treating these problems.

Mental Health Professionals

Who can help those with emotional problems? Confusion about the different professions in the mental health field is understandable. To add to the muddle, self-appointed counselors without professional training and experience have set themselves up in this field, so it is necessary to know whom to consult to obtain the best help possible.

Psychiatrists

Psychiatrists are medical doctors; that is, they have graduated from a medical school, served internships and afterwards residencies specializing in emotional disorders. They are specialists in the same way that a surgeon or an eye doctor is a specialist. Most are members of the American Psychiatric Association. They are experienced in treating medical illnesses, having done so for many years before being certified as specialists in emotional disorders. Generally they can be relied upon to adhere to the ethical and professional standards of the medical field.

The American Psychiatric Association, 1400 K St., N.W., Washington, D.C. 20005, can supply the names of members. The American Board of Psychiatry and Neurology, One American Plaza, Suite 800, Evanston, Illinois 60201, examines and certifies psychiatrists who pass its tests, so that the term "board certified" means that the psychiatrist has passed its tests. If a family physician is consulted about an emotional problem, he will often refer the patient to a psychiatrist, just as he would to any other specialist.

Psychologists

Psychologists have gone to college, majored in psychology, and most often have advanced degrees, for example, a doctorate in psychology. They are not medical doctors and may get a degree in psychology without ever working with a human being, e.g., by working in animal behavior, experimental psychology, or other fields. They may or may not have clinical training, but many acquire this training and experience with human beings. There is no guarantee that a psychologist has this background, however, without looking into the qualifications of each individual.

Psychotherapists

Psychotherapy is the general term for any treatment that tries to effect a cure by psychological rather than physical means. A psychotherapist may be a psychiatrist, or he may be a psychologist, or may have no training at all. Anyone can set up an office and call himself a psychotherapist, psychoanalyst, marriage counselor, family therapist, or anything else he desires. It is up to the patient to check on the training and background of a therapist. Any reputable therapist should be pleased to tell patients his credentials and qualifications for helping them. A psychoanalyst, for example, may be a psychiatrist with several years of additional training in psychoanalysis, or may be someone whose qualifications consist of a college psychology courses.

Social Workers

Social workers are another group of trained persons who may also counsel those with emotional problems. They may work either with individuals, families, or groups after meeting the educational requirements for the profession, which include a bachelor's degree and two years of professional training leading to a master's degree in social work.

Professionals should be associated with recognized groups of their peers, or perhaps with a medical center or hospital. Generally a person with emotional problems should consult a psychiatrist first, who will then either treat the problem or be in a good position to advise what is necessary and who can best be available for treatment.

Types of Therapy

Functional mental illnesses are treated by a variety of tools, among them psychotherapy and chemotherapy (treatment with drugs).

Psychotherapy

As noted above, psychotherapy applies to various forms of treatment that employ psychological methods designed to help patients understand themselves. With this knowledge, or insight, the patient learns how to handle his life—with all its relationships and conflicts—in a happier and more socially responsible manner.

The best known form of psychotherapy is psychoanalysis, developed by Freud but modified by many others, which seeks to lift to the level of awareness the patient's repressed subconscious feelings. The information about subconscious conflicts is explored and interpreted to explain the causes of the patient's emotional upsets.

The technique employs a series of steps beginning with *free association,* in which the patient is encouraged to discuss anything that comes to mind, including things that the patient might be reluctant to discuss with anyone else but the analyst. Other steps include dream analysis and *transference,* which is the redirection to the analyst of repressed childhood emotions.

Group therapy is a form of therapeutic treatment in which a group of approximately six to ten patients, usually under the guidance of a therapist, participate in discussions of their mental and emotional problems. The therapist may establish the direction of the discussion or may remain mostly silent, allowing the patients' interaction to bring about the special cathartic benefits of this technique.

Family therapy is much like group therapy, with an individual family functioning as a group. It is felt that the family members may be better able to discuss the problems of relating to each other within the context of a group than they would be on an individual basis with a therapist.

Psychodrama is a therapeutic technique in which a patient or a group of patients act out situations centered about their personal conflicts. The psychodrama is "performed" in the presence of a therapist and, sometimes, other people.

Children are sometimes enrolled in programs of *play therapy* in which dolls, doll houses, and other appropriate toys are made available so that they can express their frustrations, hostilities, and other feelings through play. This activity, carried on under the observation of a therapist, is considered a form of catharsis in that it often prevents the repression of hostile emotions. In the case of a maladjusted child, it can also act as a helpful diagnostic tool—revealing the source of the child's emotional problem.

Chemotherapy

The relationship between body chemistry and mental illness has been studied for over half a century. The result of this study is the therapeutic technique known as *chemotherapy,* the treatment of disease with drugs or chemicals.

Early Uses of Chemical Agents

Sedatives to provide treatment of mental diseases were used during World War I for soldiers suffering from shell shock. *Sodium amytal,* one of the early chemicals used, offered a prolonged restful sleep, after which the army patients could tolerate some form of psychotherapeutic treatment.

In the 1930s, physicians introduced *insulin shock therapy* as a method for treating psychotic patients. The patients received injections of insulin in doses large enough to produce a deep coma, after which they were revived by doses of sugar. As with the use of sodium amytal, the insulin treatment was accompanied by psychotherapy for most effective results.

Present-Day Uses of Chemical Agents

More recently, the control of mental illness has taken a giant step forward with the development of *tranquilizers* and *antidepressants.* Tranquilizers counteract anxiety, tension, and overexcitement; they are used to calm patients whose behavior is dangerously confused or disturbed. Antidepressants help to stimulate the physiological activity of depressed patients, thereby tending to relieve the sluggishness that attends depression.

The treatment of the manic-depressive psychosis has been facilitated with the use of salts derived from lithium, a metal. Lithium salts seem to control the disease without producing the undesirable emotional and intellectual effects that resulted from the previous treatment with tranquilizers and antidepressants. The medication has been found to be particularly effective in treating patients with frequent manic episodes; it is also said to be effective as a preventive measure against future manifestations of mania or depression. Lithium may have adverse side effects and must be administered carefully.

Chemotherapy does not usually cure mental illness. It does, however, improve the patient's mental state, thereby enabling him to cope more effectively with the problems of everyday life.

Electroshock Treatment

Electroshock is a form of therapy in which a carefully regulated electric current is passed through a patient's head, thereby producing convulsions and unconsciousness.

Electroshock is primarily a treatment for the manic-depressive psychosis; to a lesser extent the therapy is used on schizophrenic patients. It often shortens depressed periods, and sometimes the patient seems totally free of the symptoms of his disorder. Unfortunately, the remission may be temporary; electroshock does not prevent further attacks. Also, transitory memory impairment often occurs.

Because of the recent advances in the techniques of chemotherapy, electroshock is used much less frequently than it was in the past.

Facilities Available for the Mentally Ill

The last decade has seen a number of hopeful changes in the facilities for treatment of mental disorders in the United States. The great majority of severely ill mental patients used to be cared for in county or state mental hospitals, many of which were crowded and able to offer custodial care but very little in the way of therapeutic programs. The picture has changed, however, and the extent and quality of care in these hospitals is expanding and improving.

Patients with mental illnesses are also being treated in greater numbers at general hospitals. As a matter of fact, more patients who need hospitalization for such illnesses are being admitted to general hospitals than to public mental hospitals.

Treatment for the mentally or emotionally disturbed is also provided in other facilities, including private mental hospitals, mental health clinics, and various social agencies.

Among the new facilities for treating mental illness is one which permits many patients who would formerly have been hospitalized, perhaps for the rest of their lives, to be served by community mental health centers. These centers offer both inpatient and outpatient care. The services they provide go beyond diagnosis and treatment to include rehabilitation, thus making it possible for more and more of today's mental patients to live at home, function in a job situation, and be a part of their own community.

Results of Treatment

What can be expected from treatment? Does a person who has been through treatment emerge bland, uncaring about others, with absolutely no problems, and without guilt for his misdeeds? Absolutely not. What treatment can do, said Freud, is to change neurotic misery into common unhappiness. There will always be things in life that are disappointing or otherwise upsetting. No treatment can eliminate such problems. After successful treatment, however, one should be better able to handle these stresses with flexible and constructive responses and to see his own difficulties in relation to the problems of others.

To feel emotionally fit is to have a capacity for enjoying life, working well, and loving others. Fear, shame, and guilt about undergoing needed treatment should not prevent anyone from reaching that potential.

29

Substance Abuse

"Drug-Related Deaths up 59%." "Driving-and-Drinking Accident Claims 5 Lives." "Teen Drug Abuse—The News Is Bad."

The headlines tell a story with a moral, or lesson. The lesson is that the United States has a major health and social problem. Once called by a number of names, including *alcoholism, drug addiction,* and *drug abuse,* the problem today goes by the designation *substance abuse.* In this usage, the phrase applies to all forms of addiction or abuse, whether the substance is alcohol or such vegetation-derived drugs as marihuana, cocaine, and heroin.

In a broad sense, substances include any material aside from food that can be imbibed, injected, or taken into the body in any way and that changes or affects the body or mind. This definition covers aspirin, many medications, tobacco, and a broad range of other substances. But *substance abuse* refers to unhealthy or excessive use of any material, alcohol, or addictive drugs at an individual's discretion and not according to a physician's prescription.

The dimensions of the substance-abuse problem are almost incalculable. Americans in 1986 spent an estimated $110 billion on addictive drugs alone. At least 40 percent of all Americans between the ages of 18 and 25 had experimented with one or more illegal substances. As one authority wrote,

> Not only the poor, the uneducated, the deprived, or the shadow types are being destroyed. We're dealing with the privileged, the successful, the professional.

Alcohol Abuse

Alcohol abuse is not unique to the United States or to the twentieth century. Alcoholic beverages, and their use or abuse, have an ancient history. Long before humans began to keep records of any kind, these beverages were valued as food, medicine, and ceremonial drinks. When people today have a beer with dinner, or toast newlyweds with champagne, or share wine at a religious ritual or festival, they are continuing traditions that have deep roots in the past.

The consumption of alcoholic beverages has always been a fact of life. So has, in a sense, alcohol abuse. The immigrants who came to the United States brought their ethnic ceremonies and drinking habits with them. The frontiersmen who moved continually west found liquor to be a source of release and comfort. Inevitably, alcohol use and abuse occurred.

Most drinkers have been, and are, able to control what they are doing and are none the worse for the habit. However, of the estimated 100 million drinkers in the United States, about 10 million have some kind of problem with alcohol: they are *alcohol abusers.* The 10 million alcoholics cost the economy some $60 billion annually. Drunken drivers are implicated in about half of the nearly 50,000 traffic deaths occurring yearly.

Scientists have come to believe that habitual alcohol abuse is a disease and should be treated as such. In 1956, the American Medical Association officially termed alcoholism an illness and a medical responsibility.

Kinds of Alcohol

The alcohol in beverages is chemically known as *ethyl alcohol.* It is often called *grain alcohol.* It is produced by the natural process of *fermentation:* When certain foods such as honey, fruits, grains, or their juices remain in a warm place, airborne yeast organisms begin to change the sugars and starches in these foods into alcohol. Ethyl alcohol is in itself a food in the sense that its caloric content produces energy in the body, but it contains practically no essential nutriments.

Methyl alcohol, also called *wood alcohol,* because it is obtained by the dry distillation of maple, birch, and beech, is useful as a fuel and solvent. It is poisonous if taken internally and can cause blindness and death. Other members of the same family of chemicals, such as *isopropyl alcohol,* are also used as rubbing alcohols—as cooling agents and skin disinfectants—and are also poisonous if taken internally.

Present-Day Drinking Trends

On a per capita basis, Americans drink twice as much wine and beer as they did a century ago, and half as much distilled spirits. Where the drinking takes place has also changed. There is less hard drinking in saloons and more social drinking at home and in clubs. The acceptance of drinking in mixed company has made it more a part of social situations than it used to be.

Here are some facts about the current consumption of alcoholic beverages in the United States:

- Drinking is more common among men than among women, but the gap is closing.
- It is more common among people who are under 40.
- It is more common among the well-to-do than among the poor.
- Beyond the age of 45, the number of drinkers steadily declines.

Teenagers and Alcohol

One fact emerges clearly and consistently from all the surveys of teenage drinking in all parts of the country: the drinking behavior of parents is more related to what children do about drinking than any other factor. It is more influential than children's friends, their neighborhoods, their religion, their social or economic status, or their local laws.

Statistics on teenage (and adult) drinking vary from one ethnic group or one part of the country to another. But overall, the statistics show that about two-thirds of all Americans 18 and older consume alcoholic beverages. Some three-quarters of all students in the tenth to twelfth grade range also drink.

In general, drinking is an activity that is associated with growing up. For boys, it represents manhood; for girls, sophistication.

Kinds of Alcoholic Beverages

The way any alcoholic drink affects the body depends chiefly on how much alcohol it contains. The portion of alcohol can range from less than 1/20th of the total volume, in the case of beer, to more than one-half in the case of rum. As a general rule, distilled drinks have a higher alcohol content than fermented ones.

The five basic types of beverages are beers, table wines, dessert or cocktail wines, cordials and liqueurs, and distilled spirits such as brandy and whisky. The labels of beers and wines usually indicate the percentage of alcohol by volume. The labels of distilled spirits indicate *proof.*

Proof

The proof number is twice the percentage of alcohol by volume. Thus a rye whisky that is 90-proof contains 45 percent alcohol, 80-proof bourbon is 40 percent alcohol, and so on. The word *proof* used in this way comes from an old English test to determine the strength of distilled spirits. If gunpowder soaked with whisky would still ignite when lighted, that fact was "proof" that the whisky contained the right amount of alcohol. The amount, approximately 57 percent, is still the standard in Canada and Great Britain.

How Alcohol Affects the Body

The overall effects of alcohol on the body and on behavior vary a great deal depending on many factors. One factor should be noted at once: if the blood reaching the brain contains a certain percentage of alcohol, there are marked changes in reaction. As the percentage increases, the functioning of the brain and central nervous system is increasingly affected. As the alcohol is gradually metabolized and eliminated, the process reverses itself.

If at any given time the blood contains a concentration of about 3/100 of one percent (0.03 percent), no effects are observable. This amount will make its way into the bloodstream after you have had a highball or cocktail made with one and one-half ounces of whisky, or two small glasses of table wine, or two bottles of beer. It takes about two hours for this amount of alcohol to leave the body completely.

Twice that number of drinks produces twice the concentration of alcohol in the bloodstream (0.06 percent) with an accompanying feeling of warmth and relaxation.

If the concentration of alcohol in the bloodstream reaches 0.1 percent—when one part of every thousand parts of blood is pure alcohol—the person is legally drunk in most states. The motor areas of the brain are affected; there is a noticeable lack of coordination in standing or walking. If the percentage goes up to 0.15 percent, the physical signs of intoxication are obvious, and they are accompanied by an impairment of mental faculties as well.

A concentration of as much as 0.4 percent can cause a coma. At the level of 0.5 to 0.7 percent there may be paralysis of the brain centers that control the activities of the lungs and heart, a condition that can be fatal.

Alcohol affects the brain and nervous system in this way because it is a depressant and an anesthetic.

How Alcohol Moves through the Body

Although it is negligible as nourishment, alcohol is an energy-producing food like sugar. Unlike most foods, however, it is quickly absorbed into the bloodstream through the stomach and small intestine without first having to undergo complicated digestive processes. It is then carried to the liver, where most of it is converted into heat and energy. From the liver, the remainder is carried by the bloodstream to the heart and pumped to the lungs. Some is expelled in the breath and some is eventually eliminated in sweat and urine. From the lungs, the alcohol is circulated to the brain.

People who use good judgment when drinking rarely, if ever, get drunk. The safe and pleasurable use of alcoholic beverages depends on the drinker's weight and his or her physical condition and emotional state. Other factors include the following:

1. *The Concentration of Alcohol in the Beverage* The higher the alcohol content in terms of total volume, the faster it is absorbed. Three ounces of straight whisky—two shot glasses—contain the same amount of alcohol as 48 ounces (or four cans) of beer.

2. *Sipping or Gulping* Two shots of straight whisky can be downed in seconds or, more normally, in a few minutes. The same amount diluted in two highballs can be sipped through an entire evening. In the latter case, the body has a chance to get rid of much of the alcohol.

3. *Additional Components of the Drink* The carbohydrates in beer and wine slow down the absorption of alcohol in the blood. Vodka mixed with orange juice travels much more slowly than a vodka martini.

4. *Food in the Stomach* The alcohol concentration in two cocktails consumed at the peak of the hunger before dinner can have a nasty effect. Several glasses of wine with a meal or a brandy sipped after dinner get to the bloodstream much more slowly and at a lower concentration. The sensible drinker doesn't drink on an empty stomach.

The Hangover

The feeling of discomfort that sometimes sets in in the morning after excessive drinking is known as a hangover. It is caused by the disruptive effect of too much alcohol on the central nervous system. The symptoms of nausea, headache, dry mouth, diarrhea, fatigue, dizziness, heartburn, and a feeling of apprehension are usually most acute several hours after drinking and not while there is still any appreciable amount of alcohol in the system.

Although many people believe that "mixing" drinks, such as switching from whisky drinks to wine, is the main cause of hangovers, a hangover can just as easily be induced by too much of one type of drink or by pure alcohol. Nor is it always the result of drinking too much because emotional stress or allergy may well be contributing factors.

Some aspects of a hangover may be caused by substances called *congeners.* These are the natural products of fermentation found in small amounts in all alcoholic beverages, among them tannic acid and fusel oil. Some congeners have toxic properties that produce nausea by irritating certain nerve centers.

In spite of accumulated lore about hangover remedies, there is no certain cure for the symptoms. Neither raw eggs, oysters, alkalizers, sugar, black coffee, nor another drink has any therapeutic value. A throbbing head and aching joints can sometimes be relieved by aspirin and bed rest. Stomach irritation can be eased by bland foods such as skim milk, cooked cereal, or a poached egg. Persons seeking relief may also try analgesics such as aspirin or acetaminophen for the headache, antacids if the problem is upset stomach, or over-the-counter medications for the diarrhea.

Alcohol and General Health

As a result of new studies of the effect of alcohol on the body, many myths have been laid to rest. In general, it is known that in moderate quantities, alcohol causes the following reactions: the heartbeat quickens slightly, appetite increases, and gastric juices are stimulated. In other words, a drink makes people "feel good." But drinking does have harmful effects when consumed in large quantities.

Tissue Impairment

Habitual drinking of straight whisky can irritate the membranes that line the mouth and throat. The hoarse voice of some heavy drinkers is the result of a thickening of vocal cord tissue. As for the effect on the stomach, alcohol doesn't cause ulcers, but it does aggravate them.

There is no evidence to support the belief that port wine or any other alcoholic beverage taken in moderation will cause gout. Studies have shown that as many as 60 percent of all patients with this disease had never drunk any wine at all.

Brain Damage

Alcohol abuse continued over many years has been found to contribute to cognitive defects. These may, in turn, indicate brain impairment. Researchers do not know what the defects represent—whether greater susceptibility to the problems of aging or an actual, alcohol-caused "premature aging" effect. Whatever the case, long-term chronic alcohol abuse leads to more rapid aging of the brain. Neuropsychologically, the alcoholic's brain resembles that of an older nonalcoholic.

Long-term abuse can have many other effects. These include withdrawal symptoms beginning 12 to 48 hours after a person stops drinking, sometimes followed by *delirium tremens* (DTs), which brings hallucinations and can be fatal; the Werner-Korsakoff syndrome, a type of beriberi characterized by a lack of the B vitamins; alcoholic peripheral neuropathy, involving damage to the nerve tissue outside the brain and spinal cord; and liver damage, including alcoholic hepatitis and cirrhosis. In the latter the liver becomes hard and yellowed.

Alcohol and Immunity to Infection

Moderate drinkers who maintain proper health habits are no more likely to catch viral or bacterial diseases than nondrinkers. But heavy drinkers, who often suffer from malnutrition, have conspicuously lower resistance to infection. Even well-nourished heavy drinkers have a generally lower immunity to infection than normal. When the blood-alcohol level is 0.15 percent or higher, the alcohol appears to weaken the disease-fighting white blood cells.

Alcohol and Stroke

Studies have shown that heavy drinkers face nearly three times the teetotaler's risk of hemorrhagic stroke. Light drinkers face twice the risk. About one stroke in four occurring in the United States is hemorrhagic, but these strokes are more likely to be fatal than those caused by blood clots.

Alcohol and Life Expectancy

It is difficult to isolate drinking in itself as a factor in longevity. One study reported the shortest life span for heavy drinkers, a somewhat longer one for those who don't drink at all, and the longest for moderate drinkers. But other factors, such as general health and heredity, play important roles.

Alcohol and Sex Activity

Alcohol in sufficient quantity depresses the part of the brain that controls inhibitions. This liberating effect has led some people to believe that alcohol is an aphrodisiac, in men. This is a conclusion that is far from the truth. At the same time that alcohol increases the sexual appetite, it reduces the ability to perform.

Alcohol as an Irritant

Many otherwise healthy people cannot tolerate alcoholic beverages of any kind, or of a particular kind, without getting sick. In some cases, the negative reaction may be psychological in origin—connected with a disastrous experience with drunkenness in the early years or with an early hatred for a drinker in the family. Some people can drink one type of beverage but not another because of a particular congener, or because of an allergy to a specific grain or fruit. People suffering from such diseases as peptic ulcers, kidney and liver infections, and epilepsy should never drink any alcoholic beverages unless allowed to do so by a physician.

Uses and Hazards

At practically all times and in many parts of the world today, alcoholic beverages of various kinds have been and are still used for medicinal purposes. This should not be taken to mean that Aunt Sally is right about the curative powers of her elderberry wine, or that grandpa knows best when he says brandy is the best cure for hiccups. Today an American physician may recommend a particular alcoholic beverage as a tranquilizer, a sleep-inducer, or an appetite stimulant.

Use of Alcohol with Other Drugs

Alcoholic beverages should be avoided by anyone taking barbiturates or other sedatives. See "Drug Use and Abuse" later in this chapter for a discussion of barbiturates.

Alcohol and Driving

For many people, coordination, alertness, and general driving skills are impaired at blood-alcohol levels below the legal limit (0.15 percent). There are some people who become dangerous drivers after only one drink. Attempts are constantly being made, but so far with less than perfect success, to educate the public about the very real dangers of drunken driving.

Possible Causes of Alcohol Abuse

A popular myth holds that alcohol causes alcohol abuse. It doesn't—any more than sugar causes diabetes. Various theories have been evolved to explain what does cause alcohol abuse.

Physiological Causes

Although several physiological factors seem to be involved in the progression of alcohol abuse, no single one can be pinpointed as the cause of the disease. Among the theories that have come under investigation are the following: abnormal sugar metabolism, disorders of the endocrine glands, and dietary deficiencies.

Psychological Causes

Recent studies have pointed to a possible relationship between personality and alcohol abuse. Researchers indicate that one definable segment of the alcoholic population has the character disorder known as *antisocial personality.* Once called a *sociopath,* the person with an antisocial personality is usually charming in a social sense, manipulative, impulsive and rebellious, and egocentric. An estimated 25 percent of the alcoholic population falls in this category; in the general population the prevalence of antisocial personalities is about 3 percent.

Sociological Factors

Practically all studies of alcohol abuse in the United States indicate that ethnic groups vary dramatically in their rates of problem drinkers. A great deal of attention has therefore been focused on *learned attitudes* toward alcoholic beverages and how they are used or abused. Generally, in the low-incidence groups attitudes toward drinking are clearly defined and understood by all the members of the group. Drunkenness is consistently frowned upon. In the high-incidence groups, researchers have found extensive conflict over alcohol. The basic rules aren't clearly defined, and there are no clear-cut standards for acceptable and unacceptable drinking behavior.

Genetic Factors

Research into the genetics of alcohol abuse has led to a theory of "familial abuse." The theory holds that the person with a close relative who is alcoholic is at far greater risk of succumbing to the disease than are others without such connections. Familial abuse or "familial alcoholism" characterizes as many as three in four of all abusers. Therapy has thus begun to focus on the families of alcohol abusers—particularly young sons—as the ones most susceptible to the disease.

Recognizing the Danger Signals of Problem Drinking

The chronic alcohol abuser shows physical symptoms that a physician can recognize. Among them are hand tremors, deterioration of eye functions, reduced bladder control, liver disorders, anemia, memory lapses, and others. But there are many other symptoms that family members and friends can observe, among them these:

- Alcohol use as a way of handling problems or escaping from them
- Increased use of alcohol with repeated occasions of unintended intoxication
- Sneaking drinks or gulping them rapidly in quick succession
- Irritation, hostility, and lying when the subject of alcohol abuse is mentioned
- A noticeable deterioration in appearance, health, and social behavior
- Persistent drinking in spite of such symptoms as headaches, loss of appetite, sleeplessness, and stomach trouble

Treatment

Methods of treating alcohol abuse fall generally into three categories. Choice of any one form of treatment depends on the particular needs of a client, including the degree of dependency. The three categories include the hospital, the intermediate, and the outpatient settings. Other approaches to treatment may be geared to individual or group needs.

The family physician can in most cases provide guidance on what kind of treatment would most benefit a particular patient. The alcohol abuser may be referred first to a toxicologist for an interview and recommendations on treatment. A review of the patient's history is a typical first step in treatment. Family involvement during therapy may be critically important. More than 4,200 centers offer treatment programs; of these, many are nonprofit clinics while others are units owned by for-profit health care chains. Many centers and clinics specialize in team approaches to therapy.

The Hospital Setting

Whether undertaken voluntarily or involuntarily (for example, by court order) the treatment formats offered in a hospital can be individualized. Where some patients adjust best to inpatient care, others prefer partial hospitalization. In the latter case the patient is allowed to go home or to work at appropriate times, otherwise living in the hospital. In a hospital detoxification program, one designed to end physical addiction, the patient has a variable period, usually two weeks to a month, during which he or she undergoes a programmed regimen of activities. These may range from exercise classes to medications to bed rest and regulated diets.

The Intermediate Setting

The intermediate settings usually include at least halfway houses, quarterway houses, and residential care sites. The first of these offer not only living quarters but also job counseling, psychotherapy, and other services. In quarterway houses, the patient receives more attention in the form of counseling and psychotherapy. Residential care centers usually offer little beyond living quarters.

The Outpatient Setting

Again in the outpatient setting the patient has a range of treatment choices. Among them typically are individual counseling sessions held by a paraprofessional; individual therapy session with a professional who may have an advanced degree in social work, psychology, medicine, or a related specialty; and group therapy sessions supervised by either a paraprofessional or a professional.

Chemical Treatments

Some treatment programs utilize medications to help patients to "shake the habit." Tranquilizers may be used to reduce tensions and prepare the patient for a follow-up stage. In a program of *aversion therapy* a substance called emetine may be prescribed. Taken before an alcoholic drink, emetine causes nausea. The treatment should be undertaken only under medical supervision.

Where to Find Help

Volunteer organizations of various kinds offer the alcohol abuser and his or her family a wide range of services and programs. The best known is Alcoholics Anonymous (AA), which is supported by contributions from members. AA utilizes a group-support approach to treatment. Most larger communities have AA chapters as well as Al-Anon and Alateen units for family members, relatives, and friends of abusers. Alateen works with young people between 12 and 20 years of age. Counseling and referrals may be obtained from a local Alcoholic Treatment Center.

Information may also be obtained from the following national headquarters of organizations established to help alcohol abusers:

National Association for Children of Alcoholics
31706 Coast Highway, Suite 201
South Laguna, CA 92677
(714/499-3889)

Al-Anon Family Group Headquarters
One Park Avenue
New York, NY 10016
(212/683-1771)

National Council on Alcoholism
12 W. 21 Street
New York, NY 10010
(212/206-6770)

National Clearinghouse for Alcohol Information
P.O. Box 2345
Rockville, MD 20852
(301/468-2600)

Drug Abuse

Like alcohol abuse, drug abuse can wreck lives and break up families. But to many experts the problem of drug abuse is far more serious than alcohol abuse. The trade in addictive, harmful drugs is not only unlawful; it has grown year by year, to the point where many believe it is out of control. The U.S. government spent some $1.6 billion on efforts to combat illegal drug importation in 1986, calling on units of the military forces to join the campaign. Even so, heroin imports increased by about 10 percent and cocaine imports by about 4 percent.

The forms that drug abuse takes, and the numbers of drugs, are numerous and increasing. Many authorities believe we should examine our whole American society for the "pill-happy" context in which drug abuse occurs. Dr. Joel Fort, former consultant on drug abuse to the World Health Organization, called America

> "a drug-prone nation. . . . The average 'straight' adult consumes three to five mind-altering drugs a day, beginning with the stimulant caffeine in coffee, tea, and Coca Cola, going on to include alcohol and nicotine, often a tranquilizer, not uncommonly a sleeping pill at night and sometimes an amphetamine the next morning."

The social effects of drug abuse rank among the most alarming of all the symptoms of what has been called the drug crisis. By estimate, drugs are involved in one-third to one-half of all crimes committed in the United States in a typical year. In a single recent year, medical treatments for drug abusers cost the nation more than $2 billion. The costs of abuse to families, communities, and to abusers themselves cannot be calculated.

Making the problem of control of drug abuse unbelievably complex is the fact that literally thousands of drugs and drug combinations have basic roles in medical treatments. Legal and illicit uses may, because of the close connections, become confused. Physicians' instructions regarding use of such legal drugs as sleeping pills may be ignored or neglected. Legitimately prescribed drugs may, in some cases, unintentionally lead to abuse or dependency.

Other facts make it difficult to control drug abuse. More and more, for example, abusers are turning to multiple substance abuse. Cocaine "sniffers" may take alcohol in one form or another to soften the uncomfortable and even painful effects of cocaine withdrawal. Physicians report that "polydrug" abuse leads to progressive worsening of such medical symptoms as stomach ailments and liver problems.

Designer drugs add another complicating factor. Made in clandestine chemical laboratories, these drugs are imitations or analogs of such other drugs as cocaine, heroin, amphetamines, and many other basic substances. The new drugs are legal until declared illegal by the federal government's Drug Enforcement Administration because a chemist has altered their chemical compositions enough to take them out of the banned or controlled drug categories. Far more powerful than the basic drugs they imitate, the designer forms have been implicated in more than 200 deaths. Researchers indicate that there is no limit to the numbers of designer drugs that can be produced.

A designer drug called *new heroin* was, on analysis, found to contain the industrial chemical MPTP, a suspected causative element in cases of Parkinson's disease. A number of new-heroin abusers also had classic Parkinson's symptoms: rigidity, tremors in the arms, legs, and even the head, and slow or difficult movement. Thus new research has focused on MPTP as a possible clue to the degenerative brain processes that lead to Parkinson's.

Over-the-Counter Drugs

Americans consume over-the-counter (OTC) drugs in enormous quantities. Purchasable without a physician's prescription, these drugs have limited but real potential for abuse. They range from headache remedies to cold nostrums and from acne ointments to vitamins. In general, good practice is to use OTC drugs as seldom as possible, for short-term, minor illnesses. Medicines of proven effectiveness should be used exclusively: taking an aspirin for a headache is a good example. The U.S. Public Health Service offers these guidelines:

- Self-prescribed drugs should never be used continuously for long periods of time. . . . A physician is required for abdominal pain that is severe or recurs periodically; pains anywhere, if severe, disabling, persistent, or recurring; headache, if unusually severe or prolonged more than one day; a prolonged cold with fever or cough; earache; unexplained loss of weight; unexplained and unusual symptoms; *malaise* lasting more than a week or two. . . .

The Food and Drug Administration (FDA), a branch of the U.S. Public Health Service, is responsible for establishing the safety and usefulness of all drugs marketed in the United States, both OTC and prescription. You can be assured that OTC drugs are safe provided you take them in strict accordance with the label instructions. These indicate the appropriate dosages, among other things, and carry warnings against prolonged or improper use, such as "discontinue if pain persists," or "do not take if abdominal pain is present." This labeling information is regulated by the FDA.

Drug Classifications

In addition to alcohol, the drugs of potential abuse fall into six categories: stimulants, depressants, and narcotic preparations, all of which can have legitimate medical uses; hallucinogens; cannabinoids such as marihuana; and inhalants (or volatile inhalants) such as aerosol sprays, glues, and fuels. See the accompanying table:

Major Drug Classifications

Type	Examples
Stimulants	Amphetamines Cocaine derivatives
Depressants	Valium Seconal
Narcotics (opioids)	Morphine Codeine
Hallucinogens	LSD Mescaline Psilocybin
Marihuana (cannabinoids)	Marihuana Hashish
Inhalants	Gasoline Glue

Drug abuse can lead to at least three kinds of addiction or dependency. *Physical addiction* results in unpleasant withdrawal symptoms, including, nausea, headache, or cold sweats when the abuser does not take the drug. *Psychological addiction,* more subtle, is a stage at which the abuser believes he or she cannot cope without the drug. In *functional addiction,* the abuser grows dependent on such drugs as decongestant nasal sprays to remain free of an annoying physical condition.

Three Classes of Prescription Drugs

Among the drugs that may be prescribed for you are some that have a tremendous potential for abuse. They include *stimulants,* such as amphetamines; *depressants,* such as sleeping pills; and *narcotic* painkillers, including morphine and codeine. When abused (that is, when taken in any way other than according to a physician's strict instructions) these drugs constitute a substantial part of America's burgeoning national drug problem.

Stimulant Drugs

The legitimate use of stimulant drugs and their great capacity for abuse stem from the same property their ability to speed up the processes of the central nervous system. Physicians may prescribe amphetamines primarily to curb the appetites of patients who are dieting or to counteract mild depression. More rarely, they use stimulant drugs to treat *narcolepsy,* a disease in which the patient is subject to irresistible bouts of sleep, and to counteract the drowsiness caused by sedatives. Amphetamines and an amphetamine-like drug (Ritalin) may be used to treat some hyperactive children who are extremely excitable and easily distracted. For reasons that are imperfectly understood, the drug calms these children instead of stimulating them.

The major forms of the amphetamines are: amphetamine (Benzedrine), the more powerful dextroamphetamine (Dexedrine), and methamphetamine (Methedrine, Desoxyn). The street name for these drugs is "speed," which some abusers use to refer only to Methedrine.

Amphetamine Abuse

The consumption of amphetamines is reportedly far greater than the prescription books indicate. Some 10 billion tablets are produced in the United States annually, enough for 50 doses for every man, woman, and child. Of this amount, probably half is diverted into illicit channels. Underground laboratories manufacture even more.

Abusers of amphetamines include students cramming for exams, housewives trying to get through the day without collapsing from exhaustion, and the businessman who has tossed and turned all night in a strange hotel bedroom and needs to be alert for a conference the next morning.

Used judiciously, amphetamines can improve performance, both mental and physical, over moderate periods of time. In effect, they delay the deterioration in performance that fatigue normally produces. Required to carry out routine duties under difficult circumstances and for extended periods, some astronauts have used amphetamines under long-range medical supervision.

Amphetamines give some persons feelings of self-confidence, well-being, alertness, and an increased ability to concentrate and perform. Others may experience an increase in tension ranging from the uncomfortable to an agonizing pitch of anxiety. High doses may produce dry mouth, sweating, palpitations, and raised blood pressure. Because amphetamines only defer the effects of fatigue, the letdown can be dangerous, especially for such users as long-distance truck drivers. In addition, the feelings of self-confidence about improved performance may be highly deceptive. Some college students who have crammed for exams while on speed have turned in blank examination books, or written a whole essay on one dense line.

Amphetamine abusers quickly develop a tolerance to the drug. They may have continually to increase dosages, and may undergo different kinds of drug experiences. Psychological dependence can build rapidly.

Amphetaminelike Stimulants

Several drugs that are chemically unrelated to the amphetamines produce very similar effects on the body. They are, also, equally amenable to abuse. Among them are methylphenidate (Ritalin) and phenmetrazine (Preludin). The latter has been commonly used as a diet pill.

Cocaine

Ranked as powerful stimulants to the central nervous system, cocaine and its derivatives have become the trendy drugs of the 1980s. An alkaloid found in the leaves of the coca bush, *Erythroxylon coca,* cocaine in its crystalline form is a white powder that looks like moth flakes. It may be called *snow, girl, Coke,* or any of a number of other names. The cocaine abuser sniffs it or takes it intravenously. Abusers of cocaine may or may not develop a tolerance for the drug. But some evidence indicates that the same dose repeated frequently will not produce similar effects over a period of time.

Very little street-purchased cocaine is pure. Usually, the drug is mixed, or cut, with other drugs or with substances that resemble it, such as talcum powder or sugar. For many years a favored recipe was the *speedball,* a combination, usually, of heroin and cocaine that was injected. The shot yielded a sudden rush of sensation in the genitals or lower abdomen (from the cocaine) followed by a sense of euphoria (from the heroin).

Physical dependence on cocaine is rare. Psychological dependence is much more common. When physical dependence occurs, the withdrawal symptoms may include hunger, irritability, extreme fatigue, depression, and restless sleep. With psychological dependence, abusers come to need the feeling of euphoria induced by cocaine. When a dose wears off, the abuser may go into a period of deep depression.

The use of cocaine as a legal anesthetic need not lead to addiction. It has been used particularly in surgical operations on the mouth, eyes, and throat because it can constrict blood vessels and because it is rapidly absorbed by the mucous membranes.

Cocaine's effects as a stimulant last only a short time. Generally, the effects depend on the size of the dose. A small dose may produce sensations of euphoria and illusions of increased strength and sensory awareness. A large dose may magnify these effects. The abuser may engage in irrational behavior, and may experience such physical side effects as sweating, dilation of the pupils, and rapid heartbeat.

In extreme cases abusers may have hallucinations and feelings of paranoia and depression. They may imagine that insects are crawling over their skins (formication) and may have chest pains. Injections by needle may produce skin abscesses. Both heavy and light users may develop runny noses, eczema around the nostrils, and deterioration of the nasal cartilage. The latter occurs because cocaine is usually "snorted" into the nostrils through a straw or a roll of paper, or from a spoon.

Death results, occasionally, from overdoses of cocaine, with respiratory arrest as a prime cause. The abuser may also have high fever, heart rhythm disturbances, or convulsions.

Cocaine Freebase

By a simple process dealers in cocaine can convert cocaine in white powder form, cocaine hydrochloride, into cocaine alkaloid, called *freebase.* The process involves mixing powdered cocaine with baking soda and water to form a paste. Once the concoction hardens, it looks like lumpy, off-white granulated sugar. Unlike powdered cocaine, the drug in this form, called *crack* or *rock,* can be smoked, eliminating the need for needles. Freebase can also be made by heating ether, lighter fluid, or a similar flammable solvent with cocaine hydrochloride.

However made, crack is a purified cocaine base that is usually smoked in a special pipe with wire screens, or sprinkled on a tobacco or marihuana cigarette. The drug produces a high that may start in eight seconds and last two minutes. By contrast, snorted cocaine takes effect after about five minutes.

Crack produces a very intense euphoria along with other physical symptoms. Because the drug in this form is far more potent than powdered cocaine, the heartbeat speeds up and the abuser's blood pressure may rise. Heart-lung problems may follow, and seizures can occur. Death may ensue. Abuse of crack may lead to physical addiction in weeks, with the victim needing continually larger doses to achieve a high.

Depressant Drugs

Making up a second class of medically useful drugs that are also widely abused, the depressants act as sedatives on the central nervous system (CNS). They may also act as hypnotic, or sleep-inducing, agents.

The depressants include mainly the barbiturates, which are both sedative and hypnotic, and the tranquilizers, which can calm without producing sleep. Though they are available as main or secondary constituents of more than 80 brand name preparations, the barbiturates are readily abused. One study showed that abuse among young people, including many at the grade-school level, has increased markedly in recent years. But older people 65 years of age and older are more vulnerable to the toxic effects of barbiturates and to dependence.

Tranquilizers act selectively on the brain and the central nervous system. Divided into major and minor tranquilizers, these drugs are similar to barbiturates in many ways, including their sedative or calming effect. The major tranquilizers, called *neuroleptics* because they are useful in the treatment of mental disorders, are *haloperidol* and *chlorpromazine.* These drugs lead to virtually no addiction or dependence even in long-term therapy.

The minor tranquilizers, among them *meprobamate* (Miltown), *chlordiazepoxide* (Librium), and *diazepam* (Valium), are, by contrast, highly addictive. Abusers take such drugs to achieve euphoric states as well as to offset the effects of alcohol, amphetamines, and other drugs.

Barbiturates

Barbiturates have many legitimate uses. For example, they may be prescribed to overcome insomnia, reduce high blood pressure, alleviate anxiety, treat mental disorders, and sedate patients both before and after surgery. Barbiturates may help to bring epileptic and other convulsions under control.

Barbiturates are metabolized, or broken down chemically, by the liver. They are then eliminated by the kidneys at different speeds depending on their types: slow- or long-acting, intermediate and short-acting, or ultrashort-acting. The first of these, primarily phenobarbital and barbital, take effect on the brain in one to two hours and last for six to 24 hours. The intermediate and short-acting barbiturates, including secobarbital and pentobarbital, take effect in 20 to 45 minutes and last five to six hours. The best known of the ultra-short-acting drugs, sodium pentothal or thiopental, can produce unconsciousness in a few minutes. Used mostly in hospitals as an anesthetic, pentothal is also injected by dentists to produce instant unconsciousness.

Barbiturate Abuse

Barbiturate abusers usually select the ultra-short-acting form of the drug because of the rapid action. Abusers as a group generally fall into four categories, with some overlap.

The "silent abuser" takes sleeping pills at first to get some sleep, probably with a physician's prescription. Progressively, the drug helps the abuser to deal with tension and anxiety. Indulging at home, he or she finds the barbiturates producing an alcohol-like high, with slurred speech, confusion, poor judgment and coordination, and sometimes wild emotional swings. Eventually the abuser is obtaining the drug through illicit channels. Some may end up spending most of their time in bed.

A second group, taking barbiturates for stimulation, has already developed a high tolerance that makes drug stimulation possible. Some other abusers find that the drug releases inhibitions.

Made up mostly of young people who are experimenting with various drugs, a third group uses barbiturates to "come down" from an amphetamine high. Members of this group may find themselves in a vicious cycle of stimulation and sedation. To obtain both effects at once, some abusers take the barbiturate-amphetamine combination in the same swallow—a so-called "set-up."

A fourth group, abusers of heroin and other narcotics, uses barbiturates as a substitute when drugs of choice are not available. They may also combine barbiturates with heroin to prolong its effect. In one hospital surveyed, 23 percent of the narcotics users said they were also dependent on barbiturates.

Effects and Dangers

Barbiturate abuse is generally considered to be far more dangerous than narcotic abuse. Every year brings some 3,000 deaths from barbiturate overdose, accidental or intentional. For such reasons many physicians believe barbiturates are the most dangerous of all drugs. Chronic abuse can lead to psychological dependence and increased tolerance, followed often by physical dependence of a particularly anguishing kind.

Abrupt withdrawal from barbiturates can be much more dangerous than withdrawal from heroin. Within a day the abuser withdrawing from barbiturates may experience headaches, muscle twitches, anxiety, weakness, nausea, and blood pressure drops. If the abuser stands up suddenly he or she may faint. Delirium and convulsions may come later. The latter can be fatal. Thus the withdrawal must always be undertaken under medical supervision. Even with supervision, a withdrawal from barbiturates may take two months.

Abuse of barbiturates presents other dangers. Unintentional overdosing frequently occurs when a person takes a regular dose to get to sleep and then remains awake or awakens soon afterward; tired and confused, the person may take another or repeated doses. Death may result. Mixing barbiturates and alcohol can produce the same outcome.

Other Barbiturate-Type Drugs

Some depressants are chemically unrelated to the barbiturates but have similar effects. These include *glutethimide* (Doriden), *ethchlorvynol* (Placidyl), *ethinamate* (Valmid), and *methyprylon* (Noludar). These too lead to tolerance when abused and sometimes to psychological and physical dependence.

Tranquilizers

The minor tranquilizers are manufactured as capsules and tablets in many sizes, shapes, and colors. They may also be purchased in liquid form for injection. Used legitimately to treat emotional tension and as muscle relaxants, these tranquilizers have high abuse potential because they produce both psychological and physical dependence. Tolerance develops with prolonged abuse.

Miltown, Librium, and Valium produce effects similar to those of barbiturates. But the minor tranquilizers act more slowly and have longer duration. Once considered completely harmless, these drugs came into such vogue that in the 1970s the federal government intervened. Both Valium and Librium as well as some other drugs were placed under federal control. From 1975 on anyone requiring a prescription for these drugs was limited to five prescription refills within a six-month period following the initial prescription. If more of the medication was required after that, a new prescription had to be written.

Withdrawal from the minor tranquilizers can be as dangerous and painful as withdrawal from barbiturates. Combining the tranquilizing drugs with others, including alcohol, is a highly dangerous form of abuse. Each drug reinforces the effects of the other. The result may be greater than the combined effects of the different drugs.

Some Slang Drug Terms

Name	Slang	Form	Drug
amphetamine methamphetamine	white crosses, greenies, speed, footballs, uppers, pep pills, whites, dexies, hearts, wake-ups, beans, bennies, roses, oranges, Black bird, Black Beauties, Black Cadillacs, crystals, crank, crink, amped, cris, cristian, bombidos, copilots, bottles, jugs, b-bomb, turn abouts, chicken powder, lightning, nuggets, dynamites, splash, sparkle plenties, cross tops, peaches, marathons, cross-roads, bumble bees, thrusters, meth	capsule, pill, liquid, powder, tablet, lozenge	stimulant
barbiturate	downers, block busters, reds, barbs, blues, blue birds, blue devils, blue heaven, blue bullets, blue dots, candies, softballs, seccies, seggies, Christmas trees, Mexican Reds, green dragons, yellow jackets, yellow bullets, red bullets, reds, goof balls, devils, nebbies, nimbies, peanuts, pink lady, phennies	sleeping pills, capsules, tablets, liquid, injected	depressant, sedative
cocaine	coke, Cecil, coconut, Big C, Corrine, crack, flake, Bernice, jam, sniff, bernies, lady snow, snow, rock, white, frisky powder, incentive, dream, girl, gold dust, star dust, paradise, Carry Nation, heaven dust, nose candy, uptown, toot	white powder; sniffed or snorted, injected	stimulant, local anesthetic
hashish	hash, kif, black Russian, quarter moon, soles	resin; smoked	relaxant, euphoriant, hallucinogen (in large or strong doses)
heroin	horse, junk, H, Harry, scat, smack, scag, stuff, cat, chick, big H, thing, Mexican mud, doojee, duji, dogie, crap, brown sugar, Chinese red, brother	powder; injected, or sniffed	narcotic
inhalants (for example, gasoline, paint, glue, aerosols, amyl nitrite)	poppers, snappers, huffing, sniffing (glue, paint)	aerosols, volatile substances, solvents	
LSD (d-lysergic acid diethylamide)	acid, sugar, cubes, big D, ghost, hawk-25, beast, coffee, blue heaven, California sunshine, orange mushrooms, mellow yellows, chocolate chips, window panes, paper acid, trips, purple haze	tablet, capsule, liquid	hallucinogen (psychedelic)
marihuana, marijuana	grass, pot, dope, hemp, weed, herb, tea, Mary Jane, Acapulco Gold, Colombian, Panama Red, Panamanian gold, Zacatecas purple, Mexican green, broccoli, bush, gage, dry high, greta, Texas tea, yesca, sweet Lucy	dried leaves; smoked (joint, stick)	relaxant, euphoriant, hallucinogen (in large or doses)
mescaline	mesc, beans, buttons, cactus, moon, peyote, mescal, mescal buttons	tablet, capsule	hallucinogen
PCP	angel dust, hog, crystal, cyclone, PeaCe Pill, bad grass, super grass, elephant, killer weed (when added to marihuana cigarettes, "to dust a joint"), DOA (dead on arrival)	powder, smoked	anesthetic (used only with animals)

Narcotics (Opioids)

Narcotics are drugs that relieve pain and induce sleep by depressing the central nervous system. Under U.S. law, narcotics are addictive drugs that produce physical and psychological dependence and that include opium and such opium derivatives as heroin, morphine, and codeine. The narcotics, or *opioids,* also include the so-called synthetic opiates, among them *meperidine* and *methadone.*

Opium

The seedpods of the opium poppy, *Papaver somniferum,* produce a gummy resin that has narcotic effects when eaten or smoked. Opium has been used in many lands and many cultures since prehistoric times. It was used medicinally in ancient Egypt. But not until recently did its addictive properties become known. Of the more than two dozen active compounds, or *alkaloids,* that can be isolated from opium, the two most important are morphine and codeine.

Morphine

Morphine, named after Morpheus, the Roman god of dreams, is the chemical substance in opium that gives it sedative and analgesic properties. Isolated initially in the early 1800s, morphine was later synthesized in pure form. On the illicit drug market it appears usually as a white powder called M, dreamer, or Miss Emma.

Morphine can relieve almost any kind of pain, particularly dull, continuous pain. It may also relieve the fear and anxiety that go with such suffering. In addition to drowsiness, euphoria, and impairment of mental and physical performance, morphine may have adverse effects including nausea, vomiting, and sweating. Intravenous injections of the drug may produce an orgasmic high sensation beginning in the upper abdomen and spreading throughout the body. Taken in overdose, morphine can lead to respiratory depression that is sometimes severe enough to cause coma and death. Naloxone (Narcan) may be administered intravenously as an antidote for morphine overdose.

Codeine

Taking its name from the Greek word *kodeia,* meaning poppyhead, codeine is a mild pain-reliever that can be produced from gum opium or through conversion from morphine. The effects of codeine peak in 30 to 60 minutes; they disappear in three to four hours. Called *schoolboy* in the streets, codeine is milder than either morphine or heroin, and is an ingredient in some popular nonprescription cough syrups.

Heroin

Originally thought to be nonaddictive, heroin was for a time used as a cure for opium and morphine addiction. It was then found to be more addictive than either of those drugs. It was prohibited in the United States in 1924 and became a staple on the drug black market. Given such nicknames as H, horse, junk, and many others, heroin is several times as powerful as morphine.

The heroin abuser rapidly develops tolerance to the drug. Continually larger doses are then required to produce the same degree of euphoria. Used chronically, heroin leads to both psychological and physical dependence. The former is far more important, and is more difficult to break.

Caught in a cycle involving desperate efforts to obtain enough money, often by criminal means, and getting high, the heroin abuser is not necessarily driven by the search for escape. He or she may want, equally, to avoid withdrawal symptoms. For the chronic abuser these symptoms can be difficult and painful, and may include anxiety, sweating, muscle aches, vomiting, and diarrhea. But the experience is often no worse than recovering from a bad cold.

The explanation is that the heroin sold on the streets is cut with quinine, milk sugar, or baking soda. It may be cut several times before reaching the abuser. A *bag* or *deck* may contain only 1 to 5 percent heroin. If the addict unknowingly buys a dose containing 30 percent or more pure heroin, the higher concentration can spell grave illness or death.

All of the opiates, including heroin, produce feelings of well-being or euphoria. They also lead to dulled senses and to reduction or elimination of normal fears, tensions, and anxiety. The drug also produces sleepiness and lethargy; *nodding* is one of the characteristic symptoms of abuse. Possible side effects include nausea, flushing, constipation, slowed respiration rates, retention of urine, and, eventually, malnutrition resulting from loss of appetite.

Because heroin can be taken in different ways, the drug's narcotic effects are variable. Sniffing is the mildest form of abuse, followed by skin-popping or subcutaneous injection anywhere on the body, and mainlining, injection directly into a vein, usually the large vein inside the elbow. Abscesses at the preferred site of injection are common, and the vein may become inflamed.

Heroin use does not necessarily lead to dependence. Many persons have experimented with the drug without becoming addicted. Others "joy-pop"—use the drug on weekends, usually for recreational purposes or "kicks." A few persons can take heroin daily without becoming dependent. Of the majority of abusers who become addicted, many drop the habit spontaneously at about age 35. The reasons for such a phenomenon are not clear.

Little agreement exists regarding treatments for heroin abuse. A promising yet controversial method is the substitution of controlled doses of *methadone* for heroin. Called *Dolly* after its trade name, Dolophine, methadone is a synthetic opiate that does not produce the euphoria of heroin. The substitution can help the abuser to lead a normal life, but he or she may still be addicted—to methadone.

Other forms of treatment utilize group psychotherapy, often in live-in communities modeled after the West Coast's *Synanon.* Some experts believe that only multiple-approach treatment formats, combining chemical treatment, psychiatry, user communities, and rehabilitation, can be effective. But the five-year cure rate for heroin abusers is low—only about one-third of that for alcoholics.

Synthetic Opiates

Prescription pain-relievers such as Demerol, Dilaudid, Pantopon, and other synthetic opiates can become addicting if used indiscriminately. They occasionally appear on the illicit drug market. With the increased availability of methadone in treatment clinics, methadone itself is used illicitly, often in combination with alcohol or other drugs, and especially when heroin is in short supply.

The Hallucinogens: LSD and Others

LSD (lysergic acid diethylamide) is one of a class of drugs legally classed as *hallucinogens*—agents that cause the user to experience hallucinations, illusions, and distorted perceptions. Others include *mescaline, psilocybin* and *psilocin, PCP, DMT* (dimethyltryptamine), and *DOM* or *STP.*

A colorless, tasteless, odorless compound, LSD is a semisynthetic acid of immense potency. A single effective dose requires, on the average, only 100 millionths of a gram. A quantity of LSD equivalent to two aspirin tablets would furnish 6,500 such doses. When sold on the street, LSD is generally mixed with colored substances. It may be manufactured in capsule, tablet, or liquid form.

History of LSD

With names such as *California sunshine, acid, purple haze,* and others, LSD reached a peak of popularity in the 1960s. Today it cannot be made legally except for use in certain supervised experiments. Physicians may use it to treat alcoholism and some mental disease, but without uniformly convincing results. It may be sold illegally in sugar cubes, candy, cookies, on the surfaces of beads, even in the mucilage of stamps and envelopes. One dose may produce a 4- to 18-hour *trip,* a hallucinogenic experience.

In the 1960s this trip made LSD the drug of choice for many substance abusers. Among those who claimed that LSD and other psychedelic drugs were consciousness-expanding were well-known public figures. The drugs, in brief, were supposed to enhance the user's appreciation of everything in the environment, to increase creativity, open the gates of awareness to mind-bending mystical or religious experiences, and perhaps to bring about profound changes, hopefully for the better, in the user's personality.

While some users reported such results, various studies suggested that the improvements were illusory. Members of some groups nonetheless felt that it was "in" to be an *acidhead,* an LSD user. One authority estimates that less than 1 percent of the total population have experimented with LSD. Partly because knowledge of dangers in LSD use has become common, the drug has passed the peak of its popularity even though it can still be obtained illegally.

Addictive Aspects

Abuse of LSD is difficult; the drug produces such a spectacular high that daily ingestion is virtually out of the question. Thus LSD use does not lead to physical dependence. But the heavy user can develop a tolerance for the drug very quickly. The tolerance disappears after a few days of abstinence.

Effects

Taking LSD, the individual is usually prepared for minor physical discomforts: a rise in temperature, pulse, and blood pressure; the sensation of hair standing on end; and some nausea, dizziness, and headache. The trip begins about an hour after the drug is first taken. Vision is affected the most profoundly. Colors become more intense and more beautiful; those in a painting may seem to merge and stream. Flat objects become three-dimensional.

The LSD user's reactions are closely related to his or her expectations. Thus one trip may be mind-expanding, filled with brilliant sights and sensations as well as euphoric feelings of oneness with the universe. Another trip may bring anxiety, panic, fear, and depression verging on despair. The latter experience can be terrifying; some bad trips have ended in psychiatric wards, with the tripper suffering from a severe mental disorder, a *psychosis.* An individual's body image may be distorted; in the LSD-induced vision he or she may have no head, for example. Such psychotic episodes, or breaks, may clear up within a day or two. Others can last for months or years.

Some trips have ended in tragedy. Convinced that they could fly or float through the air, some trippers have walked through high windows to their deaths. Others have walked in front of trains or cars.

In effect, no one can predict what psychological changes LSD use will produce. One reason is that no one really knows how LSD works inside the body to affect the mind. What is known is that the drug moves quickly to the brain and throughout the body, acting on both the central and autonomic nervous systems. But all traces of the drug disappear from the brain in some 20 minutes. The effects, as noted, last many more hours.

As with all drugs, LSD should not be ingested by persons who have psychotic tendencies or who are unstable. A disquieting side effect, usually occurring after chronic or heavy use, appears in the flashback, a reexperiencing of the effects of the drug weeks or months after a trip. One theory holds that flashbacks are induced by stress or fatigue, or by resort to other drugs, but the theory remains a theory.

Studies have reported some statistical findings. One research project found that the children of LSD users are 18 times more likely to have birth defects than the children of nonusers. Some research also suggests that the drug may have toxic effects on some cells of the human body. An unproved, and possibly unprovable, theory indicates that there may be a link between LSD use and breaks in chromosomes that could conceivably lead to leukemia or to birth defects in users' children.

Other Hallucinogens

Many other substances, both natural and synthetic, are used as hallucinogens. Most of them produce effects similar to those of LSD, but are far less potent.

Mescaline

Mescaline is the active ingredient of *peyote,* a Mexican cactus that has been used by American Indians for centuries to achieve mystical states in religious ceremonies. Users consume cactus "buttons" either ground up or whole. Mescaline itself may be obtained as a powder or a liquid. It can also be synthesized in a laboratory.

Psilocybin and Psilocin

Psilocybin and psilocin are the active hallucinogenic ingredients in the Aztec mushroom *Psilocybe mexicana.* The mushroom grows in southern Mexico and has been eaten raw by the natives since about 1500 B.C. Both derivatives can be made in the laboratory.

PCP (Phencyclidine Hydrochloride)

First developed in 1959 as an anesthetic, PCP in its pure form is a white crystalline powder that is readily soluble in water or alcohol. It appears on the drug black market as tablets, capsules, and colored powders. Abusers snort, smoke, or eat PCP. They can also inject the drug, but do not usually do so. PCP appears as an adulterant in many drug mixtures—in mescaline, psilocybin, or LSD, for example. PCP reportedly has as many or more undesirable effects as positive ones, among them forgetfulness, loss of behavior control, feelings of depersonalization, paranoid episodes, hallucinations, and suicidal impulses.

DMT (Dimethyltryptamine)

Called the "businessman's high" because its effects may last only 40 to 50 minutes, DMT is similar in structure to psilocin. DMT can be smoked or injected; in either case the effect is a powerful wave of exhilaration. An ingredient of various plants native to South America, DMT has long been used by Indian tribes in the form of intoxicating drinks or snuff, often very dangerous. In the United States, DMT is synthesized from tryptamine in the laboratory.

DOM or STP

DOM or STP is a synthetic compound originally developed by the Dow Chemical Company for possible use in the treatment of mental disorders. The drug was never released. Manufactured illicitly, it was allegedly given the name STP for Serenity, Tranquillity, Peace. The drug is powerful, it produces vivid hallucinations, and it seems to last as long as LSD. It is also extremely poisonous, and can bring on fever, blurred vision, difficulty in swallowing, and occasionally death from convulsions. In some cases abusers suffer from manic psychoses lasting for days.

Marihuana (Cannabinoids)

Marihuana, or *marijuana,* is a Mexican-Spanish word originally used to refer to a poor grade of tobacco. Later it came to mean a smoking preparation made from the Indian hemp plant (*Cannabis sativa*). A tall, weedy plant related to the fig tree and the hop, cannabis grows freely in many parts of the world and in a variety of grades depending on climate and method of cultivation. The different grades produce drugs of varying strengths. Some 300 million people around the world obtain drug preparations of one kind or another from cannabis.

Drugs are obtained almost exclusively from the female hemp plants. The male plants produce the fiber for hemp. When the female plants are ripe, late in the summer, their top leaves and especially the clusters of flowers at their tops develop a minty, sticky, golden-yellow resin, which eventually blackens. This resin contains the highest concentrations of THC (tetrahydrocannabinol), the group of substances containing the active principles of the drug. The pure resin of carefully cultivated plants is the most potent form of cannabis. It is available in cakes, called *charas* in India, and as a brown powder called hashish in the Middle East.

An estimated 15,000 tons of marihuana are illegally smuggled into the United States annually. But cannabis cultivation has become a major underground business inside the United States. Most illegal shipments of the drug come from Colombia, Jamaica, and Mexico.

Abuse Potential

Marihuana has puzzling aspects. Scientists have not succeeded in establishing exactly what substances in the cannabis plant produce drug effects, or how. THC is, of course, believed to be the most important active element, but chemists believe it is not the only one.

Beyond that, marihuana seems to be in a special class as a drug. It is classed as a hallucinogen, but is less potent than the true hallucinogens. It is not a narcotic, and it resembles both stimulants and depressants in some of its effects. Its use does not lead to physical dependence, nor does the user or abuser develop tolerance. Some users, in fact, find that with regular use they need less marihuana to achieve the desired high.

Users do acquire a slight to moderate psychological dependence—less, in some experts' opinions, than do regular users of alcohol or tobacco. Thus much of the theorizing about marihuana is conjecture despite the fact that millions of persons use it regularly or occasionally.

Effects

Experimenters and newcomers to marihuana smoking may experience little at the beginning. A sense of panic may accompany early exposure to the drug. More serious reactions have been reported, however, including *toxic-psychosis* (psychosis caused by a toxic agent) with accompanying confusion and disorientation. But such reports are rare. Experimenters using large doses of marihuana, hashish, or THC have induced what they termed hallucinations and psychotic reactions.

The experienced smoker may feel halfway between elation and sleepiness. He or she may have some altered perceptions of sound or color, for example, and a greatly slowed-down sense of time. It is usually possible to control the extent of the high by stopping when a given point is reached. The smoker often experiences mild headache or nausea.

Medical Evidence

Research and medical use of marihuana have led to some relatively tentative findings. Some evidence indicates, for example, that the drug may produce genetic damage. More definitely, marihuana has been found to be effective for reducing the pressure of fluids in the eyes of patients suffering from glaucoma. In a 1976 case, the Food and Drug Administration (FDA) approved the use of marihuana for such treatment.

In 1985 the FDA licensed a small drug firm to manufacture THC for use in combating the nausea associated with cancer chemotherapy. Other studies indicated that the drug may also be useful in the treatment of such other diseases as multiple sclerosis.

The debate over full legalization of marihuana promises to continue. Few argue that all penalties for major suppliers should be dropped, at least as long as marihuana remains illegal. But many persons see a contradiction in sending a young person to prison for smoking a marihuana cigarette while his or her parents can drink three martinis every evening.

Inhalants

The inhalants as a class include solvents used in cleaning compounds, aerosol sprays, fuels, and glues. Abusers of these substances sniff or inhale the fumes for recreational and mind-altering purposes. But the substances, primarily chemical compounds, were never meant for human consumption. With some exceptions, they are available commercially and thus have appeal for persons who cannot afford or cannot obtain the more conventional drugs.

Strictly speaking, tobacco, cocaine, and marihuana could be considered inhalants. But the term more commonly refers to three categories of products: solvents, aerosols, and anesthetics. Among the solvents are commercial items such as gasoline, transmission fluid, paint thinner, and airplane cement. The aerosol products include shoeshine compounds, insecticides, spray paints, and hair spray. The type of inhalant used appears to vary according to geographic location, the ethnic backgrounds of abusers, and availability.

Anesthetics comprise a special group of inhalants. Some of them, including nitrous oxide, ether, and chloroform, were used recreationally before medical applications were found for them. Because they are not widely available, they are not abused as much as solvents and aerosols.

Abuse Patterns

Young teenagers, mostly boys, are primary inhalant abusers. But some groups or classes of adults, such as prisoners in institutions, also use inhalants. Reasons for abuse vary; among teenagers they range from hostility and lack of affection to peer pressure. Adults, say authorities, are attracted by the ready availability of many inhalants. Alcoholics may resort to inhalants while trying to forestall the symptoms of withdrawal from alcohol.

Effects

Among the active chemicals in many inhalants are toluene, naphtha, carbon tetrachloride, acetone, and others. The fumes from these chemicals enter the bloodstream quickly. They are then distributed to the brain and liver. Entering the central nervous system, the fumes depress such body functions as respiration and heartbeat.

Classed as depressants, inhalants are sometimes referred to as "deliriants." The reason is that they can produce illusions, hallucinations, and mental disturbances. These effects usually result in cases of overdose; in moderate doses, the abuser feels sedated, has changed perceptions and impaired judgment, and may experience fright or even panic. Depending on the dosage, the abuser may also feel intoxicated, and may have lowered inhibitions along with feelings of restlessness, uncoordination, confusion, and disorientation.

Prolonged abuse can lead to nausea, muscular weakness, fatigue, and weight loss. Other effects of such abuse can be extensive damage to the kidneys, bone marrow, liver, and brain. Inhalants have been implicated in some forms of cancer. A high can last from a few minutes to an hour or more. Repeated dosing can produce physical and psychological dependence; but inhalants are not considered as dangerously addictive as other depressants.

In the 1960s the many deaths resulting from glue-sniffing made inhalant abuse a matter of nationwide concern. Studies reported later that about two-thirds of these deaths came about because the abusers, usually children, put plastic bags over their heads to intensify the effect and suffocated.

Where to Find Help

Substance abuse has many disturbing aspects aside from the physical, psychological, and social damage that it can cause. With addictive medicines, the progression from a *therapeutic* dose—the amount prescribed by a physician—to a *toxic* dose may seem, to some persons, natural and even inevitable. Ingestion or injection of a *lethal* dose may follow as an unintended consequence.

Other factors are causes for concern. The proliferation of illicit street drugs, the rapidity with which dependence or addiction can develop, and the costs and complexity of treatment or detoxification programs all add to the dangers inherent in abuse as a spreading phenomenon. Researchers are discovering weapons that may help in some cases to make treatment more effective: *naloxone* (Narcan), for example, can be given intravenously to reduce the toxic effects of narcotics. But too often a drug has done irreversible harm in a human system before help arrives.

American society has begun to mobilize resources to aid those who need information, asssistance, or counsel, for themselves or others, in cases of substance abuse. A National Partnership to Prevent Drug and Alcohol Abuse has established a network of community groups to inform teenagers about narcotics and their potentially disastrous effects. Among helplines and hotlines is one operated by Fair Oaks Hospital in Summit, New Jersey, with the toll-free number 800-COCAINE. Counselors serving with 800-COCAINE are linked to a network of treatment centers and hospitals throughout the country. The addresses and telephone numbers of four national groups, including Fair Oaks Hospital and its program, are:

National Federation of Parents for Drug-Free Use
8730 Georgia Avenue, Suite 200
Silver Spring, MD 20910
800/544-KIDS

American Counsel for Drug Education
5820 Hubbard Drive
Rockville, MD 20852
301/984-5700

National Parent Resource Institute for Drug Education (PRIDE)
100 Edgewood Avenue, Suite 1216
Atlanta, GA 30303
800/241-7946

Fair Oaks Hospital
19 Prospect Street
Summit, NJ 07901
800/COCAINE

30

The Environment and Health

How pure is the soil in which the food grows? How clean is the air? How unpolluted the water? How healthy the animals that provide substantial portions of our diets?

Americans were asking such questions with increasing frequency in the 1980s. Their concern had a basis in historic fact. Newspaper reports had for years told of the spread of toxic wastes, of the threat of radiation from nuclear power plants, of seepages of poisonous chemicals, and of polluted drinking water. The Environmental Protection Agency (EPA), established in 1970, had the task of monitoring the environment, but the agency could not prevent such accidents as Three-Mile Island, leaks of toxic gases and liquids in at least four states in 1983, and a toxic gas leak at a chemical plant in West Virginia in 1985. The latter accident raised new fears concerning health that had been generated by a 1984 accident that took 2,000 lives in Bhopal, India.

It became obvious that individual and public health depended on factors that were, in part, beyond governmental control. No one suggested that the American economy should shut down until every possible source of contamination had been removed or neutralized. But because the health fears were so real and so widespread, the environment—all of it, natural and manmade—became the focus of intense interest.

Today's Challenges

Can the health hazards in the environment be reduced or eliminated without hurting the American system and without changing Americans' lifestyles? Most experts believe it is possible.

Harmful ingredients in the environment may be the result of pollution, accidental or intentional. But some toxic substances enter the environment as a result of deliberate planning. Asbestos, for example, a mineral fiber that will not burn, has been widely used to insulate and fireproof buildings. The EPA called a halt to the use of asbestos in construction in the 1970s, when researchers proved that the fiber caused diseases such as *asbestosis,* a lung ailment, and several forms of cancer. Excluding such problems, the major health hazards fall in four main categories: Air, water, and noise pollution and food contamination. Some other hazards, including toxic wastes, nuclear radiation, and workplace dangers, received special attention.

Air Pollution

Air pollutants can damage health in a number of ways. Even where little scientific proof links these pollutants to specific maladies, much statistical or circumstantial evidence suggests that air pollution can lead to various forms of respiratory disease. Some cases of air pollution outside the workplace and exclusive of nuclear radiation hazards have been documented.

Inversions

An inversion is a freak weather condition in which a mass of warm air rests like a lid on top of cooler air. The warm air traps the lower air and prevents the pollutants in it from being ventilated. The results can be deadly.

Donora, Pennsylvania, experienced an inversion in 1948. Situated in a valley, at the center of an industrial complex, the town found its air becoming more and more polluted over a six-day period. Residents eventually had difficulty breathing; more than half of the valley's 14,000 inhabitants were coughing and gasping for breath. Thousands were hospitalized. Twenty-two persons died. Physicians used adrenalin to keep older people alive. Daytime visibility dwindled to a few yards. Some residents collapsed on the streets and in their homes.

What had happened? The temperature inversion, trapping the smoke and fumes from smoldering slag heaps, trash fires, coal-fueled home heating plants, and smokestacks, had filled the valley's air with soot, sulfur dioxide, and other pollutants.

Sulfur Dioxide

Sulfur dioxide enters the air from many sources. In the main, however, it is spewed into the atmosphere when heavy fuel oil and coal are burned to provide heat, generate electricity, and provide industrial power. Large cities are especially vulnerable because of their concentrations of heavy industry.

Sulfur dioxide apparently irritates the lungs and leads to a reduction of the lungs' oxygen-handling capacity. Persons who are particularly susceptible to carbon and sulfur dioxide-filled smogs are those suffering from bronchial asthma, chronic bronchitis, and emphysema. The respiratory systems of such persons are already defective. In emphysema, for example, the elasticity of the air sacs in the lungs has progressively broken down, usually after prolonged infection or repeated bronchial irritation. Cigarette smoking can produce such irritation; the sulfur dioxide only worsens the situation.

Lead

Substantial evidence indicates that lead in the air can cause neurological harm and impair body chemistry and bone growth. Most of the airborne lead comes from auto and smelter emissions. These are inhaled directly or they may "soak" food crops. Children are most immediately affected because they have fewer natural defenses against toxic absorption than adults. But adults too may feel the effects of such absorption. They may, for example, feel tired, cramped, or confused.

Because their bodies absorb and metabolize substances rapidly, children may have rates of lead absorption four times as high as those of adults. Workers in some industries, including the ceramic, glass, and lead industries, are also at risk. One study showed that 44 percent of the lead workers in two U.S. smelters suffered from clinical poisoning.

Specific effects of lead poisoning range across a broad spectrum. The formation of red blood cells may be inhibited even by low-level exposure to lead in the air. At higher levels, lead may cause anemia. In children, bone cell growth may be stunted; in pregnant women, lead may prevent the normal development of the fetal skeleton. But lead affects the brain primarily, in some cases interfering with motor skills, auditory development, memory, and the nervous system. Children with higher levels of lead absorption have been found to have serious learning disabilities. Fortunately, lead levels may fluctuate, and the lead in blood and soft tissue may pass out of the human system four to six weeks after exposure ends. But lead remains in bone for periods lasting as long as three decades.

Other Fuel Contaminants

Auto exhausts are major sources of other air pollutants besides lead. Exhaust emissions, for example, may include nitrogen oxides, carbon monoxide, hydrocarbons, and soot. The latter is made up of visible particles of carbon suspended in the air.

How can these substances affect your health? Nitrogen oxides irritate the eyes and the respiratory tract. When nitrogen oxide and hydrocarbons mix in sunlight, they form other noxious substances in the typical photochemical smog that has a yellowish cast. The new ingredients include *ozone,* a poisonous form of oxygen, and peroxyacetyl nitrate (PAN), which is intensely irritating to the eyes. Los Angeles was the first city to experience these smogs; they now occur in many other cities as well.

Worst of all, auto exhaust hydrocarbons include varieties that are possible *carcinogens,* causes of cancer in susceptible individuals. Carbon monoxide, another major hazard, is a colorless, odorless gas that is lethal even in small concentrations because it combines with hemoglobin and thus readily replaces oxygen in the blood. In concentrations that have been measured in heavy city traffic, carbon monoxide can make you tired, headachy, drowsy, and careless.

Acid Rain

While so-called *acid rain* has not been found to harm humans directly, scientists say it has begun to damage the natural food chain in certain regions. As industrial smokestacks emit pollutants, including sulfur and nitrogen oxides, these rise into the upper atmosphere. Mixed with water vapor and other substances, the airborne chemicals are changed by sunlight, becoming tiny acid droplets. The droplets fall to earth as rain or snow, raising the acid content of freshwater lakes and damaging trees and other plants. Under conditions of extreme acidity, fish populations have disappeared; where the food web is disrupted, aquatic animals, algae, and bacteria may dwindle in number. The effects of acid rain on crops and trees are less apparent but are thought to be harmful.

To some extent, acid rain is a geographic phenomenon in North America. Factories in the midwestern industrial belt throw off most of the pollutants, which are then carried east and north. Southeastern Canada and the northeastern and eastern regions of the United States are the areas primarily affected.

Indoor Air Pollution

Reports of illness associated with office and other nonresidential buildings have given rise to what has been termed the "sick building syndrome." The causes of this syndrome, or complex of symptoms, have not been completely and precisely explained. Among the possible explanations are the following:

- Building ventilation has been reduced to conserve energy, with the result that ventilation is simply inadequate
- Indoor air has become contaminated by emissions from the building fabric and associated systems, furnishings, office equipment, or maintenance materials
- Entrainment or cross contamination has taken place, with contaminants generated in a different part of the building or in a separate building drawn in by an air-handling system
- Bioeffluents, or volatile human substances, spread throughout a building, polluting the air with pyruvic acid, lactic acid, acetaldehyde, butyric acid, carbon dioxide, and other body effluents
- Combustion byproducts from smoking tobacco have produced substances, smoke included, that contaminate indoor air
- Microorganisms or airborne particles from molds, dust mites, and other sources cause such illnesses as Legionnaires Disease

A common tendency has been to identify a public building's heating, ventilating, and air conditioning (HVAC) system as the cause of indoor air pollution. But that conclusion may be premature and overly nonspecific. The symptoms described by persons affected by the sick building syndrome should be studied closely. At least four separate illnesses have been isolated according to their symptoms and causes. Hypersensitivity Pneumonitis and Humidifier Fever usually produce such symptoms as coughing, wheezing, chest tightness, muscular aches, chills, headache, fever, and fatigue. While these conditions are rarely fatal, Legionnaires Disease, produced by the bacterium *Legionella pneumonophilae,* is notable because of its 15 to 20 percent mortality rate. Both Legionnaires Disease and the relatively less serious Pontiac Fever are identified by their pneumonialike symptoms.

Household Chemicals

Depending on its location, structural characteristics, and other factors, the typical home may have as many as 350 or more organic chemical pollutants in its interior air. Household chemical products like spray paints, insecticides, and furniture polish disperse tiny (and toxic) droplets into the air, adding the propellant to the chemicals in the basic product. Among the hazard-producing chemicals, some solvents in particular are known or suspected carcinogens. One of the worst is methylene chloride, found in paint sprays and paint strippers and in some hair sprays and insecticides. Product labels may identify methylene chloride as a "chlorinated solution" or as "aromatic hydrocarbons."

Radon

After cigarette smoking, say scientists, the second leading cause of lung cancer may be radon gas. Considered by many to be the most dangerous of all indoor air pollutants, radon, a naturally occurring radioactive gas, diffuses out of the ground into houses that happen to be built above subsurface sources.

Invading homes, according to the U.S. Environmental Protection Agency, radon causes between 5,000 and 20,000 lung cancer deaths annually. The gas breaks down into unstable elements called "radon daughters"; these become attached to particles of dust or other matter floating in the air. If breathed in, the radon daughters lodge in the linings of the lungs. Radioactive decay takes place almost at once, with the daughters emitting alpha particles that damage the adjacent lung cells, sometimes causing cancer.

Private homes can be tested for radon and, if hazardous levels are found, can be equipped with ventilation or other equipment to remove the health threat. A charcoal-based detector is available. Finally, many firms can conduct home radon checks for a fee.

Water Pollution

To an increasing extent, water pollution has prevented or limited use of many once-valuable sources of water. This progressive deterioration of the nation's water supply has resulted from years of abuse in which natural lakes and waterways were inundated with quantities of raw sewage, waste products of industrial plants and slaughterhouses, petroleum residues, poisonous herbicides and insecticides, and so on. But the pollutants generally fall into two categories: materials that change with time and contact with water, and materials that remain unchanged in form. Organic materials in sewage and such industrial wastes as pulp and paper effluents belong in the first group; inorganic salts like sodium sulfate and such inert inorganic materials as pesticides represent the second.

Where do the pollutants come from? Communities generate thousands of tons of municipal sewage daily. Industries, the greatest users of water, utilize more than half of all the water consumed in the United States for raw material, heating and cooling processes, and transporting, sorting, and washing operations. Agriculture, the second largest user, requires millions of gallons of water for irrigation and drainage; for spraying orchards and crops, often with insecticides, fungicides, or herbicides; for removal of animal and other organic wastes; and for manufacturing operations such as meat packing and canning.

Chemical Contamination

The continuing proliferation of chemicals, many of them toxic, suggests the dimensions of the problems relating to water pollution. One estimate by the EPA's Office of Toxic Substances indicated that more than 70,000 chemicals are manufactured or processed commercially in the United States. About 1,000 new chemical compounds are added annually. Literally hundreds of these compounds find their ways into the nation's water supply, some in potentially dangerous concentrations.

How directly and to what degree chemical contaminants contribute to America's health bill cannot be gauged with accuracy. But the roles of these contaminants as carcinogens is widely accepted. Federal health officials have estimated that environmental carcinogens, including those in water, account for 55 to 60 percent of all U.S. cancer cases annually. Some estimates run much higher.

Heavy Metals

Attention has focused on the heavy metals. A study by the U.S. Geological Survey reported that small amounts of seven toxic metals were present in many of the nation's lakes and streams, with dangerous concentrations occurring occasionally. The metals are mercury, arsenic, cadmium, chromium, cobalt, lead, and zinc. Aside from being generally poisonous, some of these metals are implicated in specific health problems. Cadmium, as one example, has been linked to hypertension caused by kidney malfunction. Some other substances represent special situations.

Mercury

Because mercury is heavier than water, experts thought for years that it could be dumped into lakes, the oceans, and waterways. In theory, the mercury would lie harmlessly on the bottom. In reality, bacteria can convert some of the metallic part of the element into water-soluble form. The new compound enters the food chain and ends up in fish. When dangerous levels of this form of mercury were found in some waters and in food fish, warnings were issued regarding canned tuna and swordfish. The government later announced that 97 percent of the tuna on the market was safe to eat. But lakes and rivers across the country were closed to commercial and sport fishing.

An extremely toxic substance, mercury can, even in small concentrations, produce blindness, paralysis, and brain damage. The U.S. Food and Drug Administration has established the safe limit of mercury in food at half a part per million—about the equivalent of a thimbleful in an Olympic-sized swimming pool.

PCBs

Among the chief water pollutants today are the *polycholorinated biphenyls* (PCBs), highly toxic chemicals used industrially in carbonless copying paper and as an additive in lubricants, paints, printing inks, coatings, waxes, and many other products. PCBs, which are *biodegradable* (capable of decomposing) only over a period of years, have been found in unusually large quantities in waterways downstream from manufacturing plants. The EPA banned the direct discharge of PCBs into any U.S. waterway in 1977 after tests showed that fish in some rivers, like the Hudson, had levels of PCBs far higher than the permissible levels.

No one knows what the long-term effects of ingesting small quantities of PCBs will be. But the chemical is a suspected carcinogen. PCB's have also caused severe skin and eye irritations and have been implicated in reproductive disorders, kidney damage, and liver ailments. Researchers believe that the millions of pounds of PCBs in the nation's water or in landfills will take many years to dissipate.

Sludge

Sewage treatment plants around the country also face the major health challenge of disposing of the sludge, or solid matter, that is removed from sewage in the treatment process. Sludge contains not only human wastes but the residues of petroleum products, detergents, toxic heavy metals such as cadmium, lead, and zinc, and many other contaminants. Disposal methods range from dumping on land to burning and to composting for use as fertilizer. But environmental experts maintain that the use of sludge as fertilizer constitutes a health hazard; and major food processors will not accept food grown with sludge as fertilizer. In refusing such food, the companies are following guidelines set by the National Food Processors Association, which has expressed concern for farm workers' health and for the health of the consumer.

The sludge comes from an estimated 6.8 billion gallons of sewage flushed daily into America's sewers. The sewage itself contains microorganisms that can endanger health. You may be risking gastrointestinal upsets if you swim at a beach that is posted with a sign proclaiming "polluted water." Scientists warn that the fish caught in sewage-polluted coastal waters and harbors may not only be cancerous; they may also be carcinogenic. A number of states including Michigan and New York have restricted or banned sales of tainted fish such as naturally grown carp, catfish, and striped bass.

Oil Spills

With the increasing reliance on supertankers to carry industrial and heating oil from abroad, the danger of major water-polluting oil spills in coastal areas has grown substantially. Several of these huge ships have gone aground and broken apart under heavy pounding by sea waves. Their cargoes have spilled into the oceans, where currents usually carry them many miles before they float ashore or sink to the ocean floor. The oil reaching land fouls beaches and kills water birds. Similar accidents on inland waterways have polluted rivers and lakes, killing fish and spoiling recreational areas.

Noise Pollution

"Pollution" refers generally to the various forms of physical pollution by liquids, gases, or solids. Few persons realize that we are all threatened by a pollutant so common that it tends to be overlooked: noise.

Noise assails us nearly everywhere. It fills homes with loud music or the dog's barking or the grinding of the washing machine and the workplace with the chatter of drill presses and the roar of huge engines. Neither city dwellers nor country people can live noise-free today; none of us can escape car and truck horns, motorcycles that belch sound, and the noisy throb of machinery.

Effects of Sound on the Eardrum

Noise is not just annoying; it is potentially dangerous, both physically and mentally. It has been described as "a slow agent of death." A form of energy, sound or noise is caused by anything that vibrates, that moves back and forth. Our ears receive the effects of this vibrating motion from a distance, great or small, via sound waves. These waves are successive series of regions of compressed air and partial vacuums, or areas of high and low air pressure. Sound can also travel through liquids and solids. We *hear* sound because our eardrums are moved back and forth by the changes in air pressure. The eardrum, or *tympanic membrane,* may perceive a sound that moves it only one billionth of a centimeter—the threshold of hearing. If the intensity of sound pressure becomes too great, we experience pain, and the eardrum or the delicate structures inside the ear may be damaged.

The intensity of sounds is often measured in units called *decibels,* or *db.* These units are logarithmic, that is, 10 db is ten times as powerful as 1 db, 20 db is 100 times as powerful, 30 db is 1,000 times as powerful, and so on. On this scale, 0 db is at the threshold of hearing; rustling leaves, 20 db; a quiet office, about 50 db; conversation, 60 db; heavy traffic, 90 db; a pneumatic jackhammer six feet away, 100 db; a jet aircraft 500 feet overhead, 115 db; a Saturn rocket's takeoff, 180 db.

For most people, the pain threshold is about 120 db; deafening ear damage can result at 150 db. But damage of various kinds can come from much lower exposures. Temporary hearing impairment can result from sounds over the 85 db now found in modern kitchens with all appliances going. If the ears do not get a chance to recover, the impairment will become permanent.

Damage to the Inner Ear

Although very loud noise can damage the eardrum, most physiological damage from noise occurs in the snail-shaped, liquid-filled *cochlea,* or inner ear. Sound transmitted to the cochlea produces waves in the liquid, which in turn move delicate and minute structures called hair cells or *cilia* in that part of the cochlea known as the organ of Corti. The motion of the cilia is transformed into electrical impulses that conduct the sensation of sound to the brain.

The cilia can easily be fatigued by noise, causing a temporary loss of hearing, or a shift in the threshold of hearing. If they are not given a chance to recuperate, they will be permanently damaged, and irreversible hearing loss will result. There are some 23,000 cilia in the average cochlea; different sets of cilia respond to different frequency bands. The cilia responding to sound frequencies of

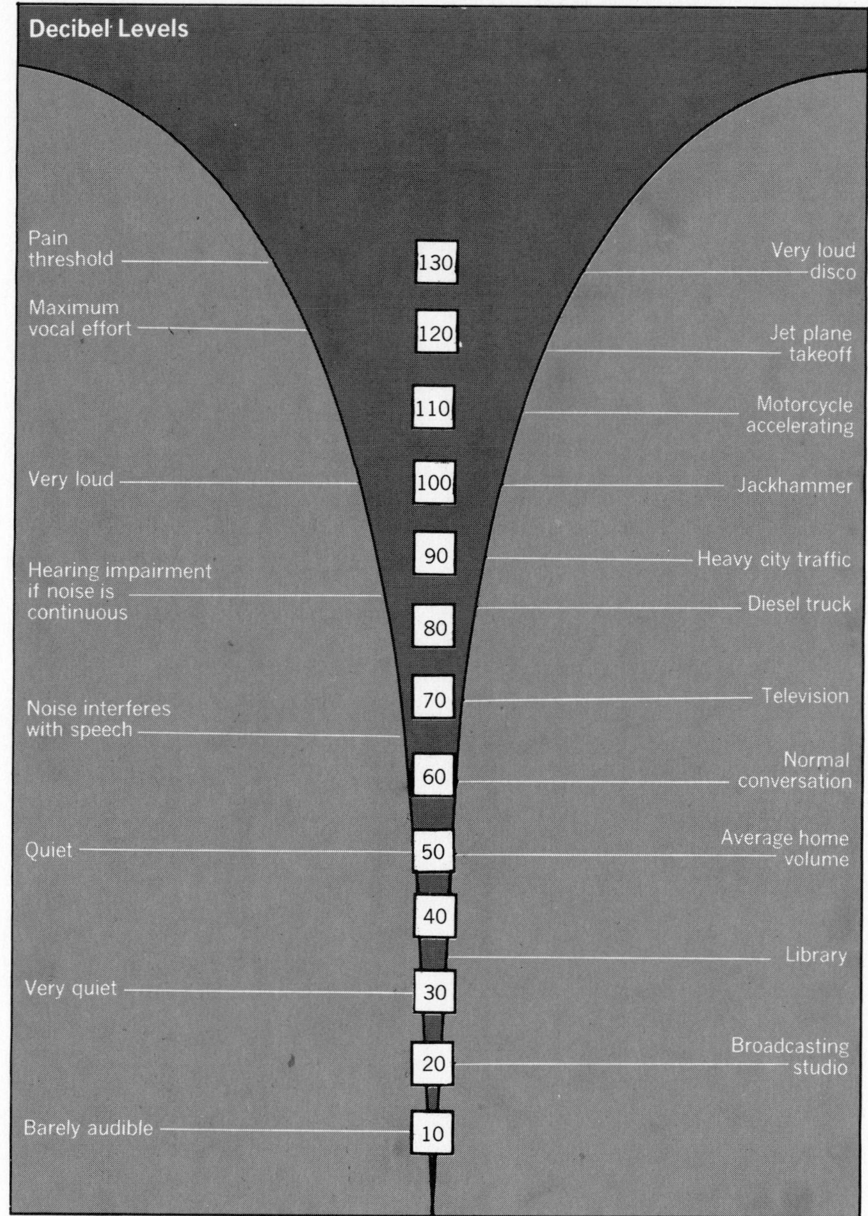

4,000 to 6,000 cps (cycles per second) are especially vulnerable to damage. The region of 85 to 95 db is generally regarded as the beginning of dangerous sound intensities. In general, the louder the noise, the longer it lasts, the higher it is, and the purer in frequency, the more dangerous it is. Thus, jet engines and powerful sirens are particularly hazardous.

Noise and Stress

The EPA has estimated that some 20 million Americans live or work at noise levels that could cause hearing losses; about 18 million have experienced at least some hearing loss because of noise exposure. But sound, or noise, can lead to physical and psychological problems ranging from irritability to migraine headaches. Linked with many such problems is stress, which has been found to cause high blood pressure, insomnia, ulcers, digestive disorders, alcoholism, anxiety, and many other ills.

Excessive noise has been implicated in such problems as adrenaline flow, elevated heart rates, and blood pressure. All are associated with heart disease. Noise can also affect children in special ways. For example, researchers believe it can retard language development and impair reading ability. Pregnant women exposed to excessive noise may show symptoms of stress and may pass on the harmful effects to their unborn babies. Studies in several countries have shown that the newborns of women living near airport runways experience a higher than normal incidence of birth defects.

Noise-related stress has a definite effect on mental well-being. No one knows exactly how, but noise can produce irritability, tension, and nervous strain. More seriously, British medical authorities have reported a significantly higher incidence of mental illness among people exposed constantly to aircraft noise.

Workplace Noise

Workplace noise presents special problems. Persons working in such industries as construction, mining, steel, lumber, and textiles are almost universally exposed to loud noises. Certain operations in other industries expose workers to high decibel levels. Overexposure takes place when employees work eight hours a day at sites with noise levels exceeding 90 decibels. Such standards, established by the government's Occupational Safety and Health Administration (OSHA), provide also that overexposure occurs where workers are subjected to higher decibel levels for shorter periods.

Workplace noise can lead to problems similar to those produced by overexposure elsewhere. But many workers have little choice as regards the places where they work. For their parts, companies may have limited options insofar as noise control or abatement is concerned. Changing the gears of a machine or building an enclosure around it may not always be feasible.

Some professional musicians find it difficult or impossible to avoid excessive noise on the job. Rock music artists, for example, spend hours at a stretch in enclosed places that magnify sound that is already greatly amplified. Such persons may be at serious risk of incurring hearing losses.

Food Hazards

Contaminants found in water often make their way into food products in the cooking and packaging processes, so that many of the comments on water pollution apply here. Some dilute water pollutants become highly concentrated as they pass up the food chain and end in fish or other foods for man. Mercury was cited earlier as one example. Contamination of food with harmful microorganisms is an everpresent concern wherever standards of cleanliness and sanitation are low.

Additives

Food entails a whole new set of problems because of the thousands of new ingredients that have been added to it, directly and indirectly, in recent years. These substances include many that have been deemed necessary because of the revolution in food technology: the rise of packaged convenience foods of all kinds. Labels on today's convenience foods list preservatives, nutrients, flavors, colors, and processing agents. The trouble with food additives is that we have had little time to learn about their long-term effects on the body. The Food and Drug Administration does set standards in this area; but in the opinion of many experts, these safeguards are inadequate.

What do the additives do and what are they? What kinds of health hazards do they present? The principal kinds are explained below.

Nutrients

Some additives are simply vitamins and minerals that increase the nutritional value of food. Iodine is added to salt as a goiter preventative; vitamins A and D go into fortified milk. The vitamin and mineral additives are generally beneficial.

Preservatives

Preservatives do what the name implies: they protect against spoilage from molds, yeasts, or bacteria, or prevent oxidation. In the first category are such substances as salt, sugar, vinegar, and—among the controversial additives—sodium nitrate, sodium nitrite, and the sulfiting agents. Where some of these substances guard against illnesses like salmonella and *Clostridium botulinum,* or botulism, a deadly form of food poisoning, the controversial types may cause serious illnesses and even cancers. For example, nitrates and nitrites can combine with the amines in protein to become nitrosamines, powerful carcinogens.

The antioxidants include lecithin from soybeans, ascorbic acid (vitamin C), and *butylated hydroxytoluene* (BHT) and *butylated hydroxyanisole* (BHA). The latter two have been studied because they appear to protect against stomach cancer and liver damage.

Flavors

Of the more than 1,500 different flavors used in food, some are natural and some synthetic. Among the natural flavors are cinnamon, vanilla, and citrus oils. The synthetics, some of which, like vanillin, have exactly the same chemical compositions as their originals, include monosodium glutamate (MSG), hydrolyzed vegetable protein, and maltol. MSG in particular has become controversial because it can cause "Chinese restaurant syndrome," with temporary headaches, dizziness, and other unpleasant symptoms.

Colors

As a group, the color additives are the most controversial. But they range from beta carotene, a yellow coloring that is used in carrots and sweet potatoes and is beneficial, to a number of coal tar dyes. The FDA has banned as unsafe more than a dozen of the latter in recent years. Others are readily available and are widely used in cereals, baked goods, ice cream, and beverages.

Processing Agents

Many useful processing agents, including yeast and baking soda, are standard kitchen items. They help to control stability, moisture, texture, and other food qualities and characteristics.

Chemical Residues

Some toxic substances found in food appear in the natural environment. An example: the trace amounts of arsenic in cow's milk. Other poisons are introduced into the environment by humans. These, including fungicides, herbicides, and pesticides, have aroused deep concern among environmentalists and a growing number of private physicians.

American farmers use more than 350 approved agricultural chemicals, including about one billion pounds of insecticides annually. Because of such heavy use, about 52 percent of the average American's diet contains one or more kinds of chemical residues. Measured often in parts-per-billion, these can collect in human bodies. Permanent damage can result, according to researchers. Among the compounds are not only weed- and bug-killers like parathion but also growth-enhancers like daminozide.

Researchers warn of other problems with contaminated food. The use of antibiotics in livestock feed, for example, promotes the development of bacteria that resist antibiotics. As one result, humans who eat beef or pork that is improperly cooked may acquire infections that resist penicillin or tetracycline.

Irradiated Foods

Consumer groups have urged further study and cautious use of irradiation as a means of preserving many foods. At least 30 countries have approved radiation exposure to retard spoilage and aging; but concerns remain. They focus particularly on the nutritional losses thay may occur if foods are exposed to more than one kind of preservative, on the effects of radiation exposure on workers handling irradiated foods, and on environmental hazards that could emerge in the transport, storage, and handling of radioactive food-processing wastes.

The possible long-term effects of irradiation have led to other concerns. Radiation kills the salmonella microorganism, but may not affect more virulent and dangerous bacteria such as those responsible for botulism and may, over time, strengthen those other organisms. Irradiation might even produce dangerous mutations of some bacteria. Researchers point out further that meat can become contaminated after irradiation, indicating that other preservatives might have to be used.

Other Hazards

Toxic Wastes

Various estimates place the number of toxic-waste disposal sites in the United States at 14,000 to 20,000. Poisonous substances left over from industrial processes are buried or simply dumped at these sites, many of which present serious health hazards. Primarily, according to scientists, the open dumps, landfills, bulk storage containers, and surface impoundments at the thousands of sites spill toxic chemicals into the surrounding soil and through it into groundwater systems. Noxious fumes and even flames burst from some sites at unpredictable moments. The wastes include a huge variety of substances, among them chlorinated solvents, aromatic hydrocarbons, pesticides, trace metals, and PCBs.

The locations of many waste disposal sites remain unknown, often, until a health or environmental problem is detected. Thus the health threats posed by waste dumps may lie dormant for years and may surface only after a container has rusted through or seepage has brought poisonous slush into contact with drinking-water sources.

Waste chemicals can enter the body through skin contact and inhalation as well as ingestion. But the latter is the most common method. Where dosage is substantial, ingestion usually leads to toxic effects on the liver and kidneys. Other parts of the body may be affected as well. Skin contact may produce lesions while inhalation can have direct respiratory effects.

Improved methods of disposing of toxic wastes have combined with public awareness and governmental action to build hopes of reduced waste problems in the future. In the meantime, as environmentalists contend, the thousands of existing toxic-waste sites pose continuing health hazards.

Nuclear Radiation

Among the most dangerous of all pollutants is nuclear or "ionizing" radiation. Made up of particles of energy, this radiation can attack the atoms that form the body's cells, causing both short- and long-term damage. Human tissues like skin, bone-marrow, and intestinal cells, all of which reproduce rapidly, feel the impact of radiation most intensely. But different isotopes in ionizing radiation concentrate in different body tissues, sometimes causing cancer or genetic mutations many years after exposure. Of the most common radioactive elements in radiation from a nuclear power plant, barium resembles calcium and therefore concentrates in the bones while iodine 131 concentrates in the thyroid.

Completely invisible, radiation reaches the earth from various natural and manmade sources. Some comes from the sun and outer space; larger amounts are given off by radioactive materials, including waste from nuclear power plants, the fallout from nuclear weapons explosions, and various electronic devices. The numbers of such devices are increasing steadily; among them are lasers, X-ray machines, TV sets, and microwave ovens.

The damage done to the human body as a result of exposure to radiation varies with the intensity of the "dose" and the isotopes involved. A dose of radiation above 1,000 rem, a unit of measurement, is always fatal. Smaller doses, with exposure over an extended period of time, may also be fatal. Victims can protect themselves to a limited degree if given time. For example, they can guard against thyroid cancer by taking potassium iodide. Ingested in pill form, the medication loads the thyroid gland with iodine, thus "blocking" the iodine 131 isotope and preventing its concentration in the thyroid.

In a simple operation physicians can transplant marrow into persons exposed to the barium isotope, and thus reduce the possibility of bone-marrow syndrome. This illness cripples the body's immune system. But donor marrow must match that of the victim, and the relatives of a victim are those most likely to supply marrow that is a genetic match. If the relatives have also been exposed to radiation, no donors may qualify.

Workplace Dangers

Air and noise pollution are, as noted, common in certain industries. The materials and machines used in manufacturing processes are the usual causes of such pollution. Many controls have been mandated by the federal Occupational Safety and Health Administration, but researchers have reported that some industries are experiencing increased health hazards, largely because of the materials they use.

High-tech microelectronics plants are especially threatened. According to scientists, many such plants use toxic chemicals that have been linked to reproductive disorders in both men and women. Among the high-tech hazards usually cited are glycol ethers, widely used as a solvent by manufacturers of printed circuit boards; arsenic, an element in the manufacture of some semiconductor chips; and lead, used in soldering and other operations. Some semiconductor plants are also employing radio-frequency radiation in potentially dangerous amounts to etch and clean silicon wafers.

31

Health Insurance

Health insurance has two basic purposes. It provides for reimbursement to families or individuals for health care costs. It may also guarantee replacement income when a person is unable to work because of sickness or injury. Reimbursement insurance can cover virtually all types of expenses connected with hospital care, medical treatment, and related services. Disability insurance usually calls for periodic payments to make up for lost income.

From another perspective, health insurance offers protection to both groups and individuals. The groups may be company work forces that have *group insurance* as a benefit. Individuals can buy insurance from as many as 1,000 commercial insurance companies offering a huge variety of plans.

Some insurers are general insurance companies. Others are hospital and medical service plans such as Blue Cross and Blue Shield, group medical prepayment plans such as health maintenance organizations (HMOs), and others.

What Health Insurance Is and Does

"Health insurance" means a number of things. It may be called "accident and health insurance" or "disability insurance." Various types of policies have other names. The different descriptions indicate that the policies vary as regards the types of expenses covered. While some policies cover hospital expenses only, others may cover virtually all kinds of medical expenses.

Two Types of Coverage

In general, private health insurance coverage is one of two kinds: *group* and *individual*. Employers, unions, and other kinds of organizations typically provide group insurance as an employee or membership benefit. An individual can buy individual insurance whether or not he or she is covered under a group policy. But a good group policy usually covers all the major health problems or contingencies that a person could face under normal circumstances.

Group insurance has a number of specific advantages over individual coverage, among them the following:

- Because a number of people can be included under a single contract, with consequent savings to the insurer in sales, administrative, and claims costs, the insurer can charge less per individual covered.
- In most cases the company, union, or organization holding the group contract pays part or all of the individual premiums.
- With group insurance the health of the individual insured person is usually not a major factor in determining eligibility. The insurance company is more interested in the average age and overall health status of the group. The health of individuals may become a selection factor, however, where small groups, 10 or fewer persons, are involved.
- Unless an individual leaves a job or gives up a membership, his or her group coverage cannot be can-

celed. Termination of the group plan itself would, of course, terminate coverage.

Despite such advantages, individual and family policies fulfill at least two fundamental needs. First, they provide coverage for persons who are not members of an insured group. Such policies may also cover those who cannot, for whatever reason, obtain group coverage. Second, the individual or family policy can provide supplementary coverage where a group plan does not meet all basic health insurance needs.

Group and individual plans differ in basic ways. Where a group policy establishes the level of benefits for all group members, the individual policy can more easily be tailored to specific requirements. With the individual policy, too, each person or family is enrolled separately. The cost of individual insurance is usually substantially higher because the insurer considers the age, health status of the insured, and other factors when setting premium rates.

Principles of Health Insurance

Private or commercial health insurance programs function according to some key principles. Primarily, these programs are based on the theory that a relatively small, regular payment, the premium, can protect the insured against what might be a sizable loss.

A companion principle holds that the insured must pay the expenses of operating an insurance system. These expenses include the costs of maintaining offices, investigating claims, and otherwise administering the system as well as paying benefits.

Two other principles underlie the operation of most health insurance programs:

- The *large-loss principle,* which holds that the insured should try to obtain protection only against those costs or losses that he or she could not bear financially. Under this principle the contract may exclude from reimbursement some specific kinds of costs. Most such policies contain a "deductible" clause specifying that the insured must pay a certain amount of initial costs.

  Major medical insurance plans probably exemplify best the large-loss, or large-risk, principle. These policies nearly always provide for a deductible. The higher the deductible, as a rule, the lower the premium.

- The *first-dollar principle,* under which the policy pays the full cost of all covered hospital and medical expenses. Policies of this kind have no deductible clauses.

  Advocates of first-dollar policies stress the need for preventive health care. The policy in theory encourages the insured to see a physician and obtain treatment before a health problem becomes worse or even unmanageable.

Kinds of Insurance Plans

Voluntary or private health insurance plans offer protection against a broad range of hospital and medical expenses. Some policies offer protection against a single illness such as cancer while others insure individuals, families, or groups against nearly all medical contingencies. Some of the many kinds of coverage are as follows:

Hospital

Blue Cross plans and most other commercial plans provide room benefits at a specified rate per day. Usually, they also cover miscellaneous hospital services, including drugs, operating room, and laboratory services up to a given cost level. Some commercial plans and most Blue Cross plans cover all costs in a semiprivate, or shared, room.

Surgical

Typically, health insurance policies cover the costs of surgery according to a schedule that establishes specified amounts for listed procedures. The insurance contract sets a payment of so many dollars for an appendectomy or a tonsillectomy, for example, with that payment going toward coverage of the surgeon's bill. In the case of Blue Shield, certain surgeons perform surgical operations for low-income subscribers for no additional charge.

Regular Medical

This is a form of insurance that provides coverage of physicians' fees in cases that do not involve surgery. The medical care may be provided in the home, in a hospital, or in a physician's office. A regular medical policy may also cover diagnostic X-ray and other laboratory expenses.

Major Medical

As noted, major medical policies usually provide for deductibles. After an insured has reached a specified hospital-medical expense level, the insurer will also pay, for example, 80 percent of all remaining expenses to a set maximum. The maximum may be $1 million or more. Some policies offer unlimited coverage. In some cases the policy sets a maximum, perhaps $5,000, $10,000, or $25,000, for a given illness in a one- or three-year period. Where an insurance company and the insured pay percentages of all costs beyond a deductible, the policy is said to be a form of "coinsurance."

Comprehensive or Comprehensive Major Medical

This kind of health policy combines hospital, major medical, and surgical coverage in one contract. Generally, little or no deductible applies to hospital and surgical charges. But the major medical coverage ordinarily comes with a deductible.

Dental

Basic or comprehensive protection, covering the costs of hospital care, surgery, and physicians' services, may also include dental insurance. A basic plan may establish a set of allowances for each procedure to an annual maximum of, for example, $500 or $1,000. A comprehensive policy would cover, typically, 80 percent of all dental expenses above a specified minimum.

Special Perils

While frowned upon by many insurance experts, "special perils" plans continue to appear. They cover such specific health hazards as cancer, polio, and vision problems.

Auto and Travel

Many insurance companies offer auto and travel policies that cover insured persons in the event of injury or death in an accident. Such policies may provide protection against almost any travel accident in various kinds of vehicles.

Income

Insurance against loss of income gives the insured person a flow of cash if, because of illness or disability, he or she cannot work. A commercial policy that limits coverage to accidental disability usually costs much less than broader coverage, or it provides for greater benefits. Accidental disability payments, usually monthly, may continue for life. Payments for disability resulting from illness are commonly limited to 6, 12, or more months depending on the terms of the contract.

Many policies provide only for *hospital income insurance.* Such insurance pays a stipulated cash payment for every day of hospitalization. Insurance companies offer these policies to individuals only, not to groups.

Basic Protection

Of the various kinds of comprehensive health insurance, the so-called "basic protection" plan ranks among the most common. Basic protection offers coverage for the costs of hospital care and services and physicians' services.

Most basic protection policies specify that hospital room and board benefits will be paid in one of two ways. One kind of policy provides for reimbursement for actual room and board charges up to a set daily maximum. Another kind offers a service type of benefit equaling the hospital's established semiprivate room and board rates. If the insured occupies a private room, he or she pays the additional room charge.

Surgical-Expense Insurance

Basic policies that provide hospital expense coverage generally offer surgical-expense benefits as well. That means coverage may extend to operations and postoperative, inpatient physicians' visits. The policy then becomes a "hospital-and-surgical-expense" or "hospital-surgical" plan.

Surgical-expense insurance normally pays benefits whether illness or accident makes the surgery necessary. Coverage may include benefits for anesthetics. A schedule of surgical procedures and specified maximum benefits for each may be part of such a policy. Physicians' fees may be covered to a "reasonable and customary" level for the particular city or region. In this case the policy would not contain a surgical schedule.

Physician's-Expense Insurance

The counterpart of the surgical-expense policy is the physician's-expense plan. This policy offers benefits to help cover the costs of nonsurgical physicians' services in a hospital, home, or office. The terms of the policy usually provide for maximum payments for specified services. The latter may include diagnostic X-ray and other laboratory expenses.

Policy Provisions

Purchasing health insurance calls for close attention to the provisions of any given policy. Little standardization exists among the hundreds of types of policies, a factor that makes the buyer's task a difficult one. In four areas in particular the buyer should scrutinize closely the "fine print" in an individual, but not a group, policy.

Provisions Relating to Other Policies

Many policies include clauses that limit or prohibit payments where the policyholder has other insurance covering the same loss or expense. In this way insurers protect themselves against overpayments for specific losses. A typical clause of this kind reduces benefits payments to the policy's prorated share of the insured person's actual expenses.

Preexisting Conditions

Most individual health insurance policies exclude preexisting conditions. That means they do not cover at all, or do not cover for a stated period, physical or health problems that existed before the policy became effective. The waiting period that must elapse before coverage for a preexisting condition begins may be 30, 60, or more days.

Cancellation and Renewal

All health policies contain cancellation and renewal provisions. One type, the most favorable to the policyholder, specifies that the insurer cannot cancel or refuse to renew the policy before the insured turns 65. The same clause may state that the premium cannot be increased. Because it provides guaranteed coverage, this kind of policy is usually the most expensive.

Many policies contain a widely used modification of the no-cancel, guaranteed renewal clause. This alternative provides that the company must continue the coverage until the insured reaches 65, but that the premium can be increased for entire groups of insured persons. In a third variation, some policies permit the insurer to cancel or refuse to renew the coverage at any time by giving written notice to the policyholder. This kind of policy is the least advantageous to the insured.

"Good-Health" Discounts

Increasingly, the disability, hospital, or medical policy provides for discounts for persons in good health. For example, the policy may specify that the applicant be a nonsmoker who exercises three to five times a week and does not have a high-risk job or hobby. Race-car driving would fall in the latter category.

Discounts of 5 to 15 percent have been available to nonsmokers since the 1960s. New discount arrangements broaden the range of qualifying factors and increase the discount levels. The new trend takes as a model the life insurance plan that may offer discounts of up to 50 percent if the applicant observes basic rules of health and safety. These include, in addition to those named, adhering to a nutritious diet, using seat belts while riding in a car, and avoiding excess salt in diet.

Meeting Special Needs

Some health insurance policies are designed to meet special needs. One common kind of coverage protects persons who are above-average risks: persons with poor health histories, existing problems or illnesses, or chronic disorders of one kind or another. Other types of policies serve other purposes.

Existing Health Problems

Because persons with existing health problems are not average risks, insurance for them may be costly. But an approach to insurance may be made in at least three ways.

1. A policy may exclude entirely the usual benefits for the specified existing condition. The insurance may then provide protection for all or many other conditions. Standard rates or premiums may be charged.

2. Charging a standard rate, the insurer may amend the policy to provide for a longer waiting period before coverage begins. In such a case standard benefits may be available.

3. The policy may call for a higher than normal premium to compensate for the greater degree of risk. Regular benefits might be available.

Some special health coverages have become relatively common. For example, dental-expense insurance helps pay for normal dental care as well as accidental damage. Insurance companies, prepayment plans, and some state dental associations make such coverage available, usually providing for a deductible and for coinsurance.

Special coverage may, finally, be provided for eye care. Many group policies have such coverage.

Insuring the Unemployed and Divorced

Most Americans have health insurance as a job-related benefit. Coverage terminates, however, if an individual quits his or her job, is laid off, or loses the job for whatever reason.

An employee who is leaving a job should find out how long, if at all, coverage will continue after employment terminates. A normal period would be 30 days. In that period the employee is usually allowed to convert the coverage from group to individual. The conversion option means the employee can remain insured by the same company while retaining, usually, reduced benefits. The premium payments generally increase, sometimes dramatically. Where a group policy permits conversion, the insured has the right to convert regardless of existing health problems. No medical examination is required.

Many group policies provide for conversion from group to individual coverage where a divorced person was dependent for protection on the former spouse's group plan. The person needing health coverage has to apply within the specified period, but cannot be rejected for health reasons.

By the middle 1980s, some 25 states had laws requiring "group continuance." By the terms of these laws a divorced spouse or unemployed person could remain in the group and receive the same benefits as before. The insured had only to assume the group cost formerly contributed by the employer for each insured individual. The effect of the group continuance laws was to make it possible for divorced or unemployed persons to retain group coverage for about half of what an individual policy would cost. With some exceptions, state laws limited group continuance periods to a year or less.

"Medigap" Insurance

An estimated 95 percent of all Americans over 65 are protected by Medicare. But the government program covers only a portion of all possible physician and hospital expenses—less than 50 percent. To help bridge the gap between Medicare and the 100 percent coverage that most persons need and want, private insurance companies have developed "medigap" policies.

What do the medigap policies cover? Their terms vary. Most help insured persons to expand existing Medicare coverages. But few offer even partial protection against hospital and medical costs that Medicare does not cover, or does not cover fully. These areas include: routine physical checkups; most prescription drugs; hearing tests and hearing aids; eye examinations and eyeglasses; most dental care, including dentures; private nursing care; and custodial home nursing care.

Because neither Medicare nor medigap insurance covers these areas thoroughly, many elderly persons remain vulnerable. But some medigap policies, including those offered by Blue Cross/Blue Shield and some associations for the elderly, provide for good hospital and physician coverage.

Congress set minimum standards for medigap insurance in 1980. But the Better Business Bureau has warned that the older person in need of additional insurance should shop carefully. Some groups, the BBB states, offer insurance as a means of building membership rolls. The BBB also advises as follows:

- Older buyers should make sure they have the Medicare medical insurance (Part B) as well as the hospital coverage (Part A).
- Insurance buyers should check the reputation of any potential private insurer with the state insurance department and the local Better Business Bureau. Insurance companies are also rated according to their financial health in *Best's Insurance Reports: Life and Health Insurance,* available in most libraries.
- The practice of switching from one insurance company to another because of premium levels can be hazardous: rates charged by any company can increase.
- As a rule, premiums should not be paid for years in advance. Your needs may change.

Five Innovative Plans

Pressures to cut the costs of medical care have given rise to basic changes in the methods of delivering such care in the United States. No longer do most persons simply call their family physicians and, if the physician so advises, go to a specific hospital. More and more, insurance plans and programs offer both choices and restrictions. Five innovative programs in particular have gained in popularity.

Health Maintenance Organizations (HMOs)

Operating clinic-style facilities, HMOs require that their subscribers pay a set monthly premium. In return the HMO provides full medical care. But members have to select their physicians from a list provided by the HMO. If hospitalization is necessary, the subscriber goes to a hospital selected by the organization.

Charging premiums that may be 10 to 20 percent lower than those for equivalent insurance coverage, HMOs provide incentives to avoid unnecessary expenses or treatments. HMOs, for example, encourage subscribers to make use of preventive care to stay healthy. Thus most HMOs offer eye and hearing checkups, as well as podiatry and dental services, at little or no cost beyond a monthly fee.

Many subscribers point to the convenience of HMOs as their major attraction. Subscribers not only have the convenience of full medical and hospital services at one facility; they pay no deductibles and have no claim forms to fill out.

HMOs have won federal support. New rules published in 1985 encouraged Medicare recipients to drop out of the government's medical insurance program and to join HMOs. The usual HMO restrictions on choices of physicians and hospitals would apply; applicants would join a central hospital facility, with its own physicians and specialties, and would be directed to specific physicians approved for HMO patients. Those who make the change have to retain the Medicare Part B coverage.

Former Medicare beneficiaries have various ways to report grievances. They can, for example, write to the U.S. Department of Health and Human Services Office of Health Maintenance Organizations, Compliance Division, Room 9-11, Parklawn Building, 5600 Fishers Lane, Rockville, MD 20857.

Preferred Provider Organizations (PPOs)

In the PPO, subscribers receive care at a discount if they go to physicians and hospitals recommended by the insurer. Generally, the insurance company underwriting the PPO allows employees in insured groups to go to a nonparticipating physician. But in such a case the costs of care rise considerably, sometimes to twice those charged by the listed physicians.

Under the PPO arrangement, physicians, hospitals, and insurers work together to keep down overall costs. A PPO hospital provides care for insured persons at reduced rates. In exchange, the hospital enjoys increased utilization of its facilities.

Managed Care

Unlike the HMO and the PPO, a managed care program gives members the freedom to pick the physicians and hospitals they prefer. But severe cost-containment rules apply. The restrictions may include the following:

- Preadmission reviews of hospital stays by panels of physicians and nurses. A panel would have to agree in all cases, except for maternity care and emergencies, that hospitalization and the proposed care are necessary.
- Reviews during hospitalization to ensure that continued inpatient care is necessary.
- Mandatory second opinions before some operations to make certain a particular procedure is necessary.
- As in some newer group plans, surgery is performed on an outpatient basis where possible.

Companies adopting managed care plans may offer HMO and PPO plans as well. An eligible employee in such a firm then has a choice of program.

Hospital Chains

Competition among health care providers has led to still another approach to both cost control and hospital utilization. Some for-profit hospital chains have bought insurance companies to obtain insurance licenses, then provided health insurance programs that required the insured to use the chain's facilities.

A variation on the HMO and PPO systems, the hospital chain approach makes possible insurance costs that are 10 to 15 percent lower than those of traditional plans. Chain officials contend that the lower charges are justified by more efficient hospital operation.

Insurance experts note characteristics of the hospital chains' programs that appear to justify caution on the part of the potential buyer. For example, the policies sold by the chains usually impose limits on lifetime benefits. Unlike the plans of such nonprofit groups as Blue Cross/Blue Shield, the chains' policies provide for the termination of certain benefits at specified ages.

Nursing Home Care

Increasingly, major insurance companies have begun to devise policies that would cover the costs of nursing home care for the elderly. Such specialized plans face a double difficulty. First, the insurance company needs to make a profit off the program of coverage. Second, nursing home costs ranging generally from $15,000 to $50,000 and more per year raise the possibility of enormous claims that could continue for years.

Long-term care insurance marks a start toward a solution. Major insurers have begun to market policies that differ on such points as home health care benefits and the right to renew. But because no actuarial figures are available to show, for example, how many younger policyholders would be needed to offset older beneficiaries, the companies have worked through organizations such as the American Association of Retired Persons (AARP). The memberships of such groups are usually numerous enough to reduce the risks of major claims.

If given a choice, the person shopping for a long-term care policy should ask at least these questions:

- Does the policy put a ceiling on benefits, and at what point?
- Exactly what does the policy cover? No such policies provide coverage for *all* the ills of aging.
- To be eligible for benefits, must the patient be hospitalized before he or she enters a long-term care facility?
- Must a patient's diagnosis cite an organic disease before eligibility can begin?
- Are "mental health" problems, possibly including Alzheimer's disease and senility, excluded from coverage?

32

Home Care of the Sick

Patients suffering from serious illnesses or from certain communicable diseases should be hospitalized. Home care facilities do not normally include the expensive and delicate medical equipment required for the complete care of these diseases.

If, however, the physician in charge of a case decides that his patient does not need hospitalization and that adequate home nursing care can be provided, the well-being of the patient can be greatly enhanced by his being cared for in the comfortable and familiar surroundings of his own home.

When the decision to treat a patient at home is made, it must be understood that the physician's orders regarding rest, exercise, diet, and medications have to be rigorously adhered to. Nursing responsibilities assigned to the patient and whoever else is tending to the patient's recovery should be carried out as conscientiously as they would be if the patient's care were entrusted to a team of medical professionals in a hospital environment.

The physician in charge of a case should, of course, be notified of any significant changes in the condition of the patient. The physician should be contacted if, for example, the patient complains of severe pain, pain of long duration, or pain that apparently is not directly related to an injury or surgical procedure. The location and characteristics of the pain should be noted, and the physician will want to know whether the pain is affected by changing the position of the patient or if it seems to be related to the intake of food or fluids.

In addition to being informed of such potentially dangerous developments, the physician should get daily or frequent reports on the patient's progress. The easiest and best way to see that this is done is to keep a written record of the following functions, symptoms, and conditions of the patient:

- Morning and evening body temperature, pulse rate, and respiration rate
- Bowel movements—frequency, consistency of stools, presence of blood
- Urination—amount, frequency, presence of burning sensation, color
- Vomiting or nausea
- The amount and kind of solid foods and liquids taken by the patient
- Hours of sleep
- Medications given (should be administered only on the instructions of the physician)
- Patient's general appearance (includes any unusual swelling, skin rash, or skin discoloration)
- General mental and psychological condition of the patient, such as signs of irritability or despondency

Checking the Pulse and Respiration

The pulse and respiration are usually checked in the morning and again in the evening; the physician may recommend other times as well.

Pulse

The home nurse should learn how to measure the pulse rate in beats per minute. A watch with a second hand or a nearby electric clock will help count the passage of time while the pulse beat is counted. The pulse can be felt on the inner side of the wrist, above the thumb; the pulse also can be checked at the temple, the throat, or at the ankle if for some reason the wrist is not conveniently accessible.

The patient should be resting quietly when the pulse is counted; if the patient has been physically active the pulse count probably will be higher than normal, suggesting a possible disorder when none actually exists. Temperature extremes, emotional upsets, and the digesting of a meal also can produce misleading pulse rates.

What is a normal pulse rate? The answer is hard to define in standard or average terms. For an adult male, a pulse rate of about 72 per minute is considered normal. The pulse of an adult woman might range around 80 per minute and still be normal. For children, a normal pulse might be one that is regularly well above 100 per minute. Also, a normal pulse may vary by a few beats per minute in either direction from the average for the individual. The home nurse with a bit of practice can determine whether a patient's pulse is significantly fast or slow, strong or weak, and report any important changes to the physician.

Respiration

The patient's respiration can be checked while his pulse is taken. By observing the rising and falling of the patient's chest, a close estimate of the rate of respiration can be made. An average for adults would be close to 16 per minute, with a variation of a few inhalations and exhalations in either direction. The rate of respiration, like the pulse rate, is higher in children.

Sometimes the respiration rate can be noted without making it obvious to the patient that there is concern about the information; many persons alter their natural breathing rate unconsciously if they know that function is being watched.

Body Temperature

A fever thermometer, available at any drugstore, is specially shaped to help the home nurse read any tiny change in the patient's temperature, such changes being measured in tenths of a degree. Instead of being round in cross-section like an ordinary thermometer, a fever thermometer is flat on one side and ridge-shaped on the other. The inner surface of the flat side is coated with a reflective material and the ridge-shaped side actually is a magnifying lens. Thus, to read a fever thermometer quickly and properly, one looks at the lens (ridged) side.

How To Take the Temperature

The usual ways of taking temperature are by mouth (oral) or by the rectum (rectal), and fever thermometers are specialized for these uses. The rectal thermometer has a more rounded bulb to protect the sensitive tissues in the anus. Normal body temperature taken orally is 98.6° F. or 37° C. for most people, but slight variations do occur in the normal range. When the temperature is taken rectally, a normal reading is about 1° F. higher—99.6° F. or about 37.5° C.—because rectal veins in the area elevate the temperature slightly.

Before a patient's temperature is taken, the thermometer should be carefully cleaned with soap and water, then wiped dry, or sterilized in alcohol or similar disinfectant. The thermometer should then be grasped firmly at the shaft and shaken briskly, bulb end downward to force the mercury down to a level of 95° F. or lower—or 35° C. or lower if the thermometer is calibrated according to the Celsius temperature scale. See the chart *Body Temperature in Degrees* for comparative values of the Fahrenheit and Celsius scales.

Body Temperature in Degrees

Fahrenheit		Celsius
105.5		40.8
105		40.6
104.5		40.3
104		40
103.5		39.7
103		39.4
102.5		39.2
102		38.9
101.5		38.6
101		38.3
100.5		38.1
100		37.8
99.5		37.5
99	Normal Range	37.2
98.6		37.0
97.8		36.6

If the temperature is taken orally, the thermometer should be moistened in clean fresh water and placed well under the tongue on one side. If the temperature is taken rectally, the thermometer should be dipped first in petroleum jelly and then inserted about one inch into the opening of the rectum. If an oral thermometer is used in the rectum, special care should be taken to make sure that the lubrication is adequate and that it is inserted gently to avoid irritating rectal tissues. Whichever method is used, the thermometer should be left in place for at least three minutes in order to get an accurate reading.

If circumstances preclude an oral or rectal temperature check, the patient's temperature may be taken under the arm; a normal reading in that area is about 97.6° F. or 36.5° C.

Above-Normal Temperature

If the patient's temperature hovers around one degree above his normal reading, the home nurse should note the fact and watch for other signs of a fever that would indicate the presence of an infection or some other bodily disorder. A mild fever immediately after surgery or during the course of an infectious disease may not be cause for alarm. Also, the normal body temperature of a mature woman may vary with hormonal changes during her menstrual cycle. But when oral temperatures rise above 100° F. the change should be regarded as a warning signal. A rise of as much as three degrees above normal, Fahrenheit, for a period of several hours or more, could be critical, and a physician should be notified immediately.

Sleep

Another item to be checked each day for the at-home medical records is the patient's sleeping habits. While there is no standard number of hours of sleep per day preferred for healthy individuals, a regular pattern of sleep is very important during recovery from disease or injury, and an obvious change from such a pattern can suggest tension, discomfort, or other problems. Typical daily sleep periods for most adults range from 7 to 9 hours, while children and infants may sleep as much as 12 to 20 hours per day and be considered normal; sleep in the form of naps should be included in total amounts per day.

Making the Patient Comfortable

A good deal of the patient's time at home will be devoted to sleep or rest, most or all of it in bed. The bed should give firm support to the body; if the mattress does not offer such support, place a thick sheet of plywood between the springs and mattress. Pillows can be placed under the head and shoulders of the patient to raise those parts of the body from time to time. When the patient is lying on his back, a small pillow can be slipped under the knees to provide support and comfort. A small pillow can also be placed under the small of the back if necessary. Additional pillows may be placed as needed between the ankles or under one foot or both feet.

If the pressure of bed clothing on the feet causes discomfort, a bridge made from a grocery carton or similar box can be placed over the feet but beneath the blankets. To help maintain muscle tone and circulation in the feet and legs, a firm barrier can be placed as needed at the foot of the bed so the patient can stretch his legs and push against the barrier while lying on his back.

Changing Position

Helping the patient change position in bed is an important home-nursing technique. Unless a definite effort is made to help the patient change positions at regular intervals, the sick person may tend to curl up into a sort of fetal position, with the hips and knees flexed and the spine curved. While this position may be preferred by the patient in order to increase body warmth or to relieve pain, the practice of staying in one position for longer periods of time can lead to loss of muscle tone and even deformities.

Moving or positioning the patient in bed should, of course, be done according to directions outlined by the doctor for the specific medical problem involved. Body movements should not aggravate any injury or other disorder by placing undue strain or stress on a body part or organ system that is in the healing stage. At the same time, the patient should be stimulated and encouraged to change positions frequently and to use as much of his own strength as possible.

If the patient is likely to need a very long period of bed rest, and the family can afford the modest expense, it may be wise to purchase or rent a hospital-type bed. The basic hospital bed is higher from the floor than ordinary beds, making the tasks of changing bed linens, taking temperatures, etc., easier for the home nurse. More sophisticated hospital beds have manual or electrical controls to raise the head and foot of the bed.

Helping the Patient Sit Up

The patient can be helped to a sitting position in bed by placing one arm, palm upward, under the patient's shoulder while the patient extends an arm around the nurse's back or shoulders. The nurse also may slip both hands, palms facing upward, under the patient's pillow, raising it along with the patient's head and shoulders. The same procedures can be used to help move a patient from one side of the bed to the other if the patient is unable to move himself.

When the patient has been raised to a sitting position, he should try to brace his arms behind him on the bed surface with elbows straightened. If the patient feels dizzy or faint as a result of the effort, he can be lowered to the back rest position again by simply reversing the procedure.

When the patient is able to support himself in a sitting position, he should be encouraged to dangle his legs over the side of the bed, and—when his strength permits—to move to a chair beside the bed and rest for a while in a seated position.

Bathing the Patient

A patient who is unable to leave the bed will require special help in bathing. When bath time comes, the nurse will need a large basin of warm water, soap, a washcloth, and several towels, large and small. A cotton blanket also should be used to replace the regular blanket during bathing, and pillows should be removed from the bed unless they are necessary at the time.

One large towel should be placed under the patient's head and another should be placed on top of the bath blanket, with part of the towel folded under the bath blanket. This preliminary procedure should help protect the bed area from moisture that may be spilled during the bathing procedure.

The bath should begin at the area of the eyes, using only clear water and brushing outward from the eyes. Soapy water can be applied to the rest of the face, as needed, with rinsing afterward. After the face, bathing and rinsing are continued over the chest and abdomen, the arms and hands, the legs and feet, and the back of the body from the neck downward to the buttocks. The external genitalia are washed last.

During the washing procedure, the nurse uses firm strokes to aid circulation and checks for signs of pressure areas or bed sores. Skin lotions or body powders may be applied, and a back rub given, after washing. The teeth may be brushed and the patient may want to use a mouthwash. After the personal hygiene routine is completed, a fresh pair of pajamas can be put on. If bed linen needs to be changed, the bathing period provides a good opportunity for that chore.

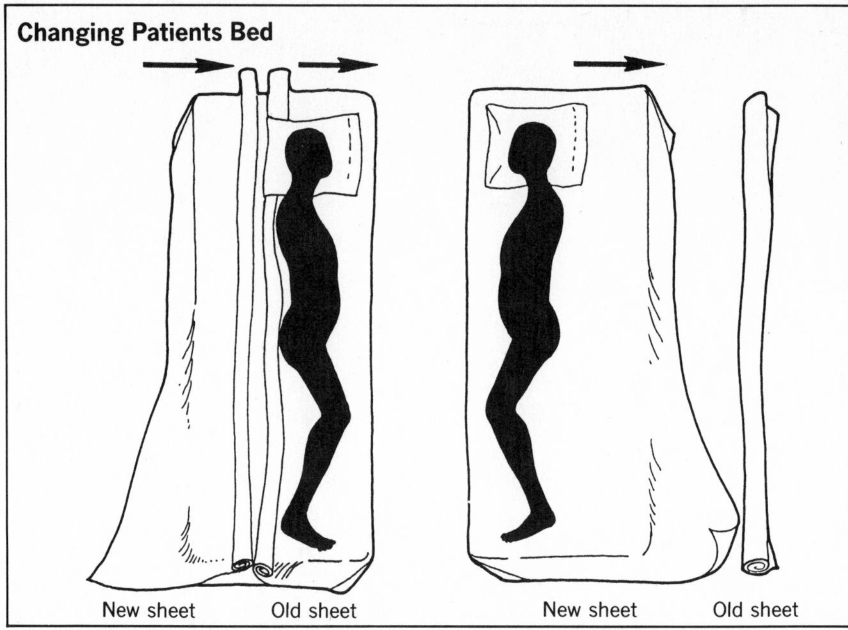

Changing the Bed Linen

Changing the bed linen while the patient is in bed can be a challenge for any home nurse. However, there are a few shortcuts that make the task much easier. First, remove all pillows, or all but one, as well as the top spread if one is used. Loosen the rest of the bedding materials on all sides and begin removing the sheets from the head of the bed, top sheet first. By letting the patient hold the top edge of the blanket, or by tucking the top edges under his shoulder, the blanket can remain in place while the top sheet is pulled down, under the blanket, to the foot of the bed. If the top sheet is to be used as the next bottom sheet, it can be folded and placed on the side with the top spread.

Next, the patient must be moved to one side of the bed and the bottom sheet gathered in a flat roll close to the patient. Then the clean bottom sheet is unfolded on the mattress cover and the edges, top, and bottom, tucked under the mattress. The rest of the clean sheet is spread over the empty side of the bed and pushed in a flat roll under the soiled sheet next to the patient's back.

The next step is to roll the patient from one side of the bed onto the clean sheet that has been spread on the other side. The soiled bottom sheets can be pulled out easily and the new bottom sheet spread and tucked in on the other side.

The new top sheet can be pulled up under the blanket, which has been used to cover the patient throughout the change of bed linens. Finally, the top spread and pillows can be replaced, after the pillow cases have been changed. A special effort should be made, meanwhile, to keep the mattress cover and bottom sheet of the patient's bed as flat and smooth as possible and to allow room for the feet to move while the sheets are firmly tucked in at the foot of the bed.

The home nurse should handle the soiled linens carefully if the patient is being treated for an infectious disease; they should never be held close to the face.

Bowel Movements and Urination

If the patient is expected to remain bedridden for a long period of time, the home nurse should acquire a bedpan and perhaps a urinal from a drugstore. A sheet of oilcloth, rubber, or plastic material should also be provided to protect the bed during bowel movements and urination.

If the patient is unable to sit up on a bedpan because of weakness, his body can be propped up with pillows. If he is capable of getting out of bed but is unable to walk to the bathroom, a commode can be placed near the bed and the patient can be helped from the bed to the commode and back. Another alternative is to use a wheelchair or any chair with casters to move the patient between the bedroom and bathroom.

Administering an Enema

Occasionally, a physician may recommend an enema to help the patient empty his bowels or to stimulate the peristaltic action associated with normal functioning of the intestinal tract.

Since enemas are seldom an emergency aspect of home nursing, there usually is time to purchase disposable enema units from a drugstore. The disposable enema contains about four or five ounces of prepared solution packaged in a plastic bag with a lubricated nozzle for injecting the fluid into the patient's rectum. The entire package can be thrown away after it has been used, thus eliminating the need to clean and store equipment. The alternative is to use a traditional enema bag filled with plain warm water or a prescribed formulation.

An enema is best administered while the patient is lying on his side with his knees drawn up toward his chest. When using the disposable enema unit, the home nurse simply squeezes the solution through the lubricated nozzle that has been inserted into the rectum. When using an enema bag, the home nurse should lubricate the nozzle before insertion. After insertion of the nozzle, the enema bag should be held or suspended above the patient so that, upon the opening of the valve that controls the flow of the enema, the liquid will flow easily into the patient's rectum.

Feeding the Patient

It may be necessary at times for the home nurse to feed a patient unable to feed himself. An effort should be made to serve meals to the patient in an attractive and, when possible, colorful manner. The bedding should be protected with towels or plastic sheeting and the patient made as comfortable as possible with his head raised.

Liquids should be offered in a spoon filled about two-thirds full with any drops on the bottom of the spoon carefully wiped off. The spoon should be held so that the area between the tip and the side touch the patient's lower lip. Then the spoon is tilted toward the tip so the liquid will run into the patient's mouth. The process takes time, and much patience is required of the nurse. The patient may be slow to swallow and in no hurry to finish the meal.

If the patient can take liquids through a glass tube or plastic straw, the home nurse should see to it that the end of the tube inserted in the container of liquid is always below the surface of the fluid so that the patient will swallow as little air as possible.

A patient who can drink liquids from a spoon or tube may be able to drink from a cup. In making the step from tube or spoon to cup, the home nurse can help the patient by holding the cup by its handle and letting the patient guide the cup to his lips with his own hands.

The nurse should always make sure the patient is fully alert before trying to put food or liquid into his mouth; a semiconscious person may not be able to swallow. The nurse also should test the temperature of the food; cold foods should be served cold and warm foods should be served warm. But foods should never be too hot or too cold for the patient. Finally, the dishes, tubes, or other devices used to feed the patient should be carefully cleaned before storing them.

Ice Bags and Hot-Water Bottles

Ice bags and hot-water bottles frequently are used in home nursing to relieve pain and discomfort. The temperature of the water in a hot-water bottle or bag should be tested before it is placed near a patient's body. The maximum temperature of the water should be about 130° F., and preferably a few degrees cooler. The hot-water container should never be placed directly against the skin of a patient; it must be covered with soft material, such as a towel, to protect the patient against burns. A patient who is receiving pain-killing medications could suffer serious tissue damage from a hot-water bottle without feeling severe pain.

When ice is the preferred method of relieving pain, it can be applied in a rubber or plastic bag sealed to prevent leakage and covered with a soft cloth. Cold applications to very young and old persons should be handled cautiously and with medical consultation, particularly if ice packs are to be applied to large body areas for long periods of time; individuals at both age extremes can lack the normal physiological mechanisms for coping with the effects of cold temperatures.

Steam Inhalators

If the at-home patient suffers from a respiratory ailment that is relieved by steam inhalation, there are several devices to provide the relief he needs. One is the commercial electric inhalator that boils water to which a few drops of a volatile medication are added to provide a pleasantly moist and warm breathing environment. If a commercial inhalator is not available, a similar apparatus can be made by fashioning a cone from a sheet of newspaper and placing the wide end of the cone over the top and spout of a teapot containing freshly boiled water. The narrow end of the cone will direct the hot water vapor toward the face of the patient. If a medication is to be added, it can be applied to a ball of cotton placed in the cone; the steam or water vapor will pick up the medication as it passes through the cone.

If medicated vapor is intended for a small child or infant, the end of the cone can be directed into a canopy or tent made of blankets placed over a crib or the head of a bed. This arrangement should produce an effective respiratory environment for the child while keeping his body safely separated from the hot teakettle.

Still another method of providing steam inhalation for a patient requires only an old-fashioned washstand pitcher and bowl plus a grocery bag. An opening is cut in one corner of the bottom of the bag which is placed upside down over the pitcher filled with hot steaming water and, if needed, a medication. The patient simply breathes the hot moist air seeping through an opening in the bag. The pitcher of steaming water is placed in a bowl or basin as a safety precaution.

Sickroom Devices

With a bit of imagination, many sickroom devices can be contrived from items already around the house. A criblike bed railing can be arranged, for example, by lining up a series of ordinary kitchen chairs beside a bed; if necessary, they can be tied together to prevent a patient from falling out of bed. The bed itself can be raised to the level of a hospital bed by placing the bed legs on blocks built from scrap lumber. Cardboard boxes can be shaped with scissors and tape into bed rests, foot supports, bed tables, or other helpful bedside aids.

Plastic bags from the kitchen can be used to collect tissues and other materials that must be removed regularly from the sickroom. Smaller plastic bags may be attached to the side of the bed to hold comb, hairbrush, and other personal items.

Keeping Health Records

The family that keeps good records of past injuries and illnesses, as well as immunization information and notes on reactions to medications, has a head start in organizing the home care of a member who suddenly requires nursing. The file of family health records should include information about temperatures and pulse rates taken during periods of good health; such data can serve as benchmark readings for evaluating periods of illness. Also, if each member of the family can practice taking temperatures and counting pulse and respiration rates during periods of good health, the family will be better able to handle home nursing routines when the need arises.

Home Care Equipment Checklist

Following is a convenient checklist of basic supplies needed for home care of the sick:

1. Disinfectants for soaking clothing and utensils used by the sick. Not all disinfectants are equally effective for every purpose. For clothing and food utensils, corrosive or poisonous disinfectants are to be avoided. Antiseptics do not kill bacteria; they only retard their growth. Among the common disinfectants that can be used in the home are:

- Alcohol, 75 percent by weight, used for disinfecting instruments and cleaning the skin
- Lysol, for decontaminating clothing and utensils
- Soap with an antibacterial agent for scrubbing the hands
- Carbolic acid (phenol) for disinfecting instruments and utensils (it is corrosive, poisonous, and very effective if used in 5 percent solution)
- Cresol in 2.5 percent solution for disinfecting sputum and feces (less poisonous than phenol and can be obtained as an alkali solution in soap)
- Boric acid, a weak antiseptic eyewash
- Detergent creams, used to reduce skin bacteria

2. Disposable rubber gloves, to be used when handling patients with open wounds or contagious diseases, as well as for cleaning feces.

3. Paper napkins and tissues for cleaning nasal and oral discharges.

4. Rectal and oral thermometers. The former is used primarily for infants, while the latter is used for adults and older children. Thermometers should always be thoroughly disinfected after use by soaking in isopropyl alcohol, and they should be washed prior to reuse.

5. Eating and drinking utensils to be used only by the patient. Disposable utensils are preferable.

6. Urinal, bedpan, and sputum cup for patients who cannot go to the toilet. After use, they should be thoroughly disinfected with cresol and washed with liquid soap containing an antibacterial agent.

7. Personal toilet requisites: face cloths and towels, toilet soap, washbasin, toothbrush and toothpaste, comb, hairbrush, razor, and a water pitcher (if running water is not accessible to the patient).

8. Measuring glass graduated in teaspoon and tablespoon levels for liquid medication.

9. Plastic waste-disposal bags that can be closed and tied.

33

Health Care Delivery

A Changing Service

Unending change has characterized American health care in recent decades. The general practitioner in private practice, once the institutionalized symbol of medical care in the United States, has largely given way to specialists of many kinds. Where the general practitioner once sent a handwritten bill for services to the family home, he or she may now send a computerized invoice to an insurance company or a government agency. The "house call" has virtually disappeared.

Technology has taken over. Hospitals and other health care institutions may pay sums in seven figures for equipment that can save lives but that also demands to be used. A "technological imperative" requires that the new approach or instrument or drug at least be tried—experimented with, proven useful or useless, and made available to those who need it. In diagnosis and therapy in particular, physicians and other professionals are continually seeking the new and better.

Some seven million people work in the American health care system. Half a million of those are physicians. The facilities in which the system's personnel work range from rural clinics to high-technology urban medical centers. On balance, the consumer dealing with this system has many choices. Understanding those choices may make the difference between a beneficial experience and a frustrating search for help.

Health care reaches the American public at three broadly defined levels. The three are primary, secondary, and tertiary care.

Primary Care

Essentially, *primary care* refers to "first contact" care as provided in physicians' offices or hospitals. Such care may also be provided in emergency rooms and outpatient clinics. The individual can obtain primary care without referral by a physician, but referrals from this level of care are generally necessary to ensure that the patient will receive treatment at the next higher level. Among the types of services provided at the primary care level are health maintenance for infants and children, screening for infectious and communicable diseases, and treatment for minor injuries.

Secondary Care

At the *secondary care* level the patient usually comes under the care of a specialist, often in a community hospital or other, similar setting. Secondary level specialties include such well-known areas of medicine as obstetrics and gynecology, dermatology, otolaryngology, and cardiology. While physicians often refer their patients for secondary level care, many persons "refer themselves."

Tertiary Care

At the tertiary care level, the patient receives highly specialized, high-technology care and treatment. Complex programs and unusual procedures, among them open heart surgery, heart or kidney transplantation, and neurological surgery, are provided by physicians with extensive training and the advantages of sophisticated equipment for diagnosis and treatment. Often, care at this level is obtainable only if the patient enters a hospital with specialized facilities. Of the various tertiary care institutions, three key ones are hospitals specializing in a certain disease or a group of diseases, hospitals associated with medical schools, and large regional referral centers. Many such institutions would be expected to have diagnostic equipment for such procedures as cardiac catheterization, nuclear magnetic resonance testing, and CT scanning.

Importantly, the three levels of care overlap. The distinctions among them are not always clearly drawn or defined. For the patient, the most important factor may be the need for referrals at some levels and not at others.

Health Care Delivery Formats

The average American visits a physician five times a year. That statistic appears in a U.S. Public Health Service survey that also defines a visit as an encounter with a physician or other health professional under a physician's direction or supervision. The "encounter" can take place in the physician's office, in the patient's home, by telephone, or in some other ambulatory care setting. The physician initiates about half of the encounters, usually as part of follow-up care.

Office and Clinic Care

In the main, the patient sees his or her physician in an office or at a site reserved for group practice; in a hospital outpatient department; in an ambulatory surgical center; or in a freestanding surgical center.

Office-Based Practice

Most physicians practice on their own; even so, the solo practice is declining as a way of medical life. The solo practitioner survives in isolated or rural areas, but hardly at all elsewhere. For the physician, solo practice is both simpler because of the independence and freedom it guarantees and more complex because the service responsibility may continue 24 hours a day, seven days a week. For the patient, the main advantage of solo practice is both the closer relationship that can develop and less fragmented care.

Partnerships

Very common today is the partnership, an agreement between two or more physicians under which the participants share office space, staff, and equipment. The physicians retain their independence in the sense that they have their own practices, but they usually share patient responsibilities under given circumstances. A physician who has to be out of contact with the office may, for example, give a patient another partner's number so as to have continuous backup. Spreading the care responsibilities and reducing the workload, each physician may also have more time for each patient.

The patient may find major advantages in the partnership. He or she can become acquainted with the physician's partner and in this way obtain personalized care at all times. Backup support may be especially important in obstetrics, where deliveries may occur without warning, and in cardiology, where emergencies are equally unscheduled.

Groups

Where three or more physicians associate in an arrangement that is normally less formal than a partnership, it is termed a *group*. The physicians belonging to the group may practice in a single specialty or in diverse fields of medicine. An example of the latter would be a group of three doctors offering internist, obstetrics-gynecological, and pediatric services. In other ways the group shares the advantages and disadvantages of the typical partnership. Like the partnership, the group has one particular advantage, however: other physicians are available for consultation and education. The group format may also make possible relatively sophisticated laboratory and other facilities.

Health Maintenance Organizations

The health maintenance organization (HMO) ranks as a special kind of group practice, one that involves a fixed monthly or annual fee system rather than a fee-for-service arrangement. The fixed fee ensures that the HMO member will receive, at no additional charge, all necessary health services, including hospitalization and the care of specialists. Preventive medicine at no extra cost to the member is a feature of the HMO that has ensured reduced usage of hospital facilities.

Preferred Provider Organizations

Like the HMO, the preferred provider organization (PPO) is at least partly a response to rising health-care costs. Forming a PPO, a group of physicians contracts individually with an insurance company or employer to provide health services for fees that are usually lower than those prevailing in the community or area. The PPO does charge on a fee-for-service basis, but employees making use of the organization's medical services save money because they avoid the copayments of conventional insurance plans and the standard deductibles. Physicians belonging to the PPO have a stable pool of employed members whose health problems may be extremely diverse. For the employer or insurance company, a particular advantage is the ability to bargain for lower fees.

Three Alternative Systems

Obviously, office and clinic care takes many forms. Three alternatives that provide relatively minor, low-level services are the hospital outpatient department, the ambulatory surgical center, and the freestanding emergency center. Each plays a particular role in the health care delivery network.

Hospital Outpatient Departments

Outpatient departments once offered free services as a means of training medical students and residents or because physicians volunteered their services for such departments. Today, outpatient departments charge for their services while delivering health care that varies broadly as regards quality. One hospital in three has an outpatient department or a clinic for ambulatory care while nine of ten community hospitals offer outpatient care in their emergency departments.

Ambulatory Surgical Centers

Sometimes called surgicenters, the ambulatory surgical center may be attached to a hospital or be completely independent. In either case, the surgicenter may be an effective alternative in the traditional situation where a patient needs an abortion, a dilatation and curettage (D & C), hernia repair, or tissue biopsy. Because they perform lower-risk procedures, ambulatory surgical centers can keep costs down. Local anesthesia is the norm, and usually the patient goes home on the day of the operation.

Freestanding Emergency Centers

Sometimes called *urgicenters,* freestanding emergency centers resemble hospital emergency departments. But private, for-profit groups usually run them. Open from 12 to 24 hours daily, they operate on a drop-in basis, meeting a definite need where a hospital emergency room is far away or when all physicians' offices have shut down for the day. Typically, emergency centers treat sprains and bruises, cuts that require stiches, and upper respiratory infections. Charges for such services usually range from visits to physicians' offices on the low side to hospital emergency rooms on the high side.

Community Health Care Facilities

Providing more evidence of the complexity of the United States' health care delivery complex, community health facilities fill a void in health services at a very basic level. At least five different modes of providing health care need to be considered as community facilities.

School and College Health Programs

Once concerned primarily with the control of communicable diseases and screenings for dental, vision, and hearing problems, school and college health programs have taken on new functions. At the elementary and high-school levels, they may help with health and sex education programs, keep vaccination records, and consult with parents. Colleges and universities generally provide infirmary services, meaning inpatient care for acute illness. At larger schools, programs may deal with contraception and pregnancy problems, substance abuse, and neuroses.

Industrial Health Programs

Treatment of work-related injuries and minor illnesses remains a key function of industrial health programs. The programs also continue to give minor physical exams and to provide general medical and dental care. But they have expanded their services in recognition of the value of preventive medicine. Newer or more modern programs offer comprehensive work-site education and screening programs, alcohol abuse counseling, stop-smoking clinics, and aerobic fitness classes.

Health Screening

Provided by local health departments and voluntary health agencies (see Chapter 36), health screening varies from community to community as regards both availability and reliability. Depending on community funding, a local health department may or may not provide tests that screen for infectious or parasitic diseases, including sexually transmitted diseases (see Chapter 17), and chronic disorders such as high blood pressure, sickle cell anemia, or diabetes. Many health departments make referrals to follow-up medical care.

Neighborhood and Primary Health-Care Centers

Neighborhood and primary health-care centers were established first in the 1960s to provide ambulatory care in underserved communities, both rural and urban. Staffed often by U.S. Public Health Service medical personnel or by nurse practitioners, the centers either limited their services according to income requirements or served specific communities. Because of cuts in federal spending, experts note, many such centers have been or are being phased out.

Women, Infant, and Child Care

Also federally funded, the women, infant, and child care program emphasizes provision of well-baby care, nutritious food, and nutrition education for pregnant women, infants, and children under three. Estimates indicate that the program saves three dollars for every dollar spent. But federal budget cuts have begun seriously to scale back the program.

Disease Prevention and Control

County or city health departments usually establish disease prevention and control programs to help control the spread of communicable diseases. Methods used include immunization, screening, and follow-up. Typical concerns include immunization for childhood diseases like diphtheria, measles, and polio; tuberculosis and sexually transmitted diseases; and influenza immunization for older persons.

Hospitals

Viewed a century ago as a deathhouse, the hospital has a new image in the 1980s. With an entirely revised role built on its ability to provide comforts and even amenities, the hospital has added a "hotel" function to its fundamental "healing" function. But the hotel role does not affect the hospital's main medical purpose: to provide, within budgetary and other limits, sophisticated, technologically up-to-date care. The hospital has become the place to go for diagnostic and therapeutic care that a physician's office cannot provide.

A basic method of classifying hospitals is by length of the patient's stay. Viewed this way, hospitals fall into two groups, long-term or extended-care institutions and short-term hospitals. The former will be discussed later; the second group includes community, teaching, and public hospitals.

Community Hospitals

Most Americans receive medical care in community hospitals. Usually quite small, with 50 to 500 beds, this kind of hospital generally provides good to excellent secondary-level care. Traditionally, community hospitals were nonprofit corporations that depended heavily on community support. Today, the community hospital is increasingly likely to be proprietary. That means it is run for profit by investor-owned groups or corporations.

The costs of medical care at a proprietary community hospital may not be significantly different from those charged by a voluntary or nonprofit hospital.

Teaching Hospitals

Ranging in size from a few hundred to a few thousand beds, teaching hospitals universally offer training for undergraduate medical students, postgraduate students, or fellows. Also, nearly all have ties to major medical schools. A state government may own a teaching hospital that is used by state medical schools; others are owned by the associated university or by a nonprofit corporation. Teaching hospitals provide care at all three levels.

Public Hospitals

Public hospitals include not only county hospitals but others supported by public funds, among them public health service hospitals, Veterans Administration (VA) hospitals, and municipal short-term-stay hospitals. Many such institutions that are owned by federal, state, or city governments are teaching hospitals, and many also have associated rehabilitation units and nursing homes.

The Elderly: Home Care

Surprisingly, most elderly persons live at home and receive care from relatives and others who may visit the home to help out. Younger family members may need home care because of illness or injury, but typically the disabled or ill older person is the one receiving such care. A number of community resources are available to make home care—or self-care for those living alone—easier. These resources include home health workers, such services as Meals-on-Wheels, and various day-care programs.

Invaluable aids for those responsible for home care for an aging relative are unskilled companions and temporary help. With this kind of assistance, the elderly person may be able to enjoy continuity of care and independence while maintaining ties with family, home, and community.

Home Health Services

Some 2,500 home health agencies operate under the general direction of physicians to provide two kinds of services: skilled and supportive. Of the many types of home health service providers, the best known are private, either profit-making or nonprofit; public health agencies such as neighborhood health centers; hospital-based services; and local or county health department or community and church programs. The nationwide Visiting Nurses Association is perhaps the most familiar.

Different communities and areas enjoy different levels and types of home health services. But most such agencies provide care to anyone who requests it. Fees vary, and may be paid by the individual or the family accepting the care. In other cases the government or individual insurance plans may reimburse the family, partially or totally, for the fees charged.

Hospital social workers or discharge-planners, the Area Agency on Aging, the local office of the Social Security Administration, day-care centers, and churches and synagogues normally provide information on home health services.

Voluntary Health Agencies

Many voluntary health agencies provide aid and support to the disabled or sick elderly person (see Chapter 36). Such groups and organizations as the American Cancer Society and the Easter Seal Society may even offer "friendly visitor" services in specific communities. Most of the groups see education of the public as functional to their roles. Thus they may provide films, lecturers, books and pamphlets, and other materials of interest to groups and organizations of many kinds. Many such agencies have specialized equipment for those who need it as well as listings of community resources.

Drugstores and Medical Supply Houses

Two other basic sources of specialized equipment and sickroom supplies, the medically oriented drugstore and the medical supply house, play important roles. In many cases the family discharging home care responsibilities can obtain wheelchairs, walkers, portable oxygen equipment, and hospital beds from one source or the other. Often, the supplier will rent or sell the specialized equipment; the choice may be the family's to make.

Community Facilities for the Aged

An entire new category of health care facilities has come into being in recent years in response to the needs of the elderly. These community facilities are designed specifically for those elderly persons living at home who are not housebound.

Adult Day Care

A broad variety of community-based centers schedule adult day-care programs for the elderly. To some extent the programs provide an alternative to institutionalization. In each case the programs are tailored to meet specific needs. Each type has a basic therapeutic objective.

Day Hospitals

Generally located at an extended-care facility or hospital, the day hospital provides medical care and supervision for persons recovering from acute illnesses. A physician's referral is normally required; fees closely parallel those charged for other hospital services. The day hospital that treats primarily patients discharged from an institution is sometimes called an aftercare clinic.

Medical Day Care

Where chronically ill or disabled persons do not require frequent or intensive medical intervention, the medical day care service may be the solution. Located usually in a long-term care institution or freestanding center, such a care service may include nursing and other supports. A physician's referral is required, and rehabilitation and maintenance are primary therapeutic goals. Reimbursement is by third-party (insurance company) payments on a sliding scale. Medicaid pays for medical day care in some states.

Mental Health Day Care

Offering a supervised environment along with mental health services to adults with organic or functional mental illness, the mental health day care service is usually located in a psychiatric institution or freestanding center. Referral by a psychiatrist is required. Three basic therapeutic goals are supervision, assistance with coping skills, and safety for the patient. Reimbursement is by third-party payment.

Social Adult Day Care

Title XX of the Social Security Act provides for funding of many social adult day care facilities, all of which are geared to the needs of adults who have difficulty functioning independently. Both families and health facilities can make referrals, but examination by a physician is normally required before admission. Third-party reimbursement is the norm. Program objectives and services vary widely, and are usually formulated by the funding source and the sponsoring organization. Program participants may attend part-days or full days five days a week; the facility may provide a midday meal and transportation within a specified area.

Nutrition Services

Nutrition ranks as a critical need for both homebound and more independent elderly persons. Meals-on-Wheels, a community service offered under voluntary auspices but funded partly by public funds, caters to the homebound. For a reasonable charge the service provides at least one hot meal daily for persons 60 and older. For the elderly attending senior centers, the Area Agency on Aging provides both adequate nutrition and a chance to socialize. Agency personnel can keep in touch with clients' physical and social situations, giving the program an important outreach and prevention dimension.

Extended-Care, Long-Term Care, Nursing Homes

Closely related, the extended-care facility, long-term care facility, and nursing home nonetheless meet different needs. A relatively recent innovation, the extended-care facility provides a service that falls between that given in an acute-care hospital and that provided in a skilled nursing facility or nursing home.

Extended-Care Facility

Despite its name, the extended-care facility provides short-term inpatient care. This type of facility is designed mainly to aid patients who have been hospitalized but no longer need the full complement of hospital services. Such patients still require professional nursing and medical supervision. Typically attached to a hospital, the extended-care facility may also serve those who are not acutely ill but who require skilled care.

Because most extended-care facilities are physically attached to hospitals, patients often simply move from one hospital wing to another. Some nursing homes also meet the standards set for qualification as extended-care facilities by the Joint Commission on the Accreditation of Hospitals (JCAH). For the most part, extended-care facilities charge much less than the typical hospital.

Long-Term Care Facilities

Patients with chronic conditions that cannot be treated effectively in a general hospital generally qualify for care in a long-term care facility. Such conditions range from tuberculosis to mental retardation. The facilities also include chronic disease hospitals, rehabilitation hospitals, and psychiatric hospitals for both children and adults.

Nursing Homes

Also falling in the category of long-term care facilities, nursing homes comprise a special group of facilities of different kinds. They offer services ranging from sheltered living arrangements to around-the-clock nursing care. All nursing homes rank as residential facilities.

The approximately 18,000 nursing homes in the United States have between 1.3 and 1.5 million beds. Three-quarters of these nursing homes are proprietary, or for-profit, institutions that house about two-thirds of all the beds. Nonprofit organizations operate 15 percent of all the nation's nursing homes and make available about 20 percent of the beds. The government operates the remaining homes.

Nursing homes accommodate persons of all ages. A few younger residents have serious congenital illnesses or disorders, or have been recently discharged from a hospital. Others are recovering from recent surgery. But most patients are the chronically ill elderly. Typically, a nursing home resident is a woman in her 80s, single or widowed. Afflicted with three or more serious chronic illnesses, she has very likely exhausted all her assets except her monthly Social Security payments.

Residential-Care Facilities

Standing at the lowest level of nursing home care, the residential-care facility is usually appropriate for the person who can no longer live alone and manage household chores. This "typical" resident does not need extensive medical attention but does require sheltered living, prepared meals, and some medical monitoring. The latter may include supervision of medications and tracking of signs and symptoms.

Intermediate-Care Facilities

The intermediate-care facility supplements typical RCF services with regular, but not round-the-clock, nursing care for residents who are unable to survive on their own. The intermediate-care facility may also make provision for social and recreational activities. Programs of physical therapy and rehabilitation, occupational therapy, speech therapy, and social work services may also be offered.

Skilled Nursing Facilities

With staffs of registered nurses, licensed practical nurses, and nurses' aides, skilled nursing facilities can provide 24-hour care. They are, thus, appropriate for persons in need of intensive nursing care and rehabilitation. Like intermediate-care facilities, skilled nursing facilities are state-certified for the most part, a factor that makes them eligible for public funds as payment for services. Lack of certification may mean that an ICF or SNF has serious deficiencies.

Hospices

Described sometimes as more a philosophy than a type of physical facility, the hospice is a form of care for the terminally ill. The family and the patient merit equal consideration in the typical hospice; the purpose is to minimize the twin fears associated with dying, fear of isolation and fear of pain. Typical palliative care involves the careful control of pain and the management of other symptoms of terminal disease or illness.

A growing number of communities have hospice facilities. But no pattern appears in the types of institutions—or sections of institutions—devoted to the care of the terminally ill. A hospice may be a wing in a hospital or simply a group of hospital beds that can be made available as needed. A hospice may also be a separate building or institution. While families provide much of the care as long as patients are at home, a team including a physician, nurses, counselors, home health aides and others may be continually on call. The team provides continuity between home and hospice when patients must be institutionalized. At all times, the individual patient's comfort is a prime consideration.

Patients enter hospice programs at their own requests. A physician's referral, indicating that the prognosis is no more than six months, may also be required.

34

Voluntary Health Agencies

Major Agencies

The establishment of more than 100 voluntary health agencies since the beginning of this century has been a major factor in the growth of health services to the American public. These agencies, whose activities are made possible by donations of time and money from the public, occasionally augmented by government grants for special projects, have the following objectives: spreading information about various diseases to the professional and lay public; sponsoring research; promoting legislation; and operating referral services on the community level to patients in need of diagnosis, treatment, and financial aid.

Some of these agencies, such as the American Diabetes Association or the Arthritis Foundation, focus on a particular disease; others deal with problems arising from related disorders, such as the National Association for Mental Health and the American Heart Association. Still others, such as Planned Parenthood and the American Social Health Association, have programs vital not only to individuals, but to society as a whole.

To coordinate the activities of these many groups, to promote better health facilities, and to establish standards for the organization and conduct of these agencies, the National Health Council was founded in 1920. Its membership includes government, professional, and community associations, as well as the 21 voluntary health agencies described below, which command a total budget of almost $1.5 billion and involve the services of almost 12 million volunteers.

All of these organizations function on the national, state, and community level. Information and literature may be obtained through local chapters or by writing to the national office of the organization. Volunteers may offer their services in a variety of ways: as office workers, fund raisers, speakers, and community coordinators.

On the following pages, voluntary health agencies are discussed under the subjects with which they are concerned; the subjects are arranged alphabetically. Following these agencies is a brief discussion of other voluntary health agencies. Because of limitations of space, however, many worthwhile organizations have had to be omitted.

Accident Prevention

The National Safety Council, 444 North Michigan Avenue, Chicago, Illinois 60611, was founded in 1913 to improve factory safety but soon broadened its activities to preventing every type of accident. The Council is now composed of groups and individuals from every part of the popúlation: business, industry, government, education, religion, labor, and law. Its main efforts are devoted to building strong support for official safety programs at the national, state, and community levels in specific areas, such as traffic, labor, and home.

The Council believes that practically all accidents can be prevented with the application of the right safeguards. These safeguards include public education and awareness of danger, enforcement of safety laws and regulations, and improved design standards for machines, farm equipment, and motor vehicles.

It maintains the world's largest library of accident prevention materials, distributes a wide variety of safety literature, and issues awards for outstanding safety achievements. It also serves as a national and international clearing house of information about the causes of accidents and how they can be prevented.

In addition to campaigning for increased safety legislation on the national and state level, the Council's current programs include a defensive driving course, which provides effective adult driver training on a mass scale; a safety training institute; environmental and occupational health and "Right-to-Know" educational materials; and several approaches to the alcohol and driving problem.

Its publication, *Family Safety and Health,* has record circulation of almost two million readers, and its manual called *Fundamentals of Industrial Hygiene* provides more than 1,000 pages of material essential to the safety of factory workers.

The Council in recent years has expanded its safety promotion work to include both on- and off-the-job safety for workers and their families, as well as 24-hour-a-day safety for all persons in all activities.

Alcoholism

The National Council on Alcoholism, 12 W. 21st Street, New York, New York 10010, is the only national voluntary health agency founded to combat alcoholism as a disease by an extensive program on the professional and community level. The Council is completely independent of Alcoholics Anonymous, although the two organizations cooperate fully.

In 184 cities where the Council has affiliates, alcoholism information centers have been established that provide referral services for alcoholics and their families as well as educational materials for all segments of the community, including physicians and nurses, the clergy, the courts, social workers, and welfare agencies. Local affiliates also help to develop labor-management programs that provide help for employees who suffer from the disease.

The NCA also sponsors research, professional training, and legislative action. Its publications department distributes more than 100 different books and pamphlets divided into special categories. Information on this literature as well as on all aspects of the Council's programs is available to anyone who writes to the national headquarters or contacts the nearest local affiliate.

Arthritis

The Arthritis Foundation, 1314 Spring Street N.W., Atlanta, Georgia 30309, was established to help arthritis sufferers and their physicians through programs of research, patient services, public health information, and education on the professional and popular level. Its long-term goal is to find the cause, prevention, and cure for the nation's number one crippling disease.

The Foundation operates local chapters throughout the United States whose chief concern is the patient who has or might have arthritits. These chapters are centers for information about the disease itself and also serve as referral centers for treatment facilities. In addition, they distribute literature and sponsor forums on the latest developments in research and patient care.

Some chapters support arthritis clinics and home care programs; most conduct patient self-help programs such as discussion groups and exercise classes. Parent groups are often maintained for parents of children with arthritis.

Two special groups work within the Foundation: the Arthritis Health Professions Association which devotes itself to continuing education for health professionals caring for arthritis patients and the American Juvenile Arthritis Organization for those with a special interest in arthritis in children. A major part of the Foundation's work at the national level is providing funds for fellowships to young physicians and scientists so that they may continue their work in arthritis research and in funding through annual grants research at major institutions throughout the United States.

Cancer

The American Cancer Society, 90 Park Avenue, New York, New York 10016, was established in 1913 by a small group of physicians and volunteer workers to inform the public about the possibility of saving lives through the early diagnosis and treatment of cancer. The Society now has 58 incorporated divisions, one in each state plus one in the District of Columbia and seven other metropolitan areas, devoted to the control and eradication of cancer. In addition to the physicians, research scientists, and other professional workers engaged in the Society's activities, more than two million volunteers are connected with its many programs.

The American Cancer Society conducts widespread campaigns to educate the public in the importance of annual medical checkups so that cancerous symptoms can be detected while they are still curable. Such checkups should include an examination of the rectum and colon and, for women, examination of the breasts and a Pap test for the detection of uterine cancer.

In another of its campaigns, the Society emphasizes the link between cigarette smoking and lung cancer. It also sponsors an extensive program to persuade teenagers not to start smoking. During its annual April Crusade against Cancer, the Society distributes approximately 40 million copies of a leaflet containing lifesaving information on early detection of cancer.

On the professional level, the major objective of the Society is to make every physician's office a cancer-detection center. To achieve this goal, it publishes a variety of literature, offers refresher courses, sponsors seminars, and cooperates closely with local and state medical societies and health departments on the diagnosis and treatment of cancer. It also arranges national and international conferences for the exchange of information on the newest cancer-fighting techniques, and finances a million-dollar-a-year clinical fellowship program for young physicians.

Among its special services to patients are sponsorship of the International Association of Laryngectomies, for people who have lost their voices to cancer; and Reach to Recovery, a program for women who have had treatment for breast cancer and who need support and guidance to return to normal living. On the community level, the American Cancer Society operates a counseling service for cancer patients and their families, referring them to the proper medical facilities and social agencies for treatment and care. Through its "loan closets," it provides sickroom necessities, hospital beds, medical dressings, and so on.

Some local divisions offer home care programs through the services of the Visiting Nurse Association or a similar agency. Although the Society does not operate medical facilities, treat patients, or pay physicians' fees, some of the chapters support cancer detection programs and professionally supervised rehabilitation services.

Cerebral Palsy

The United Cerebral Palsy Associations, 66 East 34th Street, New York, New York 10016, founded in 1948 by a small group of concerned parents, now has 203 affiliates across the country where those who have the condition may obtain treatment referral, therapy, and education. The Associations also play an important role in vocational training, job placement programs, housing, and recreational services.

The Research and Educational Foundation of this organization supports studies investigating possible causes of cerebral palsy. The Foundation also gives grants to universities and medical schools for research into the causes and prevention of cerebral palsy and new methods of therapy, for training medical and other professional personnel in the management of this condition.

Cystic Fibrosis

The Cystic Fibrosis Foundation, 6931 Arlington Road, Bethesda, Maryland 20814, was organized in 1955 by a group of concerned parents whose children were born with this lung disease. The Foundation now concerns itself with all serious lung ailments of children regardless of their medical names, and it engages in a broad program of research, medical education, public information, and the sponsorship of diagnostic and treatment centers.

The Foundation's 60 local chapters offer advice and information to parents of children with severe lung disease, and have direct connections with the 125 Cystic Fibrosis Centers throughout the country. They refer patients to sources of financial aid, make arrangements for the purchase of drugs at a discount, and lend home treatment equipment to families who cannot afford to buy it.

The national organization makes grants for research activities, conducts professional conferences, and publishes literature for physicians and the general public on various aspects of childhood lung diseases.

Diabetes

The American Diabetes Association, National Service Center, P.O. Box 25757, 1660 Duke Street, Alexandria, Virginia 22313, was established as a professional society in 1940. In recent years it has enlarged its scope so that it currently has 700 affiliated local chapters throughout the country that promote the creation of better understanding of diabetes among patients and their families; the exchange of knowledge among physicians and other scientists; the spreading of accurate information to the general public about early recognition and supervision of the disease; and the sponsorship of basic research.

Since 1948, the American Diabetes Association has conducted an annual Diabetes Detection Drive supported by widespread publicity in all news media. During this drive, approximately three million testing kits are provided to state and county medical societies to facilitate the early detection and prompt treatment of the disorder. This annual activity hopes to find the estimated 1,600,000 people who are unaware that they have diabetes.

Among the Association's publications of special interest to diabetics and their families are the *ADA Forecast,* a national magazine that presents news items on research and treatment; *Meal Planning with Exchange Lists,* prepared with the cooperation of the American Dietetic Association and the U.S. Public Health Services; and *A Cookbook for Diabetics,* which contains attractive recipes for meals that can be served to diabetics.

Other activities of the Association inlcude encouraging the employment of diabetics and providing special groups such as teachers, police, and social agencies with information on the condition. It also established a classification of the disease according to its severity. Guidelines on emergency medical care and the scientific journal *Diabetes* are available to physicians.

Drug Abuse

The American Social Health Association, which was organized originally to combat the spread of venereal disease, expanded its program in 1960 to include drug abuse education. For information about its activities in this field, see below under "Sexually Transmitted Diseases."

Eye Diseases

The National Society to Prevent Blindness, 79 Madison Avenue, New York, New York 10016, was founded in 1908 to reduce the number of cases of infants born with impaired sight. In subsequent years, it merged with the American Association for the Conservation of Vision and the Ophthalmological Foundation. The Society is now concerned with investigating all causes of blindness and supports measures and community services that will eliminate them. It also distributes information on the proper care and use of the eyes.

The organization's first and most significant victory was the adoption of laws by almost all states requiring that silver nitrate solution be routinely dropped into the eyes of all newborn babies to counteract the possibility of congenital blindness. This resulted in a dramatic drop in the number of children suffering from eye impairment dating from birth.

For almost half a century, the Society has actively campaigned to reduce the number of people suffering from glaucoma, one of the leading causes of blindness in the United States. It has also conducted a national program to educate the elderly in the ease, safety, and advantages of surgery for cataracts, the leading cause of blindness among the aged.

Since 1926, the Society has been conducting preschool vision screening programs administered by teams that travel from big cities to isolated rural communities. Current activities also include research into the cause, treatment, and prevention of eye diseases leading to blindness; assembling data and publishing reports; cooperating with community agencies to improve eye health; promoting conditions in schools and industry to safeguard vision; and advocating eye examinations in early childhood so that disorders can be properly and promptly corrected.

Family Planning

Planned Parenthood Federation of America, 810 Seventh Avenue, New York, New York 10019, is the nation's oldest and largest voluntary family planning organization. Tracing its origins to 1916, when Margaret Sanger founded the first U.S. birth control clinic in Brooklyn, New York, Planned Parenthood maintains that every individual has the fundamental right to choose when or whether to have a child.

Planned Parenthood has five key goals:

- To increase the availability and accessibility of high quality and affordable reproductive health care services and information, especially for underserved groups
- To reduce adolescent pregnancy and unwanted births to teens
- To meet the challenge of changes in health care delivery systems and maintain high-quality, efficiently run, and creative Planned Parenthood programs
- To further Planned Parenthood's role in the provision of education of human sexuality, reproduction, and population, and on the bioethical and legal implications of reproductive technology
- To increase access to safe and effective methods of voluntary fertility regulation for individuals in developing countries

Each year, more than three million individuals in 47 states and the District of Columbia obtain medical, educational, and counseling services through more than 735 clinics operated by Planned Parenthood's 186 affiliates. The organization is active in more than 100 developing countries throughout the world. In addition, Planned Parenthood conducts clinical research, provides professional training of health and education personnel, and serves as a resource to health agencies, government agencies at the state and federal levels, legislators and other policy makers, and the media.

Heart Disease

The American Heart Association, 7320 Greenville Avenue, Dallas, Texas 75231, was founded in 1924 as a professional organization of cardiologists. It was reorganized in 1948 as a national voluntary health agency to promote a program of education, research, and community service in the interests of reducing premature death and disability caused by diseases of the heart and blood vessels. The complex of heart disorders, including atherosclerosis, stroke, high blood pressure, kidney diseases, rheumatic fever, and congenital heart disturbances, is by far the leading cause of death in the United States.

Since its first Annual Heart Fund Campaign in 1949, the Association has contributed more than $150 million to research and has been a major factor in the reduction of cardiovascular mortality statistics. It has spent more than $2 million since 1959 studying human heart transplantation procedures, and has contributed to the development of an artificial heart, plastic heart valves, and synthetic arteries.

Public and professional education programs designed to reduce the risk of heart attack through avoidance of cigarette smoking, obesity, and foods high in cholesterol are conducted on a nationwide and community level by the Association's affiliates throughout the country. The local chapters are also engaged in service programs for rheumatic fever prevention, stroke rehabilitation, school health, cardiopulmonary resuscitation, and industrial health. In addition, they conduct information and referral services for patients and their families.

The American Heart Association publishes many technical and professional journals as well as material designed for the general public.

Hemophilia

The National Hemophilia Foundation, 110 Green Street, Room 406, New York, New York 10012, was established in 1948 to serve the needs of hemophiliacs and their families by ensuring the availability of treatment and rehabilitation facilities. It is estimated that there are as many as 100,000 males suffering from what is popularly known as "bleeder's disease," an inherited condition passed from mothers to sons.

The long-term goal of the Foundation is to develop a national program of research and clinical study that will provide new information about early diagnosis and effective treatment of the disorder as well as trained professional personnel to administer patient care.

The development in recent years of blood-clotting concentrates is the most important advance to date in the treatment of the disease. This development, supported in part by the Foundation's 48 chapters, makes it possible for patients to have elective surgery and dental work, and to eliminate much of the pain, crippling, and hospitalization of those suffering from hemophilia.

The need for blood supplies from which to extract the clotting factor caused the Foundation to embark on an extensive campaign for blood donations. For this purpose, it has been working closely since 1968 with the American Red Cross and the American Association of Blood Banks. It also maintains close ties with various laboratories and research groups in the development of more powerful concentrates that can be manufactured and sold at the lowest possible cost.

The organization's activities include a national network of facilities with blood banks, clinics, and treatment centers as well as referral services. It has also established a Behavioral Science Department to explore the nonmedical aspects of hemophiliacs' problems, such as education, vocational guidance, and psychological needs.

Kidney Disease

The National Kidney Foundation, Two Park Avenue, New York, New York 10016, formerly the National Nephrosis Foundation, was founded in 1950 by a group of parents whose children had a disease with no cure—nephrosis. The ultimate goal was the total eradication of all diseases of the kidney and urinary tract. Today, although there remains no cure for nephrosis, the disease is almost totally treatable. In the past two decades the National Kidney Foundation and its 50 affiliates nationwide have supported more than $20 million in research to find the answers to kidney and urinary tract related diseases.

The National Kidney Foundation and its affiliates sponsor a wide variety of programs in treatment, service, education, and prevention that are designed to aid the patient in the community. Examples of some affiliate programs include: information and referral programs for patients and their families, drug banks, support groups, summer camp programs for children on dialysis and transplantations, transportation services, counseling and screening, and direct financial assistance to needy patients.

The National Kidney Foundation seeks continually to increase the number of organs available for transplantation through its nationwide Organ Donor Program. To date, more than 50 million donor cards have been distributed by the Foundation and its affiliates. Distribution of public and professional educational materials continues to heighten public awareness of organ donation and the "Gift of Life" it can provide to thousands of people waiting for a kidney transplant.

Mental Health

The National Mental Health Association, 1021 Prince Street, Alexandria, Virginia 22314, was founded in 1909 to work toward the improved care and treatment of people with mental illnesses, the promotion of mental health, and the prevention of mental disorders. The original National Committee for Mental Hygiene merged with the National Mental Health Foundation and the Psychiatric Foundation in 1950 to create the organization as it now stands.

The association implements its service programs through its 650 affiliates (local chapters and larger state divisions) across the country. These mental health associations tailor their efforts to the needs of their communities.

The National Mental Health Association is composed of one million volunteers and supporters who have a keen interest in mental health. They include family members whose loved ones have been affected by mental illnesses, current or former consumers, mental health professionals, and lay citizens.

Recent and ongoing activities include:

- Coordinated a national coalition to address the needs of people with mental illnesses who are homeless.
- Serves as a prime source of referral and educational information on mental illnesses and mental health issues through the NMHA Mental Health Information Center.
- Assists local and state MHA affiliates in serving communities through patient and family support groups, housing programs, suicide-prevention hotlines, and school mental health education programs.
- Helped extend the civil rights protection of the 8th and 14th Amendments to the U.S. Constitution to the mentally disabled by representing persons with severe mental illnesses before the Supreme Court.
- Specified a "state-of-the-art" program to prevent severe mental and emotional disabilities in a landmark 1986 report by its National Commission on the Prevention of Mental-Emotional Disabilities.
- Serves as the public-interest policy voice for mental health issues in the Congress and state legislatures.

Multiple Sclerosis

The National Multiple Sclerosis Society, 205 East 42nd Street, New York, New York 10017, was founded in 1946 with the primary goal of supporting research on this chronic neurological disease whose cause and cure are unknown. Some 250,000 Americans are estimated to have multiple sclerosis (MS).

Research aimed at finding the cause and methods of arresting MS is being conducted worldwide. In 1985 the Society spent more than $5.4 million on grants and fellowships, bringing its cumulative research expenditures since inception to $95.6 million.

From the beginning the Society has made every effort to increase professional and public awareness of the symptoms of MS and the best ways of treating them. This is done through a network of 139 chapters and branches and some 50,000 active members. The chapters, which are either affiliated with or support 82 MS clinics around the country, provide home and hospital visits, recreational programs, referrals for medical care, job counseling, and other services. The chapters also arrange educational programs for physicians and social workers as well as for patients and their families.

The national office distributes publications for physicians and the interested public, including guides for the development of patient services and a quarterly magazine, *Inside MS*. Films, slide presentations, videocassettes and audiocassettes are available for purchase or loan.

Physical Disabilities

The National Easter Seal Society, 2023 West Odgen Avenue, Chicago, Illinois 60612, has grown from its pioneering origins in 1919 to a national organization that serves more than one million disabled people of all ages. Among its network of facilities are 83 comprehensive rehabilitation centers in 25 states; 131 treatment and diagnostic centers in 28 states; and vocational training workshops, residential camps, special education programs, and transportation services in many different parts of the country.

Because many crippled children and adults in rural areas and small communities are unaware of the services available to them, the Society gives top priority to publicizing its information, referral, and follow-up activities. In recent years, it has also established mobile treatment units in hospitals and nursing homes in rural areas.

Other innovative activities include screening and testing programs to detect hearing loss in newborns and learning disabilities in preschool children, and providing treatment and referral for those who are disabled by respiratory diseases.

The Society collaborates with federal and professional agencies in all programs designed to eliminate architectural barriers to the disabled, and was instrumental in the enactment of legislation making it mandatory that all buildings constructed with government funds be fully and easily accessible to the handicapped. It also initiates and supports significant studies in rehabilitation procedures as well as scientific research in bone transplant techniques.

Extensive literature is distributed to professionals, the public, parents, and employers. It also assembles special educational packets for parents of the handicapped.

Sexually Transmitted Diseases

The American Social Health Association, 260 Sheridan Avenue, Suite 307, Palo Alto, California 94306, was organized in 1912 to promote the control of venereal disease and to combat prostitution. Since 1960, it has also concerned itself with problems relating to drug dependence and abuse. In the mid-1980s the Association faced new challenges in the field of sexually transmitted diseases (STDs) while also developing new strategies to augment and complement existing AIDS information programs, promote attention to chlamydia, the most widespread STD in the United States, exert influence in Congress for additional federal funding for STD prevention and control programs, and place STD information in the hands of high-school students.

The Association is in close touch with government agencies such as the Public Health Service, the National Institutes of Health, and the various branches of the armed forces, as well as the Federal Bureau of Narcotics, the Children's Bureau, and the Office of Education. Through these channels, it promotes its program for STD education in the schools and for research toward the discovery of an immunizing vaccine against syphilis and gonorrhea.

In the drug field, it is the major national voluntary respository for information and consultation, and maintains the world's most comprehensive collection of source workshops, residential camps, special education programs, and materials on the misuse of narcotics, barbiturates, and the like. It constantly helps communities in diagnosing their problems and produces a number of publications for teachers, guidance counselors, and youth workers.

The Association's original sex education program has been broadened to include all aspects of family life. In literature, lectures, and conferences, it stresses the importance of introducing family life education into the curriculum of elementary and secondary schools and of establishing training programs on this subject in teachers' colleges. These efforts have resulted in the inclusion of family life education in an increasing number of school systems throughout the United States.

Tuberculosis and Respiratory Diseases

The American Lung Association, 1740 Broadway, New York, New York 10019, is the direct descendant of the first voluntary health organization to be formed in the United States. In 1904, when the National Association for the Study and Prevention of Tuberculosis was organized, this disease was the country's leading cause of death. Since 1973, with the sharp increase in the problems relating to smoking and air pollution, the association has been known by its present name, which was adopted to reflect the broader scope of its activities.

It now concerns itself not only with the elimination of tuberculosis but with chronic and disabling conditions, such as emphysema, and with acute diseases of the respiratory system, such as influenza. Through its 1,500 affiliates and nationwide state organizations, it is actively engaged in campaigns against smoking and air pollution.

The early endeavor of the association to have tuberculosis included among the reportable diseases was accomplished state by state, and since the 1920s all states have required that every case in the country be brought to the attention of local health officials.

Public awareness of better care and the development of effective drugs have dramatically reduced the number of TB patients, but the association continues to concern itself with the fact that provisional data indicate that there are still about 22,000 new cases each year.

Through its local affiliates, the American Lung Association initiates special campaigns to combat smoking and air pollution, using radio and television announcements, car stickers, posters, and pamphlets, as well as films and exhibits. Educational materials on respiratory diseases are regularly distributed by the national office to local associations for physicians, patients, and the general public. Funds raised by the annual Christmas Seal drive also support research and medical education fellowships.

Other Voluntary Health Agencies

In addition to those voluntary health agencies that are members of the National Health Council, many other organizations function on a national scale and offer specialized services as well as literature and guidance to professionals, patients, parents, and concerned families. The following is a partial list.

Alcoholics Anonymous World Services, Box 459, Grand Central Station, New York, New York 10163, is a fellowship of men and women who share their experiences and give each other support in overcoming the problem of alcoholism. Chapters exist throughout the country and offer referral services, literature, and information about special hospital programs.

Al-Anon Family Group Headquarters, Inc., One Park Avenue, New York, New York 10016, is not affiliated with Alcoholics Anonymous, but cooperates closely with it. Al-Anon, which includes Alateen for younger members, is a primary community resource and self-help fellowship for the families and friends of alcoholics. Members share their experiences, strength, and hope at regularly held meetings, and learn to cope with the effects of being close to an alcoholic. Headquarters registers, services, and provides literature to 25,000 groups worldwide, of which 18,000 are in the United States.

Asthma and Allergy Foundation of America, 1835 K Street, N.W., Suite P-900, Washington, D.C. 20006, was established to help solve all health problems related to allergic diseases by sponsoring research and treatment facilities. It also grants scholarships to medical students specializing in the study of allergy.

Alzheimer's Disease and Related Disorders Association, 70 E. Lake Street, Suite 600, Chicago, Illinois 60601, was founded in 1980 to heighten public awareness of this degenerative brain disorder, provide support for patients and their families, aid research efforts, advocate for legislation that responds to the needs of Alzheimer's disease patients and their family members, and commemorate National Alzheimer's Disease Awareness Month each November. The network includes more than 140 chapters and affiliates across the country representing over 1,000 Family Support Groups. To obtain the most up-to-date information on Alzheimer's disease legislation, research, and referral to local chapters, call the Association's toll-free information and referral number, 800-621-0379 (in Illinois only, 800-572-6037) or write to the Association.

The *American Foundation for AIDS Research* (AmFAR), 40 W. 57th Street, New York, New York 10019, was created in the fall of 1985 as a result of the unification of two not-for-profit public foundations: the AIDS Medical Foundation (AMF), incorporated in the State of New York in April 1983; and the National AIDS Research Foundation (NARF), incorporated in the State of California in August 1985. AmFar is an independent, national organization whose directors, committee members, and staff are professionals in the field of AIDS.

The Foundation has two main missions. First, it supports and facilitates laboratory and clinical research projects selected on the basis of scientific merit and relevance to achieve an understanding of the pathogenesis of AIDS, its prevention through the use of a vaccine, and its treatment. Second, the Foundation works to develop data and to serve as a source of accurate and up-to-date information about an epidemic that has profound psychosocial repercussions in our society.

American Foundation for the Blind, 15 West 16th Street, New York, New York 10011, is a national nonprofit organization working with local and national services to improve the quality of life for all blind and visually impaired persons. It stocks over 600 different consumer products and publications and has recorded and produced almost 34 million talking book records for the Library of Congress.

Through its staff of national consultants and its six regional offices, the Foundation maintains a direct liaison with state, regional, and local agencies.

The *Association for Voluntary Surgical Contraception,* 122 East 42nd Street, New York, New York 10168, was founded in 1937 to promote the right of each individual to choose sterilization as a method of birth control. A nonprofit membership organization, the AVSC has increasingly collaborated with governmental and private sector providers to ensure effective access to sterilization facilities. The Association also sponsors training, education, and program support for sterilization and family planning counselors and others; prepares annual estimates of male and female voluntary sterilizations in the United States; issues a quarterly newsletter, the *AVSC News,* and other publications, and initiates and monitors research into medical, legal, psychological, ethical, and public health aspects of voluntary sterilization.

The Epilepsy Foundation of America, 4351 Garden City Drive, Landover, Maryland 20785, is the result of a merger in 1967 of two similar organizations. At present, the Foundation has 85 local affiliates that provide information, referral services, and counseling. It conducts a research grant program for medical and psychosocial investigation and distributes a wide variety of literature on request to physicians, teachers, employers, and the interested public on such subjects as anticonvulsant drugs, insurance, driving laws, and emergency treatment. The national office also maintains an extensive research library.

The Leukemia Society of America, 733 Third Avenue, New York, New York 10017, was organized in 1949 and now has 56 chapters in 28 states. It supports research in the causes, control, and eventual eradication of the disease that, though commonly thought of as a disorder of the blood, is in fact a disorder of the bone marrow, lymph nodes, and spleen, which manufacture blood. The society has a continuing program of education through special publications directed to physicians, nurses, and the public.

Through its local affiliates, it conducts patient-aid services that provide counseling, transportation, and—to those who need financial assistance—drugs, blood transfusions, and laboratory facilities.

The Muscular Dystrophy Association, Inc., 810 Seventh Avenue, New York, New York 10019, has as a primary goal the scientific conquest of muscular dystrophy and related neuromuscular diseases. The Association supports scientific investigators worldwide. In addition, through its 170 chapter affiliates nationwide, MDA provides a comprehensive patient and community services program to individuals diagnosed with any one of 40 neuromuscular disorders. The Association maintains a network of some 240 MDA clinics coast to coast to provide diagnostic services and therapeutic and rehabilitative follow-up care as well as genetic, vocational, and social service counseling to patients and their families. MDA also sponsors a summer camping program for youngsters aged 6 to 21 as well as adult outings, with activities geared to the special needs of those with neuromuscular diseases.

The Association for Retarded Citizens of the United States, P.O. Box 6109, Arlington, Texas 76006, established in 1950, is the nation's largest voluntary organization specifically devoted to promoting the welfare of children and adults with mental retardation. It is estimated that there are six million such persons in the United States. Through its 1,500 affiliates the association conducts and supports research, sponsors employment programs, advocates for progressive public policy, and works for better community services. Counseling and referral services, as well as extensive literature for professionals and concerned families, are available on request.

The March of Dimes Birth Defects Foundation, 1275 Mamaroneck Avenue, White Plains, New York 10605, was founded in 1938 to combat infantile paralysis (polio). In the 30 years since the conquest of polio, through the development of the Salk and Sabin polio vaccines, the March of Dimes has dedicated itself to the prevention of birth defects, the nation's number one child health problem. It does this through programs of birth defects research and medical service and education that provide new knowledge and understanding of birth defects and their prevention. More than a quarter-million babies are born with one or more of the 3,000 known birth defects each year. The Foundation also has established the Salk Institute in La Jolla, California, directed by Dr. Jonas Salk, for the purpose of carrying on basic research in life processes to discover what causes birth defects and other diseases.

Special Health Services and Agencies

Many factors have contributed to the growth of the American system of health services. Specialists in various medical specialties have tried to meet needs for new types of health care. Medical care has become so effective that individual life expectancy has increased enormously; as one result, the number of Americans aged 65 and older tripled in the three-quarters of a century between 1900 and 1975. As the population of the United States has grown older, in percentage terms, the problems of the aged have received more attention. New methods and devices have been developed for the care and assistance of the ill or disabled of any age.

Special health services and agencies help to fill such needs. Many older persons have utilized the services of trained individuals who make survival possible—sometimes at home—or slow down the rate of deterioration. Other institutions and agencies perform simple maintenance tasks for the aged or the seriously ill or handicapped, or help with rehabilitation. Social service agencies and groups with health roles, for example, provide adult day care, homemaker assistance, and home health services that may include the following:

- Part-time or occasional nursing care, often under the supervision of a registered nurse
- Physical, occupational, or speech therapy
- Medical social services that help the patient and his or her family to adjust to the social and emotional conditions accompanying illness or disability of any kind
- Assistance from a home health aide, including help with such tasks as bathing and going to the bathroom, taking medications, exercising, and getting into and out of bed
- Under some circumstances, medical attention from interns or residents in training

35

Medical Emergencies

Anyone attempting to deal with a medical emergency will do so with considerably more confidence if he has a clear notion of the order of importance of various problems. Over and above all technical knowledge about such things as tourniquets or cardiac massage is the ability of the rescuer to keep a cool head so that he can make the right decisions and delegate tasks to others who wish to be helpful.

Cessation of Breathing

The medical emergency that requires prompt attention before any others is cessation of breathing. No matter what other injuries are involved, artificial respiration must be administered immediately to anyone suffering from respiratory arrest.

To determine whether a person is breathing naturally, place your cheek as near as possible to the victim's mouth and nose. While you are feeling and listening for evidence of respiration, watch the victim's chest and upper abdomen to see if they rise and fall. If respiratory arrest is indicated, begin artificial respiration immediately.

Time is critical; a human body has only about a four-minute reserve supply of oxygen in its tissues, although some persons have been revived after being submerged in water for ten minutes or more. Do not waste time moving the victim to a more comfortable location unless his position is life threatening.

If more than one person is available, the second person should summon a physician. A second rescuer can also assist in preparing the victim for artificial respiration by helping to loosen clothing around the neck, chest, and waist, and by inspecting the mouth for false teeth, chewing gum, or other objects that could block the flow of air. The victim's tongue must be pulled forward before artificial respiration begins.

Normal breathing should start after not more than 15 minutes of artificial respiration. If it doesn't, you should continue the procedure for at least two hours, alternating, if possible, with other persons to maintain maximum efficiency. Medical experts have defined normal breathing as eight or more breaths per minute; if breathing resumes but slackens to a rate of fewer than eight breaths per minute, or if breathing stops suddenly for more than 30 seconds, continue artificial respiration.

Mouth-to-Mouth and Mouth-to-Nose Artificial Respiration

Following is a description of the techniques used to provide mouth-to-mouth or mouth-to-nose artificial respiration. These are the preferred methods of artificial respiration because they move a greater volume of air into a victim's lungs than any alternative method.

After quickly clearing the victim's mouth and throat of obstacles, tilt the victim's head back as far as possible, with the chin up and neck stretched to ensure an open passage of air to the lungs. If mouth-to-mouth breathing is employed, pull the lower jaw of the victim open with one hand, inserting your thumb between the victim's teeth, and pinch the nostrils with the other to prevent air leakage through the nose. If using the mouth-to-nose technique, hold one hand over the mouth to seal it against air leakage.

Next, open your own mouth and

Mouth-to-Mouth Respiration

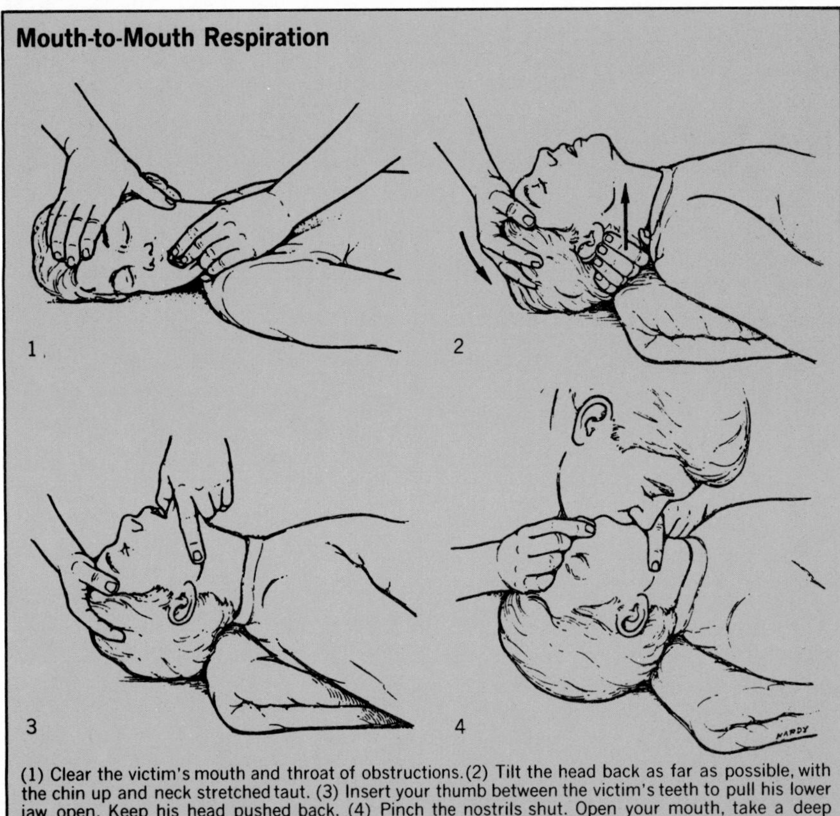

(1) Clear the victim's mouth and throat of obstructions. (2) Tilt the head back as far as possible, with the chin up and neck stretched taut. (3) Insert your thumb between the victim's teeth to pull his lower jaw open. Keep his head pushed back. (4) Pinch the nostrils shut. Open your mouth, take a deep breath, and, placing your mouth firmly against the victim's, blow forcefully. Repeat every 3 or 4 seconds.

take a deep breath. Then blow forcefully into the victim's mouth (or nose) until you can see the chest rise. Quickly remove your mouth and listen for normal exhalation sounds from the victim. If you hear gurgling sounds, try to move the jaw higher because the throat may not be stretched open properly. Continue blowing forcefully into the victim's mouth (or nose) at a rate of once every three or four seconds. (For infants, do not blow forcefully; blow only small puffs of air from your cheeks.)

If the victim's stomach becomes distended, it may be a sign that air is being blown into the stomach; press firmly with one hand on the upper abdomen to push the air out of the stomach.

If you are hesitant about direct physical contact of the lips, make a ring with the index finger and thumb of the hand being used to hold the victim's chin in position. Place the ring of fingers firmly about the victim's mouth; the outside of the thumb may at the same time be positioned to seal the nose against air leakage. Then blow the air into the victim's mouth through the finger-thumb ring. Direct lip-to-lip contact can also be avoided by placing a piece of gauze or other clean porous cloth over the victim's mouth.

Severe Bleeding

If the victim is not suffering from respiration failure or if breathing has been restored, severe bleeding is the second most serious emergency to attend to. Such bleeding occurs when either an artery or a vein has been severed. Arterial blood is bright red and spurts rather than flows from the body, sometimes in very large amounts. It is also more difficult to control than blood from a vein, which can be recognized by its dark red color and steady flow.

Emergency Treatment

The quickest and most effective way to stop bleeding is by direct pressure on the wound. If heavy layers of sterile gauze are not available, use a clean handkerchief, or a clean piece of material torn from a shirt, slip, or sheet to cover the wound. Then place the fingers or the palm of the hand directly over the bleeding area. The pressure must be *firm and constant* and should be interrupted only when the blood has soaked through the dressing. *Do not remove the soaked dressing.* Cover it as quickly as possible with additional new layers. When the blood stops seeping through to the surface of the dressing, secure it with strips of cloth until the victim can receive medical attention. This procedure is almost always successful in stopping blood flow from a vein.

If direct pressure doesn't stop ar-

Pressure Points

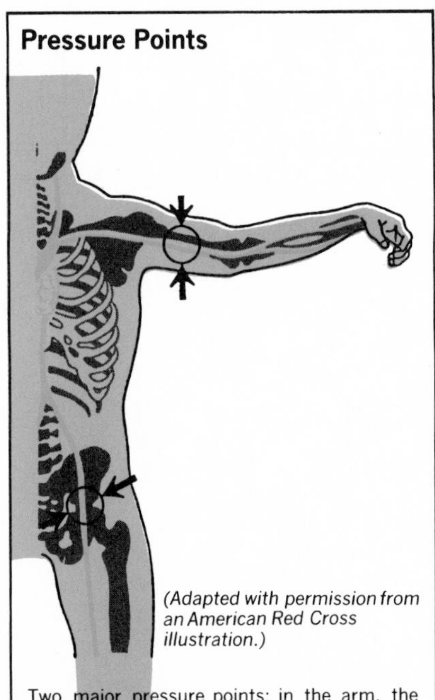

(Adapted with permission from an American Red Cross illustration.)

Two major pressure points: in the arm, the brachial artery; in the leg, the femoral artery. Continue to apply direct pressure and elevate the wounded part while utilizing pressure points to stop blood flow.

Pressure Points

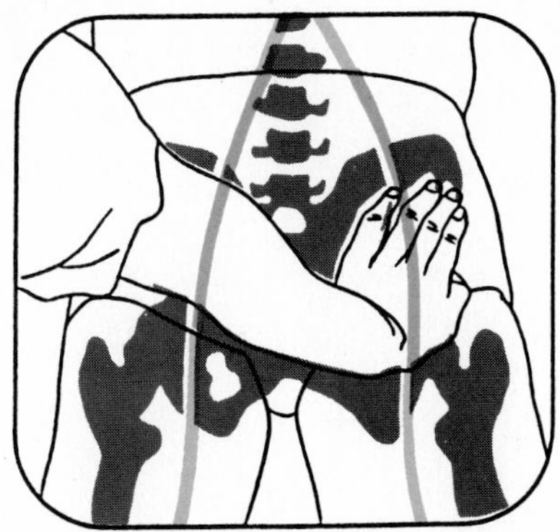

(Top) Use the femoral artery for control of severe bleeding from an open leg wound. Place the victim flat on his back, and put the heel of your hand directly over the pressure point. Apply pressure by forcing the artery against the pelvic bone. *(Bottom)* Use the brachial artery for control of severe bleeding from an open arm wound. Apply pressure by forcing the artery against the arm bone. Continue to apply direct pressure over the wound, and keep the wounded part elevated.

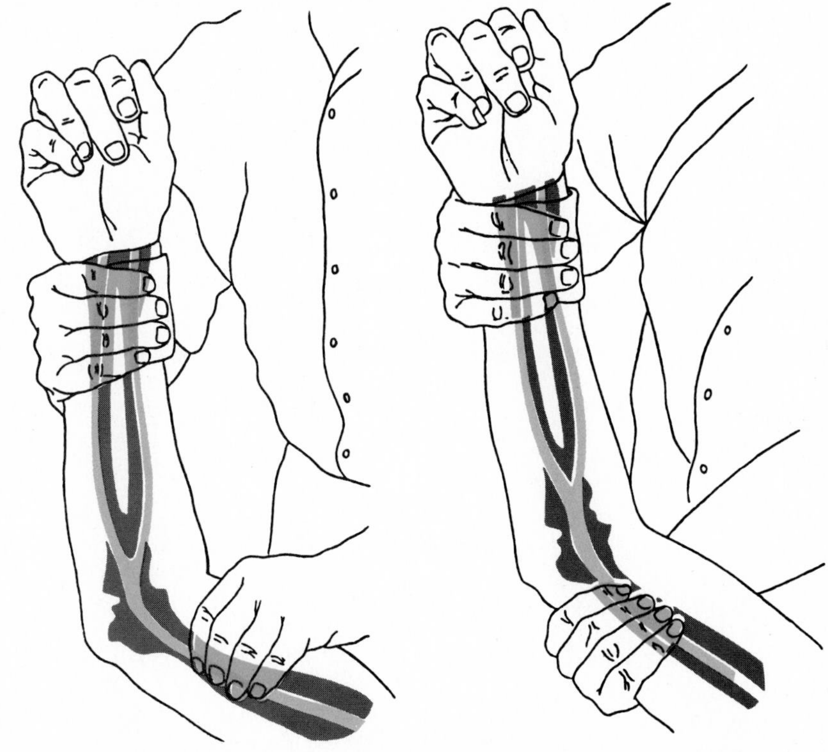

(Adapted with permission from American Red Cross illustrations.)

terial bleeding, two alternatives are possible: pressure by finger or hand on the pressure point nearest the wound, or the application of a tourniquet. No matter what the source of the bleeding, if the wound is on an arm or leg, elevation of the limb as high as is comfortable will reduce the blood flow.

Tourniquets

A tourniquet improperly applied can be an extremely dangerous device, and should only be considered for a hemorrhage that can't be controlled in any other way.

It must be remembered that arterial blood flows away from the heart and that venous blood flows toward the heart. Therefore, while a tourniquet placed on a limb between the site of a wound and the heart may slow or stop arterial bleeding, it may actually increase venous bleeding. By obstructing blood flow in the veins beyond the wound site, the venous blood flowing toward the heart will have to exit from the wound. Thus, the proper application of a tourniquet depends upon an understanding and differentiation of arterial from venous bleeding. Arterial bleeding can be recognized by the pumping action of the blood and by the bright red color of the blood.

Once a tourniquet is applied, it should not be left in place for an excessive period of time, since the tissues in the limb beyond the site of the wound need to be supplied with blood.

Shock

In any acute medical emergency, the possibility of the onset of shock must always be taken into account, especially following the fracture of a large bone, extensive burns, or serious wounds. If untreated, or if treated too late, shock can be fatal.

Shock is an emergency condition in which the circulation of the blood is so disrupted that all bodily functions are affected. It occurs when blood pressure is so low that insufficient blood supply reaches the vital tissues.

Types of Circulatory Shock and Their Causes

- *Low-volume shock* is a condition brought about by so great a loss of blood or blood plasma that the remaining blood is insufficient to fill the whole circulatory system. The blood loss may occur outside the body, as in a hemorrhage caused by injury to an artery or vein, or the loss may be internal because of the blood loss at the site of a major fracture, burn, or bleeding ulcer. Professional treatment involves replacement of blood loss by transfusion.

Arterial Bleeding

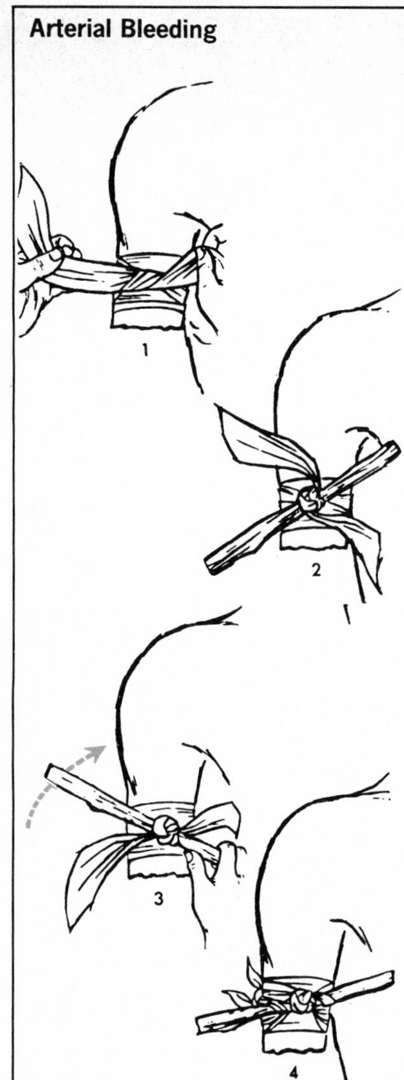

Severe arterial bleeding can be controlled by the correct application of a tourniquet. (1) A long strip of gauze or other material is wrapped twice around the arm or leg above the wound and tied in a half-knot. (2) A stick, called a windlass, is placed over the knot, and the knot is completed. (3) The windlass is turned to tighten the knot and finally, (4) the windlass is secured with the tails of the tourniquet. Improper use of a tourniquet can be very dangerous.

- *Neurogenic shock,* manifested by *fainting,* occurs when the regulating capacity of the nervous system is impaired by severe pain, profound fright, or overwhelming stimulus. This type of shock is usually relieved by having the victim lie down with his head lower than the rest of his body.
- *Allergic shock,* also called *anaphylactic shock,* occurs when the functioning of the blood vessels is disturbed by a person's sensitivity to the injection of a particular foreign substance, as in the case of an insect sting or certain medicines.
- *Septic shock* is brought on by infection from certain bacteria that release a poison which affects the proper functioning of the blood vessels.
- *Cardiac shock* can be caused by any circumstance that affects the pumping action of the heart.

Symptoms

Shock caused by blood loss makes the victim feel restless, thirsty, and cold. He may perspire a great deal, and although his pulse is fast, it is also very weak. His breathing becomes labored and his lips turn blue.

Emergency Treatment

A physician should be called immediately if the onset of shock is suspected. Until medical help is obtained, the following procedures can alleviate some of the symptoms:

1. With a minimum amount of disturbance, arrange the victim so that he is lying on his back with his head somewhat lower than his feet. (**Exception:** If the victim's breathing is difficult, or if he has suffered a head injury or a stroke, keep his body flat but place a pillow or similar cushioning material under his head.) Loosen any clothing that may cause constriction, such as a belt, tie, waistband, shoes. Cover him warmly against possible chill, but see that he isn't too hot.

2. If his breathing is weak and shallow, begin mouth-to-mouth respiration.

3. If he is hemorrhaging, try to control bleeding.

4. When appropriate help and transportation facilities are available, quickly move the victim to the nearest hospital or health facility in order to begin resuscitative measures.

5. *Do not* try to force any food or stimulant into the victim's mouth.

Cardiac Arrest

Cardiac arrest is a condition in which the heart has stopped beating altogether or is beating so weakly or so irregularly that it cannot maintain proper blood circulation.

Common causes of cardiac arrest are heart attack, electric shock, hemorrhage, suffocation, and other forms of respiratory arrest. Symptoms of cardiac arrest are unconsciousness, the absence of respiration and pulse, and the lack of a heartbeat or a heartbeat that is very weak or irregular.

Cardiac Massage

If the victim of a medical emergency manifests signs of cardiac arrest, he should be given cardiac massage at the same time that another rescuer is administering mouth-to-mouth resuscitation. Both procedures can be carried on in the moving vehicle taking him to the hospital.

It is assumed that he is lying down with his mouth clear and his air passage unobstructed. The massage is given in the following way:

1. The heel of one hand with the heel of the other crossed over it should be placed on the bottom third of the breastbone and pressed firmly down with a force of about 80 pounds so that the breastbone moves about two inches toward the spine. Pressure should not be applied directly on the ribs by the fingers.

2. The hands are then relaxed to allow the chest to expand.

3. If one person is doing both the cardiac massage and the mouth-to-mouth respiration, he should stop the massage after every 15 chest compressions and administer two very quick lung inflations to the victim.

4. The rescuer should try to make the rate of cardiac massage simulate restoration of the pulse rate. This is not always easily accomplished, but compression should reach 60 times per minute.

The techniques for administering cardiac massage to children are the same as those used for adults, except that much less pressure should be applied to a child's chest, and, in the case of babies or young children, the pressure should be exerted with the tips of the fingers rather than with the heel of the hand.

Caution

Cardiac massage can be damaging if applied improperly. Courses in emergency medical care offered by the American Red Cross and other groups are well worth taking. In an emergency in which cardiac massage is called for, an untrained person should seek the immediate aid of someone trained in the technique before attempting it himself.

Obstruction in the Windpipe

Many people die each year from choking on food; children incur an additional hazard in swallowing foreign objects. Most of these victims could be saved through quick action by nearly any other person, and without special equipment.

Food choking usually occurs because a bite of food becomes lodged at the back of the throat or at the opening of the trachea, or windpipe. The victim cannot breathe or speak. He may become pale or turn blue before collapsing. Death can occur within four or five minutes. But the lungs of an average person may contain at least one quart of air, inhaled before the start of choking, and that air can be used to unblock the windpipe and save the victim's life.

Finger Probe

If the object can be seen, a quick attempt can be made to remove it by probing with a finger. Use a hooking motion to dislodge the object. Under no circumstances should this method be pursued if it appears that the object is being pushed farther downward rather than being released and brought up.

Back Blows

Give the victim four quick, hard blows with the fist on his back between the shoulder blades. The blows should be given in rapid succession. If the victim is a child, he can be held over the knee while being struck; an adult should lie face down on a bed or table, with the upper half of his body suspended in the direction of the floor so that he can receive the same type of blows. A very small child or infant should be held upside down by the torso or legs and struck much more lightly than an adult.

The Heimlich Maneuver

If the back blows fail to dislodge the obstruction, the Heimlich maneuver should be given without delay. (Back blows may loosen the object even if they fail to dislodge it completely; that is why they are given first.) The lifesaving technique known as the *Heimlich maneuver* (named for Dr. Henry J. Heimlich) works simply by squeezing the volume of air trapped in the victim's lungs. The piece of food literally pops out of the throat as if it were ejected from a squeezed balloon.

To perform the Heimlich maneuver, the rescuer stands behind the victim and grasps his hands firmly over the victim's abdomen, just below the victim's rib cage. The rescuer makes a fist with one hand and places his other hand over the clenched fist. Then, the rescuer forces his fist sharply inward and upward against the victim's diaphragm. This action compresses the lungs within the rib cage. If the food does not pop out on the first try, the maneuver should be repeated until the air passage is unblocked.

Back Blows for Treatment of Strangulation

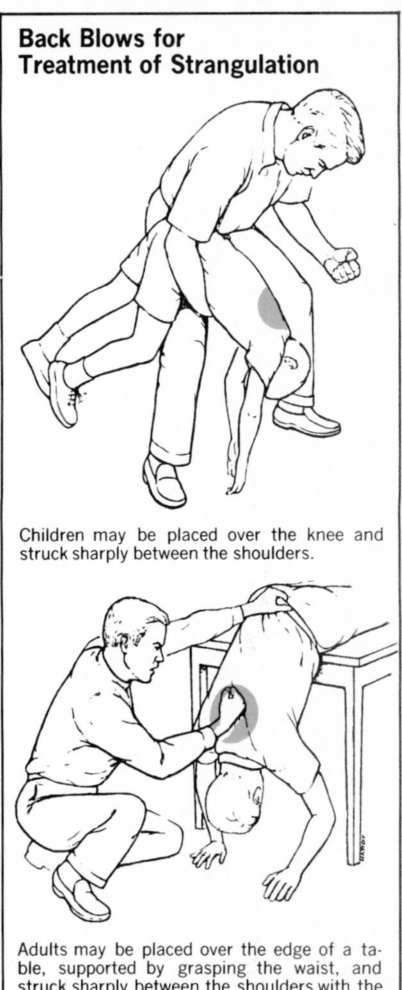

Children may be placed over the knee and struck sharply between the shoulders.

Adults may be placed over the edge of a table, supported by grasping the waist, and struck sharply between the shoulders with the fist.

The Heimlich Maneuver

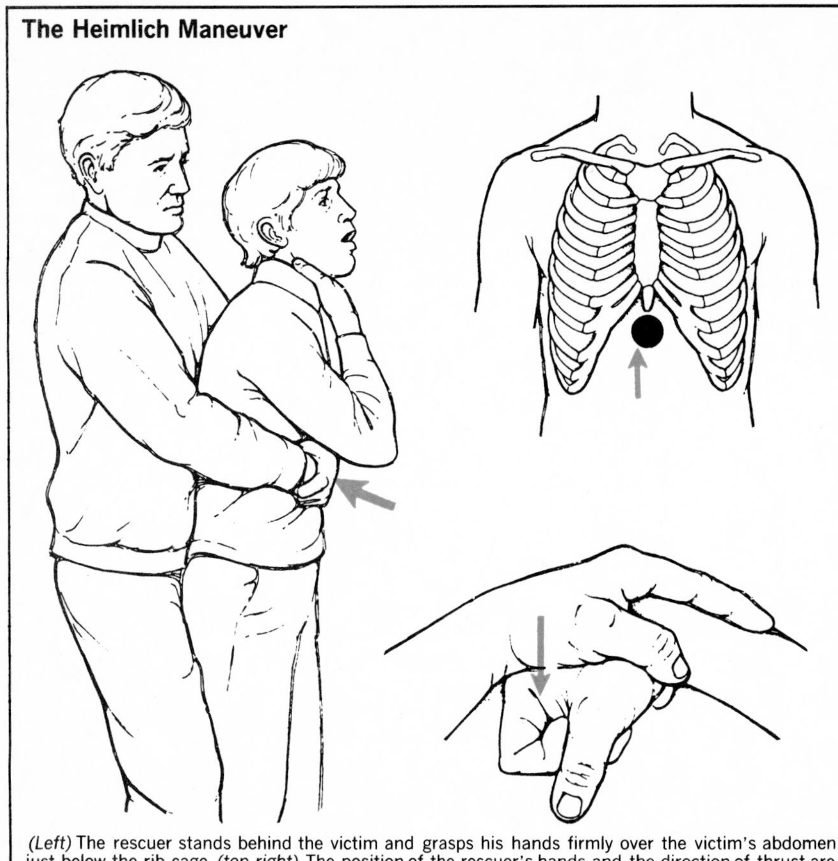

(Left) The rescuer stands behind the victim and grasps his hands firmly over the victim's abdomen just below the rib cage *(top right)*. The position of the rescuer's hands and the direction of thrust are shown at the bottom right.

When the victim is unable to stand, he should be rolled over on his back on the floor. The rescuer then kneels astride the victim and performs a variation of the Heimlich maneuver by placing the heel of one open hand, rather than a clenched fist, just below the victim's rib cage. The second hand is placed over the first. Then the rescuer presses upward (toward the victim's head) quickly to compress the lungs, repeating several times if necessary.

The Heimlich maneuver has been used successfully by persons who were alone when they choked on food; some pressed their own fist into their abdomen, others forced the edge of a chair or sink against their abdomen.

Poisoning

In all cases of poisoning, it is imperative to get professional assistance as soon as possible.

Listed below are telephone numbers for Poison Control Centers throughout the United States. These health service organizations are accessible 24 hours a day to provide information on how best to counteract the effects of toxic substances.

In the event of known or suspected poisoning, call the center nearest you immediately. Give the staff member to whom you speak as much information as possible: the name or nature of the poison ingested, if you know; if not, the symptoms manifested by the victim.

If for any reason it is impossible to telephone or get to a Poison Control Center (or a doctor or hospital), follow these two general rules:

1. If a strong acid or alkali or a petroleum product has been ingested, dilute the poison by administering large quantities of milk or water. Do not induce vomiting.

2. For methanol or related products such as window cleaners, antifreeze, paint removers, and shoe polish, induce vomiting—preferably with syrup of ipecac.

Calling for Help

Every household should have a card close by the telephone—if possible attached to an adjacent wall—that contains the numbers of various emergency services. In most communities, it is possible to simply dial the operator and ask for the police or fire department. In many large cities, there is a special three-digit number that can be dialed for reaching the police directly.

An ambulance can be summoned either by asking for a police ambulance, by calling the nearest hospital, or by having on hand the telephone numbers of whatever private ambulance services are locally available. Such services are listed in the classified pages of the telephone directory.

Practically all hospitals have emergency rooms for the prompt treatment of accident cases. If the victim is in good enough physical condition, he can be placed in a prone position in a family station wagon for removal to a hospital. However, under no circumstances should a person who has sustained major injuries or who has collapsed be made to sit upright in a car. First aid must be administered to him on the spot until a suitable conveyance arrives.

Every family should find out the telephone number of the nearest Poison Control Center (see section in this chapter) and note it on the emergency number card.

Poison Control Centers

This list of poison control and information centers is compiled by the American Association of Poison Control Centers. State or regional control centers and other centers with a 24-hour poison control staff are listed in boldface (darker) type. All centers are listed by state and are grouped alphabetically by city or town. **CAUTION:** These numbers occasionally change and smaller centers are not available at all hours of the day. If you do not get an answer from the number you call after several rings, call your local police or fire emergency number in case of a crisis in your home.

ALABAMA

Alabama Poison Center
Druid City Hospital
809 University Blvd., E.
Tuscaloosa 35401
(800) 462-0800 (statewide)
(205) 345-0600

Birmingham
Children's Hospital
1600 Seventh Ave., S. 35233
(800) 292-6678 (local)
(205) 933-9201
939-9201
939-9202

ALASKA

Anchorage
Anchorage Poison Center
Providence Hospital
3200 Providence Dr. 99504
(907) 563-3393

Fairbanks
Fairbanks Poison Control Center
Fairbanks Memorial Hospital
1650 Cowles St. 99701
(907) 456-7182

ARIZONA

Arizona Regional Poison Control System
Tucson
(800) 362-0101

Flagstaff
Flagstaff Hospital and Medical Center of Northern Arizona
1215 N. Beaver St. 86001
(602) 779-0555

Phoenix
St. Luke's Hospital Medical Center
525 N. 18th St. 85006
(602) 253-3334

Tucson
Arizona Poison and Drug Information Center
University of Arizona
Arizona Health Sciences Center
85724
(800) 362-0101
(602) 626-6016

Yuma
Yuma Regional Medical Center
Avenue A & 24th St. 85364
(602) 344-2000

ARKANSAS

Statewide Poison Control Drug Information Center
University of Arkansas for Medical Sciences
College of Pharmacy
4301 W. Markham St.
Little Rock 72201
(800) 428-8948 (statewide)
(501) 666-5532 (Pulaski County)

El Dorado
Warner Brown Hospital
Emergency Room
460 W. Oak St. 71730
(501) 863-2266

Fort Smith
St. Edward Mercy Medical Center
Emergency Room
7301 Rogers Ave. 72904
(501) 452-5100, ext. 2041

Sparks Regional Medical Center
Emergency Room
1311 S. Eye St. 72902
(501) 441-5011

Harrison
Boone County Hospital
Emergency Room
620 N. Willow St. 72601
(501) 365-2000

Helena
Helena Hospital
Emergency Room
Hi-Way 49 Bypass 72342
(501) 338-6411, ext. 340

Osceola
Osceola Memorial Hospital
Emergency Room
611 W. Lee Ave. 72370
(501) 563-7182
563-3174

Pine Bluff
Jefferson Regional Medical Center
Emergency Room
1515 W. 42nd Ave. 71601
(501) 541-7100

CALIFORNIA

Los Angeles

Los Angeles County Medical Association Regional Poison Information Center
1925 Wilshire Blvd. 90057
(213) 484-5151 (public)
664-2121 (MDs and hospitals)

Orange

University of California Poison Control Center
Irvine Medical Center
101 City Drive S., Rte. 78 92668
(714) 634-5988

Sacramento

UCDMC Regional Poison Control Center
2315 Stockton Blvd. 95817
(800) 852-7221 (Northern Calif.)
(916) 453-3692

San Diego

San Diego Regional Poison Center
University of California, San Diego, Medical Center
225 Dickinson St. 92103
(619) 294-6000

San Francisco

San Francisco Bay Area Regional Poison Center
San Francisco General Hospital
Room 1 E 86
1001 Potrero Ave. 94110
(415) 666-2845

San Jose

Central-Coast Counties Regional Poison Control Center
Santa Clara Valley Medical Center
751 S. Bascom Ave. 95128
(800) 662-9886
(408) 299-5112

Fresno

Fresno Community Hospital
Regional Poison Control Center
Fresno & R Sts. 93715
(209) 445-1222

Oakland

Children's Hospital Medical Center of Northern California
51st & Grove Sts. 94609
(415) 428-3248

Redding

Redding Medical Center
1450 Liberty St. 96099
(916) 243-4043

COLORADO

Rocky Mountain Poison Center
645 Bannock St.
Denver 80204-4507
(800) 332-3073
(303) 629-1123

CONNECTICUT

Connecticut Poison Control Center
University of Connecticut Health Center
Farmington 06032
(203) 674-3456
674-3457

Bridgeport

Bridgeport Hospital
267 Grant St. 06602
(203) 384-3566

St. Vincent's Medical Center
2800 Main St. 06606
(203) 576-5178

Danbury

Danbury Hospital
95 Locust Ave. 06810
(203) 797-7300

Farmington

Connecticut Poison Control Center
University of Connecticut Health Center
Farmington 06032
(203) 674-3456
674-3457

Middletown

Middlesex Memorial Hospital
28 Crescent St. 06457
(203) 347-9471

New Haven

Hospital of St. Raphael
1450 Chapel St. 06511
(203) 789-3464

Yale-New Haven Hospital
Department of Pediatrics
Pediatric Emergency Room
789 Howard Ave. 06504
(203) 785-2222

Norwalk

Norwalk Hospital
Department of Emergency Medicine
Maple St. 06856
(203) 852-2160

Waterbury

St. Mary's Hospital
Emergency Room
56 Franklin St. 06702
(203) 574-6011

DELAWARE

Poison Information Center
Medical Center of Delaware
Wilmington Division
501 W. 14th St.
Wilmington 19899
(302) 655-3389

DISTRICT OF COLUMBIA

National Capital Poison Center
Georgetown University Hospital
3800 Reservoir Rd.
Washington 20007
(202) 625-3333

FLORIDA

Bradenton
Manatee Memorial Hospital
206 Second St. E. 33505
(813) 748-2121

Ft. Lauderdale
Broward General Medical Center
Poison Control Center
Emergency Department
1600 S. Andrews Ave. 33316
(305) 463-3131, ext. 1955, 1956

Ft. Myers
Lee Memorial Hospital
2776 Cleveland Ave. 33902
(813) 334-5334
334-5287

Ft. Walton Beach
Humana Hospital of Ft. Walton Beach
1000 Mar-Walt Dr. 32548
(904) 863-7606

Gainesville
Shands Hospital
University of Florida 32610
(904) 392-3389

Inverness
Citrus Memorial Hospital
502 Highland Blvd. 32650
(904) 726-2800

Jacksonville
St. Vincent's Medical Center
1800 Barrs St. 32203
(904) 387-7500
387-7499 (TTY)

Leesburg
Leesburg Regional Medical Center
600 E. Dixie 32748
(904) 787-9900

Melbourne
James E. Holmes Regional Medical Center
1350 S. Hickory St. 32901
(305) 676-7199

Naples
Naples Community Hospital
350 Seventh St. N. 33940
(813) 262-3131

Ocala
Munroe Regional Medical Center
131 S.W. 15th St. 32670
(904) 351-7607

Orlando
Orlando Regional Medical Center
Orange Memorial Division
1414 S. Kuhl Ave. 32806
(305) 841-5222

Punta Gorda
Medical Center Hospital
809 E. Marion Ave. 33950
(813) 637-2529

Rockledge
Wuesthoff Memorial Hospital
110 Longwood Ave. 32955
(305) 636-4357

Sarasota
Memorial Hospital
1901 Arlington St. 33577
(813) 953-1332

Tallahassee
Tallahassee Memorial Regional Medical Center
1300 Miccosukee Rd. 32308
(904) 681-5411

Tampa
Tampa Bay Regional Poison Control Center
Tampa General Hospital
Davis Island 33606
(800) 282-3171
(813) 251-6995

Titusville
Jess Parrish Memorial Hospital
951 N. Washington Ave. 32780
(305) 268-6260

West Palm Beach
Good Samaritan Hospital
Flagler Dr. at Palm Beach Lakes Blvd. 33402
(305) 655-5511, ext. 4333

Winter Haven
Poison Control Center
Winter Haven Hospital
200 Avenue F, N.E. 33880
(813) 299-9701

GEORGIA

Georgia Poison Control Center
Grady Memorial Hospital
80 Butler St., S.E.
Atlanta 30335
(800) 282-5846
(404) 589-4400
525-3323 (TTY)

Albany
Phoebe Putney Memorial Hospital
417 Third Ave. 31705
(912) 883-1800, ext. 4150

Augusta
University Hospital
1350 Walton Way 30902
(404) 724-5050

Columbus
The Medical Center
Emergency Dept.
710 Center St. 31902
(404) 571-1080

Macon
Regional Poison Control Center
Medical Center of Central Georgia
777 Hemlock St. 31201
(912) 744-1427
744-1146
744-1000

Rome
Floyd Medical Center
Regional Poison Control Center
Emergency Dept.
Turner McCall Blvd. 30161
(404) 295-5500

Savannah
Savannah Regional EMS Poison Center
Department of Emergency Medicine
Memorial Medical Center 31403
(912) 355-5228

Thomasville
John D. Archbold Memorial Hospital
Poison Control
900 Gordon Ave. 31792
(912) 228-2000

Valdosta
South Georgia Medical Center
Emergency Dept.
2501 N. Patterson St. 31601
(912) 333-1110

Waycross
Memorial Hospital
Emergency Dept.
410 Darling Ave. 31501
(912) 283-3030

HAWAII

Hawaii Poison Center
Kapiolani-Children's Medical Center
1319 Punahou St.
Honolulu 96826
(800) 362-3585
(808) 941-4411

IDAHO

Mid-Plains Poison Control Center
Omaha, Neb.
(800) 228-9515

Boise
Idaho Emergency Medical Poison Center
State House
450 W. State St., 1st Fl. 83706
(800) 632-8000
(208) 334-2241

Idaho Falls
Idaho Falls Consolidated Hospitals
Emergency Dept.
900 Memorial Dr. 83401
(208) 522-3600

Pocatello
Idaho Drug Information Service and Poison Control Center
Pocatello Regional Medical Center
777 Hospital Way 83202
(800) 632-9490
(208) 234-0777

ILLINOIS

Chicago Area Poison Resource Center
Rush-Presbyterian-St. Luke's Medical Center
1753 W. Congress Pkwy.
Chicago 60612
(800) 942-5969
(312) 942-5969

Peoria Poison Center
St. Francis Hospital Medical Center
530 N.E. Glen Oak Ave.
Peoria 61637
(800) 322-5330
(309) 672-2334

Central and Southern Illinois Regional Poison Resource Center
St. John's Hospital
800 E. Carpenter St.
Springfield 62769
(800) 252-2022
(217) 753-3330

INDIANA

Indiana Poison Center
1001 W. 10th St.
Indianapolis 46202
(800) 382-9097
(317) 630-7351

Anderson
Community Hospital
1515 N. Madison Ave. 46012
(317) 646-5143

St. John's Medical Center
2015 Jackson St. 46014
(317) 646-8222

Angola
Cameron Memorial Hospital
416 E. Maumee St. 46703
(219) 665-2141, ext. 146

Crown Point
St. Anthony Medical Center
Main at Franciscan Rd. 46307
(219) 738-2100, ext. 1311

Columbus
Bartholomew County Hospital
2400 E. 17th St. 47201
(812) 376-5277

East Chicago
St. Catherine Hospital
4321 Fir St. 46312
(219) 392-7203

Elkhart
Elkhart General Hospital
600 East Blvd. 46514
(800) 382-9097
(219) 294-2621

Evansville
Deaconess Hospital
600 Mary St. 47710
(812) 426-3333

Welborn Memorial Baptist Hospital
401 S.E. Sixth St. 47713
(812) 426-8249

Fort Wayne
Lutheran Hospital
3024 Fairfield Ave. 46807
(219) 458-2211

Parkview Memorial Hospital
2200 Randalia Dr. 46805
(219) 484-6636, ext. 6000

St. Joseph's Hospital
700 Broadway 46802
(219) 425-3765

Frankfort
Clinton County Hospital
1300 S. Jackson St. 46041
(317) 659-4731

Gary
Methodist Hospital of Gary
600 Grant St. 46402
(219) 886-4710

Goshen
Goshen General Hospital
200 High Park Ave. 46526
(219) 533-2141

Hammond
St. Margaret Hospital
25 Douglas St. 46320
(219) 932-2300, ext. 4350

Indianapolis
Indiana Poison Center
Principal Information Center for Indiana
1001 W. 10th St. 46202
(800) 382-9097
(317) 630-7351

Kendallville
McCray Memorial Hospital
Hospital Dr. 46755
(219) 347-1100

Kokomo
Howard Community Hospital
3500 S. LaFountain St. 46902
(317) 453-8444

Lafayette
Lafayette Home Hospital
2400 South St. 47902
(317) 447-6811

Poison Control Center
St. Elizabeth Hospital Medical Center
1501 Hartford St. 47904
(317) 423-6271

LaGrange
LaGrange Hospital
Rte. 5 46761
(219) 463-2143

LaPorte
LaPorte Hospital
State & Madison Sts. 46350
(219) 326-1234

Lebanon
Witham Memorial Hospital
1124 N. Lebanon St. 46052
(317) 482-2700, ext. 241

Madison
King's Daughters' Hospital
112 Presbyterian Ave. 47250
(812) 265-5211, ext. 154

Marion
Marion General Hospital
Wabash & Euclid Aves. 46952
(317) 662-4693

Muncie
Ball Memorial Hospital
2401 University Ave. 47303
(317) 747-4321

Portland
Jay County Hospital
505 W. Votaw St. 47371
(219) 726-7131

Richmond
Reid Memorial Hospital
1401 Chester Blvd. 47374
(317) 983-3148

Shelbyville
Major Hospital
150 W. Washington St. 46176
(317) 392-3793

Terre Haute
Union Hospital
1606 N. Seventh St. 47804
(812) 238-7000, ext. 7523

Valparaiso
Porter Memorial Hospital
814 LaPorte Ave. 46383
(219) 464-8611, ext. 301, 302

Vincennes
Good Samaritan Hospital
520 S. Seventh St. 47591
(812) 885-3344

IOWA

Mid-Plains Poison Control Center
Omaha, Neb.
(800) 228-9515

University of Iowa Hospitals and Clinics Poison Control Center*
Iowa City 52242
(800) 272-6477
(319) 356-2922

Des Moines
Variety Club Poison and Drug Information Center
Iowa Methodist Medical Center
1200 Pleasant St. 50308
(800) 362-2327
(515) 283-6254

Fort Dodge
Trinity Regional Hospital
Kenyon Rd. 50501
(515) 573-7211
573-3101 (night)

Waterloo
Allen Memorial Hospital
Emergency Dept.
1825 Logan Ave. 50703
(319) 235-3893

KANSAS

Mid-American Poison Center
University of Kansas Medical Center
39th & Rainbow Blvd.
Kansas City 66103
(800) 332-6633
(913) 588-6633

Mid-Plains Poison Control Center*
Omaha, Neb.
(800) 228-9515

Atchison
Atchison Hospital
1301 N. Second St. 66002
(913) 367-2131

Dodge City
Dodge City Regional Hospital
3001 Avenue A 67801
(316) 225-9050, ext. 381

Emporia
Newman Memorial Hospital
12th & Chestnut Sts. 66801
(316) 343-6800, ext. 545

Fort Riley
Irwin Army Hospital
Emergency Room 66442
(913) 239-7776
239-7777
239-7778

Fort Scott
Mercy Hospital
821 Burke St. 66701
(316) 223-2200, ext. 135

Great Bend
Central Kansas Medical Center
3515 Broadway 67530
(316) 792-2511, ext. 115

Hays
Hadley Regional Medical Center
201 E. Seventh St. 67601
(913) 628-8251

Lawrence
Lawrence Memorial Hospital
325 Maine St. 66044
(913) 749-6100, ext. 162

Salina
St. John's Hospital
139 N. Penn St. 67401
(913) 827-3187
827-5591, ext. 112

Topeka
Northeast Kansas Poison Center
St. Francis Hospital and Medical Center
1700 W. Seventh St. 66606
(913) 295-8094

Stormont-Vail Regional Medical Center
10th & Washburn Sts. 66606
(913) 354-6100

Wichita
Wesley Medical Center
550 N. Hillside 67214
(316) 688-2277

KENTUCKY

Fort Thomas
St. Luke Hospital of Campbell County
Northern Kentucky Poison Center
85 N. Grand Ave. 41075
(800) 352-9900
(606) 572-3215

Lexington
Central Baptist Hospital
Poison Control Center
1740 S. Limestone St. 40503
(606) 278-3411, ext. 1663

Drug Information Center
University of Kentucky Medical Center 40506
(606) 233-5320

Louisville Kentucky Regional Poison Center of Kosair-Children's Hospital
40232
(800) 722-5725
(502) 589-8222

Murray
Murray-Calloway County Hospital
Poison Control Center
803 Poplar St. 42071
(502) 753-7588

Owensboro
Owensboro-Daviess County Hospital
Emergency Room
811 Hospital Ct. 42301
(502) 926-3030, ext. 180, 174, 391

Paducah
Western Baptist Hospital Poison Control
2501 Kentucky Ave. 42001
(502) 575-2105—days (8 a.m. to 8 p.m.)
(502) 575-2199—nights (8 p.m. to 8 a.m.)

Prestonburg
Poison Control Center
Highlands Regional Medical Center 41653
(606) 886-8511, ext. 132, 160

South Williamson
Williamson Appalachian Regional Hospital
Central Pharmaceutical Service
Emergency Dept.
2000 Central Ave. 41503
(606) 237-1010

LOUISIANA

Louisiana Regional Poison Control Center
1501 Kings Hwy.
Shreveport 71130
(800) 535-0525
(318) 425-1524

Monroe
St. Francis Medical Center
309 Jackson St. 71201
(318) 325-6454

MAINE

Maine Poison Control Center
at Maine Medical Center
22 Bramhall St.
Portland 04102
(800) 442-6305
(207) 871-2381 (ER)

MARYLAND

Maryland Poison Center
University of Maryland
School of Pharmacy
636 W. Lombard St.
Baltimore 21201
(800) 492-2414
(301) 528-7701

Cumberland
Tri-State Poison Center
Sacred Heart Hospital
900 Seton Dr. 21502
(301) 722-6677

MASSACHUSETTS

Massachusetts Poison Control System
300 Longwood Ave.
Boston 02115
(800) 682-9211
(617) 232-2120
277-3323 (TTY)

MICHIGAN

Poison Control Center
Children's Hospital of Michigan
3901 Beaubien
Detroit 48201
(800) 572-1655
(800) 462-6642
(313) 494-5711

Blodgett Regional Poison Center
Blodgett Memorial Medical Center
1840 Wealthy, S.E.
Grand Rapids 49506
(800) 632-2727
(616) 774-7854

Battle Creek
Community Hospital
Pharmacy Dept.
183 West St. 49016
(616) 963-5521

Flint
Poison Information Center
Hurley Medical Center
1 Hurley Plaza 48502
(800) 572-5396
(313) 257-9111

Kalamazoo
Great Lakes Poison Center
Bronson Methodist Hospital
252 E. Lovell St. 49001
(800) 442-4112
(616) 383-6409

Midwest Poison Center
Borgess Medical Center
1521 Gull Rd. 49001
(800) 632-4177
(616) 383-7070

Lansing
St. Lawrence Hospital
1210 W. Saginaw St. 48915
(517) 372-5112
372-5113

Marquette
Upper Peninsula Regional Poison Center
Marquette General Hospital
420 W. Magnetic St. 49855
(800) 562-9781
(906) 228-9440

Pontiac
Poison Information Center
St. Joseph Mercy Hospital
900 Woodward Ave. 48053
(313) 858-7373
858-7374

Saginaw
Saginaw Region Poison Center
Saginaw General Hospital
1447 N. Harrison St. 48602
(517) 755-1111

MINNESOTA

Hennepin Poison Center
Hennepin County Medical Center
701 Park Ave.
Minneapolis 55415
(612) 347-3141

Minnesota Poison Control System
St. Paul-Ramsey Medical Center
640 Jackson St.
St. Paul 55101
(800) 222-1222
(612) 221-2113

MISSISSIPPI

Regional Poison Control Center
University Medical Center
2500 N. State St.
Jackson 39216
(601) 354-7660

Hattiesburg
Forrest County General Hospital
400 S. 28th St. 39401
(601) 264-4235

MISSOURI

Cardinal Glennon Children's Hospital Regional Poison Center
1465 S. Grand Blvd.
St. Louis 63104
(800) 392-9111
(314) 772-5200

Mid-Plains Poison Control Center
Omaha, Neb.
(800) 228-9515

Kansas City
Children's Mercy Hospital
24th at Gillham Rd. 64108
(816) 234-3000

MONTANA

Rocky Mountain Poison Center
Denver, Colo.
(800) 525-5042

NEBRASKA

Mid-Plains Poison Control Center
Children's Memorial Hospital
8301 Dodge St.
Omaha 68114
(800) 642-9999 (outside Omaha)
(402) 390-5400 (Omaha)
(800) 228-9515 (Idaho, Iowa, Kan., Mo., S. Dak.)

NEVADA

Las Vegas
Southern Nevada Memorial Hospital
1800 W. Charleston Blvd. 89102
(702) 385-1277

Sunrise Hospital Medical Center
3186 S. Maryland Pkwy. 89109
(702) 732-4989

Reno
St. Mary's Hospital
235 W. Sixth St. 89520
(702) 789-3013

Washoe Medical Center
77 Pringle Way 89520
(702) 785-4129

NEW HAMPSHIRE

New Hampshire Poison Center
NH-Dartmouth Hitchcock Medical Center
2 Maynard St.
Hanover 03756
(800) 562-8236
(603) 646-5000

NEW JERSEY

New Jersey Poison Information and Education System*
Newark Beth Israel Medical Center
201 Lyons Ave.
Newark 07112
(800) 962-1253
(201) 926-8005

NEW MEXICO

New Mexico Poison and Drug Information Center
University of New Mexico
Albuquerque 87131
(800) 432-6866
(505) 277-4261

NEW YORK

Binghamton
Southern Tier Poison Center
Binghamton General Hospital
Mitchell Ave. 13903
(607) 723-8929

Buffalo
Western New York Poison Center
Children's Hospital
219 Bryant St. 14222
(716) 878-7654
878-7655

Dunkirk
Brooks Memorial Hospital
10 W. Sixth St. 14048
(716) 366-1111

East Meadow
Long Island Regional Poison Control Center
Nassau County Medical Center
2201 Hempsted Tnpk. 11554
(516) 542-2324
542-2325
542-2323 (TTY)

Elmira
Arnot Ogden Memorial Hospital
Roe Ave. & Grove St. 14901
(607) 737-4100

St. Joseph's Hospital Health Center
555 E. Market St. 14901
(607) 734-2662

Jamestown
Women's Christian Association Hospital
207 Foote Ave. 14701
(716) 487-0141
484-8648

New York
New York City Poison Center
455 First Ave. 10016
(212) 340-4494
764-7667

Nyack
Hudson Valley Poison Center
Nyack Hospital
N. Midland Ave. 10960
(914) 353-1000

Rochester
Finger Lakes Poison Center
LIFE LINE
University of Rochester
Medical Center 14620
(716) 275-5151
275-2700 (TTY)

Schenectady
Ellis Hospital Poison Center
1101 Nott St. 12308
(518) 382-4039
382-4309

Syracuse
Syracuse Poison Information Center
Upstate Medical Center
750 E. Adams St. 13210
(315) 476-7529
473-5831

Troy
St. Mary's Hospital
1300 Massachusetts Ave. 12180
(518) 272-5792

Utica
St. Luke's Memorial Hospital Center
P.O. Box 479 13503
(315) 798-6200
798-6223

Watertown
Watertown Poison Information Center
House of the Good Samaritan Hospital
Washington & Pratt Sts. 13602
(315) 788-8700

NORTH CAROLINA

Duke Poison Control Center
Duke University Medical Center
Durham 27710
(800) 672-1697
(919) 684-8111

Asheville
Western NC Poison Control Center
Memorial Mission Hospital
509 Biltmore Ave. 28801
(704) 255-4490

Charlotte
Mercy Hospital
2001 Vail Ave. 28207
(704) 379-5827

Greensboro
Moses H. Cone Memorial Hospital
Triad Poison Center
1200 N. Elm St. 27420
(800) 722-2222
(919) 379-4105

Hendersonville
Margaret R. Pardee Memorial Hospital
Fleming St. 28739
(704) 693-6522, ext. 555, 556

Hickory
Catawba Memorial Hospital
Fairgrove Church Rd. 28601
(704) 322-6649

Jacksonville
Onslow Memorial Hospital
Western Blvd. 28540
(919) 577-2555

Wilmington
New Hanover Memorial Hospital
2131 S. 17th St. 28401
(919) 343-7046

NORTH DAKOTA

North Dakota Poison Information Center
St. Luke's Hospitals
Fifth St. N. & Mills Ave.
Fargo 58122
(800) 732-2200
(701) 280-5575

OHIO

Central Ohio Poison Control Center
Children's Hospital
700 Children's Dr.
Columbus 43205
(800) 682-7625
(614) 228-1323

Southwest Ohio Regional Poison Control System Drug and Poison Information Center
University of Cincinnati Medical Center
Bridge Medical Science Bldg.
231 Bethesda Ave.
Cincinnati 45267
(800) 872-5111
(513) 872-5111

Akron
Children's Hospital Medical Center of Akron
281 Locust St. 44308
(800) 362-9922
(216) 379-8562

Cleveland
Greater Cleveland Poison Control Center
2119 Abington Rd. 44106
(216) 231-4455

Dayton
Children's Medical Center
1 Children's Plaza 45404
(800) 762-0727
(513) 222-2227

Lorain
Lorain Community Hospital
3700 Kolbe Rd. 44053
(216) 282-2220

Mansfield
Mansfield General Hospital
335 Glessner Ave. 44903
(419) 526-8200

Springfield
Community Hospital
2615 E. High St. 45505
(513) 325-1255

Toledo
Poison Information Center
Medical College of Ohio Hospital
3000 Arlington Ave. 43614
(419) 381-3897

Youngstown
Mahoning Valley Poison Center
St. Elizabeth Hospital Medical Center
1044 Belmont Ave. 44501
(216) 746-2222
746-5510 (TTY)

Zanesville
Bethesda Poison Control Center
Bethesda Hospital
2951 Maple Ave. 43701
(614) 454-4221

OKLAHOMA

Oklahoma Poison Control Center
Oklahoma Children's Memorial Hospital
Oklahoma City 73126
(800) 522-4611
(405) 271-5454

Ada
Valley View Hospital
1300 E. Sixth St. 74820
(405) 332-2323, ext. 200

Lawton
Comanche County Memorial Hospital
3401 Gore Blvd. 73502
(405) 355-8620

McAlester
McAlester Regional Hospital
1 Clark Bass Blvd. 74501
(918) 426-1800, ext. 7705

Ponca City
St. Joseph Medical Center
Emergency Room
14th St. & Hartford Ave. 74601
(405) 765-0584

OREGON

Oregon Poison Control and Drug Information Center
University of Oregon Health Sciences Center
3181 S.W. Sam Jackson Park Rd.
Portland 97201
(800) 452-7165
(503) 225-8968

PENNSYLVANIA

Allentown
Lehigh Valley Poison Center
Allentown Hospital
17th & Chew Sts. 18102
(215) 433-2311

Altoona
Keystone Region Poison Center
Mercy Hospital
2500 Seventh Ave. 16603
(814) 946-3711

Bloomsburg
Bloomsburg Hospital
549 E. Fair St. 17815
(717) 784-4241

Bradford
Bradford Hospital
Emergency Room
Interstate Pkwy. 16701
(814) 368-4143, ext. 274

Bryn Mawr
Bryn Mawr Hospital
Bryn Mawr Ave. 19010
(215) 896-3577

Chester
Sacred Heart Medical Center
Ninth & Wilson Sts. 19013
(215) 494-4400

Clearfield
Clearfield Hospital
809 Turnpike Ave. 16830
(814) 765-5341

Coaldale
Coaldale State General Hospital
Seventh St. 18218
(717) 645-2131

Coudersport
Charles Cole Memorial Hospital
RD 3, Rte. 6 16915
(814) 274-9300

Danville
Susquehanna Poison Center
Geisinger Medical Center
N. Academy Ave. 17821
(717) 271-6116

Doylestown
Doylestown Hospital
595 W. State St. 18901
(215) 345-2283

Erie
Hamot Medical Center
201 State St. 16550
(814) 452-4242

Metro Health Center
252 W. 11th St. 16501
(814) 454-2120

Millcreek Community Hospital
5515 Peach St. 16509
(814) 864-4031, ext. 442

Northwest Poison Center
Saint Vincent Health Center
232 W. 25th St. 16544
(814) 452-3232

Gettysburg
Gettysburg Hospital
147 Gettys St. 17325
(717) 334-9155

Greensburg
Westmoreland Hospital
532 W. Pittsburgh St. 15601
(412) 832-4355

Hanover
Hanover General Hospital
300 Highland Ave. 17331
(717) 637-3711

Hershey
Capital Area Poison Center
Milton S. Hershey Medical Center
University Dr. 17033
(717) 534-6111
534-6039

Jeannette
Jeannette District Memorial Hospital
600 Jefferson Ave. 15644
(412) 527-9300

Jersey Shore
Jersey Shore Hospital
Thompson St. 17740
(717) 398-0100, ext. 225

Johnstown
Conemaugh Valley Memorial Hospital
1086 Franklin St. 15905
(814) 535-5351

Lee Hospital
320 Main St. 15901
(814) 533-0109

Mercy Hospital
1020 Franklin St. 15905
(814) 535-5353

Lancaster
Lancaster General Hospital
555 N. Duke St. 17604
(717) 295-8322

St. Joseph's Hospital
250 College Ave. 17604
(717) 299-4546

Lansdale
North Penn Hospital
Medical Campus Dr. 19446
(215) 368-2100

Lebanon
Good Samaritan Hospital
Fourth & Walnut Sts. 17042
(717) 272-7611

Lehighton
Gnaden Huetten Memorial Hospital
11th & Hamilton Sts. 18235
(215) 377-1300, ext. 552

Lewistown
Lewistown Hospital
Highland Ave. 17044
(717) 248-5411

Muncy
Muncy Valley Hospital
Water St. 17756
(717) 546-8282

Nanticoke
Nanticoke State General Hospital
W. Washington St. 18634
(717) 735-5000, ext. 261

Philadelphia
Philadelphia Poison Information
321 University Ave. 19104
(215) 922-5523
922-5524

Philipsburg
Philipsburg State General Hospital
Locklomond Rd. 16866
(814) 342-3320, ext. 293

Pittsburgh
Pittsburgh Poison Center
Children's Hospital
125 De Soto St. 15213
(412) 681-6669—(emergency)
647-5600—(admin./consultation)

Reading
Community General Hospital
145 N. Sixth St. 19601
(215) 375-9115

Sayre
Robert Packer Hospital
Guthrie Sq. 18840
(717) 888-6666

Sellersville
Grand View Hospital
Lawn Ave. 18960
(215) 257-5955

State College
Centre Community Hospital
Orchard Rd. 16803
(814) 238-4351

Titusville
Titusville Hospital
406 W. Oak St. 16354
(814) 827-1851

Tunkhannock
Tyler Memorial Hospital
RD 1 18657
(717) 836-2161, ext. 180

Wilkes-Barre
NPW-Medical Center
1000 E. Mountain Blvd. 18704
(717) 826-7762

York
Memorial Osteopathic Hospital
325 S. Belmont St. 17403
(717) 843-8623

York Hospital
1001 S. George St. 17405
(717) 771-2311

PUERTO RICO

Poison Control Center
Centro Médico
Rio Piedras 00936
(809) 754-8535

RHODE ISLAND

Rhode Island Poison Center
Rhode Island Hospital
593 Eddy St.
Providence 02902
(401) 277-5906

SOUTH CAROLINA

Palmetto Poison Center
University of South Carolina
College of Pharmacy
Columbia 29208
(800) 922-1117
(803) 765-7359

SOUTH DAKOTA

Mid-Plains Poison Control Center
Omaha, Neb.
(800) 228-9515

Aberdeen
Dakota Midland Poison Control Center
57501
(605) 773-3361

Rapid City
Rapid City Regional Poison Center
353 Fairmont Blvd. 57701
(800) 742-8925
(605) 341-8222

Sioux Falls
McKennan Hospital Poison Center
800 E. 21st St. 57101
(800) 952-0123
843-0505
(605) 336-3894

TENNESSEE

Chattanooga
T. C. Thompson Children's Hospital
910 Blackford St. 37403
(615) 778-6100

Columbia
Maury County Hospital
1224 Trotwood Ave. 38401
(615) 381-4500, ext. 405

Cookeville
Cookeville General Hospital
142 W. Fifth St. 38501
(615) 526-4818

Jackson
Jackson-Madison County General Hospital
708 W. Forest Ave. 38301
(901) 424-0424, ext. 525

Johnson City
Johnson City Medical Center Hospital
Poison Control Center
400 State of Franklin Rd. 37601
(615) 461-6572

Knoxville
Memorial Research Center and Hospital
1924 Alcoa Hwy. 37920
(615) 544-9400

Memphis
Southern Poison Center
Le Bonheur Children's Medical Center
848 Adams Ave. 38103
(901) 528-6048

Nashville
Vanderbilt University Hospital
1161 21st Ave. S. 37232
(615) 322-6435

TEXAS

Texas State Poison Center
University of Texas Medical Branch
Eighth & Mechanic Sts.
Galveston 77550
(800) 392-8548
(409) 765-1420 (Galveston)
(713) 654-1701 (Houston)
(512) 478-4490 (Austin)

Abilene
Hendrick Hospital
N. 19th & Hickory Sts. 79601
(915) 677-7762

Amarillo
Amarillo Emergency Receiving Center
Amarillo Hospital District
1501 Coulter Dr. 79106
(806) 376-4292

Beaumont
Baptist Hospital of Southeast Texas
College & 11th Sts. 77701
(409) 833-7409

Corpus Christi
Memorial Medical Center
2606 Hospital Blvd. 78405
(512) 881-4559

Dallas
North Central Texas Poison Center
75235
(214) 920-2400

El Paso
El Paso Poison Control Center
R. E. Thomason General Hospital
4815 Álameda Ave. 79905
(915) 533-1244

Fort Worth
Cook Poison Center
W. I. Cook Children's Hospital
1212 W. Lancaster St. 76102
(817) 336-6611

Harlingen
Valley Baptist Medical Center
2000 Peace St. 78550
(512) 421-1860
421-1859

Laredo
Mercy Regional Medical Center
1515 Logan St. 78040
(512) 724-6247

Lubbock
Methodist Hospital
3615 19th St. 79410
(806) 793-4366

Midland
Midland Memorial Hospital
2200 W. Illinois Ave. 79701
(915) 685-1558

Odessa
Medical Center Hospital
Poison Control Center
Fourth & Allegheny Sts. 79760
(915) 333-1231

Plainview
Central Plains Regional Hospital
2601 Dimmitt Rd. 79072
(806) 296-9601

San Angelo
Shannon West Texas Memorial Hospital
120 E. Harris Ave. 76903
(915) 655-5330

Tyler
Medical Center Hospital
1000 S. Beckham St. 75701
(214) 597-8884

Waco
Hillcrest Baptist Medical Center
3000 Herring Ave. 76708
(817) 753-1412

Wichita Falls
Wichita Falls General Hospital
1600 Eighth St. 76301
(817) 322-6771

UTAH

Intermountain Regional Poison Control Center*
50 N. Medical Dr.
Salt Lake City 84132
(800) 662-0062
(801) 581-2151

VERMONT

Vermont Poison Center
Medical Center Hospital
Burlington 05401
(802) 658-3456

VIRGINIA

Alexandria
Alexandria Hospital
4320 Seminary Rd. 22314
(703) 379-3070

Arlington
Arlington Hospital
1701 N. George Mason Dr. 22205
(703) 558-6161

Blacksburg
Montgomery County Hospital
Rte. 460, S. 24060
(703) 951-1111, ext. 140

Charlottesville
Blue Ridge Poison Center
University of Virginia Hospital
22903
(800) 552-3723 (TTY: Va. only)
(800) 446-9876 (TTY: out of state)
(804) 924-5543

Danville
Danville Memorial Hospital
142 S. Main St. 24541
(804) 799-2222

Falls Church
Poison Control Center
Fairfax Hospital
3300 Gallows Rd. 22046
(703) 698-2900

Hampton
Hampton General Hospital
3120 Victoria Blvd. 23661
(804) 722-1131

Harrisonburg
Rockingham Memorial Hospital
Emergency Room
235 Cantrell Ave. 22801
(703) 433-9706

Lexington
Stonewall Jackson Hospital
Spotswood Dr. 24450
(703) 463-1492

Lynchburg
Lynchburg General-
Marshall Lodge Hospitals
Tate Springs Rd. 24504
(804) 528-2066

Nassawadox
Northampton-Accomack
Memorial Hospital 23413
(804) 442-8700

Newport News
Riverside Hospital
500 J. Clyde Morris Blvd. 23601
(804) 599-2050

Norfolk
Tidewater Poison Center
150 Kingsley Lane 23505
(804) 489-5288

Petersburg
Petersburg General Hospital
Apollo & Adams Sts. 23803
(804) 861-2992

Portsmouth
U.S. Naval Hospital 23708
(804) 398-5898

Reston
Access Emergency Center
11900 Baron Cameron Ave.
22091
(703) 437-5992

Richmond
Central Virginia Poison Center
Medical College of Virginia 23298
(804) 786-4780

Roanoke
Southwest Virginia Poison Center
Roanoke Memorial Hospital
Belleview at Jefferson St. 24033
(703) 981-7336

Staunton
King's Daughters' Hospital
1410 N. Augusta St. 24401
(703) 885-6848

Waynesboro
Waynesboro Community Hospital
501 Oak Ave. 22980
(703) 942-4096

WASHINGTON

Seattle
Seattle Poison Center
Children's Orthopedic Hospital
and Medical Center
4800 Sand Point Way, N.E.
98105
(206) 526-2121
(800) 732-6985 (statewide)

Spokane
Spokane Poison Center
Deaconess Medical Center
800 W. Fifth Ave. 99210
(509) 747-1077 (TTY)
(800) 572-5842 (statewide)
541-5624 (N. Idaho and W. Montana)

Tacoma
Mary Bridge Poison Information Center
Mary Bridge Children's Health
Center
311 S. L St. 98405
(800) 542-6319 (statewide)
(206) 594-1414

Yakima
Central Washington Poison Center
Yakima Valley Memorial Hospital
2811 Tieton Dr. 98902
(800) 572-9176 (statewide)
(509) 248-4400

WEST VIRGINIA

West Virginia Poison System
West Virginia University
School of Pharmacy
3110 McCorkle Ave., S.E.
(800) 642-3625
(304) 348-2971
348-4211

WISCONSIN

Green Bay
Green Bay Poison Center
St. Vincent Hospital
835 S. Van Buren St. 54305
(414) 433-8100

Madison
Madison Area Poison Center
University Hospital and Clinics
600 Highland Ave. 53792
(608) 262-3702

Milwaukee
Milwaukee Poison Center
Milwaukee Children's Hospital
1700 W. Wisconsin Ave. 53233
(414) 931-4114

WYOMING

Wyoming Poison Center
DePaul Hospital
2600 E. 18th St.
Cheyenne 82001
(307) 777-7955

Reaching a Physician

Emergencies are usually best handled in a hospital because they are likely to require oxygen, blood transfusions, or other services only a hospital can provide. There are many situations, however, in which a physician's guidance on the phone can be extremely helpful and reassuring.

Because there are times when the family physician may not be available by phone, it's a good idea to ask for the names and phone numbers of physicians who can be called when your own physician can't be reached. In many communities, it is also possible to get the services of a physician by calling the county medical society.

A family on vacation in a remote area or on a cross-country trip by car can be directed to the nearest medical services by calling the telephone operator. If the operator can't provide adequate information promptly, ask to be connected with the nearest headquarters of the state police.

Emergency Transport

In the majority of situations, the transfer of an injured person should be handled only by experienced rescue personnel. If you yourself must move a victim to a physician's office or hospital emergency room, here are a few important rules to remember:

1. Give all necessary first aid before attempting to move the victim. Do everything to reduce pain and to make the patient comfortable.

2. If you improvise a stretcher, be sure it is strong enough to carry the victim and that you have enough people to carry it. Shutters, doors, boards, and even ladders may be used as stretchers. Just be sure that the stretcher is padded underneath to protect the victim and that a blanket or coat is available to cover him and protect him from exposure.

3. Bring the stretcher to the victim, not the victim to the stretcher. Slide him onto the stretcher by grasping his clothing or lift him—if enough bearers are available—as shown in the illustration.

4. Secure the victim to the stretcher so he won't fall off. You may want to tie his feet together to minimize his movements.

5. Unless specific injuries prevent it, the victim should be lying on his back while he is being moved. However, a person who is having difficulty breathing because of a chest injury might be more comfortable if his head and shoulders are raised slightly. A person with a severe injury to the back of his head should be kept lying on his side. In any case, place the patient in a comfortable position that will protect him from further injury.

6. Try to transport the patient feet first.

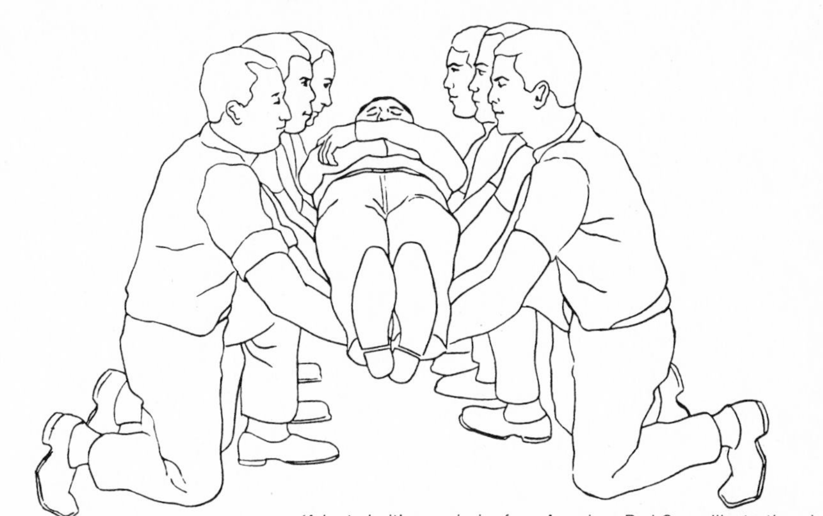

(Adapted with permission from American Red Cross illustrations.)

How to lift an injured or unconscious person to place him on a stretcher. Three bearers on each side of the victim kneel on the knee closer to the victim's feet. The bearers work their hands and forearms gently under the victim to about the midline of the back. On signal, they lift together as shown; on a following signal, they stand as a unit, if that is necessary. In lowering the victim to a stretcher or other litter, the procedure is reversed.

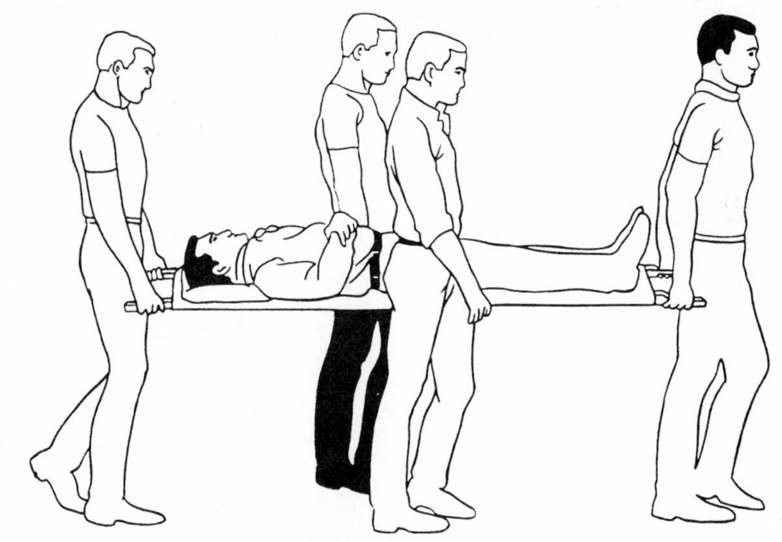

The proper way to carry a victim on a stretcher. One bearer is at the head, one at the foot, and one at either side of the stretcher. The victim should be carried feet first.

7. Unless absolutely necessary, don't try to put a stretcher into a passenger car. It's almost impossible to get the stretcher or injured person into a passenger car without further injuring him. If there is no ambulance, a station wagon or truck makes a good substitute.

8. When you turn the patient over to a doctor or take him to an emergency room of a hospital, give a complete account of the situation to the person taking charge. Tell the doctor what you've done for the patient and what you suspect might cause further problems.

Alphabetic Guide to Medical Emergencies

Abdominal Wound

Abdominal wounds can result from gunshots during hunting or working with firearms, from falling on a knife or sharp object at home or work, or from a variety of other mishaps ranging from automobile accidents to a mugging attack. Such a wound can be a major emergency requiring surgery and other professional care. Call a physician or arrange for quick transportation to a hospital as quickly as possible.

Emergency Treatment

If there is severe bleeding, try to control it with pressure. Keep the victim lying on his back with the knees bent; place a pillow, coat, or a similar soft object under the knees to help hold them in the bent position. If abdominal organs are exposed, do not touch them for any reason. Cover the wound with a sterile dressing. Keep the dressing moistened with sterile water or the cleanest water available. Boiled water can be used to moisten the dressing, but be sure it has cooled before applying.

If the victim is to be moved to a hospital or physician's office, be sure the dressing over the wound is large enough and is held in place with a bandage. In addition to pain, you can expect the victim to experience nausea and vomiting, muscle spasms, and severe shock. Make the victim as comfortable as possible under the circumstances; if he complains of thirst, moisten his mouth with a few drops of water, but do not permit him to swallow the liquid.

Abrasions

Emergency Treatment

Wash the area in which the skin is scraped or rubbed off with soap and water, using clean gauze or cotton. Allow the abrasion to air-dry, and then cover it with a loose sterile dressing held in place with a bandage. If a sterile dressing is not available, use a clean handerchief.

Change the dressing after the first 24 hours, using household hydrogen peroxide to ease its removal if it sticks to the abrasion because of clotted blood. If the skinned area appears to be accompanied by swelling, or is painful or tender to the touch, consult a physician.

Acid Burns

Among acids likely to be encountered at work and around the home are sulphuric, nitric, and hydrochloric acids. Wet-cell batteries, such as automobile batteries, contain acid powerful enough to cause chemical destruction of body tissues, and some metal cleaners contain powerful acids.

Emergency Treatment

Wash off the acid immediately, using large amounts of clean, fresh, cool water. Strip off or cut off any clothing that may have absorbed any of the acid. If possible, put the victim in a shower bath; if a shower is not available, flood the affected skin areas with as much water as possible. However, do not apply water forcefully since this could aggravate damage already done to skin or other tissues.

After as much of the acid as possible has been eliminated by flooding with water, apply a mild solution of sodium bicarbonate or another mild alkali such as lime water. Caution should be exercised, however, in neutralizing an acid burn because the chemical reaction between an acid and an alkali can produce intense heat that would aggravate the injury; also, not all acids are effectively neutralized by alkalis—carbolic acid burns, for example, should be neutralized with alcohol.

Wash the affected areas once more with fresh water, then dry gently with sterile gauze; be careful not to break the skin or to open blisters. Extensive acid burns will cause extreme pain and shock; have the victim lie down with the head and chest a little lower than the rest of the body. As soon as possible, summon a physician or rush the victim to the emergency room of a hospital.

Aerosol Sprays

Although aerosol sprays generally are regarded as safe when handled according to directions, they can be directed accidentally toward the face with resulting contamination of the eyes or inhalation of the fumes. The pressurized containers may also contain products or propellants that are highly flammable, producing burns when used near an open flame. When stored near heat, in direct sunlight, or in a closed auto, the containers may explode violently.

Emergency Treatment

If eyes are contaminated by spray particles, flush the eye surfaces with water to remove any particles of the powder mist. Then carefully examine eye surfaces to determine if chemicals appear to be imbedded in the surface of the cornea. If aerosol spray is inhaled, move the patient to a well-ventilated area; keep him lying down, warm, and quiet. If breathing fails, administer artificial respiration. Victims of exploding containers or burning contents of aerosol containers should be given appropriate emergency treatment for bleeding, burns, and shock.

The redness and irritation of eye injuries should subside within a short time. If they do not, or if particles of spray seem to be imbedded in the surface of the eyes, take the victim to an ophthalmologist. A physician should also be summoned if a victim fails to recover quickly from the effects of inhaling an aerosol spray, particularly if the victim suffers from asthma or a similar lung disorder or from an abnormal heart condition.

Alkali Burns

Alkalis are used in the manufacture of soap and cleaners and in certain household cleaning products. They combine with fats to form soaps and may produce a painful injury when in contact with body surfaces.

Emergency Treatment

Flood the burned area with copious amounts of clean, cool, fresh water. Put the victim under a shower if possible, or otherwise pour running water over the area for as long as is necessary to dilute and weaken the corrosive chemical. Do not apply the water with such force that skin or other tissues are damaged. Remove clothing contaminated by the chemical.

Neutralize the remaining alkali with diluted vinegar, lemon juice, or a similar mild acid. Then wash the affected areas again with fresh water. Dry carefully with sterile gauze, being careful not to open blisters or otherwise cause skin breaks that could result in infection. Summon professional medical care as soon as possible. Meanwhile, treat the victim for shock.

Angina Pectoris

Angina pectoris is a condition that causes acute chest pain because of interference with the supply of oxygen to the heart. Although the pain is sometimes confused with ulcer or acute indigestion symptoms, it has a distinct characteristic of its own, producing a feeling of heaviness, strangling, tightness, or suffocation. Angina is a symptom rather than a disease, and may be a chronic condition with those over 50. It is usually treated by placing a nitroglycerine tablet under the tongue.

An attack of acute angina can be brought on by emotional stress, overeating, strenuous exercise, or by any activity that makes excessive demands on heart function.

Emergency Treatment

An attack usually subsides in about ten minutes, during which the patient appears to be gasping for breath. He should be kept in a semireclining position rather than made to lie flat, and should be moved carefully only in order to place pillows under his head and chest so that he can breathe more easily. A physician should be called promptly after the onset of an attack.

Animal Bites/Rabies

Wild animals, particularly bats, serve as a natural reservoir of rabies, a disease that is almost always fatal unless promptly and properly treated. But the virus may be present in the saliva of any warm-blooded animal. Domestic animals should be immunized against rabies by vaccines injected by a veterinarian.

Rabies is transmitted to humans by an animal bite or through a cut or scratch already in the skin. The infected saliva may enter through any opening, including the membranes lining the nose or mouth. After an incubation period of about ten days, a person infected by a rabid animal experiences pain at the site of infection, extreme sensitivity of the skin to temperature changes, and painful spasms of the larynx that make it almost impossible to drink. Saliva thickens and the patient becomes restless and easily excitable. By the time symptoms develop, death may be imminent. Obviously, professional medical attention should begin promptly after having been exposed to the possibility of infection.

Emergency Treatment

The area around the wound should be washed thoroughly and repeatedly with soap and water, using a sterile gauze dressing to wipe fluid away from—not toward—the wound. Another sterile dressing is used to dry the wound and a third to cover it while the patient is taken to a hospital or physician's office. A tetanus injection is also indicated, and police and health authorities should be promptly notified of the biting incident.

If at all possible the biting animal should be indentified—if a wild animal, captured alive—and held for observation for a period of 10 to 15 days. If it can be determined during that period that the animal is not rabid, further treatment may not be required. If the animal is rabid, however, or if it cannot be located and impounded, the patient may have to undergo a series of daily rabies vaccine injections lasting from 14 days for a case of mild exposure to 21 days for severe exposure (a bite near the head, for example), plus several booster shots. Because of the sensitivity of some individuals to the rabies vaccines used, the treatment itself can be quite dangerous.

Recent research, however, has established that a new vaccine called HDCV (human diploid cell vaccine), which requires only six or fewer injections, is immunologically effective and is not usually accompanied by any side effects. The new vaccine has been used successfully on people of all ages who had been bitten by animals known to be rabid.

Appendicitis

The common signal for approaching appendicitis is a period of several days of indigestion and constipation, culminating in pain and tenderness on the lower right side of the abdomen. Besides these symptoms, appendicitis may be accompanied by nausea and a slight fever. Call a physician immediately and describe the symptoms in detail; delay may result in a ruptured appendix.

Emergency Treatment

While awaiting medical care, the victim may find some relief from the pain and discomfort by having an ice bag placed over the abdomen. Do not apply heat and give nothing by mouth. A laxative should not be offered.

Asphyxiation

See GAS POISONING.

Asthma Attack

Emergency Treatment

Make the patient comfortable and offer reassurance. If he has been examined by a physician and properly diagnosed, the patient probably has an inhalant device or other forms of medication on his person or nearby.

The coughing and wheezing spell may have been triggered by the presence of an allergenic substance such as animal hair, feathers, or kapok in pillows or cushions. Such items should be removed from the presence of the patient. In addition, placing the patient in a room with high humidity, such as a bathroom with the shower turned on, may be helpful.

Asthma attacks are rarely fatal in young people, but elderly persons should be watched carefully because of possible heart strain. In a severe attack, professional medical care including oxygen equipment may be required.

Back Injuries

In the event of any serious back injury, call a physician or arrange for immediate professional transfer of the victim to a hospital.

Emergency Treatment

Until determined otherwise by a physician, treat the injured person as a victim of a fractured spine. If he complains that he cannot move his head, feet, or toes, the chances are that the back is fractured. But even if he can move his feet or legs, it does not necessarily mean that he can be moved safely, since the back can be fractured without immediate injury to the spinal cord.

If the victim shows symptoms of shock, do not attempt to lower his head or move his body into the usual position for shock control. If it is absolutely essential to move the victim because of immediate danger to his life, make a rigid stretcher from a wide piece of solid lumber such as a door and cover the stretcher with a blanket for padding. Then carefully slide or pull the victim onto the stretcher, using his clothing to hold him. Tie the body onto the stretcher with strips of cloth.

Back Pain

See SCIATICA.

Black Eye

Although a black eye is frequently regarded as a minor medical problem, it can result in serious visual problems, including cataract or glaucoma.

Emergency Treatment

Inspect the area about the eye for possible damage to the eye itself, such as hemorrhage, rupture of the eyeball, or dislocated lens. Check also for cuts around the eye that may require professional medical care. Then treat the bruised area by putting the victim to bed, covering the eye with a bandage, and applying an ice bag to the area.

If vision appears to be distorted or lacerations need stitching and antibiotic treatment, take the victim to a physician's office. A physician should also be consulted about continued pain and swelling about the eye.

Black Widow Spider Bites

Emergency Treatment

Make the victim lie still. If the bite is on the arm or leg, position the victim so that the bite is lower than the level of the heart. Apply a rubber band or similar tourniquet between the bite and the heart to retard venom flow toward the heart. The bite usually is marked by two puncture points. Apply ice packs to the bite. Summon a physician or carry the patient to the nearest hospital.

Loosen the tourniquet or constriction band for a few seconds every 15 minutes while awaiting help; you should be able to feel a pulse beyond the tourniquet if it is not too tight. Do not let the victim move about. Do not permit him to drink alcoholic beverages. He probably will feel weakness, tremor, and severe pain, but reassure him that he will recover. Medications, usually available only to a physician, should be administered promptly.

Bleeding, Internal

Internal bleeding is always a very serious condition; it requires immediate professional medical attention.

In cases of internal bleeding, blood is sometimes brought to the outside of the body by coughing from the lungs, by vomiting from the stomach, by trickling from the ear or nose, or by passing in the urine or bowel movement.

Often, however, internal bleeding is concealed, and the only symptom may be the swelling that appears around the site of broken bones. A person can lose three or four pints of blood inside the body without a trace of blood appearing outside the body.

Some Symptoms of Internal Bleeding

The victim will appear ill and pale. His skin will be colder than normal, especially the hands and feet; often the skin looks clammy because of sweating. The pulse usually will be rapid (over 90 beats a minute) and feeble.

Emergency Treatment

Serious internal bleeding is beyond the scope of first aid. If necessary treat the victim for respiratory and cardiac arrest and for shock while waiting for medical aid.

Bleeding, Minor

Bleeding from minor cuts, scrapes, and bruises usually stops by itself, but even small injuries of this kind should receive attention to prevent infection.

Emergency Treatment

The injured area should be washed thoroughly with soap and water, or if possible, held under running water. The surface should then be covered with a sterile bandage.

The type of wound known as a puncture wound may bleed very little, but is potentially extremely dangerous because of the possibility of tetanus infection. Anyone who steps on a rusty nail or thumbtack or has a similar accident involving a pointed object that penetrates deep under the skin surface should consult a physician about the need for antitetanus inoculation or a booster shot.

Blisters

Emergency Treatment

If the blister is on a hand or foot or other easily accessible part of the body, wash the area around the blister thoroughly with soap and water. After carefully drying the skin around the blister, apply an antiseptic to the same area. Then sterilize the point and a substantial part of a needle by heating it in an open flame. When the needle has been thoroughly sterilized, use the point to puncture the blister along the margin of the blister. Carefully squeeze the fluid from the blister by pressing it with a sterile gauze dressing; the dressing should soak up most of the fluid. Next, place a fresh sterile dressing over the blister and fasten it in place with a bandage. If a blister forms in a tender area or in a place that is not easily accessible, such as under the arm, do not open it yourself; consult your physician.

The danger from any break in the skin is that germs or dirt can slip through the natural barrier to produce an infection or inflammation. Continue to apply an antiseptic each day to the puncture area until it has healed. If it appears that an infection has developed or healing is unusually slow, consult a doctor. Persons with diabetes or circulatory problems may have to be more cautious about healing of skin breaks than other individuals.

Blood Blisters

Blood blisters, sometimes called hematomas, usually are caused by a sharp blow to the body surface such as hitting a finger with a hammer while pounding nails.

Emergency Treatment

Wash the area of the blood blister thoroughly with soap and water. Do not open it. If it is a small blood blister, cover it with a protective bandage; in many cases, the tiny pool of blood under the skin will be absorbed by the surrounding tissues if there is no further pressure at that point.

If the blood blister fails to heal quickly or becomes infected, consult a physician. Because the pool of blood has resulted from damage to a blood vessel, a blood blister usually is more vulnerable to infection or inflammation than an ordinary blister.

Boils

Boils frequently are an early sign of diabetes or another illness and should be watched carefully if they occur often. In general, they result from germs or dirt being rubbed into the skin by tight-fitting clothing, scratching, or through tiny cuts made during shaving.

Emergency Treatment

If the boil is above the lip, do not squeeze it or apply any pressure. The infection in that area of the face may drain into the brain because of the pattern of blood circulation on the face. Let a physician treat any boil on the face. If the boil is on the surface of another part of the body, apply moist hot packs, but do not squeeze or press on the boil because that action can force the infection into the circulatory system. A wet compress can be made by soaking a wash cloth or towel in warm water.

If the boil erupts, carefully wipe away the pus with a sterile dressing, and then cover it with another sterile dressing. If the boil is large or slow to erupt, or if it is slow to heal, consult a physician.

Bone Bruises

Emergency Treatment

Make sure the bone is not broken. If the injury is limited to the thin layer of tissue surrounding the bone, and the function of the limb is normal though painful, apply a compression dressing and an ice pack. Limit use of the injured limb for the next day or two.

As the pain and swelling recede, cover the injured area with a foam-rubber pad held in place with an elastic bandage. Because the part of the limb that is likely to receive a bone bruise lacks a layer of muscle and fat, it will be particularly sensitive to any pressure until recovery is complete.

Botulism

The bacteria that produce the lethal toxin of botulism are commonly present on unwashed farm vegetables and thrive in containers that are improperly sealed against the damaging effects of air. Home-canned vegetables, particularly string beans, are a likely source of botulism, but the toxin can be found in fruits, meats, and other foods. It can also appear in food that has been properly prepared but allowed to cool before being served. Examples are cold soups and marinated vegetables.

Emergency Treatment

As soon as acute symptoms—nausea, diarrhea, and abdominal distress—appear, try to induce vomiting. Vomiting usually can be started by touching the back of the victim's throat with a finger or the handle of a spoon, which should be smooth and blunt, or by offering him a glass of water in which two tablespoons of salt have been dissolved. Call a physician; describe all of the symptoms, which also may include, after several hours, double vision, muscular weakness, and difficulty in swallowing and breathing. Save samples of the food suspected of contamination for analysis.

Prompt hospitalization and injection of antitoxin are needed to save most cases of botulism poisoning. Additional emergency measures may include artificial respiration if regular breathing fails because of paralysis of respiratory muscles. Continue artificial respiration until professional medical care is provided. If other individuals have eaten the contaminated food, they should receive treatment for botulism even if they show no symptoms of the toxin's effects, since symptoms may be delayed by several days.

Brown House (or Recluse) Spider Bites

Emergency Treatment

Apply an ice bag or cold pack to the wound area. Aspirin and antihistamines may be offered to help relieve any pain or feeling of irritation. Keep the victim lying down and quiet. Call a physician as quickly as possible and describe the situation; the physician will advise what further action should be taken at this point.

The effects of a brown spider bite frequently last much longer than the pain of the bite, which may be comparatively mild for an insect bite or sting. But the poison from the bite can gradually destroy the surrounding tissues, leaving at first an ulcer and eventually a disfiguring scar. A physician's treatment is needed to control the loss of tissue; he probably will prescribe drugs and recommend continued use of cold compresses. The victim, meanwhile, will feel numbness and muscular weakness, requiring a prolonged period of bed rest in addition to the medical treatments.

Bruises/Contusions

Emergency Treatment

Bruises or contusions result usually from a blow to the body that is powerful enough to damage muscles, tendons, blood vessels, or other tissues without causing a break in the skin.

Because the bruised area will be tender, protect it from further injury. If possible, immobilize the injured body part with a sling, bandage, or other device that makes the victim feel more comfortable; pillows, folded blankets, or similar soft materials can be used to elevate an arm or leg. Apply an ice bag or cold water dressing to the injured area.

A simple bruise usually will heal without extensive treatment. The swelling and discoloration result from blood oozing from damaged tissues. Severe bruising can, however, be quite serious and requires medical attention. Keep the victim quiet and watch for symptoms of shock. Give aspirin for pain.

Bullet Wounds

Bullet wounds, whether accidental or purposely inflicted, can range from those that are superficial and external to those that involve internal bleeding and extensive tissue damage.

Emergency Treatment

A surface bullet wound accompanied by bleeding should be covered promptly with sterile gauze to prevent further infection. The flow of blood should be controlled as described under "Severe Bleeding" in this chapter. *Don't* try to clean the wound with soap or water.

If the wound is internal, keep the patient lying down and wrap him with coats or blankets placed over and under his body. If respiration has ceased or is impaired, give mouth-to-mouth respiration and treat him for shock. Get medical aid promptly.

Burns, Thermal

Burns are generally described according to the depth or area of skin damage involved. First-degree burns are the most superficial. They are marked by reddening of the skin and swelling, increased warmth, tenderness, and pain. Second-degree burns, deeper than first-degree, are in effect open wounds, characterized by blisters and severe pain in addition to redness. Third-degree burns are deep enough to involve damage to muscles and bones. The skin is charred and there may be no pain because nerve endings have been destroyed. However, the area of the burn generally is more important than the degree of burn; a first- or second-degree burn covering a large area of the body is more likely to be fatal than a small third-degree burn.

Emergency Treatment

You will want to get professional medical help for treatment of a severe burn, but there are a number of things you can do until such help is obtained. If burns are minor, apply ice or ice water until pain subsides. Then wash the area with soap and water. Cover with a sterile dressing. Give the victim one or two aspirin tablets to help relieve discomfort. A sterile gauze pad soaked in a solution of two tablespoons of baking soda (sodium bicarbonate) per quart of lukewarm water may be applied.

For more extensive or severe burns, there are three first-aid objectives: (1) relieve pain, (2) prevent shock, (3) prevent infection. To relieve pain, exclude air by applying a thick dressing of four to six layers plus additional coverings of clean, tightly woven material; for extensive burns, use clean sheets or towels. Clothing should be cut away—never pulled—from burned areas; where fabric is stuck to the wound, leave it for a physician to remove later. Do not apply any ointment, grease, powder, salve, or other medication; the physician simply will have to remove such material before he can begin professional treatment of the burns.

To prevent shock, make sure the victim's head is lower than his feet. Be sure that the victim is covered sufficiently to keep him warm, but not enough to make him overheated; exposure to cold can make the effects of shock more severe. Provide the victim with plenty of nonalcoholic liquids such as sweetened water, tea, or fruit juices, so long as he is conscious and able to swallow.

To prevent infection, do not permit absorbent cotton or adhesive tape to touch the wound caused by a burn. Do not apply iodine or any other antiseptic to the burn. Do not open any blisters. Do not permit any unsterile matter to contact the burn area. If possible, prevent other persons from coughing, sneezing, or even breathing toward the wound resulting from a burn. Serious infections frequently develop in burn victims from contamination by microorganisms of the mouth and nose.

Long-Term Treatment

A highly effective method of treating serious burns involves, first, removal of samples of uninjured skin from victims' bodies. Laboratory workers then "grind up" the healthy skin samples and separate them into groups of cells. Placed in flasks and bathed in a growth-stimulating solution, the cells grow rapidly; while the colonies are small, they double in size every 17 hours. New skin appears. The procedure can be repeated until enough has been grown to cover the burned areas.

Because the "test-tube skin" is developed from samples of a victim's own skin, the body does not reject it. It can be grafted onto a burned area in patches until the entire burn is covered. The new skin has no hair follicles or sweat glands, and is thinner than normal skin. But it offers hope to some 10 to 15 percent of those persons who are hospitalized with burn injuries.

See also CHEMICAL BURNS OF THE EYE.

Carbuncles

Carbuncles are quite similar to boils

except that they usually develop around multiple hair follicles and commonly appear on the neck or face. Personal hygiene is one factor involved in the development of carbuncles; persons apparently susceptible to the pustular inflammations must exercise special care in cleansing areas in which carbuncles occur, particularly if they suffer from diabetes or circulatory ailments.

Emergency Treatment

Apply moist hot packs to the boil-like swelling. Change the moist hot packs frequently, or place a hot-water bottle on the moist dressing to maintain the moist heat application. Do not handle the carbuncle beyond whatever contact is necessary to apply or maintain the moist heat. The carbuncle should eventually rupture or reach a point where it can be opened with a sterile sharp instrument. After the carbuncle has ruptured and drained, and the fluid from the growth has been carefully cleaned away, apply a sterile dressing.

Frequently, carbuncles must be opened and drained by a physician.

Cat Scratch Fever

Although the scratch or bite of a house cat or alley cat may appear at first to be only a mild injury, the wound can become the site of entry for a disease virus transmitted by apparently healthy cats. The inflammation, accompanied by fever, generally affects the lymph nodes and produces some aches and pains as well as fatigue. Although the disease is seldom fatal, an untreated case can spread to brain tissues and lead to other complications.

Emergency Treatment

Wash the scratch thoroughly with water and either soap or a mild detergent. Apply a mild antiseptic such as hydrogen peroxide. Cover with a sterile dressing.

Watch the area of the scratch carefully for the next week or two. If redness or swelling develop, even after the scratch appears healed, consult your physician. The inflammation of the scratch area may be accompanied by mild fever and symptoms similar to those of influenza; in small children, the symptoms may be quite serious. Bed rest and antibiotics usually are prescribed.

Charley Horse

A charley horse occurs because a small number of muscle fibers have been torn or ruptured by overstraining the muscle, or by the force of a blow to the muscle.

Emergency Treatment

Rest the injured muscle and apply an ice pack if there is swelling. A compression dressing can be applied to support the muscle. Avoid movement that stretches the muscle, and restrict other movements that make the victim uncomfortable. If pain and swelling persist, call a physician.

During the recovery period, which may not begin for a day or two, apply local heat with a hot water bottle or an electric heating pad, being careful not to burn the victim. A return to active use of the muscle can begin gradually as pain permits.

Chemical Burns of the Eye

Emergency Treatment

Flush the victim's eye immediately with large quantities of fresh, clean water; a drinking fountain can be used to provide a steady stream of water. If a drinking fountain is not available, lay the victim on the floor or ground with his head turned slightly to one side and pour water into the eye from a cup or glass. Always direct the stream of water so that it enters the eye surface at the inside corner and flows across the eye to the outside corner. If the victim is unable, because of intense pain, to open his eyes, it may be necessary to hold the lids apart while water pours across the eye. Continue flushing the eye for at least 15 minutes. (An alternate method is to immerse the victim's face in a pan or basin or bucket of water while he opens and closes his eyes repeatedly; continue the process for at least 15 minutes.)

When the chemical has been flushed from the victim's eye, the eye should be covered with a small, thick compress held in place with a bandage that covers both eyes, if possible; the bandage can be tied around the victim's head. **Note:** Apply nothing but water to the eye; do not attempt to neutralize a chemical burn of the eye and do not apply oil, ointment, salve, or other medications. Rush the victim to a physician as soon as possible, preferably to an ophthalmologist.

Chemicals on Skin

Many household and industrial chemicals, such as ammonia, lye, iodine, creosote, and a wide range of insecticides can cause serious injury if accidentally spilled on the skin.

Emergency Treatment

Wash the body surface that has been affected by the chemical with large amounts of water. Do not try to neutralize the chemical with another substance; the reaction may aggravate the injury. If blisters appear, apply a sterile dressing. If the chemical is a refrigerant, such as Freon, or carbon dioxide under pressure, treat for frostbite.

If the chemical has splashed into the eyes or produces serious injury to the affected body surface, call a physician. The victim should be watched closely for possible poisoning effects if the chemical is a pesticide, since such substances may be absorbed through the skin to produce internal toxic reactions. If there is any question about the toxicity of a chemical, ask your doctor or call the nearest poison control center.

Chigger Bites

Emergency Treatment

Apply ice water or rub ice over the area afflicted by bites of the tiny red insects. Bathing the area with alcohol, ammonia water or a solution of baking soda also will provide some relief from the itching.

Wash thoroughly with soap, using a scrub brush to prevent further infestation by the chiggers in other areas of the body. Rub alcohol over the surrounding areas and apply sulfur ointment as protection against mites that may not have attached themselves to the skin. Continue applications of ice water or alcohol to skin areas invaded by the insects. Clothing that was worn should be laundered immediately.

Chilblains

Emergency Treatment

Move the victim to a moderately warm place and remove wet or tight clothing. Soak the affected body area in warm—but not hot—water for about ten minutes. Then carefully blot the skin dry, but do not rub the skin. Replace the clothing with garments that are warm, soft, and dry.

Give the victim a stimulant such as tea or coffee, or an alcoholic beverage, and put him to bed with only light blankets; avoid the pressure of heavy blankets or heavy, tight garments on the sensitive skin areas. The victim should move the affected body areas gently to help restore normal circulation. If complications develop, such as marked discoloration of the skin, pain, or blistering and splitting of the skin, call a physician.

Cold Sores/Fever Blisters

Emergency Treatment

Apply a soothing ointment or a medication such as camphor ice. Avoid squeezing or otherwise handling the blisters; moisture can aggravate the sores and hinder their healing. Repeated appearances of cold sores or fever blisters, which are caused by the herpes simplex virus, may require treatment by a physician.

Concussion

See HEAD INJURIES.

Contusions

See BRUISES.

Convulsions

Emergency Treatment

Protect the victim from injury by moving him to a safe place; loosen any constricting clothing such as a tie or belt; put a pillow or coat under his head; if his mouth is open, place a folded cloth between his teeth to keep him from biting his tongue. Do not force anything into his mouth. Keep the patient warm but do not disturb him; do not try to restrain his convulsive movements.

Send for a physician as quickly as possible. Watch the patient's breathing and begin artificial respiration if breathing stops for more than one minute. Be sure that breathing actually has stopped; the patient may be sleeping or unconscious after an attack but breathing normally.

Convulsions in a small child may signal the onset of an infectious disease and may be accompanied by a high fever. The same general precautions should be taken to prevent self-injury on the part of the child. If placed in a bed, the child should be protected against falling onto the floor. Place him on his side—not on his back or stomach—if he vomits. Cold compresses or ice packs on the back of the neck and the head may help relieve symptoms. Immediate professional medical care is vital because brain damage can result if treatment is delayed.

See also EPILEPTIC SEIZURES.

Cramps

See MUSCLE CRAMPS.

Croup

Croup is a breathing disorder usually caused by a virus infection and less often by bacteria or allergy. It is a common condition during childhood, and in some cases, may require brief hospitalization for proper treatment.

The onset of a croup attack is likely to occur during the night with a sudden hoarse or barking cough accompanied by difficulty in breathing. The coughing is usually followed by choking spasms that sound as though the child is strangling. There may also be a mild fever. A physician should be called immediately when these symptoms appear.

Emergency Treatment

The most effective treatment for croup is cool moist air. Cool water vaporizers are available as well as warm steam vaporizers. Another alternative is to take the child into the bathroom, close the door and windows, and let the hot water run from the shower and sink taps until the room is filled with steam.

It is also possible to improvise a croup tent by boiling water in a kettle on a portable hot plate and arranging a blanket over the back of a chair so that it encloses the child and an adult as well as the steaming kettle. A child should never be left alone even for an instant in such a makeshift arrangement.

If the symptoms do not subside in about 20 minutes with any of the above procedures, or if there is mounting fever, and if the physician is not on his way, the child should be rushed to the closest hospital. Cold moist night air, rather than being a danger, may actually make the symptoms subside temporarily.

Diabetic Coma and Insulin Shock

Diabetics should always carry an identification tag or card to alert others of their condition in the event of a diabetic coma—which is due to a lack of insulin. They also should advise friends or family members of their diabetic condition and the proper emergency measures that can be taken in the event of an onset of diabetic coma. A bottle of rapid-acting insulin should be kept on hand for such an emergency.

Emergency Treatment

If the victim is being treated for diabetes, he probably will have nearby a supply of insulin and a hypodermic apparatus for injecting it. Find the insulin, hypodermic syringe, and needle; clean a spot on the upper arm or thigh, and inject about 50 units of insulin. Call a physician without delay, and describe the patient's symptoms and your treatment. The patient usually will respond without ill effects, but may be quite thirsty. Give him plenty of fluids, as needed.

If the victim does not respond to the insulin, or if you cannot find the insulin and hypodermic syringe, rush the victim to the nearest physician's office.

Insulin shock—which is due to a reaction to too much insulin and not enough sugar in the blood—can be treated in an emergency by offering a sugar-rich fluid such as a cola beverage or orange juice. Diabetics frequently carry a lump of sugar or candy that can be placed in their mouth in case of an insulin shock reaction. It should be tucked between the teeth and cheek so the victim will not choke on it.

If you find a diabetic in a coma and do not know the cause, assume the cause is an insulin reaction and treat him with sugar. This will give immediate relief to an insulin reaction but will not affect diabetic coma.

Diarrhea

Emergency Treatment

Give the victim an antidiarrheal agent; all drugstores carry medications composed of kaolin and pectin that are useful for this purpose. Certain bismuth compounds also are recommended for diarrhea control.

Put the victim in bed for a period of at least 12 hours and withhold food and drink for that length of time. Do not let the victim become dehydrated; if he is thirsty, let him suck on pieces of ice. If the diarrhea appears to be subsiding, let him sip a mild beverage like tea or ginger ale; cola syrup is also recommended.

Later on the patient can try eating bland foods such as dry toast, crackers, gelatin desserts, or jellied consomme. Avoid feeding rich, fatty, or spicy foods. If the diarrhea fails to subside or is complicated by colic or vomiting, call a physician.

Dizziness/Vertigo

Emotional upsets, allergies, and improper eating and drinking habits—too much food, too little food, or foods that are too rich—can precipitate symptoms of dizziness. The cause also can be a physical disorder such as abnormal functioning of the inner ear or a circulatory problem. Smoking tobacco, certain drugs such as quinine, and fumes of some chemicals also can produce dizziness.

Emergency Treatment

Have the victim lie down with the eyes closed. In many cases, a period of simple bed rest will alleviate the symptoms. Keep the victim quiet and comfortable. If the feeling of dizziness continues, becomes worse, or is accompanied by nausea and vomiting, call a physician.

Severe or persistent dizziness or vertigo requires a longer period of bed rest and the use of medicines prescribed by a physician. While recovering, the victim should avoid sudden changes in body position or turning the head rapidly. In some types of vertigo, surgery is required to cure the disorder.

Drowning

Victims of drowning seldom die because of water in the lungs or stomach. They die because of lack of air.

Emergency Treatment

If the victim's breathing has been impaired, start artificial respiration immediately. If there is evidence of cardiac arrest, administer cardiac massage. When the victim is able to breathe for himself, treat him for shock and get medical help.

Drug Overdose (Barbiturates)

Barbiturates are used in a number of drugs prescribed as sedatives, although many are also available through illegal channels. Because the drugs can affect the judgment of the user, he may not remember having taken a dose and so may take additional pills, thus producing overdose effects.

Emergency Treatment

If the drug was taken orally, try to induce vomiting in the victim. Have him drink a glass of water containing two tablespoons of salt. Or touch the back of his throat gently with a finger or a smooth blunt object like the handle of a spoon. Then give the victim plenty of warm water to drink. It is important to rid the stomach of as much of the drug as possible and to dilute the substance remaining in the gastrointestinal tract.

As soon as possible, call a physician or get the victim to the nearest hospital or physician's office. If breathing fails, administer artificial respiration.

Drug Overdose (Stimulants)

Although most of the powerful stimulant drugs, or pep pills, are available only through a physician's prescription, the same medications are available through illicit sources. When taken without direction of a supervising physician, the stimulants can produce a variety of adverse side effects, and when used frequently over a period of time can result in physical and psychological problems that require hospital treatment.

Emergency Treatment

Give the victim a solution of one tablespoon of activated charcoal mixed with a small amount of water, or give him a glass of milk, to dilute the effects of the medication in the stomach. Then induce vomiting by pressing gently on the back of the throat with a finger or the smooth blunt edge of a spoon handle. Vomiting also may be induced with a solution made of one teaspoonful of mustard in a half glass of water. Do not give syrup of ipecac to a victim who has been taking stimulants.

As soon as possible call a physician or get the victim to the nearest hospital or physician's office. If breathing fails, administer artificial respiration.

Earaches

An earache may be associated with a wide variety of ailments ranging from the common cold or influenza to impacted molars or tonsillitis. An earache also may be involved in certain infectious diseases such as measles or scarlet fever. Because of the relationship of ear structures to other parts of the head and throat, an infection involving the symptoms of earache can easily spread to the brain tissues or the spongy mastoid bone behind the ear. Call a physician and describe all of the symptoms, including temperature, any discharge, pain, ringing in the ear, or deafness. Delay in reporting an earache to a doctor can result in complications that require hospital treatment.

Emergency Treatment

This may incude a few drops of warm olive oil or sweet oil held in the ear by a small wad of cotton. Aspirin can be given to help relieve any pain. Professional medical treatment may include the use of antibiotics.

Ear, Foreign Body in

Emergency Treatment

Do not insert a hairpin, stick, or other object in the ear in an effort to remove a foreign object; you are likely to force the object farther into the ear canal. Instead, have the victim tilt his head to one side, with the ear containing the foreign object facing upward. While pulling gently on the lobe of the ear to straighten the canal, pour a little warmed olive oil or mineral oil into the ear. Then have the victim tilt that ear downward so the oil will run out quickly; it should dislodge the foreign object.

Wipe the ear canal gently with a cotton-tipped matchstick, or a similar device that will not irritate the lining of the ear canal, after the foreign body has been removed. If the emergency treatment is not successful, call a physician.

Electric Shocks

An electric shock from the usual 110-volt current in most homes can be a serious emergency, especially if the person's skin or clothing is wet. Under these circumstances, the shock may paralyze the part of the brain that controls breathing and stop the heart completely or disorder its pumping action.

Emergency Treatment

It is of the utmost importance to break the electrical contact *immediately* by unplugging the wire of the appliance involved or by shutting off the house current switch. **Do not touch the victim of the shock while he is still acting as an electrical conductor.**

If the shock has come from a faulty wire out of doors and the source of the electrical current can't be reached easily, make a lasso of dry rope on a long sturdy dry stick. Catch the victim's hand or foot in the loop and drag him away from the wire. Another way to break the contact is to cut the wire with a dry axe.

If the victim of the shock is unconscious, or if his pulse is very weak, administer mouth-to-mouth respiration and cardiac massage until he can get to a hospital.

Epileptic Seizures

Epilepsy is a disorder of the nervous system that produces convulsive seizures. In a major seizure or *grand mal,* the epileptic usually falls to the ground. Indeed, falling is in most cases one of the principal dangers of the disease. Then the epileptic's body begins to twitch or jerk spasmodically. His breathing may be labored, and saliva may appear on his lips. His face may become pale or bluish. Although the scene can be frightening, it is not truly a medical emergency; the afflicted person is in no danger of losing his life.

Emergency Treatment

Make the person suffering the seizure as comfortable as possible. If he is on a hard surface, put something soft under his head, and move any hard or dangerous objects away from him. **Make no attempt to restrain his movements, and do not force anything into his mouth.** Just leave him alone until the attack is over, as it should be in a few minutes. If his mouth is already open, you might put something soft, such as a folded handerchief, between his side teeth. This will help to prevent him from biting his tongue or lips. If he seems to go into another seizure after coming out of the first, or if the seizure lasts more than ten minutes, call a physician. If his lower jaw sags and begins to obstruct his breathing, support of the lower jaw may be helpful in improving his breathing.

When the seizure is over, the patient should be allowed to rest quietly. Some people sleep heavily after a seizure. Others awake at once but are disoriented or confused for a while. Treat the episode in a matter-of-fact way. If it is the first seizure the person is aware of having had, advise him to see his physician promptly.

Eye, Foreign Body in

Emergency Treatment

Do not rub the eye or touch it with unwashed hands. The foreign body usually becomes lodged on the inner surface of the upper eyelid. Pull the upper eyelid down over the lower lid to help work the object loose. Tears or clean water can help wash out the dirt or other object. If the bit of irritating material can be seen on the surface of the eyeball, try very carefully to flick it out with the tip of a clean, moistened handkerchief or a piece of moistened cotton. Never touch the surface of the eye with dry materials. Sometimes a foreign body can be removed by carefully rolling the upper lid over a pencil or wooden matchstick to expose the object.

After the foreign object has been removed, the eye should be washed with clean water or with a solution made from one teaspoon of salt dissolved in a pint of water. This will help remove any remaining particles of the foreign body as well as any traces of irritating chemicals that might have been a part of it. Iron particles, for example, may leave traces of rust on the eye's surface unless washed away.

If the object cannot be located and removed without difficulty, a small patch of gauze or a folded handkerchief should be taped over the eye and the victim taken to a physician's office—preferably the office of an ophthalmologist. A physician also should be consulted if a feeling of irritation in the eye continues after the foreign body has been removed.

Fever

Emergency Treatment

If the fever is mild, around 100°F. by mouth, have the victim rest in bed and provide him with a light diet. Watch closely for other symptoms, such as a rash, and any further increase in body temperature. Aspirin usually can be given.

If the temperature rises to 101° F. or higher, is accompanied by pain, headache, delirium, confused behavior, coughing, vomiting, or other indications of a severe illness, call a physician. Describe all of the symptoms in detail, including the appearance of any rash and when it began.

Fever blisters

See COLD SORES.

Finger Dislocation

Emergency Treatment

Call a physician and arrange for inspection and treatment of the injury. If a physician is not immediately available, the finger dislocation may be reduced (put back in proper alignment) by grasping it firmly and carefully pulling it into normal position. Pull very slowly and avoid rough handling that might complicate the injury by damaging a tendon. If the dislocation cannot be reduced after the first try, go through the procedure once more. But do not try it more than twice.

Whether or not you are successful in reducing the finger dislocation, the finger should be immobilized after your efforts until a physician can examine it. A clean flat wooden stick can be strapped along the palm side of the finger with adhesive tape or strips of bandage to hold it in place.

Fingernail Injuries/Hangnails

Emergency Treatment

Wash the injured nail area thoroughly with warm water and soap. Trim off any torn bits of nail. Cover with a small adhesive dressing or bandage.

Apply petroleum jelly or cold cream to the injured nail area twice a day, morning and night, until it is healed. If redness or irritation develops in the adjoining skin area, indicating an infection, consult a physician.

Fish Poisoning

Emergency Treatment

Induce vomiting in the victim to remove the bits of poisonous fish from the stomach. Vomiting usually can be started by pressing on the back of the throat with a finger or a spoon handle that is blunt and smooth, or by having the victim drink a solution of two tablespoons of salt in a glass of water.

Call a physician as soon as possible. Describe the type of fish eaten and the symptoms, which may include nausea, diarrhea, abdominal pain, muscular weakness, and a numbness or tingling sensation that begins about the face and spreads to the extremities.

If breathing fails, administer mouth-to-mouth artificial respiration; a substance commonly found in poisonous fish causes respiratory failure. Also, be prepared to provide emergency treatment for convulsions.

Food Poisoning

Emergency Treatment

If the victim is not already vomiting, try to induce it to clear the stomach. Vomiting can be started in most cases by pressing gently on the back of the throat with a finger or a blunt smooth spoon handle, or by having the patient drink a glass of water containing two tablespoons of salt. If the victim has vomited, put him to bed.

Call a physician and describe the food ingested and the symptoms that developed. If symptoms are severe, professional medical treatment with antibiotics and medications for cramps may be required. Special medications also may be needed for diarrhea caused by bacterial food poisoning.

Fractures

Any break in a bone is called a fracture. The break is called an *open* or *compound fracture* if one or both ends of the broken bone pierce the skin. A *closed* or *simple fracture* is one in which the broken bone doesn't come through the skin.

It is sometimes difficult to distinguish a strained muscle or a sprained ligament from a broken bone, since sprains and strains can be extremely painful even though they are less serious than breaks. However, when there is any doubt, the injury should be treated as though it were a simple fracture.

Emergency Treatment

Don't try to help the injured person move around or get up unless he has slowly tested out the injured part of his body and is sure that nothing has been broken. If he is in extreme pain, or if the injured part has begun to swell, or if by running the finger lightly along the affected bone a break can be felt, *do not* move him. Under no circumstances should he be crowded into a car if his legs, hip, ribs, or back are involved in the accident. Call for an ambulance immediately, and until it arrives, treat the person for shock.

Splinting

In a situation where it is imperative to move someone who may have a fracture, the first step is to apply a splint so that the broken bone ends are immobilized.

Splints can be improvised from anything rigid enough and of the right length to support the fractured part of the body: a metal rod, board, long cardboard tube, tightly rolled newspaper or blanket. If the object being used has to be padded for softness, use a small blanket or any other soft material, such as a jacket.

The splint should be long enough so that it can be tied with a bandage, torn sheet, or neckties beyond the joint above and below the fracture as well as at the site of the break. If a leg is involved, it should be elevated with pillows or any other firm support after the splint has been applied. If the victim has to wait a considerable length of time before receiving professional attention, the splint bandaging should be checked from time to time to make sure it isn't too tight.

In the case of an open or compound fracture, additional steps must be taken. Remove that part of the victim's clothing that is covering the wound. Do not wash or probe into the wound, but control bleeding by applying pressure over the wound through a sterile or clean dressing.

Frostbite

Emergency Treatment

Begin rapid rewarming of the affected tissues as soon as possible. If possible, immerse the victim in a warm bath, but avoid scalding. (The temperature should be between 102°F. and 105°F.) Warm wet towels also will help if changed frequently and applied gently. Do not massage, rub, or even touch the frostbitten flesh. If warm water or a warming fire is not available, place the patient in a sleeping bag or cover him with coats and blankets. Hot liquids can be offered if available to help raise the body temperature.

For any true frostbite case, prompt medical attention is important. The depth and degree of the frozen tissue cannot be determined without a careful examination by a physician.

Gallbladder Attacks

Although gallstones can affect a wide variety of individuals, the most common victims are overweight persons who enjoy rich foods. The actual attack of spasms caused by gallstones passing through the duct leading from the gallbladder to the digestive tract usually is preceded by periods of stomach distress including belching. X rays usually will reveal the presence of gallstones when the early warning signs are noted, and measures can be taken to reduce the threat of a gallbladder attack.

Emergency Treatment

Call a physician and describe in detail the symptoms, which may include colic high in the abdomen and pain extending to the right shoulder; the pain may be accompanied by nausea, vomiting, and sweating. Hot water bottles may be applied to the abdomen to help relieve distress while waiting for professional medical care. If the physician permits, the victim may be allowed to sip certain fluids such as fruit juices, but do not offer him solid food.

Gas Poisoning

Before attempting to revive someone overcome by toxic gas poisoning, the most important thing to do is to remove him to the fresh air. If this isn't feasible, all windows and doors should be opened to let in as much fresh air as possible.

Any interior with a dangerous concentration of carbon monoxide or other toxic gases is apt to be highly explosive. Therefore, gas and electricity should be shut off as quickly as possible. **Under no circumstances should any matches be lighted in an interior where there are noxious fumes.**

The rescuer needn't waste time covering his face with a handkerchief or other cloth. He should hold his breath instead, or take only a few quick, shallow breaths while bringing the victim to the out-of-doors or to an open window.

Emergency Treatment

Administer artificial respiration if the victim is suffering respiratory arrest. Arrange for medical help as soon as possible, requesting that oxygen be brought to the scene.

Head Injuries

Accidents involving the head can result in concussion, skull fracture, or brain injury. Symptoms of head injury include loss of consciousness, discharge of a watery or blood-tinged fluid from the ears, nose, or mouth, and a difference in size of the pupils of the eyes. Head injuries must be thought of as serious; they demand immediate medical assistance.

Emergency Treatment

Place the victim in a supine position, and, if there is no evidence of injury to his neck, arrange for a slight elevation of his head *and* shoulders. Make certain that he has a clear airway and administer artificial respiration if necessary. If vomitus, blood, or other fluids appear to flow from the victim's mouth, turn his head gently to one side. Control bleeding and treat for shock. Do not administer stimulants or fluids of any kind.

Heart Attack

A heart attack is caused by interference with the blood supply to the heart muscle. When the attack is brought on because of a blood clot in the coronary artery, it is known as *coronary occlusion* or *coronary thrombosis*.

The most dramatic symptom of a serious heart attack is a crushing chest pain that usually travels down the left arm into the hand or into the neck and back. The pain may bring on dizziness, cold sweat, complete collapse, and loss of consciousness. The face has an ashen pallor, and there may be vomiting.

Emergency Treatment

The victim ***must not be moved*** unless he has fallen in a dangerous place. If no physician is immediately available, an ambulance should be called at once. No attempt should be made to get the victim of a heart attack into an automobile.

Until help arrives, give the victim every reassurance that he will get prompt treatment, and keep him as calm and quiet as possible. Don't give him any medicine or stimulants. If oxygen is available, start administering it to the victim immediately, either by mask or nasal catheter, depending on which is available.

If the victim is suffering from respiratory arrest, begin artificial respiration. If he is suffering from cardiac arrest, begin cardiac massage.

Heat Exhaustion

Heat exhaustion occurs when the body is exposed to high temperatures and large amounts of blood accumulate in the skin as a way of cooling it. As a result, there is a marked decrease in the amount of blood that circulates through the heart and to the brain. The victim becomes markedly pale and is covered with cold perspiration. Breathing is increasingly shallow and the pulse weakens. In acute cases, fainting occurs. Medical aid should be summoned for anyone suffering from heat exhaustion.

Emergency Treatment

Place the victim in a reclining position with his feet raised about ten inches above his body. Loosen or remove his clothing, and apply cold, wet cloths to his wrists and forehead. If he has fainted and doesn't recover promptly, smelling salts or spirits of ammonia should be placed under his nose. When the victim is conscious, give him sips of salt water (approximately one teaspoon of salt per glass of water), the total intake to be about two glasses in an hour's time. If the victim vomits, discontinue the salt solution.

Heatstroke/Sunstroke

Heatstroke is characterized by an acutely high body temperature caused by the cessation of perspiration. The victim's skin becomes hot, dry, and flushed, and he may suffer collapse. Should the skin turn ashen gray, a physician must be called immediately. Prompt hospital treatment is recommended for anyone showing signs of sunstroke who has previously had any kind of heart damage.

Emergency Treatment

The following measures are designed to reduce the victim's body temperature as quickly as possible and prevent damage to the internal organs:

Place him in a tub of very cold water, or, if this is not possible, spray or sponge his body repeatedly with cold water or rubbing alcohol. Take his temperature by mouth, and when it has dropped to about 100°F., remove him to a bed and wrap him in cold, wet sheets. If possible, expose him to an electric fan or an air conditioner.

Hiccups

Emergency Treatment

Have the victim slowly drink a large glass of water. If cold water is not effective, have him drink warm water containing a teaspoonful of baking soda. Milk also can be employed. For babies and small children, offer sips of warm water. Do not offer carbonated beverages.

Another helpful measure is breathing into a large paper bag a number of times to raise the carbon dioxide level in the lungs. Rest and relaxation are recommended; have the victim lie down to read or watch television.

If the hiccups fail to go away, and continued spastic contractions of the diaphragm interfere with eating and sleeping, call a physician.

Insect Stings

Honeybees, wasps, hornets, and yellow jackets are the most common stinging insects and most likely to attack on a hot summer day. Strongly scented perfumes or cosmetics and brightly colored, rough-finished clothing attract bees and should be avoided by persons working or playing in garden areas. It should also be noted that many commercial repellents do not protect against stinging insects.

Emergency Treatment

If one is stung, the insect's stinger should be scraped gently but quickly from the skin; don't squeeze it. Apply Epsom salt solution to the sting area. Antihistamines are often helpful in reducing the patient's discomfort. If a severe reaction develops, call a physician.

There are a few people who are critically allergic to the sting of wasps, bees, yellow jackets, or fire ants. This sensitivity causes the vocal cord tissue to swell to the point where breathing may become impossible. A single sting to a sensitive person may result in a dangerous drop in blood pressure, thus producing shock. Anyone with such a severe allergy who is stung should be rushed to a hospital immediately.

A person who becomes aware of having this type of allergy should consult with a physician about the kind of medicine to carry for use in a crisis.

Insulin Shock

See DIABETIC COMA AND INSULIN SHOCK.

Jaw Dislocation

The jaw can be dislocated during a physical attack or fight; from a blow on the jaw during sports activities; or from overextension of the joint during yawning, laughing, or attempting to eat a large mouthful of food. The jaw becomes literally locked open so the victim cannot explain his predicament.

Emergency Treatment

Reducing a dislocated jaw will require that you insert your thumbs between the teeth of the victim. The jaw can be expected to snap into place quickly, and there is a danger that the teeth will clamp down on the thumbs when this happens, so the thumbs should be adequately padded with handkerchiefs or bandages. Once the thumbs are protected, insert them in the mouth and over the lower molars, as far back on the lower jaw as possible. While pressing down with the thumbs, lift the chin with the fingers outside the mouth. As the jaw begins to slip into normal position when it is pushed downward and backward with the chin lifted upward, quickly remove the thumbs from between the jaws.

Once the jaw is back in normal position, the mouth should remain closed for several hours while the ligaments recover from their displaced condition. If necessary, put a cravat bandage over the head to hold the mouth closed. If difficulty is experienced in reducing a jaw dislocation, the victim should be taken to a hospital where an anesthetic can be applied. A dislocated jaw can be extremely painful.

Jellyfish Stings

Emergency Treatment

Wash the area of the sting thoroughly with alcohol or fresh water. Be sure that any pieces of jellyfish tentacles have been removed from the skin. Aspirin or antihistamines can be administered to relieve pain and itching, but curtail the use of antihistamines if the victim has consumed alcoholic beverages. The leg or arm that received the sting can be soaked in hot water if the pain continues. Otherwise, apply calamine lotion.

If the victim appears to suffer a severe reaction from the sting, summon a doctor. The victim may experience shock, muscle cramps, convulsions, or loss of consciousness. Artificial respiration may be required while awaiting arrival of a doctor. The physician can administer drugs to relieve muscle cramps and provide sedatives or analgesics.

Kidney Stones

Emergency Treatment

Call a physician if the victim experiences the agonizing cramps or colic associated with kidney stones. Discuss the symptoms in detail with the doctor to make sure the pain is caused by kidney stones rather than appendicitis.

Comforting heat may be applied to the back and the abdomen of the side affected by the spasms. Paregoric can be administered, if available, while waiting for medical care; about two teaspoonsful of paregoric in a half glass of water may help relieve symptoms.

Knee Injuries

Emergency Treatment

If the injury appears to be severe, including possible fracture of the kneecap, immobilize the knee. To immobilize the knee, place the injured leg on a board that is about four inches wide and three to four feet in length. Place padding between the board and the knee and between the board and the back of the ankle. Then use four strips of bandage to fasten the leg to the padded board—one at the ankle, one at the thigh, and one each above and below the knee.

Summon a physician or move the patient to a physician's office. Keep the knee protected against cold or exposure to the elements, but otherwise do not apply a bandage or any type of pressure to the knee itself; any rapid swelling would be aggravated by unnecessary pressure in that area. Be prepared to treat the patient for shock.

Laryngitis

Laryngitis is associated with colds and influenza and may be accompanied by a fever. The ailment can be aggravated by smoking, and it is possible that the vocal cords can be damaged if the victim tries to force the use of his voice while the larynx is swollen by the infection.

Emergency Treatment

Have the victim inhale the warm moist air of a steam kettle or vaporizer. A vaporizer can be improvised in an emergency by pouring boiling water into a bowl and forming a "tent" over the steaming bowl with a large towel or sheet, or by placing a large paper bag over the bowl and cutting an opening at the closed end of the bag so the face can be exposed to the steam. The hot water can contain a bit of camphor or menthol, if available, to make the warm moist air more soothing to the throat, but this is not necessary.

Continue the use of the vaporizer for several days, as needed. The victim should not use the vocal cords any more than absolutely necessary. If the infection does not subside within the first few days, a physician should be consulted.

Leeches

Emergency Treatment

Do not try to pull leeches off the skin. They will usually drop away from the skin if a heated object such as a lighted cigarette is held close to them. Leeches also are likely to let go if iodine is applied to their bodies. The wound caused by a leech should be washed carefully with soap and water and an antiseptic applied.

Lightning Shock

Emergency Treatment

If the victim is not breathing, apply artificial respiration. If a second person is available to help, have him summon a physician while artificial respiration is administered. Continue artificial respiration until breathing resumes or the physician arrives.

When the victim is breathing regularly, treat him for shock. Keep him lying down with his feet higher than his head, his clothing loosened around the neck, and his body covered with a blanket or coat for warmth. If the victim shows signs of vomiting, turn his head to one side so he will not swallow the vomitus.

If the victim is breathing regularly and does not show signs of shock, he may be given a few sips of a stimulating beverage such as coffee, tea, or brandy.

Motion Sickness

Emergency Treatment

Have the victim lie down in a position that is most comfortable to him. The head should be fixed so that any view of motion is avoided. Reading or other use of the eyes should be prohibited. Food or fluids should be restricted to very small amounts. If traveling by car, stop at a rest area; in an airplane or ship, place the victim in an area where motion is least noticeable.

Drugs, such as Dramamine, are helpful for control of the symptoms of motion sickness; they are most effective when started about 90 minutes before travel begins and repeated at regular intervals thereafter.

Muscle Cramps

Emergency Treatment

Gently massage the affected muscle, sometimes stretching it to help relieve the painful contraction. Then relax the muscle by using a hot water bottle or an electric heating pad, or by soaking the affected area in a warm bath.

A repetition of cramps may require medical attention.

Nosebleeds

Emergency Treatment

Have the victim sit erect but with the head tilted slightly forward to prevent blood from running down the throat. Apply pressure by pinching the nostrils; if bleeding is from just one nostril, use pressure on that side. A small wedge of absorbent cotton or gauze can be inserted into the bleeding nostril. Make sure that the cotton or gauze extends out of the nostril to aid in its removal when the bleeding has stopped. Encourage the victim to breathe through the mouth while the nose is bleeding. After five minutes, release pressure on the nose to see if the bleeding has stopped. If the bleeding continues, repeat pressure on the nostril for an additional five minutes. Cold compresses applied to the nose can help stop the bleeding.

If bleeding continues after the second five-minute period of pressure treatment, get the victim to a physician's office or a hospital emergency room.

Poison Ivy/Poison Oak/Poison Sumac

Emergency Treatment

The poison of these three plants is the same and the treatment is identical. Bathe the skin area exposed to poison ivy, poison oak, or poison sumac with soap and water or with alcohol within 15 mintues after contact. If exposure is not discovered until a rash appears, apply cool wet dressings. Dressings can be made of old bed sheets or soft linens soaked in a solution of one teaspoon of salt per pint of water. Dressings should be applied four times a day for periods of 15 to 60 minutes each time; during these periods, dressings can be removed and reapplied every few minutes. The itching that often accompanies the rash can be relieved by taking antihistamine tablets.

Creams or lotions may be prescribed by a physician or supplied by a pharmacist. Do not use such folk remedies as ammonia or turpentine; do not use skin lotions not approved by a physician or druggist. Haphazard application of medications on poison ivy blisters and rashes can result in complications including skin irritation, infection, or pigmented lesions of the skin.

Rabies

See ANIMAL BITES.

Rape

Rape has been defined as any unlawful sexual intercourse or sexual contact by force or threat. Most commonly, men commit rape against women; but homosexual rape involving men only may occur, for example, in a prison.

Of the million or more Americans who are raped each year, one in five is under the age of 12. Boys are the victims of sexual assault as often as girls. In seven to ten percent of all reported adult cases, men are the victims.

Emergency Response

The victim of rape may not always be able to help him- or herself. Because violence may accompany the rape, the victim may find it impossible to seek help at once. But where possible, the recommended course of action is to go to a hospital for physical examination. Reporting to a hospital in itself may reduce the feelings of shock, depression, anxiety, and revulsion that generally follow a sexual assault. The physical examination that takes place at the hospital may produce evidence that could be important in a court trial if the rapist is later apprehended. Victims are also advised to report the rape to the police as soon as possible.

For additional information on ways to avoid rape and what to do if it occurs, see "The Rape Victim" in Ch. 25, *Women's Health.*

Sciatica/Lower Back Pain

Although lower back pain is frequently triggered by fatigue, anxiety, or by strained muscles or tendons, it may be a symptom of a slipped or ruptured disk between the vertebrae or of a similar disorder requiring extensive medical attention.

Emergency Treatment

Reduce the pressure on the lower back by having the victim lie down on a hard flat surface; if a bed is used there should be a board or sheet of plywood between the springs and mattress. Pillows should be placed under the knees instead of under the head, to help keep the back flat. Give aspirin to relieve the pain, and apply heat to the back. Call a physician if the symptoms do not subside overnight.

Scorpion Stings

Emergency Treatment

Apply ice to the region of the sting, except in the case of an arm or leg, in which event the limb may be immersed in ice water. Continue the ice or ice-water treatment for at least one hour. Try to keep the area of the sting at a position lower than the heart. No tourniquet is required. Should the breathing of a scorpion sting victim become depressed, administer artificial respiration. If symptoms fail to subside within a couple of hours, notify a physician, or transfer the victim to a doctor's office or hospital.

For children under six, call a physician in the event of any scorpion sting. Children stung by scorpions may become convulsive, and this condition can result in fatal exhaustion unless it receives prompt medical treatment.

Snakebites

Of the many varieties of snakes found in the United States, only four kinds are poisonous: copperheads, rattlesnakes, moccasins, and coral snakes. The first three belong to the category of pit vipers and are known as *hemotoxic* because their poison enters the bloodstream. The coral snake, which is comparatively rare, is related to the cobra and is the most dangerous of all because its venom is *neurotoxic.* This means that the poison transmitted by its bite goes directly to the nervous system and the brain.

How to Differentiate among Snakebites

Snakes of the pit viper family have a fang on each side of the head. These fangs leave characteristic puncture wounds on the skin in addition to two rows of tiny bites or scratches left by the teeth. A bite from a nonpoisonous snake leaves six rows—four upper and two lower—of very small bite marks or scratches and no puncture wounds.

The marks left by the bite of a coral snake do not leave any puncture wounds either, but this snake bites with a chewing motion, hanging on to the victim rather than attacking quickly. The coral snake is very easy to recognize because of its distinctive markings: wide horizontal bands of red and black separated by narrow bands of yellow.

Symptoms

A bite from any of the pit vipers produces immediate and severe pain and darkening of the skin, followed by weakness, blurred vision, quickened pulse, nausea, and vomiting. The bite of a coral snake produces somewhat the same symptoms, although there is less local pain and considerable drowsiness leading to unconsciousness.

If a physician or a hospital is a short distance away, the patient should receive professional help *immediately.* He should be transported lying down, either on an improvised stretcher or carried by his companions—with the wounded part lower than his heart. He should be advised to move as little as possible.

Emergency Treatment

If several hours must elapse before a physician or a hospital can be reached, the following procedures should be applied promptly:

1. Keep the victim lying down and as still as possible.

2. Tie a constricting band *above* the wound between it and the heart and tight enough to slow but not stop blood circulation. A handkerchief, necktie, sock, or piece of torn shirt will serve.

3. If a snakebite kit is available, use the knife it contains; otherwise, sterilize a knife or razor blade in a flame. Carefully make small cuts in the skin where the swelling has developed. Make the cuts along the length of the limb, not across or at right angles to it. The incisions should be shallow because of the danger of severing nerves, blood vessels, or muscles.

4. Use the suction cups in the snakebite kit, if available, to draw out as much of the venom as possible. If suction cups are not available, the venom can be removed by sucking it out with the mouth. Although snake venom is not a stomach poison, it should not be swallowed but should be rinsed from the mouth.

5. This procedure should be continued for from 30 to 60 minutes or until the swelling subsides and the other symptoms decrease.

6. You may apply cold compresses to the bite area while waiting for professional assistance.

7. Treat the victim for shock.

8. Give artificial respiration if necessary.

Splinters

Emergency Treatment

Clean the area about the splinter with soap and water or an antiseptic. Next, sterilize a needle by holding it over an open flame. After it cools, insert the needle above the splinter so it will tear a line in the skin, making the splinter lie loose in the wound. Then, gently lift the splinter out, using a pair of tweezers or the point of the needle. If tweezers are used, they should be sterilized first.

Wash the wound area again with soap and water, or apply an antiseptic. It is best to cover the wound with an adhesive bandage. If redness or irritation develops around the splinter wound, consult a physician.

Sprains

A sprain occurs when a joint is wrenched or twisted in such a way that the ligaments holding it in position are ruptured, possibly damaging the surrounding blood vessels, tendons, nerves, and muscles. This type of injury is more serious than a strain and is usually accompanied by pain, sometimes severe, soreness, swelling, and discoloration of the affected area. Most sprains occur as a result of falls, athletic accidents, or improper handling of heavy weights.

Emergency Treatment

This consists of prompt rest, the application of cold compresses to relieve swelling and any internal bleeding in the joint, and elevation of the affected area. Aspirin is recommended to reduce discomfort. If the swelling and soreness increase after such treatment, a physician should be consulted to make sure that the injury is not a fracture or a bone dislocation.

Sting Ray

Emergency Treatment

If an arm or leg is the target of a sting ray, wash the area thoroughly with salt water. Quickly remove any pieces of the stinger imbedded in the skin or flesh; poison can still be discharged into the victim from the sting-ray sheath. After initial cleansing of an arm or leg sting, soak the wound with hot water for up to an hour. Apply antiseptic or a sterile dressing after the soak.

Consult a physician after a sting-ray attack. The physician will make a thorough examination of the wound to determine whether stitches or antibiotics are required. Fever, vomiting, or muscular twitching also may result from an apparently simple leg or arm wound by a sting ray.

If the sting occurs in the chest or abdomen, the victim should be rushed to a hospital as soon as possible because such a wound can produce convulsions or loss of consciousness.

Strains

When a muscle is stretched because of misuse or overuse, the interior bundles of tissue may tear, or the tendon that connects it to the bone may be stretched. This condition is known as strain. It occurs most commonly to the muscles of the lower back when heavy weights are improperly lifted, or in the area of the calf or ankle as the result of a sudden, violent twist or undue pressure.

Emergency Treatment

Bed rest, the application of heat, and gentle massage are recommended for back strain. If the strain is in the leg, elevate the limb to help reduce pain and swelling, and apply cold compresses or an ice bag to the area. Aspirin may be taken to reduce discomfort.

In severe cases of strained back muscles, a physician may have to be consulted for strapping. For a strained ankle, a flexible elastic bandage can be helpful in providing the necessary support until the injured muscle heals.

Stroke

Stroke, or apoplexy, is caused by a disruption of normal blood flow to the brain, either by rupture of a blood vessel within the brain or by blockage of an artery supplying the brain. The condition is enhanced by hardening of the arteries and high blood pressure, and is most likely to occur in older persons. A stroke usually occurs with little or no warning and the onset may be marked by a variety of manifestations ranging from headache, slurred speech, or blurred vision, to sudden collapse and unconsciousness.

Emergency Treatment

Try to place the victim in a semireclining position, or, if he is lying down, be sure there is a pillow under his head. Avoid conditions that might increase the flow of blood toward the head. Summon a physician immediately. Loosen any clothing that may be tight. If the patient wears dentures, remove them.

Before professional medical assistance is available, the victim may vomit or go into shock or convulsions. If he vomits, try to prevent a backflow of vomitus into the breathing passages. If shock occurs, do not place the victim in the shock position but do keep him warm and comfortable. If convulsions develop, place a handkerchief or similar soft object between the jaws to prevent tongue biting.

Sty on Eyelid

Sties usually develop around hair follicles because of a bacterial infection. Like cold sores, they are most likely to develop in association with poor health and lowered resistance to infection.

Emergency Treatment

Apply warm, moist packs or compresses to the sty for periods of 15 to 20 minutes at intervals of three or four hours. Moist heat generally is more penetrating than dry heat.

The sty should eventually rupture and the pus should then be washed carefully away from the eye area. If the sty does not rupture or is very painful, consult a physician. Do not squeeze or otherwise handle the sty except to apply the warm moist compresses.

Sunburn

Emergency Treatment

Apply cold wet compresses to help relieve the pain. Compresses can be soaked in whole milk, salt water, or a solution of cornstarch mixed with water. The victim also may get some relief by soaking in a bathtub filled with plain water. Soothing lotions, such as baby oil or a bland cold cream, can be applied after carefully drying the skin. Don't rub the burn area while drying. Avoid the use of "shake" lotions, like calamine, which may aggravate the burn by a drying action. The victim should, of course, avoid further exposure to sunlight.

If pain is excessive, or extensive blistering is present, consult a physician. Avoid application of over-the-counter topical anesthetics that may cause allergic skin reactions.

A severe or extensive sunburn is comparable to a second-degree thermal burn and may be accompanied by symptoms of shock; if such symptoms are present the victim should be treated for shock. See also BURNS, THERMAL.

Sunstroke

See HEATSTROKE.

Tick Bites

Emergency Treatment

Do not try to scrape or rub the insect off the skin with your fingers; scraping, rubbing, or pulling may break off only part of the insect body, leaving the head firmly attached to the skin. Rubbing also can smear disease organisms from the tick into the bite. To make the tick drop away from the skin, cover it with a heavy oil, such as salad, mineral, or lubricating oil. Oil usually will block the insect's breathing pores, suffocating it. If oil is not readily available, carefully place a heated object against the tick's body; a lighted cigarette or a match that has been ignited and snuffed out can serve as a hot object.

Carefully inspect the bite area to be sure that all parts of the tick have been removed. Use a pair of tweezers to remove any tick parts found. Then carefully wash the bite and surrounding area with soap and water and apply an antiseptic. Also, wash your hands and any equipment that may have come in contact with the tick. Consult a physician if symptoms of tick fever or tularemia, such as unexplained muscular weakness, occur following a bite.

Toothaches

Emergency Treatment

Give an adult one or two aspirin tablets; a young child should be given no more than one-half of an adult tablet. The aspirin should be swallowed with plenty of water. Do not let it dissolve in the mouth or be held near the aching tooth. Aspirin becomes effective as a painkiller only after it has gone through the digestive tract and into the bloodstream; if aspirin is held in the mouth, it may irritate the gums.

Oil of cloves can be applied to the aching tooth. Dip a small wad of cotton into the oil of cloves, then gently pack the oil-soaked cotton into the tooth cavity with a pair of tweezers. Do not let the tweezers touch the tooth.

If the jaw is swollen, apply an ice bag for periods of 15 minutes at a time, at intermittent intervals. Never apply heat to a swollen jaw when treating a toothache. Arrange to see your dentist as soon as possible.

Tooth, Broken

Emergency Treatment

Apply a few drops of oil of cloves to the injured tooth to help relieve pain. If oil of cloves is not available, give an adult one to two regular aspirin tablets. One-half of a regular tablet can be given to a young child.

Make an emergency filling from a wad of cotton containing a few drops of oil of cloves. An emergency filling also can be made from powdered chalk; it is important to protect the cavity from infection while providing pain relief.

If the tooth has been knocked out of the socket, retrieve the tooth, because it can be restored in some cases. Do not wash the tooth; ordinary washing can damage dental tissues. A dentist will take care of cleaning it properly. Wrap the tooth in a damp clean handkerchief or tissue or place the tooth in a container of slightly salty warm water for the trip to the dentist.

Unconsciousness

Unconsciousness is the condition that has the appearance of sleep, but is usually the result of injury, shock, or serious physical disturbance. A brief loss of consciousness followed by spontaneous recovery is called *fainting*. A prolonged episode of unconsciousness is a *coma*.

Emergency Treatment

Call a physician at once. If none is available, get the victim to the nearest hospital. If the loss of consciousness is accompanied by loss of breathing, begin mouth-to-mouth respiration. If the victim is suffering cardiac arrest, administer cardiac massage. Don't try to revive the victim with any kind of stimulant unless told to do so by a physician.

Vertigo

See DIZZINESS.

36

Commonly Prescribed Generic Drugs

Name	Action	Prescribed for
Trade Names	**(CD = combined drug)**	
Acetaminophen	Believed to reduce concentration of chemicals involved in production of pain, fever, and inflammation (analgesic; antipyretic)	Relief of mild to moderate pain; reduction of fever
Anacin-3 Datril Tylenol Acetaco (CD) Algisin (CD) Amacodone (CD) Amaphen (CD) Anoquan (CD) Bancap (CD) Capital (CD) Chlorzone Forte (CD)	Codalan (CD) Co-Gesic (CD) Compal (CD) Comtrex (CD) Congesprin (CD) Co-Tylenol (CD) Darvocet-N (CD) Dia-Gesic (CD) Dolacet (CD) Dolprn (CD) Dorcol (CD) Dristan (CD) Duradyne (CD) Empracet (CD) Esgic (CD) Excedrin (CD) Hycomine (CD) Hyco-Pop (CD) Korigesic (CD) Lorcet (CD) Midrin (CD) Migralam (CD) Pacaps (CD)	Parafon Forte (CD) Percocet (CD) Percogesic (CD) Penaphen (CD) Phenate (CD) Phrenilin (CD) Protid (CD) Repan (CD) Sinarest (CD) Sine-Aid (CD) Singler (CD) Sinubid (CD) Sinutab (CD) Stopayne (CD) Supac (CD) Talacen (CD) Two-Dyne (CD) Tylox (CD) Vanquish (CD) Vicodin (CD) Wygesic (CD)
Amitriptyline	Believed to restore to normal levels the constituents of brain tissue that transmit nerve impulses (antidepressant)	Relief of emotional depression; gradual improvement of mood
Elavil Endep Etrafon (CD)	Limbitral (CD) Triavil (CD)	
Ampicillin	Interferes with ability of susceptible bacteria to produce new protective cell walls as they grow and multiply (antibiotic)	Elimination of infections responsive to action of this drug
Amcill Omnipen Polycillin	Principen SK-Ampicillin	

Name	Action	Prescribed for
Trade Names	**(CD = combined drug)**	
Antacids (Aluminum Hydroxide) (Calcium Carbonate) (Sodium Bicarbonate)	Neutralizes stomach acid; reduces action of digestive enzyme pepsin (relief from gastric hyperacidity)	Relief of heartburn, sour stomach, acid indigestion, and discomfort associated with peptic ulcer, gastritis, esophagitis, hiatal hernia
Absorbable: Sodium bicarbonate:	Alka-Seltzer Brioschi Bromo-Seltzer Less absorbable: Aluminum	hydroxide: Amphojel Calcium carbonate: Alka-2 Amitone
Aspirin (Acetylsalicylic Acid)	Dilates blood vessels in skin, thus hastening loss of body heat (antipyretic); reduces tissue concentration of inflammation and pain (analgesic; antirheumatic)	Reduction of fever; relief of mild to moderate pain and inflammation; prevention of blood clots, as in phlebitis, heart attack, stroke
Bayer Easprin Empirin Eneaprin St. Joseph's Children's Aspirin Verin Zorpin	A.P.C. (CD) Alka-Seltzer (CD) Anacin (CD) Ascriptin (CD) Axotal (CD) Buff-A Comp (CD) Bufferin (CD) Congespirin (CD) Cosprin (CD) Darvon with A.S.A. (CD) Darvon-N with A.S.A (CD) Dia-Gesic (CD) Dolprn #3 (CD) Equagesic (CD)	Excedrin (CD) 4-Way Cold Tablets (CD) Fiorinal (CD) Hyco-Pap (CD) Midol (CD) Norgesic (CD) Percodan (CD) Robaxisal (CD) Saleto (CD) Soma Compound (CD) Supac (CD) Synalgos-DC (CD) Talwin (CD) Vanquish (CD)
Atropine (Belladonna, Hyoscyamine)	Prevents stimulation of muscular contractions and glandular secretions in organ involved (antispasmodic [anticholinergic])	Relief of discomfort associated with excessive activity and spasm of digestive tract; irritation and spasm of lower urinary tract; painful menstruation
Antrocol (CD) Arco-Lase Plus (CD) Bellergal (CD)	Donnagel-PG (CD) Donnatal (CD) Donnatal Extendtabs (CD) Donnazyme (CD) Festalan (CD) Ru-Tuss (CD)	Trac-Tabs 2X (CD) SK-Diphenoxylate (CD) Urised (CD) Wigraine-PB (CD)
Bendroflumethiazide	Increases elimination of salt and water (diuretic); relaxes walls of smaller arteries, allowing them to expand; combined effect lowers blood pressure (antihypertensive)	Elimination of excessive fluid retention (edema); reduction of high blood pressure
Naturetin	Corzide (CD) Rautrax-N (CD)	Rauzide (CD)
Brompheniramine	Blocks action of histamine after release from sensitized tissue cells, thus reducing intensity of allergic response (antihistamine)	Relief of symptoms of hay fever (allergic rhinitis) and of allergic reactions of skin (itching, swelling, hives, rash)
Dimetane Veltane	Bromfed (CD) Bromphen (CD) Dimetapp (CD) Dura Tap-PD (CD)	E.N.T. Syrup (CD) Poly-histine-DX(CD) S-T Decongest (CD) Tamine S.R. (CD)
Butabarbital	Believed to block transmission of nerve impulses (hypnotic; sedative)	Low dosage: relief of moderate anxiety or tension (sedative effect); higher dosage: at bedtime to induce sleep (hypnotic effect)
Buticaps	Butisol Pyridium (CD)	Quibron Plus (CD)
Caffeine	Constricts blood vessel walls; increases energy level of chemical systems responsible for nerve tissue activity (cardiac, respiratory, psychic stimulant)	Prevention and early relief of vascular headaches such as migraine; relief of drowsiness and mental fatigue
No-Doz A.P.C. (CD) Amaphen (CD) Anacin (CD) Anoquan (CD)	Buff-A Comp (CD) Cafergot (CD) Cafetrate-PB (CD) Compal (CD) Dia-Gesic (CD) Esgic (CD) Excedrin Extra Strength (CD) Fiorinal (CD) Korigesic (CD)	Maximum Strength Midol (CD) Migralam (CD) Pacaps (CD) Two-Dyne (CD) Vanquish (CD) Wigraine (CD)

Name	Action	Prescribed for
Trade Names	**(CD = combined drug)**	
Carisoprodol	Believed to block transmission of nerve impulses and/or to produce a sedative effect (muscle relaxant)	Relief of discomfort caused by spasms of voluntary muscles
Rela Soprodol Soma (CD)	Soma Compound (CD)	
Chloral Hydrate	Believed to affect wake-sleep centers of brain (hypnotic)	Low dosage: relief of mild to moderate anxiety or tension (sedative effect); higher dosage: at bedtime to relieve insomnia (hypnotic effect)
Noctec SK-Chloral Hydrate		
Chloramphenicol	Prevents growth and multiplication of susceptible bacteria by interfering with formation of their essential proteins (antibiotic)	Elimination of infections responsive to action of this drug
Chloromycetin Ophthochlor Ophthocort		
Chlordiazepoxide	Believed to reduce activity of some parts of limbic system (tranquilizer)	Relief of mild to moderate anxiety and tension without significant sedation
Libritabs Librium SK-Lygen	Clipoxide (CD) Librax (CD)	
Chlorpheniramine	Blocks action of histamine after release from sensitized tissue cells, thus reducing intensity of allergic response (antihistamine)	Relief of symptoms of hay fever (allergic rhinitis) and of allergic reactions of skin (itching, swelling, hives, rash)
Chlor-Trimeton Polaramine Teldrin		
Chlorpromazine	Believed to inhibit action of dopamine, thus correcting an imbalance of nerve impulse transmission thought to be responsible for certain mental disorders (antiemetic; tranquilizer)	Relief of severe anxiety, agitation, and psychotic behavior
Thorazine		
Codeine	Believed to affect tissue sites that react specifically with opium and its derivatives (antitussive; narcotic analgesic)	Relief of moderate pain; control of coughing
A.P.C. with Codeine (CD) Acetaco (CD) Actifed with Codeine (CD) Amaphen with Codeine (CD) Anacin-3 with Codeine (CD) Ascriptin with Codeine (CD) Bancap c̄ Codeine (CD) Bromanyl (CD)	Bromphen DC (CD) Buff-A Comp No. 3 (CD) Capital with Codeine (CD) Codalan (CD) Codimal PH (CD) Conex with Codeine (CD) Deproist (CD) Dimetane-DC (CD) Dolprn #3 (CD) Empirin with Codeine (CD) Fiorinal with Codeine (CD) Guiatuss A-C (CD) Iophen-C (CD) Naldecon-CX (CD) Novahistine DK (CD) Nucofed (CD) Pediacof (CD) Phenaphen with Codeine (CD)	Phenergan with Codeine (CD) Phrenilin with Codeine (CD) Robitussin A-C (CD) Ru-Tuss (CD) Soma Compound (CD) Stopayne (CD) Triafed-C (CD) Triaminic with Codeine (CD) Tussar (CD) Tylenol with Codeine (CD)

Name	Action	Prescribed for
Trade Names	**(CD = combined drug)**	
Dexamethasone	Believed to inhibit several tissue mechanisms that induce inflammation (adrenocortical steriod [anti-inflammatory])	Symptomatic relief of inflammation (swelling, redness, heat, pain)
Decadron Dalalone Dexasone	Hexadrol Neodecadron	
Dextroamphetamine (d-Amphetamine)	Increases release of nerve impulse transmitter (central stimulant); this may also improve concentration and attention span of hyperactive child (primary calming action unknown); alters chemical control of nerve impulse transmission in appetite control center of brain (appetite suppressant [anorexiant])	Reduction or prevention of sleep epilepsy (narcolepsy); reduction of symptoms of abnormal hyperactivity (as in minimal brain dysfunction); suppression of appetite in management of weight reduction
Dexedrine	Obetrol Biphetamine (CD)	
Diazepam	Believed to reduce activity of some parts of limbic system (tranquilizer)	Relief of mild to moderate anxiety and tension without significant sedation
Valium		
Dicyclomine	Believed to produce a local anesthetic action that blocks reflex activity responsible for spasm (antispasmodic)	Relief of discomfort from muscle spasm of the gastrointestinal tract
Bentyl		
Digitoxin	Increases availability of calcium within the heart muscle, thus improving conversion of chemical energy to mechanical energy; slows pacemaker and delays transmission of electrical impulses (digitalis preparations [cardiotonic])	Improvement of heart muscle contraction force (as in congestive heart failure); correction of certain heart rhythm disorders
Crystodigin	Purodigin	
Digoxin	Same as above	Same as above
Lanoxicaps	Lanoxin	
Diphenhydramine	Blocks action of histamine after release from sensitized tissue cells, thus reducing intensity of allergic response (antihistamine)	Relief of symptoms of hay fever (allergic rhinitis) and of allergic reactions of skin (itching, swelling, hives, rash)
Allerdryl Benadryl Ambenyl (CD)	Benylin (CD) Bromanyl (CD) Dytuss (CD) Ziradryl (CD)	
Doxylamine	Same as above	Same as above
Unisome Nighttime Cremacoat 4 (CD) Nyquil (CD)		
Ephedrine	Blocks release of certain chemicals from sensitized tissue cells undergoing allergic reaction; relaxes bronchial muscles; shrinks tissue mass (decongestion) by contracting arteriole walls in lining of respiratory passages (adrenergic [bronchodilator])	Prevention and symptomatic relief of bronchial asthma; relief of congestion of respiratory passages
Efed II (Yellow) Primatene Mist Bronkaid (CD) Bronkolixir (CD)	Bronkotabs (CD) Derma Medicone-HC (CD) Marax (CD) Mudrane (CD) Nyquil (CD) Primatene (CD) Quadrinal (CD)	Quelidrine (CD) Quibron Plus (CD) Rynatuss (CD) Tedral (CD) T.E.H. (CD) T-E-P (CD) Theozine (CD) Wyanoids (CD)

Name	Action	Prescribed for
Trade Names	**(CD = combined drug)**	
Ergotamine	Constricts blood vessel walls, thus relieving excessive dilation that causes pain of vascular headaches (migraine analgesic [vasoconstrictor])	Prevention and early relief of vascular headaches such as migraines or histamine headaches
Cafetrate-PB Ergomar Ergostat	Medihaler Ergotamine Wigrettes Bellergal (CD) Cafergot (CD) Wigraine (CD)	
Erythrityl Tetranitrate	Acts directly on muscle cells to produce relaxation which permits expansion of blood vessels, thus increasing supply of blood and oxygen to heart	Management of pain associated with angina pectoris (coronary insufficiency)
Cardilate		
Erythromycin	Prevents growth and multiplication of susceptible bacteria by interfering with formation of their essential proteins (antibiotic)	Elimination of infections responsive to action of this drug
A/T/S E.E.S. E-Mycin Eryc	Eryderm Erymax Eryped Ery-Tab Erythrocin Ethril Ilosone Ilotycin	Pediamycin Staticin/T-Stat Wyamycin E Wyamycin S SK-Erythromycin Pediaxole (CD)
Estrogens (Estrogenic Substances) Conjugated Estrogens, Esterified Estrogens (Estrone and Equilin)	Prepares uterus for pregnancy or induces menstruation by cyclic increase and decrease in tissue stimulation; when taken regularly, blood and tissue levels increase to resemble those during pregnancy, thus preventing pituitary gland from producing hormones that induce ovulation; reduces frequency and intensity of menopausal symptoms (female sex hormone)	Regulation of menstrual cycle; prevention of pregnancy; relief of symptoms of menopause
Conjugated Estrogens Estrocon	Estratab Premarin Estratest (CD) Menrium (CD) Milprem (CD)	
Griseofulvin	Believed to prevent growth and multiplication of susceptible fungus strains by interfering with their metabolic activities (antibiotic; antifungal)	Elimination of fungus infections responsive to actions of this drug
Fulvicin-U/F Fulvicin P/G Grifulvin V	Grisactin Gris-PEG	
Hydralazine	Lowers pressure of blood in vessels by causing direct relaxation and expansion of vessel walls—mechanism unknown (antihypertensive)	Reduction of high blood pressure
Apresoline Apresazide (CD) Apresoline-Esidrex (CD) H-H-R (CD)	Ser-Ap-Es (CD) Serpasil-Apresoline (CD) Unipres (CD)	
Hydrochlorothiazide	Increases elimination of salt and water (diuretic); relaxes walls of smaller arteries, allowing them to expand; combined effect lowers blood pressure (antihypertensive)	Elimination of excessive fluid retention (edema); reduction of high blood pressure
Esidrix HydroDIURIL Oretic Thiuretic Aldactazide (CD)	Aldoril (CD) Apresazide (CD) Apresoline-Esidrix (CD) Dyazide (CD) Esimil (CD) H-H-R (CD) Hydropres (CD) Hydroserpine (CD)	Inderide (CD) Maxzide (CD) Moduretic (CD) SK-Hydrochlorothiazide Spironazide (CD) Timolide (CD) Unipres (CD)

Name	Action	Prescribed for
Trade Names	**(CD = combined drug)**	
Hydrocortisone (Cortisol)	Believed to inhibit several tissue mechanisms that induce inflammation (adrenocortical steroid [anti-inflammatory])	Symptomatic relief of inflammation (swelling, redness, heat, pain)
Aeroseb-HC Alphaderm Carmol HC Cortef Cortril Cort-Dome Cortifair Eldecort	F-E-P Hydrocortone Hytone Penecort Pro-Cort Synacort Texacort Vanoxide-HC Vioform-Hydrocortisone VōSoL HC Allersone (CD) Corticaine (CD) Cortisporin (CD) Derma-Sone (CD) Di-Hydrotic (CD)	Hill Cortac (CD) Hysone (CD) Iodo-Cortifair (CD) Octicair (CD) Otic-HC (CD) Oticol (CD) Otobiotic (CD) Otocort (CD) Pedi-Cort V (CD) Pyocidin-Otic (CD) Vytone (CD)
Hydroxyzine	Believed to reduce excessive activity in areas of brain that influence emotional health (antihistamine; tranquilizer)	Relief of anxiety, tension, apprehension, and agitation
Atarax Durrax Nevcalm	T.E.H. Theozine Vistaril Marax (CD)	
Insulin	Facilitates passage of sugar through cell wall to interior of cell (hypoglycemic)	Control of diabetes
Humulin N Humulin R Iletin I	Iletin II Insulatard NPH Lente Insulin Mixtard Novolin L Novolin N	Novolin R NPH Insulin Regular Insulin Semilente Insulin Ultrlente Insulin
Isonizaid	Believed to interfere with several metabolic activities of susceptible tuberculosis organisms (antibacterial; tuberculostatic)	Prevention and treatment of tuberculosis
INH Nydrazid Rifamate (CD)		
Isopropamide	Prevents stimulation of muscular contraction and glandular secretion in organ involved (antispasmodic [anticholinergic])	Relief of discomfort from excessive activity and spasm of digestive tract
Darbid Combid (CD) Ornade (CD)	Prochlor-Iso (CD) Pro-Iso (CD)	
Isoproterenol/ Isoprenaline	Dilates bronchial tubes by stimulating sympathetic nerve terminals (Isoproterenol: adrenergic [bronchodilator]; Isoprenaline: sympathomimetic)	Management of acute bronchial asthma, bronchitis, and emphysema
Aerolone Isuprel Medihaler-Iso Norisodrine Vapo-Iso	Duo-Medihaler (CD) Isuprel Compound (CD)	
Isosorbide Dinitrate	Acts directly on muscle cells to produce relaxation which permits expansion of blood vessels, thus increasing supply of blood and oxygen to heart (coronary vasodilator)	Management of pain associated with angina pectoris (coronary insufficiency)
Dilatrate Iso-Bid	Isochron Isordil Isotrate Sorate	Sorbide Sorbitrate

Name	Action	Prescribed for
Trade Names	**(CD = combined drug)**	
Levodopa	Believed to be converted to dopamine in brain tissue, thus correcting a dopamine deficiency and restoring more normal balance of chemicals responsible for transmission of nerve impulses (anti-Parkinsonism)	Management of Parkinson's disease
Larodopa Sinemet		
Liothyronine (T-3)	Increases rate of cellular metabolism and makes more energy available for biochemical activity (thyroid hormone)	Correction of thyroid hormone deficiency (hypothyroidism)
Cytomel Euthroid (CD) Thyrolar (CD)		
Lithium	Believed to correct chemical imbalance in certain nerve impulse transmitters that influence emotional behavior (antidepressant)	Improvement of mood and behavior in chronic manic-depression
Eskalith Libalith-S Lithane	Lithobid Lithotabs	
Meclizine	Blocks transmission of excessive nerve impulses to vomiting center (antiemetic)	Management of nausea, vomiting, and dizziness associated with motion sickness
Antivert Bonine Ru-Vert-M		
Meperidine/ Pethidine	Believed to increase chemicals that transmit nerve impulses (narcotic analgesic)	Relief of moderate to severe pain
Demerol Mepergan (CD)		
Meprobamate	Not known (tranquilizer)	Relief of mild to moderate anxiety and tension (sedative effect); relief of insomnia resulting from anxiety and tension (hypnotic effect)
Equanil Miltown SK-Bamate Tranmep	Deprol (CD) Equagesic (CD) Mepro Compound (CD)	PMB (CD) Pathibamate (CD)
Methacycline	Prevents growth and multiplication of susceptible bacteria by interfering with formation of their essential proteins (antibiotic)	Elimination of infections responsive to action of this drug
Rondomycin		
Methadone	Believed to increase chemicals that transmit nerve impulses (narcotic analgesic)	Treatment of heroin addiction; sometimes for relief of moderate to severe pain
Dolophine		
Methyclothiazide	Increases elimination of salt and water (diuretic); relaxes walls of smaller arteries, allowing them to expand; combined effect lowers blood pressure (antihypertensive)	Elimination of excess fluid retention (edema); reduction of high blood pressure
Aquatensen Enduron	Diutensen (CD) Enduronyl (CD)	

Name	Action	Prescribed for
Trade Names	**(CD = combined drug)**	
Methylphenidate	Believed to increase release of nerve impulse transmitter, which may also improve concentration and attention span of hyperactive child (primary action unknown) (central stimulant)	Management of fatigue and depression; reduction of symptoms of abnormal hyperactivity (as in minimal brain dysfunction)
Ritalin		
Nicotinic Acid/ Niacin	Corrects a deficiency of nicotinic acid in tissues; dilation of blood vessels is believed limited to skin—increased blood flow within head has not been demonstrated; reduces initial production of cholesterol and prevents conversion of fatty tissue to cholesterol and triglycerides (vitamin B-complex component; cholesterol reducer)	Management of pellagra; treatment of vertigo, ringing in ears, premenstrual headache; reduction of blood levels of cholesterol and triglycerides
Nico-400 Nicobid	Nicolar Cardioguard (CD) Nicotinex Elixir Lipo-Nicin (CD)	
Nitrofurantoin	Believed to prevent growth and multiplication of susceptible bacteria by interfering with function of their essential enzyme systems (antibacterial)	Elimination of infections responsive to action of this drug
Furadantin Macrodantin		
Nitroglycerin	Acts directly on muscle cells to produce relaxation which permits expansion of blood vessels, thus increasing supply of blood and oxygen to heart (coronary vasodilator)	Management of pain associated with angina pectoris (coronary insufficiency)
Nitrobid Nitrodisc Nitro-Dur	Nitroglyn Nitrong Nitrol Nitrospan Nitrolin Nitrostat	Transderm-Nitro Tridil
Nystatin	Prevents growth and multiplication of susceptible fungus strains by attacking their walls and causing leakage of internal components (antibiotic; antifungal)	Elimination of fungus infections responsive to action of this drug
Korostatin Mycostatin	Nilstat O-V Statin Nystex Mycolog (CD)	Myco-Triacet (CD) Nystraform (CD) Mytrex (CD) Nyst-olone (CD)
Oral Contraceptives	Suppresses the two pituitary gland hormones that produce ovulation (oral contraceptives)	Prevention of pregnancy
Ovcon Brevicon Demulen Enovid-E	Loestrin Nordette LO/Ovral Norinyl Micronor Norlestrin Medicon Nor-Q.D.	Ortho-Novum Ovrette Ovulen Tri-Norinyl
Oxycodone	Believed to affect tissue sites that react specifically with opium and its derivatives (narcotic analgesic)	Relief of moderate pain; control of coughing
Percocet (CD) Percodan (CD) SK-Oxycodone with Acetaminophen (CD)	SK-Oxycodone with Aspirin (CD) Tylox (CD)	

Name	Action	Prescribed for
Trade Names	**(CD = combined drug)**	
Oxytetracycline	Prevents growth and multiplication of susceptible bacteria by interfering with their formation of essential proteins (antibiotic)	Elimination of infections responsive to action of this drug
Oxymycin Terramycin Urobiotic (CD)		
Papaverine	Causes direct relaxation and expansion of blood vessel walls, thus increasing volume of blood which increases oxygen and nutrients (smooth muscle relaxant; vasodilator)	Relief of symptoms associated with impaired circulation in extremities and within brain
Cerespan Pavabid Pavatym		
Paregoric (Camphorated Tincture of Opium)	Believed to affect tissue sites that react specifically with opium and its derivatives to relieve pain; its active ingredient, morphine, acts as a local anesthetic and blocks release of chemical that transmits nerve impulses to muscle walls of intestine (antiperistaltic)	Relief of mild to moderate pain; relief of intestinal cramping and diarrhea
Donnagel-PG (CD) Parepectolin (CD)		
Penicillin G	Interferes with ability of susceptible bacteria to produce new protective cell walls as they grow and multiply (antibiotic)	Elimination of infections responsive to action of this drug
Bicillin C-R Crysticillin	Pentids Pfizerpen	SK-Pencillin G Wycillin
Penicillin V	Same as above	Same as above
Betapen-VK Pen-Vee K Ledercillin	Robicillin VK SK-Pencillin VK	V-Cillin K Veetids
Pentaerythritol Tetranitrate	Acts directly on muscle cells to produce relaxation which permits expansion of blood vessels, thus increasing supply of blood and oxygen to heart (coronary vasodilator)	Management of pain associated with angina pectoris (coronary insufficiency)
Duotrate Pentritol	Peritrate Miltrate (CD)	
Pentobarbital	Believed to block transmission of nerve impulses (hypnotic; sedative)	Low dosage: relief of mild to moderate anxiety or tension (sedative effect); higher dosage: at bedtime to induce sleep (hypnotic effect)
Nembutal Wigraine P-B (CD) WANS (CD)		
Phenacetin (Acetophenetidin)	Believed to reduce concentration of chemicals involved in production of pain, fever, and inflammation (analgesic; antipyretic)	Relief of mild to moderate pain; reduction of fever
A.P.C. (CD) Bromo-Seltzer (CD)	Empirin Compound (CD)	Percodan (CD) Sinubid (CD)

Name	Action	Prescribed for
Trade Names	**(CD = combined drug)**	
Phenazopyridine	Acts as local anesthetic on lining of lower urinary tract (urinary-analgesic)	Relief of pain and discomfort associated with acute irritation of lower urinary tract as in cystitis, urethritis, and prostatitis
Pyridium Azo Gantanol (CD)	Thiosulfil-A (CD) Urobiotic (CD)	
Pheniramine	Blocks action of histamine after release from sensitized tissue cells, thus reducing intensity of allergic response (antihistamine)	Relief of symptoms of hay fever (allergic rhinitis) and of allergic reactions of skin (itching, swelling, hives, and rash)
Triaminic Citra Forte (CD) Dristan (CD) Fiogesic (CD)	Poly-Histine-D (CD) Robitussin AC (CD) Ru-Tuss with Hydrocodone (CD) S-T Forte (CD)	Triaminicin (CD) Tussagesic (CD) Tussirex (CD)
Phenobarbital/ Phenobarbitone	Believed to block transmission of nerve impulses (anticonvulsant; hypnotic; sedative)	Low dosage: relief of mild to moderate anxiety or tension (sedative effect); higher dosage: at bedtime to induce sleep (hypnotic effect); continuous dosage: prevention of epileptic seizures (anticonvulsant effect)
SK-Phenobarbital Solfoton Antispasmodic Capsules (CD)	Antrocol (CD) Arco-Lase Plus (CD) Bronkolixir (CD) Bronkotabs (CD) Chardonna-2 (CD) Mudrane (CD) Mudrane GG (CD) Phazyme-PB (CD) Primatene (CD)	Pro-Banthīne with Phenobarbital (CD) Quadrinal (CD) T-E-P (CD)
Phentermine	Believed to alter chemical control of nerve impulse transmitter in appetite center of brain (appetite suppressant [anorexiant])	Suppression of appetite in management of weight reduction
Adipex-P Fastin	Ionamin Oby-Trim Teramine Tora	
Phenylbutazone	Believed to suppress formation of chemical involved in production of inflammation (analgesic; anti-inflammatory; antipyretic)	Symptomatic relief of inflammation, swelling, pain, and tenderness associated with arthritis, tendinitis, bursitis, superficial phlebitis
Azolid Butazolidin		
Phenylephrine	Shrinks tissue mass (decongestion by contracting arteriole walls in lining of nasal passages, sinuses, and throat, thus decreasing volume of blood (decongestant [sympathomimetic])	Relief of congestion of nose, sinuses, and throat associated with allergy
Bromphen (CD) Codimal (CD) Comhist (CD) Congespirin (CD) Coryban-D Cough Syrup (CD) Dallergy (CD) Dimetapp (CD) Donatussin (CD)	Dristan, Advanced Formula (CD) Dura-Tap/PD (CD) Dura-Vent/PD (CD) E.N.T. (CD) Entex (CD) Extendryl (CD) 4-Way Nasal Spray (CD) Histalet (CD) Histaspan-D (CD) Histor-D (CD) Hycomine (CD) Korigesic (CD) Naldecon (CD) Neo-Synephrine (CD)	P-V-Tussin (CD) Pediacof (CD) Phenergan VC (CD) Protid (CD) Quelidrine (CD) Ru-Tuss (CD) Rynatan (CD) Rynatuss (CD) Sinarest (CD) Singlet (CD) S-T Decongest (CD) S-T Forte (CD) Tamine S.R. (CD) Tussar DM (CD) Tussirex (CD) Tympagesic (CD)

Name	Action	Prescribed for
Trade Names	**(CD = combined drug)**	
Phenylpropanolamine	Same as above	Same as above
Help Propagest Rhindecon Alka-Seltzer Plus (CD) Allerest (CD) Appedrine, Maximum Strength (CD) Bayer Children's Cold Tablets (CD) Bayer Cough Syrup for Children (CD)	Bromphen (CD) Codimal Expectorant (CD) Comtrex (CD) Conex (CD) Congesprin (CD) Contac (CD) Control (CD) Coryban-D (CD) CoTylenol Children's Liquid (CD) Cremacoat 3 (CD) Dehist (CD) Dexatrim (CD) Dieutrim (CD) Dimetane (CD) Dimetapp (CD) Dura-Tapp/PD (CD) Dura-Vent (CD) Dura-Vent/A (CD) E.N.T. (CD) Entex (CD) 4-Way (CD) Fiogesic (CD) Heat & Chest (CD)	Histalet (CD) Hycomine (CD) Korigesic (CD) Kronohist (CD) Naldecon (CD) Nolamine (CD) Ornacol (CD) Ornade (CD) Phenate (CD) Poly-Histine (CD) Prolamine, Extra Strength (CD) Quadrahist (CD) Resaid (CD) Rescaps (CD) Rhinolar (CD) Ru-Tuss (CD) S-T Decongest (CD) S-T Forte (CD) Sinubid (CD) Sinulin (CD) Sinutab (CD) Tamine S.R. (CD) Tavist-D (CD) Triaminic (CD) Triaminicin (CD) Triaminicol (CD) Tuss-Ade (CD) Tuss-Ornade (CD)
Phenytoin (formerly Diphenylhydantoin)	Believed to promote loss of sodium from nerve fibers, thus lowering their excitability and inhibiting spread of electrical impulse along nerve pathways (anticonvulsant)	Prevention of epileptic seizures
Dilantin		
Pilocarpine	Lowers internal eye pressure (antiglaucoma [miotic])	Management of glaucoma
Almocarpine Isopto Carpine Pilocar		
Potassium	Maintains and replenishes potassium content of cells (potassium preparations)	Management of potassium deficiency
Kaon Kay Ciel	K-Lor Kaochlor Klorvess Pima Syrup	
Prednisolone	Believed to inhibit several mechanisms that induce inflammation (adrenocortical steroid [anti-inflammatory])	Symptomatic relief of inflammation (swelling, redness, heat, and pain)
Delta-Cortef Hydeltra-T.B.A.	Metimyd Metreton Predate	
Prednisone	Same as above	Same as above
Deltasone Liquid Pred	SK-Prednisone Sterapred	
Probenecid	Reduces level of uric acid in blood and tissues; prolongs presence of penicillin in blood (antigout [uricosuric])	Management of gout
Benemid SK-Probenecid ColBENEMID (CD)	Col-Probenecid (CD) Polycillin-PRB (CD)	
Promethazine	Blocks action of histamine after release from sensitized tissue cells, thus reducing intensity of allergic response (antihistamine); blocks transmission of excessive nerve impulses to vomiting center (antiemetic); action producing sedation and sleep is unknown (sedative)	Relief of symptoms of hay fever (allergic rhinitis) and of allergic reactions of skin (itching, swelling, hives, rash); prevention and management of nausea, vomiting, and dizziness associated with motion sickness; production of mild sedation and light sleep
Phenergan Promet Remsed	Mepergan (CD) Synalgos-DC (CD)	

Name	Action	Prescribed for
Trade Names	**(CD = combined drug)**	
Propantheline	Prevents stimulation of muscular contraction and glandular secretion within organ involved (antispasmodic [anticholinergic])	Relief of discomfort associated with excessive activity and spasm of digestive tract
Norpanth Pro-Banthine SK-Propantheline		
Propoxyphene	Increases chemicals that transmit nerve impulses, somehow contributing to the analgesic effect (analgesic)	Relief of mild to moderate pain
Darvon Darvon-N Darvocet-N (CD) Darvon Compound (CD)	Lorcet (CD) SK-65 APAP (CD) SK-65 Compound (CD) Wygesic (CD)	
Pseudoephedrine (Isoephedrine)	Shrinks tissue mass (decongestion) by contracting arteriole walls in lining of nasal passages, sinuses, and throat, thus decreasing volume of blood (decongestant [sympathomimetic])	Relief of congestion of nose, throat, and sinuses associated with allergy
Sudafed Actifed (CD) Ambenyl-D (CD) Anafed (CD) Anamine (CD) Brexin (CD) Bromfed (CD) Cardec DM (CD)	Chlorafed (CD) Codimal-L.A. (CD) Congess SR & JR (CD) CoTylenol Cold Medication (CD) Deconamine (CD) Dimacol (CD) Dorcol (CD) Extra-Strength Sine-Aid (CD) Fedahist (CD) Gunifed (CD) Histalet (CD) Isoclor (CD)	Kronofed-A (CD) Novafed (CD) Novahistine (CD) Nucofed (CD) Phenergan (CD) Poly-Histine-DX (CD) Respaire-SR (CD) Robitussin-DAC (CD) Sine-Aid (CD) Triafed (CD) Tussend Expectorant (CD) Zephrex (CD)
Pyrilamine/ Mepyramine	Blocks action of histamine after release from sensitized tissue cells, thus reducing intensity of allergic response (antihistamine)	Relief of symptoms of hay fever (allergic rhinitis) and of allergic reactions of skin (itching, swelling, hives, and rash)
Albatussin (CD) Citra Forte (CD) Codimal (CD) 4-Way Nasal Spray (CD)	Fiogesic (CD) Histalet (CD) Kronohist (CD) Mydol PMS (CD) P-V-Tussin (CD) Poly-Histine-D (CD) Primatene-M (CD) Ru-Tuss (CD) Triaminic (CD)	Triaminicin (CD) Triaminicol (CD) WANS (CD)
Quinidine	Slows pacemaker and delays transmission of electrical impulses (cardiac depressant)	Correction of certain heart rhythm disorders
Cardioquin Cin-Quin Duraquin	Quinaglute Quinidex Quinora SK-Quinidine	
Rafampin	Prevents growth and multiplication of susceptible tuberculosis organisms by interfering with enzyme systems involved in formation of essential proteins (antibiotic; tuberculostatic)	Treatment of tuberculosis
Rifadin Rimactane		
Reserpine	Relaxes blood vessel walls by reducing availability of norepinephrine (antihypertensive; tranquilizer)	Reduction of high blood pressure
Sandril Serpasil SK-Resperine Chloroserpine (CD)	Demi-Regroton (CD) Diupres (CD) Diutensen-R (CD) H-H-R (CD) Hydro-Fluserpine (CD) Hydromox R (CD) Hydropres (CD)	Hydroserpine (CD) Metatensin (CD) Naquival (CD) Regrotin (CD) Salutensin (CD) Ser-Ap-Es (CD) Unipres (CD)

Name	Action	Prescribed for
Trade Names	**(CD = combined drug)**	
Secobarbital	Believed to block transmission of nerve impulses (hypnotic; sedative)	Low dosage: relief of mild to moderate anxiety or tension (sedative effect); higher dosage: at bedtime to induce sleep (hypnotic effect)
Seconal Tuinal (CD)		
Sulfamethoxazole	Prevents growth and multiplication of susceptible bacteria by interfering with their formation of folic acid (antibacterial)	Elimination of infections responsive to action of this drug
Gantanol Azo Gantanol (CD)	Bactrim (CD) Septra (CD) Cotrim (CD) Sulfatrim (CD)	
Sulfisoxazole	Same as above	Same as above
Gantrisin SK-Soxazole Azo Gantrisin (CD) Pediazole (CD)		
Tetracycline	Prevents growth and multiplication of susceptible bacteria by interfering with their formation of essential proteins (antibiotic)	Elimination of infections responsive to action of this drug
Achromycin V Cyclopar Panmycin Robitet SK-Tetracycline	Topicycline Sumycin Achrostatin V (CD) Mysteclin-F (CD)	
Theophylline (Aminophylline, Oxtriphylline)	Reverses constriction by increasing activity of chemical system within muscle cell that causes relaxation of bronchial tube (bronchodilator)	Symptomatic relief of bronchial asthma
Accurbron Bronkodyl Constant-T Elixicon LABID Lodrane Respbid	Somophyllin Theon Sustaire Theo-Organidin Synophylate Theophyl Theobid Aerolate (CD) Theoclear Amesec (CD) Theo-Dur Aquaphyllin (CD) Theolair Brondecon (CD)	Bronkolixir (CD) Quibron (CD) Bronkotabs (CD) Slo-bid (CD) Elixophyllin (CD) Slo-Phyllin (CD) Marax (CD) T.E.H. (CD) Mudrane (CD) T-E-P (CD) Primatene (CD) Tedral (CD) Quadrinal (CD) Theozine (CD)
Thyroid (Thyroid Preparations)	Makes more energy available for biochemical activity and increases rate of cellular metabolism by altering processes of cellular chemicals that store energy (thyroid hormones)	Correction of thyroid hormone deficiency (hypothyroidism)
Armour Thyroid Cytomel	Euthroid Proloid Levothroid S-P-T	Synthroid Thyrolar
Thyroxine (T-4)	Same as above	Same as above
Choloxin Euthroid	Levothroid Synthroid L-Thyroxine Thyrolar (CD)	
Tolbutamide	Stimulates secretion of insulin by pancreas (hypoglycemic)	Correction of insulin deficiency in adult diabetes
Orinase		
Tridihexethyl	Prevents stimulation of muscular contraction and glandular secretion in organ involved (antispasmodic [anticholinergic])	Relief of discomfort from excessive activity and spasm of digestive tract
Pathilon Milpath (CD) Pathibamate (CD)		

Name	Action	Prescribed for
Trade Names	**(CD = combined drug)**	
Trimethoprim	Prevents growth and multiplication of susceptible organisms by interfering with formation of proteins (antibacterial)	Elimination of infections responsive to action of this drug
Proloprim Trimpex	Bactrim (CD) Cotrim (CD)	Septra (CD) Sulfatrim (CD)
Triprolidine	Blocks action of histamine after release from sensitized tissue cells, thus reducing intensity of allergic response (antihistamine)	Relief of symptoms of hay fever (allergic rhinitis) and of allergic reactions of skin (itching, swelling, hives, and rash)
Actidil Actifed (CD) Actifed-C (CD)	Triafed (CD) Trifed (CD)	
Vitamin C (Ascorbic Acid)	Believed to be essential to enzyme activity involved in formation of collagen; increases absorption of iron from intestine and helps formation of hemoglobin and red blood cells in bone marrow; inhibits growth of certain bacteria in urinary tract; enhances effects of some antibiotics (vitamin)	Prevention and treatment of scurvy; treatment of some types of anemia; maintenance of acid urine
Cetane Cevalin		

CHAPTER 36

Encyclopedic Guide to the Body, Health, and Medicine

AA *See* ALCOHOLICS ANONYMOUS.

abdominal pain Acute pain or persistent ache in the region between the chest and the pelvis is a symptom that may be difficult to diagnose. Since the abdominal cavity contains the stomach, liver, spleen, gallbladder, kidneys, appendix, intestines, ovaries, and during pregnancy the expanding uterus, a disorder, dysfunction, or infection of any of these organs may be the source of the discomfort.

Pain that disappears within a few hours and doesn't recur may be due to indigestion. If accompanied by nausea and diarrhea and it subsides within a day or two, it may be due to a comparatively harmless virus infection of the intestinal tract.

Two possible causes of severe upper abdominal pain are the onset of a heart attack and food poisoning; both require emergency medical treatment. The formation of gallstones leading to gallbladder inflammation will produce pain ranging from mild and recurrent to acute enough to require hospitalization. A serious gallbladder which has affected the liver may produce symptoms of jaundice and hepatitis and pain that occurs only when pressure is applied to the upper right side of the abdomen.

An acute pain accompanied by a cough may be a symptom of pleurisy or pneumonia. Although these diseases cause inflammation in the chest, the pain may travel along the nerve pathway to the upper abdomen. Colitis is likely to produce abdominal cramps and attacks of diarrhea; a peptic ulcer manifests itself in a burning pain a few hours after meals. Gastritis, an inflammation of the stomach wall, may be a temporary condition caused by tension, overeating, or too much alcohol, and its characteristically severe pain may subside with a return to a normal routine. However, the chronic pains of gastritis associated with alcoholism or emotional disturbance require accurate diagnosis and systematic treatment.

Cramps in the lower abdomen sometimes occur immediately before or during the first day of menstruation, and for some women menstrual pain may spread to the back and down the leg. Among other causes of lower abdominal pain are endometriosis or endometritis (disorders of the uterus), infection of the fallopian tubes, ectopic pregnancy, and intestinal obstruction.

Persistent pain localized in the lower right part of the abdomen is a characteristic signal of the onset of appendicitis. Self-treatment of appendicitis may worsen the condition. Enemas, laxatives, heating pads, and unprescribed medicines should be avoided in favor of a call to the doctor.

abortion, spontaneous The expulsion of a dead embryo or fetus from the body of a pregnant woman; also known as miscarriage. Since many miscarriages are not recognized, it is difficult to estimate the number of pregnancies that terminate in this way. Doctors, however, estimate the figures at one in ten. Of these, most occur between the sixth and tenth week of pregnancy. At least half of the total of spontaneously aborted fetuses are abnormal in some way. The abnormalities may be caused by genetic defect, poor health of the mother, maternal infections of syphilis, medications, a serious accident, and an emotional trauma affecting hormone production. Evidence is accumulating that excessive caffeine intake in coffee and cola beverages, excessive alcohol, and heavy smoking during the early months of pregnancy may cause the type of fetal damage that leads to miscarriage. The typical symptom is vaginal bleeding with or without cramps. If the blood flow is only a matter of staining, the embryo or fetus may still be alive and miscarriage not inevitable; if it is heavy, miscarriage is probably inevitable. In either case, the doctor should be called at once. If there is a possibility of averting the miscarriage, absolute bed rest may be ordered and sedatives administered until the crisis is past. If a miscarriage does occur, the uterus should be scraped clean of all retained products of conception by dilatation and curettage (D&C). This is essential if infection is to be prevented. In most cases, any subsequent pregnancy is a normal one. Women who have experienced more than one spontaneous abortion should consult a gynecologist to attempt to determine and correct the underlying causes. *See also* "Pregnancy and Childbirth."

abscess An accumulation of pus in an area where healthy tissue has been invaded and broken down by bacteria. An abscess may form anywhere in the body that might be vulnerable to bacterial infection–around a hangnail or splinter, around an infected tooth, in the breast, in the middle ear, in the lung. Many abscesses can be cured with antibiotics, but some require surgical incision and draining.

When harmful bacteria begin to destroy tissue, blood rushes to the spot to provide the white blood cells and antibodies necessary for fighting off the infection. The resulting mixture of blood cells, bacteria, and dead tissue is called pus. Pain is caused by the inflammation of adjacent tissues and the accumulation of pus pressing against the adjoining nerves. The blood concentration causes redness.

A simple abscess beneath the skin may break through the surface, drain, and heal itself. A skin abscess should never be squeezed or cut open by an untrained person. A doctor or the emergency services of the nearest hospital must be consulted at once if the redness that surrounds an abscess begins to travel in a visible line towards a gland.

Achromycin Brand name of one of the tetracycline group of antibiotics.

acidity and alkalinity Acids and alkalies (alkalies are also called bases) are produced by the body for various metabolic purposes. For example, the stomach produces hydrochloric acid which is essential in protein digestion; the kidneys produce the alkali ammonia to neutralize body chemistry. An upset in the acid-base balance of the body may produce symptoms that require medical attention. Seemingly harmless medication is sometimes responsible for a serious imbalance. Small amounts of the alkali sodium bicarbonate (bicarbonate of soda, baking soda) can remedy mild hyperacidity of the stomach, but an overdose can cause metabolic alkalosis. The overuse of diuretics as a way of losing weight may result in excessive loss of acids through the urine. An overdose of aspirin may cause salicylate (acid) poisoning. The balance may also be disturbed by conditions of the body such as kidney malfunction or loss of essential chemicals due to diarrhea.

Like most body tissues, the lining of the vagina is normally acid. It becomes alkaline at the time of ovulation in order to keep the alkaline sperm alive. In cases of infertility caused by an invariable acid environment of the vagina, chemicals are prescribed to produce vaginal alkalinity.

acne A skin disorder occurring mainly in association with the hormonal changes of adolescence. The increased amounts of androgen produced by both the male and female sex glands stimulate the sebaceous (oil) glands of the hair follicles to produce an increased amount of the fatty substance called *sebum* which is normally discharged through the pores to lubricate the skin. The overproduction of sebum results in oily skin. The characteristic pimples, pustules, and blackheads of acne are formed when the pores become plugged by the sebum that has backed up, mixed with the skin pigments, and leaked into surrounding areas.

Acne is not caused by junk food or faulty hygiene; the chief cause is the onset of puberty combined with the hereditary factors that govern the oiliness of the skin. The condition may be controlled–not cured–by keeping the skin clean and avoiding any particular food that seems to make it flare up. Mild cases of acne usually clear up by themselves. Emotional upsets, the onset of the menstrual period, and humid weather often cause the symptoms to worsen. Vitamin A acid cream (resorcinol), sun lamp treatments, and tetracycline pills may be prescribed by the doctor with beneficial results.

If acne has left scars and blemishes, a dermatologist can be consulted about the advisability of removing them by the skin-planing technique known as dermabrasion.

ACTH Adrenocorticotrophic hormone, a hormone secreted by the anterior lobe of the pituitary gland; also known as adrenocorticotrophin and trophin. ACTH is carried by the blood to the adrenal glands. When it reaches the outer layer or cortex of these glands, the adrenals secrete a number of vital hormones grouped together as corticoids. Since the development of adrenal steroids which can be taken orally and have fewer side effects, ACTH is rarely used for treatment, but it is sometimes used in a diagnostic test of adrenal function.

acupuncture A therapeutic technique based on the theory that key points in the body are related to specific disorders or pain elsewhere in the body and that these conditions can be healed by stimulation at the key points by the insertion and rotation of needles. Acupuncture has been practiced for at least 5,000 years in the Orient and is now gaining increased acceptance for certain purposes among Western doctors.

Although cures of various ailments have been reported, the most verified benefits of acupuncture have been in the field of anesthesia and analgesia. American medical teams who have witnessed major operations performed by Chinese hospitals have been impressed by the effectiveness of acupuncture as a means of controlling pain reception without inducing unconsciousness. These analgesic properties are currently being explored, with varying degrees of success, in many hospitals in the United States and Europe, especially in pain-control experiments.

Before embarking on acupuncture treatment for any disorder, it is advisable to examine the practitioner's medical credentials and legal status. State-chartered acupuncture centers in various parts of the United States will provide detailed information about their activities on request.

acute symptom A symptom of a disorder which has a sudden onset and runs a comparatively brief course such as an "acute" asthma attack as opposed to a persistent, or chronic, manifestation of a disorder. "Acute" should not be confused with "fatal."

addiction Physical dependence on a drug; adaptation of the body to the presence of a drug so that its continued use is required by the user just to feel well and to continue to function physiologically.

Addison's disease A rare disorder whose immediate cause is failure of the adrenal glands. It was first identified by the English physician Dr. Thomas Addison (who also identified pernicious anemia) in the mid-nineteenth century. The disease usually occurs in people in their twenties or thirties. The glandular underfunction is sometimes the result of tuberculosis. Other causes may be a tumor, hemorrhage, or any injury that interferes with hormone production. The hormones produced by the adrenal cortex are involved in a variety of life processes, chiefly the regulation of the body's supply of water and salts and consequently of muscle function and blood pressure. Thus degeneration of this gland produces wide-ranging symptoms: extreme fatigue on slight exertion, dramatic weight loss, lowering of blood pressure, and conspicuous darkening of the skin. Addison's disease, once fatal, is now treated with cortisone and other forms of hormone replacement therapy in the same way that diabetes is treated with insulin.

adenoma A usually benign tumor composed of glandular tissue.

adhesion The union of two internal body surfaces that are normally separate. The term also refers to the formation of the fibrous, or scar, tissue that connects them. The scar tissue that forms around a surgical wound during the healing process may cling to adjoining areas causing them to fuse. Lung adhesions may occur after inflammation and scarring of the pleural membrane; abdominal adhesions may occur following peritonitis. Although most adhesions are painless and without consequence, they may occasionally cause an obstruction or malfunction that requires surgical correction. The incidence of postoperative adhesions has dramatically diminished as a result of early ambulation after surgery.

adoption Adoption should be approached through a qualified agency. Only an irresponsible doctor or lawyer would suggest considering the so-called blackmarket babies. Adoption laws differ from state to state, and only an accredited agency can advise you about the circumstances and qualifications that govern a legal adoption in your state. The agencies, whose chief concern is the well-being of the child in their trust, carefully investigate the economic, social, and emotional status of prospective parents. If a marriage seems shaky, if only one of the pair is strongly interested in parenthood, if there are sharply divergent attitudes toward child-rearing, if there is disagreement about the preferred sex of the child—all these factors and many others are weighed by the agency. Persons eager to offer the child warmth and acceptance into the family are always preferred to those who talk only about privileges and luxuries. Agencies do not approve of too great an age disparity—no more than forty years—between parents and child.

As soon as a congenial pairing has been worked out, the adoption must be legalized by the courts. This can take six months to a year, and during this "trial period" the agency provides help and advice to the family. During all court proceedings, adoptive parents should have the counsel of a reputable lawyer so that future legal complications will be avoided.

adrenal glands A pair of glands situated at the upper part of the kidneys. The adrenals, like other components of the endocrine system, secrete hormones into the bloodstream for transportation to other parts of the body. Each adrenal consists of two separate glands that manufacture different classes of hormones: the cortex, or outer shell, secretes adrenocorticosteroids or corticoids for continuous regulation of bodily processes such as fluid and salt balance, protein metabolism, antibody formation, and the repair of damaged tissue; the medulla, or inner core, secretes epinephrine (adrenalin) and norepinephrine which are released in stress situations, mobilizing the body to deal with combat or flight at maximum efficiency.

adrenalin One of the hormones produced by the medulla or inner core of the adrenal glands; also known as epinephrine. This hormone maximizes the body's physiologic response to stress. The large quantities of stress-secreted adrenalin result in increased heart rate and blood pressure. By transforming the glycogen in the liver into glucose, the adrenalin also provides the muscles with a quick source of energy so that they can perform effectively without suffering fatigue. Adrenalin dilates the pupils of the eyes for more effective vision and expands the bronchial tubes for more effective respiration. When the body sustains a wound, adrenalin increases the clotting capacity of the blood.

Adrenalin was originally extracted from animal glands, but it is now produced synthetically and is widely prescribed as an emergency medication in heart arrest, acute asthma and other allergy attacks, shock, and severe bleeding.

afterbirth *See* PLACENTA.

air pollution *See* POLLUTION.

air sickness *See* MOTION SICKNESS.

Al-Anon An organization which, though separate from Alcoholics Anonymous, provides the same kind of help, support, and therapy for the family of the alcoholic that AA provides for the alcoholic. Alcoholism is considered a family disease because the alcoholic affects the mental and physical health of other members and their response in turn affects the alcoholic.

A person who suspects that any member of the household, including teenage children, is an alcoholic may find that going to Al-Anon meetings is an effective first step toward recognizing the illness for what it is and beginning to deal with it in a realistic way.

Alateen, a subsidiary of Al-Anon, is a fellowship for the adolescent children of alcoholics. Further information about both organizations is available by writing to Al-Anon Family Group Headquarters, P.O. Box 182, Madison Square Station, New York, NY 10010.

alcohol Any of a group of related chemical compounds derived from hydrocarbons. Ethyl alcohol, also called ethanol or grain alcohol, is the intoxicating ingredient of fermented and distilled beverages. Methyl alcohol, also known as wood alcohol or methanol, is widely used in industry as a solvent and a fuel. Taken internally, it is a poison that can lead to blindness and death. Rubbing alcohol, used on the skin as a cooling agent or disinfectant, may be ethyl alcohol made unfit for consumption by the addition of chemicals known as denaturants (denatured alcohol) or it may be another compound called isopropyl alcohol.

alcoholic beverages Drinks that contain ethyl alcohol, the substance that results naturally from the fermentation of carbohydrates (sugars, such as those in grape mash, molasses, and apples, or starches, such as those in wheat, rice, barley, and other grains). Hard cider, beer, and ale contain about 3 to 5 percent alcohol; table wines about 10 percent; fortified wines like sherry about 20 percent. Beverages of higher alcoholic content, such as vodka, bourbon, and brandy, are called liquors or "hard" liquors and are produced by distilling the alcohol from the fermented mash. Liqueurs like Benedictine or Cointreau may contain as much as 35 percent alcohol, and whiskey and rum as much as 50 percent. The concentration of alcohol in a beverage is usually given in terms of "proof." Half of the proof number is the percentage of alcohol by volume; thus a 90-proof vodka is 45 percent alcohol, with the remainder made up of water, flavoring, and other ingredients. In assessing alcohol intake, it should be kept in mind that a 12-ounce can of beer contains four-fifths as much alcohol as a 1½-ounce jigger of 80-proof whiskey, 6 ounces of wine equals 1½ ounces of vodka, and 6 ounces of sherry contains almost twice as much alcohol as a 1½-ounce jigger of whiskey.

Alcohol is metabolized to produce a substance that provides high energy, but no other nutritional value. It enters the bloodstream very quickly, and unless it is consumed very slowly and in combination with food, the alcoholic content of the blood rises rapidly. It is a depressant and sedative that has a marked effect on the central nervous system. Intoxication occurs when the alcohol concentration in the blood is about $\frac{1}{10}$ of 1 percent; a concentration of twice that amount results in marked intoxication; and at $\frac{4}{10}$ of 1 percent the drinker usually passes out.

It is estimated that about 80 million Americans drink alcoholic beverages and about 10 percent of these suffer from alcoholism. However, in terms of health and safety, all people who drink at all should observe certain rules and precautions. Anyone with chronic gastrointestinal disorders shouldn't drink unless allowed to do so on special occasions by their doctors. Anyone taking tranquilizers, antidepressants, or barbiturates should observe *to the letter* the doctor's and pharmacist's instructions about alcoholic intake. A hostess should never offer a last drink "for the road" to the guest who is about to drive a car. Anyone on a weight reduction diet should cut down on or eliminate alcohol; a glass of whiskey contains 120 calories with no nutritional value, and alcoholic beverages simultaneously increase the appetite and weaken the will to diet. Alcohol in any form generally should not be given as a first aid measure or as emergency treatment unless a doctor has issued the instruction.

Alcoholics Anonymous A worldwide community resource for dealing with the problem of alcoholism. AA is a fellowship of men and women who help each other stay sober and who share their recovery experience freely with all those who have the desire to stop drinking. It is an integral part of the tradition that no member may violate another member's anonymity. Although its members may cooperate with other organizations that help alcoholics, AA is not affiliated with any sect, denomination, political group, or institution.

Membership is estimated at about 1 million people. Since 1971 one out of every three new members is a woman. Approximately 28,000 local groups meet in 92 different countries. Meetings are held once or twice a week, and each group is self-supporting through voluntary contributions.

The telephone directory of most towns and cities contains an AA listing. Where such information is not available, write to General Service Office, P.O. Box 459, Grand Central Station, New York, NY 10017. This name, rather than any AA designation, will appear on the wrapper containing the requested material.

alcoholism Compulsive drinking, now recognized as a disease—not a moral disorder—by the American Medical Association, the U.S. Public Health Service, and the World Health Organization. The National Council on Alcoholism estimates that there are at least 5 million women alcoholics in the United States. Experts agree that the qualitative difference between the "heavy" or "hard" drinkers and alcoholics is that the former, unlike alcoholics, can control their drinking if and when they choose to. Another way of expressing the difference is: social and heavy drinkers like alcohol but can do without it; alcoholics need alcohol, and their addiction becomes progressively worse.

The National Council has reported a number of significant facts in regard to women alcoholics. Regardless of their life style, women drink primarily in relation to life crises and to relieve loneliness, inferiority feelings, and conflicts about their sex role. Women alcoholics tend to become involved with other drugs such as tranquilizers. Just as many teenage females drink as teenage males. Maternal alcoholism can harm fetal development and cause addiction to alcohol in the newborn. The husband and children of a woman alcoholic are more likely to "protect" her (and themselves) from public exposure than to encourage her to seek help. The woman alcoholic is abandoned by her husband in nine out of ten cases, whereas the male alcoholic is abandoned by his wife in only one out of ten.

Although many theories have been advanced for the cause of alcoholism, it is now generally agreed that there is no single explanation and that the disorder is usually the result of a combination of physical, psychological, and circumstantial factors. Current research also indicates that once a person develops an addiction to alcohol, the body chemistry becomes different from that of a nonalcoholic, and that even though the disease can be treated, the alcoholic can never return to "normal" drinking.

Even though alcoholism, like peptic ulcers, may be evidence of psychological stress, it must be understood that, also like peptic ulcers, alcoholism itself can be fatal. Fortunately, many of the physical effects of alcoholism—on the liver, heart, and kidneys and on resistance to infection—are reversible through sobriety and rehabilitation therapy.

Medical care may involve the doctor's supervision of diet, vitamins, and, in some cases, drugs to ease the transition to total abstention. Psychotherapy, especially in groups whose members are mutually supportive, helps the alcoholic face problems and deal with them realistically. Membership in AA is recommended by most specialists, and since the role of the family is extremely important in the treatment of the alcoholic, participation in groups such as Al-Anon can be very helpful.

Because alcoholism is now recognized as one of this country's major public health problems, the U.S. Department of Health and Human Services has established the National Institute on Alcohol Abuse and Alcoholism. Information on all aspects of the disease, as well as state-by-state listings of most public and private counseling and treatment facilities may be obtained by writing to the Institute's National Clearing House for Alcohol Information, P.O. Box 2345, Rockville, Maryland 20852.

allergy Hypersensitivity to a substance such as food, pollen, animal dander, or medicine or to a climatic condition such as sunshine or low temperature which in similar amounts is harmless to most people. Literally the word means an altered capacity to react. It is known that allergy can occur anywhere in the body: on the skin, in the eyes, in the lungs, and so on. The offending substance contains an allergen that signals the body of the allergic person to manufacture antibodies as a defense. In this process chemicals known as histamines are released into the bloodstream, and these chemicals are the immediate cause of the allergic symptoms. Histamine can produce two main effects. First, by increasing the permeability of the small blood vessels, it causes the fluid portion of the blood or serum to leak into the tissues. Second, it causes spasm of particular muscles, especially in the bronchial tubes. The first condition produces swelling, blisters, and irritation of some tissues such as the eyes, nose, and skin; the second produces labored breathing and asthmatic episodes. In extreme cases hypersensitivity to penicillin or nonhuman antitoxin serum or to the venom in an insect sting produces sudden shock (anaphylactic reaction) which can be fatal.

Most allergies are treated by identifying the offending substance and avoiding it. This is relatively simple in the case of a cosmetic that causes a rash or a cantaloupe that brings on diarrhea or a long-haired pet that produces an asthma attack. In many instances, however, identification can be extremely difficult. Specialists have evolved various scratch tests and patch tests that are painless, time-consuming, and not always helpful.

For cases in which avoidance is not possible and relief from symptoms is necessary there are desensitizing treatments that can build up a resistance to the allergen once it is identified. Medicines such as antihistamines, cortisone, ephedrine, and aminophylline, alone or in combination, may be effective in controlling the symptoms and reducing discomfort. Self-medication with any of these drugs, prior to identifying the problem, is always inadvisable. Because emotions play a prominent part in many allergies, some reactions, especially asthmatic attacks, may be eliminated by psychotherapy.

alveoli The smallest air sacs of the lungs. Each alveolus is a microscopic structure covered by a capillary wall through which oxygen in the air and carbon dioxide in the blood are exchanged in the respiratory process. The hundreds of millions of alveoli form grapelike clusters. When their function is disordered by bronchitis, pneumonia, or a cardiocirculatory attack associated with heart failure, treatment is essential.

AMA *See* AMERICAN MEDICAL ASSOCIATION.

amenorrhea The absence of the menstrual flow. Primary amenorrhea is the failure of menstrual periods to begin by the age of 18. The cause is usually endocrine (glandular) in nature. Secondary amenorrhea is the cessation of menstrual periods after they have begun. It occurs normally during pregnancy, nursing, and following the menopause. When none of these circumstances accounts for the interruption of menstruation, it may be a symptom of malnutrition, alcoholism, glandular disturbance, or tumors. It may also be psychogenic in origin and related to a severe emotional disturbance, to a prolonged psychotic episode, or to an emotional condition such as anorexia nervosa (obsessional refusal to eat resulting in extreme weight loss, usually occurring in young women). When there is no obvious explanation for either primary or secondary amenorrhea, a doctor should be consulted.

American Medical Association (AMA) A professional organization made up of county and state units, with approximately 210,000 members—about 75 percent of all practicing physicians. It was founded in 1847 with the purpose of improving medical education and eliminating quackery. Together with the American College of Surgeons and the American Hospital Association, it accredits hospitals, inspects medical schools, and approves residency and intern-training programs.

The AMA publishes the American Medical Directory which lists the professional credentials of all licensed physicians, including nonmembers. The directory, organized by states, is usually available in the reference collection of local libraries.

In recent decades, the AMA has been increasingly criticized for its outspoken opposition to practically all government-initiated public health programs as well as to the extension of social security benefits, health insurance plans, and group medical practice.

amnesia Loss of memory. Amnesia may be partial or extensive, temporary or permanent. With total amnesia (very rare), practically all mental functions would necessarily cease. Memory loss may result from brain damage caused by injury, tumor, arteriosclerosis, stroke, or alcoholism. It may also be caused by the psychological mechanism of repression. Amnesia following an accident or acute emotional shock may cause the victim to black out and forget the event itself, but remember all details leading up to it. When serious memory lapses due to an overriding anxiety neurosis interfere with normal functioning, some form of psychotherapy may be helpful. Except for the amnesia associated with senility, memory loss that wipes out past identity occurs more frequently in fiction than in fact.

amniocentesis A diagnostic procedure in which a small amount of the amniotic fluid that surrounds the fetus during pregnancy is withdrawn and examined to assess genetic and other disorders. The technique, developed in the 1960s, is accurate and relatively safe and requires only a local anesthetic. A needle similar to a hypodermic needle is inserted through the abdomen into the womb. The extracted fluid contains cells shed by the fetus, and when these cells are grown in laboratory cultures, it is possible to detect fetal chromosomal abnormalities.

Amniocentesis may be performed for a variety of reasons. If either parent is known to have a transmissible defect for certain diseases, amniocentesis can determine if that defect has been transmitted to the fetus. When a mother is 35 years of age or over and therefore is at increased risk of having a child with Down's syndrome (trisomy 21 or mongolism), amniocentesis can determine if the fetus is normal. It is also done to assess Rh complications and fetal maturity. To protect both fetus and mother, amniocentesis should be done by medically accredited specialists.

amnion The tough-walled membrane that forms the protective sac in which the embryo is contained within the uterus during pregnancy. The amnion and its contents (amniotic fluid) are commonly known as the bag of waters. During labor contractions the bag generally breaks and the fluid leaks out. When the amnion remains intact and envelops the head of the newborn baby, it is known as a caul. It then has to be broken by the person delivering the baby. A caul was once regarded as an indication of great good fortune for the offspring.

amphetamine A category of drugs, including Benzedrine, Dexedrine, and Methedrine, which act as stimulants to the central nervous system. Formerly prescribed somewhat indiscriminately as antidepressants and aids in overcoming obesity, the widespread abuse of amphetamines in the form of "pep" pills and diet pills, the increased tolerance developed by some users, and the freak aftereffects experienced by athletes, dancers, students, and others who seek to perform at the peak of their powers through amphetamine intake have led to a greater control over the use and availability of these drugs. Their therapeutic use should be limited to cases of narcolepsy and to counteracting the effects of an overdose of sedatives.

ampicillin Generic name of one of the forms of penicillin.

analgesic Substance that temporarily reduces or eliminates the sensation of pain without producing unconsciousness. The most common over-the-counter analgesics are aspirin and acetaminophen (such as Tylenol). Narcotic analgesics derived from opium, such as codeine and morphine, as well as similar synthetic substances should be prescribed with caution since they are habit-forming. Analgesia may be produced by means other than drugs such as hypnosis and acupuncture. *See* ANESTHESIA.

analysis *See* PSYCHOANALYSIS.

androgens The male sex hormones that determine the secondary sex characteristics of men. Although the two chief androgens, testosterone and androsterone, are manufactured mainly by the male testes, they are also produced to a lesser extent by the adrenal glands of both sexes and by the female ovaries. In males they are responsible for the deepening of the voice and the development of the beard at puberty, and they account in part for the greater size and muscular development of men since they also stimulate the growth of muscles and bones. An overproduction of androgen in women accounts for the presence of these essentially male characteristics. The administration of androgens in postmenopausal anticancer therapy is an extremely complex matter and should be approached warily by both doctor and patient. The hormones are used in replacement therapy for men suffering from testicular malfunction.

androgynous Having both male and female sex characteristics. True androgyny is extremely rare and can be corrected in part by a combination oi hormone therapy and surgery.

anemia A condition in which there is a deficiency in the number of red blood cells, hemoglobin, or the total amount of blood. Anemia, whether acute or chronic, is not a disease in itself, but rather the result of an underlying disorder: chronic malnutrition, industrial poisoning, bone marrow disease, heavy bleeding, intestinal parasites, kidney disease, or a defect in the body's ability to absorb iron. Since treatment varies according to the cause, accurate diagnosis is extremely important. The symptoms of a mild deficiency may be vague: listlessness, general lack of vitality, and fatigue following little effort. When the condition is more severe, the inability of the anemic blood to supply oxygen to body tissues can result in shortness of breath, rapid pulse, and the sensation that the heart is working harder or faster. Visible indications are the paleness of the lining of the eyelids and of the area under the fingernails. When the blood has sufficient hemoglobin, these parts of the body are a healthy pink.

Anemia should never be self-diagnosed for the purpose of self-treatment with tonics, vitamins, pills, or herbal remedies. It is a specific condition which can be diagnosed accurately only by laboratory analysis of blood samples. In these tests the number, size, color, and shape of the red blood cells are determined, and the amount of hemoglobin in the sample is measured. When anemia is clearly present, other tests may follow. A sample of bone marrow may be taken in order to find out whether defective cells are produced at the source. Other laboratory procedures may be used to establish the fragility of the cells. If there is suspicion of bleeding within the body, usually within the gastrointestinal tract, additional tests may be essential.

There are several types of anemia. The most common form, deficiency anemia, is a deficiency of iron essential for the body's manufacture of hemoglobin. It may result from insufficient iron in the diet or from chronic blood loss from excessive menstrual flow or internal bleeding due to an ulcer or some other gastrointestinal disorder. When diet deficiency is the cause, foods high in iron content as well as supplementary medicine containing iron will correct the anemia. When chronic bleeding is involved, the basic cause must be dealt with if the anemia is to be corrected.

Pernicious anemia, also known as Addison's anemia, is a serious disease characterized by a breakdown in the mechanism of red blood cell formation, usually traceable to a deficiency of vitamin B_{12}. In addition to the symptoms of deficiency anemia, this disorder produces the following symptoms: the skin becomes pale yellow, the tongue is bright red and sore, and a resulting malfunction in the nervous system may produce a chronic tingling sensation in the fingers and toes. The disease is most often a result of the absence in the body of the substance necessary for the absorption of vitamin B_{12}. Therapeutic amounts of the vitamin with or without folic acid (another B complex vitamin) are administered for a lifetime. The disease may also result from a dietary deficiency of vitamin B_{12}, although this is rare because the amount required by the body is easily obtained from small amounts of animal products. It may sometimes occur among the strictest vegetarians unless their diet is supplemented by the vitamin in capsule form.

Hemolytic anemia results from the destruction of red blood cells, which may occur because of Rh incompatibility, mismatched blood transfusions, industrial poisons, or hypersensitivity to certain chemicals and medicines. This type of anemia may also accompany other diseases, especially certain types of cancer. Severe cases require immediate hospitalization for determination of the underlying cause and suitable treatment, including blood transfusions.

Aplastic anemia is caused by a disease of the bone marrow, the part of the body where red blood cells are manufactured. While some cases result from bone marrow cancer, others follow excessive radiation exposure or contact with a long list of substances that have the same destructive effect (the chemicals in certain insecticides, antibiotics, medicines containing bismuth and other heavy metals). In addition to the usual symptoms of anemia, this type results in dark discolorations of the skin and, in extreme cases, bleeding from the nose and mouth. Hospitalization is mandatory, with prompt treatment of blood transfusions and in some cases cortisone injections.

Hemoglobinopathies are forms of anemia of genetic origin. Included in this category are sickle cell anemia, thalassemia (Cooley's anemia), and hemoglobin C disease. When such a congenital trait is known to exist, genetic counseling is advised before pregnancy.

anesthesia Partial or total loss of sensation or feelings. Analgesia, one category of anesthesia, refers specifically to loss of sensation of pain. The great advances in surgery have gone hand in hand with modern methods of anesthesia and the discovery of a variety of anesthetics (substances capable of producing anesthesia). Until the nineteenth century opium and alcohol were the only available painkillers. Ether, nitrous oxide (called "laughing gas" because it produces a kind of euphoria), and chloroform were all discovered in the 1840s, and since that time many more effective and less dangerous methods have been perfected. The study of these substances and their application is known as anesthesiology. An anesthesiologist is a doctor who specializes in this branch of medical science. An anesthetist is not a doctor, but usually a nurse with advanced training.

The following are among the procedures that produce anesthesia and analgesia. They may be used separately or in combination. *Intravenous injection* of sleep-producing drugs such as sodium pentothal produces light anesthesia. The injection of light anesthetics often precedes the use of longer lasting methods when major surgery is involved. *Inhalation* of gases such as nitrous oxide, cyclopropane, or Halothane is used to anesthetize the whole body. *Spinal injection* of one of the cocaine derivatives does not produce sleep, but deadens the nerves in a specific part of the body. *Rectal administration* by a light enema of paraldehyde, a sleep-inducing drug that is quickly absorbed by the body, is used for patients who are especially difficult to deal with, such as alcoholics, psychotics, or those who are extremely apprehensive. More limited procedures are *local freezing, nerve block,* such as the injection of procaine for dental surgery, and *surface or topical analgesia,* such as the use of cocaine-related drugs for eye surgery. *Hypnosis* is being used successfully in situations such as childbirth and pediatric dentistry. *Acupuncture* is being evaluated scientifically for its analgesic applications.

aneurysm An abnormal widening or distension of an artery or vein, forming a sac which is filled with blood. Aneurysms may be congenitally caused by a deficiency in the vessel walls, or they may be acquired through injury or disease, especially atherosclerosis and the late stages of syphilis. When the sac wall is composed of one or more intact layers of the blood vessel tissue, it is known as a true aneurysm; when the whole vessel has given way and the blood is contained by the surrounding fibrous tissues, the condition is known as false aneurysm.

Both kinds may exist for many years without any symptoms and may be detected only as a result of an X ray taken for some other reason. Aneurysms in the arteries of the brain or in the aorta may make themselves known by pressure in the surrounding area, for example on the optic nerve or on an organ in the chest.

When the swelling is detected in a small artery or vein, the vessel can be tied off so that the flow of blood is redirected to healthier channels. The repair of larger vessels has recently been made possible by organ banks that provide vascular replacements, both plastic and those available from smaller mammals. Rupture of an aneurysm requires emergency hospitalization and treatment.

angina pectoris Literally, pain in the chest, and the signal of an interference (generally reversible) with the supply of oxygen to the heart muscle. The pain is rarely confused with any other; it characteristically produces a feeling of tightness and suffocation beginning under the left side of the breastbone and sometimes spreading to the neck, throat, and down the left arm. Angina pectoris is more common among men than women, but women, especially in their late fifties and sixties, may suffer from the condition, especially if they smoke or are overweight, hypertensive, or diabetic.

The onset of an angina attack is likely to follow strenuous exercise, exposure to cold and wind, eating and digesting a heavy meal, or a strong emotional experience such as a quarrel or a frightening dream. In such circumstances the heart works harder and pumps faster and therefore needs an extra supply of blood and oxygen. When circulation is impaired in any way, especially by atherosclerosis, the blood supply does not reach the heart muscle cells quickly enough. The resulting lack of oxygen is the immediate cause of the pain.

An angina attack is usually brief and subsides upon resting. Nitroglycerine in the form of quickly dissolving tablets is an effective medication available by prescription. The nitroglycerine promptly dilates the smaller coronary vessels, thus increasing the supply of blood and oxygen to the heart. Since angina pectoris is a signal that the heart is under stress, the underlying causes should be explored and corrected or minimized wherever possible.

angiography A diagnostic procedure in which radiopaque substances are injected into the blood vessels so that any abnormalities or displacements are visible on an X-ray film. This type of radiological picture is called an angiogram.

animal bites Any animal bite, even by a family pet, that breaks the surface of the skin requires attention. It should be washed at once with soap under running water. Medical attention should be sought for deep or severe bites and for any bite by a wild animal. Although rabies and tetanus are comparatively rare, they should never be excluded. Not only dogs and cats, but squirrels, horses, mice, bats, foxes, and other warm-blooded animals are capable of spreading diseases through bites. If the offending animal can be caught, it should not be killed, but rather turned over to a veterinarian or a health authority. *See* RABIES.

ankles, swollen The tissues around the ankle may swell for various reasons: heart disease, kidney or liver malfunction, and pregnancy. Women who spend lots of time on their feet, such as salespeople, artists, waitresses, housewives, are especially susceptible to this complaint in hot weather, not because of disease but because of insufficient venous return. When the puffy condition persists in spite of sitting with the feet extended and raised or a warm bath before bedtime, a doctor should be consulted.

Antabuse Brand name of the drug disulfiram developed in Denmark for the treatment of alcoholism. Antabuse affects the metabolism of alcohol so that the patient becomes so sick after drinking that he or she may stop taking alcohol. A responsible doctor does not use Antabuse alone in treating alcoholism. At best it is an emergency measure that should be combined with more basic and supportive therapy.

antacid A substance that relieves acidity. *See* ACIDITY and ALKALINITY.

antibiotic A chemical substance produced during the growth of various fungi and bacteria that has the capacity to kill other bacteria or inhibit their growth. Since the discovery of penicillin in 1929 and its mass application during World War II, literally thousands of antibiotic substances have been isolated and studied. As disease-causing bacteria develop strains that are resistant to a particular antibiotic, new drugs are developed to counteract the adaptation.

While antibiotics have saved many lives, there is increasing concern about their indiscriminate prescription by doctors who rely on drug advertising rather than the more objective information in scientific journals. Surveys indicate that doctors most up-to-date about how to prescribe antibiotics are those most recently graduated from medical school and those who see only a few patients a day. Authorities agree that antibiotics are overprescribed and incorrectly prescribed to an alarming degree in the United States and that one of the best correctives to this situation is the informed self-interest of the patient. The correct application of antibiotics is the treatment of *bacterial* infections. They are ineffective against viral infections. They should not be prescribed as a preventive medicine, except for a few special conditions.

The following is a list by their generic names of the more commonly prescribed antibiotics and their application. You have every right as a patient to ask the physician if there is any reason not to prescribe a generic drug and if there are differences in effects among brands. Generic drugs are likely to be less expensive than brand-name products.

The penicillin group of antibiotics includes penicillin G potassium, penicillin V, and ampicillin. The first two drugs are both most frequently prescribed for streptococcus infections of the ear and throat, sinus infections, gonorrhea, syphilis, pneumococcal pneumonia. Ampicillin is prescribed for middle ear and urinary infections. Allergic reactions to penicillin may range from a mild rash, diarrhea, or nausea to severe shock. Any history of adverse reactions to penicillin in any form should be pointed out to a doctor, especially in an emergency situation involving a possible injection.

The tetracycline group includes tetracycline HCL (hydrochloride), chlortetracycline, oxytetracycline, and some new drugs in the same family. These are commonly prescribed under various brand names for bronchitis, acne, pneumonia, and, in cases of penicillin allergy, for syphilis and gonorrhea.

Erythromycin is an antibiotic developed for those patients who are allergic to penicillin or who should not be given tetracycline because of pregnancy or possible side effects on bone development.

Chloramphenicol is sold under the brand name of Chloromycetin. It should be prescribed only for typhoid fever and a few other special situations since it has been found in some cases to interfere with the production of blood cells in the bone marrow.

antibody A component of the immune system produced by cells called plasmocytes in the presence of an antigen (any substance foreign to the body) to destroy or neutralize that antigen; a specific antibody is produced for each antigen. This specificity is the basis of immunization by vaccination; the introduction of a controlled amount or variety of a disease-producing organism stimulates the plasmocytes to develop the antibodies necessary to fight the organism in advance of an uncontrolled invasion of the body. In addition to warding off disease and controlling infection, antibody activity also results in the rejection of grafts, transplants, and prostheses and in Rh disease in which Rh negative maternal antibodies destroy Rh positive fetal blood cells.

antidepressant A class of mood-changing drugs which counteract some of the immobilizing effects of depressive illness. While antidepressants do not cure mental illness, they have largely replaced electroshock therapy as a means of helping certain withdrawn or hysterical patients benefit from psychotherapy. In cases of agitated depression or hysteria antidepressants may be combined with tranquilizers. They may also be prescribed to stabilize a suicidal patient.

These medications were once prescribed and used with a lack of discrimination that constituted a major health hazard. Unfortunately, many women still think of antidepressants as handy pills to have around when they feel "low." Although antidepressants are not known to be physically addictive, they can establish a psychological dependency that may be more difficult to deal with than the circumstances that caused the depression in the first place. Antidepressants of any kind–as well as all other medication –should not be taken during pregnancy except under doctor's orders.

antidote Any substance that counteracts the effect of another substance, usually a poison. There are very few specific antidotes, and since ridding the body of a poison is a complicated matter, a local poison control center should be consulted immediately for emergency care.

antigen Any substance that stimulates the production of antibodies. Antigens are present in bacterial toxins, pollens, immunizing agents, blood, and other substances.

antihistamine Any of various drugs that minimize the discomfort of hay fever, hives, and other allergic reactions caused by the body's release of chemicals known as histamines. Depending on the nature of the allergy, antihistamines may be prescribed in the form of drops for the nose or eyes, a salve or topical ointment to be used on the skin, or pills to be taken orally. They may also be an effective remedy for motion sickness. Whether antihistamines are helpful in relieving the symptoms of a cold is debatable. Many researchers feel that such relief is the result of a placebo effect or is an indication that an allergic situation coexists with the cold.

Continuous and indiscriminate use of these drugs may have unpleasant effects and should be avoided. Since antihistamines produce drowsiness, caution is advisable while driving a car and when alertness at a job or at household tasks is essential for proper functioning and well-being. They should not be used by pregnant women for morning sickness. Nonprescription "daytime sedatives," widely advertised for their effectiveness in diminishing tension and anxiety, actually contain little more than an antihistamine that causes drowsiness and perhaps serious adverse consequences.

antiperspirant A mixture of chemicals that diminish the amount of perspiration that reaches the skin and reduce the rate of growth of the odor-creating bacteria. (Deodorants only reduce the speed with which bacteria multiply). Antiperspirants are considered drugs and their ingredients must be listed on their containers. They may contain irritants to the skin so it may be necessary to experiment with different brands to find one that does not produce a rash. Those packaged in spray cans contain propellants harmful to the lungs and should be rejected in favor of a cream or roll-on product.

antiseptic A substance that inhibits or slows down the growth of microorganisms; in more recent usage the term conveys the meaning of bactericide, that is, a substance that kills bacteria. Disinfectants are included under the general heading of antiseptics, although they are too strong to be applied to body tissues and are meant to make surfaces germ-free in kitchens, bathrooms, and sickrooms. The English surgeon Joseph Lister's application of the principle of antisepsis to surgery was one of the major medical accomplishments of the nineteenth century, eliminating a significant number of fatalities caused by infection.

antitoxin A type of antibody that neutralizes the specific toxin released by a disease-causing agent. Antitoxins may be manufactured by the body's immune system or they may be injected as a defense against diseases such as tetanus, diphtheria, or botulism.

anus The opening at the end of the alimentary canal (at the end of the rectum, which is the last segment of the large intestine). The action of the anus in bowel evacuation is controlled by valves of two ringlike voluntary muscles known as anal sphincters.

anxiety A feeling of threat or danger in which the threat cannot be clearly identified; a response to stress in which the condition creating stress is not fully known.

aorta The largest and most important artery, carrying blood from the heart to be distributed throughout the body. The aorta begins at the left ventricle of the heart, curves over and downward into the chest, and then penetrates the diaphragm for entry into the abdomen where it ends opposite the fourth lumbar vertebra. The branches of the aorta supply arterial blood to all parts of the body.

aphasia Loss of speech (motor aphasia) or the ability to comprehend speech (sensory aphasia). Aphasia is usually the result of damage by disease or injury to those parts of the brain concerned with language formulation rather than comprehension. Since brain function rather than mind function (the formulation of thoughts and ideas) is involved, rehabilitation of speech can be accomplished in many instances, especially if the patient, the therapist, and the family are optimistic and persistent. When aphasia occurs as a form of hysteria, psychotherapeutic techniques, including hypnotism, can be effective in restoring the ability to speak.

aphrodisiac A substance that purportedly increases sexual desire and potency. Aphrodisiacs may be celebrated in song, story, overheated imaginations, and "health food" literature, but scientific investigation has yet to validate the claims of any of them. Where sexual incapacity exists, a good physician should be consulted for treatment.

apoplexy *See* STROKE.

appendicitis Inflammation of the appendix, the 3- to 6-inch appendage or sac that lies in the lower right portion of the abdominal cavity at the junction of the small and large intestine. Appendicitis accounts for at least half the abdominal emergencies that occur between the ages of 10 and 30. The critical aspect of an attack of acute appendicitis is that the inflammation may result in a rupture leading to peritonitis (infection of the abdominal lining).

Appendicitis is not caused by swallowing fruit pits or nut shells. However, hard bits of matter in food being digested, intestinal worms, or some undetermined element may plug up the tubelike appendix, hindering normal drainage and increasing the likelihood of bacterial infection. If the body's defenses do not stop the multiplication of colon bacilli and streptococci, inflammation results, causing three main symptoms: pain in the lower right side, nausea or vomiting, and fever. If one or all of these symptoms persist, see a doctor promptly.

If they become acute and no doctor is available, call an ambulance to take you to the nearest hospital's emergency room. Under no circumstances should anything be taken by mouth without professional instructions: no food, no fluid, no medicines, and especially *no laxative or cathartic*. Self-treatment with an enema or a hot-water bottle is equally ill-advised.

An appendectomy performed under the best medical conditions has a very low mortality rate. Even when postoperative complications occur, they can be overcome with antibiotics.

So-called chronic appendicitis is considered to be a designation with little medical validity. Constant complaints of discomfort in the lower right part of the abdomen should be investigated for the correct cause.

appetite The natural desire for food, usually conditioned by psychological factors such as eating habits, pleasant memories, and the stimuli of the sight and smell of particular foods. Hunger, on the other hand, is a physiological phenomenon resulting from the contractions of an empty stomach. An infant's cries for food are an expression of hunger, not appetite.

When appetite is active and intense beyond the apparent physical needs of the body, diabetes or a thyroid disorder may be responsible. More frequently, an insatiable appetite that leads to compulsive overeating may originate in an emotional problem that requires attention.

People occasionally experience a loss of appetite in the presence of unattractive surroundings or uncongenial company. Emotions such as fear, anger, or anxiety affect the flow of stomach juices and diminish the appetite. A continuing loss of appetite, technically known as chronic *anorexia* (not to be confused with anorexia nervosa), may indicate kidney malfunction or cancer. When a lack of interest in food occurs in old age, it may be related to depression and withdrawal from life.

A doctor's guidance is advised when someone's appetite needs to be stimulated or reduced.

areola Any round, colored area surrounding a raised center, such as the inflamed area surrounding a pustule or the pigmented area of the breast in which the nipple is centered.

arteriosclerosis A disease of aging, also called hardening of the arteries, in which the walls of the arteries thicken and lose their elasticity. It is more prevalent among men than women. *See* ATHEROSCLEROSIS.

arthritis Inflammation of a joint. The term is broadly used to cover almost 100 different conditions many of which do not necessarily involve inflammation, but do result in aches and pains in the joints and connective tissues all over the body. The designation rheumatism is often incorrectly used for such aches and pains. The Arthritis Foundation estimates that about 20 million Americans suffer from some form of arthritis severe enough to require medical attention and that among the sufferers women far outnumber men.

Arthritis is a chronic condition, but it may be less of a problem if its symptoms are recognized early enough for prompt and proper treatment. The typical warning signs of the onset of one of the arthritic diseases are: stiffness and pain in the joints on getting up in the morning; tenderness, soreness, and swelling in one or several joints; tingling sensations in the fingers and toes; fatigue and weakness unconnected with any other disorder. Authorities emphasize that the mountain of misinformation about arthritis has been the cause of a great deal of unnecessary suffering and mismanagement of the various arthritic diseases. It is *not* true that most women have arthritis as they get older and there's nothing to be done about it. It is *not* true (loud and persistent claims to the contrary) that diet is an important factor in arthritis. It is *not* true that home treatments are just as effective as professional medical care. This last misconception is the most dangerous of all since it can lead to a delay in getting an accurate diagnosis and effective treatment early enough to avoid irreversible joint damage.

Rheumatoid arthritis is the most serious—and the most mysterious—of the arthritic diseases. Although no one is immune to it, 80 percent of all cases occur between the ages of 25 and 50, with three times as many women affected as men. The current theory about the cause is that virus-like organisms remain dormant in the body until they are triggered into destructive activity by some infection, injury, or emotional shock. No two cases are the same: in some the symptoms become progressively worse and disabling, while in many others the pain and swelling are severe for several months and then vanish forever.

The disease chiefly affects the joints of the hands, arms, hips, legs, and feet, although the inflammation may attack connective tissue anywhere in the body. Since rheumatoid arthritis has so many variations, it must be treated on an individual basis by a specialist who is aware of all the possible forms of therapy: medication, rest, exercise, heat, surgery, and any combination of treatments to keep the inflammation from spreading, to eliminate as much pain as possible, to prevent the occurrence of irreversible deformities, and to maintain as much joint movement and function as possible. Analgesics such as aspirin (which also is anti-inflammatory) are helpful in mild cases. Corticosteroids are used for their anti-inflammatory effect in more severe cases. The use of combinations of these drugs plus newer, more powerful ones in very severe cases may require hospitalization. Recent developments in surgical techniques—plastic surgery, fusions, and artificial implants—are achieving good results in overcoming deformities and disabilities.

Osteoarthritis, also known as degenerative joint disease, is the most common form of arthritis, usually an accompaniment to aging and rarely disabling. Mild aches and stiffness are likely to settle in those joints that have received the most use and weight stress; women are especially vulnerable to osteoarthritis of the hip, knee, big toe, and the end (or distal) joints of the fingers. Overweight is clearly a contributing cause since it places an added burden on the hip and knee joints; joints that have been injured in falls or have taken constant abuse in athletics may be the source of arthritic discomfort; heredity seems to be a factor that predisposes some women to osteoarthritis in the small joints of the fingers and toes; tension that takes its toll in muscle fatigue is one of the factors that has led some specialists to call osteoarthritis one of the self-punishing diseases.

In many cases the disorder will show up in an X-ray before it has caused much discomfort. Typically, the symptoms are localized soreness, a constant pain of varying intensity resulting from pressure on nerve endings, or some difficulty in moving the joint easily, for example, a stiff knee or pains in the hip ("creaking joints"). While there is no cure for osteoarthritis, a doctor can recommend various procedures to ease the discomfort and to prevent further deterioration of tissue.

The national office of The Arthritis Foundation, 3400 Peachtree Road NE, Suite 1101, Atlanta, Georgia 30326, supplies information on request about local specialists and treatment centers. It also offers free literature covering many aspects of the disease and current research activities.

artificial insemination The transfer of semen into the vagina by artificial means for the purpose of conception. The procedure known as AIH (artificial insemination by the husband) is used in cases where normal sexual intercourse and ejaculation cannot be achieved. The husband's semen is injected into the vagina by syringe on three or four successive days around the time of ovulation. If the husband is sterile, the same procedure may be followed with semen from a donor.

artificial respiration Any of several techniques whereby air is forced into and out of the lungs when natural breathing has ceased. None of the techniques requires special equipment, so they are first aid measures that almost anyone can master. Since brain death occurs four to six minutes after breathing has stopped, artificial respiration must be administered at once in such circumstances as a near-drowning, an almost lethal electric shock, suffocation from smoke inhalation. It is therefore crucial to learn the techniques *before* the need arises in order to function swiftly and competently. Local Red Cross chapters or other community organizations should be contacted for information about courses that cover instruction in first aid for common emergencies.

ascorbic acid Chemical designation of vitamin C.

aspirin Common name for the pure chemical acetylsalicylic acid; originally the brand name invented by the Bayer Drug Company, but now a generic term. Aspirin is always aspirin no matter what company packages it; therefore, there's no reason not to buy the least expensive brand. Aspirin is one of the greatest discoveries of all times because of its many benefits. It is a painkiller (analgesic); it lowers fever (antipyretic); it reduces some of the destructive consequences of arthritis (anti-inflammatory); and recently it has been reported to play a role in controlling the mechanism that causes blood to form clots (anticoagulant).

The addition of certain chemicals to aspirin may be profitable to the manufacturer, but of questionable value to the consumer. Aspirin combined with caffeine? It probably costs less to have plain aspirin with a cup of coffee. With phenacetin? In large doses this is an ingredient likely to produce stomach upsets and kidney problems.

Aspirin itself can be a stomach irritant and should be avoided by anyone with ulcers or gastritis. It can be "buffered" by combining it with an alkalizer such as a bicarbonate of soda pill or a half glass of milk. When aspirin causes an allergic response, acetaminophen (Tylenol or other aspirinlike analgesics) should be substituted.

Children should be given a recommended dose of plain aspirin, not "candied" aspirin. Medicine is medicine and candy is candy. Confusing the two has caused many tragedies.

Headaches, ringing in the ears, and drowsiness are signs of aspirin overdose. Severe cases of aspirin poisoning, with symptoms of vomiting and delirium, require emergency treatment.

asthma A respiratory disorder in which the air tubes of the lungs are constricted by tightened muscles, mucous plugs, and inflamed tissue, causing breathing to be mildly or severely labored; technically known as bronchial asthma. While most asthma victims are children, it is also common among adults, with men and women affected in equal numbers. Asthma is a disease that occurs in "attacks" or "episodes." Asthmatics are said to have lungs that are abnormally sensitive to certain stimuli, ranging from cat hairs to chemicals to sudden changes in temperature to virus infections. The offending stimulus (in most cases an allergen that causes the body to produce histamines) triggers muscle tightening, mucous secretion, and tissue swelling in the bronchial passages that transport oxygen into the lungs. The victim of the attack begins to wheeze, cough, and gasp for air. An attack may subside in a few minutes or it may continue intermittently for hours.

Asthmatics who know exactly what substances or circumstances precipitate an attack but cannot easily avoid the stimulus should be desensitized. If the episodes are of mysterious origin, the American Lung Association recommends that a doctor be consulted before taking any medicines. Since no environment is pollen-free, pollutant-free, dust-free, or mold-free year round, moving is rarely a final solution. For some the answer is as simple as avoiding other people's cigarette smoke; for others it is as difficult as giving up smoking themselves.

Attacks that are triggered by tension or anxiety may be eliminated after a period of productive psychotherapy.

astigmatism A defect in the curved surface of the lens or the cornea that results in blurred vision. When the refracting surface is not truly spherical, rays of light coming from a single spot are not brought into sharp focus. Astigmatism is a common disorder of vision that is easily corrected with properly fitted eyeglasses.

atherosclerosis A thickening and decreased elasticity of the arteries combined with the formation of fatty deposits (plaquer) on or beneath their inner walls. When these plaques become large enough to block the flow of blood, the tissue beyond the block dies (infarcts). This blockage of blood flow is what causes the brain damage in most strokes and the heart muscle damage (myocardial infarction) in most heart attacks. Similar blockage may occur in other blood vessels, resulting in such conditions as kidney failure and gangrene in the legs. Atherosclerosis is the major cause of cardiovascular disease which is the immediate cause of about half of the deaths in the United States each year.

The causes of atherosclerosis are not sharply defined. Because the disease is rare in undernourished populations, some specialists blame overeating, especially of animal fats. Because the disorder is not a major problem in agricultural countries, other specialists blame the stresses of industrial society, especially since its incidence is greatest among male business executives. Because between the ages of 35 and 40 the death rate from atherosclerosis is almost 500 percent higher for men than for women, researchers have begun to explore the role of sex hormones in its development.

Although simple hardening of the arteries (arteriosclerosis) is a concomitant of aging, the fatty deposits (atheromas) are not. Medical science has recently discovered special constituents, known as HDL (high density lipoproteins), in the blood of certain people that seem to break down cholesterol instead of allowing it to remain and clog the arteries.

Yearly checkups should include diagnostic blood tests as insurance against the sudden onset of a preventable disease. One of the recently developed diagnostic procedures for assessing arterial disease is phonoangiography. This procedure records the noise produced by the blood flow in a constricted artery and feeds the sound into a small computer for analysis. The loudness and pitch indicate the degree of narrowing caused by the fatty deposits. Phonoangiography can be conducted on an out-patient basis as a screening test when dangerous degrees of atherosclerosis are suspected.

athlete's foot *See* FUNGUS INFECTIONS.

atrophy The wasting away, degeneration, or shriveling up of any part of the body through disuse or lack of nourishment. A healthy muscle will atrophy if the nerve that controls its function is irreversibly damaged.

Aureomycin Brand name of one of the tetracycline group of antibiotics.

auscultation A means of examining the body by listening. A doctor may do this by placing his or her ear against various parts of the body or, more commonly, by using a stethoscope which makes binaural listening possible without the distraction of outside sounds. Auscultation is used to determine the condition of the heart and lungs, to discover possible disorders within the abdominal cavity, to determine the health of the fetal heart, and to make a prenatal determination of twins.

autoimmune responses The body's production of antibodies against its own tissues. The autoimmune mechanism is one of the most important areas of present-day medical research because it is thought to be responsible for various diseases such as rheumatoid arthritis and for many allergic responses. If the autoimmune mechanism is triggered by an infection such as mumps, it may explain the onset of encephalitis. Since this response is also the cause of rejected grafts of tissue that are essential in successful transplants, a better understanding of autoimmunity will represent an important medical advance.

backache The discomfort of backache, sometimes called lumbago, can in most cases be reduced by appropriate exercises and by rectifying such causes of the problem as poor posture, ill-fitting shoes, an improper mattress. Upper back pain can often be traced to stress and anxiety, and lower muscles may be strained for many reasons such as lifting heavy objects. Backache may be connected with osteoporosis of the spine in older women, with premenstrual internal pressures in younger ones, and with a kidney disorder or an ovarian cyst in some cases.

When acute back pain interferes with normal activity and all efforts have been made to eliminate apparent external causes, a doctor should be consulted.

bacteria Single-cell microscopic organisms, essentially a form of plant life without chlorophyl, that occur everywhere in nature. Some bacteria are harmless, many are useful, and some cause disease. Bacteria are classified by their shape: bacilli are rod-shaped, spirochetes spiral, vibrios hooklike, and cocci round. Cocci are also classified by the way they are grouped: diplococci occur in pairs, streptococci run together in a chain, and staphylococci are clustered.

The development of antibiotics was based on the observation that there are substances in nature, produced by microorganisms and fungi, that can destroy disease-producing bacteria.

bacterial endocarditis A serious infection of the lining of the heart. The internal chambers and valves of the heart are lined with a delicate tissue called the endocardium. Normal endocardium is usually immune to bacterial infection, but where abnormalities exist, either congenital or caused by rheumatic fever, the danger of endocarditis is a particularly serious threat. Women with such a heart disability should discuss prophylactic antibiotic therapy with their oral surgeon before a tooth extraction and with other surgeons before any procedure. Otherwise the bacteria, usually streptococci, that escape into the bloodstream may cause subacute bacterial endocarditis, which can be fatal.

bag of waters *See* AMNION.

baldness Loss or absence of hair; technically called alopecia. Although women may temporarily lose hair as a result of an acute fever, anticancer chemotherapy, tuberculosis, thyroid disorder, or pregnancy, they are spared the characteristically male baldness that is permanent. When women's hair begins to thin out with age, hormone replacement is not effective. Although chemicals in hair dyes or constant "permanents" may cause hair to break off, unless the root is destroyed, hair will grow back.

barbiturate A class of sedative and hypnotic medicines derived from barbituric acid that have a depressant effect on the central nervous system. Depending on the type and amount prescribed, barbiturates produce sedation, sleep, or anesthesia. An overdose may result in coma, respiratory failure, and death.

Short-action barbiturates such as sodium pentothal are injected intravenously as anesthetics. Sodium pentobarbital (Nembutal) and sodium secobarbital (Seconal) are slower acting; an oral dose of 100 mg produces about six hours of sleep. Phenobarbital, one of the slowest acting barbiturates, may be prescribed with other drugs for the control of epileptic seizures.

The indiscriminate prescribing of barbiturates and their consequent overuse have come under severe criticism. Sedatives and sleeping pills that contain no barbiturates have become available in recent years. Barbiturates should be used only when and as prescribed and should be prescribed only when there is an authentic need for them. These drugs not only can be physically and psychologically addictive, but can produce the kind of confusion responsible for accidental overdose. The combination of alcohol and barbiturates can be lethal. Sudden and total withdrawal can also be lethal and should *never* be attempted without medical supervision.

The victim of acute barbiturate poisoning should be given strong, black coffee at once and hospitalized for emergency treatment. Low-level chronic poisoning may be evident in poorly coordinated movements, sluggishness, memory lapses, and slurred speech. If these symptoms appear, professional help is essential.

barium test A diagnostic test for the exploration of gastrointestinal disorders by X ray. Barium sulfate, a harmless chalky substance, is administered to the patient. The opacity of the barium causes the gastrointestinal (GI) tract to stand out in a white silhouette on the fluoroscope or X-ray plate, making visible to the diagnostician ulcers, tumors, and various other disorders of the stomach, duodenum, or intestines. The barium, mixed with water and a drop of flavoring, is taken orally for an examination of the upper tract. A barium enema is administered for an X-ray examination of the lower bowel and colon.

Bartholin's glands A pair of glands situated on each side of the vaginal opening. They are named after the Danish anatomist who first described them. Their function is not known, but they are presumed to provide some of the lubricating liquid that facilitates intercourse. These glands cannot be seen or felt unless they become inflamed or abscessed.

basal metabolism test A procedure for measuring the body's energy output by recording its rate of oxygen intake and consumption. The test for BMR (basal metabolism rate) measures the rate at which the body uses energy in order to carry on its basic life processes such as respiration, circulation, and temperature maintenance. The test calculates this rate by measuring the oxygen intake and comparing its consumption with a norm based not on weight, but on age, sex, and body surface area. The results of the test express the BMR as a percentage indicating its variation from the normal rate for a woman of the same age and size. Thus a result of minus 20 means that the patient's BMR is 20 percent slower than average, plus 5 that it is 5 percent faster. The BMR is no longer the most accurate indicator of the proper functioning of the thyroid gland and is seldom used for that purpose.

bed sore Patch of degenerating skin tissue, technically called decubitus ulcer, caused by prolonged and uninterrupted pressure of the bedding on the skin of a patient immobilized during an illness or postoperative convalescence. Elderly women and women with diabetes or heart disease are especially susceptible. The parts of the body most vulnerable are the area over the heels, the shoulders, the elbows, the buttocks, and the ankles. The first symptom of the sore is redness of the skin; continued interference with circulation produces a blue appearance of the affected area and then the formation of ulcers. Preventive measures are advisable as bed sores heal with great difficulty and are susceptible to infection. Bed linens should be soft, smooth, and dry. The patient's skin should be washed and powdered each day and the vulnerable areas cushioned with cotton pads. If possible, the bedridden patient should change body position every few hours.

bee stings *See* INSECT STINGS AND BITES.

Bell's palsy Paralysis of the muscles of one side of the face caused by inflammation of the facial nerve to a point where it becomes incapable of transmitting impulses. It generally is caused by an inflammation of the ear canal with resultant pressure on the facial nerve. The condition causes loss of the blink reflex, inability to close the eyelids, a flow of tears from the affected eye, and the dribbling of saliva from the immobilized side of the mouth. Food may also collect inside the cheek.

Recovery is based in part on treating the cause, if known, or stimulating the nerve electrically. Until the blink reflex is restored, the eye must be protected from excessive dryness and foreign particles. In most cases the condition subsides in a few weeks. At its very worst the deformity caused by Bell's palsy can be partially corrected by cosmetic surgery.

Benadryl Brand name of an antihistamine.

Benzedrine Brand name of an amphetamine.

bifocals *See* EYEGLASSES.

bile A yellow-brown fluid with a greenish tinge secreted by the liver and concentrated and stored in the gallbladder until needed for the digestive process, especially for the digestion of fats. The channel known as the biliary duct carries bile into the small intestine for this purpose. When the gallbladder has been removed, bile passes directly from the liver into the duodenum through the biliary duct. Among the constituents of bile are cholesterol, bile salts, some proteins, and the emulsifier lecithin. When the balance of these contents is upset, a common type of gallstones, which are actually a precipitate of cholesterol, may form. In some instances such gallstones can be treated medically by dissolution rather than surgically. Blockage of bile ducts by inflammation or other abnormal circumstances is one of the causes of discoloration of the skin and whites of the eyes that characterize jaundice.

biofeedback A still largely experimental technique, also called biomedical feedback, whereby a person learns how to achieve a state of relaxation that minimizes arteriolar constriction in her body in order to ward off headaches, particularly vascular headaches, and other symptoms of stress. A sensitive device that measures skin temperature, which in turn reflects blood flow, is used in biofeedback training.

biopsy The microscopic examination of small fragments of tissue cut from an organ of the body. The term is usually applied to the removal and evaluation of cells to determine whether they are cancerous.

birth control *See* "Contraception and Abortion."

birth defect Any disorder or disease which is either genetically determined (inborn or inherited) or congenitally caused by chemicals, drugs, virus infection, injury, or malnutrition that affect the normal physical and mental development of the fetus before birth.

birth injuries Damages sustained by a baby during the birth process, beginning at the onset of labor and ending when the newborn has been delivered. Thanks to new obstetrical procedures, new medicines, and new monitoring techniques of blood and oxygen supply to the baby, the number of birth injuries has been dramatically reduced. Ultrasonic apparatus can determine the exact placement of the fetus and position of the head, so that complications of delivery can be anticipated. Electronic monitors can record the fetal heartbeat during labor and any cutoff in oxygen supply is immediately corrected before brain damage can occur. Injuries and fatalities to the newborn that result from heavy sedation of the mother during labor have also been reduced. Advances in anesthesiology and the increasing number of women taking courses in childbirth have combined to hold sedation in the delivery room to a minimum.

birthmarks Congenital skin blemishes visible from birth. The most frequent type of birthmark, commonly called a strawberry mark and technically known as a hemangioma, is a collection of small red or purplish blood vessels appearing on the skin surface. Most of these marks disappear by the time a child is 3 or 4. If they do not or if they grow and ulcerate, they can be removed by radiotherapy or surgery. The mark known as a port wine stain is formed by a combination of blood vessel clusters and erratic pigmentation. This blemish does not disappear spontaneously, but it may be treated with diathermy or effectively hidden under cosmetics prepared for this purpose.

bisexuality Sexual attraction to both men and women. An increase in the number of people who consider themselves bisexual may be due to the fact that more men and women feel free to acknowledge their bisexual feelings.

black eye Discoloration, swelling, and pain of the tissues around the eye, usually caused by a bruise that has ruptured tiny blood vessels under the skin. An icepack or cold compress applied immediately after the blow will slow subcutaneous bleeding, thus reducing the symptoms. A warm, wet compress applied on the following day will help absorb the discoloring fluids. If a blow to the eye is followed by persistent blurring of vision or severe pain, an ophthalmologist should be consulted promptly.

blackhead A skin pore in which fatty material secreted by the sebaceous glands has accumulated and darkened, not because of dirt, but because of the effect of oxygen on the secretion itself. Blackheads usually accompany the acne of adolescence and may occasionally trouble older women whose skin is oily. Their occurrence may be reduced by keeping the skin clean and dry. When blackheads do appear, the temptation to squeeze them should be resisted in order to avoid infection. Blackheads can be removed with a device designed for this purpose and available at most drugstores.

bladder disorders The urinary bladder is joined to the kidneys by tubes called ureters and to the outside of the body by the urethra. Cystitis, the technical term for infection of the bladder, is caused by multiplication of bacteria in the urine. Women are more prone to bladder infections than men because the female urethra is shorter, facilitating the entry of bacteria, particularly from the rectal area. Although the condition is rarely serious, it can be very annoying. It has a tendency to recur intermittently and the symptoms are a burning sensation during urination, a frequent feeling of having to urinate when the bladder is practically empty, and a nagging pain in the lower abdomen. It is important that the causing organism be identified by urinalysis and treated with an appropriate antibiotic or other antibacterial agent.

To prevent cystitis women should use toilet paper only in a front-to-back motion after a bowel movement and wash their genital area daily. Since bacteria can enter the urethra during sexual contact, it is a good idea to urinate afterward to "flush" them out.

Blood-streaked urine unaccompanied by pain may be an indication of a tumor in the bladder or kidney or of kidney stones. Although the tumor may be nonmalignant, surgical removal may be recommended to eliminate discomfort. Surgery is also the only way of removing stones that are not passed with urination since there is, as yet, no medical way of dissolving them.

Surgical correction is the usual procedure for dealing with the type of hernia resulting from a difficult delivery during which the weakening pelvic tissues have allowed the bladder to protrude into the vagina.

bleeding *See* HEMORRHAGE.

blister A collection of fluid (lymph), usually colorless, that forms a raised sac under the skin surface. A common cause of blisters is friction on the skin. Improperly fitted shoes should be stretched or discarded and gloves should be worn to protect the skin when using tools which may blister the hands. Mild burns, such as overexposure to the sun and scalding with steam or hot water, will cause the skin to blister. Minor injuries that do not break the skin may rupture a tiny blood vessel beneath the skin and cause a blood blister. Blisters are also associated with various allergic reactions such as poison ivy sensitivity and eczema, with infections caused by the herpes simplex virus (fever blisters or cold sores), and with fungus invasions such as ringworm.

Blisters caused by an illness usually vanish as the illness improves. Small surface blisters should be left to heal by themselves since the unbroken skin protects against infection. A large and painful blister may be drained in the following way: sterilize a needle by placing it in a flame, swab the area with soap and water, prick the outer margin of the blister, press the inflated skin surface gently with a sterile gauze to remove the fluid, and apply a sterile bandage. Any inflammation or accumulation of pus around a blister that has ruptured is a sign of bacterial infection and should be examined by a doctor.

blood The principal fluid of life; the medium in which oxygen and nutrients are transported to all tissues and carbon dioxide and other wastes are removed from tissues. Blood maintains the body's fluid balance by carrying water and salts to and from the tissues. It contains antibodies that fight infection, delivers hormones from the endocrine glands to the organs they influence, and regulates body temperature by dispersing heat in the form of perspiration. Every adult body contains about 1 quart (1,000 cc) of blood for every 25 pounds of weight. About 45 percent of blood composition consists of red cells that contain hemoglobin, white cells that fight infection, and platelets essential for the clotting process. The remaining 55 percent of blood composition is plasma. Blood plasma consists of water (over 90 percent) and proteins, hormones, enzymes, and other organic substances. Dissolved in the plasma are such proteins as globulins, fibrinogen, and albumin. *See also* BLOOD SERUM, HEMOGLOBIN. Blood diseases are discussed under the specific headings: ANEMIA, HEMOPHILIA, LEUKEMIA.

blood clotting The coagulation or solidification of blood. Many complicated chemical changes occur in the clotting process during which blood proteins and platelets combine to seal a break in the circulatory system. One of the plasma proteins indispensable in the clotting process, AHF (the *a*nti*h*emophilic *f*actor), is missing from the blood of hemophiliacs. Medicines known as coagulants are available to hasten clotting in the case of hemorrhaging; vitamin therapy may be necessary in those cases where diet deficiencies or faulty metabolism interfere with normal clotting.

Blood clots that form within the cardiovascular system are a major hazard because they impede circulation and can deprive vital organs of oxygen necessary for survival. Anticoagulants are used to counteract the formation of dangerous blood clots that may accompany diseases of the veins (phlebitis) or arteries (arteriosclerosis). Heparin, a drug until recently used only in high doses to reduce the possibility of clotting in high-risk patients after surgery, injury, or childbirth, is now being used preoperatively in low doses by some surgeons. It has also been discovered that aspirin, in addition to its many other properties, is an anticoagulant since it depresses platelet activity.

blood pressure The amount of pressure exerted against the arterial walls when the heart contracts (systolic pressure) and when it relaxes between beats (diastolic pressure). These measurements vary according to changes in the rate at which the heart beats and changes in the dilation or constriction of the blood vessels. The pumping action of the heart and the efficiency of the arteries in circulating the body's five quarts of blood are affected by many factors: general health of the heart muscle, elasticity and smoothness of the arterial walls, emotional stress, overweight, ingestion of drugs, alcoholic intake, time of day, and so on.

Blood pressure is measured by a device called a sphygmomanometer. It consists of a rubber cuff which can be blown up by squeezing an attached rubber bulb. The cuff is connected to a mercury-filled glass tube or to a gauge calibrated in millimeters. The cuff is wrapped around the brachial artery of the upper arm and inflated. As the cuff begins to put pressure on the artery, the mercury indicator rises. The doctor or nurse places a stethoscope on the crook of the elbow where the sound of the arterial pulse can be heard, while continuing to inflate the cuff until the arterial blood flow is momentarily halted. The air pressure in the cuff is then released so that the blood flow resumes, producing a rhythmic tap. As soon as this tap is heard, the pressure registered on the gauge is recorded. This number is the systolic pressure. The cuff is then deflated slowly until the sound becomes so faint that it can scarcely be heard. The number registered by the gauge at this moment is the diastolic pressure.

The figures 120/80 are sometimes called an average reading, but they should not be considered a rigid norm. Normal readings for age ranges are: 17 to 40 years, up to 140/90; 41 to 60 years, up to 150/90; 61 years and older, 160/90. Lower limits of both systolic and diastolic pressures vary and their significance, if any, must be individually determined. When the readings go up and stay up for several months, medicines may be prescribed to reduce them.

blood pressure, high *See* HYPERTENSION.

blood serum The clear, yellowish liquid which separates from whole blood when it clots. It contains proteins, enzymes, hormones, and chemicals such as glucose and sodium—in fact all the constituents of whole blood except hemoglobin and fibrinogen. Albumin protein can be fractionated out from the serum (or plasma) of human blood and used to treat people who need more albumin in their blood. Also, protein antibodies (gamma globulins) present in the blood naturally or subsequent to active immunization can be fractionated out from serum, concentrated, and injected intramuscularly into another person to provide passive (short-lived, not more than 6 months) immunization against such diseases as hepatitis and measles. The general term for serum from humans used for this purpose is Immune Serum Globulin (Human). Serum from people who are convalescing, or have been immunized recently against a specific disease is given a more specific name, for example, Tetanus Immune Globulin (Human), Measles Immune Globulin (Human). The more specific the preparation, the more effective it is. Animal serum also is used, but many people are allergic to it.

blood test Laboratory analysis of the blood which provides information for the diagnosis of a disorder or disease. If only a small amount of blood is required, it is taken from the fleshy cushion of a finger. When a large amount is needed for several different laboratory tests, blood is usually taken from a vein in the crook of the arm.

A patient entering the hospital for surgery is often given several blood tests. These are necessary for diagnostic purposes as well as to establish the patient's blood type in the event a transfusion is required during or after the operation. Blood tests for hemoglobin, cholesterol, and glucose are among the routine procedures of a comprehensive annual checkup. Blood tests can indicate the presence of diabetes, anemia, kidney disorder, or glandular disorder.

blood transfusion The infusion of blood into the veins of a patient from an outside source. Transfusions had unpredictable results until the beginning of the twentieth century when blood groups were discovered. The accurate matching of blood is necessary for a successful transfusion.

The replenishment of blood is a lifesaving measure in such circumstances as hemorrhage resulting from accident, tissue injuries caused by severe burns, or blood loss attendant on surgery. While whole blood may be desirable in most cases, it may not be essential in instances of shock, when the crucial requirement is blood plasma or serum. These components can be accumulated without regard to type since they are universally compatible. They can be stored frozen in large amounts and drawn on in emergencies involving large numbers of victims, such as a plane crash.

Among the most recent developments in blood transfusion are two techniques with broad application. Plateletpheresis involves taking blood from a healthy donor, removing the platelets which are the component essential for clotting, and immediately returning the remainder—the red cells, white cells, and plasma—to the donor. The transfusion of platelets can extend the lives of patients with certain types of anemia, leukemia, and other malignant diseases for whom bleeding episodes might otherwise be fatal. This procedure in no way endangers the donor's blood supply since platelets in the body of a healthy person are automatically replaced within two days. The second innovation in transfusion is a technique whereby white blood cells can be supplied to cancer patients who are receiving drugs that temporarily suppress the ability of the bone marrow to manufacture them. In this way patients undergoing anticancer chemotherapy are provided with the white cells necessary for fighting infection.

blood types For many years it had been observed that some blood transfusions were successful and some were not, but it was not until the twentieth century that the riddle of incompatibility was solved. It is now known that the blood of all humans, regardless of skin color, race, country of origin, or sex, can be classified under four main groupings: A, B, AB, and O. Blood type O (the "O" stands for zero) is composed of red cells that can blend with any type of plasma. Because of this compatibility, a person with O type blood is a universal donor. Conversely, anyone with AB type blood is a universal recipient. Of each 100 individuals, approximately 45 will be type O, 40 will be type A, 10 will be type B, and 5 will be type AB. There are many minor subtypes which are inconsequential for most people. *See also* RH FACTOR.

body odors Natural odors associated with the human body. Fresh perspiration from a healthy body is practically odorless. Most unpleasant body odors are caused by the presence of bacteria or fungi that multiply in areas where perspiration can accumulate, such as the genital area, the armpits, and between the toes, and by stale perspiration absorbed by clothing. Regular scrubbing with soap and water and regular changes of clothes should keep the body clean and odorless. It should be noted that vaginal sprays can be quite harmful to the delicate membranes they are supposed to deodorize.

boil A painful bacterial infection, usually staphylococcal, of a hair follicle or sweat gland, often occurring on the face, neck, shoulders, breast, or buttocks. The infected lump, technically called a *furuncle,* may be as small as a cherry pit or quite large. Since the infection can easily spread, a boil should be treated promptly. Moist, hot compresses should be applied several times a day. The boil should then be covered with an antibiotic salve such as bacitracin ointment and protected by a sterile gauze bandage. A boil should never be squeezed, especially one on the nose, ear, or upper lip, since some of the bacteria may invade the bloodstream, instead of going to the lymph glands or being exuded to the skin surface, leading to possible blood poisoning. Boils that do not drain naturally following the application of heat and moisture may have to be incised surgically. Those that occur in groups (carbuncles) or that recur may be the result of faulty habits of personal hygiene, low resistance, diabetes, or a strain of bacteria requiring a newer antibiotic. Such cases should be treated by a doctor.

bone The hard tissue that forms the major part of the skeleton. The 206 bones in the human body are connected by ligaments at the joints and are activated into movement by muscles secured to the bones by tendons. Bones are covered by a thin fibrous membrane called periosteum which sheathes and protects them and supports the adjacent tendons. The periosteum stops at the joints which are covered by a layer of cartilage. The fibrous layer of tissue directly under the periosteum gives bones their elasticity. Next are the dense hard layers called compact tissue within which are encased the porous materials known as spongy tissue. The innermost cavity of bone contains the marrow, which is the source of red blood cell production. Every layer of bone is crisscrossed by blood vessels. Bone tissue also contains a large number of nerves.

The hardness and strength of the skeleton result from the mineral content—calcium phosphate. This mineral, plentiful in milk, is essential for the transformation of cartilage into the calcified part of bone during childhood and adolescence. Bone tissue, even when fully formed in adulthood, constantly renews itself, but since the rate of renewal slows with age, the bones of the elderly become more brittle as they become more porous and less elastic.

The health of bones may be impaired by dietary deficiency of the mother during pregnancy or of the child during the years of growth, by infectious diseases (osteomyelitis), degenerative diseases (osteoporosis, osteoarthritis), tumors, and a rare form of primary cancer (sarcoma). The most common bone injury is a fracture, and bones may also bleed internally after sustaining a severe bruise.

boric acid An antiseptic in the form of a powder dissolved in water and once commonly used as an eyewash or for application to minor skin irritations. Since it is highly poisonous when swallowed, it should be discarded in favor of equally effective and less dangerous substances.

botulism A form of food poisoning caused by bacteria that produce a toxin that attacks the nervous system. The causative bacterium, *Clostridium botulinum,* thrives in low-acid, low-sugar substances where there is no oxygen. It is typically found in improperly preserved foods, such as canned vegetables, meat, or smoked fish, and the contaminated food rarely smells, tastes, or looks spoiled. Faulty procedures in home canning are responsible for a significant number of cases, as many as half of which are fatal. Diagnosis is simplified by the fact that several people, including household pets, are likely to be affected at the same time.

Nausea and vomiting occur generally in less than 24 hours and may or may not precede the central nervous system symptoms which are caused by the toxin and whose onset usually is from 12 to 36 hours after eating. These symptoms are double vision, puffy or drooping eyelids, and paralysis that impedes swallowing and breathing. The victim must be hospitalized at once for treatment to nullify the toxin and to prevent respiratory failure. Anyone who has eaten the spoiled food must be treated without delay with botulinus antitoxin.

With more and more families growing and preserving their own vegetables, the U.S. Department of Agriculture has issued warnings about the dangers of careless food processing. The department issues bulletins on home canning that are often available in libraries and can be ordered by mail.

brain The central organ of the nervous system, interpreting all sense impressions, controlling the activities of over 600 of the body's voluntary muscles, regulating the autonomic nervous system, and through its capacity for storing and recalling the messages received by its billions of cells, functioning as the memory bank that we call the mind.

The human brain is made of soft, convoluted, pinkish-gray tissue that weighs about 3 pounds and fits within the confines of the skull. Enveloping the brain and separating it from its bony encasement are three tough membranes, collectively called the meninges, which also sheathe the spinal cord. Between two of these membranous layers is the cerebrospinal fluid which may be tapped for accurate diagnosis of such diseases as cerebrospinal meningitis. The portion of the brain that has come to be synonymous with the mind is the cerebrum whose outer layer, the cerebral cortex, is fissured, furrowed, and wrinkled into "gray matter." The deepest fissure divides this part of the brain into two distinct halves: the nerves in the right hemisphere control the left side of the body and vice versa. Emerging from the cerebrum at the middle of the skull and extending down the back of the neck into the spinal cord is the brain stem; on either side of the brain stem are the two halves of the cerebellum. The cerebellum is the portion of the brain whose essential function is the coordination of muscular activities.

Because the activities of the brain are manifested by the transmission of electrical impulses, normal and abnormal brain wave patterns can be charted by an instrument called an encephalograph. This enables neurologists to diagnose such disorders as epilepsy and tumors and to explore the various stages of sleep by the different brain wave patterns they produce. The brain responds to electrical stimulation from the outside, thus revealing the particular function of different areas.

The brain also functions as a gland, manufacturing substances similar in chemical composition to morphine which have the same effect on the body as synthetic painkillers. These hormonelike substances are called endorphins and enkephalins. The amounts in which they are produced and released are presumed to define the body's sensations of pain and pleasure as well as to account for the symptoms of some forms of mental illness.

Epilepsy is the most common disease that originates in disordered electrical impulses of the brain without affecting the function of the mind. Parkinsonism is a disease originating in an abnormality of brain function in which, for the most part, the mind remains unaffected also. However, in the degenerative hardening of the arteries of the brain or in cerebrovascular stroke, both brain physiology and mind physiology are intimately involved. Brain/mind function may also be irreversibly damaged by the late stages of alcoholism, by tertiary syphilis, or by a hemorrhage within the skull. Many brain tumors which were previously untreatable or inoperable can now be reduced by radiation or completely removed due to advances in the techniques of hypothermia and microsurgery. Legal death is now often defined not by the cessation of the heartbeat, but by the death of the brain resulting from oxygen deprivation.

breast In the human female, the milk-producing glands and surrounding duct, fat, and connective tissue.

breech delivery Childbirth in which the baby emerges buttocks or feet first instead of head first.

Bright's disease An obsolescent term for nephrosis, or the nephrotic syndrome. *See* KIDNEYS AND KIDNEY DISORDERS, GLOMERULONEPHRITIS.

bromides Compounds of bromine which until recently were used as anticonvulsants in the treatment of epilepsy, as sedatives to reduce tension, and as headache remedy. Bromides have largely been replaced by medicines that are equally effective and less likely to cause unpleasant side effects in the form of rashes and boils. Another reason for eliminating bromides is that use over a long period has a cumulative toxic effect. Bromine poisoning is a condition characterized by mental confusion, listlessness, and, in serious cases, hallucinations.

bronchitis Inflammation of the lining of the bronchial tubes, the air passages that connect the windpipe and the lungs. In its acute form the inflammation may be an extension of an upper respiratory viral infection or may be caused by a bacterial infection following an upper respiratory illness. Such an attack is accompanied by fever and coughing up of the excess mucus secreted by the inflamed membranes. Bed rest and an expectorant medicine that loosens the sputum rather than one that suppresses the cough are the standard treatment. Antibiotics are used if the infection is diagnosed as bacterial. Chronic bronchitis is a much more serious matter, since the recurrent or persistent coughing and spitting up can lead to irreversible lung injury and an increased vulnerability to emphysema and heart disease. The American Lung Association estimates that of the approximately 6½ million Americans who suffer from this debilitating disease, the great majority are smokers. The typical sufferer is a middle-aged male (men are three times as likely as women to have the disease), who lives in a city where respiratory problems are exacerbated by pollutants in the air. The victim coughs and spits up yellow mucus, especially in the morning and evening, and eventually the condition becomes irreversible. Too many patients take early symptoms for granted and wait until the disease approaches a disabling stage before seeing a doctor. The first and indispensable aspect of treatment is to stop smoking. In some cases rehabilitation may involve a change of job. In others the symptoms may gradually disappear after strict adherence to a wholesome regimen: proper diet, mild exercise, rest and relaxation, and avoidance of lung irritants.

bruise An injury in which small subcutaneous blood vessels are damaged, but the skin surface remains intact; also called a *contusion*. When the skin is broken, the injury is called an abrasion or a *laceration*. In a bruise the escape of blood into the surrounding tissues causes pain and swelling as well as the characteristic discoloration of the skin. The effects of a bruise may not be visible when a blow is sustained by a muscle, a bone or an ear. Healing is usually hastened and pain reduced by the use of cold compresses just after the injury to slow down the bleeding. An injured arm or leg will cause less discomfort and mend more quickly if it is elevated. The application of heat to the bruised area the following day is likely to hasten the reabsorption of the blood. If symptoms increase rather than abate, a doctor should be consulted, especially where deeper internal bruises are suspected.

Some women bruise more easily than others; some parts of the body look worse than they feel when bruised, for example, a black eye or a puffy lip. Since constant bruising and slow healing may be an indication of an arterial disorder, a disturbance in the blood-clotting mechanism, or a vitamin deficiency, the condition should be discussed with a doctor.

bunion A deformity of the foot that occurs when the big toe deviates from its natural position because of inflammation at the joint connecting the toe to the foot. Continuing pressure results in the hard swelling at the base of the toe and the development of the bunion. Discomfort is best relieved by correcting the footwear that causes the problem. In mild cases, with shoes that fit properly, the condition may be eliminated without further treatment. When the pain is severe enough to interfere with normal functioning even when wearing shoes with an orthopedic correction, surgery may be the only practical solution.

burns Injuries resulting from contact with dry heat (fire), moist heat (scalding by steam or liquid), electricity, chemicals, or the ultraviolet rays of the sun or a sunlamp. Whatever the cause, the injury is classified according to the extent of tissue damage. A first-degree burn is one in which the skin turns visibly red; a second-degree burn causes the skin to blister; a third-degree burn damages the deeper skin layers and may destroy the growth cells in the subcutaneous tissues. Even a first-degree burn is potentially dangerous if a large area of the body has been affected, especially if the victim is very young or very old. Until professional help is available a person who has sustained a serious burn should lie down and liquids should be administered, but only if they can be consciously swallowed. Ice cold water can be gently applied to the burned area. *Do not* give any alcoholic beverage. *Do not* disturb blisters. *Do not* attempt to remove clothing adhering to burnt skin. *Do not* apply oily salves or ointments or antiseptic sprays except in cases of superficial burns involving a small area.

bursitis Inflammation of a bursa, one of the small fluid-filled sacs located at various joints throughout the body for the purpose of minimizing friction. Bursitis most commonly occurs at the joints receiving the most wear and tear: at the hip, shoulder, knee, and elbow. "Housemaid's knee" and "tennis elbow" are the result of bursa inflammation. A bunion is the result of inflammation of the bursa that lubricates the joint between the big toe and the foot. An acute, and acutely painful, attack of bursitis may occur after an accident, following unusual exertion connected with moving heavy objects, or as a concomitant of a systemic infection. Although such an attack may be self-healing within a week or ten days, the process can be eased and hastened by taking aspirin or some other analgesic and immobilizing the affected joint in a sling or a flexible bandage. When the sudden onset of bursitis is connected with bacterial infection, antibiotic treatment usually eliminates the discomfort. Chronic bursitis is best treated by reviewing the circumstances that bring it about and modifying them.

caffeine A drug that stimulates the central nervous system, the heart, and the kidneys.

calcium A metallic element essential to life.

Improper metabolism of calcium during the growing years may result in osteoporosis, a disorder in which the bones are excessively brittle and weaker than normal. This condition commonly occurs during aging, especially in women, and is caused by the loss of calcium associated with the cessation of estrogen production. A diet deficient in calcium and vitamin D, during pregnancy or at other times, may cause muscle cramps, especially in the legs. If the symptom persists in spite of proper nutrition, it may indicate faulty calcium metabolism, necessitating the injection of the calcium or the vitamin directly into the bloodstream. This particular malfunction may be due to underactivity of the parathyroid glands. Overactivity of the glands may cause excessive amounts of calcium in the bloodstream, which in turn may encourage the formation of kidney stones and increase the likelihood of bone fractures. In either case diagnostic blood tests are a guide to proper treatment.

calculus Technical term for stone formation in the body. Calculi may develop in the gallbladder or in the kidneys. Gallstones are usually composed of cholesterol, minerals, and bile pigments. Stones in the kidneys, which may migrate to the urinary tract, are composed of mineral salts. Cholesterol stones can now be disposed of with medicines; kidney stones still have to be removed surgically.

calendar rhythm method A means of contraception based on the avoidance of sexual intercourse during those days of the month when a woman is most likely to conceive.

callus An area of the skin that has thickened as a protection against repeated friction; also an irregular bump on a bone that has formed when the recalcification process closes a fracture. The calluses that form on the hands as a result of constant friction or repeated pressures can best be prevented by wearing protective gloves. Most of those that form on the soles of the feet or around the outer rim of the heels can be eliminated by wearing proper footwear. Calluses of this type become painful when they are thick enough to transfer pressure exerted on them to a bone. Calluses can be reduced by rubbing them with pumice or an emery board, or they can be carefully shaved after softening them by soaking in warm, soapy water. The shaving should not be attempted by anyone with diabetes or a circulatory disturbance.

A callus on the bone originates when the bone-forming cells multiply in order to repair a break in the tissue. This "knitting" of the bone takes about a month, after which the callus decreases and the bone resumes its normal shape. The bump formed by the bone callus may become permanent if a fracture is improperly set or if the break or splinter of the bone was so minor as to escape attention.

calorie A unit of energy measurement used in both physics and in the study of nutrition. Food is the fuel that provides the body with the energy essential for carrying on the life processes. The potential energy provided by various foods as they are metabolized by the body is measured in calories. In dietetics 1 calorie is equal to the amount of heat (energy) required to raise the temperature of 1 kilogram of water by 1 degree centigrade.

cancer The general term for a disease process in which the cells in a particular part of the body grow and reproduce with abnormal rapidity. This defect in the controls that govern normal cell growth characterizes about 200 different diseases known as cancers, most of which are also called malignancies or malignant tumors. Cancers that are created by disordered epithelial cells and arise on the surface of the lining of a tissue or within a duct are carcinomas. Malignancies that originate in bones and muscles are known as sarcomas. Those that originate in the blood-forming organs are called leukemias. Those that start in the lymphatics are called lymphomas. Malignancies created by the cells that carry the dark pigment melanin are called melanomas.

A cancer is said to be localized when the diseased cells remain clumped together, even if the group of cells grows into a visible mass large enough to invade underlying or surrounding tissue. When some of the diseased cells break away and make their way into the bloodstream or the lymphatics, eventually reaching other parts of the body, the cancer is said to have metastasized. *See also* CARCINOMA, SARCOMA, LEUKEMIA, METASTASIS.

canker sore An ulceration of the mucous membrane at the corner of the mouth or inside the lips or cheeks. The cause of canker sores is uncertain, but it may be virus infection, stress, sensitivity to particular foods, or mechanical irritation by a rough-edged tooth or filling or ill-fitting dentures. Most canker sores are occasional and self-healing. Recurrent canker sores of unknown origin should be discussed with a physician.

car sickness *See* MOTION SICKNESS

carbohydrates Any of a number

of chemical substances, including starches, sugars, cellulose, and gums, containing only carbon, hydrogen, and oxygen in varying amounts with the ratio of hydrogen to oxygen usually being two to one as in water. Carbohydrates are present in many foods, primarily in grains and potatoes as starch and in fruits and vegetables as sugar. They are an indispensable source of animal (human) energy. Dietary starch and polysaccharide (complex) sugars–maltose, sucrose, and lactose–are converted into glucose in the digestive tract and are absorbed in that form into the bloodstream. Monosaccharide (simple) sugars–glucose, fructose, and galactose–are absorbed into the blood unchanged. Some of these absorbed monosaccharides are used immediately to provide energy. The rest are converted into glycogen by the liver and stored primarily in the liver and muscles for later energy or are converted into fat. Many factors, including diseases, influence the rate and amount that is absorbed. The most common disease which interferes with normal carbohydrate metabolism is diabetes mellitus. *See* DIABETES, GLUCOSE, SUGAR.

carcinogen Any agent (tobacco smoke, X-rays, asbestos fibers, DES) capable of causing changes in cell structure (mutagenesis) and therefore a potential cause of cancer.

carcinoma One of the two main groups of cancers; the other is sarcoma. A carcinoma originates in epithelial cells located in glandular structures, mucous membranes, and skin. Practically all malignancies of the skin, tongue, stomach, uterus, and breast come under this heading.

cardiologist *See* DOCTORS

cardiopulmonary resuscitation (CPR) An emergency lifesaving technique in which oxygenated blood is sent to the brain and other tissues of the victim of cardiac arrest by the simultaneous administration of artificial respiration and external manipulation of the heart. CPR must be initiated at once following a heart attack, electric shock, or any other circumstance in which the lack of circulation has begun to deprive the brain of oxygen. Because of its proven effectiveness when administered by a properly trained individual, the Red Cross and the American Heart Association are encouraging ordinary citizens, including teenagers, to take the six- to twelve-hour CPR courses being offered under their auspices. Authorities in first aid techniques stress the fact that anyone who weighs 90 pounds or more can accomplish a rescue once the skills have been mastered.

carotene A plant pigment especially plentiful in carrots and also found in yellow, orange, and red fruits and vegetables in smaller amounts. Carotene is essential in the diet since it is converted into vitamin A in the body. It is also one of the weaker pigments in human skin. Its yellowish tone is generally masked by the melanin pigment in dark-complexioned women, but a fair complexion will take on an orange hue if the diet contains an excessive amount of carrots.

cartilage The tough, whitish elastic tissue which, together with bone, forms the skeleton. There are three different types of cartilage. Hyaline cartilage forms the extremely strong slippery surface of the ends of the bones at the joints, acting as a shock absorber. It is also the material of which the nose and the rings of the trachea are made. Fibrocartilage is densely packed with fibers and forms the disks between the spinal vertebrae. Elastic cartilage is the most flexible, forming the external ear and the larynx. The stiffness in the joints that characterizes osteoarthritis is associated with a deterioration of cartilage. A knee injury resulting in severe damage to the two sections of cartilage at the edges of the joint may cause the knee to lock in one position. This condition, sometimes referred to as a trick knee, may require surgical repair or removal of the torn cartilage.

cataract Opacity or cloudiness that develops in the crystalline lens of the eye. When the lens becomes so opaque that light can no longer reach the retina, loss of vision results. Fortunately, restoration of eyesight is accomplished safely and successfully in 95 percent of the hundreds of thousands of cataract operations performed every year in the United States. Although a few types of cataracts are congenital or are caused by injury or infection, the largest number by far are senile or degenerative cataracts, those that develop after the age of 60. They are one of the leading causes of blindness among the aged.

In many instances the cloudiness develops so slowly that no significant change in vision is detectable. Annual visits to an ophthalmologist for a glaucoma check after the age of 40 are the best way to find out about incipient cataracts and to plan ahead for their removal. However, for most people the first awareness of a cataract comes with blurred or dimmed vision, double images, and a scattering of light beams when looking directly at a street lamp or at the headlights of an approaching car. As soon as any of these symptoms occur, an ophthalmologist should be consulted. The only effective treatment for the condition is surgery. Since there is as yet no magical method for "dissolving" cataracts with "special medicines," all such claims should be regarded as quackery and, if possible, reported to the proper authorities for investigation.

A cataract operation consists of the removal of the degenerated lens and its replacement with an artificial lens in the form of eyeglasses, contact lens, or more recently, for certain patients, an intraocular lens. Whether the surgery is the conventional method that removes the cataract by lifting it out in one piece or the newer method that pulverizes the lens with an ultrasonic probe, recovery is considerably faster today than in the past. Even in cases where there is some difficulty in adjusting to the artificial lens, it rarely takes more than a few months for the transition to occur.

Since people who develop a cataract in one eye are likely to have the same problem with the other eye, it is considered advisable to schedule early treatment of the damaged eye without waiting for the cataract to develop fully, so that the unaffected eye can provide unimpaired vision following the operation.

cathartic Any medicine in liquid, tablet, or suppository form that stimulates intestinal activity for the purpose of bowel evacuation. Cathartics, also known as physics and purgatives, are stronger than laxatives and should never be used to treat constipation without a doctor's recommendation. They should be avoided when there is the slightest suspicion of appendicitis. A cathartic should not be used as a countermeasure against poisoning without consulting a doctor.

catheterization The procedure in which a tube is inserted through a passage in the body for the purpose of withdrawing or introducing fluids or other materials. Catheters have been used for centuries, but since the introduction of plastics they are less costly to manufacture and give minimal discomfort to the patient. In the more common applications, a catheter is introduced into the urethra for draining urine from the bladder; an intravenous catheter is used for "tube-feeding" following surgery; a nasogastric tube is used for withdrawing samples of material from the stomach as a diagnostic clue. Catheterization is essential in the administration of oxygen through the nose, and it can effectively remove stones lodged in the ureter, the passageway connecting the kidney and the bladder. Cardiac catheterization is routinely used to detect and measure critical abnormalities caused by circulatory disorders.

cauterization The burning away of infected, unwanted, or dead tissue by the application of caustic chemicals or electrically heated instruments. Cryosurgery used in the treatment of certain types of tumors is a form of cauterization; the removal of surface moles with an electrical needle is another. Cauterization of cervical tissue to prevent the spread of erosion is a common gynecological practice.

cavities *See* DENTAL CARIES.

cell The structural unit of which all body tissues are formed. The human body is composed of billions of cells differing in size and structure depending on their function. In spite of these differences every cell includes the same basic components, chiefly, an outer limiting membrane which regulates the transport of chemical substances into and out of the cell; a mass of cytoplasm containing substances involved in metabolism and genetic transmission; a nucleus whose membrane contains the concentration of RNA and which encloses the DNA that determines the hereditary transmission of genetic characteristics. The study of normal cell structure and behavior is basic to cancer research, since all cancers are characterized by aberrational cell growth and reproduction.

cerebrovascular accident *See* STROKE.

cervix The neck or narrow portion of any organ, but generally used to refer to the hollow end of the uterus that forms the passageway into the vaginal canal. The cervix is approximately 2 inches in length. Under normal circumstances it has the diameter of a quarter with an opening (*os*) which has the diameter of a drinking straw. At the time of delivery the cervix dilates to a diameter usually given as 10 centimeters or five fingers. Dilatation to this size marks the end of the first stage of labor; the baby is ready to come down the birth canal, and the cervical opening has become large enough to permit passage of the infant's head.

Women who use a diaphragm should be aware of the position of the opening of the cervix, since the diaphragm is inserted across this opening as a barrier against the passage of sperm toward the ovum.

During pregnancy natural processes deposit a thick layer of mucus across the cervical entrance, sealing off the womb against invasion by infectious organisms.

Infections of the cervix—cervicitis—are quite common at other times. Among the chief causes are viruses, fungi, and bacteria, especially gonococci. In some women cervical tissue may be chronically inflamed by the use of birth control pills. The first symptom of cervicitis is likely to be a vaginal discharge that becomes more abundant immediately following menstruation. Other signs may be bleeding, pain during intercourse, a burning sensation during urination, or lower back pain. Such symptoms should be brought to the attention of a gynecologist. Examination of the cervix by insertion of a speculum usually indicates the source of the trouble. A culture of the discharge may be necessary to identify the infectious agent, especially if the infection does not respond to antibiotic medicines or fungicides. Where tissue erosion has occurred, cauterization by electricity, chemical application, or freezing may be necessary.

Another cause of bleeding, especially in middle-aged women with a history of cervical infections, is the presence of fleshy growths called polyps. Although these growths are easily removed and generally benign, a tissue biopsy is performed to rule out the possibility of cancer. The best safeguard against cervical cancer, one of the leading causes of cancer deaths in women over 40, is an annual pap test. This simple and painless procedure is based on the microscopic examination of a cervical smear to identify abnormalities before they produce any symptoms.

cesarean section A surgical procedure in which an incision is made into the uterus through the front of the abdominal wall to facilitate the delivery of the baby. At a time when many women feel that conscious participation in the birth experience is an inalienable right and when many fathers want to share as much of the experience as the hospital will allow, cesarean deliveries sometimes cause feelings of deprivation, depression, and guilt. A Massachusetts-based organization has been formed with chapters across the country to provide literature, films, and, above all, supportive reassurance to those women who are concerned about having a cesarean section or who want more information about it. The organization is called C/SEC (Cesarean/Support, Education, Concern) and is located at 66 Christopher Road, Waltham, MA 02154. It offers information on local chapters and will mail literature on receipt of a request which includes a stamped self-addressed envelope.

chafing Inflammation of the skin caused by the friction of one body surface against the other or of clothing against a body surface. Chafing is especially common in hot weather when sweating increases irritation, particularly in the fleshier parts of the body.

The chafed area is likely to itch and burn, and without treatment the inflamed skin may crack or blister, increasing the possibility of bacterial or fungoid infection. Diabetics and obese women are particularly vulnerable to chafing. The irritation can be relieved by medicated powders to promote dryness, topical ointments to reduce itching, or cold compresses to alleviate the inflammation. In acute cases the doctor may prescribe a cortisone salve and a sterile dressing. The most effective way to prevent chafing is to keep the skin clean and dry, especially in hot weather, and to wear clothing that is loose and comfortable.

chancre An ulcerated sore in the area of bacterial invasion that is the first sign of the primary stage of syphilis.

chapping Irritation and cracking of the skin, usually due to dryness resulting from overexposure to cold or wind. In cold weather the lubricating glands of the skin are less active, and as the outer layer of the skin loses its oily secretion, it becomes dry and vulnerable to cold and to the irritating effects of strong soaps and detergents. Chapping can be prevented or reduced by the use of protective creams, lotions, and bath oils. Once the irritation has occurred, the chapped areas of the skin should be cleansed with a mild soap substitute and tepid water and blotted dry with a soft towel. A layer of lotion or cream containing lanolin should be applied before bedtime, and exposure to irritating housecleaning chemicals should be kept to a minimum until the chapped skin has healed.

chemotherapy The treatment of illness by the use of specific chemicals. The term was used originally to describe the use of medications effective against particular organisms with minimal damage to the patient. One of the earliest such treatments was the use of quinine against the malarial parasite. This was followed by Dr. Paul Ehrlich's discovery in 1910 that salvarsan effectively destroyed the spirochete that causes syphilis and by later development of sulfa drugs and antibiotics. More recently, the meaning of the term chemotherapy has been expanded to include the use of the medication to relieve the effects of disease, for example, the application of such drugs as chlorpromazine in controlling some of the symptoms of mental illness.

At present treatment of various cancers by chemotherapy has increased survival rate in a significant number of cases. Especially dramatic results have been achieved by postsurgical multiple-combination chemotherapy in cases of advanced breast and ovarian cancers and by chemotherapy combined with radiation in the treatment of certain types of cancer. Pharmacologists and medical chemists are concerned in their research not only with finding new chemical agents to combat disease, but with minimizing adverse side effects, mainly, destruction of healthy tissue. In order to do so it is necessary to find the right agent and the critical dose that will cure without causing secondary complications.

chest pains Discomfort in any part of the thorax, usually caused by a disorder of one of the organs within the thoracic cavity enclosed by the rib cage, by an injury to a rib, or by a strained muscle. The site of a disorder may be the heart, lungs, large blood vessels, esophagus, or part of the trachea. Any viral or bacterial infection of the respiratory system may be accompanied by pain which may become acute when constant coughing is involved. Various allergies to mold, dust, animal dander, chemical pollutants may be another cause. Pain might be referred to the chest by the nervous system from areas outside the thoracic cavity. For example, certain types of indigestion produce a pain that may be mistaken for a heart attack. In most cases, however, the pain resulting from cardiovascular problems is the feeling of tightness and suffocation characteristic of angina pectoris. Almost all chest pains that originate in respiratory or circulatory disorders are intensified by smoking. Persistent chest pains should always be diagnosed and treated by a doctor.

chilblains Inflammation of the skin, accompanied by burning and itching, usually caused by exposure to cold. Special vulnerability to chilblains may result from poor circulation, inadequate diet, or an allergic response to low temperatures. The affected areas are commonly the face, hands, and feet and less frequently the ears. The areas swell and turn reddish-purple.

The condition is easier to prevent than to treat. Anyone sensitive to the cold should always wear warm clothes, especially woolen or partly woolen socks (never 100 percent synthetic), fleece-lined boots, and woolen gloves. Wet garments should be removed at once on coming indoors and the skin dried gently (never rubbed or massaged) with a soft towel. When chilblains have occurred, no attempts should be made to "stimulate" circulation by applying extreme heat or cold to the affected areas. In most cases a warm dry environment will bring about a return to normal. If the symptoms persist or if blisters form on the skin surface, a doctor should be consulted for further instructions.

chills A sudden onset of shivering or shaking, accompanied by the sensation of cold and by uncontrollable chattering of the teeth; the technical term for the condition is rigor. It should not be confused with feeling "chilly" because of a sudden draft or drop in the temperature. Chills are usually followed by fever as a symptom of infection, most commonly by the bacteria that cause pneumonia, "strep" throat, food poisoning, or kidney infection. They are also associated with various tropical diseases, especially malaria. Since chills and fever are a warning of a disorder that may need prompt treatment, the doctor should be called. Until a regimen is prescribed, the patient should get into bed, remain under the covers, and keep a record of temperature readings.

chiropodist *See* PODIATRIST.

chiropractor A practitioner of a therapeutic system based on the theory that disease is caused by subluxations, that is, partial dislocations, of the vertical bones that cause pinching of the nerves emanating from them. The pinching of the nerves impairs the function of vital organs and is corrected by spinal adjustment. Chiropractors are licensed to practice in all 50 states, but since they are not medical doctors, they are forbidden by law to write prescriptions. Chiropractic fees can be reimbursed through Medicare and in most states through Medicaid and Workmen's Compensation. Although many people claim to have found relief from various symptoms, particularly back pain, through chiropractic treatment, this specialized approach to disease has yet to be scientifically proven right or wrong.

chlorine A chemical element widely used to purify public water supplies and disinfect swimming pools because it is cheap, easily manufactured, and effective against bacteria, viruses, and fungi. An excessively chlorinated swimming pool will cause temporary eye discomfort. Household bleaches containing chlorine should be kept out of the reach of children since they can cause serious damage to the membranes of the mouth and stomach if swallowed.

chloroform An easily inhaled, volatile, colorless liquid introduced as a general anesthetic around 1850 and in widespread use until replaced by equally effective and less damaging substances.

Chloromycetin Brand name of the antibiotic chloramphenicol. *See also* ANTIBIOTICS.

chlorpromazine The first of a new class of drugs now categorized as major tranquilizers. Chlorpromazine (brand name, Thorazine) was discovered in 1949 in connection with antihistamine research and successfully used in 1952 by two French doctors as a means of forestalling the onset of acute psychotic episodes in schizophrenic and manic-depressive patients. It has since been widely used in the treatment of mentally ill patients, not as a cure, but to control their disturbance. This application of chemotherapy has largely replaced electroshock treatments, previously used for the same purpose. Although chlorpromazine was also used at one time as an antidepressant, it has been replaced for this purpose by other more effective drugs.

A patient taking Thorazine on a regular basis must be given periodic tests to ascertain whether the liver is being affected adversely, whether there is any white cell aberration, and whether other negative side effects are evident. None of these effects seems to be irreversible; however, close medical supervision is necessary with the use of this medication.

choking Obstruction of the air passage in the throat by a swallowed object that has gone into the windpipe instead of into the esophagus. When food is being swallowed, an automatic mechanism closes the flap at the top of the trachea (windpipe). It is not unusual, however, for a morsel of food or, in the case of a small child, a foreign object such as a button to "go down the wrong way." This is apt to happen when a sudden intake of breath caused by laughing, talking, or coughing occurs while a person has food in her mouth. The immediate signs of choking are an inability to speak or breathe. In minutes the skin turns bluish, and unless emergency assistance is prompt, the results can be fatal.

If an infant is choking, hold the body upside down by the torso and strike its back lightly several times between the shoulder blades. For an older child or an adult use the Heimlich maneuver, a lifesaving technique illustrated below. *See* HEIMLICH MANEUVER.

cholesterol A crystalline fatty alcohol found in animal fats, blood, bile, and nerve tissue. Cholesterol is synthesized in the liver and is the material from which the body's steroids, including the sex hormones, are manufactured. It is also one of the chief constituents of biliary gallstones which can now be dissolved by a drug that reduces the liver's synthesis and secretion of cholesterol.

It has been demonstrated that very high levels of cholesterol in the blood serum increase the likelihood of atherosclerotic disease and the possibility of heart attack. However, these levels can be determined only on the basis of an individual blood test, and until a doctor recommends that animal fats or eggs be eliminated from the diet, no one need eliminate these foods. Too little fat in the diet can be as harmful as too much. Recent studies indicate that the crucial blood component that acts to prevent the accumulation of cholesterol deposits within the artery walls is a material known as HDL (for high density lipoproteins). HDL, which is plentiful in the blood of some people and scarce in others, seems to have the ability to remove cholesterol from arterial walls and from other tissues where it might accumulate in dangerous amounts and to direct it to the liver for excretion. This interaction has opened up the possibility of raising an individual's HDL level by artificial means, thus counteracting the dangers of cholesterol accumulation.

chorea A disorder of the nervous system characterized by involuntary jerking movements (the term comes from the Greek word meaning "dance" as in choreography); also known as St. Vitus's dance. There are two types of the disease, each named for the doctor who described it. Sydenham's chorea is an acute disease of childhood often associated with rheumatic fever, but usually there is no known explanation. Huntington's chorea is an incurable hereditary disease in which the motor disturbances usually become manifest in middle age and are associated with mental deterioration. When there is a family history of Huntington's chorea, genetic counseling is advisable before considering having children.

chromosomes Stringlike structures within the cell nucleus that contain the genetic information governing each person's inherited characteristics. Normal human body cells contain 46 paired chromosomes composed of DNA (deoxyribonucleic acid). An ovum contains 22 autosome and 1 sex (X) chromosomes. A sperm contains 22 autosome and 1 sex (X or Y) chromosomes so that when they combine during reproduction the offspring cell receives its full complement of 46 "message carriers."

The sex of an offspring is determined by the combination of the sex chromosomes designated as X and Y. If an egg is fertilized by a sperm carrying the X chromosome, the offspring will have two X chromosomes and will therefore be female (XX). If an egg is fertilized by a Y-bearing sperm, the offspring will have one of each and will be male (XY).

Chromosomal abnormalities vary in significance, the more serious ones being responsible for birth defects, mental retardation, and spontaneous abortion.

The possibility of abnormalities severe enough to warrant abortion can be determined through prenatal genetic counseling. Research in recent years indicates that environmental and occupational exposure to various chemicals can cause irreversible damage to chromosomes, leading to genetic mutations in the offspring.

chronic symptom Symptom of a disorder that lasts over a long period of time, sometimes for the remainder of the patient's life, such as the fatigue associated with most cancers or the joint pains characteristic of rheumatoid arthritis.

circulatory system The heart and network of blood vessels throughout the body.

cirrhosis Degenerative disease of an organ, in rare cases the heart or kidney, but generally the liver, in which the development of fibrous tissue with consequent hardening and scarring causes the loss of normal function. Cirrhosis of the liver is most frequently associated with chronic alcoholism. However, the condition may also occur after infectious hepatitis or, more rarely, as a consequence of toxic hepatitis in which liver cells are damaged because of sensitivity to such drugs as chlorpromazine (Thorazine) or chloramphenicol (Chloromycetin).

Cirrhosis is insidious because it may be asymptomatic until it has resulted in irreversible damage. When symptoms are manifest, they include abdominal swelling with fluid, soreness under the rib cage, swollen ankles, weight loss, and general fatigue. In advanced cases the signs are jaundice evident in the yellowing of the skin and the eyes and possible vomiting of blood leading to collapse. When alcoholic cirrhosis is treated promptly at an early stage, the liver may repair and rehabilitate itself. Total abstention from alcohol and a diet rich in proteins and supplementary vitamins are essential to recovery.

claustrophobia An irrational, persistent, and often insurmountable fear of enclosed places such as elevators, windowless rooms, and the like.

climacteric The time in a woman's life when her childbearing capabilities come to an end; the menopause. The so-called male climacteric is characterized by the psychological stresses that accompany aging rather than the loss of reproductive potential.

clinics Medical establishments that offer treatment on an outpatient basis. A clinic may be publicly supported or privately owned; it may be free-standing or part of a hospital's many services. Special clinics exist for special functions, for example, prenatal and baby care, eye and ear, abortion, psychiatric. Medicaid clinics exist to provide treatment for the indigent.

clitoris The female genital organ located at the upper end of the vulva. The clitoris is the counterpart of the male penis and although it may vary in size and placement, it is a direct source of orgasm for most women. During sexual intercourse it becomes firm and engorged with blood. Penile, oral, manual, or other manipulation of the clitoris may be essential to the achievement of orgasm.

coagulation *See* BLOOD CLOTTING.

cobalt A metallic element that produces the radioactive isotope cobalt 60 used with beneficial effect in some types of cancer radiation therapy. It is also one of the elements essential in infinitesimal amounts for the healthy functioning of the body's chemistry, but is toxic in larger amounts.

cocaine A drug with stimulating properties derived from an alkaloid found in the coca tree's leaves.

codeine A mild narcotic drug derived from opium. Codeine is prescribed in tablet form as a painkiller, especially by dentists after a tooth extraction or periodontal surgery. A federal law requires that pharmacists keep records of their sales of codeine-containing medicines to prevent their being bought in large quantities for narcotic purposes. Some women find codeine the most effective analgesic for premenstrual pain; others find that it produces side effects of nausea and constipation.

coffee *See* CAFFEINE.

coitus interruptus The withdrawal of the penis before ejaculation as a means of preventing pregnancy. As a contraceptive method its failure rate is high.

cold sores *See* HERPES SIMPLEX.

colitis Inflammation of the colon (large intestine). The type most frequently encountered is mucous colitis, also known as spastic colon. Mucous colitis produces lower bowel spasms with or without cramps, accompanied by an alteration of diarrhea and constipation. Since in such cases the bowel itself has no organic impairments, the disorder is called functional colitis. A far more serious condition is ulcerative colitis, in which there is tissue impairment. A mucus and blood mixture is often found in the feces of persons with ulcerative colitis. The onset of this form of the disease typically occurs among young adults of both sexes, eventually producing disabling attacks of diarrhea. Cancer of the colon or rectum develops in up to 10 percent of those who have had colitis for ten years or more.

The cause of colitis in any of its manifestations is presumed to be emotional stress produced by anxiety. Unfortunately, it is an illness in which cause and effect produce a vicious circle, making it difficult to treat medically. In practically all cases of ulcerative colitis psychotherapy in one form or another is indispensable to the abatement of the more disturbing symptoms. Since patterns of remission and relapse are usual, the disease must be treated with patience and care, including supervision of diet, bed rest, and elimination of as many tension-producing factors as possible. Where complications of weight loss, anemia, or infections develop, medicines with the least number of adverse side effects must be administered. In extreme cases removal of the diseased portion of the bowel is essential as a lifesaving measure.

colon *See* INTESTINES.

colostomy A surgical procedure by which an artificial anal opening is created in the abdominal wall. A colostomy may be performed as a temporary measure after bowel surgery or it may have to be a permanent procedure. Patients who have undergone a colostomy usually must regulate their diets to control the character of their stool.

colostrum The thin, pale yellow substance exuded by the breasts late in pregnancy and immediately following delivery. Colostrum contains proteins, minerals, and antibodies and provides adequate nourishment for the newborn baby before breast milk becomes available, usually about the third day after birth. Mothers who do not wish to breast-feed their babies should discuss with their doctor the importance of providing them with colostrum for the two days following delivery.

colposcopy A diagnostic procedure in which a magnifying device (colposcope) is used to examine the cervix and vagina. Colposcopy requires no anesthesia and can be done in a doctor's office.

coma Deep unconsciousness resulting from, among other circumstances, injury to the brain, stroke, poisoning by barbiturates or alcohol, overdose or underdose of insulin, coronary thrombosis, or shock. Expert care should be obtained without delay, and if the victim is suffering cardiac arrest, cardiopulmonary resuscitation should be initiated.

common cold The designation for any of a large number of brief and relatively mild virus infections of the upper respiratory tract which may produce uncomfortable symptoms in the nose (rhinitis), throat (pharyngitis), or voice box (laryngitis). Since allergies to grasses and pollens produce certain overlapping symptoms, they are often mistakenly labeled "summer colds." The development of a cold vaccine has so far proved impractical because the symptoms are caused by more than 150 different viruses.

Scientific investigations have exploded many myths about colds: the infection is less contagious than once thought, taking a laxative does not dispose of cold germs, sweating does not drive the germs out of the pores of the skin, staying in bed is not a cure. Most important: an ordinary cold should *not* be treated with antibiotics. These medicines are ineffective against viruses and may cause undesired side effects such as changes in normal bacteria.

There are no sure ways of preventing or curing a cold. There are, however, practical measures that can minimize the discomforts and reduce the likelihood of secondary infection. A cold accompanied by a cough, a fever of over 100°, or a painful sore throat can be more than a common cold and should be diagnosed by a doctor. The ordinary upper respiratory viral infection may produce any or all of the following symptoms in combination: stuffed or running nose, mildly scratchy throat, teary eyes, heavy breathing, fits of sneezing, some impairment of the sense of taste and smell, mild headache, and a general feeling of lassitude. Many healthy adults do not bother to treat these symptoms and go about their business until the cold goes away, usually within three or four days. Others buy over-the-counter medicines containing antihistamines, often exchanging drowsiness for unclogged nostrils and dry eyes. The occasional use of nasal decongestants may be harmless and somewhat helpful, but overuse can have a destructive effect on delicate mucous membranes.

Whether vitamin C taken daily is effective to prevent colds is an unsettled issue. The dose usually taken for this purpose is 1 to 4 grams per day for several days. It appears that the action of vitamin C is similar to that of interferon, a substance produced in the body which suppresses virus growth. It is this protein substance that scientists hope to synthesize eventually as the most generalized and effective method of fighting the many viruses that produce common cold symptoms.

compulsion The expression of inner emotional stress through the involuntary and repetitious performance of a particular action. Compulsive behavior generally provides a certain relief from the anxiety generated by unconscious, and therefore unexpressed, feelings of rage against an individual or repressed sexuality.

conception The fertilization of the ovum by the sperm.

condom A protective sheath, generally made of thin rubber, that is used to cover the penis during sexual intercourse as a way of preventing sperm from entering the vagina and also as protection against venereal disease.

conjunctivitis Inflammation of the conjunctiva, the thin membrane that lines the eyelid and covers the front of the eye. The disorder is commonly called pink eye. Conjunctivitis may be caused by bacteria or a virus or it may be an allergic response to a new brand of eye makeup, a reaction to a chemical pollutant in the air or water, or the result of irritation from an ingrown eyelash in the lower lid. An inflammation caused by bacteria or a virus is highly contagious, and precautions should be taken to prevent its spread to others and to minimize self-reinfection. For example, the patient should use disposable paper towels to dry the face after washing. When an infectious organism is the cause, an ophthalmic antibiotic ointment is usually the effective treatment. In some cases the application of hot wet compresses several times a day will eliminate the inflammation. If it persists or shows no sign of improvement within a few days, the condition should be treated by a doctor.

consciousness-raising groups Informally organized sessions at which discussion is directed toward disclosing and confronting feelings and problems previously buried or suppressed. In the exchange of ideas and airing of emotions the participants often achieve a sense of shared purpose as well as a clearer sense of who they are, what they want, and how best to achieve it.

consent laws State legislation that covers the following circumstances. (1) *The age of consent:* the age of a woman before which sexual intercourse with her is considered statutory rape whether or not she has given her consent to the act. (2) *Consent to an abortion:* some states require the written consent of a parent before a legal abortion can be performed on an unwed minor. Other laws require the consent of the husband. These are being struck down by various courts. (3) *Hospital consent forms:* a patient undergoing surgery or some other potentially hazardous procedure must sign a statement consenting to the operation. In the case of a child (defined differently in different states) or an incapacitated adult the form must be signed by a responsible member of the family. In an emergency responsibility is assumed by the hospital staff after consultation.

constipation A condition in which the fecal matter contained in the bowels is too hard to eliminate easily or in which bowel movements are so infrequent as to cause physical discomfort. The body may take from 24 to 48 hours to transform food into waste matter, and the frequency with which this waste is normally eliminated may vary from once a day to once a week, depending among other things on age, diet, amount of exercise, emotional health, and general personality traits.

The most common causes of chronic constipation unaccompanied by any organic disorder are faulty diet, insufficient exercise, emotional tension caused by the repression of anger and resentment, and chronic dependence on laxatives. Attention to these factors will generally prevent its occurrence. When constipation does occur, a cleansing enema is usually more effective than a dose of a laxative. However, the regular use of enemas or laxatives is likely to be self-defeating since it causes the bowel to depend on artificial stimulation rather than on natural signals.

The feelings of bloat, nausea, and general malaise that usually accompany constipation have nothing to do with the body's absorption of "poisons"; they are caused by messages from the nervous system reacting to a distended rectum. When these symptoms persist after elimination or when constipation itself persists in spite of all common sense treatments, the possibility of an organic disease or obstruction should be investigated by a doctor.

contact dermatitis Any skin disorder produced by substances that come in contact with the skin and cause redness, swelling, itching, hives, or other symptoms of allergic response. When the offending substance touches the skin, the blood vessels dilate, becoming more and more porous and permitting cellular fluid to seep under the skin surface. This accumulation of fluid forms blisters which eventually break. As the area dries out, crusts are formed which thicken and then flake off. Less extreme cases involve no more than a rash that itches and burns.

The first step in treatment is to eliminate the substance causing the response. Once the irritant has been removed, the skin heals eventually. In severe cases, especially where the skin is broken and vulnerable to infection, the affected surface should be covered with an antibiotic salve or ointment containing corticosteroids. If the symptoms persist even with this treatment, the doctor may prescribe cortisone to be taken orally.

contact lenses Corrective lenses placed directly on the eyeball. There are two types of contact lenses–hard and soft. Both are designed in such a way that the natural flow of tears to the surface of the cornea is unimpeded. Of the two types, hard lenses correct a larger number of sight disorders, are simpler to care for, and cost less; soft lenses are more comfortable and the wearer usually adapts to them more quickly. Because soft lenses follow the natural curve of the eye, there is less chance that foreign bodies will reach the cornea than when the cornea is covered by a hard lens. The disadvantages of soft lenses, in addition to the greater expense, are their fragility and the complicated disinfecting routine they require. An ophthalmologist or an optometrist fits contact lenses, explains exactly how they should be used, and informs the wearer as to what services and follow-up procedures are covered by the professional fee. The occasional need for small adjustments requires frequent checkups in order to safeguard the health of the eye.

contraception The prevention of conception following coitus; birth control.

contraceptives Chemical or mechanical means to prevent conception following coitus. Chemical methods are hormonal (oral contraceptive) or spermicidal (foam, cream, jelly, vaginal suppository, and the medicated intrauterine device). Mechanical methods are the condom, diaphragm, and nonmedicated intrauterine device.

contraction The action of the muscular walls of the uterus by which the infant is propelled from the uterus through the birth canal.

convalescence The transitional period between an operation, injury, or illness and the reestablishment of normal health, strength, and emotional equilibrium. Many convalescents try to push themselves beyond their actual stage of endurance. They may do so to prove to others that they are well or because they feel guilty about not being able to accomplish daily activities for which they are normally responsible. It is most important not to try to do too much as it only postpones or jeopardizes full recovery. The doctor is the one who should decide when a normal routine can be resumed.

A prolonged convalescence following a critical illness, major surgery, or an accident often requires special attention and long periods of bed rest. A visiting nurse or a nurse's aide may be needed to provide sufficient home care, but should the convalescent require constant supervision, an extended care facility connected with the hospital may be a more practical solution. A woman in charge of the convalescence of another family member should work out ways of sharing responsibilities, explaining to each person exactly what is expected.

convulsions Violent and abnormal muscular contractions or spasms that seize the body suddenly and spontaneously, usually ending with unconsciousness. Convulsions are almost always a symptom of a serious disorder and they are the classic manifestation of the grand mal seizures of epilepsy. They are not uncommon among children during infections of the nervous system or during generalized infections that cause a very high fever. Convulsions in late pregnancy are a sign of the toxemia known as eclampsia and usually are preceded by other warning signs. Convulsions are one of the critical consequences of unsupervised and sudden withdrawal from barbiturates following heavy and habitual use. They may also occur in adulthood from a tumor or from diseases that attack the brain and central nervous system, especially encephalitis and meningitis.

At first sign of seizure the mouth should be opened (forced open if necessary) and something (a knotted handkerchief, a wadded piece of sheet, or a smooth stick) put between the upper and lower teeth to keep the mouth open so that an airway can be maintained and to keep the patient from biting his tongue. If the tongue is swallowed, keep the mouth wide open and free the tongue with a finger. Then seek medical attention.

cornea The transparent tissue that forms the outer layer of the eyeball, covering the iris and the lens through which vision is achieved. It is a continuation of the tough sclera (the "white" of the eye). The most serious disease that affects the cornea is herpes simplex keratitis; it causes more loss of vision in the Western world than any other corneal infection. When this virus attacks the tissues, painful ulcers form and to date there is no successful cure for the condition. The infection may recur frequently causing progressive impairment each time.

Corneal dystrophy is an inherited disease in which there is a progressive loss of vision resulting from an increasing cloudiness of the tissue. Corneal dystrophy as well as vision impairment caused by damage to the cornea can be corrected by a corneal transplant.

corneal transplant The removal of an impaired cornea and its replacement with a clear, healthy one. This operation, which originated in the 1920s, is the most successful of all tissue transplants. Ideally, a cornea should be removed within 6 hours of death and transplanted within 24 hours. The Eye Bank for Sight Restoration, of which there are chapters throughout the world, receives donor eyes through bequests and can preserve them for 2 to 3 days. Most large cities have ophthalmological specialists who can perform corneal transplants. Some operations are scheduled well in advance; others are performed under emergency conditions. The patient is given either local or general anesthesia before the transplant and full vision is usually restored no more than three days after surgery.

corns An area of thickened skin (callus) that occurs on or between the toes. There are two types of corns: hard corns which are usually located on the small toe or on the upper ridge of one of the other toes; soft and white corns which are likely to develop between the fourth and fifth toe. The hard core of both types of callus points inward and when pressed against the surrounding tissue causes pain. Corns are the result of wearing shoes that are too tight, and unless proper footwear is worn they will recur.

Treating corns at home with razor blades or with strongly medicated "removers" can injure surrounding tissues, resulting in additional discomfort and sometimes in serious infection. The sensible course is a visit to a podiatrist.

coronary artery disease *See* HEART ATTACK.

corpus luteum The ovarian follicle after it releases its ovum. The corpus luteum produces the hormone progesterone which prepares the lining of the uterus for possible implantation of a fertilized ovum and is essential to the maintenance of pregnancy. If conception occurs, the corpus luteum continues to produce progesterone for a short time until the placenta takes over this function. If conception does not occur, the progesterone level drops, the corpus luteum degenerates, and menstruation starts.

corticosteroids A group of hormones produced from cholesterol by the adrenal cortex; now also synthesized in the laboratory. The original biochemical designation for these hormones was adrenocorticosteroids. At least 30 of these substances have been identified, of which the best known is cortisone. Among their many functions are regulation of the water and salt balance of body fluids and assistance in protein metabolism, antibody formation, and repair of damaged tissue.

The fact that these steroids suppress inflammation of the joints and reduce the destructive effects of rheumatic fever and kidney inflammations has provided successful treatment for a large number of disorders formerly unresponsive to drug therapy. For people suffering from Addison's disease (nonfunction of the adrenal cortex) they play the same vital role in lifetime replacement therapy as insulin does for some diabetics. Overproduction of cortical hormones causes Cushing's syndrome.

cosmetics Preparations designed to enhance the appearance. Cosmetic preparations must meet the standards of the Food and Drug Administration for health protection. On occasion there is a justifiable concern over an ingredient in a particular product: a potential cancer-causing red dye found in a lipstick, dangerous amounts of asbestos dust in an expensive dusting powder, a lung-damaging chemical in a spray-on hair lacquer. The purchaser should make a habit of reading the fine print and warnings that appear on all packages and in the enclosed printed material. This is usually the only way to find out whether the manufacturer has been required by the FDA to indicate that some ingredient "may be harmful to health."

Cold creams, cleansing creams, lubricating lotions, and moisturizers should be judged on their merits and individual suitability, not on their cost or expensive packaging. Cosmetics advertised as containing "secret formulas" or special medications should be checked out with a knowledgeable person or doctor to make certain the product is not harmful. Any product which produces an allergic reaction, such as a rash or puffy eyelids, should, of course, not be used. Special hypoallergenic cosmetics and soaps are available for those who require them. Since infections can be spread by powder puffs, lipsticks, or makeup brushes, articles of this type should not be borrowed or lent.

coughing A reflex action for the purpose of clearing the lining of the air passages of an excessive accumulation of mucus or disturbing foreign matter. A cough is achieved by the following mechanism: a deep breath is drawn; the glottis which controls the passage of air through the windpipe is closed; pressure is built up in the chest by the contraction of muscles; the glottis suddenly opens causing an explosive release of air to sweep through the air passages. The air expulsed carries with it foreign irritants such as dust, particles of food, or abnormal secretions that are irritating the larynx, trachea, or bronchial tubes. Coughing may also be a psychological manifestation of boredom or a means of attracting attention.

Medicines that loosen the secretions resulting from an inflammatory condition of the mucous membranes and make it easier to cough them up are called expectorants. The congestion may also be loosened and coughed up after treatment with hot tea, hot lemonade and honey, or steam inhalation. It is advisable to rid the air passages of the accumulated mucus by coughing it up, but if coughing interferes with sleep, the doctor may decide that a cough suppressant is necessary. Suppressant medicines often contain codeine or some other opiate which requires a prescription.

Coughs associated with common colds may last two to three weeks after all other symptoms have disappeared. A cough that lasts longer or causes pain in the chest is the sign of a chronic condition that should be discussed with a doctor. Early diagnosis of the underlying cause of a chronic cough followed by proper treatment and no smoking can help prevent the onset of emphysema, lung cancer, or other respiratory disease.

crabs Parasites, also known as pubic lice, that infest the genital and anal hairs, causing extreme itching and irritation.

cramps *See* ABDOMINAL PAIN.

cryosurgery Operations in which tissues are destroyed by freezing them, usually with supercold liquid nitrogen or carbon dioxide. Cryosurgery is frequently used for the removal of hemorrhoids, warts, and moles and for treatment of cervical erosion. Cryosurgical instruments are also used successfully in certain types of delicate brain surgery.

curettage A procedure in which the walls of a body cavity are scraped with an instrument called a curette in order to remove a tissue sample for examination or to remove unwanted tissue.

Cushing's syndrome A group of symptoms caused by the presence in the body of an excess of corticosteroid hormones. Formerly, Cushing's syndrome was a rare disorder resulting in most cases from overactivity of the adrenal cortex because of a glandular tumor or from hyperfunction of the pituitary gland. It has become more common now, resulting from the side effects of medication containing steroids prescribed as long-term therapy for chronic diseases of the kidneys, the joints, etc.

Early symptoms include weakness, facial puffiness ("moon" face), and fluid retention, followed by general obesity and an interruption of menstruation.

When Cushing's syndrome is attributable to glandular malfunction caused by a tumor, surgery is essential. If total removal of the gland is indicated, replacement therapy of the corticosteroid hormones is necessary for the remainder of one's life.

cyanosis A blue appearance of the blood and mucous membranes caused by an inadequate amount of oxygen in the arterial blood. A cyanotic appearance is one of the first signs of a number of respiratory diseases in which lung function is so impaired that the blood cannot take up a sufficient amount of oxygen. Cyanosis is also a characteristic of certain heart diseases characterized by abnormal shunting of blood. The cyanotic characteristic of the so-called blue baby is due to a congenital heart defect that leads to an excess of unoxygenated arterial blood. Surgery often is helpful in correcting such defects.

cyst An abnormal cavity filled with a fluid or semifluid substance. While some cysts do become malignant, most are harmless and are often reabsorbed by the surrounding tissues, leaving no trace of their existence. A benign cyst that interferes with the proper functioning of an adjacent organ, such as a gland, is removed in an operation called a cystectomy.

There are several categories of cysts. Retention cysts occur when the opening of a secreting gland is blocked, causing the secretion to back up and form a swelling. In this category are several different types. Sebaceous cysts cause a lump to appear under the skin. Mucous cysts are commonly found in the mucous membranes of the mouth, nose, genitals, or inside the lips or cheeks. Breast cysts may result from a chronic mastitis that causes the ducts leading to the nipples to be blocked by the development of fibrous tissue. Kidney cysts are a congenital defect eventually proliferating to the point where they interfere with kidney function.

Pilonidal cysts form in the cleft between the buttocks. They are called "pilonidal," which means literally resembling a "nest of hair," because the folding over of the skin in the cleft between the buttocks results in ingrown hairs that block the pores of the ducts leading outward from the sebaceous glands. When the retained secretions accumulate and back up, the affected area becomes swollen and painfully inflamed. When the cyst is small, treatment need be no more complicated than warm sitz baths to open and drain the abscess. The open cyst is covered with an antibiotic ointment to prevent the complication of bacterial invasion. A pilonidal cyst that becomes chronic and recurs with uncomfortable frequency may require surgical removal.

When a retention cyst develops in the Bartholin's glands in the vagina, infection and inflammation may occur blocking the gland and its secretions and surgical removal of the gland may be recommended to prevent the development of an abscess. Other cysts are formed by the slow seepage of blood into a tissue, forming a pocket similar to a tumor. These are called hematomas and can be under the skin, under a fingernail, in a muscle, or elsewhere.

Parasitic cysts are caused by certain types of tapeworms which enter the body in the form of eggs. Once the eggs hatch in the intestines, the microscopic embryos settle in the kidneys or liver, forming cysts large enough to be dangerous and to require prompt surgical removal. Parasites, such as those responsible for amebic dysentery and trichinosis do not cause a cyst to develop in the tissues of the human host, but form and encase themselves in their own cysts as part of their life cycle.

The category referred to as ovarian cysts includes a variety of different types.

cystic fibrosis An inherited, disabling respiratory disease of early childhood. The disease is genetically transmitted to offspring when both parents are carriers; when only one parent is a carrier, some of the offspring may also be carriers. Although there is no known cure for cystic fibrosis, new treatments have increased the life expectancy of patients with the disease. Prenatal genetic counseling can detect the presence of the disease in the fetus, thus giving the parents the option of an induced abortion at an early stage of the pregnancy.

cystocele A hernia in which part of the bladder protrudes into the vagina. A cystocele causes a feeling of discomfort in the lower abdomen and may produce bladder incontinence. The abnormal position of the bladder results in an accumulation of residual urine that increases the possibility of bacterial infection. Surgical correction is therefore advisable.

cystoscopy A diagnostic procedure in which the inner surface of the bladder is examined by an optical instrument called a cystoscope. The procedure, usually performed by a specialist known as a urologist, consists of passing the cystoscope through the opening of the urethra into the bladder. The doctor can detect inflammation, tumors, or stones by means of an illuminated system of mirrors and lenses and can obtain tissue samples. If diagnostic X-rays are to be taken during a cystoscopy, a catheter may be passed through the hollow tube of the instrument in order to inject radiopaque substances into the bladder.

D&C *See* DILATATION AND CURRETAGE.

D&E *See* DILATATION AND EVACUATION.

DTs *See* DELIRIUM TREMENS.

dandruff A scalp disorder characterized by the abnormal flaking of dead skin. The underlying cause of the condition is not known, but it is directly related to the way in which the sebaceous glands function. There is no evidence that dandruff is triggered by an infectious organism.

Normal skin constantly renews itself as dead skin cells are shed. Oily dandruff is the result of overactivity of the tiny oil glands at the base of the hair roots, accelerating the shedding process. The hair becomes greasy and the skin flakings are yellowish and crusty, similar to the flakings that characterize "cradle cap" in infants. A dry type of dandruff occurs when the sebaceous glands are plugged, causing the hair to lose its natural gloss and the flaking to be dry and grayish. In either type of dandruff it is important not to scratch the scalp, as broken skin may lead to infection.

There are several medicines that can control dandruff and sometimes eliminate it. If over-the-counter shampoos containing tar, salicylic acid, or sulfur prove ineffective, treatment by a prescribed medication may be necessary.

deafness *See* HEARING LOSS.

death Traditionally, the end of life was presumed to have occurred when breathing ceased and the heart was still. The increasing technological means for prolonging life and the concern of the medical profession as to precisely when a donor's organs should be removed for transplantation have created a compelling need for a "redefinition" of death in terms acceptable to both the legal and medical professions. Various state legislatures have statutes in which death is equated with the irreversible cessation of brain function. The criteria for brain-death are generally accepted by the medical profession throughout the world. The creation of similar state laws is essential for the prevention of civil or criminal liability suits against a hospital or a doctor that signs a patient's death certificate. Passage of brain-death legislation has the active support of the three major religious denominations as well as the most prestigious organizations of the legal and medical professions.

Following the lead of California, several states are enacting a "right-to-die" law which gives people the opportunity to make out living wills prohibiting the use of unusual or artificial devices to prolong their lives if they become terminally ill. More and more frequently, doctors are discussing the subject of dying among themselves, with their patients, and with the families of terminally ill patients. Many communities have organized patients' rights movements and death-with-dignity organizations to facilitate the passage of laws like the California law. Group activity of this type can be gratifying and a means for the living to confront their own mortality.

deficiency disease A disorder caused by the absence of an essential nutrient in the diet. Not until the twentieth-century discovery of the vital role of vitamins was this category of disease understood, although before that time people had discovered through trial and error what foods or extracts appeared to prevent particular disabilities, such as the control of rickets with cod liver oil (rich in vitamin D) and the control of scurvy with citrus juice (rich in vitamin C). Pellagra was once prevalent in areas where meat, eggs, or other foods containing niacin were precluded, due to poverty, from the diet. This deficiency disease has practically disappeared through the use of synthesized niacin as an additive in commercially processed foods. Certain types of blindness and skin ulcers, once thought to be infectious ailments, were discovered to be the result of diets deficient in liver, eggs, and other foods rich in vitamin A. Margarine and many other widely used items are now fortified with vitamin A. Beriberi, a deficiency disease that produces gastrointestinal and neurological disturbances, is caused by a lack of fresh vegetables, whole grains, and certain meats, all of which contain vitamin B_1 (thiamine). Mild beriberi symptoms are likely to appear among people on restricted diets, among alcoholics, and among crash dieters who fail to take supplementary doses of this essential nutriment. All of these deficiency diseases, however, are rare in the United States, in large part due to the multivitamin fortification of bread.

degenerative disease A category of disorders having in common the progressive deterioration of a part or parts of the body, leading to increasing interference with normal function. Among the more common of the degenerative diseases are the various forms of arthritis, cerebrovascular disabilities caused by the dystrophy diseases that impair neuromuscular function, arteriosclerosis, and the many disorders connected with progressive malfunction of the heart and lungs.

dehydration An abnormal loss of body fluids. Deprivation of water and essential electrolytes (sodium and potassium) for a prolonged period can lead to shock, acidosis, acute uremia, and, especially in the case of infants and the aged, to death. Under normal circumstances water accounts for well over half the total body weight. The adult woman loses about 3 pints of fluid a day in urine; the amount of water in feces is variable, but may account for another 3 or 4 ounces; vaporization through the skin (perspiration) and the lungs (breath expiration) account for another 2 pints. Normal consumption of food and water generally replaces this loss. A temporary increase in the loss of body fluid due to heat, exertion, or mild diarrhea is usually accompanied by extreme thirst or a dry tongue and can be rectified simply by drinking an additional amount of liquid. Salt pills are not necessary as an aid to fluid retention unless a doctor specifically recommends them.

The body becomes dehydrated if the daily fluid intake cannot compensate for fluid loss. Dehydration may become a problem if there is an extraordinary loss of fluids for reasons such as accident or illness; excessive perspiration through fever, extreme heat, or overactivity; or excessive production of urine due to the use of diuretics. Severe dehydration may require intravenous fluid replenishment. The fever, diarrhea, and vomiting that are characteristic in cases of gastroenteritis and cholera (and, to a lesser degree, dysentery) can cause dehydration that is severe enough to be fatal if it is not treated by intravenous fluid and electrolyte replacement. Dehydration that accompanies the acidosis signaling the onset of diabetic coma or of certain kidney diseases requires prompt hospitalization and treatment. Any serious signs of dehydration should be reported to a doctor for proper medical attention.

delirium tremens (DTs) Literally, a trembling delirium; a psychotic state observed in chronic alcoholics as a result of withdrawal of alcohol. The condition is characterized by confusion, nausea, vivid hallucinations, and uncontrollable tremors. The victim of delirium tremens may become obstreperous and therefore should be hospitalized for self-protection as well as for the treatment of chronic alcoholism. Until a doctor or ambulance arrives, the victim should be confined to a well-lighted room that is free of sharp or breakable objects and calmly reassured that help is imminent.

delusions False and persistent beliefs contrary to or unsubstantiated by facts or objective circumstance; one of the symptoms of mental illness. Delusions are false beliefs, as differentiated from hallucinations which are false sense impressions. As an example, an individual suffering from paranoid schizophrenia may have delusions of being destroyed by people who are thought to be enemies. In true paranoia the delusion becomes the focus of all activity. Some delusions are difficult to recognize and the person is merely thought of as an eccentric. When a delusion takes the form of ordering the individual to commit an inappropriate act, hospitalization is mandatory.

Demerol Brand name of the sedative and analgesic drug meperidine, a synthesized crystalline narcotic.

dental care The strength or weakness of one's teeth begins with one's genetic inheritance combined with the prenatal health and diet of one's mother. (Pregnant women please note.) However, good health, good habits of oral hygiene, and periodic dental checkups are the most important factors in preventing the decay of teeth. Tooth decay is incurable and irreversible, and prompt treatment of cavities is essential. A cavity should be filled before decay advances beyond the enamel. Otherwise bacteria may penetrate the dentin and attack the pulp chamber of the tooth. This may produce an infection that not only kills the tooth, but, in extreme cases, may spread throughout the body causing bacteremia and possibly bacterial endocarditis, a serious inflammation of the lining of the heart.

A vaccine immunizing against tooth decay is one of the long-range goals of the National Institute of Dental Research. Until such a vaccine is available, the most effective means of preventing dental caries is through regular visits to the dentist for checkups and cleanings and proper home hygiene. X-rays should be taken only when absolutely necessary. The American Dental Association makes the following recommendations. Rinse your mouth thoroughly after eating anything containing starch or sugar. Plain water will do, or you may use a mouthwash of ¼ teaspoon of baking soda or ½ teaspoon of salt dissolved in ½ glass of water. Deposits of food should be removed after each meal or, at the very least, before bedtime by using a brush with properly resilient bristles to clean every surface of every tooth and by using unwaxed floss to remove accumulations between the teeth.

dental caries Tooth decay, in particular cavities caused by bacteria. *Streptococcus mutans,* a microorganism that induces cavities, is related to the bacterial agent that causes strep throat. Some people appear to inherit an immunity to caries. The decay results from bacteria feeding on sugar and producing a corrosive acid. There are billions of bacteria in the saliva, but only *S. mutans* appears capable of creating an adhesive out of sucrose that adheres to the enamel tooth surface gradually destroying it. *See* DENTAL CARE.

dentin The hard calcified tissue that forms the body of a tooth under the enamel surface. When bacterial decay spreads from the enamel into the dentin, a toothache is likely to occur. If this symptom is ignored, the bacteria will eventually invade the pulp and increase the probability of the death of the tooth.

dentures Artificial teeth used to replace some or all natural teeth. Dentures may be removable or permanently attached to adjacent teeth. While preventive dentistry has reduced the number of women who need dentures at an early age, the loss of some teeth is almost inevitable with advancing age. Teeth should be replaced promptly to avoid the possibility of a chewing impairment, a speech impediment, or the collapse of facial structure caused by the empty spaces. In addition, missing teeth imperil the health of the adjacent natural ones. Dental materials and techniques used today make it virtually impossible to distinguish between a person's artificial and natural teeth.

deodorants Over-the-counter products containing chemicals that slow down the bacterial growth in perspiration, thus diminishing the likelihood of unpleasant body odor. Unlike antiperspirants, deodorants do not inhibit the amount of perspiration itself. Vaginal deodorants advertised for "feminine daintiness" should be avoided because of their irritating effect on tissue. Daily use of a pleasantly scented mild soap is a safer, cheaper, and sufficiently effective way of keeping the genital area clean.

depressant A category of drugs that produce a calming, sedative effect by reducing the functional activity of the central nervous system.

depression A feeling that life has no meaning and that no activity is worth the effort; profound feelings of sadness, discouragement, or self-deprecation.

dermabrasion A procedure in which the outermost layers of the skin are removed by planing the skin with an abrasive device.

dermatitis Inflammation of the skin, often accompanied by redness, itching, swelling, and a rash. Inflammation caused by direct contact with an irritant is called contact dermatitis; inflammation caused by psychological stress is called neurodermatitis. Types caused by viruses, bacteria, fungi, or parasites are called infectious dermatitis; they are discussed under entries entitled BOIL, FUNGUS INFECTIONS, HIVES, and IMPETIGO. Other forms appear under the headings CHILBLAINS, FROSTBITE, and HIVES. *See also* CONTACT DERMATITIS, RASHES.

DES (diethylstilbestrol) A synthetic nonsteroidal estrogen hormone. DES was first prescribed in the 1950s to prevent miscarriage. In 1971 it was discovered to be the specific cause of a rare type of vaginal cancer found at a young age in a few female offspring of women who took the hormone. This cancer, previously rare in women under 50, is called adenocarcinoma; it is an *iatrogenic* cancer, that is, a cancer inadvertently caused by prescribed medication.

Approximately 4 to 6 million people (mothers, daughters, sons) were exposed to DES, mainly in the 1950s. Of the daughters born to these women ("DES daughters"), about 1.4 per 1,000 to 10,000 developed clear cell adenocarcinoma of the vagina or cervix. Less than 200 such cases (often effectively treatable) have been identified in the United States. Other DES daughters, perhaps about the same number, may develop squamous cell cancer of the vagina or cervix. A larger number of DES daughters have developed minor vaginal abnormalities, called adenosis, which apparently have no functional or other effect on the women. Some of these daughters have uterine conditions that cause miscarriages and problems during labor. DES daughters should be examined periodically by a gynecologist starting in their early teens. The possible effects of DES on the male offspring of DES mothers are not completely understood, but seem to be related to an abnormal urethra. Some of these sons have reduced fertility. For DES mothers, there is a suspected risk of breast and gynecologic cancers. For further information on DES contact DES Registry, Inc., 5426 27th Street, NW, Washington, D.C. 20015.

desensitization A process whereby an individual allergic to a particular substance is periodically injected with a diluted extract of the allergen in order to build up a tolerance to it.

detoxification A form of therapy, usually conducted in a hospital, whereby the patient is deprived of an addictive drug and given a substitute one in diminishing doses. Alcohol detoxification produces severe withdrawal symptoms which can be eased by the use of sedatives on a transitional basis. When detoxification has been accomplished, a program of physical and psychological rehabilitation is usually essential.

Dexedrine Brand name for dextroamphetamine, a drug that has a greater stimulating effect on the central nervous system than amphetamine by itself.

dextrose A variant of glucose. *See* GLUCOSE.

diabetes A chronic hereditary disease characterized by the presence of an excess of glucose in the blood and urine due to an inability to metabolize glucose normally, usually as a result of an insufficient production of insulin by the pancreas. Although the basic cause of diabetes is still unknown, the condition can be controlled if treated correctly. The full name of the disease is diabetes mellitus, roughly translatable from the Greek and Latin as "a passing through of honey."

According to the American Diabetes Association, the number of diabetics is increasing, with approximately 10 million Americans being affected at this time. Of this number, 6 million are aware of having the disease and are under treatment; the other 4 million are unaware of their diabetic condition or are not being treated for it. Adult onset diabetes is the direct cause of at least 38,000 deaths a year and is considered to be the indirect cause of an additional 300,000 deaths. Thus it can be considered the third highest cause of death in the United States. Concern about this major health problem has resulted in the allocation by the federal government in recent years of about $75 million in annual research grants to determine its cause and to find a cure.

Symptoms of the disease are easily recognized and once the diagnosis has been confirmed, most diabetics, given the proper treatment, are able to live normal lives. The increased life expectancy of diabetics, particularly in the case of women over 30, is largely due to the discovery of insulin by two Canadian scientists in 1921–22. This hormone, produced by the pancreas, regulates the body's use of sugar by metabolizing glucose and turning it into energy or into glycogen for storage for future use. Glucose is a form of sugar derived from carbohydrates during the digestive process. An insufficiency of insulin or other abnormalities not fully understood results in the diabetic's inability to metabolize or store glucose, thus leading to its accumulation in the bloodstream in amounts large enough to spill over into the urine. This metabolic aberration causes the characteristic symptoms of diabetes: frequent urination due to the abnormal amount of urine produced to accommodate the excess glucose that the kidneys filter out of the blood, chronic thirst, an excessive hunger. Dramatic weight loss occurs because, being unable to use glucose, the diabetic must use body fat and protein as a source of energy. In order to reach the proper balance of insulin production and glucose conversion, which is constantly being regulated by the normal body, each diabetic must be individually stabilized through a controlled regimen of medication, diet, and energy output.

In addition to the previously mentioned symptoms, other symptoms that indicate the possibility of diabetes are drowsiness and fatigue; changes in vision; repeated infections of the kidneys, gums, or skin; intense itching without a known cause; and cramps in the extremities. Any woman with symptoms suggesting diabetes should have a urine and blood sugar test. There is also a simple laboratory procedure, the glucose tolerance test, that can identify prediabetics, thus alerting the doctor and patient to the possible onset of the disease.

When medication is essential to maintain normal blood sugar levels, the amount of insulin needed is determined initially by the level of glucose in the blood. Thereafter it usually can be determined by the level of glucose in the urine which is tested regularly by the patient. Variations in the results of the urine tests are the guide to necessary adjustments in diet, medication, and exercise. The use of oral drugs that stimulate the pancreas to produce its own insulin is now being reevaluated, especially since many of these drugs have been removed from the market by the FDA after a significant number of fatalities resulted from their side effects.

With the combined efforts of patient and doctor, satisfactory control can be attained and is reflected in the patient's general feeling of well-being, the maintenance of normal blood sugar and negative urine tests, and a minimal fluctuation of weight. Many authorities now believe that less severe cases of diabetes can be controlled successfully by diet and exercise alone.

Control is essential in order to avoid two specific reactions: hypoglycemia, a condition in which the blood sugar level is too low, and hyperglycemia, in which it is too high.

Hypoglycemia is likely to occur if the diabetic does not eat additional food to compensate for physical exertion, skips a meal, or takes too much insulin. Onset is sudden, the symptoms being nervous irritability, moist skin, and a tingling tongue. The situation can be corrected quickly by promptly eating or drinking anything containing sugar—a spoonful of honey, a glass of orange juice, a piece of candy, or a lump of sugar.

Hyperglycemia accompanied by acidosis and diabetic coma was the chief cause of early death in diabetics before the discovery of insulin. While rare today, hyperglycemic reaction does occur when the diabetic fails to take the necessary amount of insulin. Blood sugar builds up to a point at which the body begins to burn proteins and fats, a process that ends in the formation of chemicals known as ketones. When the accumulation of ketones leads to a critical imbalance in the body's acid concentration, the result can be diabetic coma. This condition is characterized by a hot dry skin, labored breathing, abdominal pain, and drowsiness. The patient should be hospitalized immediately so that the correct doses of insulin can be administered. A diabetic should carry cubes of sugar and wear a diabetic identification tag or bracelet at all times. *See* MEDIC ALERT.

A woman with diabetes may be concerned about whether she can or should become pregnant. While fertility is generally unaffected, once conception occurs, the blood sugar level of a diabetic woman may rise precipitously and behave erratically throughout the pregnancy. It is therefore essential that urine tests be made three or four times a day and that the blood sugar level be checked during prenatal visits as a guide to adjusting the dose of insulin. If the mother-to-be takes proper care of herself, there is every reason to expect a normal, healthy baby. Although diabetes is a genetic disease, the pattern of inheritance appears more complicated than originally assumed, making it impossible to predict the likelihood of transmission. Genetic counseling can be most helpful in this regard.

Diabetes that develops after having a baby or at middle age may not present the usual symptoms of urine frequency, thirst, and excessive appetite, but may be discovered because of a persistent skin infection or in some other way. In women over 60 a comparatively asymptomatic diabetes may lead to arteriosclerosis and in turn to a stroke or heart attack. Related disorders of vision, kidney function, and the nervous system may also develop in cases of delayed or improper control of diabetes.

Most diabetics lead a productive and fulfilling life, both on a personal and professional level. Women applying for jobs are protected by a federal law which prevents employers from discriminating against applicants solely on the basis of this disorder. Diabetics should be in touch with their local chapter of the American Diabetes Association. This organization provides information on current research, job options, travel possibilities, summer camps, and international affiliations. It publishes a bimonthly magazine called *Diabetes Forecast* containing practical material on menu planning and medical equipment and providing a forum for an exchange of ideas on living as a diabetic or with one. If there is no listing in the telephone directory, write directly to American Diabetes Association, 600 Fifth Avenue, New York, N.Y. 10020.

diabetic retinopathy An abnormal condition in the retina occurring among diabetics who have had the disease for a prolonged period of time. Diabetic retinopathy was practically unknown until the lives of diabetics were extended by the use of insulin. Leakage of blood and fluid from the retina's tiny blood vessels is the cause of the condition and the degree of vision impairment depends on the extent of the leakage. If the retinal hemorrhage is extensive and leads to a proliferation of "new" vessels and obstructive fibrous tissue, surgery is essential to prevent sight deterioration. Photocoagulation is a new treatment still somewhat in the experimental stage. In this procedure a laser beam is directed at the diseased retinal tissue in an attempt to destroy it and prevent it from activating new obstructive tissue growth.

dialysis The separation of waste matter and water from the bloodstream by mechanical means in cases of kidney failure. This form of "blood washing" prolongs the life of many thousands of patients who might otherwise die of renal failure. The dialysis machine, which may be installed in the home of the patient or used at a hospital or special clinic, is connected to the body by a complex arrangement of tubes. Blood containing impurities and wastes, that would normally be filtered out by healthy kidneys, runs through one set of tubes past a thin membrane. On the other side of the membrane is a solution which extracts salt wastes, excess water, and other substances from the blood by osmotic pressure. The cleansed blood is then returned to the body through another set of tubes. This procedure is routinely followed at least three times a week and takes about four hours per treatment.

The machine that serves as an artificial kidney to accomplish this procedure is costly, and patients using it require medical supervision for the rest of their lives. There are over 22,000 people in the United States on dialysis programs. The number increased considerably after Congress passed a law in 1973 amending the Social Security Act to extend Medicare funds to anyone under 65 suffering from kidney failure.

diaphragm A rubber, dome-shaped cap inserted over the cervix to prevent conception.

diaphragm The large muscle that lies across the middle of the body, separating the thoracic and abdominal cavities. The diaphragm is convex in shape when relaxed. Approximately 20 times a minute, upon receiving signals from the area of the brain that controls the respiratory process, it tenses and flattens so that the thoracic cavity enlarges, thus enabling the lungs to expand each time a breath is taken.

Many nerves pass through this muscle and it also contains large openings to accommodate the aorta, the thoracic duct, and the esophagus. When there is a weakening of the muscle structure that surrounds the esophagus, the stomach may push upward into the hole, causing the disorder known as a diaphragmatic or hiatus hernia. Involuntary spasms of the diaphragm are the cause of hiccups.

diarrhea Abnormally frequent and watery bowel movements usually related to an inflammation of the intestinal wall. The inflammation may follow infection caused by microorganisms that produce food poisoning or dysentery. Causes of diarrhea may be food, alcohol, a new medication, too strong a cathartic, an allergy, excitement or emotional stress. Some women have mild diarrhea with the onset of menopause, and practically all women have diarrhea before the onset of labor. At times it is accompanied by stomach cramps, nausea, vomiting, and a feeling of debility due to loss of body fluids and salt.

Chronic diarrhea may be a symptom of any of the following: thyroid disturbance, especially hyperthyroidism, nonspecific ulcerative colitis, a cyst or tumor of the bowel, low level chemical poisoning, and alcoholism.

The weakening effects of a brief siege of diarrhea can be remedied by the replacement of lost fluids and a bland diet. If the condition persists, the doctor may request a stool sample for laboratory analysis. If no infectious agent is discovered, diagnosis may involve internal examination with a proctoscope (a lighted tube which is passed into the rectum) or sigmoidoscope (a similar device for examining the sigmoid colon), blood tests, or a barium test.

diathermy Treatment by heat generated within the body by tissue resistance to the passage of high frequency electric current. The machines that produce the current are designed with various attachments shaped to fit the parts of the body that need treatment. Medical diathermy makes use of slight heat for purposes of muscle rehabilitation and tissue healing as one of the aspects of physical therapy. Surgical diathermy generates enough heat to coagulate and destroy body cells. As a procedure for removing warts and moles or for cauterizing cervical erosion, it has largely been replaced by cryosurgery.

diethylstilbestrol *See* DES.

dieting The systematic attempt to lose weight by cutting down on caloric intake. It is generally agreed by health authorities that any woman who weighs 20 percent more than the norm for her age and body build ought to go on a diet. Reducing need not be supervised by a doctor unless the individual is extremely overweight or special medical circumstances are involved, such as diabetes. The most effective weight reduction program is a self-motivated change in eating habits sustained over a protracted period of time.

digestion The transformation of food into nutrients that can be absorbed into the blood and assimilated by the cells; the digestive, or gastrointestinal system involves the alimentary canal and related organs (liver, gallbladder, and pancreas).

Digestion may be temporarily impaired or chronically affected by obstructions, bacterial or chemical poisoning, alcoholism, and infections such as dysentery, typhoid fever, cholera, and influenza. Emotional states of fear, excitement, anxiety, and anger are all known to be causes of acute or chronic digestive disorders, ranging from an attack of nausea to the development of a peptic ulcer. Any abdominal pain of an unknown nature should be brought to the attention of a doctor for proper diagnosis and treatment.

digitalis A substance derived from the dried leaves of the foxglove flower (*Digitalis purpurea*) and used in the treatment of heart disease. For several hundred years digitalis has been used effectively as a means of stimulating the action of the failing heart muscle, while at the same time slowing down the heartbeat. Digitalis is chemically purified so that doses can be measured with meticulous accuracy. Patients in need of immediate results may be given a dose that is close to being toxic; others may be placed on a daily maintenance program. Since the medication may have to be increased or decreased over a patient's lifetime, continuing medical supervision is mandatory. Symptoms suggestive of toxicity such as nausea, loss of appetite, headache, diarrhea, and irregular pulse should be reported to a doctor promptly.

dilatation and curettage (D&C) The expansion of the cervix by the use of surgical dilators and the removal of tissue from the lining of the uterus with a curette. The D & C procedure is used in early pregnancy as an abortion method; following a miscarriage to remove unexpelled tissue; in diagnosing uterine cancer, abnormal bleeding, or other discharge; and in certain cases of infertility to improve the general condition of the uterus.

dilatation and evacuation (D&E) The expansion of the cervix with surgical dilators and the removal of the contents of the uterus by suction.

disc, slipped The dislocation or herniation of one of the gellike, cartilaginous rings that separate the spinal vertebrae from each other. The column of 33 bones that make up the spine bears much of the body's weight above the hips. The vertebrae themselves are constantly being subjected to stress and sudden shock due to lifting, bending, and performing other activities that are part of one's daily routine. The discs between the vertebrae are the built-in shock absorbers. These resilient and somewhat spongy structures are held in place by rings of tough, fibrous tissue. When one of the discs slips out of position, it may press on a spinal nerve, causing acute pain to spread through the pathway of the nerve. In some cases the pain may radiate from the lower back into the buttocks, through the thighs and calves, and into the feet. When the pressure on the nerve is not as intense, the symptom may be restricted to lower back discomfort.

The point at which the pain originates is located by X-rays of the spine. The first aspects of treatment usually consist of bed rest on a hard mattress, analgesics to mute the pain, and traction. The condition may also be substantially improved by wearing an individually adjusted surgical corset with a back brace or a neck collar. In about 20 percent of slipped disc cases relief sufficient to make mobility possible can be achieved only by an operation known as a laminectomy; a piece of the vertebra is removed and the protruding piece of the disc that is causing the pressure is eliminated. Recovery is usually complete in a couple of weeks. A more radical operation is a spinal fusion involving bone graft. This procedure requires a long stay in the hospital and the use of a body cast and brace until fusion has been accomplished. It is an operation that is performed only as an alternative to painful disability.

discharge An abnormal emission signifying an infection or disorder, such as pus from a boil or an ear infection or the leukorrhea that characterizes cervical erosion. Normal emissions, such as the waste matter of the menstrual flow or the lubricating secretions of the vaginal membranes during sexual excitation, are not usually called discharges. Discharges of various composition are usually the first sign of vaginal infection. The color, odor, and consistency of the discharge depends on the nature of the infection. When the organism is a yeastlike fungus as in candidiasis, the emission is thick and white and has a yeasty smell. When the inflammation is caused by the parasite responsible for trichomoniasis, a greenish-gray discharge with a strong unpleasant odor is characteristic. Bacterial infections of the cervix, vagina, or other genital areas produce a foul-smelling yellowish discharge compounded of mucus, pus, and sometimes streaks of blood. Any unusual discharge should be called to a doctor's attention for evaluation, analysis, and treatment.

dislocation Specifically, the displacement of a bone from its normal position in the joint; also called subluxation. Dislocations most commonly occur in the fingers and shoulder and less frequently in the elbow, knee, hip, and jaw. A dislocation does not necessarily involve a break in the bone, but it almost always involves some damage, either slight or serious, to the surrounding ligaments and muscles. Anyone may experience a dislocation as a result of a fall or a blow, but it is a routine hazard among dancers and athletes. Dislocations are also more apt to occur to women whose joints are flexible rather than stiff, who consider themselves to be "double-jointed." Once the displacement occurs, particularly if the site is the shoulder or elbow, it is likely to recur because of the stretching of the sac and the ligaments that hold the joint in place. After several recurrences surgery is usually recommended to tighten the tissues.

A sudden dislocation can be extremely painful, and since the possibility of fracture as well as injury to surrounding nerves and blood vessels must be taken into consideration, prompt medical attention is essential to ensure restoring normal function. To minimize pain and swelling, cold compresses should be applied to the injured area. The injured joint should be immobilized while transporting the victim to the doctor or hospital.

The layman should never attempt to reset a dislocated joint; such an effort can result in serious irreversible injury.

diuretic Any drug that increases urinary output. The increase is called diuresis. Diuretics are indispensable in the treatment of heart failure to prevent fluid accumulation. They are often used in treating high blood pressure and certain kidney and liver disorders. Since diuresis involves the loss of vital salts such as potassium as well as water, patients receiving a daily dose of this type of medication are advised to consume extra potassium. Common substances such as coffee and alcohol have a diuretic effect.

diverticulosis The presence of diverticula, an abnormal mucous membrane pouch, in any part of the gastrointestinal tract, but especially in the colon. Diverticulosis may be entirely without symptoms and is most commonly found in middle-aged and elderly women with a history of chronic constipation. Since the diverticula formations are visible in X-rays following a barium enema, accurate diagnosis of diverticulosis is comparatively simple.

Diverticulitis is the inflammation of diverticula and it may produce cramps and muscle spasms in the lower left side of the abdomen. (Appendicitis produces similar pains in the lower right side.) Treatment should be prompt to prevent the serious consequences of fistula development or complete intestinal obstruction. Bed rest, a bland low-residue diet, and antibiotics are usually successful therapy. In severe cases of diverticulitis, where a rupture of the colon may lead to peritonitis, surgery should be performed without delay.

dizziness *See* VERTIGO.

DNA One of the basic components of all living matter; the molecular material in the nuclear chromosome of the cell responsible for the transmission of the hereditary genetic code. The designation DNA stands for the chemical compound deoxyribonucleic acid, the molecules of which are connected in an arrangement known as the double helix. The discovery in 1962 of the molecular composition of DNA is the foundation on which the comparatively new field of genetic medicine is based.

doctor The term doctor or physician designates persons who have either the degree of Doctor of Medicine (M.D.) or Doctor of Osteopathy (D.O.). The term doctor, but not physician, is also used to designate persons who have completed training and earned a degree in specific areas of treatment such as chiropractic, podiatry, and optometry. In order to practice medicine, a doctor must be licensed by the state in which the office is to be located.

Physicians usually work as hospital interns for one or two years before they become general practitioners (GPs). Most doctors who intend to specialize remain in an accredited hospital as resident physicians for several additional years in order to gain the necessary experience for certification in the specialty. This certification involves passing an examination given by a board of specialists in the selected branch. It is unfortunate—and a warning to the unwary—that any doctor may set himself or herself up as a specialist without having received certification through examination.

Information about a doctor's special qualifications is conveyed in the initials that follow the M.D. designation on a bill or prescription form. The designations indicate further credentials and peer recognition. The more common initials are:

F.A.C.C.	Fellow of the American College of Cardiology
F.A.C.P.	Fellow of the American College of Physicians
F.A.C.G.	Fellow of the American College of Gastroenterology
F.A.C.O.G.	Fellow of the American College of Obstetrics and Gynecology
F.A.C.R.	Fellow of the American College of Radiology
F.A.C.S.	Fellow of the American College of Surgeons

The most recent designation is P.C. which stands for Professional Corporation and must appear after the other credentials attached to the name of any doctor whose medical practice has been incorporated.

Although there are now as many as 50 different specialties, all with subdivisions, the medical profession officially certifies specialists in these fields.

Anesthesiology. The anesthesiologist is a physician who is responsible for choosing the proper means for the safe and effective anesthetizing of a patient before and during surgery. This choice is based on an assessment of detailed information of the patient's medical history and present condition. An anesthetist is not an M.D., but a specialized nurse who may administer the anesthesia under an anesthesiologist's direction.

Family practice. The specialist in family practice is trained to give basic and comprehensive medical care to any individual of any age. This is one of the most recent areas of specialization for which there is approved hospital-residency training and certification. The development of training programs for this specialty is an updating of the concept of the general practitioner.

Internal medicine. An internist (not to be confused with an intern, a medical school graduate practicing under supervision to acquire practical experience) is trained in all areas of medical diagnosis and treatment. This practitioner may, however, refer a patient to another doctor who is a specialist in the treatment of a specific ailment. Most internists develop their own subspecialization, and they may limit their practice to a particular field. Among the best known of the subspecialists are: allergist, endocrinologist (glandular and hormonal problems), hematologist (disorders of the blood), cardiologist (heart disease), and gastroenterologist (digestive disorders).

Neurology. A neurologist diagnoses and treats organic disorders and diseases of the nervous system, spinal cord, and brain.

Obstetrics and gynecology. The obstetrician is concerned with pregnancy and delivery; the gynecologist with disorders of the female reproductive system and with matters relating to birth control. A doctor who has had specialized training in both areas may decide to practice in both fields or in only one.

Ophthalmology. The ophthalmologist specializes in diagnosis and treatment involving the structure, function, and diseases of the eye. This specialist not only prescribes corrective lenses and eye medicines, but also performs all types of eye surgery.

Orthopedics. The orthopedist is trained to handle all diseases and injuries affecting the skeletal system, including joints, muscles, ligaments, tendons, and bones.

Otolaryngology. Commonly known as an ENT specialist (for ear, nose, and throat), the otolaryngologist is trained in the medical and surgical treatment of these particular organs as well as the cavities of the head, excluding those containing the brain (the skull) and the eyes (the eye sockets). An otolaryngologist is the specialist who usually performs tonsillectomies.

Pathology. The pathologist is essentially involved with the causes and behavior of particular diseases as revealed in laboratory research. They investigate bodily reactions to disease in tests on tissue, blood, urine, and other specimens. They do the tissue analysis in biopsies and also perform autopsies.

Pediatrics. The pediatrician is a specialist in child care, including immunization. Some pediatricians treat patients until their late teens; others consider the onset of puberty as the time young people should transfer to a family practitioner. A recent subspecialty in the pediatric field is neonatology. A neonatologist, usually a member of a hospital's staff, specializes in the care of the newborn, especially premature infants and those born with birth defects.

Physical medicine and rehabilitation. This specialist works to rectify disabilities of patients who have had a stroke, an injury, or a disease that affects the normal function of a certain part of the body.

Plastic surgery. The plastic surgeon deals with the repair, restoration, or replacement of malformed, damaged, or missing parts of the body resulting from injury or from congenital defect, for example, repair of cleft palate, skin grafting after major burns, reconstruction of facial bones damaged in an accident, and replacement of a joint or limb with a prosthesis. Cosmetic surgery is that branch of plastic surgery concerned with changing appearance solely for esthetic reasons.

Preventive medicine. This specialist is usually associated with community health programs and public health measures involving the anticipation and prevention of disease and injuries.

Proctology. The proctologist specializes in medical and surgical treatment of disorders of the anus and rectum.

Psychiatry. The psychiatrist is a medical doctor who deals with the mind and feelings. There are many categories of psychotherapists, but among them only those who are licensed M.D.s are legally permitted to write prescriptions for medication. A psychoanalyst is a psychotherapist who bases therapy on Freudian principles and who may or may not be a medical doctor. A psychologist is a person who has an academic degree in psychology. Psychologists with a Ph.D. may be called doctor, but they are not medical doctors nor are they legally permitted to dispense prescription medication. The term psychotherapist or therapist is a catchall for anyone from a psychiatrist to someone with no professional training or recognized credentials.

Radiology. A qualified radiologist uses X-rays, sonography, radioactive substances, and other forms of radiant energy in the diagnosis and treatment of disease.

Surgery. A general surgeon is qualified to perform any type of operation. Most surgeons specialize in a particular type of operation. For example, the thoracic surgeon performs operations involving the lungs and heart. Neurosurgeons are called upon for the removal of brain tumors, repair of nerves following injury, and similar operations.

Urology. A urologist specializes in medical and surgical treatment of disorders of the urinary tract.

dog bites *See* ANIMAL BITES.

dopamine A substance in the brain that is essential to the normal functioning of the nervous system. A decreased concentration of dopamine is assumed to be the underlying cause of Parkinsonism. Symptoms of this disorder are dramatically alleviated by chemotherapy with dopamine in the synthesized form known as L-dopa.

douche *See* VAGINAL CARE.

Down's syndrome A form of inherited mental retardation caused by defective chromosomal development in the embryo. It is also referred to as mongolism due to the downward curve of the affected offspring's inner eyelids and as Trisomy 21 because there are 3 instead of 2 number 21 chromosomes. In addition to retardation, these children often suffer eye disorders and have a tendency to develop leukemia.

The incidence of Down's syndrome increases with the age of the mother from 1 birth in 1,000 among women between 20 and 25 years of age, to 1 birth in 100 among 40-year-olds, to 3 births in 100 among women 45 years old or older. The role of the father is uncertain. Amniocentesis is advised for women at risk to determine if the defect is present.

Dramamine Brand name of the chemical dimenhydrinate, an antihistamine effective against motion sickness and vertigo. Since it induces drowsiness, it should never be taken before driving or engaging in any activity requiring mental alertness.

duodenal ulcer An open sore in the mucous membrane lining of the duodenum, the portion of the small intestine nearest to the stomach. *See also* ULCER.

dysentery An infectious inflammation of the lining of the large intestine characterized by diarrhea, the passage of mucus and blood, and severe abdominal cramps and fever. There are two types: bacillary dysentery is caused by several different types of bacterial strains; amebic dysentery is caused by amebae. Both types are endemic in parts of the world where public sanitation is primitive. Dysentery is spread from person to person by food or water that is contaminated by infected human feces and by houseflies that feed on human excrement containing the infectious agent. It may also be spread by food handlers who transmit the disease by way of unwashed hands.

When bacillary dysentery is diagnosed in the very young or very old or in anyone with diabetes or some other chronic condition, hospitalization is usually recommended so that dehydration can be prevented or treated. In milder forms of dysentery, rest combined with a prescribed dose of an antibiotic or other medication is a common course of treatment. Close supervision is important in the case of amebic dysentery since the infection can become chronic if amebic abscesses are formed in the liver.

Travelers to parts of the world where infection is an everpresent hazard should take the necessary precautions against dysentery by drinking only bottled water or other bottled beverages, avoiding raw fruit and vegetables, and, if possible, inspecting the facilities where food is prepared to make sure that the premises are screened against flies. If symptoms of the disease occur, a local doctor should be consulted promptly.

dysmenorrhea Painful menstruation. The discomfort is usually felt in the lower abdomen, extending into the lower back, and in some cases into the lower part of the legs. Dysmenorrhea may occur with or without headaches and may be the result of tension.

Gynecologists distinguish between spasmodic dysmenorrhea, characterized by cramps resulting from uterine contractions in sloughing off the unneeded lining of the uterus, and congestive dysmenorrhea, characterized by a dull achiness. In many cases the crampy discomfort subsides following pregnancy. The achy type might persist through the menopause. Women who are troubled by mild menstrual pain may find relief in a mild analgesic rather than in a tranquilizer. Adolescents and younger women should not be ridiculed for what is often termed "imaginary" pains, since the discomfort is very real no matter what the cause may be. A doctor should be consulted when the pain is sufficiently severe to be immobilizing or when menstruation suddenly becomes painful. In some instances minor corrective surgery or hormone therapy is recommended to relieve the condition.

dyspareunia Painful sexual intercourse caused by physical or psychogenic factors or a combination of both. Women for whom intercourse is so painful that it interferes with their sexual life should consult a gynecologist. Among the many organic reasons for the pain are endometriosis, cervicitis, cystitis, and cysts in the Bartholin's glands.

One of the most common circumstances resulting in coital pain is the first occasion of penetration when the penis may cause lacerations of vaginal tissue due to insufficient natural lubrication. In such cases the difficulties are compounded by the involuntary spasm of the vagina that follows the original trauma. Older women may experience the gradual onset of discomfort during or following intercourse as a consequence of the degeneration of vaginal tissues and a drying out of the lubricating mucus. An organic anomaly, such as a tipped uterus, may turn out to be the underlying factor. When there appears to be no organic explanation for the pain and no sign of infection, a woman should seek psychological counseling either with or without her sexual partner.

dyspepsia *See* INDIGESTION.

dysplasia An aberration of cellular development that may occur in the cervix, lung, and other places. In the cervix it is diagnosed by a pap smear. Although cervical dysplasia usually does not progress to cancer, women in whom it has been diagnosed need to be examined regularly. Some cases of dysplasia clear up without treatment; others require cauterization or other treatment.

dyspnea Labored breathing; the feeling of being "out of breath." Dyspnea is a symptom or sign of insufficiently oxygenated blood resulting from an obstruction in the air passages such as occurs in chronic respiratory diseases; a reduction in the capacity of the lungs to carry on the normal oxygen-carbon dioxide exchange because of areas of scar tissue; certain forms of heart failure in which the lungs fill with fluid; chronic anemia. An acute breathlessness may accompany asthma, bronchial pneumonia, the sudden onset of an allergic response that causes the swelling of the windpipe, and myocardial infarction. It is also one of the most distressing manifestations of an anxiety attack. Shortness of breath that often accompanies obesity can be rectified by loss of weight. When dyspnea is accompanied by chest pain or when it is chronic, medical evaluation is indicated.

ear The organ of hearing and equilibrium. The ear is divided into three parts: the outer ear consists of the visible fleshy auricle that collects the sound waves which are then transmitted through the ear canal; the middle ear contains the three bones of hearing; the inner ear is the site of the organ of hearing and the organ of balance. The thin layer of tissue known as the eardrum, also called the tympanus or tympanic membrane, forms the barrier between the outer ear and the middle ear. The bones of hearing in the middle ear, called the ossicles, are named for their respective shapes —the hammer, anvil, and stirrup. They are connected to the bone surrounding the middle ear by ligaments. When loud noises strike the eardrum, tiny muscles attached to the ossicles limit the vibrations of the eardrum by contracting, thus protecting it and the inner ear from damage. Equal pressure is maintained on both sides of the eardrum because the eustachian tube connects the middle ear to the upper rear part of the throat. The organ of hearing within the inner ear is called the cochlea, a spiral-shaped organ whose name means "snail" in Latin. The cochlea covers the nerves that sort out various sound messages and sends them on to the auditory center of the brain. The organ of balance, made up of the three semicircular canals situated in three different planes of space within the inner ear, maintains the body's equilibrium in relation to gravitational forces. Any disturbance or infection of the semicircular canals results in vertigo and imbalance.

The hearing process works in the following way. Any vibrating object that pushes air molecules at a rate ranging from 15 to 15,000 vibrations per second (the range of human audibility) causes waves to enter the ear canal and strike the eardrum. The vibrations are transmitted by the eardrum to the middle ear where their intensity is magnified by the ossicles. The waves are then sent through a membranous window behind the third bone, and are transmitted through the fluid within the cochlea. Hairlike structures within the cochlea communicate with the auditory nerves in such a way that a sound of a particular pitch and volume is perceived by the brain.

ear disorders Diseases, infections, mechanical difficulties, and pressure problems that affect the ears. The disorders directly responsible for the onset of deafness are discussed under the headings HEARING LOSS and OTOSCLEROSIS.

Discomfort within the ear may range from irritation due to dermatitis of the outer ear to a feeling of pressure caused by congestion in the eustachian tube to acute pain resulting from bacterial infection of the middle ear. Until the discomfort is diagnosed, it may be temporarily relieved with aspirin and the application of heat. Any sharp pain in the ear, an earache that lasts more than a day, an earache accompanied by a discharge, or chronic pain resulting from exposure to dangerous sound levels should be investigated by a doctor immediately.

Because the ears are directly connected to the nose and throat by the eustachian tube, a head cold is likely to cause the ears to feel "stuffed." The symptom may be remedied by the supervised use of nosedrops. Precautions should be taken to prevent the entrance of infectious material into the ear through the eustachian tube. Nostrils should not be held closed when blowing the nose, because closing both at once may force such material into the ear. Similar precautions should be taken while swimming. Air should be breathed in through the mouth and exhaled through the nose; if the mouth or nose fills with water, it should not be swallowed, but rather sniffed into the back of the throat and spat out. Earplugs may be worn. If water enters the ear, it can usually be drained by the force of gravity when lying down with the ear to the ground.

Otomycosis, a fungus infection of the outer ear, results from swimming in polluted waters and causes itching, swelling, and pain. It is often accompanied by crusted sores that must be kept dry in order to cure the condition. Fungicidal ointments and antibiotic salves are usually effective treatment.

Infections of the middle ear, more common in childhood than in later years, can be brought under control by antibiotics.

An earache caused by sinusitis or a diseased tooth will usually diminish as the underlying condition is treated. An infection that spreads from the middle ear to the inner ear will affect the sense of balance and cause vertigo. Several ear disorders are accompanied by a temporary "ringing in the ears" known as tinnitus.

The eardrum is susceptible to damage. A sudden and dramatic change in air pressure as occurs in an airplane or while swimming at great depths may lead to a ruptured or perforated eardrum. Probing the ear to remove wax or to relieve itching with any object, other than a twisted wad of cotton, may also cause perforation of the eardrum. This condition is usually accompanied by pain and bleeding and should be attended to without delay. The chief danger of a perforated eardrum is that it increases the possibility of middle ear infections. Anyone with this condition should be especially careful about protecting the ears while swimming.

echogram A recording produced on an oscilloscopic screen that shows the difference between the wave patterns of healthy and diseased tissue which cannot be distinguished by X-rays. Echocardiograms provide tracings of the ultrasonic waves reflected back from the internal heart tissues. The echoencephalogram provides similar material for the diagnosis of brain disorders.

eclampsia An acute condition occurring during pregnancy characterized by elevated blood pressure, convulsions, and coma; also known as toxemia of pregnancy.

ectopic pregnancy The implantation of the fertilized ovum in a fallopian tube, the cervix, or the abdomen instead of within the uterus.

eczema A skin disorder characterized by itching, a rash, and scaling. The eczematous symptoms may result from an allergy to a particular food, medicine, or pollen or from contact dermatitis. Eczema is also associated with varicose veins, since this circulatory disturbance can be responsible for local hypersensitivity of the skin, particularly of the ankles. Eczema is treated by eliminating the underlying cause and by topical creams that reduce discomfort and hasten healing. When flareups are traced to emotional stress, psychotherapy may be helpful.

edema Swelling caused by the abnormal accumulation of fluid in the tissues. The archaic term for edema is dropsy, derived from the Greek word *hydrops* from *hydros,* meaning "water." Edema is a symptom of various disorders, many of which require immediate treatment. The edema that accompanies heart failure or circulatory impairments usually takes the form of swollen ankles, but it may occur in the more serious form of accumulation of fluid in the lungs. Edema may also be caused by kidney and liver diseases. Puffy eyelids and ankles are among the symptoms of pre-eclampsia, a condition that afflicts pregnant women. Fluid retention and a bloated feeling are common problems among women troubled by premenstrual cramps, headaches, and other aspects of dysmenorrhea. When no organic disorder is detected, the symptoms, including the edema, vanish with the onset of menstrual flow. If the edema persists between periods, it should be checked by a doctor.

EEG *See* ELECTROENCEPHALOGRAM.

egg *See* OVUM.

ejaculation The reflex action by which semen is expelled during the male orgasm. Premature ejaculation, usually psychogenic in origin, is a circumstance in which the male reaches orgasm relatively rapidly and sooner than he or his partner desires. Rapid ejaculation may occur occasionally because of stress, a long period of abstinence, or several other factors. When it is chronic, a reputable therapist specializing in such problems should be consulted by both partners.

EKG *See* ELECTROCARDIOGRAM.

elastic stockings Hosiery reinforced with elastic thread in order to provide support for or to help prevent the formation of varicose veins. Elastic stockings are often recommended where circulation in the legs is affected by pregnancy or by work that necessitates standing in one place for long periods of time.

elective surgery *See* SURGERY.

electrical injury Any accident involving the transmission of electrical current through the body, either by a conductive apparatus or by being struck by lightning. If the voltage is sufficiently high, a fatal cardiac arrest can occur. To prevent electrical injuries in the home, electrical equipment should be inspected on a regular basis.

electrocardiogram (EKG) A tracing that represents the electrical impulses, that is, changes in electrical potential, generated by the heart as measured by an instrument called an electrocardiograph. The instrument magnifies the current about 3000 times. This magnified current provides the power to propel a lever in contact with a moving paper on which the wave pattern is recorded. The pattern indicates the rate of the heart rhythm, tissue damage that may have occurred following a heart attack, the effect of various medications on the heart muscle, and other valuable information for the diagnosis of cardiac disorders.

electroencephalogram (EEG) A tracing by an electroencephalograph of the electrical potential produced by the brain. Electrical impulses picked up by electrodes attached to the scalp surface are amplified so that they are strong enough to move an electromagnetic pen to make a record of brain wave patterns. This procedure is quick and painless. It is used routinely to diagnose tumors, brain damage, and neurological disorders such as epilepsy.

electrolysis *See* HAIR REMOVAL.

electroshock therapy A procedure in which a controlled amount of electric current is passed through the frontal area of the brain of a mentally ill patient. The physical response is convulsions and unconsciousness. Electroshock is not a cure for any form of mental illness, but when treatments are given in series, they may temporarily relieve some of the more anguishing emotional symptoms and thereby make the patient accessible to other forms of psychotherapy. It has largely been replaced by antidepressant drugs and tranquilizers.

elephantiasis Abnormal swelling of the legs and abdomen that occurs as a late stage of the tropical and subtropical disease filariasis, caused by a parasitic worm that invades the lymphatic system.

embolism Obstruction of a blood vessel by material carried in the bloodstream from another part of the body. The material, or embolus, is most often a blood clot, but it may also be a fat globule, air bubble, segment of a tumor, or clump of bacteria.

embryo The term by which the developing human organism is known from conception to the end of the eighth week of pregnancy. After that time and until delivery, it is known as the fetus.

emetic Any substance that causes vomiting. A safe and fast emetic is a mixture of 2 tablespoons of salt in a glass of warm water.

emphysema A severe respiratory disease, incurable but treatable, characterized by the air-filled expansion of the lungs. Emphysema is more prevalent among men than women and is most commonly observed in heavy cigarette smokers living in an area with a high level of air pollution. The disease develops gradually and is usually preceded by a chronic cough and intermittent bouts of bronchitis. Symptoms often become apparent between the ages of 50 and 70, as the lung's functioning surface area is progressively diminished by the destruction of the walls that separate the air spaces. This creates a disruption in the exchange of oxygen and carbon dioxide so that the lungs become inflated by an accumulation of stale air. Cigarette smoking aggravates emphysema since it places a burden on the lungs to oxygenate the blood. A first sign of the disease is difficulty in breathing after a minimum amount of exertion. As breathing becomes more labored, the heart is forced to work harder to increase the blood supply to the lungs.

To counteract the debilitating effect of emphysema, proper breathing techniques must be established in order to enhance lung capacity. Other aspects of treatment include a proper diet to counteract weight loss, supplementary oxygen, elimination of environmental irritants, immunization against respiratory infections, and medications that dilate the bronchial passages. Above all, people suffering from emphysema should never smoke cigarettes.

empyema A collection of pus within any body cavity; generally used to describe pus in the pleural spaces around the lungs as a consequence of infection. Pus within the chest cavity may follow pleurisy, pneumonia, pulmonary tuberculosis, or a chest wound or tumor. When possible, the fluid is drained off by a technique called thorocentesis: a hollow needle attached to a syringe is inserted into the pleural cavity and the pus withdrawn by suction. When the pus is too thick, surgical drainage may be required. In either case antibiotics are prescribed to halt the further development of abscesses.

encephalitis Inflammation of the tissues covering the brain. One form of the disease, encephalitis lethargica, was epidemic from 1915 to 1926 and was generally called sleeping sickness. The brain inflammation may be associated with such virus infections as measles, mumps, and herpes. It may be produced by lead poisoning, or it may follow the infectious bite of certain ticks and mosquitos. The disease may occur at any age. Typical symptoms are fever, vomiting, headache, and in some cases convulsions. Correct diagnosis is made by laboratory tests of the blood, spinal fluid, and stools and by an electroencephalogram. There is no specific cure. Treatment consists of bed rest, medication to keep the fever down, and antibiotics in cases where the infectious agent is bacterial.

endocrine system A physiological system that includes the ductless glands whose secretions, the hormones, are delivered directly into the bloodstream.

endometrial aspiration A technique in which suction is applied to remove the lining of the uterus (the endometrium).

endometriosis A condition in which tissue normally found in the lining of the uterus (the endometrium) begins to grow in the ovaries, fallopian tubes, bladder, or between the rectum and vagina.

endometritis Inflammation of the endometrium (the lining of the uterus), caused by bacterial infection which may follow a normal delivery, a cesarean section, an induced or spontaneous abortion, or irritation resulting from an IUD. Symptoms include pain in the lower abdomen, discharge, and fever. Acute endometritis is usually treated with antibiotics. Where the condition is caused by an IUD, a reevaluation of birth control methods should be considered. Chronic cases that do not respond to medication may require curettage.

endoscopy Examination of a hollow

cavity or an internal organ with an illuminated optical instrument (endoscope). Among the more commonly used instruments are the cystoscope for examining the bladder, the proctoscope for examining the lower portion of the intestine and rectum, and the bronchoscope for locating the origin and extent of respiratory disorders.

enema The injection of a fluid into the lower bowel by means of a tube inserted into the rectum; also, the fluid injected. A barium enema is administered prior to X-rays of the lower gastrointestinal tract, a sedative enema may be used for a calming effect, and a warm water or special solution enema is often recommended in special cases of constipation. The habitual use of enemas as a means of bowel evacuation is not recommended because they are apt to impair the natural responses involved in the normal process of elimination. Disposable enema units are a convenient substitute for the more traditional equipment which must be washed and stored.

energy The capacity for activity. Energy may take mechanical, electrical, chemical, or thermal form. All fuel is stored energy, and the body's fuel is food. The chemical energy stored in food is transformed by the metabolic process. The three essential sources of human energy are proteins, fats, and carbohydrates. "Lack of energy" may be traced to faulty diet, chronic illness, or emotional conflict.

Enovid Brand name of a contraceptive pill containing a very high amount of estrogen.

ENT The initials that designate *e*ar, *n*ose, and *t*hroat as an area of medical specialization. The doctor who is an ENT specialist is known as an otolaryngologist.

enterocele A hernia in which a loop of the small intestine protrudes into the vaginal wall. The condition may reveal itself when X-rays are taken to diagnose pain. Surgical correction is the usual treatment.

enuresis Involuntary bedwetting while sleeping; more specifically, by a child past the age at which bladder sphincter control is expected. Faulty bladder control by an adult during wakefulness is called urinary incontinence and may result from a variety of causes.

enzyme An organic substance, usually protein, manufactured by the cells of all living things and acting as a catalyst in the transformation of a complex chemical compound into a simple or different one. The human body produces hundreds of different enzymes, each with a specific function: some are related to the chemistry of muscle function; three main groups of digestive enzymes are essential for the normal metabolic processing of proteins, fats, and carbohydrates; particular enzymes are involved in maintaining normal respiratory function.

ephedrine A chemical derived from an Asian shrub, ephedra, or produced synthetically. For centuries the Chinese have recognized its medicinal properties which include dilating air passages, shrinking mucous membranes of the nose and throat, increasing blood pressure, and speeding up the heartbeat. In its synthesized form ephedrine is a component of various medicines that relieve nasal congestion and counteract the effects of an asthmatic attack. It must be used with discretion by anyone with a heart condition or with high blood pressure.

epiglottis The leaf-shaped flap of cartilage covered with mucous membrane that lies between the back of the tongue and the entrance to the larynx and the trachea (windpipe). In the act of swallowing, the epiglottis folds back over the opening of the larynx which contains the vocal apparatus (in the glottis) and channels the food from the back of the tongue to the esophagus. The disruption of this mechanism, such as by a person's laughing while eating, may allow food to enter the windpipe, leading to a coughing spell and in more serious cases to choking.

epilepsy A disorder of the nervous system in which an imbalance in the electrical activity of brain circuitry leads to convulsive spasms, loss of consciousness, and in some cases abnormal behavior. The seizures vary in magnitude and duration. There are approximately 4 million epileptics in the United States. The disorder is not contagious nor is intelligence affected. Some epilepsy is attributed to brain injury, but usually the basic cause of the disorder is unknown. It cannot be cured, but the seizures can be controlled in approximately 80 percent of all cases with anticonvulsant medicines.

Temporal-lobe epilepsy is a form of the disorder that may cause abnormal behavior without the characteristic seizures. When this form of the disease exists, it is important that the cause of the aberrant behavior be properly diagnosed as physical rather than psychological so that it can be treated medically or surgically rather than with psychotherapy.

Through its local affiliates, the Epilepsy Foundation of America, whose national office is located at 1828 L Street, Washington, D.C., 20036, will supply information through literature, films, and speakers on all aspects of the disorder including how to recognize a seizure and deal with it in an emergency.

episiotomy An incision made in the perineum from the vagina downward toward the anus during the final stage of labor.

epithelioma A tumor composed of epithelial cells, usually benign; the former term for skin cancer. One of the more common causes of this type of growth is overexposure to sunlight, especially among women with fair complexions. Another cause is overexposure to X-rays. Where the epitheliomas are confined to the outermost layers of the skin, they may seem to be no more than scaling patches. When they are more deeply buried, they appear to be pimples. Any such growth, especially if it suddenly begins to enlarge and is also bounded by a shiny border, should be removed. Even though this type of tumor is not generally cancerous, its continuing growth may interfere with the normal function of other vital organs.

Equanil Brand name of a chemical compound meprobamate, prescribed as a tranquilizer for the control of mild anxiety. It may produce side effects of drowsiness and a skin rash.

There are indications that Equanil (or Miltown, another brand name of the same chemical) taken during the first twelve weeks of pregnancy increases the possibility of birth defects.

erection The swelling and stiffening of the penis or increase in length, diameter, and firmness of the clitoris resulting from sexual arousal. The stimulus may be psychological (sexual fantasies), visual (the sight of a sexually appealing person), or physical (touch).

There is no correlation between the size of the flaccid penis and the same penis in erection, which may range on the average from 5 to 7 inches. There is no correlation between body size and the size of the erect penis nor between the size of the erect penis and sexual prowess. Inability to have an erection is called impotence.

erogenous zone Any area of the body, especially the oral, genital, and anal, that is the source of sexual arousal when stimulated by touch.

erysipelas An acute streptococcal skin infection, formerly called St. Anthony's fire because of the bright red patches that appear on the affected areas. While erysipelas may affect any part of the body, it usually originates through a lesion on the face or hands; once contracted, it is virulent and dangerous, especially to the very young or old. In addition to the changed appearance of the skin, other symptoms include headache, fever, and vomiting. Untreated, the red patches swell, spread, and cause the adjacent skin to blister. Erysipelas is a disease that requires prompt administration of antibiotics and a supervised regimen including lots of liquids, simple foods, and bed rest until recovery is complete.

erythema The reddening of the skin resulting from a dilation of the capillaries. An erythematous condition may be caused by allergy, bacterial or viral infection, superficial burns, chafing or chapping, or response to certain medication. Blushing is an erythematous response to an emotional situation.

erythrocytes The red blood cells. Each cubic millimeter of blood normally contains about 5 million erythrocytes. They are the smallest cells in the body and are constantly being manufactured in the bone marrow. Erythrocytes live for about 100 days. Any change in their number, size, shape, color, or density, which can be determined by microscopic examination, indicates a deviation from the normal health pattern.

erythromycin Generic name for an antibiotic commonly prescribed to patients with a penicillin allergy and to pregnant women and young children when the tetracycline antibiotics are considered inadvisable.

esophagus The muscular tube that transmits food from the mouth to the stomach; the gullet. This portion of the alimentary canal is approximately 10 inches long; it extends from the pharynx through the chest and connects with the stomach just below the diaphragm. Between the esophagus and the stomach is a muscular ring, the cardiac sphincter, that opens to permit food to leave the esophagus and descend into the stomach.

estrogen A sex hormone, primarily a female hormone, which is produced in the ovary, adrenal gland, and placenta. Males also produce estrogen in much smaller amounts in their adrenals. Estrogen regulates the development of the secondary sex characteristics in women and is involved in the menstrual cycle and the implantation and nourishment of a fertilized ovum. Synthetic estrogen is widely used in birth control pills and in estrogen replacement therapy to treat symptoms of menopause.

eustachian tube The canal that connects the middle ear with the back of the throat and equalizes the pressure on either side of the eardrum. Swallowing is the mechanism by which air is forced into the tube, correcting the stuffy sensation in the ears produced by a change in air pressure as occurs in an elevator or airplane. The eustachian tube is also the pathway through which infection may travel from the nasal passages into the middle ear.

eye The organ of vision. The eyes are contained in bony sockets of the skull. The extent of their movements depends on six delicate muscles attached to the top, sides, and bottom of each eyeball. The movements of the lids, which serve to protect the eyes, are controlled by other muscles that are both voluntary and involuntary.

The front of the eyeball is covered by the translucent tissue called the cornea. It is a continuation of the tough fibrous sclera, the white of the eye that protects the delicate structures within. Under the cornea is a middle, pigmented layer that forms the iris which is responsible for the color of the eyes and which is densely supplied with blood vessels. The iris functions in much the same way as the diaphragm of a camera, narrowing or widening in response to varying light conditions to expand or contract the pupil, the opening through which light enters the eye. The dilation of the pupil is influenced by various chemicals as well as by light intensity.

The light that passes through the pupil is focused on the retina, the expanded end of the optic nerve extending into the middle of the brain. Within the retina are the nerve cells, the light- and color-sensitive rods and cones, and the many connections that supply information to the occipital lobes of the brain where stimuli are transformed into the images called "seeing." The information the eyes continuously send to the brain may be acted upon immediately or may be stored away as memory for future recall.

The main part of the eyeball is filled with a transparent jelly called the vitreous humor, and the area in front of the lens is filled with a watery substance called the aqueous humor. The eyes are constantly lubricated, cleansed, and protected from infection by the tears secreted through the lacrimal ducts.

Among the more common disorders of vision are astigmatism, farsightedness, and nearsightedness, all of which can be corrected by prescribed lenses. Cataracts and glaucoma, the two main causes of blindness in this country, can be treated surgically. A cornea damaged by disease or accident can now be replaced by a transplant.

Foreign objects in the eye should

be dealt with by an eye doctor. Except for washing the eye with an irrigating solution contained in a dropper or an eye cup, no untrained person should attempt to treat any eye discomfort. Eye makeup and especially the brushes used to apply it should never be borrowed or lent as a precaution against the spread of infection.

eye examinations Any variation of vision, no matter how minor, should be evaluated. An ophthalmologist, a physician specializing in the eye, can diagnose or treat any disorder that might be affecting vision. Optometrists can check visual acuity and prescribe corrective lenses, but cannot diagnose organic eye disease. (An optician makes the prescription lens.)

eyeglasses Lenses ground to individual prescription for the correction of defects in vision, such as nearsightedness, farsightedness, and astigmatism. Bifocals are worn when both short-range and long-range vision require correction. If vision is impaired at the middle distance as well, a second pair of glasses or trifocals may be necessary.

eyestrain A feeling of tiredness in the eyes often accompanied by headache. The problem may exist with no apparent impairment of vision and is commonly the result of using one's eyes under poor lighting conditions.

It is important that the illumination come from the side and the rear in such a way that no shadow is cast on the object on which the eye is focused. It is also recommended that 60 or 75 watt light bulbs be used for reading. Office workers who suffer from chronic eyestrain due to poor lighting should make every effort to see that the condition is corrected. If the eyes tire before the completion of a task, they can be rested by closing the lids or by gazing into the distance. Television will not cause eyestrain if the set is properly adjusted and the viewer at a distance of approximately 6 feet from the picture. While it is advisable to have light in the room, it is important that it does not bounce off the TV screen into the viewer's eyes.

facial tic *See* TIC.

fainting A brief loss of consciousness caused by a temporary lack of oxygen to the brain; technically called syncope. (Fainting should not be confused with shock which is an emergency situation resulting from a critical loss of body fluids.) Fainting is usually preceded by lightheadedness, weakness, pallor, and a cold sweat. Circumstances that may reduce the brain's oxygen supply are a sudden emotional trauma, an excess intake of alcohol, and standing up for the first time after an illness. Standing still increases the chances of fainting because the blood supply to the brain is temporarily diminished. When one feels faint it is best to lie down or sit down with one's head lowered between the knees until the dizziness subsides. To help someone who has fainted, loosen all clothing and make certain that there is an adequate amount of fresh air to be breathed. Alcohol should not be administered as a means of reviving someone who has fainted. If consciousness is not regained within a minute or two, a doctor should be summoned.

Recurrent fainting spells should be reported to a physician to determine the cause. Heart disease, anemia, or diabetes may be a contributing factor.

fallopian tubes Two tubes, each approximately 4 inches long, extending from the ovaries to the uterus.

false pregnancy A condition in which overt signs of pregnancy exist, such as swelling of the breasts and the cessation of menstruation, but conception has not occurred; also known as pseudocyesis.

family history Facts concerning the health conditions, both mental and physical, of a patient's blood relatives. Some diseases are clearly inherited; others that do not necessarily have a genetic foundation may run in the family. With the increasing recognition of inheritance and predisposition as determinants of many diseases, every woman should be aware of her family's past and present medical history and should give this information to her doctor in detail. In describing a grandfather's diabetes or another relative's Duchenne muscular dystrophy, for example, the patient is providing the doctor with information that may be a clue for the early diagnosis of a condition.

family practitioner *See* DOCTOR.

farsightedness A disorder of vision in which only distant objects are seen clearly; technically called hyperopia. Farsightedness occurs when the lens of the eye focuses the image behind the retina rather than directly on it because the eyeball is shorter than normal from front to back. This disorder is corrected by wearing a convex lens that bends the light rays to the center of the retina.

fats An essential nutrient, found in both plant and animal food, composed of fatty acids (organic compounds of chains of carbon atoms with many hydrogen and some oxygen atoms added on).

feet The underlying cause of most foot problems is often improperly fitted shoes. Shoes and hosiery should be selected carefully in regard to proper fit, comfort, and support. Natural leather is preferred over other shoe materials since it allows the feet to "breathe" and has flexibility. Extremely high heels are inadvisable for those who walk a great deal since they place a strain on the foot and calf muscles and often cause problems with posture. Support hosiery is helpful in cases where constant standing places extra pressure on the blood vessels of the feet and legs. Any blister that does occur must be given prompt attention to avoid the possibility of infection.

Feet can be pampered by elevating them for a short period of time; circulation problems can be helped by immersing the feet in hot water and then rinsing with cold water. Exercises may keep feet limber and counteract the effects of poor circulation. These exercises may be simple ones such as wriggling the toes or picking up small objects with the toes. Walking barefoot on lawns or beaches is also helpful in keeping feet in good condition.

For chronic foot problems, consult a podiatrist (formerly called a chiropodist).

fertility The ability to conceive offspring.

fetus The organism in the uterus

after the eighth week of pregnancy. Prior to that time it is called an embryo. Some time around the eighteenth week the fetal heartbeat can be detected by placing an ear or a stethoscope against the mother's abdomen, and "quickening" or fetal movement also begins at about this time. By the twenty-fourth to twenty-seventh week a fetus is considered viable and, if born, may be kept alive with special hospital equipment and intensive care.

fever Body temperature that rises significantly above 98.6°F or 37°C, presumably due to a change in metabolic processes. A 1-degree variation is well within the normal range, since temperature rises this much after exercise, after a heavy meal, during hot weather when the body must work harder to rid itself of heat, or during ovulation when the increase in the secretion of progesterone affects the body processes.

A high fever usually results from a bacterial or viral infection; other causes may be heat stroke, brain injury, shock, or any occurrence affecting the brain center that regulates the balance between heat loss and heat production. Chills often precede or alternate with a high fever. As the temperature rises, the patient feels achy and thirsty, skin becomes hot and dry, urine is scant, and, depending on the cause, vomiting may take place. Until a doctor is consulted, a person with a high fever should stay in bed, drink lots of liquids, and take 10 grains of aspirin every four hours while awake. It should be kept in mind that the temperature reading on a rectal thermometer is usually 1 degree higher than the reading on a mouth thermometer. It should also be kept in mind that the seriousness of an illness cannot be judged by the presence or absence of fever.

fever sores *See* HERPES SIMPLEX.

fiber Cellulose or roughage in food. Fiber cannot be digested by humans. However, in small amounts it has a stimulating effect on the peristaltic action of the intestines and thus is useful in preventing sluggish digestive action and constipation. In larger amounts it acts as an irritant and can lead to unpleasant gastrointestinal disturbances. A balanced diet containing whole grain breads and cereals and cooked and raw vegetables provides sufficient fiber.

fibrillation A condition in which the fibers of a muscle contract in groups or singly, rather than in unison, thus causing parts of the muscle to twitch in rapid succession. When fibrillation occurs in the ventricles of the heart, the muscle cannot contract in a coordinated way, and the heart stops beating. A patient in the intensive coronary care unit of a hospital who experiences ventricular fibrillation after a heart attack has a 90 percent chance of survival if treatment begins within one minute. Treatment consists of the use of a machine called a defibrillator, which attempts to jolt the heart back into its proper rhythmic pattern by means of electric current. Monitoring equipment in coronary care units can anticipate the onset of fibrillation by the characteristic EKG pattern of skipped ventricular beats. This monitoring system enables the doctor to prescribe medication that helps to prevent impending danger.

fibroadenoma A benign tumor composed of fibrous tissue.

fibroid tumor *See* TUMOR.

first aid Emergency treatment administered to the victim of an accident or unexpected illness prior to the arrival of medical assistance. Instruction in the fundamentals of first aid are available under the auspices of local Red Cross chapters, hospitals, or community organizations. Such instruction enables the potential rescuer to provide emergency treatment in the event of a crisis. First aid can be effectively and promptly administered if the proper supplies are on hand. Every home should have the following first aid supplies available:

roll of 2-inch wide sterile gauze
individually packaged gauze squares
cotton-tipped swabs
aspirin tablets
antihistamine tablets
oral and rectal thermometers
adhesive strip bandages, assorted sizes
sterile absorbent cotton
roll of adhesive tape
baking soda (bicarbonate of soda)
rubbing alcohol
surgical scissors and tweezers

fissure A crack in a mucous membrane. Fissures at the corner of the mouth are called cheilosis and result from a riboflavin (vitamin) deficiency. An anal fissure caused by chronic constipation may lead to the further inhibition of bowel movements due to the severity of pain accompanying the passage of stools. Another type of fissure, cracked nipples, is often found in nursing mothers. It can best be prevented by the use of lubricating cream. Since fissures may be a source of infection, a doctor should be consulted for proper treatment.

fistula An abnormal opening leading from a cavity or a hollow organ within the body to an adjacent part of the body or to the skin surface. Anal fistulas that occur because of a lesion or abscess in the anal canal or the rectum eventually become painful enough to require surgical removal. A fistula between the urethra and the vagina that results from damage to the organs during childbirth or during surgery may cause incomplete bladder control and urinary incontinence. A fistula between the vagina and the rectum may also occur after an operation. Both conditions should be evaluated for surgical correction.

flat feet A condition in which there is no arch between the toes and the heel; the imprint of the sole on a level surface is seen to rest flat. Flat feet may be hereditary, a consequence of obesity, a fractured heel bone, or arthritis, or the result of having worn archless or no shoes throughout childhood. Many women who walk long distances on hard surfaces or spend a great deal of time standing may develop flat feet because of stretched ligaments that cause bones to lose their normal position. Since flat feet can lead to fatigue and backaches, an orthopedist should be consulted in regard to special shoes and therapeutic exercises.

flu *See* INFLUENZA.

fluids The maintenance of proper fluid balance within the body is essential. An excessive loss through diarrhea, vomiting, hemorrhage, or perspiration leads to dehydration. The presence of salt and potassium and other electrolytes is essential for normal cellular use of fluids. People using diuretics must have regular tests to determine whether the salt and potassium level is sufficent. The condition of edema, or the abnormal fluid retention manifested in puffiness or swelling of the eyelids, ankles, or other parts of the body, is a symptom of an underlying condition that should be diagnosed by a doctor and corrected.

fluoridation The addition of a fluoride (a chemical salt containing fluorine) to public drinking water. There is still controversy over this practice, but health authorities, including the U.S. Public Health Service, the American Dental Association, the American Medical Association, and the World Health Organization, have not found significant evidence of harmful effects and have found that fluoridation is related to a decrease in dental decay among children. There is no question that the incidence of cavities is much lower where fluorides occur naturally in the water supply than elsewhere.

fluoroscope An X-ray machine that projects images of various organs of the body in motion, as well as bones, when the patient is placed between the X-ray tube and a fluorescent screen. Fluoroscopy can provide the doctor with an immediate picture of a functional disturbance of the heart, an incipient sign of respiratory distress (as the patient breathes), the exact location of a foreign object lodged in the windpipe, and other information that increases the possibility of achieving an accurate diagnosis.

folic acid One of the B-complex vitamins.

food additives Various chemicals combined with foods when they are being processed for distribution and consumption. Among the earliest additives were preservatives that kept bread fresh. When it was discovered in the 1920s that iodine was the essential trace element in the diet for the prevention of goiter, iodized salt began to appear on grocery shelves. Many deficiency diseases such as rickets, anemia, and pellagra, once endemic in parts of the United States and among the urban and rural poor, have all but disappeared thanks to the addition of such nutrients as vitamin D to milk, vitamin A to margarine, and niacin, riboflavin, thiamine, and iron to bread. Under the regulations of the FDA intentional additives are permissible if: they upgrade the nutritional value of food, improve its quality, prolong its freshness, or make it more readily available and more easily prepared.

The subject of food additives is somewhat controversial due to the 1958 Delaney amendment which states in part that no additive is permissible in any amount if tests have shown it to be cancer-producing. Women who are concerned about the chemicals that are added to foods for the purpose of artificial coloring, artificial flavoring (monosodium glutamate), or to prevent spoilage (sodium nitrite) should read the labels of processed foods as a means of determining whether certain products contain potentially hazardous ingredients. It is also helpful to scan newspapers and magazines for any results of food tests conducted by the FDA. Local libraries often provide consumer action pamphlets and reference material on this subject.

food poisoning (food-borne illness) The general term for any acute illness, usually gastrointestinal, which is caused by the ingestion of contaminated food or of uncontaminated food which is poisonous in and of itself. The term "ptomaine poisoning" is incorrect. The most common symptoms include nausea, vomiting, abdominal cramps, and diarrhea. Food can be contaminated by bacteria (salmonella, staphylococci, *Clostridium botulinum* which causes botulism, among others), viruses (hepatitis), chemicals (such as sodium fluoride, monosodium gluconate), parasites, plankton, and poisonous plants eaten by milk-producing cows. Salmonella and staphylococci are the most common contaminants. Salmonella are not unusual contaminants of meat, but are killed by proper cooking. When not killed and if present in sufficient numbers, they infect the eater and cause abdominal cramps and diarrhea some ten or more hours after ingestion. Staphylococci, if present, multiply in foods such as salads containing mayonnaise which are left at warm temperatures for several hours. They produce a toxin which causes nausea and vomiting three to six hours after being eaten. Proper cooking and refrigeration are the best ways to prevent disease from these two bacteria. Fortunately, most victims recover quickly and spontaneously from illnesses caused by both of these bacteria, although infants and elderly people can become extremely ill and die.

Poisonous foods include certain mushrooms, fish, berries, and nuts.

Food poisoning can produce serious illness and death especially if the central nervous system is affected as happens in botulism and mushroom poisoning. Any one believed to be ill from food poisoning (usually recognized because several people become ill simultaneously), who has symptoms other than mild nausea, vomiting, abdominal cramps, and diarrhea, should seek medical attention promptly as should those who possibly have been exposed to botulism or poisonous plants. *See also* BOTULISM, WORMS.

fracture A crack or complete break in a bone. A closed or simple fracture is one in which the skin remains intact. An open or compound fracture is one in which the skin is ruptured because the broken bone has penetrated it or because whatever caused the fracture also opened the skin. A complex or comminuted fracture is one in which the bone has been broken into many pieces or part of it has been shattered. Fractures often involve damage to surrounding ligaments and blood vessels. Immobilization, preferably by splinting, is the safest way to manage a fracture until professional treatment is available. In many cases a simple fracture may be indistinguishable from a sprain except by X-ray.

frigidity The term used to describe sexual dysfunction in the sense of inability to derive erotic pleasure from physical sexual activity and absence of any sexual feelings; although the term generally has been applied primarily to women, the condition exists among men as well. Frigidity is called primary when the condition has always been present and secondary if it is of sudden onset. The term was used in the past to describe a nonorgasmic woman, but such women are now said to be suffering from orgasmic dysfunction. While the two conditions are considered separate entities, frigid women are often nonorgasmic. Where clinical frigidity exists, whether because of some physical aberration or for psychological reasons, it should be investigated. A woman or a couple considering a program of sex therapy should consult a doctor about reputable and qualified therapists. In the absence of local professional practitioners, sex manuals may be helpful in guiding couples who are concerned about the woman's inability to achieve an orgasm.

frostbite Injury to a part of the body resulting from exposure to subfreezing temperature or wind-chill factor. Since the affected tissue can be irreversibly destroyed, frostbite is an emergency situation. The parts of the body normally exposed to extreme cold are the ears, nose, hands, and feet. When the blood vessels in these parts become so constricted that the blood supply is cut off, there is no longer sufficient internal warmth to prevent the exposed tissue from freezing and eventually becoming gangrenous. The first signs of frostbite are a tingling sensation and then numbness and a bluish-red appearance of the skin. If countermeasures are not taken at this stage, the affected areas begin to burn and itch as in chilblains, there is a total loss of sensation, and the skin turns dead white. Since the frostbitten area is extremely vulnerable to further injury, any clothing that may be an additional constraint to circulation, such as boots, socks, or tight gloves, should be removed as gently as possible. If circumstances permit, the injured parts of the body should be immersed quickly in warm—not hot—water. If this is not practical, the patient should be wrapped in blankets. If the feet are involved, walking should be forbidden. If an arm or a leg is involved, the victim should be encouraged to elevate it. Absolutely no attempt should be made to massage the affected parts, rub them with snow, or apply heat. Keep the victim comfortable by offering hot beverages and a sedative and painkiller. Smoking is forbidden since the nicotine will constrict the already impaired circulation. A dry sterile dressing should be used to prevent infection. If there is no visible return of circulation after these measures have been taken and the person's condition appears to be deteriorating, medical care should be obtained.

fungus infections Diseases caused by fungi and their spores that invade the skin, mucous membranes, and lungs and may even attack the bones and the brain. These diseases are known as mycoses. Fungi are parasites that may feed on dead organic matter or on live organisms. Fungi and their airborne spores or seeds are everywhere. Of the countless varieties, some cause mold and mildew, some are indispensable in the formation of alcohol and yeast, and a small number cause infection.

The more common fungus disorders are those confined to the skin, such as ringworm which results in red, scaly patches that itch and may form into blisters. Ringworm is highly contagious and can be passed on by household pets as well as by contaminated articles such as towels and bed linens. To prevent its spread from person to person and from one part of the body to another, ringworm should be treated promptly with suitable antifungicides. Athlete's foot (tinea pedis) is a form of ringworm that can be difficult to cure once it takes hold. The fungus usually lodges between the toes, multiplying rapidly in the warm, damp, dark environment and eventually causing the skin to crack and blister. To control a chronic case, feet should be kept meticulously clean and as dry as possible, a fungicidal powder should be sprinkled in the shoes, and a medicated ointment should be spread between the toes. If athlete's foot persists despite these measures, professional attention should be sought. The same fungus sometimes affects the nails (onychomycosis) and usually requires professional care.

Thrush is an oral fungus infection that attacks the mucous membranes of the mouth and tongue, and where resistance to infection is low, especially where the diet is deficient in vitamin B, it may spread into the pharynx. It is characterized by the formation of white patches that feel highly sensitive. Similar patches may also appear in the vagina and rectum (moniliasis or candidiasis). Where only the mouth is involved, mouthwashes containing gentian violet may be recommended. In cases of moniliasis medicated suppositories are usually prescribed.

It is thought that a regimen of certain antibiotics increases vulnerability to various fungus infections, since the medicines kill off not only the bacteria causing a particular disease, but also the benign ones whose presence guards against the growth of fungi. In recent years the medical profession and public health authorities have been concerned with a group of fungus infections that attack the lungs and can eventually invade other organs. Of these, histoplasmosis and "cocci" or coccidioidomycosis (also known as desert fever) are the result of breathing in certain spores that float freely in clouds of dust. The spores are harmless, if swallowed, but those that find their way into the air sacs of the lungs begin to grow and multiply, spreading inflammation through the respiratory system and eventually into other parts of the body. Typical symptoms include a chronic cough, fever, and other manifestations that may be confused with pneumonia or tuberculosis. When tests produce the correct diagnosis, hospitalization may be required for the administration of a specific medication called Amphotericin-B.

gallbladder A membranous sac, approximately 3 inches long, situated below the liver. The gallbladder drains bile from the liver, stores and concentrates it, and eventually sends it on to the duodenum. The alkalinity of the bile is essential for neutralizing the acidity of the digested material leaving the stomach. Its component juices transform fatty compounds into simpler nutrients that can be absorbed by the intestines. A system of ducts controlled by sphincters releases bile when it is needed and forces the excess back into the gallbladder for storage.

In some cases the concentrated bile forms into gallstones. Inflammation of the gallbladder, technically called cholecystitis, may be acute or chronic.

In its acute form it usually follows bacterial infection or a sudden blockage of one of the ducts by a tumor or a large stone. Symptoms of an attack are nausea, vomiting, sweating, and sharp pain in the upper right part of the abdomen under the ribs, possibly extending to the shoulder. Jaundice may also be present. If the acute phase of the attack does not subside, emergency surgery may be necessary to prevent the danger of a rupture. The gallbladder is not usually removed unless X-rays indicate that the condition cannot be cured by routine medical treatment. Chronic gallbladder disease may cause gassiness and discomfort following a meal containing fatty foods. Abdominal pain may be brief but recurrent. In many cases the condition can be alleviated by a low-fat diet. When a low-grade infection of the bile ducts is the source of the discomfort, antibiotics may be prescribed.

gallstones Solid masses that form within the gallbladder or bile ducts. The lithogenicity or stone-forming tendency of bile results in three different types of stones: those composed of a combination of calcium, bile pigments, and cholesterol, those that are pure cholesterol, and those rare formations that are made of bile pigments only. Gallstones of the first two types are especially prevalent following pregnancy and are most common in both men and women after the age of 40. Following many years of research at the Mayo Clinic and elsewhere, it was discovered that cholesterol gallstones can be dissolved medically with a chemical compound similar in composition to natural human bile acid, thus eliminating the necessity for surgery to remove them if they cause an acute gallbladder attack.

gamma globulin The portion of the blood richest in antibodies. It is produced mainly by the lymphocytes in the lymphoid tissues and is one of the body's strongest defenses against infectious disease. Gamma globulin in one of two forms may be injected to confer passive (temporary) immunity to certain diseases. Immune serum globulin is derived from blood taken from donors who have an immunity to a specific disease either naturally or subsequent to active immunization. A specific preparation, such as measles immune globulin, is derived from donors who are convalescing from the disease or who have been recently immunized against it.

gangrene A condition in which tissue dies primarily due to loss of blood supply. Gangrene usually involves the extremities, but may occur in any part of the body where circulation has been cut off or in which massive infection has caused the affected tissue to putrefy. Among the circumstances leading to most gangrene are severe burns, frostbite, accidents involving contact with corrosive chemicals, untreated ulcerated bedsores, a carelessly applied and improperly attended tourniquet, or any other condition that cuts off circulation. When blood supply fails, infection by gas gangrene bacteria sets in. These bacteria live on dead tissue and produce toxins that poison surrounding live tissue. The dry gangrenous condition that occurs due to atherosclerosis, whether or not diabetes is present, most commonly affects the extremities. In such cases a toe or finger will shrink and turn black, and there will be a distinct line of demarcation between the healthy and gangrenous tissues. It is now possible to prevent the spread of gangrene with antibiotics and surgery. Should circumstances indicate the possibility of tissue death, particularly if numbness and discoloration of the extremities are apparent in a diabetic, it is the sign that emergency treatment is necessary.

gastrointestinal disorders Any number of conditions affecting the normal functions of digestion and elimination of food as it passes through the alimentary canal. Disorders may result from an infection caused by bacteria, viruses, or parasites, an obstruction due to a tumor, ulcers, hernias, allergies, food-borne illnesses, metabolic defects, or emotional stress. Symptoms may include mild to severe abdominal pain, constipation, diarrhea, rectal bleeding, jaundice, weight loss, nausea, vomiting, loss of appetite. Diagnosis of many disorders of the esophagus, stomach, small intestines, lower bowel, and rectum is based on X-rays. The diagnosis of other gastrointestinal disorders may require laboratory tests of blood and stools. Depending on the findings, treatment may involve a specific medication, a special diet, or surgery.

general practitioner *See* DOCTOR.

genetic counseling The National Institute of General Medical Sciences estimates that some 12 million Americans bear the risk of transmitting hereditary disorders. For this group of people genetic counseling has become an important medical service. Counseling involves educating the parents-to-be about the factors associated with genetic diseases, including diagnosis, the usual course of the disorder, and the risk of its occurrence or recurrence. Counseling also explores alternatives that take these factors into account and at the same time conform with the individuals' ethical principles and religious convictions.

Any woman who is interested in finding out whether she is a potential carrier of a genetic illness or how to prevent a genetic illness should ask her doctor for the name of an appropriate counseling agency or write to the National Genetics Foundation, Inc., 555 West 57th Street, New York, New York 10019, which acts as a clearinghouse for information concerning genetic counseling centers located at leading medical institutions throughout the United States. This advisory and referral service is free. Another source of information is the National Foundation–March of Dimes, Box 2000, White Plains, New York 10602.

geriatrics The branch of medical science that deals with the diseases and the health maintenance of the aged. It is related to gerontology which studies not just medical problems, but all aspects of aging–biological processes, environmental factors, social problems, and so forth. Medical researchers have turned their attention to the three most notable diseases of aging: atherosclerosis, heart disease, and cancer. Gerontologists are concerned not only with genetic factors and proper regimens of diet and exercise that influence longevity, but also with the importance of people participating as fully as possible in community life.

German measles *See* RUBELLA.

gingivitis Inflammation of the gums due to a tissue-destroying enzyme that stems from bacteria that cause the formation of cavities. Inflammation usually starts in the gingival crevice, a groove between the gum and tooth. Since untreated gingivitis may result in the destruction of bone tissue and the loosening or loss of teeth, prompt efforts should be made to control gum inflammation. The dental specialist who treats gingivitis is a periodontist. The form of treatment varies from scraping away the accumulation of plaque and calculus deposits at and below the gumline to oral surgery for the removal of pocket formations in which food and bacteria have collected. Gingivitis is most prevalent in women who smoke, whose diet is deficient in a particular nutrient, and who have been negligent in the dental care of their gums and teeth. Proper oral hygiene is the most effective way to prevent gingivitis or to limit its recurrence. A dentist should be consulted as to the correct way to brush and floss teeth.

glands Any organ that produces and secretes a specific chemical substance. There are two categories of glands: the ductless or endocrine glands, whose secretions are delivered directly into the bloodstream, and the exocrine glands, whose ducts transport their secretions to a precise location.

The most important exocrines are the following. The salivary glands produce the saliva that moisturizes the food in the mouth at the beginning of the digestive process. The sebaceous glands, found under the skin, produce an oil essential for its health. The sweat glands maintain the body's temperature and are part of the excretory system. The pancreas, liver, stomach, and small intestines secrete vital digestive juices. The lachrymal or tear glands are closely involved with emotional response and essential for the cleansing and lubrication of the eyes. The female exocrine glands include the vestibular glands (Bartholin's glands) located on either side of the vaginal opening, and Skene's glands, located on either side of the urethral opening. The mammary glands in the breasts supply milk for offspring. The prostate gland in men produces a secretion related to the reproductive process.

The structures sometimes referred to as lymph glands are not glands and are properly called lymph nodes. *See* LYMPH NODES.

glaucoma An eye disease that leads to progressive impairment of vision due to increased fluid pressure against the retina. Glaucoma is a leading cause of blindness in the United States, affecting approximately 2 million people. While there is no known means of preventing glaucoma, there is a test that can diagnose the disease in its earliest stages. The test should be done on a regular basis after age 40 and at an earlier age if there is a family history of glaucoma or diabetes.

The onset of glaucoma may be insidious and usually occurs in middle age. Symptoms, which persist even after many changes in eyeglass prescriptions, are blurring of vision, difficulty in focusing, loss of peripheral sight, and slow adaptation to darkness. The machine used for testing glaucoma is called a tonometer. It is a noncontact instrument that measures the pressure within the eyes. Marginal cases may require intermittent tests to establish whether the disease actually exists, since pressure within the eye can be affected by various chemicals found in food and alcoholic beverages or by other circumstances. The disease can also be precipitated or aggravated by medications, especially by antihypertensive drugs and cortisone.

While the glaucoma test can be administered by an optometrist, only an ophthalmologist can treat the symptoms. Irreversible damage to vision may be prevented by medication or surgery. The medication usually prescribed is eyedrops that reduce the pressure within the eye or that facilitate the draining away of the fluid before it accumulates in sufficient quantity to damage the optic nerve. In a minority of cases drainage can be accomplished only by surgery.

The National Society to Prevent Blindness, with chapters in many parts of the United States, provides information about the disease. If there is no local chapter, inquiries may be directed to the Society's national office, 79 Madison Avenue, New York, New York 10016.

globus A lump or mass, commonly associated with the term globus hystericus, the sensation often known as "a lump in the throat" that makes it difficult to swallow. The feeling is a manifestation of anxiety neurosis.

glomerulonephritis A kidney disease that affects the coiled clusters of capillary vessels, the glomeruli, through which the fluid content of the blood is partially filtered before it turns into urine. Each kidney consists of approximately a million of these filters. The capillaries may become inflamed following several varieties of bacterial infection, especially following a strep infection in the throat or elsewhere. Since acute nephritis may develop if the initial infection is not successfully treated with antibiotics, it is extremely important to consult a doctor immediately about any painful sore throat accompanied by a high fever. When glomerulonephritis occurs, the body retains fluid due to a collapse in the kidney's filtering capacity. Typical symptoms of the condition are puffy eyelids, swollen ankles, headaches, and decrease in urinary output. Once the correct diagnosis is made on the basis of red blood cells present in the urine, a regimen of bed rest, special diet, and fluid restriction is the usual procedure.

glucose A sugar that occurs naturally in honey and in most fruit, and the one into which starches and polysaccharide (complex) sugars are converted by the digestive process. Glucose is a major source of body fuel. Because it can be absorbed from the stomach, it is one of the quickest sources of energy. Glucose, or its variant dextrose, is also the nutrient usually administered intravenously when a patient cannot eat normally.

Glucose is present in human blood (blood sugar) at concentrations of 70 to 120 milligrams per 100 cubic centimeters of blood. Higher or much lower concentrations may indicate the presence, respectively, of diabetes or hypoglycemia. Glucose is normally not present in the urine; its presence there may indicate diabetes. The glucose tolerance test (GTT) measures the rate at which the body removes glucose from the blood. After the patient drinks a sugar solution or glucose is given intravenously, a series of blood and urine sugar tests are made during the next three to four hours. The GTT is a more refined screening technique than a single test for glucose in urine or blood and is used to identify disease when these tests provide ambiguous or inconclusive results.

glycogen A starchlike substance derived largely from glucose and stored in various organs of the body. It is converted back to glucose by various enzymes under hormonal influence, including insulin, when needed for body fuel.

goiter An enlargement of the thyroid gland. This endocrine gland, located at the base of the neck, extracts the iodine absorbed by the blood from food and drinking water and uses it for the production of the hormone thyroxin. Thyroxin is stored in the glandular follicles and released into the bloodstream as needed for the regulation of the metabolic rate. The body's iodine requirements are no more than a few millionths of an ounce, and since iodine is generally present in the soil, in most areas the requisite amounts occur naturally in food and water. Certain regions of the United States, mainly inland, are deficient in iodine and these areas have become known as the goiter belt. People living in these areas often have an enlargement of the thyroid gland, unless the deficiency is compensated for by the use of iodized salt. The enlargement occurs because the thyroid's cells increase in number in order to satisfy the body's demand for thyroxin. Eventually the gland may develop nodules or lumps. The danger of goiter is that it may press on the surrounding organs, leading to difficulty in swallowing or breathing.

When properly treated with iodine or with thyroxin itself, the goiter usually subsides. Goiter is much more common among women than men because their bodies require considerably more thyroxin during puberty, the menstrual cycle, and pregnancy. A pregnant woman must be sure that her diet contains the iodine essential for the baby's healthy prenatal development.

A goiter is often accompanied by an overactive thyroid gland (hyperthyroidism). In cases where treatment of the hyperthyroidism and the goiter by medication or radioactive iodine is unsuccessful, surgery may be necessary. The scar resulting from such an operation usually fades almost completely.

A less common type of goiter is characterized by an oversized thyroid gland incapable of manufacturing enough thyroxin (hypothyroidism). A baby born to a hypothyroid mother is likely to suffer from the permanent impairment of mental and physical development known as cretinism if the baby is not treated immediately. Successful treatment of hypothyroidism is accomplished easily by taking thyroid hormone extract by mouth. This corrects the underactive thyroid and usually the goiter as well.

Occasionally the thyroid gland enlarges because it becomes inflamed or infected (thyroiditis). Specific treatment is sometimes necessary and recovery usually complete.

gonads *See* OVARY, TESTICLE.

gonorrhea A sexually transmissible disease caused by the bacterium *Neisseria gonococcus,* which thrives in the warm moist linings of the genitourinary tract.

gout A form of arthritis resulting from a change in uric acid metabolism. This metabolic aberration may be inherited or may arise from the use of diuretics. It causes the uric acid naturally produced by the body to accumulate in the joints in the form of crystals, leading to acute inflammation and swelling. Joints affected by gout include those in the big toe and fingers and the ankle, elbow, and wrist. Pain in the big toe is most common because of the pressure of body weight on the foot. In chronic gouty arthritis the uric crystals spread and all the joints may be sore and stiff. There is also a possibility that the spreading crystalline deposits will accumulate in the kidneys in the form of stones.

Only recently have medicines been developed for the effective treatment of gout. The treatment, which controls rather than cures the disease, consists of two types of drugs: those that stimulate the elimination of uric acid and those that reduce its production. While the victims of gout are usually men, the disease sometimes attacks women, typically after the menopause. Women who feel "aches in the joints" or discomfort in the big toe or observe the beginnings of swellings of the finger joints, especially after dieting or using diuretics, should consult their doctor about the possible onset of gout. A simple blood test for uric acid content can diagnose the presence of the condition.

granuloma inguinale A sexually transmissible disease most commonly found in southern or tropical regions and caused by a specific organism, the bacillus *Donovania granulomatis.*

group therapy A psychotherapeutic technique in which interaction among several patients, supervised by a trained person, is used as a means of clarifying certain behavior patterns.

gums The fleshy fibrous tissue that covers the areas of the upper and lower jaw in which teeth are anchored. The mucous membrane that covers the gums forms a network of vessels that carry blood and lymph from the jaws to the face. Healthy gums are pink, firm, somewhat stippled, and form a collar around the neck of each tooth.

Practically all gum inflammation, or gingivitis, starts between the gum and the tooth in a shallow groove called the gingival crevice. It must be treated promptly by a dentist. A gum disease, commonly known as trench mouth and technically called Vincent's angina, is an infection of the mucous membrane. If permitted to spread, it may reach the lips and tongue. It is caused by a particular strain of bacteria, *Borrelia vincentii,* normally present in the mouth. When general health is good the bacteria are usually inactive, but when resistance is low and dental hygiene poor, these organisms, combined with other bacteria, often cause the disease. Its symptoms are inflamed gums, foul breath, and painful ulcers that not only bleed easily but may interfere with swallowing. It may be accompanied by swollen glands, sore throat, and fever. The disease usually clears up when treated with an antibiotic and can best be prevented from recurring by maintaining good health and proper oral hygiene.

The gums can be kept in good condition by brushing the teeth slowly from the gumline upward for the bottom teeth and from the gumline downward for the top teeth. Brushing the teeth horizontally is not correct since it does not stimulate the gums. Food particles lodged between the teeth and at the gumline should be dislodged by unwaxed floss, and tartar deposits should be scraped off by a dentist twice a year. Since improperly fitted dentures may affect gums adversely, dentures should be checked for necessary adjustments from time to time.

gynecologist *See* DOCTOR.

hair A specialized body growth consisting of dead skin cells that are filled with a tough protein material called keratin which is also the main constituent of the nails. Aside from the palms of the hand and the soles of the feet, hair covers almost the entire body surface to protect various areas of the body and to help to retain heat. Conservation of heat is accomplished by the reflex response whereby individual hairs stand erect and diminish the loss of body warmth ("gooseflesh"). Color, texture, and distribution of hair are inherited. Color depends on the amount of the pigment melanin contained in the hair core; the less melanin, the lighter the color. Curly hair is oval in cross-section; straight hair is cylindrical. The average woman's head may contain as many as 125,000 hairs. Each hair root is encased and nourished by a follicle buried under the skin. The growing shaft is lubricated by the oily secretions from a sebaceous gland opening into each follicle. Hair grows at an average rate of approximately half an inch a month.

Hair gradually turns gray as the melanin pigment is depleted. The age at which this occurs is a factor of inheritance. The growth and nourishment of hair are controlled by hormone secretions and the general state of one's health. The application of creams, lotions, vitamins or minerals does not affect the growth and thickness of hair in a healthy individual.

Hair should be shampooed on a regular basis, the frequency depending on a number of factors such as climate or whether the hair is dry or oily. Thorough rinsing is essential to remove all surface matter. Brushing the hair between shampoos eliminates surface dirt and also distributes the natural oils. A brush made with natural bristles is not apt to cause damage to the hair. It should be kept scrupulously clean in order to prevent an infection of the scalp.

Products used on the hair should be selected carefully to avoid any which irritate the skin, contain chemicals that might damage hair or skin, or might clog the pores of the scalp. Hair sprays should not be inhaled. Chemical hair dyes have been subjected to increasingly close scrutiny because of their potentially carcinogenic contents. Warnings in beauty shops and on home products should be evaluated carefully before deciding whether to dye one's hair. The decision may also be affected by consumer advocate reports and medical recommendations.

Women who wear wigs should select them for proper fit and porousness to allow the scalp to "breathe" and to avoid profuse sweating. Hair covered by a wig should be washed often enough to eliminate the inevitable accumulation of sweat. The wigs themselves should be kept scrupulously clean.

hair loss *See* BALDNESS.

hair removal Temporary or permanent elimination of unwanted hair; technically called depilation. The method used depends on the area and amounts involved, whether the removal is to be temporary or permanent, the amount of time and money required, and whether the hair is to be removed at home or by a trained technician. The simplest and least expensive method for removal of unwanted hair from the legs and underarms is shaving after applying cream or a lather of soap. This method does not cause the hair to grow back in increasing amounts, as the number of hair follicles one is born with remains constant unless the hairs are removed by electrolysis. Sparse face hair or unwanted hair between the breasts can be removed with tweezers. While somewhat painful, waxing has become increasingly popular as a hair removal method and with proper training can be done at home. Hot wax is applied to the skin and covered with cloth strips; when the wax has hardened, the strips are yanked off, removing both the wax and the embedded hairs. Prior to application, the wax should be tested on the back of the hand to make certain it will not burn the skin. Any skin irritation following the removal of the strips should be soothed with calamine lotion. Hair may also be removed by a depilatory containing chemicals that dissolve the hair at the surface of the skin. A patch test should precede the use of a depilatory to rule out the possibility of an allergic response to the product. Depilatories should be used with caution on the face and never applied immediately after a bath or shower while skin pores are still open. For the same reason they should be removed with cool rather than warm water.

Permanent hair removal is achieved when each hair bulb is destroyed electrically. The procedure is expensive and time-consuming and must be performed by a trained operator. Electrolysis is the older and more conventional method of permanent hair removal. A more recent version, based on the same principle, is called Depilatron. It supposedly eliminates pain, thus enabling the operator to cover a greater area of skin at each session.

halitosis The technical term for bad breath. The most common cause is poor oral hygiene and health; abscessed teeth, gingivitis, dirty dentures. Food particles trapped between the teeth, and fungus infections of the mouth are sources of decaying matter in the mouth in which microorganisms that cause the odor can grow. Bad breath on arising is characteristic in people who drink or smoke excessively. Halitosis may also be a symptom of certain respiratory, digestive, or kidney disorders, so it is important to determine whether the cause is of dental or medical origin. In the absence of a physical disorder and with normal attention to dental cleanliness and health, the breath of most people is quite acceptable. Mouthwashes and other preparations are helpful in temporarily masking bad breath.

hallucination The perception of a sound, sight, smell, or other sensory experience without the presence of an external physical stimulus. Hallucinations are produced by certain drugs. Hallucinatory episodes may be associated with such organic conditions as hardening of the arteries of the brain (cerebral arteriosclerosis) or brain tumor and with exhaustion, sleep deprivation, or prolonged solitary confinement or isolation from normal stimuli. Such experiences are also characteristic of delirium tremens, some forms of mental illness, and psychotic interludes following sudden withdrawal from barbiturates.

hallucinogens A category of consciousness-altering substances chemically related to each other; more popularly known as psychedelic drugs.

hand care *See* SKIN CARE.

hangover Symptoms of headache, queasiness, thirst, or nausea occurring the morning after drinking alcohol; also feelings of disorientation and befuddlement following the use of sleeping pills containing barbiturates. The amount of alcohol that will create a hangover varies from person to person and from time to time for the same person. It may result from having had very little to drink while one was tense, angry, or tired, or hungry. Some experts believe that the miseries of a hangover are a self-punitive mechanism caused by guilt feelings after excessive drinking. Many moderate drinkers have discovered that they are more likely to have hangovers after drinking scotch, gin, or bourbon than after drinking vodka and that wine or brandy can be deadly even in small amounts. This may be because of all alcoholic drinks, vodka contains the fewest of the complicated chemicals known as congeners. Since the circumstances that cause the malaise are so varied, each woman must figure out for herself how to prevent its occurrence.

The physiological mechanisms that cause the symptoms originate in the disruptive effects of alcohol on body chemistry. Its diuretic properties result in thirst, irritation of the lining of the gastrointestinal tract causes nausea, and dilation of blood vessels leads to throbbing headache. If a remedy is necessary, aspirin will help a headache and an alkalizer may soothe the queasiness.

hay fever *See* ALLERGIES.

headache Any pain or discomfort in the head; one of the most common complaints and a symptom for which medical science has itemized upwards of 200 possible causes. While it may be difficult to pinpoint a cause in a particular case, it should be comforting to know that 90 percent of all headaches are not caused by structural defects.

Some familiarity with the structures of the head is helpful in understanding why headaches occur. The bony structure of the skull contains the orbits of the eyes, the nasal cavities, the eight nasal accessory cavities, known as sinuses, and the teeth. Two of the sinuses are in the cheekbone (the antra), two above the eyebrows (the frontal sinuses), and four more at the base of the skull. Within the skull and protected by its rigid bony surface is the brain which itself has no pain receptors, but is surrounded by extremely sensitive tissues. It is covered by membranes known as meninges; the cerebrospinal fluid that acts as a cushion between the brain and the skull and also circulates between the brain and its membranous layers as well as around and within the spinal cord. A network of blood vessels interlace the coverings of the brain to supply oxygen and other essential nutrients to the brain and to transport the depleted blood back to the heart. It is not difficult to imagine how many chemical, physical, psychological, neurological, bacteriological, viral, and other variables can lead to changes, usually temporary, in the structures just described, most of which are sensitive to pain. For example, swelling of the blood vessels, inflammation of the nerve endings, or muscular contractions at the base of the skull, will cause the head to pound, throb, or ache.

Headaches can be classified as simple recurring, nonsimple recurring, or acute nonrecurring. Simple headaches occur at varying intervals and may be annoying or mildly disabling. Most simple recurring headaches are generally known as tension headaches. The immediate cause of the pain is the stiffening of the muscles at the base of the skull which sets up a cycle of contraction in response to pain and causes further pain because of the contractions. The usual reason for the stiffening of the muscles is emotional stress. In some cases, a muscle contraction headache may originate in a simple physical circumstance: a draft from a fan or airconditioner, straining to see or hear, or a response to pain elsewhere in the body. Such headaches may be mild or severe. When they respond favorably to over-the-counter analgesics and occur rarely, they can be viewed as one of life's nuisances.

When the headaches recur with debilitating frequency, further exploration into their cause is essential. They may be caused by injuries to the head or neck, reactions to certain pharmacologic agents, including alcohol, incorrect refraction of vision, or a variety of diseases such as high blood pressure, diabetes mellitus, and hyper- or hypothyroidism. In trying to identify the cause of these headaches, women should not overlook the possibility that they might be triggered by a response to the chemicals in hairsprays, perfumes, room deodorizers, cleaning fluids, insecticides, and the like. It is also useful to discard certain myths. Constipation does not cause headaches; both conditions are caused by tension, anxiety, or suppressed feelings. Worrying about high blood pressure is a more common cause of headaches than high blood pressure itself. Menopausal headaches are likelier to result from anxieties about aging than from a drop in estrogen levels.

Treatment must be directed primarily toward the underlying cause, but as an interim measure, some relief may be achieved by the injection of drugs that act as muscle-relaxants or local anesthetics. One of the most recent developments in the treatment of certain kinds of chronic headaches is biofeedback. Many hospitals now have established centers that use biofeedback techniques based on the patients' awareness of tension and relaxation mechanisms and how to control them.

Nonsimple recurring headaches differ from simple ones in several ways. They cause more severe symptoms, and they generally are caused by dilation of the blood vessels in the brain for which there is no explanation, as well as by contraction. The most widely known of these vascular headaches are the classic migraine headache and the common migraine headache. The classic migraine tends to be familial, is pulsating in nature, affects only one side of the head at a time, may be preceded more or less immediately by loss of vision, flashing lights, or varying neurological symptoms, and is often accompanied by nausea and vomiting. The pain is most severe during the first hour and then subsides. Frequency tends to increase during stress and to decrease with age. Treatment varies and is varyingly successful. The common migraine headache is more common. Symptoms are less specific than those of classic migraine. Mood changes usually precede it and may last several hours or days before the headache starts. The headache, also on one side of the head, may last several days. Again treatment varies and is varyingly successful. A third type of vascular headache is called the cluster headache. It is a series of closely spaced headaches, each of 20 to 90 minutes duration, continuing for several days, and then often followed by months or years of no such attacks. It may be triggered by certain foods and chemicals, such as caffeine in coffee, tea, and cola drinks; nicotine in cigarettes; monosodium glutamate in various cooked and processed foods; nitrites added to smoked meats; congeners in certain alcoholic beverages; and estrogen in certain contraceptive pills. Treatment for vascular headaches includes drugs such as ergotamine, various analgesics, including narcotics, and biofeedback techniques.

The acute nonrecurring headache usually has a sudden onset. It may be caused by a specific disease or condition which may or may not be serious or it may represent a change in the individual's pattern of simple recurring headaches. It may accompany a generalized infection, such as influenza, infectious mononucleosis, gastritis, sinusitis, otitis media (middle ear), or abscessed tooth, or it may be part of an infection of the central nervous system, such as meningitis, encephalitis, poliomyelitis, or brain abscess. It may also be caused by a brain tumor, aneurysm, or hemorrhage. The hemorrhage may be caused by an injury (contusion, concussion, or skull fracture) or be unrelated to injury. One particular type of headache is associated with a medical procedure called a lumbar puncture or spinal tap. It can be extremely severe, is usually worse when standing or sitting up and subsides in several days. Unless the headache subsides in a few hours a medical diagnosis should be sought so that the proper therapy can be initiated.

hearing aids Electronic instruments that amplify sounds. The instrument may be built into the temple piece of eyeglasses, fit inside the ear, or have a microphone behind the ear or worn on the clothing and a receiver inside the ear. A hearing aid must be fitted and regularly adjusted by a trained specialist (audiologist) after an ear specialist (otologist) has determined that some of the hearing loss can be restored in this way. Under no circumstances should a hearing aid be bought directly from a retail dealer. Community health centers or a doctor can supply the address of a nonprofit hearing aid clinic where the degree and type of deafness is accurately determined, recommendations are made for the type of instrument, if any, best suited to individual needs, and instruction is given in the most effective way to use the aid, including courses in lipreading if that skill might contribute to optimum results.

hearing loss Interruption at any point along the path traveled by sound vibrations before the information can reach the brain for processing. Hearing loss may be partial or total, temporary or permanent, congenital or acquired. The two major causes are disorders of conduction, which generally result in a loss of low-pitched sounds, and nerve defects, which generally result in a loss of high-pitched sounds. When both conditions are present, the disability is called mixed deafness. Conduction deafness may be a consequence of any of the following: obstruction by wax accumulation, inflammation of the middle ear, fluid accumulation, damaged eardrum, infection of the eustachian tube, and otosclerosis. Otosclerosis, most common among the elderly, is a progressive disease that freezes one of the three bones of hearing (the stapes) into immobility by imbedding it in a bony growth, thus preventing the soundwaves from being transmitted to the inner ear.

Nerve deafness may be caused by severe head injury, chronic infection that disables the auditory nerve, tumor, prolonged exposure to damaging noise levels ("boilermaker's deafness"), or drugs taken for some other condition.

Ringing in the ears (tinnitus) that interferes with hearing may be caused by arteriosclerosis, hypertension, or medicines containing quinine. It may also be a symptom of Menière's disease.

Since one of the causes of congenital deafness is presumed to be the mother's exposure to rubella (German measles) during the early months of pregnancy, such exposure should be reported promptly to the doctor in charge of prenatal care to determine what course of action to take.

Any indications of the onset of hearing loss should be investigated by an ear specialist. Conductive hearing loss is more susceptible to correction than nerve impairment and may be treated medically and surgically. New techniques of microsurgery have enabled specialists to restore hearing by a procedure called fenestration which opens up a new path at the inner end of the middle ear along which sound waves can travel when the normal one is obstructed. Another ingenious operation is the stapedectomy in which the otosclerotic growth and the immobilized stapes are removed and replaced by plastic and wire that conduct the sound vibrations.

hearing tests The determination of hearing acuity by the use of diagnostic instruments and procedures. Anyone who suspects a hearing loss, no matter how slight, should arrange to have her hearing tested by a physician. One of the oldest and most accurate tests measures the subject's responses to the vibrations of the stem and prongs of a tuning fork. The test can reveal whether the patient is suffering from nerve deafness or conduction deafness. A more accurate record of deviation from normal hearing is achieved by examination with an audiometer. The machine tests each ear for sensitivity to different frequencies and intensities of sounds and plots the subject's responses on an audiogram. With the results of other examinations, the audiogram is evaluated by the specialist to determine whether the hearing loss can best be corrected medically, surgically, or by a particular type of hearing aid.

heart The muscular organ that controls the circulation of the blood. It is approximately the size and shape of a fist, weighs about three-quarters of a pound, and lies in the mid-left section of the chest near the breastbone. The heart is actually two pumps lying side by side: the right side collects the venous blood and sends it to the lungs for the removal of carbon dioxide and addition of oxygen. The freshly oxygenated blood then enters the left side of the heart and is pumped out through the aorta for recirculation. The heart is nourished by its own vessels, the coronary arteries. The muscular pumping action consists of a rhythmic contraction (systole) followed by relaxation (diastole). The heart is protected by a tough membrane known as the pericardium. Its inner chambers are lined with endocardium. There are four chambers within the heart; the two upper chambers are the atria, the two lower ones, the ventricles. The atrium and ventricle on each side of the heart form a self-contained unit; there is no connection between the two so that pulmonary and systemic blood flows cannot be mingled. The upper and lower portions of each side are separated by valves, and the blood leaves the heart through two other valves: the pulmonary valve that opens into the pulmonary artery from the right ventricle and the aortic valve that opens into the aorta from the left ventricle. When the doctor listens to the heart with a stethoscope, the sounds made by the valves as they open and close are indications of health or impairment. The normal sound is heard as "lub-dup." Variations in this sound, some of which are called murmurs, are caused by leaks that occur because the valves do not open and close as they should, usually because of a congenital defect or because of damage during rheumatic fever.

Within the muscle tissue of the heart is a dense network of interwoven fibers which include a part known as the pacemaker because it is responsible for transmitting the electrical impulses that initiate the rhythmic contractions of the heartbeat throughout the network. These impulses, normally transmitted 70 to 80 times a minute, and the contractions are portrayed in an electrocardiogram. One of the greatest medical advances of modern times is the development of an artificial pacemaker which can be embedded in the chest wall and attached to the heart when the natural one can no longer work efficiently.

heart attack A condition ranging from mild to severe in which one or more of the arteries that supply blood to the heart are blocked or occluded by a clot; also called myocardial infarction, coronary occlusion, or coronary thrombosis. The chief cause of a heart attack is the cardiovascular condition known as atherosclerosis. The deprivation of blood supply results in a sudden and severe pain in the center of the chest. In some cases the chest pain radiates into the shoulders, back, and arms and is accompanied by pallor, nausea, and sweating, followed by shortness of breath. When these symptoms occur, particularly in the case of an angina patient, and do not disappear with the administration of nitroglycerin or other prescribed medication, an ambulance should be summoned immediately since the first hour after the attack is the period of greatest danger. Most doctors feel that if a heart attack victim reaches a hospital quickly, the therapeutic measures taken in the intensive coronary care unit can be effective. These measures combine the use of electronic monitoring and nuclear scanning with chemotherapy to reduce pain, decrease clotting, and strengthen the heart muscle. Whether or not coronary bypass surgery should be undertaken, should the cause be atherosclerosis of the coronary artery, is decided later on the basis of the patient's age, general health, and other individual factors.

A heart attack may occur at any time under a variety of physical or emotional circumstances. While men are more vulnerable to heart attacks than women, the risk increases in women after the menopause. Women over 40 who use the contraceptive pill bear a risk five times greater than women of the same age who do not use the pill. In the 30 to 40 age group the risk is three times greater. However, it should be kept in mind that in these age ranges, the pregnancy death rate is higher than the heart attack death rate. Widespread attention has been given to the warnings issued by the FDA that there is a substantial increase in the risk of heart attack or stroke in women on the pill who smoke. Women who fall into this category are ten times likelier to die because of a cardiovascular disability than women who neither smoke nor use the pill.

On a statistical basis and especially in men, the following conditions in one or another combination are responsible for most coronary attacks: obesity, diabetes, high blood-cholesterol, hypertension, sedentary life style, smoking, and emotional stress in the form of suppressed anger, perfectionism, and anxiety. One of the variables that acts as a powerful counterforce against heart attacks is a blood component known as HDL (high density lipoprotein) which appears to remove cholesterol from the arteries and transmit it to the liver for excretion. This component is likely to be higher in women than in men. It is also higher in nonsmokers than in smokers and in those who weigh too little rather than too much. The role of heredity is uncertain.

heart disease, hypertensive A heart muscle condition in which chronic hypertension impairs the functioning of the heart by causing it to pump with increased force. The abnormal demands cause the heart muscle to enlarge and increase the likelihood of heart failure.

heart failure Weakening of the heart muscle to the point where it is unable to pump efficiently enough to maintain a normal circulation of the blood; also called cardiac insufficiency or congestive heart failure. This does not mean that the heart has stopped beating. Heart failure causes the blood reentering the heart to slow down and back up into the veins. The consequent congestion in the blood vessels results in the expulsion of some of the fluid through the vessels' walls into the tissues. This seepage produces edema, which in turn leads to swollen ankles, fluid in the lungs, and other signs of excess fluid retention. Many women who have had heart failure can recover and lead relatively normal lives with proper medical supervision, a salt-restricted diet, the use of diuretics supplemented with potassium where necessary, and suitable amounts of digitalis. Where obesity, diabetes, or hypertension exist as an underlying cause, they must be treated simultaneously.

heart-lung machine A device that takes over the job of circulating and oxygenating the blood so that the heart can be bypassed and opened for surgical repair while it is relatively bloodless. The machine also facilitates operations on the lungs and major blood vessels as well as other types of surgery for high-risk patients.

heartburn A burning sensation in the lower esophagus. The discomfort, which may be concentrated below the breastbone, has nothing to do with the heart. It is the consequence of regurgitation by the stomach of a part of its contents upward into the esophagus. Since this partially digested matter contains gastric acid, it acts as an irritant. Heartburn may be associated with eating spicy foods, a hangover, a hiatus hernia, or emotional stress. It is not uncommon during the late stages of pregnancy. The catchall explanation of "hyperacidity" is far from correct and has caused many women to consume vast amounts of alkalizers in self-treatment. Where a hernia is the underlying cause and the heartburn is accompanied by spitting up food, surgical correction may be advisable. Most cases of occasional heartburn can be minimized by a sodium bicarbonate tablet and avoided by cutting down on rich, highly seasoned food, alcohol consumption, and tension-producing circumstances during and after mealtime.

heat exhaustion The accumulation of abnormally large amounts of blood close to the skin in an attempt to cool the surface of the body during exposure to high temperature and humidity. This disturbance of normal circulation deprives the vital organs of their necessary blood supply. The smaller vessels constrict, causing the victim to become pale and eventually to perspire heavily. Pulse and breathing may be rapid, and dizziness and vomiting may follow, but the body temperature remains normal. Fainting may be forestalled by lowering the head to increase blood circulation to the brain. First aid consists of placing the victim in the shade if possible and providing sips of salt water in the amount of half a cup every quarter of an hour for an hour (the solution should consist of 1 teaspoon of salt per 1 cup of water, or 0.25 grams salt per 8 ounces water). Feet should be elevated, clothing loosened, and as soon as it is practical to do so, cool wet compresses should be applied. If the condition does not improve or if the victim is elderly, has diabetes, or has a heart condition, emergency hospital treatment is necessary.

heat stroke A grave emergency in which there is a blockage of the sweating mechanism that results in extremely high body temperature; also known (mistakenly) as sunstroke and not to be confused with heat exhaustion. The victim of heat stroke is more likely to be male than female, old rather than young, and, not infrequently, an alcoholic. The condition is often precipitated by high humidity and may follow unusual physical exertion. Since fever may go as high as 106°F, irreversible damage may be done to the brain, kidneys, and other organs if treatment is not initiated immediately. The skin will be hot, red, and dry. If the face turns ashen, circulatory collapse is imminent. An ambulance must be summoned and in the meantime efforts must be made to bring the victim's temperature down. All clothes should be removed, and the bare skin sponged with cool water. If possible, the victim should be placed in a tub of cold (not iced) water until there are indications of recovery. No stimulants of any kind should be given. Drying off and further cooling with fans should follow the immersion. Since return to normal is likely to be slow and require close medical supervision, hospitalization after emergency treatment is usually recommended.

height The growth hormone of the pituitary gland controls growth during childhood and adolescence. When maximum adult height is reached during adolescence, at about age 16 for girls and 18 for boys, this mechanism stops. Although heredity and hormones determine body build, eventual height may be influenced to a degree by environmental factors such as diet, disease, and activity. With improvements in diet and immunization against many childhood diseases, the average height of Americans increased steadily for about 100 years until around 1914 and since then has remained relatively stable. According to the National Center for Health Statistics, the average stature for a young woman of 18 is 5 feet 4½ inches.

Heimlich maneuver A lifesaving technique used in cases of choking to dislodge whatever is blocking the air passages. An obstruction that cannot be loosened and coughed up following a few sharp blows on the back is likely to be ejected by the Heimlich maneuver. This is accomplished by squeezing the victim's body in such a way that the volume of air trapped in the lungs acts as a propulsive force against the obstruction, causing it to pop out of the throat. The rescuer stands behind the victim and places both hands just above the victim's abdomen. A fist made with one hand is grasped by the other hand and quickly and firmly pressed inward and upward against the victim's diaphragm. The pressure on the diaphragm compresses the lungs and expels the air. If you are choking and no one else is present, you may perform the maneuver on yourself by making a quick upward jab at the diaphragm with your fist.

hemangioma *See* BIRTHMARKS.

hematoma A collection of blood that has escaped from the blood vessels into the tissues, forming a local swelling. Hematomas are often associated with ruptured blood vessels that result from a blow. They are likely to accompany a fracture and frequently occur beneath the skull following a serious head injury. Bleeding that occurs after a minor mishap is usually reabsorbed into the blood vessels without forming a hematoma and without further consequences.

hematuria The presence of blood in the urine. The bleeding may originate in any portion of the urinary tract, and depending on the cause, may be trivial and temporary or may indicate the need for prompt medical treatment. The cause of hematuria is usually diagnosed by X-rays and cystoscopy. Among the more common causes are cystitis, a stone in the kidney, ureter, or bladder, inflammation of the urethra, or a type of tumor often found in the bladder known as a papilloma. Urine samples taken during a gynecological checkup will reveal the presence of hematuria. Any change in the appearance of urine from a clear, pale yellow liquid to one that is brownish or cloudy should be discussed with a doctor.

hemigastrectomy Surgical removal of a large portion (possibly as much as half) of the stomach. This operation may be necessitated by chronic peptic ulceration, by the presence of scar tissue causing an obstruction, or by stomach cancer.

hemochromotosis A rare metabolic disturbance of unknown origin in which large deposits of iron pigments accumulate in the liver, pancreas, or other vital organs, leading to their deterioration. The condition is almost exclusively found in men and is usually accompanied by cirrhosis of the liver and diabetes. Hemochromotosis may be controlled by the periodic withdrawal of whole blood combined with plasma replacement. Due to the characteristic skin color produced by the disorder, it is sometimes referred to as "bronzed diabetes."

hemoglobin The red pigment in red blood cells; a combination of the iron-containing *heme* and the protein-containing *globin.* This substance carries oxygen to the tissues and removes carbon dioxide from them. The amount of hemoglobin in the blood can be determined by a simple test. A less than normal amount indicates anemia; excess indicates polycythemia.

hemophilia An inherited blood disorder characterized by a deficiency of those chemical factors in blood plasma involved in the clotting mechanism; also known as bleeders' disease. It is a sex-linked genetic disorder; the gene is carried by the female, but only male offspring have the disease. The sons of hemophiliacs are normal (assuming marriage is with a noncarrying female). Transmission occurs through one of the mother's two sex chromosomes: 50 percent of her sons will be hemophiliacs and 50 percent of her daughters will be carriers. Thus, while the disease runs in families, the pattern of transmission may cause it to skip several generations. Hemophilia varies in severity. It is not curable, but when bleeding occurs, it can be treated by the infusion of clotting components that are separated out from normal blood plasma. Such transfusions may also be used prior to surgery and may be administered regularly as a preventive measure against hemorrhaging. Carrier screening and genetic counseling are available to those women who wish to be checked for the chromosomal defect.

hemorrhage Abnormal bleeding following the rupture of a blood vessel. Hemorrhage may be internal or external; it may come from a vein, artery, or capillary. Subcutaneous hemorrhage follows a bruise or a fracture; blood may appear in the sputum, urine, stools, or vomit. When its source is arterial, it is bright red and spurts forth with the heartbeat; when it is venous, it is wine-colored and oozes out in a steady stream. Any untoward bleeding or signs of blood in the body's discharges should be called to a doctor's attention. Other than the bleeding that results from an accident, hemorrhaging may also follow surgery, even a simple tooth extraction; it may occur during childbirth; it may also be a sign of a disorder that ruptured a blood vessel, such as an ulcer, tumor, kidney stone, or tuberculosis. Any diseases which affect the clotting mechanism, especially leukemia or hemophilia, are characterized by hemorrhage.

hemorrhoids Varicose veins in the area of the anus and the rectum; also called piles. External hemorrhoids are located outside the anus and are covered with skin; internal hemorrhoids develop at the junction of the rectum and the anal canal and are covered with mucous membrane. Among the causes are chronic constipation, obesity, pregnancy, and, less commonly, a rectal tumor. There is some evidence that the disorder may be hereditary. Typical symptoms are intermittent bleeding during the passage of stools, itching, and when thrombosis (clotting) occurs, acute pain. The hemorrhoids that develop during pregnancy are caused by the increased pressure on the veins of the lower part of the body; and are likely to diminish and disappear soon after delivery if other causative factors, such as overweight and constipation, are not also present. Treatment depends on severity: warm sitz baths are soothing, medication can reduce itching, injections of chemicals can control bleeding and shrink the swollen veins, and, if necessary, an operation can remove the diseased veins by cryosurgery. Any frequent discharge of bright red blood from the anus, even when unaccompanied by pain, should be brought to a doctor's attention.

heparin An anticoagulant substance found in the mucosal linings of the liver and other tissues. In synthetic form it is used medically and surgically to prevent clotting and to treat clotting disorders (thrombosis and vascular embolism).

hepatitis Inflammation of the liver; generally designates a viral infection of the liver caused by one of two related but somewhat different viruses, A (infectious hepatitis) and B (serum hepatitis). Recently a third type of viral hepatitis (non-A–non-B) has been identified. Victims excrete the virus in their saliva, feces, and urine and also carry it in their blood for various periods of time. Thus they can transmit it, directly or indirectly, to others. The virus enters the victim via the gastrointestinal tract (mouth) with contaminated food, water, or saliva or via the bloodstream when a contaminated needle is used to inject medicine or street drugs or when contaminated fluids, usually blood, are injected.

The incubation period for hepatitis A is about a month; for hepatitis B, about three months. Hepatitis A is twice as common as hepatitis B and occurs in about 15 per 100,000 people in the United States each year. It is more common in countries with poor sanitary facilities. Some victims are never ill clinically and have only abnormal blood tests indicative of impaired liver function for a few weeks. Most, however, are sick in varying degrees for several weeks or months and then recover completely. A few become life-time carriers of the virus and, although well, cannot donate their blood. The signs and symptoms of the disease are jaundice, dark urine and light-colored stools, fever, loss of appetite, and fatigue. A few people develop chronic hepatitis with varying degrees of liver involvement. About 1 percent of patients under 45 years of age and 3 percent of those 45 and over die during the acute phase.

Other forms of hepatitis can occur without direct infection of the liver. Diffuse bacterial infections (septicemia) can cause a toxic hepatitis. Certain chemicals, such as carbon tetrachloride, can cause hepatitis in anyone who is exposed sufficiently, and certain medications, such as phenylbutazone, cincophen, and halothane, can cause hepatitis in those who, for unknown reasons, are sensitive to them.

There is no specific treatment. However, when gamma globulin is given to a victim soon after exposure, it is effective in preventing or minimizing the disease by creating a temporary (passive) immunity. Immunization to provide permanent (active) immunity may soon be available. Those who have had hepatitis develop permanent immunity to hepatitis caused by the same virus.

heredity The transmission of characteristics from one generation to another, from parents to offspring, through the genetic information carried in the chromosomes. Geneticists are providing medical researchers with the tools for exploring the role of heredity in sickness and in resistance to disease. It is hoped that the dissemination of information about genetic disorders and the availability of genetic counseling will bring about a dramatic reduction in the medical, psychological, and economic problems created by hereditary diseases.

Among the more prevalent inherited diseases are: Tay-Sachs, Niemann-Pick, and Gaucher's disease, all three caused by faulty enzyme function and commonly associated with families of middle European Jewish ancestry; sickle-cell anemia, a blood disorder most common among blacks; Cooley's anemia, a more acute blood disease formerly called thalassemia; Huntington's chorea, a degenerative disorder of the central nervous system; hemophilia; several types of muscular dystrophy; galactosemia; phenylketonuria (PKU); cystic fibrosis, the most common genetic disease among Anglo-Saxons, carried by 1 in 20 whites or approximately 10 million Americans. Research on inherited immunities that seem to make some families immune to certain diseases is expected to yield information about resistance to disease in general. This research is still in an early stage of development. *See also* GENETIC COUNSELING.

hernia The protrusion of all or part of an organ, most commonly, an intestinal loop or abdominal organ, through a weak spot in the wall of the surrounding structure; also called a rupture. A hernia, which may be acquired or congenital, is classified according to the part of the body in which it occurs. The inguinal hernia, occurring in the groin, accounts for about 75 percent of all hernias and is much more common among men than women. The umbilical hernia is more common among infants than among adults; some cases are self-correcting and some require surgery. Incisional or ventral hernias may develop after abdominal surgery in cases of unsatisfactory healing or because a chronic cough or obesity subjects the weakened tissue to extra strain. The esophageal or hiatus hernia is more common among the middle-aged than the young. In this condition a portion of the stomach protrudes through the opening for the esophagus in the diaphragm, producing symptoms that range from mild indigestion and heartburn to serious breathing difficulties and regurgitation of food after each meal. In less severe cases the discomfort can be eased by eating small and frequent meals of bland food and sleeping with the body propped up by extra pillows. Most hernias can be corrected by surgical repair of the weakened tissue.

heroin A narcotic drug derived from opium by altering the chemical formula of morphine.

herpes simplex One of several diseases caused by a particular virus or variants of it. The seriousness of the disease depends on the area of infection and the particular strain of the virus. In all cases the symptom is an eruption of painful blisters. When the eruption occurs around the mouth, the cause is usually herpes simplex virus type I (HSV-1) and the disease is often referred to as "cold sores" or "fever blisters." This virus is also responsible for ulceration of the cornea (herpetic keratitis) that can result in scarring of the tissue and loss of vision unless treated promptly. The disorder seems to be activated by exposure to extremes of temperature or by another infection. No cure exists, but the discomfort can be eased by medicated creams or salves.

Type II of the herpes simplex virus (HSV-2) is usually responsible for an infection of the mucous membranes of the genital or anal area and may or may not be spread by sexual contact.

herpes zoster A painful virus infection of the sensory nerves causing inflammation of the skin along the nerve pathway (herpes zoster means "blister girdle"); commonly called shingles and very closely related to the virus which causes chickenpox. Herpes zoster is far less contagious than herpes simplex. What activates the virus is not clearly understood. Inflammation typically occurs above the abdomen and less often along the path of the cranial nerve on the face and near the eye, with a potential for damage to the cornea. Sensitivity of the involved nerves (neuritis) and blisters may take several weeks to disappear, and in stubborn cases the patient may be left with acute neuralgia. There is no specific cure, but various medicines are available to reduce pain.

hiccups (hiccoughs) Involuntary spasmodic contractions of the diaphragm that force the glottis to close at the same time that a breath is taken in, thus producing the characteristic clicking sound. The common cause is a minor irritation of the diaphragm itself or of some part of the digestive or respiratory system. In more serious cases hiccups may be associated with uremia or encephalitis. Although the typical attack of hiccups is self-limiting, there are remedies for quick relief: sipping water slowly, holding the breath, or breathing into a paper bag. If hiccups persist, a doctor should be called. In all but the most extreme cases, a tranquilizer or a sedative will end the discomfort.

high altitude sickness A condition associated with the ascent to altitudes of 8,000 feet above sea level or higher, where the reduced concentration of oxygen in the air (rarefied air) leads to oxygen deprivation in the blood. When the red blood cells are unable to absorb a full supply of oxygen as they pass through the lungs, breathing becomes increasingly quick and labored. Giddiness, headache, nausea, and disorientation are among the warning signals of high altitude sickness. Tourists who plan to visit high altitudes and mountain climbers or skiers who intend to reach higher altitudes than customary should have a medical checkup to make sure that their heart and lungs can tolerate the stress. Tourists in high altitudes should eliminate smoking and drinking for the first two days and keep physical exertion to a minimum until the body has adjusted to the environment.

high blood pressure *See* HYPERTENSION.

histamine A chemical compound found in all body tissues, normally released as a stimulant for the production of the gastric juices during digestion and for the dilation of the smaller blood vessels in response to the body's adaptive needs. Under certain conditions some people produce excessive amounts of histamine as an allergic reaction, causing the surrounding tissues to become swollen and inflamed. For such allergic responses, antihistamine medicines are available. Antihistamines should not be used indiscriminately since they cause drowsiness.

hives Irregularly shaped red or white elevations of the skin accompanied by itching and burning, usually caused by an allergic response involving the release of histamine; technically called urticaria. Hives may occur on any part of the body or in the gastrointestinal tract, and in some cases the weals may be as large as an inch in diameter. A topical anesthetic ointment or lotion may provide relief, but an antihistamine drug is usually prescribed to prevent additional eruptions. When hives occur for the first time, an effort should be made to identify the cause, especially if some medication is suspected, to avoid a more serious recurrence.

Hodgkin's disease A disorder of the lymphatic system characterized by the progressive enlargement of the lymph nodes throughout the body, especially of the spleen. It is a type of cancer that typically attacks young adults; men are twice as vulnerable as women. If the disease is localized, a 95 percent cure rate can be achieved by radiation treatment. If the disease spreads to the point where vital organs are endangered, various types of chemotherapy have proved effective. Hodgkin's disease may be caused by a virus. Since it seems to have a family pattern, there may be a hereditary lack of immunity.

holistic medicine An approach to health and healing that views each patient as a psychobiological unit in a particular physical and psychosocial environment. The term holistic conveys the sense that each individual has a reality that is more important than and independent of the sum of his or her parts. Similar views have been propounded in the past, especially by doctors who focus on psychosomatic medicine on the assumption that the mental and physical aspects of a patient are inextricably bound together. The holistic attitude also takes into account the role played by the person's environment, family history, interpersonal situation, occupational factors, exposure to potential carcinogens, and the like.

Practitioners of holistic medicine stress the importance of patient involvement in the healing process, pointing out that passivity on the part of the patient encourages the view that "medicine is magic." The form that this involvement takes includes self-help wherever possible, self-awareness in recognizing messages from one's feelings and one's body, and open-mindedness about the validity of types of therapy other than those that are part of conventional medical practice in the Western world.

homosexuality Sexual and emotional attraction to a member of one's own sex; called lesbianism among women. Extensive research on the subject of homosexuality still has not provided a concrete explanation as to its cause, but it is perhaps associated with hormonal balance or complex emotional factors related to a parent. Today, many people consider homosexuality to be as natural to some people as heterosexuality is to most people.

hormone Chemical product mainly of endocrine glands, but also of other organs such as the placenta, secreted directly into the bloodstream for transport to various organs for the regulation of life processes. Hormones normally control growth and sexual maturation and affect emotional response, digestion, metabolism, and other vital functions. Many hormones have been synthesized or extracted from other mammals. Their availability has made replacement treatment possible for certain types of hormone deficiencies. Doctors who specialize in this branch of medicine are called endocrinologists. *See also* ENDOCRINE SYSTEM.

hospital Hospitalization is necessary when specialized treatment or diagnostic procedures require equipment, personnel, or full-time services not available in a doctor's office or on an outpatient basis. In a medical emergency it is usually more practical to get to a hospital than to go to a local doctor. Emergencies may require oxygen, transfusions, intensive care, and on-the-spot laboratory tests as well as other lifesaving services.

If you have a choice among hospitals, a teaching hospital (one associated with a university medical school) is to be preferred. If there is none in your area, every effort should be made to choose an institution that is accredited by the Joint Commission on the Accreditation of Hospitals. This independent nongovernmental organization conducts regular inspections to see that hospitals conform to federal standards for cleanliness, fire protection, competence of nursing services, adequacy of equipment, and professional record-keeping. Also, unaccredited hospitals are ineligible for Medicare and Medicaid funds.

In hospitalization, as in all aspects of health care, every woman should take the time to know her rights. Various consumer-advocate publications of the rights of patients, including the Hospital Bill of Rights, are usually available at a local library.

hot flash The most commonly reported symptom of the menopause; a disturbance of temperature regulation connected with the decrease in the body's supply of estrogen.

hymen The membrane that partially closes the entry to the vagina; also known as the maidenhead. The hymen varies in size, shape, and toughness. The opening in the hymen allows for the discharge of menstrual flow. While it may remain intact until penetration during the first sexual intercourse, it is by no means unusual for it to be stretched or ruptured by athletic activities or by tampons before any intercourse. In cases where the membrane is so thick or tough that intercourse cannot be accomplished without severe pain or in rare cases in which it completely seals the vaginal opening, it can be cut under a local anesthetic in the gynecologist's office.

hyperglycemia Excess amounts of sugar in the blood. This condition is one of the chief signs of diabetes. Milder cases that develop after the age of 50 may be treated by one of the oral hyperglycemic drugs. *See also* DIABETES.

hypertension High blood pressure. Hypertension occurs more frequently among women, but it is more deadly to the male. Where hypertension exists, the smallest arteries (arterioles) constrict, causing the heart to have to pump harder in order to distribute blood throughout the body. Since the heart is a muscle, the harder it works, the bigger it gets. An enlarged heart in a hypertensive person is therefore a result, not a cause, of high blood pressure.

The causes of what is technically called organic hypertension are detectable, and if they are corrected, hypertension is reduced. Common causes are arteriosclerosis and atherosclerosis, glomerulonephritis, and hyperthyroidism. The more widespread and insidious type of high blood pressure, which typically affects people in their early thirties, is called essential hypertension and is of unknown origin. While the organic type is generally acquired, the essential type is presumed to be inherited. The genetic factor appears to explain why large numbers of infants and children are now known to have high blood pressure. Organic hypertension tends to progress unless treated, eventually attacking a vulnerable organ: the blood vessels of the brain (stroke), the kidneys (uremia), the coronary arteries (heart attack), the organs of vision (eye hemorrhage). Essential hypertension may have no noticeable symptoms, but the increasing blood pressure can gradually damage the heart, blood vessels, and kidneys.

When hypertension of either type is mild or borderline, it is usually treated without medication unless its cause can be treated. Recommendations include weight loss if necessary, low-salt low-sugar diet, stopping or restricted smoking, moderate alcohol intake (any more than two drinks on a regular basis will increase risks), and a contraceptive other than the pill. It is considered normal for blood pressure to rise somewhat during the menopause and with advancing age, probably due to increased stress, increased weight, hormonal changes, and increased atherosclerosis. There is no indication that estrogen replacement therapy helps hypertension as much as do weight reduction and lowered salt intake.

When the cause of the hypertension cannot be eliminated and treatment is necessary, several types of medication are available. The antihypertensive drugs can produce undesirable long-range side effects: depression, immobilizing headaches, chronic constipation, liver damage, parkinsonism, and diabetes. It is therefore essential that any woman embarking on drug therapy remain in close touch with a physician for the adjustment of doses and changes in type of medication when necessary. For some patients surgical correction of an atherosclerotic obstruction is the most effective treatment.

Any woman whose family history includes hypertension should have an annual blood pressure check. This can conveniently be done at the same time that she has the pap test. Prompt detection and proper treatment help avoid unnecessary complications.

hyperthyroidism Overactivity of the thyroid gland. Typical symptoms include restlessness and weight loss in spite of overeating. In some cases goiter is present. Diagnosis of the condition is based on blood tests and other clinical procedures. Treatment usually consists of medicine or radioactive iodine that reduces the gland's excess secretion of thyroxin and its size or, less frequently, surgery.

hyperventilation Loss of carbon dioxide from the blood caused by abnormally rapid or deep breathing. Hyperventilation produces symptoms of dizziness, muscle spasms, and chest pains and is one of the most common signs of an anxiety attack. Since the symptoms are an additional cause of anxiety, the condition may worsen to the point where it appears to be an emergency. Effective treatment consists of breathing into and out of a paper or plastic bag so that the exhaled carbon dioxide is reinhaled until the proper blood level is achieved, at which point the symptoms vanish.

hypnosis A trancelike state psychically induced by another person or by concentration on an object, during which the subject's consciousness is altered for purposes of responding to the suggestions of the hypnotist. The trance may be so shallow that the subject is scarcely aware of a change in mental state, or it may be so deep as to have all the appearances of sleep. Approximately one person in five may be successfully hypnotized, and practically no one can be a successful subject without prior consent and trust in the hypnotist. The mechanism by which the hypnotic state is achieved is not precisely understood, but the technique has accepted medical applications when used by trained and reputable practitioners. Freud's theory of the unconscious evolved from the successful use of hypnosis for the treatment of hysteria. Hypnosis is now used instead of or together with mild anesthesia to facilitate childbirth; it is being taught to pediatric dentists (hypnodontia); and it has been used with some success by psychiatrists to get patients to stop smoking or nail-biting.

hypochondria An obsessive preoccupation with the symptoms of illness and supposed ill health. Any suggestion that physical checkups indicate normal organic health is greeted with resentment and disbelief. It is a malady in itself, since it is usually an expression of psychic distress. Hypochondria can sometimes be relieved by psychotherapy.

hypoglycemia An abnormally low level of sugar in the blood; a clinical condition of sudden onset characteristic of pre-diabetes and other diseases. It also occurs in diabetics when they have too much insulin or too large a dose of a hypoglycemic agent. Untreated, it can lead to confusion, sleepiness, or in extreme cases unconsciousness. "Low blood sugar" is not a common condition, and no one should embark on a special diet before consulting a doctor and arranging for blood tests. The confusion about hypoglycemia is partially due to the fact that its symptoms–sweating, palpitations, trembling hands–are similar to those produced by an anxiety attack.

hypothalamus The master gland of endocrine activity located in the base of the brain directly above the pituitary gland.

hypothermia Abnormally low body temperature. Hypothermia may occur naturally as a consequence of prolonged exposure to extreme cold, especially when temperature regulation is affected by aging, disease such as pneumonia, or the ingestion of certain drugs and alcohol. The symptoms of hypothermia in such cases are slow breathing, weak pulse, and semiconsciousness. Body heat can be slowly restored by covering the patient. No other treatment should be administered without instructions from a doctor.

Hypothermia can also be artificially induced in order to reduce the tissues' oxygen needs and to slow down the circulation of the blood, thus making certain types of operations possible. Hypothermia allows the surgeon to reach parts of the body that might otherwise be inaccessible in the performance of delicate operations on the brain and heart.

hysterectomy Surgical removal of the uterus.

hysteria In the psychiatric sense, a condition of uncontrolled excitability, intense anxiety sometimes accompanied by sensory disturbances (such as hallucinations) and general disorientation. Conversion hysteria is the unconscious simulation of organic disability, such as blindness, deafness, loss of the faculty of speech or locomotion.

hysterotomy Surgical opening of the uterus, similar to a cesarean section. A hysterotomy is done to remove foreign bodies, such as IUDs; occasionally to remove a mole; and for abortion only when other methods are contraindicated because of the age of the fetus.

iatrogenic disease Any disorder or disease caused by a physician's medical treatment. Among the less serious examples of iatrogenic disturbances due to side effects of medication are rashes, cramps, dizziness, itching; among the more serious are birth defects (Thalidomide), cancer (DES), shock (penicillin), hemolytic anemia (chloramphenicol), liver damage (Thorazine). It has been estimated that approximately 300,000 people are hospitalized each year in the United States because of an adverse drug reaction. Iatrogenic conditions are therefore one of the ten leading causes of hospitalization in this country. Women can partially protect themselves by questioning the doctor about the possible side effects of any prescribed medication; by keeping records of any unusual responses (such as allergic reactions) to particular drugs so that drug can be avoided, if possible; and by avoiding the use of any antibiotic for a virus infection except under special conditions. In cases where a particular treatment carries with it a risk potentially equal to the condition being treated, the patient has a right to have this explained so that she can make a responsible choice.

ileitis Inflammation of the lower portion of the small intestine (ileum); also known as Crohn's disease. The typical victim of this disorder is a young adult with a low threshold for psychic stress. Ileitis seems to run in families, and some specialists believe that its underlying cause is an inherited antibody-antigen reaction. The symptoms are similar to those of colitis: diarrhea and abdominal pain. A strict regimen of combined medications and a high-protein diet may be prescribed. When the inflammation cannot be controlled by medication or when intestinal obstruction persists, surgical removal of the diseased part of the intestine may be the only alternative.

ileostomy A surgical procedure to create an artificial anus to bypass the colon by bringing the ileum (the lowest part of the small intestine) through an opening made in the abdominal wall. An ileostomy is performed when ulcerative colitis, cancer, or other disease requires the removal of the colon (large intestine). It may also be performed as a temporary measure so that an obstruction in the colon can be removed without removing the colon itself.

immunity and immunization Immunity is a biologic state of being resistant to or not susceptible to a disease or condition, usually, and here specifically, due to the presence of antibodies against the causative agent (antigen). The immunity may be congenital (acquired from the mother and present at birth but not long lasting), natural (resulting from an infectious disease which produces antibodies), or induced by immunization (inoculation).

It was proved that immunity could be induced by artificial means almost 200 years ago when Edward Jenner immunized (vaccinated) people against smallpox. Active immunization is a long-term resistance to an antigen induced by introducing a controlled amount of the antigen into the body in order to stimulate antibody formation. The antigens may be dead viruses (Salk polio vaccine), modified live viruses (Sabin polio vaccine and mumps vaccine), or chemically altered toxins produced by bacteria (tetanus toxoid). Active immunization against some diseases may require periodic boosters to maintain the immunity; against others the initial immunization may last a lifetime.

Passive immunization is achieved by introducing antibodies, rather than antigens, into the body. Antibodies are introduced by the injection of blood serum obtained from humans who have a natural immunity, have been actively immunized, or are convalescing from a particular disease. Serum from actively immunized animals also can be used. Immunity occurs immediately, but lasts only a few weeks at best.

Some vaccines (for example, BCG for tuberculosis) also sometimes are used in the treatment of certain malignant diseases such as melanomas.

impetigo A highly contagious skin disease caused by staphylococcus bacteria and characterized by blisters that rupture and form yellow crusts. The areas most frequently affected are the face, neck, and scalp and less frequently the arms and legs. Impetigo may be secondary to another skin condition that causes lesions, especially a fungus infection. The disease is spread from one person to another and from one part of the body to another through contact with the liquid discharged by the sores. Care should be exercised to prevent reinfection of the patient and infection of other members of the household through contamination of towels or bed linens. Household pets may also transmit the disease and if infected should receive treatment to curtail its spread. Antibiotic ointments are usually effective in treating impetigo.

impotence Inability of the male to achieve and maintain an erection (erectile impotence); also, inability to achieve orgasm following erection (ejaculating impotence). Almost all men experience impotence at some time in their lives. It may be occasional and temporary or it may be chronic. The cause in over 90 percent of cases is psychological, resulting from conflicts that may arise from guilt, unacknowledged homosexuality, anxiety, distrust of women, or self-punishment. It may also be related to physical causes of fatigue, general poor health, and organic conditions such as diabetes, hormonal aberration, or inherited disorders of the genitals. Alcoholism, drug addiction, and certain prescribed drugs and tranquilizers are other causes. When impotence exists, psychiatric counseling or a sex therapy clinic should be considered only after a complete medical checkup has been conducted.

incest Sexual intercourse between a male and female who are not permitted by their society to marry; the proscription may be based on consanguinity (close blood relationship) or affinity (relationship by marriage). Incest is a punishable offense (with varying legal definitions) in the United States.

indigestion Any disturbance in the digestive process that results in discomfort; also called dyspepsia. An acute attack of indigestion may be sufficiently severe and disabling to require treatment by a doctor. Alkalizers are often ineffective and potentially damaging, particularly if the condition is caused by emotional stress. In most cases of indigestion the cause is not organic and can be corrected without medication. Digestive complaints are often due to eating too much too quickly, failure to chew food properly, poorly prepared food, excessive drinking of iced or carbonated beverages including beer, eating while one is upset or angry, overuse of such medications as aspirin or tranquilizers, eating too much raw food, or changing to a new diet. When indigestion persists in spite of corrective measures, a gastrointestinal study known as a barium X ray or blood tests should be administered to determine the underlying cause.

induced labor Artificial stimulation of the birth process; often referred to as programmed labor or elective induction. Labor may be induced either by the injection of a synthetic hormone (oxytocin) that stimulates, speeds up, and intensifies uterine contractions or by a surgical procedure called amniotomy, the artificial rupture of the amniotic sac below the fetus. Except in the case of life-threatening emergencies, such as eclampsia or hemorrhage, no woman should agree to induced labor before weighing the advantages and disadvantages of such a procedure. Most doctors feel that induced labor for the purpose of a planned delivery does not warrant the potential risks involved.

infantile paralysis *See* POLIOMYELITIS.

infertility The inability to conceive or beget children.

influenza A contagious respiratory disease caused by a virus; generally known as the flu and previously called the grippe. All strains of the flu virus are airborne, and the infection is spread in the coughs, sneezes, and exhaled breath of the affected person. The disease may reach epidemic proportions rapidly, especially since natural or artificially acquired immunity against one particular strain of the virus provides no guaranteed protection against another strain.

Symptoms may range from mild to severe. Typical manifestations are inflammation of the membranes that line the respiratory tract causing a running nose, scratchy throat, and mucous congestion that causes coughing. Fever may not be present or temperature may go as high as 104°F. Aching joints, appetite loss, and general malaise characterize even the mildest cases. Even when symptoms clear up, usually within ten days, the flu patient may feel weak and tired for some time. The cough may be persistent, and relapses may occur as a result of lowered resistance and premature resumption of normal activities. Lowered resistance to bacterial infection is the most serious complication of the flu. When a healthy adult has the illness, the usual treatment is bed rest, aspirin, lots of fluids, and as much sleep as possible. A cough medicine containing an expectorant may be prescribed to facilitate the hawking up of the accumulated phlegm. For flu patients who may be vulnerable to complications, such as people over 65, diabetics, very young children, or anyone with a heart, lung, or kidney disorder, antibiotics may be prescribed.

Many doctors believe that people who are highly susceptible to serious complications should be vaccinated each year with a vaccine made from the killed viruses of the current strains responsible for the disease. Adverse responses to this form of immunization range from a slightly sore and swollen spot in the area of the vaccination, to a low fever and headache of several days' duration, to an uncomfortable response presumed to be allergic, to a 1 in 100,000 risk of severe reaction that affects the nervous system. Anyone contemplating a flu vaccination should ask the advice of his or her doctor.

inguinal glands A group of lymph nodes located in the groin. Any painful swelling or persistent soreness in this area should be brought to a doctor's attention.

inner ear *See* EAR.

insect stings and bites While usually no more than a nuisance, the bite of an insect can at times cause disease or life-threatening emergencies. The stinging insects–hornets, wasps, yellow jackets, and bees–do not transmit disease, but the venom they inject may cause a severe allergic response known as anaphylactic shock. Ordinarily, however, the sting results in no more than swelling, redness, and localized pain. In the case of a bee sting the skin should never be squeezed in order to extricate the stinger, since this only forces the venom farther into the tissues. Instead, the stinger should be removed with a pair of tweezers held flat against the skin. Any sign of a systemic response to a sting, such as body swelling or respiratory distress, indicates the need of immediate professional attention. Women who are extremely hypersensitive to the venom should be desensitized by an allergist and continue the maintenance treatments usually necessary four or five times a year. Even after desensitization emergency adrenalin should be carried when there is the threat of a sting.

Biting and bloodsucking flies and mosquitos can transmit serious diseases. The common housefly does not bite, but may be a carrier of infection. Aside from diseases endemic to the tropics, such as yellow fever and malaria, encephalitis can be transmitted by certain local mosquitos. Horseflies are also harmful since they can transmit rabbit fever (tularemia). Among dangerous parasites which are found in several parts of the world are fleas that transmit bubonic plague and typhus. It should be noted that the ticks that cause Rocky Mountain spotted fever are not indigenous to the West and may be found in other parts of the country. Immunization is available against all the above infections and should be taken into consideration by anyone planning a trip to an area of high-risk exposure. A parasite common in the rural South, known as the chigger, is the larval stage of the mite that causes scabies. While chiggers are not disease-bearing, their bite irritates the skin thereby leading the way toward a secondary infection. Once bitten, the victim can be relieved of the itching by the application of a paste of baking soda and water or calamine lotion.

While most spiders and other arachnids are harmless, there are three or four that inflict bites that must receive prompt attention: the scorpion found in the Southwest, the black widow spider (identifiable by its shiny black body whose underside is marked with a red hourglass shape), and a species of hairy tarantula found near the Mexican border. The aggressive fire ant is a more recent menace that is spreading its way through the Southern states. Its attack can be easily identified since it inflicts multiple stings around the original bite. The bite of a fire ant can cause severe systemic response in certain people. Anyone living in an area where fire ants exist should consider the advisability of desensitization.

Certain practical measures can reduce the hazards and discomforts of bites and stings without the use of insecticides that pollute the environment with dangerous chemicals. A few suggestions are the application of insect-repellent lotions containing such effective chemicals as diethyl-meta-toluamide, dimethyl phthalate, or butopyronoxyl on exposed parts of the body several times a day; wearing protective clothing during walks in the country; avoiding the use of perfumes, lotions, sprays, and jewelry since scents and colors attract stinging insects; burning insect-repellent candles or incense sticks at picnics when food is exposed; keeping foods covered; and using screens for indoor protection. Women who own or rent vacation houses in the country should heed the warnings of local health authorities as to insect-borne diseases and the precautions one can take to combat them.

insomnia Sleeplessness, either chronic or occasional. Judging from the many millions of sleeping pill prescriptions filled each year, the overuse of habit-forming barbiturates appears to be prevalent in the United States. Since it is generally believed that dependence on sleeping pills will only intensify insomnia, anyone trying to cope with the situation should try to find another solution for sleeplessness. It is perfectly normal to spend sleepless hours due to a worrisome problem, but when loss of sleep becomes a chronic condition, a person should try to deal with the underlying cause before resorting to sleeping pills. It is interesting to note that medical researchers who monitor sleep patterns have discovered that people who describe themselves as insomniacs actually sleep a good deal more than they think they do.

Sleeplessness may be caused by any one of many factors that are easily corrected, such as eating rich food or drinking beverages containing caffeine within two hours of bedtime, watching overly exciting television programs, sleeping in a poorly ventilated room or on an uncomfortable mattress. When snoring and other noises interfere with sleep, ear plugs can often relieve the problem. Daytime exercise, a hot bath in the evening, and a glass of warm milk before retiring require little effort, but are helpful. Scientists have found that an amino acid, L-triptophane, contained in certain foods, including milk, seems to act as a sedative. When insomnia is a result of depression or anxiety, the cause of the emotional distress should be explored before resorting to medication.

insulin A hormone secreted by the groups of cells in the pancreas called the islets of Langerhans. Insulin performs several vital functions and is especially critical in stabilizing the body's metabolism of sugars and starches. The isolation of insulin by Canadian scientists in 1921–22 inaugurated the successful treatment of diabetes.

insulin shock therapy The earliest and most widely used shock treatment for mentally ill patients unresponsive to other forms of therapy. Treatment consisted of producing a hypoglycemic coma by injecting insulin into the muscles. While electroshock has largely replaced insulin shock, both treatments generally have been superseded by tranquilizing and antidepressant drugs.

intelligence quotient (IQ) A number indicating an individual's relative intelligence. The figure is calculated by dividing mental age by chronological age and multiplying by 100. The mental age is determined by comparing the individual's score on standardized tests with statistical average scores at different chronological age levels. Many people question the accuracy of this form of testing since it is generally agreed that intelligence takes many forms that cannot be measured by a single test or represented by a single number and that many current test instruments measure culturally determined acquired knowledge rather than inborn intellectual or creative ability.

intercourse *See* SEXUAL INTERCOURSE.

interferon A cellular protein produced by white blood cells and fibroblasts which suppresses viral DNA reproduction. Until recently only small amounts of it could be produced in a laboratory for use in humans. Interferon may prove to be effective in treating certain viral diseases and perhaps some cancers.

internist *See* DOCTOR.

intestines The section of the alimentary canal from the stomach to the anus. The small intestine, which begins where the stomach ends, is approximately 20 feet of coiled tube. The large intestine, which is about 5½ feet long, consists of the cecum to which the appendix is attached, the colon, and the rectum.

iritis Inflammation of the iris, the ciliary body, or the choroid, the three structures that comprise the middle layer of the eyeball. The onset of iritis may be sudden, acute, and accompanied by intense pain, blurred vision, and extreme sensitivity to light. Iritis may also be chronic, with less dramatic, but persistent symptoms. In either case the eye reddens and the pupil contracts into an irregular shape. Unless the cause is obvious, as it is when there is an injury to the eye, it may be difficult to isolate. Iritis may be associated with diabetes, syphilis, abscessed teeth, or sudden systemic infections. It must be treated promptly by a doctor to prevent scarring of the eyeball tissues and irreversible damage to vision. The problem of recurring iritis can be solved only by discovering and dealing with the underlying cause.

iron One of the minerals that is an essential micronutrient.

A deficiency of iron in the diet is the direct cause of the most common type of anemia, iron-deficiency anemia. There is no such thing as a tendency to anemia; it is a clinical condition measurable by laboratory examination of a blood sample. An iron deficiency may occur temporarily if surgery or other conditions make a restricted diet necessary or during pregnancy when iron stored in the body is depleted by the demands of fetal development. To supply supplemental iron in such cases the preparation known as ferrous sulfate is considered therapeutically superior to tonics advertised for "tired blood"; it is also less expensive. Iron pills or tonics should never be taken unless prescribed by a doctor after a blood test, since excessive amounts may be damaging in the absence of anemia. Only where there is a need to obtain a rapid response or where oral preparations cause gastric upset is iron given by injection.

irritability Impatience, crankiness, oversensitivity to annoyances and frictions of daily life. No one is even-tempered all the time, but anyone who is irritable most of the time should try to find out why. Temporary crankiness may result from a variety of reasons such as a determined effort to stop a bad habit, apprehension connected with an illness, the effects of the contraceptive pill, an unbalanced diet, premenstrual tension, or overwork; such problems usually diminish with time. Assuming physical reasons for the emotional edginess have been ruled out, chronic irritability is usually due to a dissatisfaction with one's self. Since irritability can place a strain on relationships with friends and family, counseling is often advisable.

itching An irritation of the skin; technically called pruritis. Among the most common causes are insect bites, fungus infections, allergies, or contact dermatitis. Itching in the anal region may be caused by worms or hemorrhoids; in the vaginal area it may occur spontaneously or follow the use of certain antibiotics. Severe itching around the pubic hair may indicate the presence of crabs. Among other causes are an accumulation of dried body secretions under the arms, in the crotch, on the scalp, or between the toes; vaginal discharges; the drying out of the vaginal mucous membranes that occurs during menopause; exposure to cold temperatures; new skin growth following sunburn or scar healing; chafing by one body surface against another (e.g., under the breasts) or by tight clothing; emotional stress. A doctor may refer to local or generalized itching as neurodermatitis if no specific cause can be found. Certain serious disorders are accompanied by itching: diabetes, anemia, leukemia, jaundice, gout, liver malfunction, and cancer. Diseases in which an itching rash is a characteristic symptom include chickenpox, measles, and rubella.

The impulse to relieve itching by energetic scratching should be controlled since the irritation will only become more intense and the nails may cause breaks in the skin leading to secondary bacterial infection. Sometimes it is necessary to wear gloves. If topical medication provides no relief, medication taken orally or by injection may be necessary to relieve the itching until the underlying cause can be diagnosed and eliminated. The disorder that has the distinction of being called "the itch" is discussed under scabies.

jaundice A yellowish appearance of the skin and the whites of the eyes resulting from an excessive amount of bile in the blood. As a sign of a disorder of the liver or the biliary tract, jaundice may be accompanied by diarrhea, abdominal pain caused by liver enlargement, bitter-tasting greenish vomit, and itching in various parts of the body. Among the usual underlying causes, the most common is infectious hepatitis; others are gallstones, cirrhosis, hemolytic anemia, and tumors that obstruct the normal circulation of bile. The treatment of jaundice depends on the diagnosis of the condition.

joint diseases *See* ARTHRITIS, BURSITIS, etc.

kidneys and kidney disorders The kidneys are twin organs, each about 4 inches long, located on either side of the spinal column at the back wall of the abdomen approximately at waist level. As the lungs expand and contract during respiration, the kidneys move up and down. Examined in cross-section under a microscope, the functional units of the organ—the nephrons—are seen to consist of clusters of blood vessels, the glomeruli, which act as filters. The vital process in which the kidneys are indispensable is the continuous filtering of the blood to remove wastes and excess fluid while retaining or reabsorbing other materials. The kidneys also secrete hormones involved in the regulation of blood pressure and the red blood cell count. In order to understand how certain disorders originate, it is helpful to have some idea of how the kidneys work. As arterial blood enters the kidneys from the heart, it passes through the millions of nephrons. The waste materials go by way of the ureter into the bladder for eventual elimination through the urethra in the form of urine. The cleansed and filtered blood goes back into circulation through the veins, returning to the heart for recirculation. With a combined weight of only about ⅔ of a pound, the kidneys process more than 18 gallons of blood every hour and filter about 60 percent of all the fluid taken into the body, excreting as much as 2 quarts of urine each day.

The kidneys are subject to a number of disorders, some merely temporary, others potentially fatal. The most common problem is infection and the most common infection is pyelonephritis, an infection of the kidney's urine collecting ducts. It may occur with no significant symptoms, or it may be accompanied by back pain, fever, and chills. An acute attack of pyelonephritis occurs in about 1 in 500 pregnancies and usually requires antibiotic treatment to prevent recurrences. Kidney obstructions in the form of stones, cysts, or other abnormalities can lead to improper drainage, inflammation, and damage to surrounding tissues. The disease commonly called nephritis, but accurately known as glomerulonephritis, is an inflammation of the filtering vessels. Nephrosis, also known as the nephrotic syndrome, is a group of symptoms frequently accompanying some other condition. It is characterized by the leakage of large amounts of protein into the urine and leads to generalized swelling, especially a marked puffiness under the eyes. Kidney disease may also result from untreated hypertension, gout, and diabetes or as a consequence of chemical poisoning or prolonged shock. When any disorder reaches the point where the kidneys can no longer function, uremia (accumulation of urea nitrogen in the blood) occurs. Acute kidney failure may be helped by short-term dialysis. When irreversible damage to both kidneys has occurred, long-term dialysis or tissue transplant can prevent fatal consequences.

Any signs of kidney disease should be taken seriously, especially during pregnancy. Symptoms may include back pain below the rib cage; a change in the color or composition of urine or discomfort during urination; puffiness of any part of the body, especially the area around the eye. Treatment depends on the results of blood tests and X-rays and may only require changes in the diet and the use of diuretics. Antibiotics are often prescribed for bacterial infection. In the case of an obstruction, surgery may be necessary. *See also* GLOMERULONEPHRITIS.

knee disorders The knee is one of the largest and strongest joints in the body, formed by the junction of the tibia (shinbone), the femur (thighbone), and the patella (kneecap). The bones are bound by ligaments and tendons and cushioned by cartilage and fluid-filled sacs called bursas. "Housemaid's knee," so called because it usually results from frequent kneeling on hard surfaces, is a form of bursitis. "Water on the knee" is a condition in which there is an excessive accumulation of the lubricating fluid secreted by the membranous lining of the ligaments that bind the knee joints together. This oversecretion, which may follow an injury or infection or may accompany arthritis, causes the kneecap to be raised and the surrounding tissue to become painful. Keeping the knee raised and rested is usually sufficient treatment. Chronic inflammation of the joint may occur during arthritis and can be relieved by medication and other forms of therapy. Because of the exposure of the knee and the stresses to which it is subject, it is especially vulnerable to injury. Scrapes, minor bruises, or superficial cuts which do not damage anything except the skin around the knee are not usually a problem of any magnitude. A fall or athletic injury that results in soreness and swelling will benefit from the prompt application of ice to minimize internal bleeding and an elastic bandage for support against further strain. The application of heat on the day following the injury can hasten healing. If the pain and swelling increases, the knee should be examined and probably X-rayed.

labia The Latin word for "lips," used to designate the labia majora, the two folds of skin and fatty tissue that form the outer part of the vulva and that cover the labia minora, the two smaller lips or folds of mucous membrane that form the protective hood of the clitoris.

labor The rhythmic contractions of the muscles in the uterus which transport the baby through the birth canal and out of the mother's body; also called parturition.

lacrimal ducts Three sets of ducts involved in the flow of tears: 6 to 12 tiny openings that lead from the lacrimal (tear) gland at the upper, outside rim of the eye to the conjunctival sac; the lacrimal duct that leads from the inner corner of the eye to the lacrimal sac; and the nasolacrimal duct that leads from the lacrimal sac to the nose. When these ducts are overloaded by an abnormally heavy flow of tears, caused by strong feelings or by chemical or mechanical irritants, the excess liquid runs down the cheeks or through the nose. When the duct in the nose is blocked or swollen by allergy or inflammation during a respiratory infection, the eyes become watery. The dry, itchy eyes that may afflict the elderly result from a partial drying up of the lacrimal glands and a consequent decrease in the fluid that keeps the eye surface moist.

lactation The production of milk in the mother's breasts, beginning about three days following childbirth; also, the period of weeks or months during which the baby is breast-fed.

Lamaze method A system of preparation for childbirth named after its originator, Dr. Ferdinand Lamaze. The method consists in educating both parents-to-be about the birth process, teaching the pregnant woman breathing, relaxation, and concentration exercises, and training the father (or a close friend or relative) to act as a coach who will be present during labor and delivery. Increasing numbers of obstetricians are trained in the Lamaze method, and more and more hospitals are inviting the father to participate in his baby's birth.

laryngitis Inflammation of the mucous lining of the larynx, affecting both breathing and voice production. The condition may be chronic or acute, occurring because of a virus or bacterial infection, an allergic response, an irritation of the membrane by chemicals, dusts, or pollens, or recurrent misuse of the voice. The symptoms of milder cases usually include a dry cough, a tickling sensation in the throat, and hoarseness or a complete loss of voice, all of which result from swelling of the vocal cords. Fever may be present when laryngitis is produced by the flu or by a heavy chest cold. The most effective treatment is silence. The condition is also helped by a day or so of bed rest in a room where the temperature is warm and even and the humidity is high enough to prevent irritating dryness, if necessary through the use of a humidifier or a vaporizer. Spicy foods, hot soups, smoking, or any other irritants should be eliminated. Chronic laryngitis may be the result of long-time exposure to such irritants as alcohol, smoking, or industrial fumes. Since hoarseness may also accompany the development of tuberculosis or cancer, it should be investigated by a doctor if it persists for more than a few weeks.

larynx A cartilaginous structure which contains the vocal cords and is held together by ligaments and moved by attached muscles; also called the voice box. It is located in front of the throat and is lined with mucous membrane continuous with the pharynx and the trachea. The larynx is the source of sound that emanates in speech and is also part of the respiratory system, being the passageway for air between the pharynx and the lungs. The largest ring of laryngeal cartilage characteristically protrudes in the male throat as the Adam's apple. The epiglottis at the base of the tongue forms the lid that closes the larynx during swallowing, thus preventing food and drink from going down "the wrong way" and causing choking. Obstruction of the larynx may occur because of an abscess in the cartilage lining or because of an injury. Tumors are not uncommon and are removed surgically, even if benign. Singers and politicians, due to the professional use of their voices, are more likely to develop nodes on their vocal cords than other people. Such growths may also be eliminated by surgery. Cancer of the larynx, which is more common in men than women, is associated with heavy smoking. If examination with a laryngoscope and various laboratory tests including a biopsy verify the presence of an obstructive malignancy unresponsive to radiation treatment, a laryngectomy, the surgical removal of part or all of the larynx, is performed. The surgery itself is not complicated, but since it involves removal of the voice box, the patient must undergo postoperative rehabilitation in order to learn a new speech process.

laxative Preparation that encourages evacuation by loosening the contents of the bowel. A dependence on laxatives for the treatment of constipation is likely to worsen the condition since it deprives the colon of its natural muscle tone. Under no circumstances should a laxative be taken if there is cause to believe that the abdominal pain is due to an inflamed appendix. *See also* CATHARTIC, CONSTIPATION.

L-dopa The most effective medication for parkinsonism; also called levodopa. L-dopa is an amino acid extracted from certain beans. When taken orally in carefully supervised doses, it increases the brain's amount of dopamine, the natural substance essential for the normal transmission of nerve messages. The loss of this substance causes the tremors and rigidity characteristic of the disease. L-dopa compensates for this loss in approximately 75 percent of all cases.

Leboyer The French obstetrician, Dr. Frederic Leboyer, author of the book *Birth Without Violence* and proponent of a method of delivery that supposedly eases the birth trauma by creating a comforting environment from the instant the newborn baby emerges into the world.

lesbian Woman whose emotional and sexual needs are directed toward other members of her own sex.

leukemia A group of neoplastic diseases characterized by a proliferation in the bone marrow and lymphoid tissue of white blood cells whereby their excessive production interferes with the manufacturing of normal red cells. Different types of white cells are involved in the various forms taken by the disease. Acute lymphocytic leukemia, the most common form of childhood cancer and at one time almost always fatal, is now being controlled by a combination of radiation and chemotherapy. One type of acute granulocytic leukemia can occur at any age; the chronic leukemias (myeloid and lymphocytic among others) are unlikely to occur before middle age, with men contracting the disease more frequently than women. While there is no accepted theory about the cause of leukemia, it is assumed that its rising incidence results from increased exposure to radioactivity in its many manifestations: industrial pollution, food contamination, too many diagnostic X-rays over too short a period, or radiation therapy for some other disease. Whatever the age and circumstances of the victim, leukemic symptoms are generally the same: unexplained weight loss, low energy, fever, subcutaneous hemorrhaging, various signs of anemia, and lowered resistance to infection because of the destruction of normal cells. As the disease progresses, especially in its myeloid form, the spleen becomes visibly enlarged and in chronic lymphatic leukemia the lymph nodes swell and become sore. Diagnosis of all leukemias is based on microscopic examination of blood samples, bone marrow, or lymph tissue. Treatment consists of a combination of anticancer drugs, corticosteroids, radiation, antibiotics, and transfusions of hemoglobin and platelets. Several of the leukemias, which were formerly fatal, have gone into remission as a result of the effectiveness of the new drugs, the use of generalized radiation, and the transplanting of healthy bone marrow.

leukorrhea An abnormal vaginal discharge. When the discharge is heavy, when it contains pus and has an unpleasant odor, or when it causes itching or burning of the vagina or the vulva, a diagnosis of the underlying condition should be made. Among the circumstances leading to leukorrhea are: mechanical irritation by a diaphragm, tampon, or IUD; chemical irritation by excessive douching or the use of vaginal deodorant sprays; vaginal infection by bacteria or fungi, especially candidiasis or trichomoniasis; venereal disease, especially gonorrhea; benign growths such as polyps or fibroid tumors. Heavy discharge may also be a sign of diabetes or cervical cancer. In most cases it can be cleared up by finding the cause and initiating proper treatment.

libido The sexual drive; in psychoanalytic terms, a form of psychic energy that expresses erotic instincts and feelings in different ways at various stages of life.

Librium Brand name of one of the tranquilizing drugs (chlordiazepoxide) that induces a feeling of calm without causing sleepiness. Since it blunts the edge of anxiety and provides some relief from tension, it is one of the most widely prescribed medicines in the United States. Librium should never be taken in combination with alcohol and prolonged use can create a psychological dependence.

life expectancy The number of years a person of a given age may be expected to live, based on statistical averages. Current calculations for the life expectancy in the United States of white females at birth is placed between 75 and 76 years. This is 23 years longer than life expectancy for the same group born in 1900. However, there has been little change in the life expectancy of women over 60, that is, an adult woman of 65 in 1900 had a life expectancy of 13 more years and a woman of 65 today can expect to live 15 more years. This lack of improvement is balanced by the fact that more and more women live to be 60, thanks to progress in the prevention of death during childbirth, the control of infectious diseases, and improvements in public health. These advances also account in some measure for the fact that while the average length of life for women born in 1900 exceeded that of males by only two years, in our own time women live at least eight years longer than men on the average. Studies by the World Health Organization on this differential indicate that urban life lowers life expectancy for men and raises it for women. In underdeveloped countries, where women are often overworked, underfed, and frequently pregnant and where there is an age-old prejudice against female children typical of agrarian societies, the death rates for women are much higher than they are for men.

ligament Band of tough fibrous tissue that connects and stabilizes bones at the joints. An injury resulting in the stretching or tearing of ligaments is called a sprain.

lipoma A benign tumor composed of fat cells. This type of growth usually occurs close to the skin surface, and while it may reach the size of a golf ball, removal, if necessary or desired, is rarely complicated.

lithium carbonate A chemical compound of the element lithium, used in the treatment of manic-depressive illness; not to be confused with lithium chloride, another of the salts of lithium and no longer available for patients on low-sodium diets because of its dangerous side effects. Lithium carbonate is considered by specialists to be the first drug effective against a major psychosis. It is also being used increasingly for patients whose lives are disrupted by unaccountable mood swings originating in one of the depressive illnesses. Properly administered in supervised doses, it results in the emotional stabilization of many patients who have not responded well to treatments combining heavy sedation with tranquilizers, electroshock, and antidepressants.

liver The body's largest internal organ, dark red, wedge-shaped, weighing from 3 to 4 pounds, and located underneath the lower right side of the rib cage. Among its many vital functions are: the production of bile essential for fat digestion; the production and storage of glycogen for conversion to glucose; the synthesis of protein and the formation of urea; the storage of vitamins A, D, E, and K; the production of several blood components including the clotting factors; the neutralization of poisons such as carbon tetrachloride, arsenic, and others that may enter the body from without as well as of those created from within. Inflammation of the liver (hepatitis) may be caused by chemical poisons, by sensitivity to drugs such as Thorazine and Chloromycetin, and by disease agents, especially the viruses that cause the several types of hepatitis. If the infection is severe, the cells that are affected may be replaced by scar tissue, causing cirrhosis of the liver. A nourished liver that contains stored amounts of vitamins, proteins, and other nutrients is less likely to suffer irreversible harm from alcohol than a liver that is undernourished. The liver may also be adversely affected by disorders of the gallbladder, especially by gallstones. The signs and symptoms of liver disorder may include the following depending on the severity of the disease: a gradual swelling of the abdomen and sensitivity to pressure below the rib cage, clay colored stools, dark urine, and vomiting of blood. When disorders are treated promptly and a wholesome regimen is followed, recovery is usually complete.

liver spots Irregularly shaped reddish brown skin blemishes once mistakenly attributed to malfunctioning of the liver. The spots, which are concentrations of melanin pigment similar to but larger than freckles, are not due to aging as such, but rather to long exposure to sun and wind, to minor metabolic disturbances, and in some women to systemic changes that occur during pregnancy. The spots are generally harmless and can either be covered with a special cosmetic preparation or caused to fade by the use of an ointment that inhibits melanin production. If such a blemish suddenly thickens and hardens or if the surrounding tissue feels sore, a dermatologist should be consulted.

lobotomy A psychosurgical operation which severs the nerve fibers that connect the frontal lobe of the cerebrum to the rest of the brain, thereby producing a profound personality change that approaches a form of docility. Frontal lobotomies were once performed as a last resort in controlling violent patients or in handling psychoses unresponsive to any other treatment. Today lobotomies have been almost universally replaced by drug therapy in the form of tranquilizers and antidepressants.

longevity *See* LIFE EXPECTANCY.

low blood sugar *See* HYPOGLYCEMIA.

lower back pain *See* BACKACHE.

LSD Lysergic acid diethylamide, a hallucinogenic drug.

lung One of two spongelike structures, each enclosed in a pleural sac, which together with the bronchial tree, make up the lower respiratory system. Each lung is divided into lobes—three in the right lung and two in the left. Each lobe is divided into segments that have their own segmental bronchi and their own blood supply. The lungs are the organs in which the respiratory exchange of gases takes place. Under normal circumstances a signal reaches the brain approximately 16 to 20 times a minute indicating the need for an adjustment of the oxygen–carbon monoxide balance within the body. At this signal the diaphragm is thrust downward, increasing the chest capacity, making negative pressure and causing air to rush in to fill the pressure void, leading to the expansion of the lungs. This oxygen-laden atmospheric air travels through the airway passages until it reaches the alveoli. It is through the delicate membranes of the alveoli that the carbon dioxide in the blood of the pulmonary capillaries is exchanged for oxygen. The freshened blood then recirculates; a signal from the brain causes the diaphragm to relax, the negative pressure is reduced, the carbon dioxide is exhaled and the lungs compress.

While some lung disorders can be diagnosed accurately by listening to the breathing sounds through a stethoscope or by sounding the chest wall by tapping one finger against it and hearing the effects of the percussion, the state of the lungs can best be assessed by more refined techniques. Ordinary X-rays and those taken after radiopaque materials have been instilled in the bronchial tree can disclose many different types of lung tissue damage. With the use of a bronchoscope, foreign bodies, parts of tumors, or even an entire growth can be localized and removed. Other laboratory procedures for defining lung disorders involve sputum examinations that can identify a bacterial invader, fungus, or dust that may be causing progressive lung damage and examination of pleural fluid. Collapse of a lung (pneumothorax) may be partial, as may occur because of bronchial obstruction by a blood clot, tumor, or plug of mucus, or it may be complete, affecting a lobe or an entire lung damaged by a bullet wound, tuberculosis, or cancer. Spontaneous pneumothorax is a comparatively rare condition that occurs when there is a sudden air leak from the lung into the chest cavity without apparent cause. This spontaneous collapse is accompanied by the onset of chest pain and breathlessness. When the air that has collected in the space between the thorax and the lung is removed by suction, the affected lung expands to its normal capacity. The disorder is rarely serious, but when recurrences are a problem, surgical correction is recommended.

lupus erythematosus An inflammatory disease that may involve various parts of the body and cause permanent tissue damage. Typical victims are women of childbearing age. In its milder discoid form it affects the skin only, producing a butterfly-shaped rash that spreads across the nose to both sides of the face. The rash may be accompanied by fever and weight loss, as well as by arthritic pains in the joints. In its more serious form systemic lupus erythematosus involves the kidneys and the blood vessels. The cause is unknown and the disease may flare up unexpectedly, leaving the patient exhausted and weak. Recent research indicates that the disorder may occur or worsen when a latent virus is activated by overexposure to sunlight, emotional stress, or an unrelated infection. The symptoms have been explained as an aberration in the body's autoimmune system during which disease-fighting cells go awry and devour healthy tissue.

Lupus is a condition requiring long-term supervision. Special medications that control the disorder, especially heavy therapeutic doses of anti-inflammatory drugs, corticosteroids, and other drugs, may produce adverse side effects. The prescribed regimen must be carefully followed and readjusted from time to time depending on individual reactions. Patients with this disease should use a contraceptive other than the pill; if they do become pregnant, special management is needed. In all cases including the mildest, exposure to extreme sunlight should be avoided.

lymph nodes Glandlike organs located throughout the body that manufacture the disease-fighting cells known as lymphocytes. These cells are collected in the lymphatic vessels and delivered to the circulatory system in the fluid called lymph. Lymph is part of the blood's plasma. Among the most important lymph nodes and the ones that are superficially located are those found behind the ears, at the angle of the jaw in the neck, in the armpit, and in the groin. When reference is made to "swollen glands," it is the nodes that are involved, since in addition to their providing the system with protective lymphocytes, they also filter foreign bodies and bacteria out of the lymphatic fluid. Other masses of lymphatic tissue that produce specialized white cells for counteracting infection are the tonsils, thymus gland, and spleen. The general term for inflammation of lymphatic tissue, of which tonsillitis is an example, is lymphadenitis; a tumor of this tissue is a lymphoma, and a malignancy of the lymph nodes is a lymphosarcoma.

lymphogranuloma venereum A sexually transmissible disease caused by a viruslike organism.

macrobiotic diet A food regimen, supposedly derived from Zen Buddhism. The basis of the diet is brown rice and tea. The macrobiotic diet may cause a number of serious deficiency diseases and is not recommended.

malaria An infectious disease caused by several species of protozoa (parasites) which are transmitted by a mosquito which has bitten a diseased person, become infected, and then bitten another person. Occasionally it is transmitted by a blood transfusion. The natural disease occurs almost only in underdeveloped tropical areas where mosquitos are prevalent and people are readily exposed to them. It destroys red blood cells and causes bouts of severe chills, fever, and sweating daily, on alternate days, or at two day intervals, depending on the particular parasite involved. Medications are available to prevent it and to treat it, but the most important approach is to eliminate the mosquito population in tropical areas. Malaria is probably the most prevalent disease in the world and certainly is the most serious parasitic disease.

malignant A term used to describe a tumor or growth which spreads to surrounding tissues or migrates through the lymphatics or bloodstream to more distant tissues and whose natural course is usually fatal.

malnutrition Inadequate nourishment resulting from a substandard diet or a metabolic defect. Among common causes unrelated to the availability of adequate food are alcoholism, unnecessary vitamins substituted for essential foods, and crash dieting. Symptoms of malnutrition depend on the missing nutrients. In rare cases where a metabolic aberration, such as abnormal enzyme production or glandular malfunction, is the underlying cause, replacement therapy is usually effective. *See* DEFICIENCY DISEASES, ANEMIA, etc.

mammography Specialized X-ray examination of the breasts to detect abnormal growths, especially cancer, at an early stage.

manic-depressive illness A mental disturbance characterized by periods of overenergized and overconfident elation followed by profound depression; also known as bipolar depression. Attacks may be severe and cyclic, with varying periods of normalcy occurring between onsets of the illness. Lithium carbonate administered at the beginning of the manic phase has a stabilizing effect on many people suffering from this disorder.

marijuana A mild hallucinogenic drug derived from the hemp plant (*Cannabis sativa*).

marriage counseling A technique in which a qualified psychologist or other specialist trained in the complexities of human relationships helps a husband and wife to understand and resolve the problems that threaten the continuance of their marriage. A family doctor, clergyman, psychiatrist, or social service agency can usually provide referrals to counselors with proper professional standing.

massage Kneading, rubbing, pressing, stroking various parts of the body with the hands or with special instruments for the purpose of stimulating circulation, relaxing muscles, relieving pain, reducing tension, and improving general well-being. Massage does not cause weight loss. It is one of the most ancient forms of therapy and plays an indispensable role in the rehabilitation program for victims of stroke, disabling arthritis, and other conditions in which muscle health has been impaired by disuse. In such cases a trained physical therapist works under the supervision of a doctor. While massage is most commonly done with the hands, electric vibrators and whirlpool baths (hydrotherapy) may be recommended for certain purposes. Family members can learn how to be helpful in relieving a tension headache or an aching shoulder by kneading the affected area rhythmically. An alcohol rubdown or massage can provide comfort following prolonged athletic exertion. Women who wish a body massage should locate a licensed masseuse through their doctor or a nurse.

mastectomy The surgical removal of breast tissue.

mastitis Inflammation of the breast. Mastitis may be mild or severe, chronic or acute, and is usually the result of infection or of a hormonal change. One of the most common types of mastitis is called fibroadenosis. It is often referred to as having a "lumpy" breast due to the way the tissue feels when touched. The disorder may also produce cysts which tend to enlarge before the onset of menstruation. Any accompanying soreness usually can be relieved by wearing a properly fitted brassiere for support. Since the lumps produced by fibroadenosis are hard to distinguish from tumors during self-examination of the breasts, routine checkups by a physician knowledgeable in diseases of the breast is important. Acute mastitis may occur after delivery and during nursing when it is called puerperal mastitis. This is usually caused by bacterial infection introduced by way of the cracked skin of the nipples. Antibiotics normally cure this condition. If nursing is not to be continued, the breast must be emptied manually and lactation reduced by other medication. In rare instances chronic mastitis may follow an acute inflammation, and in still rarer cases the condition is caused by tuberculosis.

mastoid Relating to the cells in the temporal bone that forms the part of the skull situated directly behind the ear. Inflammation of these cells, known as mastoiditis, usually results from an untreated infection of the middle ear. It may also occur as a consequence of a severe respiratory infection or of a disease such as measles or scarlet fever. Before antibiotic therapy mastoiditis was one of the most serious diseases of childhood because infection could spread quickly from the mastoid bone to the brain. It generally was treated by surgery. An ear infection can usually be halted before it reaches the mastoid area by administering an antibiotic.

masturbation Manipulation of the genitals exclusive of intercourse for the achievement of sexual gratification. Children masturbate as a means of exploring their bodies and sexual responses. Neither physical nor psychological harm results from masturbation, although guilt and anxiety are sometimes associated with the act. Mutual masturbation is commonly practiced as a form of foreplay preceding sexual intercourse.

measles A childhood disease, also called rubeola, against which there is an effective immunizing vaccine. It should not be confused with German measles, called rubella, and discussed under that heading.

Medic Alert A three-part system for emergency medical protection consisting of a metal emblem worn on the wrist or around the neck which identifies otherwise hidden medical problems, a wallet card with additional information, and an emergency toll-free telephone answering service to provide still further information. Lifetime membership is provided for $15 by the Medic Alert Foundation International (a voluntary, nonprofit organization), Turlock, Calif. 95380.

medical records Personal data; information compiled during visits to the doctor, dentist, hospital, and clinics. Immunization shots, known allergies, X-ray and electrocardiogram reports, blood test results, and other pertinent information should be recorded by the doctor and filed away for future reference. Women should keep their own personal records for use in the event of a change in doctors.

meditation A discipline of concentration or contemplation practiced in the East by yogis and Zen Buddhists and becoming increasingly popular in the United States as a means of relaxation. The system with the largest following in this country is known as transcendental meditation (TM). As taught by practitioners trained by Maharishi Mahesh Yogi, the developer of the system, the technique consists in devoting two periods a day of about 20 minutes each to practice. Sitting in a comfortable position with eyes closed, the individual allows a particular sound, thought, or some other individually selected concept to enter the mind in such a way that it is "freely experienced" causing thought to rise "to a more creative level in an easy and natural manner." This description of the process by an experienced practitioner is affirmed by the hundreds of thousands of women and men who are finding it a helpful method of dealing with daily stress.

Meditation as practiced by Oriental experts has long been known to produce physiological effects involving control of breath, pulse, and other body processes. It now appears that even among newcomers to the technique, brain waves are modified during meditation. Subjects monitored by an electroencephalograph demonstrate a sustained production of alpha waves, the brain waves that occur during the relaxed state. According to an extensive study of meditating subjects, the technique induces what is technically called a wakeful hypometabolic state (slowed-down metabolism). This state, not to be confused with sleep or hypnosis, may have applications in those medical circumstances where the patient would benefit from self-induced relaxation without the use of drugs.

melanin The pigment that determines the color of a person's skin, hair, and eyes. Melanin is produced by specialized cells called melanocytes whose number is the same in all races. Color differences are caused by the quantity of melanin produced and how it is distributed.

melanoma A tumor composed of cells heavily pigmented with melanin. A malignant melanoma, also known as black cancer, is the most treacherous and the rarest type of skin cancer since the diseased cells invade other parts of the body through the circulatory system. Melanomas rarely develop before middle age, typically in women rather than men. Any changes in the size or appearance of a mole or any bleeding or itching in the tissues that surround it should be diagnosed by a doctor immediately.

menarche The first menstrual period.

Menière's disease A disturbance of the labyrinth of the inner ear resulting in vertigo, nausea, hearing loss, and tinnitus (ringing in the ears). The basic cause is not known. The symptoms may recur frequently or as seldom as every three months. An attack may be mild and last for only a few minutes, or it may be severe, with disabling vomiting and dizziness lasting for several hours. Menière's disease, which characteristically affects one ear, is more common among men than among women, especially after the age of 40. Since the immediate cause of the symptoms is a distention of the endolymphatic system of the inner ear, and since there are many causes for this, treatment is varied and includes the use of diuretics, antihistamines, drugs that dilate the blood vessels and speed up the circulatory flow, dietary changes that reduce cholesterol blood levels, lithium carbonate, and various tranquilizers. When all else fails and the condition seriously interferes with normal functioning, an operation on the labyrinth of the inner ear may be the only way to provide relief. Since this operation may result in a degree of permanent hearing loss, all other combinations of treatment are usually tried first.

meningitis Inflammation of the meninges, the membranes that surround the brain and spinal cord; also known as cerebrospinal meningitis. The inflammation may be caused by a virus or bacteria. Children are more susceptible than adults, but both sexes and all ages are vulnerable; epidemics are more likely to occur in temperate than in tropical climates. The most common, the most acute, and the most contagious form of the disease is meningococcal meningitis. It is caused by meningococci bacteria transmitted by contact with an infected person or in the expelled breath of a person carrying the bacteria. Viral meningitis, also called aseptic, may accompany other virus infections, especially mumps, measles, herpes simplex, and the milder forms of polio. Whatever the source of the inflammation, the symptoms are the same: severe and persistent headaches accompanied by vomiting; where the swelling of the meninges causes critical pressure on the brain, delirium and convulsions may also occur. It is characteristic for the patient to hold the neck stiff, since movements of the head intensify the already acute pain. Any signs that indicate the onset of meningitis should be checked immediately by a doctor who can make a definitive diagnosis following laboratory examination of a sample of cerebrospinal fluid. Prompt treatment with antibiotics and other suitable medications usually brings about an early recovery in bacterial meningitis. In the case of tubercular meningitis a longer course of therapy is necessary using the newer anti-tubercular drugs. The outcome of viral meningitis is varied.

menopause The span of time during which the menstrual cycle gradually wanes and finally ceases; also called the female climacteric or change of life.

menorrhagia The excessive loss of blood during menstruation. Among the causes are local or general infection, benign or malignant tumors of the uterus, hormonal imbalance, emotional stress, and hematologic disease. The condition may be said to exist when the amount of blood is excessive compared to usual periods. A thorough gynecological examination should be scheduled so that any abnormalities may be ruled out or treated. If menorrhagia goes untreated for several months, it is likely to be the direct cause of anemia.

menstruation The periodic discharge through the vagina of blood and sloughed off tissue from the uterus; the discharged matter is technically known as the menses.

mental illness Any of a group of psychobiological disturbances, generally categorized as psychoses (as distinct from neuroses) and characterized by such symptoms as severe and pervasive mood alterations, disorganization of thought, withdrawal from social interaction into fantasy, personality deterioration, hallucinations and delusions, bizarre behavior often without a loss of intellectual competence. While there is disagreement about the basic causes and mechanisms of severe mental disorders, one of the greatest advances in treating them has been the use of drugs that make seriously disturbed patients more accessible to other forms of therapy. In evolving current chemotherapy, basic research in the biochemistry of the brain has yielded important evidence to support the theory that psychotic disorders have a physiological foundation in errors of brain metabolism. There is also accumulating evidence that some mental illnesses, especially the syndrome known as schizophrenia, has a genetic basis. *See* DEPRESSION, MANIC-DEPRESSIVE ILLNESS, PSYCHOSIS, SCHIZOPHRENIA, SENILITY, etc.

mercury A silver-white metallic element that remains fluid at ordinary temperatures; also called quicksilver. It is used as the medium of measurement in fever thermometers because of its response to heat and in sphygmomanometers, the instruments that measure blood pressure, because of its weight. Mercury was once the only treatment for syphilis, and until its dangerous side effects became obvious, it was widely used in combination with other drugs as a cathartic, a diuretic, and a pesticide. It is still one of the ingredients in certain contraceptive jellies and creams and may be the source of vaginal irritation.

The dumping of industrial wastes containing mercury has irreversibly polluted many bodies of water in the United States and has so contaminated the fish in them that they are dangerous to eat. Poisoning caused by eating meat that came from animals whose feed was contaminated by pesticides containing mercury became such a health hazard that in 1976 the Environmental Protection Agency outlawed this particular use. Mercury poisoning continues to be a potential danger to anyone exposed to industrial fumes containing the chemical.

metabolism The combined processes involved in the production and maintenance of the substances essential for carrying on the activities of life. Metabolism occurs within each cell where groups of enzymes catalyze and control the chemical reactions that must occur during the normal absorption of oxygen and nutrients. The metabolic activity depends on the performance of specific functional tasks by specialized enzymes. Many diseases, previously mysterious, are now known to be caused by genetically determined enzymatic aberrations in the metabolic process. Metabolism is also adversely affected by diabetes and disorders of the thyroid gland.

metastasis The spreading of a cancerous growth by extension to surrounding tissue (direct metastasis) or by the breaking away of clumps of diseased cells which invade other parts of the body (blood borne or lymphatic metastasis) where they settle and form secondary tumors. The invasive tumors are called metastatic growths.

methadone A synthetic narcotic used as a substitute for morphine and in the United States as a substitute for heroin in supervised centers for the treatment of heroin addiction. Methadone, which is also addictive, but in a less debilitating way than heroin, is theoretically the bridge to the achievement of a drug-free condition. The purpose of the therapy is to diminish the doses of methadone until there is no longer a need for the drug. The brand name of methadone is Dolophine which accounts for its being known as "Dolly."

Methedrine Brand name of methamphetamine hydrochloride.

middle ear *See* EAR.

midwife *See* NURSE-MIDWIFE.

migraine *See* HEADACHE.

milk An essential food containing a good balance of fats, carbohydrates, and proteins, as well as a major source of essential minerals and vitamins A and B_2. Since pasteurization destroys the vitamin C content, other sources for this nutrient, such as citrus fruits and juices, are recommended. Practically all processed milk is enriched with vitamin D and is homogenized for uniform fat distribution. An adult woman should include the equivalent of two cups of milk in her daily diet (this amount may take the form of yogurt or cottage cheese). It is inadvisable for any person to drink raw unpasteurized milk since it may cause undulant fever (brucellosis). When taking antibiotic medication containing tetracycline, milk should not be ingested at the same time since the calcium in the milk interferes with the proper absorption of the medicine.

Miltown Brand name of meprobamate, one of the most widely prescribed tranquilizing chemicals. Another brand name for the same chemical is Equanil. Both these drugs suppress anxiety without causing drowsiness.

miscarriage *See* ABORTION, SPONTANEOUS.

mole A raised pigmented spot on the upper layers of the skin, usually brown and sometimes hairy. Moles may also have a blue appearance when buried more deeply, although the pigmentation is still brown. Yellowish rough-textured bumps produced by an abnormally active oil-secreting gland are called sebaceous moles. Any of these may be present from birth or they may appear early and disappear spontaneously. When such a blemish suddenly begins to itch, to grow, or especially to bleed, it should be examined by a dermatologist. While almost all moles are harmless, a few are malignant and should be removed promptly. The technical name for such skin tumors is melanoma.

moniliasis Infection caused by a yeastlike fungus, *Candida albicans;* also known as monilia, candidiasis.

mononucleosis, infectious A virus infection that causes an abnormality of and increase in the number of white blood cells containing a single nucleus; also called glandular fever. The symptoms are somewhat similar to those of the flu: fever, very sore throat, general malaise, and swollen lymph nodes. The infection is diagnosed by simple blood tests. Since the infectious agent, known as the EB virus (Epstein-Barr), is present in the throat and saliva, it is transmitted by mouth-to-mouth contact, explaining why younger people call mononucleosis the "kissing disease." The swelling of the lymph nodes is caused by the fact that the virus stimulates the number and size of the white blood cells known as lymphocytes which then become ineffective in carrying out their disease-fighting function. While the patient may suffer from extreme fatigue and complications such as a jaundiced liver, enlargement of the spleen, or a secondary infection of the throat, hospitalization generally is not necessary. The chief dangers of mononucleosis are possible rupture of the spleen and involvement of the brain.

The treatment is usually no more than bed rest, but it is important that a doctor be in charge of the patient so that any appropriate therapy can be introduced and progress monitored in general. Limited activity is advised until all symptoms disappear. Sometimes cortisone medication is used. Other medications are prescribed for secondary conditions. Since anyone who has had mononucleosis develops EB virus antibodies, it is presumed that one attack confers lifetime immunity.

mons veneris The mount of Venus; the triangular pad of fatty tissue and skin that covers the pubic bone; also known as the mons pubis or pubic mount. It is covered with hair from puberty onward.

morning sickness A feeling of queasiness and nausea often experienced upon arising during the first few months of pregnancy. Vomiting may or may not occur. The cause is assumed to be the increase in estrogen supply to which the body adjusts in time. While more than half of pregnant women suffer from morning sickness, it rarely continues beyond the twelfth week. Starting the day with an unsalted biscuit or dry toast, eliminating fried and highly seasoned food, and having smaller meals at frequent intervals will usually minimize the discomfort.

morphine The active constituent in opium and the basis of the pain-killing effects of all opiates, of which codeine (methyl morphine) is the weakest. The application of morphine in current practice is largely restricted to terminal patients and severe accident cases, but the use in these cases may eventually be superseded by other drugs.

motion sickness Nausea and vomiting resulting from a disturbance in the balancing mechanism of the inner ear. The discomfort may occur in a car, train, airplane, or elevator, but it is most common on a ship that is simultaneously pitching and rolling. Anyone who has ever been seasick is familiar with the symptoms of dizziness, headache, pallor, and cold sweating followed by vomiting. There are various antinauseant medications that can be taken in advance of a trip. A doctor can advise on which medicine might be most suitable for the particular circumstance and what the possible side effects might be. Antihistamines combined with sedatives can be helpful when taken at the first sign of discomfort. The effects of airsickness can be minimized by closing the eyes and lying almost prone in one's seat. Car sickness is rarely experienced by the driver and is less likely to occur to a passenger sitting in the front seat with the window open.

mucous membrane Thin layers of tissue that line a body cavity, separate adjacent cavities, or envelop an organ and contain glands that secrete mucus. The membrane is actually a mixture of epithelial tissue and its underlying connective tissue. The mucus, a watery exudate or slimy secretion, keeps the tissue moist. The discharge of mucus which may occur during infections of the nose, throat, and other parts of the body helps to rid the inflamed area of some of the infectious materials. Sexually transmissible diseases are spread through direct contact with infected mucous membrane.

multiple sclerosis A chronic degenerative disease of the central nervous system and the brain. The cause is not known, although evidence indicates that a factor such as an allergy or a virus triggers an autoimmune response in which the body's defense system turns against its own tissues. There is a progressive destruction of the fatty material known as myelin that sheathes the nerves. The designation "multiple" is used because, while the disease attacks mainly the nerves of the spinal cord and the brain, there is no special order or pattern to the destruction. In some people the first symptom may be eye dysfunction, in others a coronary disorder or a locomotion problem. When the nerve endings of the brain are attacked, symptoms include speech changes and emotional swings.

Multiple sclerosis is prevalent mainly in temperate climates; an estimated 1 in 5,000 persons living in northern United States and 1 in 20,000 living in southern United States are affected by it. The disease commonly appears between the ages of 20 and 40, with women twice as susceptible as men. Because the symptoms are easily confused with other disorders, multiple sclerosis is often very difficult to diagnose. Research has therefore been directed not only toward finding the specific cause, but to developing an accurate blood test that would unequivocally identify the disease and rule out all other possibilities. Treatment must be adjusted to individual cases and continually supervised, since one of the characteristics of multiple sclerosis is that it may subside for months or even years and then flare up suddenly with serious effects. Relief is usually provided by anti-inflammatory medication, corticosteroids, antispasmodics, and muscle relaxant drugs. Physical therapy, bed rest, and special diets are other forms of treatment.

mumps A contagious disease generally occurring in childhood. It is caused by a virus which affects the salivary glands, primarily the parotids (in front of and under each ear) and often the submaxillary (at the lower jaw) and the sublingual (under the tongue) glands. It may also affect the gonads. In a typical case the glands swell and become painful; in many instances, however, symptoms are so mild as to go undetected. Mumps is a serious matter only when secondary complications develop. These are primarily meningoencephalitis in children, a viral infection of the nervous system, and mumps orchitis in postpubescent males, an inflammation of the testicles that is rarely serious and rarely results in sterility. The involvement of the ovaries in adult women who contract mumps is extremely rare. However, when a pregnant woman with no acquired immunity is exposed to this infection and contracts the disease, there is a possibility of miscarriage, premature labor, or congenital defects. The doctor in charge of prenatal care should be informed at once so that proper precautionary measures can be taken. Long-term immunization of children, especially prepubescent boys, is now considered standard procedure.

muscles Bundles of fibers that have the ability to contract.

Common disorders are muscle fatigue, which results when fibers exhaust their supply of glycogen and other productive substances; spasms and cramps, which occur when a muscle is deprived of sufficient oxygen because of some failure in circulation; strains caused by overstretching; twitching or tic resulting from fatigue or tension. Muscles may also be impaired or immobilized by one or another type of muscular dystrophy and by diseases such as poliomyelitis, multiple sclerosis, or cerebral palsy.

muscular dystrophy Any of a group of chronic inherited diseases characterized by the progressive deterioration of the muscles. The particular designation of the dystrophy is based on the muscle groups first affected, the age of the patient at the onset of symptoms, and the rate at which the degeneration proceeds. While a dystrophic disease may affect anyone at any time, it occurs five times more often among males than females. No form of the disorder is contagious, and while no cure has yet been found, various types of treatment, including special orthopedic devices, can relieve the debilitating symptoms.

The most common and most crippling of the dystrophic diseases is Duchenne muscular dystrophy. It is named for the French neurologist who categorized it in 1861 as a disease characterized by the apparent enlargement (pseudohypertrophy) of the various muscles, beginning with those in the calf of the leg. The enlargement is caused by the abnormal increase in the fatty and connective tissues that replace the wasting muscles. Of all the dystrophies, the Duchenne is the only one known to be transmitted entirely by female carriers, the sons with a 50 percent likelihood of being affected by the disease and the daughters a 50 percent chance of becoming carriers. Fortunately for women who are aware of the presence of the disease in their family, there is a blood test for the detection of carriers of Duchenne MD. The test is available free of charge at any of the Muscular Dystrophy Association, Inc. clinics. If such a facility is not listed in the local telephone directory, referral information may be requested by mail from the national office, located at 810 Seventh Avenue, New York, New York 10019.

myasthenia gravis A comparatively rare neuromuscular disease characterized by abnormal weakness and fatigue following normal exertion. Depending on the muscles affected, symptoms include drooping eyelids, double vision, difficulty in locomotion, incapacity in chewing and swallowing, and, in the most threatening cases, inability of the muscles controlling respiration to function. Myasthenia gravis may occur spontaneously in anyone at any time (there are approximately 11,000 cases in the United States). The disease may be triggered by an infection, pregnancy, or a tumor of the thymus gland or it may be due to an inherited fault in the body's autoimmune system. Whatever the basic reason for the disturbance, the immediate cause appears to be an aberration in the neuromuscular production of the chemical acetylcholine, essential for stimulating the muscle fibers to contract. Successful treatment for some patients has consisted of medicines that help transmit nerve impulses to the muscles; others have been helped by surgical removal of the thymus gland (thymectomy); and most recently still others have been treated with an effective procedure called plasmapheresis. This involves the pumping out of the patient's blood so that it can be cleansed of destructive antibodies (such as would exist in cases of faulty immunologic response). While this procedure is expensive, a course of about six treatments on an outpatient basis seems to return many myasthenia gravis patients to normalcy for long periods of time without the further use of medication.

mycoses *See* FUNGUS INFECTIONS.

Mycostatin Brand name of the fungicidal chemical mystatin; frequently prescribed in vaginal tablet form for candida vaginal infections.

myocardial infarction A type of heart attack in which a portion of the heart muscle dies because its blood supply has been cut off by an obstruction in a coronary artery.

myomectomy Surgical removal of a fibromyoma, a usually benign tumor consisting of muscle fibers.

myopia *See* NEARSIGHTEDNESS.

nail Extension of the outermost skin layer of the fingers and toes. Nails are formed from the fibrous protein substance called keratin that also forms the hair that grows outward from the scalp. This elastic horny tissue (actually made up of dead cells) is pushed upward from the softer living matrix of the nail below the cuticle. It takes about six months for a nail to be replaced from the base of the cuticle to the tip of the finger. The general well-being of nails is best maintained by good hygiene and diet.

Healthy nails should be pale pink, smooth, and shiny. Variations in their appearance may be indications not only of local disorders, but of serious diseases. When nails are bluish and the fingertips clubbed, they are a sign of a circulatory or respiratory disorder; spoon-shaped nails are a sign of anemia; split or deformed nails may occur when there is arthritic inflammation of the finger joints; bitten nails indicate a response to emotional stress or simply a habit. White spots on the nails may develop after a nail has been bruised or injured or when too much pressure is exerted at the cuticle during manicuring. A more serious injury may lead to severe pain and the loss of the nail. Unless the nail bed from which the nail grows has been crushed, the new nail that grows back will be normal in all ways.

Fingernails and toenails are vulnerable to fungus infections, particularly to ringworm which can spread quickly into the nails from their free edge, causing discoloration and deformity. The most effective treatment consists in keeping the fingers and toes as clean and dry as possible and using the antibiotic griseofulvin over a period of many months or until the diseased nail has been replaced by a healthy one. Peeling or splitting may be a sign of poor nutrition or a reaction to a particular brand of detergent or nail polish; the use of nail-hardening preparations may have an adverse effect, especially in chronic or extreme cases, and it may be advisable to consult a dermatologist.

Ingrown toenails are common among women whose shoes are too tight. It is usually the nail of the big toe that is forced to grow forward into the toe's nail bed at one or both corners. This distorted growth can be extremely painful, and it can also lead to infection. Self-treatment is possible, if undertaken early, by inserting a tiny cotton swab under the nail edge, thus lifting up the nail so that it is less painful and can grow forward more easily. During treatment comfortable low-heeled shoes should be worn, since high heels throw body weight against the toes. If there is any sign of redness or pain in the area, a podiatrist or medical doctor should be consulted without further delay. Ingrown toenails are best prevented by cutting the nails straight across rather than in an oval arch and by wearing shoes that fit properly.

Manicuring and pedicuring too often is likely to be damaging, and if nail lacquer is regularly used, it should not extend to the base of the nail since the live tissue there should be exposed rather than constantly covered.

Among the more common diseases associated with the nails are infections of the fingers or toes resulting from cuts, hangnails, or any lesions that permit bacterial invasion. The application of a softening cream will decrease the likelihood of cracked cuticles and hangnails. Such infections, called paronychia, can be extremely painful because of the pus and inflammation at the side of the nail. When soaking does not lead to drainage, it may be necessary to have the infected area lanced. Antibiotics are usually prescribed, especially if there is any danger of the spread of the infection.

narcolepsy A neurological abnormality of the brain that leads to a disruption of sleep and the various components of sleep. The disorder is characterized by four symptoms which may occur singly or in any combination. The most common symptom is constant fatigue combined with attacks of sleep at inappropriate times. The second is a loss of muscle tone (catalepsy) triggered by a strong emotional response such as anger, laughter, or astonishment. The onset of catalepsy causes total body paralysis even though the mind is alert and awake. Such an attack may occur many times in one day or only once or twice a year. The other symptoms are the occurrence of frighteningly real hallucinations immediately before falling asleep or immediately after arising and the experience of complete momentary paralysis at the same times. Narcolepsy was first described over a century ago, but until recently it had been assumed to be a psychological rather than a physical abnormality. It is still so often diagnosed incorrectly that anyone who suspects he or she has the illness should arrange for a simple and accurate laboratory test, in which brain wave patterns and eye movements are monitored during sleep. While narcolepsy is not yet curable, various treatments are available for the different symptoms. The disease is under continuing study at the increasing number of sleep disorder clinics that are a part of hospital research centers. The organization that serves as a clearing house for information about such clinics and about other aspects of this particular disorder is the American Narcolepsy Association, Box 5846, Stanford, Calif. 94305.

narcotics A drug characterized by its ability to alleviate pain, calm anxiety, and induce sleep, such as opium and its derivatives or synthesized chemicals.

natural childbirth Any one of several methods of delivery in which the mother is a conscious and cooperative participant in the birth of her child. Some of these methods are based on preparation for labor by a schedule of breathing and relaxing exercises in which the father-to-be or some other family member participates as a coach. Systems of natural childbirth usually eliminate all general anesthesia and provide sedation only when requested. Many hospitals are now encouraging this type of delivery and are giving the father-to-be the option of being present at the birth of his baby. *See also* LAMAZE METHOD.

nausea The feeling that signals the possible onset of vomiting. Nausea occurs when the nerve endings in the stomach and in various other parts of the body are irritated. This irritation is transmitted to the part of the brain that controls the vomiting reflex, and when the signals are strong enough, vomiting does occur. Nausea may be triggered by psychological as well as physical conditions. Many people are nauseated by the sight of blood, unattractive sights and smells, strong feelings of fear or excitement, severe pain, or nervous tension. Nausea may be due to physical problems such as infectious disease, gallbladder inflammation, ulcer, appendicitis, and, most typically, indigestion, motion sickness, and irritation of the inner ear. In some women nausea is a side effect of contraceptive pills. The symptom may be relieved by taking the pill at bed time rather than in the morning. When nausea is a chronic condition unrelated to any specific cause, emotional stress is a likely explanation. For the queasiness associated with the early months of pregnancy, *see* MORNING SICKNESS.

nearsightedness A structural defect of the eye in which the lens brings the image into focus in front of rather than directly on the retina so that objects at a distance are not seen clearly; also called myopia. This aberration of vision is usually inherited and occurs when the eyeball is deeper than normal from front to back. Nearsightedness manifests itself at an early age, becomes increasingly worse until adulthood, then remains stable until it is likely to be compensated for by the changes in vision that occur during the aging process. It can be corrected by glasses prescribed by an ophthalmologist or an optometrist; the prescription should be checked regularly for necessary adjustments. There is no conclusive evidence that eye exercises can cure nearsightedness, nor is there any reason to presume that the condition is aggravated by reading, watching television, or any other activity that would not affect the normal eye.

neck, stiff Absolute or relative inability to move one's head without experiencing neck pain. The immediate cause in severe cases is inflammation of the nerve endings related to the spinal vertebrae. In less acute cases it may be muscle fatigue, tension, or intermittent exposure to blasts of cold air. It may follow a whiplash injury or it may be an early symptom of a bacterial or viral infection of the meninges such as polio, meningitis, and other diseases affecting the nervous system. It also can be a symptom of cervical osteoarthritis. When the pain is no more than a "crick" in the neck, it usually can be alleviated by aspirin and a heating pad.

Nembutal Brand name of sodium pentobarbital, a barbiturate drug that induces sleep. In addition to its addictive aspects, Nembutal and other drugs in the same category may be dangerous to the fetus when administered to the mother during labor. It can cause death when combined with alcohol.

neomycin An antibiotic obtained from the streptomyces group of bacteria and especially effective in treating ear and eye infections. It is also the active ingredient in creams, ointments, and powders prescribed for certain skin disorders.

neoplasm The general term for any new and abnormal tissue growth; a tumor, either malignant or benign.

nephritis *See* GLOMERULONEPHRITIS.

nephrosis *See* KIDNEY DISORDERS.

nerve The basic unit of the nervous system; any one of the cordlike structures carrying messages between the brain, the spinal cord, and all parts of the body. Each nerve is composed of bundles of fibers along which messages are transmitted by electrochemical processes. These signals control all the body's activities.

nervous breakdown *See* DEPRESSION.

nervous system The brain, spinal cord, and nerves—the parts of the body that control and coordinate all activities of the body.

neuralgia Pain in the form of a sharp intermittent spasm along the path of a nerve, usually associated with neuritis. The term is considered imprecise except when it designates the disorder trigeminal neuralgia.

neuritis Inflammation of a nerve or a group of nerves. The symptoms vary widely from decreased sensitivity or paralysis of a particular part of the body to excruciating pain. Treatment varies with the cause of the inflammation. Generalized neuritis may result from toxic levels of lead, arsenic, or alcohol, from particular deficiency diseases, from bacterial infections such as syphilis, or from a severe allergy response. Among the disorders that are caused by neuritis in a particular group of nerves are Bell's palsy, herpes zoster, sciatica, and trigeminal neuralgia.

neurologist *See* DOCTOR.

neuromuscular diseases A category of disorders affecting those parts of the nervous system that control muscle function. Among these disorders are cerebral palsy, parkinsonism, Bell's palsy, multiple sclerosis, and myasthenia gravis.

neurosis A form of maladjustment in relationship to oneself and to others; usually a manifestation of anxiety which may or may not be expressed in chronic or occasional physical symptoms; also called psychoneurosis.

neurosurgeon *See* DOCTOR

nipples The round or cone-shaped protuberances normally located in the lower outer quadrant of the breasts near the center, and surrounded by an area of darker tissue called the areola. During puberty, when the female sex hormones stimulate the development of the secondary sex characteristics, the breasts increase in size and the milk ducts branch out from the nipple through the rest of the tissue. From this time onward, the nipples also become a prime area of sexual excitation, being densely supplied with nerve endings. During pregnancy the nipples may require special care. They should be gently cleansed of any accumulation of secretions, and if they are tender or the skin is dry, the doctor may recommend the use of emollient creams to prevent cracking. In many women, inversion of the nipples is a normal condition. However, if this happens suddenly and in one breast only, it is a sign that requires prompt attention. The best way to discover nipple retraction is by raising the arms during self-examination of the breasts. Any itching or ulceration of the nipples should be called to a doctor's attention.

nodule A localized swelling or protuberance; also called a node. Fibrous nodules develop on the finger joints as one of the characteristics of osteoarthritis and are usually painless. Nodules at the elbow and along the surface of the long bones are typical of rheumatoid arthritis and rheumatic fever and are likely to be painful when touched. Verrucous dermatitis, a fungus infection more prevalent among men than among women, takes the form of warty nodules that grow into ulcerating clusters. This disorder is usually treated surgically in its early stages. Multiple nodes sometimes develop on the thyroid gland, especially among women over 30. Such growths are rarely malignant and are likely to disappear with medical treatment. A single thyroid node that increases in size or resists medical therapy may need to be removed surgically because of possible malignancy. Any nodules that develop on the skin surface, especially those that itch or bleed, should be checked by a doctor.

noise Strictly speaking, any unwanted sound. The unit that expresses the relative intensity of sound is the decibel. On the decibel scale 0 represents absolute silence and 130 is the sound level that causes physical pain to the ear. A civilized two-way conversation measures about 50 decibels. The background noises in major American cities measure more than 70 decibels. Rock and disco music are usually played at about 110 decibels.

High intensity sounds cause physiological damage. The cells that make up the organ of Corti in the cochlea, which transmits sound vibrations to the auditory nerve, are hairlike structures that break down either partially or totally when subjected to abnormally strong sound vibrations. In the cochlea of retired steelworkers, for example, these hair cells are almost totally collapsed, and it is estimated that 60 percent of workers exposed to high intensity on-the-job noise will have suffered significant hearing loss by age 65 in spite of such safety precautions as ear plugs, ear muffs, "soundproofed" enclosures, and the like.

The Environmental Protection Agency estimates that more than 16 million people in the United States suffer from hearing loss caused by sonic pollution and another 40 million are exposed to potential health hazards without knowing it. The dangers to the emotional and physical well-being of individuals, families, and communities are in many cases obvious, but in even more instances they are insidious and cumulative. Here are some facts that trouble environmentalists and health experts. According to the National Institute for Occupational Health and Safety, two or three years of daily exposure to 90 decibel sounds will result in some loss of hearing. Constant exposure to moderately loud noise (over 75 decibels) increases the pulse rate and respiration and may eventually cause tinnitus, ulcers, high blood pressure, and mental problems associated with stress. A daylong ride in a snowmobile can irreversibly damage the organ of hearing. Many young people who wear earphones when they listen to loud music have already sustained some permanent hearing loss; according to an extensive survey of students entering college, 60 percent have some impairment of hearing. Steady, moderately loud noise (power mowers, dishwashers, washing machines, vacuum cleaners, power tools, garbage disposal units) can cause the equivalent in housewives of battle fatigue in soldiers: constricted blood vessels, increased activity of the adrenal glands, irritability, dizziness, and distorted vision. People who are subjected to or subject themselves to high intensity sound are nastier and more aggressive than those who live and work in quiet surroundings. Children who live within earshot of the acoustical overload produced by the traffic on a superhighway are found to have more learning problems than a similar sampling of children whose nervous systems do not have to cope with constant background noise.

If exposure to noise is occasionally unavoidable, the use of ear plugs is recommended. If these are not available in an unexpected situation imperiling one's hearing, the ears should be covered with one's hands or fingers. Elements in the immediate environment that make unnecessary noise should be eliminated or toned down wherever possible. In addition, the Environmental Protection Agency encourages local community groups to establish noise complaint centers empowered to investigate and eliminate all sources of unnecessary noise.

nosebleed Bleeding, either mild or profuse, from the rupture of blood vessels inside the nose; technically called epistaxis. Nosebleeds may be caused by injury, disease, blowing one's nose too hard, strenuous exercise, or sudden ascent to high altitudes. Other causes are tumors and hypertension. Many women experience nosebleeds during pregnancy. They may also occur for no discernible reason and with no ill effect. Bleeding can usually be controlled by holding the head back and pressing the soft flesh directly above the nostril against the bone for a few minutes. If this method is ineffective, the nostril may be packed with sterile cotton gauze which should remain in place for several hours. If the bleeding cannot be stopped promptly, emergency hospital treatment is advisable. It may be necessary to tie or coagulate the bleeding vessel. Any bleeding from the nose or mouth following an accident or a bad fall requires immediate medical attention.

nuclear medicine A special branch of radiology that applies the advances in nuclear physics to the diagnosis and treatment of disease. One of the most important applications is the use of radioactive isotopes to irradiate abnormalities within the body so that they become visible on scanning machines. Radioactive chemicals are widely used in treating certain cancers and hyperthyroidism, and radioactive needles have made delicate nerve surgery possible.

nurse-midwife Registered nurses who have completed an organized program of study and clinical experience recognized by the American College of Nurse-Midwives. This advanced study qualifies them to extend their practice to the care of pregnant women and eventually their infants as long as their prenatal and postnatal progress is recognized as normal.

obesity Overweight in excess of 20 percent more than the average for one's age, height, and skeletal structure.

obsession A recurrent, repetitive, and persistent theme that takes control of the conscious mind. It frequently is combined with compulsive behavior, that is, the recurrent, repetitive, ritualistic performance of certain acts. Obsessions are considered to be an expression of anxiety originating in an unconscious desire unacceptable to the conscious self. Obsessive-compulsive behavior may take a form that seems bizarre (the woman who can never throw anything away and is finally imprisoned by old newspapers, bottles, rags, etc.) or it may take a form that is so completely in accord with cultural standards that it escapes detection (the woman obsessed with keeping her house spotlessly neat and clean or with buying "bargains" that she neither needs nor wants).

obstetrician *See* DOCTOR.

Oedipus complex The Freudian designation for the suppressed hostility that a son feels toward his father in competing with him for his mother and the continuance into adulthood of sexual desire for his mother if the conflict is unresolved. The term is derived from the Greek legend about the prince Oedipus who, abandoned in infancy and unaware of his true identity, murders his father and marries his mother. The parallel Freudian designation for the unresolved female attachment to the father is the Electra complex.

onychia Inflammation of the tissue surrounding the fingernails and toenails; also called onychitis.

oophorectomy An operation for the removal of one or both ovaries.

ophthalmologist *See* DOCTOR.

opiate Any drug derived from opium, the dried juice of the unripened seed pods of the poppy known as *Papaver somniferium.* All opiates have the effect of depressing the central nervous system to a greater or lesser degree, acting as a painkiller, producing euphoria, and inducing sleep. Morphine is the strongest of the naturally derived opiates; heroin is one of its semisynthetic derivatives; codeine, the weakest of the opiates, is derived from morphine or may be produced directly from gum opium. Paregoric, once widely used as a tranquilizer for babies, is an anise-flavored tincture of opium similar to laudanum, another opiate more widely used in the nineteenth century than aspirin is now. All opium derivatives are addictive and their use is strictly controlled by law.

optician A person trained to measure and grind optical lenses as prescribed by an ophthalmologist or an optometrist. An optician does not examine eyes or write prescriptions for corrective lenses.

optometrist A professional trained to measure the eye for the purpose of prescribing lenses to correct visual irregularities. Many optometrists are now equipped to test their patients for glaucoma and for the early signs of cataracts, but since they are not medical doctors, they must refer people with such disorders and other diseases affecting the eyes to an ophthalmologist for treatment. Some states have accorded this profession the right to use certain medications to facilitate lens prescription. All optometrists must be licensed by the state in which they practice.

oral sex Sexual stimulation by mouth and tongue of the female genitals, called cunnilingus, and sexual stimulation by mouth and tongue of the male genitals, called fellatio. Oral-genital contact is widely practiced as part of sexual foreplay and as a way of achieving orgasm. While it is a guaranteed method of avoiding pregnancy, it by no means eliminates the possibility of communicating sexually transmissible diseases.

orgasm The climax of sexual excitement, accompanied in women by vaginal contractions and in men by the ejaculation of semen.

Orinase Brand name of an oral antidiabetic medicine containing the chemical tolbutamide, which stimulates insulin production by the pancreas. Orinase is one of the hypoglycemic medications for diabetics whose symptoms are not severe enough to require insulin shots.

orthodontia The branch of dentistry that specializes in the correction of malocclusion, irregularities in the way upper and lower teeth come together when the jaw is closed. Although orthodontia is often undertaken for cosmetic reasons, dentists agree that gross malocclusions should be corrected for reasons of health: chewing is improved, cleaning is simplified, and gum disease is less likely to occur. Corrections in adults are slower and more painful to achieve than in children and adolescents, but in some cases they may be worthwhile to improve the health of the mouth.

The orthodontist takes a series of X rays of the mouth and jaw and studies them to determine the extent and nature of the correction advisable. Plaster casts are made, and then various appliances for repositioning the teeth are selected to achieve the correction. These include braces, wires, plastic or metal brackets, neckbraces, rubber bands, and retainer plates. The appliances are readjusted regularly to keep pace with the slow shifting of the teeth.

Before embarking on extensive orthodontia, a prospective patient should, in discussion with the family dentist and the orthodontist, compare the relative benefits of the treatment with any disadvantages, such as adverse effects on teeth, discomfort, time, and expense.

orthopedist *See* DOCTOR.

osteoarthritis A chronic degenerative disease affecting the joints of men and women equally, in most cases after the age of 40; also called degenerative joint disease. *See* ARTHRITIS.

osteopathy A type of therapy practiced by osteopaths (Doctors of Osteopathy) which utilizes generally accepted principles of medicine and surgery, but which emphasizes the importance of normal body mechanics and manipulation of the body to correct faulty body structure. In the United States today there actually is little difference between the way doctors of osteopathy and of medicine diagnose and treat disease.

osteoporosis Degenerative porousness of the bones, causing them to fracture more easily and to heal more slowly. Osteoporosis is a more common ailment of aging women than of aging men and is assumed to be related to the decrease in estrogen production following the menopause. In some cases it may be the result of a diet deficient in calcium salts. When osteoporosis affects the spinal vertebrae, they weaken and collapse, leading to the spinal curvature and decrease in stature characteristic of some older women. Estrogen replacement therapy over a strictly limited and medically supervised period can sometimes slow the progress of this disorder. Another treatment that may be effective is additional calcium intake in tablets or in milk consumption.

otolaryngologist *See* DOCTOR.

otosclerosis A condition in which one of the three bones of hearing, the stirrup, becomes immobilized by abnormal bony deposits. Otosclerosis, a more common cause of deafness among women than among men, can sometimes be corrected by surgery. *See* HEARING LOSS.

ovary The female sex organ whose function is the production of eggs and the female sex hormones estrogen and progesterone.

ovulation The process by which an egg cell or ovum is released from the surface of the ovary to travel through the fallopian tube for possible fertilization.

ovum The female germ cell which when fertilized by the male sperm develops into the human embryo; the Latin word for "egg"; the plural is ova. The ovum is the largest cell produced by the human body. All the ova released by the female throughout her life are present in her ovaries at the time of her birth. At birth the ovaries contain several hundred thousand immature ova of which only several hundred come to maturity from the onset of puberty to the cessation of menstruation. Each ovum contains the genetic information to be inherited by the offspring from the matrilineal line.

oxygen A colorless, odorless gas that makes up about 20 percent of the air and is essential for the maintenance of life. Combined with two parts hydrogen (H_2O) it forms water. When carbon is added to hydrogen and oxygen, the three elements in various molecular combinations become the chemical foundation for most organic matter. In the respiratory process, air is brought into the lungs where the oxygen is withdrawn for passage into the bloodstream and delivered to the cells throughout the body as fuel for essential metabolic activities. By the time the blood supply has circulated back to the lungs, it is carrying the carbon dioxide and wastes to be expelled in the exhalation of breath. The rapid breathing that accompanies unaccustomed physical exertion is the body's mechanism for keeping the oxygen demand and supply in working balance and eliminating CO_2.

In circumstances when sustained high energy expenditure is required, as in running away from danger or in athletic competition, more oxygen may be demanded than the lungs can supply to the muscles. At this point, an "oxygen debt" occurs in which the muscles borrow oxygen from the other tissues. The "debt" is repaid by the continued panting for air during the rest that follows overexertion. Any tissue deprived of oxygen because of circulatory failure, as occurs in a heart attack caused by a coronary artery occlusion, is irreversibly damaged. Tissue death or gangrene occurs because of oxygen deprivation when the blood supply is cut off altogether by disease or by such conditions as frostbite. Deficiency of oxygen, technically called anoxia, may occur in high altitudes or in certain diseases of the heart and lungs that produce cyanosis, a condition in which the lips and the extremities turn blue. Various chemicals–carbon monoxide and cyanide in small amounts and barbiturates in overdoses–are fatal because they interfere with the body's normal use of oxygen.

To prevent respiratory collapse following surgery under anesthesia oxygen is administered by an oxygen mask so that the air sacs of the lungs are expanded to their normal capacity. Oxygen at high pressure, provided by the device known as a hyperbaric oxygen chamber, is used in the emergency treatment of victims of carbon monoxide poisoning, gas gangrene, or accidents that have caused potentially fatal damage to arteries. Another procedure for oxygen administration is the oxygen tent, an enclosure or transparent plastic that surrounds the bed and the patient. The release of a continuous and controlled oxygen supply into the enclosure facilitates respiration in cases of lung damage.

oxytocin A pituitary hormone naturally secreted under the normal circumstances of delivery for the stimulation of uterine contractions and of the secretion of milk. Synthetic oxytocin (Pitocin) may be given by injection or in pills to induce labor or to speed up contractions in a prolonged and painful labor.

pacemaker, artificial A transistorized device implanted under the skin in the area of the shoulder and connected by wires to electrodes implanted in heart tissue for the purpose of supplying a normal beat when the natural pacemaker has been irreversibly damaged or destroyed by disease. The effectiveness of artificial pacemakers is based on the fact that the heart naturally generates electrical impulses which cause the normal contractions of the blood-pumping mechanism. The implantation operation is safe and simple. The device with all its components weighs less than half a pound, and recent models last for about five years. It is tested regularly by telemetry so that operational defects can be corrected. Experimental pacemakers powered by nuclear energy are expected to last 20 years; however, their use will be limited until there is definitive proof that they do not affect the wearer adversely in some secondary way after several years.

Paget's disease Two unrelated disorders named after the British surgeon who first identified them. In the first, Paget's disease of the bone, also called osteitis deformans, various parts of the skeleton become softer and larger through a loss of calcium and eventually become lumpy and deformed. The bones most commonly affected are those of the pelvis, the legs, and the skull. The disease is rare, occurring mostly in elderly men, although it is not entirely unknown in postmenopausal women. In a number of cases symptoms are so mild as to remain undetected until an X ray taken for some other purpose reveals the skeletal deterioration. The cause is unknown and there is no specific cure, but X-ray treatments, physical therapy, and one of the newer antibiotics can halt some of the disabling effects. The second disorder, Paget's disease of the nipple, is a type of breast cancer the onset of which is characterized by ulceration and soreness of the nipple and areola.

pain A distress signal from some part of the body, usually of brief duration and originating in the largest number of cases in a traceable disorder. Pain–throbbing, aching, pulsating, stabbing–arises in two different ways. Peripheral pain resulting from a cut finger or an abscessed tooth begins in nerve fibers located in the extremities or around the body organs; central pain, usually caused by injuries or disorders affecting the brain or central nervous system such as a tumor, stroke, or slipped disk, originates in the spinal cord or the brain itself. When this type of pain is chronic, it is the most difficult to assuage. Both types of impulses eventually reach the brain stem and thalamus where pain perception takes place.

One of the mysteries of pain is the subjective way in which it is perceived by different people and by the same people at different times. Research indicates that the brain produces certain chemical compounds that are the body's own opiates against pain perception. It is therefore assumed that people who have a low pain threshold and are extremely sensitive to any discomfort may manufacture too few of these compounds. Another complicating factor in pain studies is that in many cases the mere expectation of relief is enough to minimize the suffering. The use of placebos has proven effective in such varied circumstances as angina attacks, migraine headaches, and postoperative wounds.

Where pain is chronic and severe, medical science continues to explore unconventional methods that provide relief: acupuncture, electrical stimulation, hypnosis. The chief dangers connected with the use of chemicals for minimizing severe or persistent pain are serious adverse effects of a particular chemical itself or in combination with other drugs and the possibility of drug addiction.

palpitations A condition in which the heartbeat is so strong, irregular, or rapid that it calls attention to its abnormal behavior. This occurrence is almost always associated with anxiety and is rarely associated with any disability of the heart itself. In a few instances rapid heartbeat may be caused by a disease or may be a side effect of a strong dose of certain chemicals, such as caffeine or medication containing amphetamines. Where palpitations occur with intrusive frequency, they should be discussed with a doctor, and if anxiety is indeed the cause, alternatives to tranquilizers should be explored as treatment.

pancreas The large, mixed gland situated below and in back of the stomach and the liver. The pancreas is about 6 inches long. Its function is two-fold. One is the secretion of pancreatic juice which contains the enzymes that flow into the digestive tract and are essential for the continuing breakdown in the duodenum and small intestine of fats, carbohydrates, and proteins. The second function is the secretion of insulin, produced by almost a million clusters of specialized cells called the islands of Langerhans.

When these cells produce insufficient insulin for the body's needs, the result is diabetes. Other disorders of the pancreas include the formation of stones and of benign and malignant tumors, both treated surgically. Inflammation of the pancreas, pancreatitis, may be acute or chronic. Acute pancreatitis is a grave condition in which one of the enzymes begins to devour the tissue itself, leading to hemorrhage, vomiting, severe abdominal pain, and collapse. It may be associated with overdrinking, gallbladder infection, gallstones, or trauma. Chronic pancreatitis may be the result of recurrent acute pancreatitis. It is characterized by abdominal and back pain, diarrhea, and jaundice. When these symptoms exist, exploratory surgery is usually recommended to rule out the possibility of cancer.

pap test A diagnostic procedure used chiefly for detecting the first signs of cancer of the cervix and sometimes the uterus. The test is named for Dr. George Papanicolaou, the American anatomist who discovered that cancerous cells are shed by uterine tumors into the surrounding vaginal fluid and can therefore be detected when a sample is examined microscopically. The procedure is simple and painless: while the speculum dilates the vagina, the doctor inserts a flat stick and scrapes some cells from the cervical canal, the outer cervix, and the pooled secretions in the vagina. These "smears" are transferred to three glass slides and stained. They are then inspected under a microscope for the presence of any abnormal cells. The value of the test is that it can reveal the presence of cervical cancer long before any symptoms appear, thus making effective treatment possible at the earliest moment. However, the test in and of itself is not definitive. In many cases where cellular anomalies are found in the sample, further examination in a biopsy may indicate that the existing condition is cervical erosion, cervical inflammation, or some other benign condition rather than cancer. This test occasionally reveals cancer of the uterus, but cell washings from the uterus obtained by another technique are better.

Medical opinions vary concerning how often a woman should have a pap test.

paralysis Permanent or temporary impairment of muscle power caused by damage through disease or injury of a part of the nervous system. The extent and nature of paralysis depend on what part of the nervous system has been affected. If the brain and spinal cord are involved, central paralysis occurs, that is, the limb as a whole is immobilized rather than any individual muscle. This involvement may cause hemiplegia (paralysis of one side of the body), paraplegia (paralysis of both legs and the trunk), or quadriplegia (paralysis of all four limbs). The most common cause of central paralysis other than an injury is a cerebrovascular stroke in which the blood supply to a part of the brain is cut off. Other causes are brain tumors, the ingestion of certain poisons, and infectious diseases, especially poliomyelitis, late syphilis, and tuberculosis.

Impairment of any part of the peripheral nervous system (the nerves that connect the central nervous system with various parts of the body) can cause dysfunction of individual muscles, the reception of sensation on the skin surface, vision, and the normal behavior of various organs. Peripheral paralysis may be caused by nerve inflammation or neuritis as occurs in Bell's palsy or sciatica. It may result from such neuromuscular diseases as myasthenia gravis, or from infectious diseases, chiefly polio. One of the results of birth injury can be paralysis associated with cerebral palsy.

Hysterical paralysis is a condition in which deeply buried emotional conflict takes a physical form, such as the inability to swallow or to walk. Such episodes may be no more than a fleeting psychogenic conversion, as in the inability to move the fingers when taking a written examination, but when conversion hysteria is chronic, some type of psychotherapy is advisable.

Many types of paralysis can be overcome partially or totally by prompt treatment. Physical therapy in its many aspects can rehabilitate disabled muscles, and supportive efforts in other areas can restore confidence and competence to victims of a paralyzing accident or illness.

paranoia A mental disturbance characterized by delusions of persecution and sometimes accompanied by feelings of power and grandeur. A clinically paranoiac person may not suffer from personality disintegration and may appear to be living a normal life, but it is not unusual for the disturbance to erupt into psychotic behavior. The term paranoid may be used to describe a general mental state that is not psychotic, but is characterized by distrustfulness, suspiciousness, and a tendency toward persecution of others.

parkinsonism A mild or severe disorder of body movement characterized by slow mobility, stiffness, and tremor; also known as Parkinson's disease. Most of the estimated million and a half victims of the disorder are over 60. Symptoms similar to those of Parkinson's disease may set in after encephalitis lethargica (once called "sleeping sickness"), may result from a stroke or a brain tumor, or may be a reversible side effect of tranquilizers such as Thorazine or antihypertensives such as Serpasil. True parkinsonism is a disorder of a particular group of brain cells that normally release a substance called dopamine which is essential to the regulation of normal body movement. In most cases the debilitating aspects of the disease are now controlled by dopamine medications in combination with other drugs. Surgery, physical therapy, and supportive psychotherapy are additional forms of treatment that can reduce the damaging effects on the body as well as on the personality of victims. Since patients over 60 are likely to be on medication for some other condition, the supervising doctor should be expected to make a regular check of all prescriptions being filled so that a dangerous combination of drugs can be avoided.

patch test A diagnostic procedure for determining hypersensitivity to a particular allergen by applying it to the surface of the skin in a diluted solution or suspension. A positive allergic response is indicated by the appearance of a raised welt or hive caused by the body's histamine production. A similar test injects the attenuated allergen between the layers of the skin.

pathologist *See* DOCTOR.

penicillin The first of the antibiotics, discovered in 1929 by Sir Alexander Fleming in its natural form in the mold *Penicillium notatum;* now used to designate a group of related chemicals obtained from several molds or produced synthetically in various forms. The widespread application of penicillin is based on its ability to destroy bacteria harmful to humans without harming humans themselves. In some few cases, however, penicillin sensitivity rules out its use in favor of some other antibiotic. Any possibility of adverse effects should always be reported to the doctor and should especially be transmitted to hospital personnel in an emergency situation in which massive doses might create the greater emergency of anaphylactic shock.

pediatrician *See* DOCTOR.

penis The external male organ through which semen is ejaculated and urine is passed.

peptic ulcer *See* ULCER.

perineum The triangular layer of skin between the vulva and the anus in the female and between the scrotum and the anus in the male. Beneath the perineum in the female are the muscles and fibrous tissues that must stretch sufficiently to accommodate the passage of the baby during childbirth. To prevent the danger of tearing, a simple surgical incision called a perineal episiotomy is often performed.

peritonitis Inflammation of the peritoneum, the membrane that lines the abdominal cavity and covers the organs within it. Peritonitis may be chronic or acute. Chronic peritonitis is a comparatively rare condition associated with tuberculosis. The cause of acute peritonitis is usually the perforation or rupture of the appendix with a consequent spread of bacteria and interference of circulation. Symptoms are immobilizing abdominal pain, shallow breathing, and clammy skin. The condition is an emergency requiring prompt hospitalization and a more precise diagnosis on the basis of X-rays, blood tests, and physical exploration. Surgery is almost always inevitable: the peritoneal cavity is opened and drained of infectious material, and the cause of the problem, for example, a diseased appendix, is removed. Postoperative care involves intravenous feeding, antibiotics, and in some cases blood transfusions. When the stomach and intestines become dilated by the accumulation of gas, relief may be provided by a procedure called nasogastric suction.

perspiration The process by which the salty fluid (99 percent water and 1 percent urea and other wastes) is excreted by the sweat glands of the skin; also the fluid itself. The body has approximately 2 million sweat glands located in the lowest layers of the skin. They are connected with the outer skin layer, the epidermis, by tiny spiral-shaped tubes. The largest sweat glands are located in the groin and the armpit. The sweat glands normally produce about 1½ pints of sweat a day in a temperate climate. The chief function of perspiration is to maintain constant body temperature despite variation in environmental conditions or energy output. Thus, when the internal or external temperature goes up, sweat can be seen on the skin surface where it cools the body by evaporation. At the same time the blood in the superficial capillaries is cooled before it recirculates within the body. The sweating process is controlled by the hypothalamus at the base of the brain. Since this gland is also responsive to emotional stress, fear and excitement will cause an increase in perspiration. "Breaking out in a cold sweat" is a common phenomenon.

Any disturbance in the functioning of the sweat glands is likely to be a symptom of some other disorder. Excessive perspiration may be due to a disease that also produces a high fever such as malaria or one that produces a chronic rise in temperature such as tuberculosis. Excessive sweating and urinating are possible symptoms of untreated diabetes. The hot flashes of the menopause are often accompanied by heavy sweating. Excessively sweaty palms or soles of the feet is usually psychogenic in origin. While perspiration contains certain antibacterial chemicals that protect the skin surface, it can also be an irritant to tender skin. Prickly heat rash occurs when the sweat glands become blocked and the ducts leading to the skin surface rupture. The condition is usually a consequence of unaccustomed and profuse perspiration that keeps the skin damp. While prickly heat is more common among babies than among adults, clothing that chafes can cause it in adults as well. Fresh perspiration does not have an unpleasant odor.

pessary A device, often in the shape of a ring, worn inside the vagina to support a prolapsed uterus; also a vaginal suppository and sometimes another term for a contraceptive diaphragm.

pH A measure of the degree of alkalinity or acidity of a given solution; the letters derive from *pouvoir Hydrogène* ("hydrogen power" in French), since the concentration of the hydrogen ion determines the pH number. Acidity is indicated by pH values from 0 to 7; pH 7.0 is neutral, and pH values above 7 indicate alkalinity.

pharyngitis Inflammation, either acute or chronic, of the pharynx, the tube of muscles and membranes that forms the throat cavity extending from the back of the mouth to the esophagus. Infection is most commonly viral, occurring as a minor sore throat. In more serious cases the cause is bacterial, as in streptococcus or strep throat, and results in high fever, severe discomfort when swallowing, and a stiff neck. It is extremely important that a sore throat or tonsillitis accompanied by fever over 100°F be checked by a doctor to prevent serious complications. Chronic pharyngitis and hoarseness is usually the result of the misuse of the voice, regular exposure to irritating vapors or fumes, or heavy intake of alcohol. Even mild pharyngitis is aggravated by smoking.

phenobarbital A mild, slow-acting barbiturate prescribed as an anticonvulsant for some cases of epilepsy and as a sedative to relieve anxiety and induce sleep. Like all barbiturates, it is habit-forming and dangerous when abused. Evidence has accumulated to indicate that it is one of the tranquilizing medicines that may cause birth defects when taken during the early months of pregnancy.

phlebitis Inflammation of the vein walls, most commonly of the legs, and especially where varicosities exist. Phlebitis in a superficially located vein is usually accompanied by tenderness, redness, and swelling. The inflammation is potentially more serious when it develops in a deep vein. Clotting may occur on the damaged wall, a condition known as thrombophlebitis, and it may impede circulation or may break away from the wall and circulate as an embolism. Simple phlebitis may be caused by overweight or by progressive arterio- or atherosclerosis; it may follow an illness such as pneumonia or a long convalescence in bed. A phlebitis that affects the large vein of the thigh may occur about a week after childbirth. The condition is familiarly called "milk leg" and like most inflammations of this type can be counted on to heal if the leg is raised for part of the day and support hosiery is worn. When phlebitis is so severe as to be disabling, or if there is a strong possibility of clot formation, surgery may be recommended.

phobia An irrational and exaggerated fear of an object or condition, usually related to an anxiety neurosis. Everyone experiences fear as a response to what each perceives as present or impending danger, but phobic response may be so encompassing as to be immobilizing. In severe anxiety attacks the victim may experience dizziness, palpitations, profuse sweating, and in some cases a tendency toward suicide. Although almost any object or situation may elicit phobia in different individuals, several have been identified as common sources of phobic response, for example, agoraphobia, the fear of being in open places; acrophobia, the fear of heights; ailurophobia, the fear of cats; and claustrophobia, the fear of being confined in small areas.

Neurotic fear is a form of mental illness that is difficult to cure. In some cases the phobia may decrease as a result of life experiences that resolve the underlying conflict; in other cases psychotherapy can be helpful in diminishing a particular phobia.

physical examination A part of a medical evaluation, the results of which provide information as to the general and specific condition of a person's health. In order to perform a comprehensive medical evaluation, the doctor must obtain the medical history, perform routine diagnostic tests, and do a careful physical examination of the various parts of the body, including an internal pelvic examination. It is extremely important to have periodic examinations so that any changes from previous evaluations can be recognized and treated if necessary.

physical therapy Treatment by physical rather than by medicinal or surgical means of various disorders caused by disease or injury. The chief goals of physical therapy are the achievement of normal mobility through the relief of pain and the rehabilitation of impaired muscle function. Where irreversible disablement is present, treatment also consists in training the patient to accomplish essential tasks in alternative ways to achieve the greatest possible degree of autonomy in the participation of normal life. Techniques and means depend on the patient's needs. Exercises designed to strengthen specific muscles or to coordinate the movements of a group of muscles may be active or passive. In passive exercise the therapist moves the affected parts until the patient is able to do so alone. In hydrotherapy the patient exercises in water which, because of its buoyancy, requires a smaller expenditure of energy. When patients are entirely immobilized as may occur in a stroke, physical therapy is begun in bed with massaging and applying heat. Physiotherapists, who are trained in schools approved by the American Medical Association, usually work under the supervision of doctors in hospitals and clinics that have rehabilitation programs for both inpatients and outpatients.

physician *See* DOCTOR.

pilonidal cyst A fluid-filled sac that develops under the skin at the base of the spine. *See* CYST.

pituitary gland The pituitary gland, no larger than a pea, is situated at the base of the brain directly above the back of the nose. It is controlled in part by the hypothalamus and in part by the hormones from the various endocrine glands (biofeedback), and it in turn controls the hormone production of all the other endocrine glands.

placebo A preparation or procedure without pharmacologic or physiologic properties, which is administered for psychological benefit; literally, Latin for "I shall please." While usually no more than water with sugar flavoring, placebos are known to cause a measurable difference in how patients feel. They are also used as a control in testing the efficacy of a new therapeutic drug.

placenta The organ that attaches to the wall of the uterus during pregnancy and through which the developing fetus is nourished by the mother because it serves as an exchange between the mother's and the fetus's vascular systems; also known as afterbirth.

plantar wart Warts that develop in the sole of the foot. Such growths often are especially painful because they grow inward and thus interfere with walking. All such warts are technically called verrucae and are assumed to be caused by virus infection. Treatment is often surgical. Postoperative care involves several days of immobility to permit the tissue to heal before pressure is put on it by walking.

plaque A flat patch; most commonly, dental plaque, which refers to an accumulation of food and other organic material on the surface of a tooth. This accumulation inevitably provides a medium for the bacterial growth that leads to the destruction of tooth enamel and cavity formation. Dental plaque should be routinely removed by brushing the teeth, using unwaxed floss according to the dentist's instructions, and having a professional cleaning twice a year.

plastic surgery Operations in which damaged or abnormal tissue is repaired and rebuilt. Such damages or abnormalities may be congenital, as a hare lip, or they may be acquired, as disfiguring scars caused by burns or other injuries. Growths that are extensive enough to require skin grafting once they have been removed are also the province of the plastic surgeon. Another aspect of this specialty is the reconstruction of missing tissue with a prosthesis, a substitute manufactured of metals and plastics rather than of organic materials taken from another part of the body. Artificial limbs, jaws, breasts, and ears are some of the more customary prosthetic replacements. Change in appearance for esthetic reasons where no striking malformation exists, such as a face lift or nose reshaping, is called cosmetic surgery. The benefits of such elective surgery should be carefully weighed against the inconvenience and risks of surgery.

platelets Round or oval disks in the blood that contain no hemoglobin and are essential to the clotting process; also called thrombocytes. Platelet deficiencies occur in a number of diseases (leukemia, myeloma, lymphoma), as a result of certain drugs, and spontaneously (idiopathic thrombocytopenic purpura). This latter mainly affects women and children. Platelets can be transferred fresh or frozen.

pleurisy Inflammation of the pleura, the double membrane that lines the chest cavity and encloses the lungs. The membrane consists of two layers of pleurae separated only by a lubricating fluid. Under normal conditions this double membranous structure permits the lungs to expand freely within the chest. However, under certain adverse circumstances two different disorders can occur: wet pleurisy, in which because of an inflammation of the pleura, abnormal fluid accumulates between the pleural layers; and dry pleurisy, in which the pleura is inflamed, but there is no abnormal fluid. Pleurisy may or may not be acutely painful, but it always requires prompt treatment. Any chest pains, especially a stabbing sensation accompanying the intake of breath or a persistent cough accompanied by weakness and loss of appetite should be investigated by a doctor. Dry pleurisy (pleurodynia) is caused by several viruses and is usually self-limiting. Wet pleurisy is caused by direct infection, cancer, congestive heart failure, or the spread of infection from another respiratory disturbance, such as pneumonia, bronchitis, lung abscess, or tuberculosis. Pus accumulation is called empyema (not emphysysema) and usually needs surgical drainage. *See* EMPYEMA.

pneumonia An acute infection or inflammation of one or both lungs, causing the lung tissues and spaces to be filled with liquid matter. Pneumonia, which may be a primary infection or a complication of another disorder, has three main causes: bacteria, viruses, and mycoplasmas. Inflammation may also be caused by fungus infections or by the aspiration of certain chemicals, of irritant dusts, or of food or liquids while unconscious due to anesthesia, intoxication, or other causes. The latter type is called aspiration pneumonia. Among the bacteria, the pneumococci are by far the most common cause; there are over 80 different types responsible for approximately 500,000 cases of the disease each year. Streptococcal pneumonia is less common; staphylococcal pneumonia usually is contracted in a hospital and has a high mortality rate; victims of pneumonia caused by the klebsiella bacteria also have poor chances of recovery. The pneumonias that are viral in origin account for about half of all cases. While in some cases recovery may be spontaneous without treatment or special precautions (many people have had "walking pneumonia" without realizing it), the disease known as primary influenza virus pneumonia is extremely serious, especially because the infectious organism multiplies with practically no accompanying sign of disease in the lung. Mycoplasmas, which were identified during World War II, are microorganisms smaller than bacteria, larger than viruses, and sharing characteristics of both. Mycoplasma pneumonia typically involves older children and young adults and is usually mild in its symptoms and brief in duration. Pneumonia that involves a major part or an entire lobe of a lung is known as lobar pneumonia, and when both lungs are involved, double pneumonia. Bronchopneumonia, which affects a smaller area, is slower to develop and is localized in the bronchial tubes, with patches of infection reaching the lungs. While rarely fatal, bronchopneumonia is insidious because it may recur and resist conventional treatment.

In all cases of bacterial pneumonia, but especially in cases where resistance is low because of age, debility, or alcoholism, treatment with antibiotics must be initiated at once. In general, at the first sign of any of the following manifestations, a doctor's evaluation is mandatory: shaking chills, high fever, chest pains, dry cough, breathlessness, bluish cast to the lips and nail beds, expectoration of rust-colored or greenish sputum when coughing. Some cases may require hospitalization, while others may be supervised at home. According to the American Lung Association, prompt treatment with antibiotics almost always cures bacterial and mycoplasma pneumonia. While there is as yet no effective treatment for viral pneumonia, adequate rest, proper diet, and sufficient time devoted to convalescence usually result in full recovery. Since 1977 an immunizing vaccine has been available that offers protection against some types of pneumococci. It is administered on an individual basis to those considered especially vulnerable to infection—people over 50, anyone in a nursing home, and anyone of any age suffering from chronic diseases of the heart, lungs, and kidneys and from diabetes and other metabolic disorders. One injection of the vaccine is supposed to provide immunity for three years. The use of the vaccine is especially important since many strains of pneumococci have developed a resistance to previously effective antibiotics.

podiatrist A practitioner who specializes in the care and treatment of the feet; formerly called a chiropodist. While not a physician, a podiatrist is entitled to be called "Doctor" as the recipient of the degree of Doctor of Podiatric Medicine (D.P.M.), conferred by independent, state-accredited podiatric colleges. Holders of the degree are licensed by the state to prescribe medications and to perform minor surgery. A medical doctor might refer a patient to a podiatrist for the treatment of flat feet, ingrown toenails, bunions, or disorders resulting from daily running in the wrong shoes. When foot disorders are the result of such systemic problems as circulatory failure, the podiatrist usually refers the patient to a physician.

poison Any substance which can severely damage or destroy living tissue. Certain substances are harmful in any amount, while others, which are harmless or even beneficial in supervised doses, are poisonous in excessive amounts. Poisons can be absorbed through the skin, injected into the bloodstream, or inhaled, but the largest number of poisonings result from swallowing dangerous substances in small amounts or taking medications in overdoses. The most frequent victims are children under 5, and of these, more than half the fatalities occur following an overdose of a medicine (usually aspirin), often disguised as "candy." Among adults the greatest numbers of poisonings are also caused by an overdose of medicine, either swallowed accidentally or in a suicide attempt.

Poisons are usually classified by their destructive effects within the body. Blood toxins, such as carbon monoxide and rattlesnake venom, deprive the blood of the oxygen essential for nourishing the brain and other tissues or cause other blood problems like hemolysis. Nerve toxins, especially alcohol, barbiturates, and various opiates, destroy the nerves and interfere with normal cell processes. Corrosives, such as lye, ammonia, phenol, destroy the tissues directly. Irritants, such as arsenic, lead salts, copper sulfate, and zinc, cause inflammation of the mucous membranes. The most effective action to take in the event of poisoning is to call the nearest poison control center at once for emergency instructions. Since prompt action can make the difference between life and death, every member of the family, including children from the earliest possible age, should know that the number of this agency is posted next to the telephone with other emergency numbers. Local telephone directories usually list the number under poison control. When no such listing appears, efforts should be made *before* a crisis occurs to locate the closest agency by consulting the telephone operator, the nearest hospital, or the Red Cross chapter or by writing to the Division of Poison Control, U.S. Department of Health and Human Services, 5600 Fishers Lane, Rockville, Md. 20852.

poison control center A service organization on the community level that can be consulted 24 hours a day for information about the toxicity of a particular substance and the most effective countermeasures to take against it. The FDA provides these centers with up-to-date information on all potentially dangerous products. The centers are listed in telephone directories under poison control. The number of the nearest one should be immediately accessible at the home phone for quick use in a crisis.

poison ivy, oak, and sumac Plants containing a poisonous chemical, urushiol, to which a majority of people in the United States eventually become sensitive. It is extremely unwise to assume that insensitivity to these plants is permanent. The chemical, which is contained in all parts of the plants—leaves, berries, roots, and bark—produces contact dermatitis in those allergic to it. In cases of hypersensitivity the itching and blistering rash may develop not only when the skin has touched the plant directly, but also when a part of the body touches a piece of contaminated clothing or a dog or cat whose coat is contaminated by the allergen. Since the chemical can be spread by smoke from burning the plant, it should never be burned, but destroyed by a suitable herbicide. When exposure does occur, contaminated clothing should be removed at once and the potentially affected parts of the body washed with a strong, alkaline laundry soap. These preventive measures should be undertaken as soon as possible to limit the spread of the poison. When the rash appears, the discomfort can be reduced by the application of preparations recommended by a pharmacist or a doctor. In severe cases cortisone may be recommended as well as antihistamines to reduce the itching. The best way to prevent contact is to make a serious effort to learn what the plants look like so that they can be scrupulously avoided.

poliomyelitis An acute infectious disease caused by a virus that attacks the central nervous system and causes partial and temporary muscular paralysis when the nerve cells are injured and complete permanent paralysis when the nerve cells are totally destroyed; also known as polio and infantile paralysis. While any part of the body (except the brain) may be damaged, the muscles most often affected are those of the legs. Milder cases may produce symptoms so slight they go undetected. A severe attack causes stiffness in the neck accompanied by pain and tenderness in the leg muscles which begin to deteriorate in a few weeks. In its gravest form, bulbar polio, the disease attacks the spinal cord and cranial nerves. The disease invades the body through the mouth; the viruses enter the bloodstream and, after they produce symptoms of varying degrees of severity, are eventually excreted. Infection is spread by contaminated sewage or human excrement that in turn contaminates the drinking water supply, the community swimming pool, or food or by indirect transfer from the soiled fingers of a previous patient to the food of a potential victim. While polio has always been more widespread among children than among adults because adults have had time to develop natural immunity through asymptomatic infection, it can attack anyone at any age. In asymptomatic cases no serious signs of the disease are observable, but in fact antibodies have been formed. Symptomatic cases may or may not produce paralysis.

The disease has practically been eliminated in the United States as a result of immunization of most children when the vaccines were first introduced in 1954. It is important that children born since then be immunized. Since polio epidemics are not uncommon in areas with primitive sanitation, anyone planning a trip to such a place should be immunized or re-immunized.

polyp A smooth, tubelike growth, almost always benign, that projects from mucous membrane. Such growths are of two main types: pedunculate polyps, that are attached to the membrane by a thin stalk, and sessile polyps, that have a broad base.

While polyps may occur in any body cavity with a membranous lining, they are most commonly found in the nose, uterus, and cervix. Those that develop in the nasal canal or sinuses may result from such irritations as frequent colds or allergies. While rarely dangerous, they can interfere with breathing and with the sense of smell; they may also be the cause of chronic headaches. Surgical removal is recommended in such cases, but there is no guarantee that the underlying irritation will not produce them again. Uterine polyps may cause irregular or excessive menstrual flow and may also be one of the causes of sterility. They can usually be removed without the need for hospitalization. The presence of cervical polyps may be manifested by bleeding between menstrual periods, after menopause, or with intercourse or they may be "silent," only discovered during a routine gynecological checkup. Removal is considered advisable, with a biopsy to rule out the possibility of cancer. When polyps form anywhere along the alimentary canal, they are usually benign, but since there is always an outside possibility of their becoming malignant, they should be removed surgically as soon as their presence is discovered, either through an X-ray for some other reason or because of the symptoms they produce. A stomach polyp, for example, may be painless, but if the stalk is long enough so that if it is drawn into the duodenum, it will make its presence known. Intestinal polyps may cause no symptoms unless they become ulcerated and eventually bleed. Such growths, as well as polyps in the colon or the rectum, are likely to cause discomfort in the lower abdomen, diarrhea, as well as blood and mucus in the stools.

posture The natural position or carriage of the body when sitting or standing. Good posture is the unconscious result of mental and physical health. While a rigidly held neck or a sunken chest may be second nature by the time adulthood arrives, poor posture can be improved by suitable exercise. Women who sit at a desk or typewriter for a large part of the day should have a posture chair that discourages slouching and supports the spine. For women who are on their feet a great deal, poor posture and attendant backaches may result from wearing ill-fitting shoes or shoes with heels that are too high or too low for comfort and healthy carriage. A critical review of footwear, office furniture, and posture when doing household chores may go a long way to eliminating back pain. Good posture during pregnancy is especially important, since the growth of the fetus and the enlarged abdomen place an extra strain on the spine. Standing against a wall several times a day with head up, shoulders back, belly sucked in, and buttocks tucked under can develop posture that will eliminate back discomfort before and after delivery.

potassium A chemical element which, in combination with other minerals, is essential for the body's acid-base balance and muscle function. Most foods contain a supply of potassium adequate for the body's needs. However, vomiting or diarrhea may create a temporary deficiency. Interference with potassium metabolism may also result from corticosteroid medication, diuretic medication, or a disorder of the adrenal glands known as Cushing's syndrome. Since all cells, but especially those that form muscle tissue, require a high blood-potassium level, a critical deficiency results in weakness (even paralysis), lethargy, rapid pulse, and a tingling sensation. Following a diagnosis based on blood tests, the condition is corrected by oral medication containing potassium salts.

pre-eclampsia A condition of pregnancy characterized by abnormal retention of water, elevated blood pressure, and large amounts of protein in the urine, signaling the possible onset of convulsions (eclampsia).

premature ejaculation *See* EJACULATION.

proctologist *See* DOCTOR.

progesterone The hormone secreted by the corpus luteum each month at the time of ovulation to prepare the lining of the uterus for embedding and nourishing of the fertilized egg. It is produced by the placenta during pregnancy and is important for the maintenance of pregnancy. Diminishing progesterone secretions is one of the changes that occurs during menopause. In its synthetic form this hormone is the sole ingredient of a type of contraceptive pill, and it is also released in tiny amounts into the uterus by one of the newer, medicated IUDs. The long-term effect of the progesterone IUD, which must be replaced each year, is not yet known. Progesterone may also be prescribed in replacement therapy when a deficiency is responsible for certain menstrual disorders connected with infertility.

progestin Umbrella term for various types of progesterone.

prolactin A hormone secreted by the pituitary gland which initiates and maintains lactation after pregnancy.

prolapse The downward or forward displacement of a part of the body; most commonly, the dropping of the uterus. A prolapsed womb is a consequence of impaired muscle support, which most often results from the stress of childbirth, but is not unknown among women who have never had children. Dropping of the uterus may occur after menopause when muscle tone diminishes or when the cumulative effect of a lifetime of hard physical work takes its toll. The symptoms of uterine prolapse are frequent and painful urination, low backache, vaginal discharge, and a feeling of pressure on the vagina. Lying down provides relief from this last discomfort. When the prolapse is severe enough to cause the cervix to protrude through the vagina, special support in the form of a pessary may be a satisfactory alternative to surgery.

prostaglandin A hormonelike substance composed of unsaturated fatty acids and found in almost every tissue and body fluid. Prostaglandins are being identified in increasing numbers as indispensable for normalizing blood pressure, kidney processes, the reproductive system, gastrointestinal activity, and the release of sex hormones. Of those specifically isolated, the prostaglandins manufactured by the endometrium increase considerably just before the onset of the menstrual period. Since they cause strong uterine contractions, they are responsible perhaps for the premenstrual cramps suffered by some women. This stimulating action on the uterus can induce menstrual flow and may be the cause of some spontaneous abortions. Prostaglandin is now available in solution and as a suppository for inducing abortion. Continuing studies of this group of prostaglandins may result in a pill that will bring about abortion.

prostate gland In the male genitourinary system, the gland surrounding the neck of the bladder and the beginning of the urethra. As a sexual organ, its function is the manufacture of prostatic fluid, a component of seminal fluid in which the sperm cells are mixed to create semen.

protein One of several complex substances composed of combinations of amino acids; the basic substance of which living cells are composed; essential nutrient in the diet of all animal life.

The symptoms of protein deficiency are physical weakness, poor resistance to disease, and fluid accumulation in the legs and abdomen. Liver disease and certain other disorders may interfere with normal protein metabolism. Over-the-counter medications for "tired blood" will not correct protein deficiencies.

The classification of *serum proteins* includes globulin and albumin. Globulin, which is divided into alpha, beta, and gamma globulin, is an essential component of the blood. Since gamma globulin is the richest in antibodies, it is often used to provide passive immunity to such infectious diseases as hepatitis. Albumins are serum proteins found in all living matter. Among the most important ones are egg albumin found in eggwhite; fibrinogen and hemoglobin in blood; myosin in meat; caseinogen in milk; casein in cheese, and gluten in flour.

pruritis *See* ITCHING.

psoriasis A common skin disease of unknown cause, characterized by excessive production of cells of the outermost skin layer which produces scaly red patches. As the new cells proliferate, they cover the patches with a silvery scale, and as the scales drop off, the area below is revealed as tiny red dots. Psoriasis is neither contagious nor dangerous. Symptoms may appear for the first time in early childhood, in adolescence, or not until later in life. The condition may be chronic or intermittent; it may be triggered by injury, illness, emotional stress, or exposure to excessive cold.

The red patches may or may not be accompanied by itching. The parts of the body most often affected are the scalp, chest, elbows, knees, abdomen, palms, and soles of the feet. About 10 percent of patients have an associated arthritis.

In spite of advertising claims to the contrary, there is no cure for psoriasis. Professionally prescribed treatments which have been somewhat effective have had unfortunate side effects in many instances or have required weeks of hospitalization. The most recent treatment to show promising results is known as photochemotherapy. It combines oral medication with a photoactive drug followed by exposure to ultraviolet radiation.

psychiatry The medical specialty that deals with the diagnosis and treatment of disorders of the mind and the emotions. *See* DOCTOR.

psychoanalysis A method originated by Dr. Sigmund Freud for treating mental illness and emotional disturbances. The method is based on certain assumptions about the development from infancy onward of the human psyche or the mind as an entity with a life of its own that governs the total organism in all its relationships with others and with the environment. Psychoanalysts may be psychiatrists as Freud himself was, or they may be lay practitioners.

psychoneurosis *See* NEUROSIS.

psychosis Any mental illness characterized by disorganization of personality and a disordered contact with reality, combined with bizarre behavior consisting of unpredictable mood swings and garbled speech, and accompanied by hallucinations, delusions, and disconnected thoughts.

psychosomatic illness Any disorder that is functional in nature and that may be ascribed wholly or partly to emotional stress.

psychotherapy The treatment of mental disorder.

puberty The period of development during which sex organs begin to function, that is, become capable of reproduction, and secondary sex characteristics develop. In females it is marked by the onset of menstruation (menarche), commonly any time from age 11 to 14.

puerperal Relating to childbirth. Puerperal fever is an obsolete term for a formerly widespread and often fatal infection of the vagina and uterus just after delivery. Such infections are rare nowadays thanks to aseptic medical procedures. When there is any sign of such infection, it is usually controllable by antibiotics.

pulse The beat of the heart as felt through the expansion and contraction of an artery, especially through the radial artery at the wrist below the fleshy mound of the thumb. The best way to take the pulse is to place the three middle fingers on this artery with sufficient pressure to detect the beat, but not so heavily as to suppress it. Pulse rate is the term for the number of beats felt in 60 seconds. The normal adult rate ranges from 60 to 100 beats a minute. An abnormally slow pulse (brachycardia) may be caused by an overdose of digitalis, abnormal pressure within the skull, the onset of thyroid deficiency, or a crisis involving heart malfunction. An abnormally fast pulse (tachycardia) may result from high altitude sickness, congestive heart failure, hyperthyroidism, fever, excitement, or too much caffeine, alcohol, smoking, amphetamines, thyroid extract, or antispasmodics. The rhythm of the pulse in a normally healthy person is regular. Where perceptible irregularity exists, it may be associated with thyroid disease or it may be caused by auricular fibrillation, a symptom of chronic heart failure. If the pulse is not perceptible at the wrist, it may be felt through the carotid artery at the side of the neck.

pus The thick yellowish or greenish liquid that develops during certain infections. Pus is composed of white blood cells, tissue decomposed by bacteria or other microorganism, and the destroyed organism that caused the infection. It is often contained in an inflamed swelling called an abscess.

pyorrhea The discharge of pus; especially pyorrhea alveolaris, a condition in which the chronic discharge of pus from diseased gums causes deterioration of the bone and the eventual loss of teeth. *See* GINGIVITIS.

Q fever An acute infectious disease with symptoms similar to those of influenza and caused by microorganisms known as rickettsiae. The disease normally infects cattle and sheep and is passed from animal to animal and from animals to humans by tick bites, contaminated milk, and contaminated dust which may be inhaled or ingested in food. Mild cases last for less than a week, with fever, chills, headache, muscle pains, and some respiratory symptoms. Recovery is usually complete following bed rest, aspirin, and light diet. Antibiotics may be given when the fever stays dangerously high and there is the possibility of heart and lung involvement.

quarantine The isolation of people who might be incubating a communicable disease. The word itself derives from the Latin "forty," which was the number of days that a ship with contaminated passengers, crew, or livestock was kept in port before debarkation was permitted. Nowadays the quarantine period is as long as the incubation period of the particular disease in question. This public health measure, less frequent in modern times, is usually enforced to protect the general public from infection by members of a group returning by plane, ship, or other conveyance from places where they or the conveyances were in contact with yellow fever, cholera, and the like.

quickening The stage of pregnancy in which the mother becomes aware of fetal movements within the womb; also, the fetal movements themselves. Quickening usually occurs some time around the eighteenth week of pregnancy, at which time the fetal heartbeat is first detectable.

rabies An almost always fatal disease of the central nervous system caused by the rabies virus. It occurs in warm-blooded mammals such as humans, foxes, dogs, bats, and skunks. It is transmitted by the bite of an infected animal because the virus is present in saliva. The virus is occasionally transmitted to humans by intimate contact with an infected human or animal and by inhalation of air in caves housing infected bats.

The wound from any animal bite should be allowed to bleed and be scrubbed and flushed with soap and water; then, if possible, it should be washed with zephiran chloride or some other substance (alcohol) of proven lethal effect on the virus. Suturing the wound is not advised. Whether the victim of the bite has been exposed to rabies depends, of course, on whether the biting animal is infected. This is more likely if the bite was not provoked and if the animal was wild. Further, the more severe the wound, especially if the bite was on bare skin, the more likely the victim is to get rabies if the animal was infected. The animal should be observed, caged if necessary, for approximately 10 days to see if it is sick, gets sick, or dies. If it has to be killed to be captured, care should be taken not to shoot it in the head because an examination of the brain is essential to determine if it is rabid. If the victim has been exposed or probably exposed to rabies, it is essential that rabies vaccine and probably antirabies serum be administered. Judgment must be used in deciding about the use of vaccine and serum since there are hazards associated with both.

The incubation period of rabies in humans varies from 10 days to 12 months, the average is about 42 days, and is characterized initially by fever, headache, and general malaise and then by a variety of central nervous system signs such as spasms of the muscles of the mouth, pharynx, and larynx on drinking. This symptom explains another name for rabies, hydrophobia (the fear of water). Death usually is caused by paralysis of the respiratory muscles. There is no specific treatment for the disease.

radiologist *See* DOCTOR.

radiotherapy The treatment of disease with X-rays and with rays from such radioactive substances as cobalt, iodine, and radium; also called radiation therapy or irradiation. The effectiveness of radiotherapy, which is the special province of the radiologist, is constantly being increased by the invention of new machines and techniques that minimize the dangers of radiation exposure to healthy tissues at the same time that enough irradiation can be provided to benefit tissue already diseased. Radiotherapy is used in the treatment of inoperable cancers and localized skin malignancies and in combination with chemotherapy or alone as a postoperative means of halting the progress of metastasis or of cancer recurrence.

radium A highly radioactive metal that spontaneously gives off rays affecting the growth of organic tissue. Radium was isolated from pitchblende ore by Marie Curie in 1898, and since that time has been used to halt the progress of certain types of cancer, especially those that are inoperable. In the form of needles or tiny glass tubes, radium is embedded within the diseased tissues where the emanation of gamma rays may have a therapeutic effect. Body exposure, inhalation, or ingestion of radium may produce burns as well as several kinds of cancer, especially of the lungs, blood, and bones.

rale Any abnormal sound that accompanies the normal sound of breathing when perceived through a stethoscope or by the ear placed against the chest; pronounced *rahl.* Rales are said to be either moist or dry depending on the lung disorder or disease that produces them.

rapid eye movement (REM) A phenomenon that accompanies a particular phase of sleep during which there is also an intensification of body processes. During this phase, known as REM sleep, sleep is deep, blood pressure rises, heartbeat quickens, and there is an increase in the rate of electrical impulses produced by the brain. When perceptible rapid eye movements during sleep were reported by researchers in 1953, they were assumed to be an accompaniment of dreaming. It is now known that one process does not inevitably involve the other.

rash A skin eruption often accompanied by discoloration and itching and in most cases a temporary symptom of a particular infectious disease, allergy, or parasitic infestation. Rashes may be flat or raised, some run together into large blotches, and others turn into blisters. Many of the diseases of which rashes are a symptom, such as measles and rubella, are on the wane because of widespread immunization. Prickly heat, contact dermatitis, hives, and allergic responses to poison ivy, oak, and sumac are common causes of rashes. Rashlike symptoms usually accompany infections caused by funguses, parasites, and rickettsial organisms such as ticks. Virus diseases (mononucleosis) and sexually transmissible diseases, especially secondary stage syphilis, are characterized by rashes. Any skin eruption accompanied by fever or other acute symptoms such as a sore throat or tender swollen glands should be examined by a doctor.

rectocele The protrusion of the rectum into the vagina. This type of hernia causes difficulty in emptying the bowel and leads to constipation. It can be corrected by surgery.

rectum The lowest portion of the large intestine before the anal opening to the exterior of the body. It consists of the rectal canal, 5 to 6 inches long in crescent-shaped folds, and the anal canal, 1 to 1½ inches long. When the rectum is filled with feces as the solid wastes of digestion are pushed downward by intestinal action, nerve impulses send messages to the brain signaling the need to defecate. The rectum may be affected by various disorders, most commonly hemorrhoids, polyps, prolapse, pruritis, and cancer. Proctitis (inflammation of the rectum) can be one of the consequences of gonorrhea. A rectal examination, called a proctoscopy, is usually considered advisable for diagnosis of such symptoms as constipation alternating with diarrhea, rectal bleeding, and a constant feeling of pressure in the lower bowel.

REM *See* RAPID EYE MOVEMENT.

remission The decrease or disappearance of signs and symptoms during the course of a disease or a chronic disorder. The term spontaneous remission is used when there appears to be no therapeutic explanation for the abatement of the symptoms.

repression In Freudian terms the refusal of the conscious mind to acknowledge unacceptable impulses, thoughts, and feelings and their relegation to the unconscious where they find expression in dreams, anxiety, and various mechanisms such as sublimation and transference. If an individual fails to develop effective ways of dealing with the repressed feelings, they may be expressed in anxiety neurosis or physical illness. The purpose of a Freudian analysis is to uncover the repressed desires which stand in the way of normal functioning. Many other types of psychotherapy also attempt to help the patient get in touch with her feelings so that she can deal with them without anxiety and guilt.

reproductive system The organs and processes involved in the generation of reproductive cells, conception, gestation, and childbirth.

reserpine An alkaloid extracted from the Southeast Asian plant *Rauwolfia serpentina.* The substance known as rauwolfia was extracted from the root of the plant and used as a tranquilizer for centuries in India. Its active chemical component, reserpine, was later isolated. After World War II it was widely used in the treatment of schizophrenia and manic-depressive illness, but it has since been superseded by drugs with fewer negative side effects. Reserpine has also been one of the standard medicines for reducing hypertension. Since it has been suggested that it is associated with the development of breast cancer, its prescription as an antihypertensive is open to question.

resistance The body's ability to ward off or minimize disease either through genetic capability, the presence of antibodies produced by immunization or environmental exposure, or a high enough level of physical and psychological health to combat infection without succumbing to it. An example of inherited resistance is the fact that the darker a woman's skin, the less likely she is to develop skin cancer because of overexposure to the sun. Resistance to many of the infectious diseases caused by various organisms, especially viruses, in a particular environment may result from the presence of antibodies developed against one or another strain of the disease-bearing agent. However, should a different strain be brought into the environment from some other part of the world, as has occurred over and over again with various types of flu, epidemics are likely to result. Resistance is also a variable capacity at different times of one's life. When the body is young, it operates with considerably more efficiency and rallies its protective forces more quickly than when it is aged. Thus for the elderly, whose metabolism is inevitably slower and whose cardiovascular system has deteriorated somewhat, loss of resistance to hot weather and resultant heat stroke is more common than in younger persons. Some people find it difficult to grasp the concept that many illnesses are contracted not from other people but from themselves. Many people have been infected by the virus that causes cold sores (herpes labialis) which remain dormant after the cold sore heals. When resistance is lowered by malnutrition, too little sleep, too much stress, or a generally debilitated physical condition, the virus can become activated and the cold sore reappears. The most efficient way to produce resistance to an increasing number of infectious diseases is by immunization.

respiratory disorders *See* ASTHMA, BRONCHITIS, etc.

retina The innermost layer of cells at the rear of the eyeball; a membrane consisting of the light-sensitive rods and cones that receive the image formed by the lens and transmit it through the optic nerve to the brain. Retinal disease of one kind or another is the chief cause of blindness in the United States. With the extension in the life span of diabetics through the use of insulin a disease called diabetic retinopathy has come to the attention of medical science. According to the National Eye Institute, it threatens the vision of more than 300,000 people. This impairment of the retina through spontaneous bleeding from retinal vessels affects, to some degree, 95 percent of the diabetics who have been on insulin therapy for 25 years or more. Many cases are successfully treated with the technique called photocoagulation in which finely focused beams of intense light are directed into the eye in such a way that miniscule burns are caused on the retina. These burns destroy the abnormal blood vessels, and the minute scars that result do much less harm to vision than the disease.

Photocoagulation may also be used to treat some patients with macular degeneration. This is a disorder of unknown cause which affects the macula, the tiny orange-yellow portions in the center of the retina through which the color and detail of daytime vision are received. While this is chiefly a disease of the elderly, it may occur at any time, depriving the victim of reading vision. When a hole or tear develops in the retina or when an eye infection or tumor forces an excess of the vitreous fluid to seep between the retinal layers, the result can be a retinal detachment which can result in a permanent loss of eyesight. There is an increased risk that this condition may occur in people with severe myopia. Thanks to photocoagulation and new microsurgical techniques, restoration of vision is accomplished in a large number of cases.

Rh factor A group of genetically determined antigens found in the red blood cells of most people. The designation comes from the rhesus monkey involved in the original experiments. About 15 percent of the Caucasian population lacks this inherited blood substance, and this group is therefore known as Rh negative. Its absence in other races is much rarer. When the substance is missing, the blood is described as Rh negative, regardless of whether the major blood type is A, B, AB, or O. It is vitally important that Rh compatibility be established before a transfusion, especially when the recipient is a woman who may want children in future years. The reason for checking the Rh factor during pregnancy is to avoid the complications that ensue when the woman is Rh negative and the man is Rh positive. The mixing of the two bloods can have serious consequences so it is imperative to determine early in pregnancy if the Rh negative problem exists.

rheumatic fever A disease of the growing years triggered by a group A beta hemolytic streptococcus infection and characterized by inflammation, swelling, and soreness of the joints. During rheumatic fever a condition known as rheumatic heart disease may develop. If the valves of the heart are affected and become so inflamed that they are distorted by the eventual formation of scar tissue, the efficiency with which they shut is permanently impaired. The impairment results in a backspill of blood that can be heard through a stethoscope as the so-called heart murmur. Anyone with this type of heart disability is especially vulnerable to further indirect valve damage subsequent to recurrence of rheumatic fever or to direct valve damage secondary to bacterial infection elsewhere (called subacute bacterial endocarditis). To avoid this complication, it is important that the proper precautions be taken against bacterial invasion of the bloodstream that may occur when a tooth is extracted, during urinary tract surgery, etc. Fortunately, antibiotics started prior to such procedures have eliminated this grave complication in most cases.

rheumatism A nonscientific designation for any painful disorder or disease of the joints, muscles, bones, ligaments, or nerves. *See* ARTHRITIS, BURSITIS, etc.

rheumatoid arthritis *See* ARTHRITIS.

rhinitis Inflammation of the mucous membranes that line the nasal passages, caused by viral or bacterial infection, allergy, or inhalation of irritants. Acute rhinitis, the technical medical term for the nasal disturbance of the common cold, is its most common form. In some cases viral rhinitis is complicated by bacterial invasion which may reach the ears and the throat. When streptococcus, staphylococcus, or pneumococcus bacteria are involved, the nasal discharge will be thick and yellowish with pus instead of being practically colorless, loose, and runny. Another form of inflammation is caused by an allergic reaction to grass, trees, dog hair, or other substances.

Rhinitis may become prolonged or chronic because of constant inhalation of noxious dusts, heavy smoking, constant exposure to excessively dry air, low resistance to infection by cold viruses, or constant bouts of sinusitis. Under these circumstances, the nasal membranes may thicken and swell to the point where breathing is impaired, headaches and postnasal drip are chronic, and the sense of smell is damaged. Also associated with chronic rhinitis is the development of polyps and of a separate disorder known as ozena in which the erosion of the mucous membrane results in a thick malodorous discharge that creates heavy crusts impeding proper breathing and attempts at nose-blowing.

Obvious symptoms of chronic rhinitis should be treated by a doctor. When rhinitis is associated with fever or other manifestation of bacterial infection, antibiotic therapy may be advisable. However, the typical stuffed or runny nose characteristic of an ordinary cold is likely to clear up as the cold runs its course. Nosedrops should be used only on the doctor's recommendation, since they often contain ingredients that may further irritate the nasal membranes.

riboflavin A component of the vitamin B complex; also known as vitamin B_2. When a deficiency exists, as may occur in liver disease, alcoholism, or an improperly balanced diet, the early signs are a reddening and soreness of the tongue, painful cracks in the skin at the side of the mouth, and eye inflammation that affects vision. Therapeutic doses, usually combined with other vitamins, will correct these disorders.

ribonucleic acid *See* RNA.

rickettsial diseases A category of infectious diseases caused by microorganisms larger than viruses, smaller than bacteria but with characteristics of both, called rickettsiae after their discoverer, the pathologist H. T. Ricketts (1871–1910). Rickettsiae inhabit certain rodents as parasites and are transmitted to humans and animals by the bites of ticks, mites, fleas, and lice. The rickettsial diseases, which range from mild to extremely serious, commonly produce a rash and a fever. While they are comparatively rare in places where public health practices keep rodents and carrier insects at a minimum, epidemic outbreaks of Rocky Mountain spotted fever and Q fever have occurred in various parts of the United States. The incidence of these diseases as well as of typhus fever, the most serious of the rickettsial infections, has been considerably reduced by the availability of effective immunization. When a particular rickettsial disease is accurately diagnosed on the basis of laboratory findings, it is usually treated with antibiotics. (This group of diseases should not be confused with rickets, a vitamin D deficiency disease.) *See* Q FEVER, ROCKY MOUNTAIN SPOTTED FEVER, TYPHUS.

ringworm *See* FUNGUS INFECTIONS.

RNA Ribonucleic acid, the chemical compound contained in the cytoplasm of all cells and the carrier of genetic information provided by DNA to the ribosomes, the structures that synthesize amino acids into proteins. Through the information transmitted by RNA, inherited characteristics make their way from one generation to the next.

Rocky Mountain spotted fever An infectious disease transmitted to humans by the bite of the American dog tick in the Eastern states and from rodents to humans by the wood tick in Western states; also called tick fever or Eastern spotted fever. This is one of the rickettsial diseases that produces fever, headache, aching muscles, and a rash. One of the distinguishing characteristics of the disease is that the rash begins on the palms of the hands and the soles of the feet, spreading upward during the course of the illness, which, if untreated, may lead to serious respiratory complications. Other symptoms include sensitivity to light, abdominal cramps, and vomiting. Tetracycline halts the progress of the infection. Vacationers should find out if warnings of tick infestation have been issued in their location. Dogs should not be permitted to roam in tick-infested surroundings; where, in an attempt to eliminate ticks, areas have been sprayed with chemicals harmful to people and their pets, precautions should be taken against potentially dangerous contact. Another precaution against tick bites is suitable clothing: long pants in a light color and sturdy shoes.

root canal The passageway through the root of a tooth for the nerve. When tooth decay has proceeded unchecked from the enamel into the dentin that surrounds the pulp chamber and the root canal, the only treatment that can prevent the loss of the tooth by extraction is known as root canal therapy. This consists in removing the nerve and the diseased pulp, sterilizing the chamber, and filling the area with an inert substance. The specialist who performs this type of treatment is called an endodontist.

rubella An acute virus infection accompanied by fever and a rash, a common contagious disease of childhood; also known as German measles. In spite of the fact that long-lasting immunization against this disease is available, many young women reach childbearing age without vaccination against it and without natural immunization from infection during childhood. Rubella immunity precludes the potentially harmful fetal consequences from exposure to the disease during the early months of pregnancy. Such consequences include brain damage, blindness, and other deformities in as many as 50 percent of the affected offspring. It is therefore of the utmost importance that a woman who is planning a pregnancy or who thinks that she is pregnant already be tested for rubella immunity. Vaccination against rubella is strongly recommended in any case. Pregnant women without immunization should avoid exposure to rubella.

Rubin test A diagnostic procedure used in cases of infertility to discover whether the fallopian tubes are obstructed; also known as tubal insufflation. Carbon dioxide gas is carefully blown through the cervix into the uterus. If the passage is normal, the gas will escape through the fallopian tubes into the abdominal cavity. In cases in which mucous congestion or minor scar tissue has blocked the tubes, the pressure of the gas may open them sufficiently to make conception possible. When the pressure gauge indicates insurmountable blockage, other procedures are used to solve the problem.

rupture A popular term for a hernia. *See* HERNIA.

saccharin A chemical coal tar derivative, used as a sugar substitute and approximately 500 times sweeter than cane sugar by weight. Saccharin had been used routinely by diabetics and by people on low calorie diets, until recent scientifically controlled experiments conducted with laboratory animals pointed to carcinogenic properties in saccharin. However, debate continues about the validity of these tests when applied to human consumption since no such controlled experiments can be duplicated with humans. A sugar substitute is by no means necessary for weight reduction; women concerned about controlling their weight might use sugar in small quantities or use no sweeteners at all.

sacroiliac The cartilaginous joint that connects the sacrum at the base of the spinal column to the ilium, the open section on either side of the hipbone. Low back pain can sometimes be ascribed to arthritis in this joint.

sadism In the clinical sense, a perversion in which sexual gratification can be achieved only through inflicting pain on the partner. The term, derived from the perversities described in the writings of the Marquis de Sade, has come to be used loosely to characterize excessive cruelty or pleasure derived from inflicting physical or mental pain. Sadomasochism is a condition in which sexual or more generalized pleasure is achieved by alternately inflicting and receiving physical or mental pain.

saline abortion A procedure, performed under local anesthesia, in which a pregnancy is terminated by the withdrawal of amniotic fluid from the uterus and the injection of a concentrated salt solution into the amniotic fluid space.

saliva The secretion of the salivary glands in the mouth. The largest of these, the parotids, are situated in front of and below each ear and discharge saliva through openings in the cheeks opposite the lower back teeth. The saliva secreted into the floor of the mouth comes from the sublingual glands below the tongue and from the submaxillar glands inside the lower jaw. Saliva not only keeps the mouth and tongue moist to facilitate speech and swallowing, it also softens food and through its enzymes initiates the digestive process by chemically changing the carbohydrates in the mouth into simpler sugars. Since the flow of saliva is activated by the nervous system, stimuli of sight, smell, taste, and even mental images of food will increase salivation. For the same reason, fear and anxiety will inhibit the flow, leading to the "dry mouth" sensation that accompanies some types of stress situations. Nutritional deficiencies and some medicines may also result in an uncomfortable decrease of saliva.

salmonella A group of rod-shaped bacteria especially irritating to the intestinal tract and responsible for most cases of acute food poisoning as well as for paratyphoid and typhoid fever. Abdominal cramps and diarrhea are the typical symptoms of salmonella infection.

salpingectomy The surgical removal of one or both of the fallopian tubes. This operation is usually necessary when surgery is done for a tubal ectopic pregnancy.

salpingitis Inflammation of the fallopian tubes. It is usually caused by gonococci or other bacteria that ascend from the cervix, but may also be caused by tuberculosis. Acute salpingitis, especially when it is recurrent, can result in scar tissue that obstructs the tubes (chronic salpingitis), thereby becoming a possible cause of sterility. Any acute pain on both sides of the lower abdomen accompanied by a vaginal discharge and frequent and uncomfortable urination should be diagnosed promptly for treatment with antibiotics.

salt The chemical compound sodium chloride (NaCl); also called table salt. The average daily U.S. diet contains 7 to 13 grams of sodium. While a certain amount is essential for maintaining the body's chemical balance, it is advisable for people suffering from hypertension and certain types of heart or kidney disease to restrict their salt intake, since too much sodium may cause fluid retention. Modern food processing makes this difficult, since practically all processed foods, including frozen vegetables, contain salt; all baked goods, cake mixes, breads, and soft drinks contain salt, and the nitritex used to preserve cold cuts and smoked meat is sodium nitrite which has the same water-retention effect as sodium chloride. Anyone who must restrict sodium intake might find some help in cookbooks that specialize in low-salt recipes and menu planning. When the body loses too much fluid, as in a long siege of diarrhea or heavy sweating, a salt deficiency may occur, manifested in muscle cramps, nausea, fatigue, and in extreme cases collapse. Prompt replenishment can be accomplished by eating salted crackers or nuts or by swallowing a sodium chloride tablet with some orange juice. However, salt tablets should not be taken routinely during hot and humid weather unless the recommendation is made by a doctor. How much salt, if any, a pregnant woman should eliminate from her diet to reduce the likelihood of edema is a matter to be discussed with the physician in charge of her prenatal regimen.

sarcoma A malignant tumor composed of connective tissue such as bone or of muscle, lymph, or blood vessel tissue; one of the two main groups of cancer, the more common being carcinoma (cancer of epithelial or gland cells). A sarcoma usually metastasizes rapidly, either through the bloodstream or through the lymphatics. While treatment is difficult, a combination of chemotherapy, radiation, and surgery can be effective in halting the progress of different types of sarcoma.

scabies An infestation of the skin by insectlike parasites; also known as "the itch." The scabies mites burrow under the skin, usually between the fingers, in the groin, under the breasts, or in the armpits, to lay their eggs. When the eggs hatch, they produce new adult parasites that work their way to the skin surface and begin the cycle again. The severe itching accompanied by a rash begins about a week after the initial infestation and is especially acute at night. Constant scratching during sleep may result in lesions that are vulnerable to bacterial infection. Scabies may spread quickly through an entire family and may also be contracted during sexual contact. Treatment should therefore be simultaneously undertaken by all those who have been exposed to contamination. A doctor usually identifies the itch mite by microscopic examination. A daily change of underclothing, towels, and bed linens is advisable until the eggs and the parasites have been eliminated by laundering from anything that might be in contact with the skin. Topical medicines are usually prescribed to kill the eggs under the skin and to minimize the itching. Hot baths before bedtime may also be helpful.

scanning machines Diagnostic equipment by means of which parts of the body that cannot be examined by conventional X ray can be seen and analyzed. Scanners use radioactive materials, special cameras, and new techniques made available by nuclear medicine. One of the most widely used of these machines is called a CAT (computerized axial tomography) scanner, also known as a brain scanner. While being rotated around the patient's head, it records information about layers of the brain and feeds the information into a computer that creates a composite picture in which it is possible to locate a tumor or some other disorder previously invisible in an X-ray picture.

schizophrenia A general term for mental disorders classified as psychotic rather than neurotic, in which the victim suffers from severely disturbed patterns of thinking and feeling that lead to bizarre behavior. The schizophrenic syndrome, for which there is no known direct cause and no specific cure, is most likely to occur in early adulthood, although no age is immune. Common parlance has given the term the sense of a split personality, but this popular definition actually has very little to do with the psychiatric diagnosis of mental illness. As with the manic-depressive psychosis, schizophrenic symptoms may be periodic, sometimes so immobilizing the victim that hospitalization is necessary, at other times mild enough to liberate the patient for a comparatively normal life. Among the most striking symptoms of the condition are auditory hallucinations; delusions, usually of grandeur or of persecution (paranoia); obsessive-compulsive behavior; distinct personality changes and mood swings without visible cause; and, above all, loss of control over fantasies. While there are many theories about the cause of the illness, circumstances that trigger its onset, and reasons for its remission, no single explanation is definitively convincing. Among the areas of current research are constitutional predisposition in the form of an inherited recessive gene or a combination of genes; constitutional predisposition associated with oxygen deprivation of the brain during birth, triggered by a metabolic aberration, or related to a prenatal protein deficiency; environmental circumstances that create an atmosphere of anxiety and hostility and especially a conflict between parents or extreme parental disapproval and criticism.

When the disease is suspected, diagnosis is usually based on a complete physical examination, a series of psychiatric interviews, an electroencephalogram, and standard psychological tests. Conventional treatment may begin with chemotherapy combined with psychotherapy which may involve the family. Environmental therapy, involving residence in a halfway house rather than a hospital, is used in many cases. This form of therapy conditions or reconditions the schizophrenic for participation in the normal world even though some symptoms are ineradicable. Megavitamin therapy is used by some doctors, but since conclusive evidence of its effectiveness has not yet been provided, this approach is not sanctioned by the profession as a whole. In cases where the more immobilizing symptoms cannot be alleviated in any other way, electroshock may be used as a last resort.

sciatica Pain extending along the sciatic nerve which is the largest nerve in the body and which supplies sensation from the back of the thigh, along the outer side of the leg, and into the foot and toes. The most common cause of sciatica is a slipped or herniated disk of the lower spine. Osteoarthritis is another cause. In some cases the pain is accompanied by a paralysis of some of the associated muscles of the thigh and leg. Inflammation of the sciatic nerve (sciatic neuritis), while rare, may be a consequence of diseases such as alcoholism or diabetes or of vitamin deficiencies. Sciatica may vanish unaccountably as it arrives, but in cases where it is persistently painful and immobilizing, efforts should be made to discover the underlying cause. Until the cause can be treated, relief may be provided by physical therapy, a surgical girdle, or support tights.

scopolamine A chemical similar to belladonna, derived from a plant of the nightshade family and used medically as a sedative and painkiller; also known as "twilight sleep." It induces stupor, forgetfulness (pain is experienced but not remembered on awakening), and in some cases physical agitation. When given with barbiturates and tranquilizers in the early stages of labor, it may produce respiratory suppression in the newborn baby and transitory postpartum depression in the mother.

scrotum *See* SEX ORGANS, MALE.

scurvy A deficiency disease resulting from an insufficiency of vitamin C in the diet. Vitamin C requirements are between 10 and 20 milligrams daily. Considerably more than that amount is provided by a conventional diet that contains citrus fruits and juices and various green vegetables both raw and gently cooked. While scurvy is now a rare disease, it may occur from an improperly balanced diet; infants who are not given supplementary ascorbic acid may also suffer from scurvy. Signs of the disorder are bleeding gums, ruptured blood vessels, and eventual anemia and bone changes. Treatment consists of therapeutic doses of vitamin C in the form of ascorbic acid tablets or, in extreme cases of metabolic disorder, by injection.

sebaceous glands The oil-secreting glands situated in the epidermal layer of the skin, lubricating the surface and protecting it from the harmful effects of absorbing too much or too little moisture. The number of these glands, which may be as many as 12 to the square inch, varies from person to person and from one part of the body to another. The sebaceous glands secrete sebum which constantly seeps upward through the pores. Too little sebum production results in dry skin, too much in oily skin. During adolescence and pregnancy hormonal changes may affect the activity of the glands, leading to acne. Another condition resulting from sebaceous disorder is dandruff.

Seconal Brand name of a drug in the barbiturate family. Seconal is a central nervous system depressant prescribed in small doses as a sedative and in larger doses to induce sleep. Like other barbiturates, it creates a dependency. There are strong indications that Seconal and similar medications should not be administered during labor since they may have a depressant effect on the fetal brain and respiration.

sedative A category of drugs that in small doses reduce excitability, irritability, and nervousness by depressing the central nervous system and in larger doses induce sleep. This category includes barbiturates, tranquilizers, and bromides, as well as chloral hydrate and alcohol. If used regularly or abused even over short periods, practically all sedatives produce dependencies of one kind or another that can lead to addiction.

semen The thick, whitish fluid produced and secreted by the male organs of reproduction and containing the sperm cells. A single ejaculation of semen contains 300 to 500 million spermatazoa in a little less than a teaspoon of fluid. One of the diagnostic procedures in infertility cases is analysis of semen to determine the shape, number, and motility of the sperm.

seminal vesicles *See* SEX ORGANS, MALE.

senescence The normal process of growing old.

senility A manifest and abnormal deterioration of mental function associated with aging and caused by physical or mental disease or a combination of both. While damage to brain function by arteriosclerosis and stroke are among the conspicuous causes of senility, psychological and social factors that lead to personality deterioration may be equally responsible. Among the most prominent of these factors are withdrawal from normal life, lack of interpersonal relationships, feelings of worthlessness aggravated by familial and social neglect, unrelieved anxieties about disease and death. *Senile* is a clinical term and should never be used to describe anyone who is going through the normal aging process which may involve a slower rate of activity and response.

serum *See* BLOOD SERUM.

sex-linked abnormalities Inherited disorders transmitted by a genetic defect in the X chromosome. Women have two X chromosomes and men have one X chromosome paired with a Y chromosome. Since the presence of a Y chromosome determines maleness, fathers always transmit their X chromosome to their daughters and their Y chromosome to their sons. Because of these factors, defective genes in the X chromosome follow a particular pattern of heredity. If in a female an inherited disordered X chromosome is balanced by a normal X chromosome, she will carry the disease trait without having the disease itself. If a male offspring of the female carrier inherits her genetically abnormal X chromosome, since it is his only X chromosome, he will have the disease. When a mother is a carrier, there is therefore a fifty-fifty chance that her male offspring will inherit her abnormal X choromosome and have the disease. Female offspring have a fifty-fifty chance of inheriting the abnormal chromosome and therefore a fifty-fifty chance of being carriers. Among the sex-linked abnormalities are such diseases as hemophilia, Duchenne muscular dystrophy, and the metabolic disorder known as the Lesch-Nyhan syndrome. The relatively new field of genetic counseling seeks to inform a couple of the likelihood of having a genetically defective child so that they can make educated decisions.

sex organs, male The male reproductive organs. One of the most obvious differences between the reproductive organs of the male and the female is that whereas the scrotum and penis are visible, the female counterparts are hidden from view. Another major difference is that for the male, an erotic response in the form of an erection is generally essential for the reproductive role of the penis, but no such psychophysiological requirement exists for the procreative function of the female. The male sex organs consist of the penis, scrotum, testicles, and several glands, including the prostate. Within the testicles, which are loosely contained in the scrotum, are structures called the seminiferous tubules in which sperm cells are manufactured from puberty onward. The spermatozoa are conveyed from the tubules into the epi didymis, part of the sperm conduction system, where they are stored temporarily until they make their way into the seminal duct (vas deferens) and from this duct into the seminal vesicles which secrete a viscous material that keeps them viable. The urethra, which also carries urine from the bladder, is enveloped by the prostate gland. The prostate manufactures another fluid that mixes with the sperm and the seminal fluid to form the combination known as semen. The urethra passes through the length of the penis. When the penis is in a state of erection, muscular spasms send the semen through the urethra in the act of ejaculation that immediately follows the male orgasm. Any traces of urine that might be present in the urethra are neutralized during sexual excitation by an alkaline secretion from two tiny organs known as Cowper's glands. This chemical process is critical since spermatazoa cannot remain viable in an acid environment. Because of the dual role of the urethra and its location, the male reproductive channel is also called the genitourinary tract.

sexual intercourse In conventional parlance, the entry of the penis into the vagina, usually preceded by sufficiently stimulating foreplay to cause an erection in the male and the flow of lubricating secretions in both partners; also called coitus. Extravaginal intercourse is also a common practice, involving anal entry and oral sex (fellatio and cunnilingus) that give satisfaction as foreplay or may be another means of achieving orgasm. Painful sexual intercourse for the female (dyspareunia) may result from inflammation of any part of the genitourinary system, prolapsed uterus, abnormal vaginal contractions, or psychogenic causes.

shingles *See* HERPES ZOSTER.

shock A disruption of circulation which may be fatal if not promptly treated; not to be confused with electrical shock or insulin shock. The immediate cause of circulatory shock is the sudden drop in blood pressure to the point where the blood can no longer be effectively pumped through the vital organs and tissues. Among the circumstances leading up to this crisis are: low-volume shock following severe hemorrhage as occurs in multiple fractures, bleeding ulcers, major burns, or any accidents in which so much blood and plasma are lost that there is an insufficiency for satisfying vital needs; neurogenic shock in which the nervous system is traumatized by acute pain, fear, or other strong stimulus that deprives the brain of oxygen and results in a temporary loss of consciousness; allergic shock, also called anaphylactic shock, following the injection into the bloodstream of a substance to which the recipient may be fatally hypersensitive; cardiac shock in which the pumping action of the heart is impeded by an infarction or by fibrillation; septic shock resulting from the toxins introduced into the circulatory system by various harmful bacteria. Whatever the circumstances, shock produces similar symptoms in different degrees of swiftness: extreme pallor, profuse sweating combined with a feeling of chill, thirst, faint speedy pulse, and, as the condition intensifies, increasing weakness and labored breathing. Immediate hospitalization is mandatory. If shock is the result of a serious accident or of a heart attack, the patient should not be moved except by people professionally trained to do so.

shock treatment *See* ELECTROSHOCK TREATMENT.

sickle cell disease An inherited disease characterized by the substitution of 90 to 100 percent of normal hemoglobin by an abnormal hemoglobin, called hemoglobin S. When exposed to normal but low oxygen tension, red blood cells containing this much hemoglobin S acquire the shape of a sickle. These red blood cells are destroyed more rapidly than normal red blood cells and a hemolytic anemia results. In addition, the sickled red blood cells occlude blood vessels, thus depriving various body cells of their oxygen supply, causing them to die and producing rather widespread disease. There is as yet no cure.

A variant of sickle cell disease is sickle cell trait in which only 25 to 45 percent of normal hemoglobin is replaced by hemoglobin S. Persons with sickle cell trait may have a mild anemia, but only rarely have other problems. A simple blood test identifies the presence and quantity of hemoglobin S. Hemoglobin S is found almost exclusively in black persons of African origin. In the United States about 8 percent of Afro-Americans have the trait and about 0.2 percent have the disease. Because hemoglobin S is transmitted genetically both parents must have either the disease or the trait for any of their children to have the disease. If only one parent has the disease or the trait, none of their children will have the disease, though some will have the trait. *See* GENETIC COUNSELING.

silicone implantation A surgical procedure in which one of the silicone compounds in the form of a gel or a saline solution enclosed in a bag is inserted into the breasts in order to augment their size; also a similar procedure for the purpose of reconstructing breast tissue removed in a mastectomy.

sinuses Cavities within bones or other tissues; in ordinary usage, the paranasal sinuses, the eight hollow spaces within the skull that open into the nose. These cavities are symmetrically located in pairs. The maxillary sinuses are in the cheekbones, the frontal sinuses are above the eyebrows in the part of the skull that forms the forehead, the ethmoid sinuses are behind and below these, and the sphenoid sinuses are behind the nasal cavity. The sinuses act as resonating chambers for the voice; they help to filter dust and foreign materials from the air before it reaches the lower airway passages; and they lighten the weight of the skull on the vertebral bones of the neck that balance and support the head. Since all the sinuses are lined with mucous membrane, they are vulnerable to infection, to inflammation by allergens, and to the formation of polyps.

sinusitis Inflammation of the mucous membranes that line the sinuses. The passageway that connects the sinuses to the nasal cavity is narrow and therefore susceptible to obstruction because of colds, allergies, or the presence of polyps. Such obstruction prevents free drainage of the sinuses, causes an entrapment of air that cannot escape through the nostrils, and leads to an accumulation of mucus which can become a locus of viral or bacterial infection. Infectious organisms may be transported into the sinuses through the nose when an individual is swimming in contaminated water or may invade the maxillary sinuses by way of an abscessed tooth in the upper jaw. The characteristic symptom of sinusitis is a severe headache and face pain in the location of the affected sinus. Fever, swelling, discomfort in the neck, earache, and a stuffed nose are other symptoms.

Acute sinusitis usually clears up in a few days of bed rest; aspirin or other analgesic, limited use of nosedrops, steam inhalation, and air filters can make the recovery period more comfortable. If secondary bacterial infection develops in the sinuses the doctor may prescribe antibiotics.

When sinusitis becomes chronic, every effort should be made to find out the cause. If it can be traced to nasal polyps, consideration should be given to having them removed. When an allergy is responsible, precautions may require the use of an antihistamine combined with other medications that will keep the nasal passages clear. Heavy smoking is another cause as well as a contributing factor when other causes already exist. Irritation by the chlorinated water in swimming pools is yet another cause. Aside from the pain that accompanies chronic sinusitis, there is the remote danger of eventual complication in the form of osteomyelitis or meningitis. Since surgical drainage is advisable only in extreme cases, chronic sufferers should do what they can for themselves: smoking should be minimized, air conditioners and humidifiers installed, and the environment indoors kept as free of dusts and pollens as possible by using air filters.

skin The body's outer surface and its largest organ, covering an area of approximately 25 square feet and weighing about 6 pounds. The skin envelops the body completely and is also a continuation of the mucous membranes of the mouth, nose, urethra, vagina, and anus. Among its many vital functions are the following. It provides a barrier against invasion by infectious agents; offers the delicate tissues beneath it a large measure of protection against injury from the outside; regulates body temperature by the expansion and contraction of its supply of capillaries and by the activities of the sweat glands; and participates in the excretion of some of the body's wastes. Through its production of melanin, it wards off some of the damage of the sun's ultraviolet rays, and it also helps transform sunshine into essential vitamin D. In addition, the skin is one of the body's most delicate sense organs: through its vast network of nerve fibers, it transmits messages of pain, pleasure, pressure, and temperature.

What is commonly identified as "the skin" is merely its visible portion or the outermost layer of the epidermis. The epidermis is made of several layers of living cells and an outer horny layer of dead cells constantly being shed and requiring no nourishing blood supply from below. This is the comparatively tough layer that provides a shield against germs as long as it remains unbroken. The same nonliving skin cells form the hair and nails. Beneath the epidermis lies the dermis or true skin, bright red in appearance and containing the nerve endings and nerve fibers, sweat and sebaceous glands, and hair follicles. Beneath the dermis is a layer of fatty tissue, called subcutaneous tissue, which helps to insulate the body against heat and cold and which contains the fat globules which through a pattern of distribution give individuality to the features of the face and determine the contours of the body. Also within the subcutaneous tissue are the muscle fibers responsible for the subtle changes of facial expression.

skin care For a healthy woman skin care need consist of rituals no more complicated or costly than cleansing with soap and water to remove accumulated grease, perspiration, dirt, and dead cells and maintaining a proper balance of the protective oils on the skin surface to prevent drying, scaling, and chapping. Medicated soaps are inadvisable unless recommended by a doctor, and when dryness is a chronic problem, detergent preparations may be less dehydrating and less irritating than true soap. Cleansing lotions, cleansing creams, or cold creams removed with tissues will never leave the skin as clean as rubbing a lather over it with a soft washcloth and removing the suds with warm water. All makeup should be removed before going to bed. The cheapest cleansing cream will do, followed by washing with soap and water.

Whether or not the skin is naturally oily or dry is an inherited factor. A vaporizer or humidifier is the best aid to counteracting the drying effects of central heating or air conditioning. Animal fat, especially lanolin which comes from sheep wool, is the oil closest to human sebum and is therefore the best thing to use when skin begins to flake or crack at the knees, elbows, or fingers. It is to be preferred to mineral oil or vegetable oil for the purpose of lubrication. A sensible regimen of diet, rest, exercise, and good habits of personal hygiene are all the care that the average woman's skin should require. Attempts at correcting various skin disturbances by using cosmetic preparations, medicated soaps, and the like are not advisable.

skin diseases *See* ACNE, CONTACT DERMATITIS, PSORIASIS, etc.

sleep The period during which the body withdraws from wakeful participation in the environment, but is by no means in a continuous state of rest and repose. Sleep and dream research has yielded a great deal of interesting information. Of the time spent in sleep (one-third of the average human life), at least one-fifth is spent in dreaming. Two different states alternate during sleep in cycles: longer periods during which all body functions slow down and recuperate from the day's activity and briefer periods, called REM (rapid eye movement) sleep, when the heartbeat quickens, pulse rises, and all processes speed up as if to be at the alert. It is during

REM sleep that most dreaming occurs, but they do not always occur together. For reasons which are unclear, both types of sleep are essential for wakeful well-being. One of the dangers of barbiturate and alcohol addiction is that these drugs suppress REM sleep and also suppress dreaming.

A normal state of health is characterized by as well as promoted by good sleeping patterns, and when sleeping problems exist over a considerable period or when they arise suddenly without visible explanation, they should be investigated; the solution to the problems cannot be found in immediate recourse to hypnotics or barbiturates. Unaccustomed sleepiness or drowsiness may be a temporary phenomenon resulting from a wide variety of causes: overexposure to the sun; too much alcohol, especially in an overheated room; poor ventilation; too many tranquilizers; antihistamines; hangover effects of sedatives, tranquilizers, or sleeping pills; and low-grade infection. Chronic sleepiness may be due to thyroid deficiency, anemia, hardening of the arteries of the brain, or in rare cases the disorder known as narcolepsy. Escape into sleep rather than sleeplessness may be a sign of the onset of depression.

slipped disc *See* DISC, SLIPPED.

smallpox An acute, severe, highly infectious virus disease, characterized by multiple blisters appearing first on the face, neck, and upper extremities. Enforced vaccination throughout the world has led to the extinction of this disease. Since there are no silent carriers and no source of infection other than human carriers, and since the last human case, other than a laboratory infection, was reported in 1977, it is assumed by the World Health Organization that the virus has been eliminated everywhere. This is the only communicable disease over which immunization can record apparent total success. While vaccination against smallpox is no longer relevant as a health measure, the federal government's Communicable Disease Center, together with similar laboratories in other countries, maintains a stockpile of smallpox virus to make smallpox vaccine in the event of some future outbreak of the disease.

smegma A sebaceous secretion of a cheeselike consistency that accumulates near the clitoris and under the foreskin of the penis. Unless scrupulously washed off, it is likely to be retained and cause irritation under the foreskin of the uncircumcised male, leading to inflammation and pain.

smoking Among the health hazards unequivocally connected with inhaled tobacco smoke are increased vulnerability to lung cancer, chronic respiratory infection, heart attack (especially when combined with the use of the contraceptive pill), emphysema, and fetal damage leading to stillbirth, miscarriage, or chronic respiratory illness during infancy and early childhood. Cigarette smoke is much more likely to be inhaled than cigar and pipe smoke and therefore is more dangerous.

snoring The sound made during sleep by the vibration of the soft palate when air is inhaled through the open mouth. Snoring is a likely consequence of breathing through one's mouth when sleeping flat on one's back. The sound itself becomes louder with advancing age because of the sagging of the muscle tissue at the back of the mouth. Unless it is merely the temporary result of a stuffed nose or an allergy that has closed up the nasal passages, snoring is difficult to overcome.

soap A substance compounded of fatty acids and alkali, usually with the addition of a pleasant scent. Although all soaps are antiseptic, some contain stronger chemicals than others and may cause contact dermatitis on sensitive skin. Deodorant soaps can effectively slow down the multiplication of bacteria, even though they do not kill them. Soaps containing lanolin are helpful in lubricating dry skin, and medicated soaps contain ingredients that can promote the healing of cracked skin. The vegetable fat in cocoa butter soap is not as effective a lubricant as lanolin.

sodium chloride *See* SALT.

spasm An involuntary contraction of a muscle or group of muscles, usually the consequence of irritation of a nerve. Spasms in which there is an alternation of muscle contraction and relaxation, as occurs in hiccups, are called clonic spasms. When uncontrollable and repetitive spasms are without apparent cause, they are known as tics. Such tics, accompanied by pain, occur in trigeminal neuralgia. Any spasm that affects the entire body is called convulsive, as in the convulsions that accompany some epileptic seizures or that may occur when a high fever irritates the brain.

speculum A metal or plastic instrument with rounded blades which dilate a body passage or cavity to facilitate examination. During a gynecological checkup the speculum is inserted into the vagina and opens and holds the walls to permit the doctor to examine the vagina and cervix for infection, lesions, cervical discharge, abnormal growths, or other evidence of disorder. The pap test is done with a speculum in place.

speech disorders Abnormalities in spoken word formation which may be the result of organic anomalies, medication, disease, or emotional stress. For example, disordered speech may be caused by a cleft palate or severe malocclusion, overmedication with tranquilizers or an addictive use of barbiturates, diseases such as parkinsonism or cerebral palsy, conditions such as cumulative hearing loss, and normal occasions of emotional tension resulting in "stammering with embarrassment" or "sputtering with rage." Mild speech defects, such as a lisp or an inability to articulate the *r* or *l* sound correctly, may be a sufficient source of self-consciousness to require concentrated corrective therapy, especially if the defect causes a curtailment of such activities as speaking in public or produces difficulties during job interviews. A pronounced stutter can be agonizing. New audiovisual biofeedback techniques are being used in some speech therapy clinics with varying success depending on the seriousness of the disability. For adult stutterers corrective procedure may combine psychotherapy, medication, and disciplined reeducation of the tempo of word production as well as counseling for family members in how to help the stutterer. Anyone who wishes to consult an accredited speech pathologist can receive helpful information free of charge by writing to the American Speech-Language-Hearing Association, 10801 Rockville Pike, Rockville, Maryland, 20852.

sperm The male germ cell that must penetrate and fertilize the female ovum in order to accomplish conception. Sperm cells, technically called spermatozoa, are produced by the testicles under the stimulation of gonadotropins from the pituitary gland. The cells are carried in the semen which is ejaculated during the climax of sexual intercourse (orgasm). Each sperm cell resembles a translucent tadpole and is about 1/5000 of an inch long, with a flat elliptical head containing a complete set of chromosomes and an elongated tail by which it propels itself through the cervical canal in the direction of the ovum. Of the millions that move upward into the uterus, only a few live long enough to reach the fallopian tubes. If an ovum is available, fertilization may occur. Only one sperm cell ordinarily penetrates. The single penetration barricades the ovum against further penetration, and the processes of reproduction are initiated. Where male infertility exists, the main cause is poor sperm production, either because of testicular disease, general ill health, radiation exposure, dietary deficiency, alcohol, emotional stress, or overheated testicles.

sperm bank The storage of spermatozoa for future use in artificial insemination. Sperm banks are sometimes used by men who have had vasectomies, but this practice, never widespread to begin with, is on the decline since the increasing success of vasectomy reversal surgery. It is considered unlikely that stored sperm continue to be viable and otherwise biologically normal for more than 18 months.

spinal cord Tissue of the central nervous system that extends downward through the spinal column from the medulla oblongata of the brain to the second lumbar vertebra. The cord is protected by the bony projection of each vertebra, by the thin membranous meninges, and by the cerebrospinal fluid that serves as a shock absorber. The 31 pairs of nerves that extend from the spinal cord control practically all of the body's muscles and transmit sensory impulses to the brain. Thus the consequences of spinal injury or disease depend on the part of it that has been damaged: total paralysis and loss of sensation may occur because of a broken neck, but crushed lumbar bones may not affect the spinal cord at all.

spinal tap Withdrawal of a sample of cerebrospinal fluid by the insertion of a sterile hollow needle, usually between the third and fourth lumbar vertebrae; also called a lumbar puncture. The fluid sample is subjected to various laboratory analyses that can provide clues to such disorders of the brain or other parts of the nervous system as tumors, encephalitis, meningitis, or polio. A spinal tap is not usually performed unless other diagnostic measures are inconclusive.

spleen A flattened, oblong organ located behind the stomach in the lower left area of the rib cage. It is purplish red in color and weighs approximately 6 ounces. The spleen acts as a reservoir for red blood cells which it supplies to the bloodstream in any emergencies that diminish oxygen content. Through a network of white cells called phagocytes, the spleen also cleanses the blood of parasites, foreign substances, and damaged red cells. In its paler lymphatic tissue it manufactures the white cells known as lymphocytes which ward off infection. When removal of the spleen is essential because of hemorrhage following an injury, because it is affected by malaria, tuberculosis, or other diseases, or to control thrombocytopenia (shortage of blood platelets) or other diseases, its functions are taken over by the liver and bone marrow.

spotting Irregular or recurrent nonmenstrual bleeding from the uterus, cervix, or vagina. The most common cause of spotting prior to menopause is hormonal imbalance, either natural or resulting from taking oral contraceptives. Causes after menopause are fibroids, endometrial cancer, excess synthetic estrogen. Spotting that occurs after strenuous exercise or sexual intercourse may indicate the presence of cervical polyps or erosions or small vaginal tears. Spotting should be investigated promptly with a pelvic examination, pap smear, and perhaps a D&C. When it occurs during pregnancy, it may signal the onset of a spontaneous abortion. The occurrence should be called to the doctor's attention at once, since a prompt regimen of bed rest may be all that is necessary to prevent the abortion.

sprain An injury to the soft tissues around a joint. Ligaments can be torn or stretched, with damage to associated tendons, blood vessels, and nerves. The severity of a sprain depends on how badly the joint was twisted or wrenched. In some cases the pain is immobilizing and there is considerable swelling accompanied by a large area of discoloration. Since the symptoms are practically indistinguishable from those of a simple fracture, it is sensible to have the injured part X-rayed. If this procedure must be delayed, the following first aid measures should be observed. The injured joint should be elevated and rested on pillows or on a folded blanket. If the site of the sprain (or possible fracture) is in the wrist or elbow, the arm should be supported by a neck sling improvised from a large scarf or a torn sheet. No attempt should be made to strap the joint except by someone properly trained to do so. Rest, application of cold compresses, and aspirin should provide relief from pain and reduce swelling until the doctor can be consulted. In milder injuries the healing process may be hastened by the application of heat the next day, the intermittent application of heat for short periods of time thereafter, and the use of an elasticized bandage.

staphylococcus infection A category of diseases caused by various strains of staphylococcus bacteria, so named for their tendency to grow in grape-like clusters (staphylo) and their round shape (coccus). They are responsible for some types of food poisoning; they produce skin disorders such as impetigo, boils, and sties; and they are also a cause of osteomyelitis, an inflammation of the bones. Staph infections present a particular problem in hospitals, where they are known to cause epidemics among the newborn. Many of these bacteria are now difficult to eradicate because they have developed strains resistant to penicillin and other antibiotics.

stethoscope A diagnostic instrument which amplifies the sounds produced by the lungs, heart, and other organs; used by doctors during the listening part of an examination known as auscultation.

sterility *See* INFERTILITY.

sterilization Any process that removes the organs of reproduction or makes them incapable of functioning effectively.

steroids *See* CORTICOSTEROIDS.

stillbirth The delivery after the twentieth week of pregnancy of a baby that shows no sign of life.

stimulant A category of drugs that temporarily increase the activity of a particular part of the body.

stomach The pouchlike digestive organ into which food is emptied from the esophagus. The stomach, which leads directly into the duodenum, lies below the diaphragm in the upper left portion of the abdomen, hanging more or less freely and moving with the intake and exhalation of breath. It is composed of three layers of different types of muscle fibers which respond to the need for expansion as the stomach fills with food and are responsible for the rhythmic contractions of peristalsis during which the digestive juices are mixed with the partially digested food and churned into a semiliquid consistency. The full stomach holds about 2½ quarts; when empty, its walls lie flat against each other. The mucous membrane lining contains the glands that secrete hydrochloric acid and the digestive enzymes. The normal functioning of these glands is controlled by the actual presence of food in the stomach and by the neurological reflexes activated by the expectation or the sight of food. Like all glands, those of the stomach can be adversely affected by strong feelings. Anger especially increases the gastric secretion leading to a "churning" sensation and which, if chronic, may eventually be the cause of an ulcer. A sudden attack of anxiety or of acute fear may actually cause paralysis of the muscular wall of the stomach so that it dilates and drops to a lower part of the abdominal cavity resulting in a sinking sensation. Stomach disorders include mild indigestion, chronic or acute gastritis, and ulcers as well as tumors, both benign and malignant.

strain A mild injury to a muscle, usually caused by subjecting it to unaccustomed tension, as occurs through overexertion or an accident; also called a pulled muscle. (A sprain is more serious, involving stretched or torn ligaments.) Among the most common are twisted ankles caused by a misstep and strained back muscles caused by lifting a heavy weight incorrectly. Wrist muscles may also be strained in various athletic endeavors. The best treatment is rest of the affected part, heat application, an elasticized bandage for support, and a mild painkiller if necessary. Most strained muscles recover in a day or two without further discomfort.

streptococcus infection A category of diseases caused by strains of streptococcus bacteria, so named for their chainlike arrangement (strepto) and their round shape (coccus). Among the strep-caused disorders are pharyngitis (strep throat), scarlet fever, puerperal fever, and some pneumonias. Rheumatic fever and glomerulonephritis sometimes follow certain strep infections. The species *Streptococcus viridans,* which is normally present in the mouth and harmless for most people, is a cause of subacute bacterial endocarditis in people who have damaged heart valves. Since this species also surrounds the roots of abscessed teeth and since they may enter the bloodstream following the extraction of the tooth, a prophylactic dose of antibiotic medicine, usually penicillin, before a tooth is pulled is always advisable for those who have damaged heart valves.

streptomycin An antibiotic discovered in the 1940s, widely used in the following decades because of its effectiveness against tuberculosis, and more recently abandoned in favor of other medications because of its negative side effects.

stress Physical, chemical, or emotional factors that constrain or exert pressure on body organs or processes and on mental processes; in contemporary, popular usage, psychological pressures.

stretch marks Subcutaneous red streaks that eventually turn into silvery, slightly sunken lines; technically called striae. These marks are usually the result of ruptured skin fibers caused by an excess of subcutaneous fat, by prolonged use of steroids, or in some cases by the distension of the abdomen in pregnancy. Stretch marks typically appear wherever layers of fat are likely to accumulate: on the thighs, abdomen, breasts, and upper arms. When goiter is present, they will also appear on the neck.

stroke A discontinuity or interruption of the flow of blood to the brain causing a loss of consciousness and, depending on the severity and length of the circulatory deprivation, resulting in partial or complete paralysis of such functions as speech and movement: also known as a cerebrovascular accident and sometimes still called apoplexy. The processes leading to a stroke are cerebral thrombosis, cerebral embolism, and cerebral hemorrhage. When the blood vessels of the brain have been damaged and constricted by atherosclerosis, the formation of a clot may completely block circulatory flow. A similar blockage may occur because an embolus of air, fat, or other foreign matter impedes blood flow to the brain. The chief underlying cause of cerebral hemorrhage is a preexisting condition of hypertension, especially in combination with arteriosclerosis or atherosclerosis. The consequences of a stroke, short of being fatal, depend on what part of the brain has been deprived of oxygen and for how long. The deprivation may be so brief as to be inconsequential, an arm or a leg may be paralyzed, speech may be impaired, or the victim may go into a coma. Hospitalization in an intensive care unit must be prompt, since the correct treatment immediately following the stroke and for the first few days afterward is crucial to the amount of recovery achieved by the patient. Physical therapy for the rehabilitation of the affected muscles should begin while the patient is still in bed. A team of medical experts as well as regularly scheduled counseling by the hospital's psychotherapy staff can lead to successful partial rehabilitation.

stuttering *See* SPEECH DISORDERS.

sty An infection of a sebaceous gland at the rim of the eyelid, usually at the root of an eyelash. The infection, which results in inflammation and abscess, is usually caused by staphylococcus bacteria. If it does not respond to home treatment of hot compresses applied for about fifteen minutes every two hours and the use of ophthalmic ointment that can be bought without prescription, a doctor should be consulted. The most likely causes of frequently recurring sties are a generally poor state of health with low resistance to ever-present germs and the careless habit of rubbing the eyes with unwashed hands. Unclean or borrowed articles of eye makeup may also carry infection resulting in sties.

sugar Any of the following sweet carbohydrates found in various foods or chemically derived: sucrose (beets, cane, maple syrup); lactose (milk); maltose (malt products); glucose and dextrose (fruit, honey, corn syrup); fructose (honey, fruit juices); galactose and mannose (do not appear in free form in food); and ribose, xylose, and arabinose (do not appear in free form in foods, but are derived from meat products and seafood). *See also* CARBOHYDRATES, GLUCOSE.

suicide The act of taking one's own life. Since an action intended to result in one's death may be camouflaged as an accident, statistics are incomplete. However, in the United States in 1977 there were 28,681 documented deaths by suicide, making it the ninth leading cause of death. This is an overall rate of 13.3 per 100,000 people, but it ranges from 0.5 for persons aged 5 to 14, to 13.6 for persons 15 to 24, to 21.5 for persons 75 to 84. There are three times as many male suicide deaths as female. In addition to these deaths by suicide there are a large number of suicide attempts, more frequent among women than men, which do not result in death. These are often referred to as "cries for help." Most people who commit suicide are severely depressed for fairly long periods of time prior to taking their lives. Prevention involves recognition of the depression, sometimes by the depressed individual but usually by another, and getting psychiatric help. Anyone who talks seriously about suicide must be considered to be at real risk of suicide and needs help. "Hot lines" for emergency suicide prevention counseling listed in the telephone directory are one source of help. Some people consider activities such as cigarette smoking, high-speed automobile driving, and excessive consumption of alcohol to be self-destructive behavior and therefore related to suicide.

sulfonamides A group of medicines, known as sulfa drugs, that inhibit the growth and reproduction of various bacteria. Because many of these drugs have negative side effects, they have largely been replaced by antibiotics. However, some sulfa drugs, especially sulfadiazine, may be prescribed, often in combination with other sulfa drugs, for meningococcal, *E. Coli,* and other infections.

sunburn Inflammation of the skin caused by overexposure to the ultraviolet rays of the sun or a sunlamp. The lighter the skin, the more quickly it burns. The condition may be limited to a reddening or it may be equivalent to a second-degree burn with blisters and a fever. The best treatment for a mild burn is to avoid the sun for a while and to leave the burned area alone or apply cold, wet dressings to reduce swelling and discomfort. A severe burn may require professional medical attention.

Excessive exposure to sun or a sunlamp does more harm than good for almost everyone. Irrefutable conclusions of medical research indicate that prolonged exposure increases the risks of skin cancer and of wrinkles. For the elderly and anyone with a heart condition, lupus erythematosus, or high blood pressure, the sun can be downright dangerous, especially if there is any possibility of the onset of heat stroke. Women taking certain medicines either for indefinite or short-term therapy should be aware of the fact that overexposure to the sun may produce skin eruptions. While reactions differ in individual cases, the following drugs should be suspected as a possible cause when a rash appears following a period of sitting or lying in the sun: birth-control pills, antihistamines, oral medication for diabetes, diuretics, antibiotics, fungicides, and tranquilizers.

When exposure is unavoidable, sensible precautions should be taken: protective clothing, a brimmed hat, a heavy umbrella, and the use of a cream or lotion containing para-aminobenzoic acid, listed in the contents of over-the-counter sunscreens as PABA in alcohol.

suppositories Medicated substances in solid form, usually conical or cylindrical in shape, to be inserted into the rectum or vagina. The medication is contained in glycerin or fatty material which is melted and diffused by body heat. Suppositories may be recommended as a temporary way of dealing with constipation, especially in order to lubricate feces that have caked within the rectum. Vaginal suppositories containing spermicidal chemicals are available without prescription. They are less reliable contraceptives than creams, jellies, and foams (which are themselves not the last word in reliability), because the effective chemicals in suppositories are not likely to be evenly distributed when they finally diffuse. Vaginitis may be relieved by suitably medicated suppositories; rectal suppositories containing a surface anesthetic may be recommended to relieve the discomfort of pruritis or hemorrhoids.

surgery Operations that repair, remove, remodel, replace, or explore the body's tissues, organs, and cavities using such processes as X-ray, ultrasonics, cautery, and laser beams, as well as such instruments as scissors, knives, and tweezers. Surgery may involve organ transplants (kidneys, corneas, coronary arteries); implants (pacemakers, silicone bags, intraocular lenses), and prosthetic attachments. An operation may be elective, that is, a matter of some degree of choice as in the repair of a hiatus hernia, a tonsillectomy, or the removal of nasal polyps, or it may be a nonelective, often lifesaving or essential, measure as in a crisis dealing with a ruptured appendix, a perforated ulcer, or an ectopic pregnancy. Of the 25 million operations performed in the United States each year, only about 20 percent are considered unequivocally essential. Reasons given for the remaining 80 percent include the prevention of a more complicated problem, pain relief, and improvement of appearance.

Consumer advocates, health insurance companies, and professional medical organizations, including the American College of Surgeons, make the following suggestions about evaluating the need for elective surgery and selecting a surgeon. If the family doctor or an internist suggests a visit to a surgeon based on diagnosis of a particular problem, select, if possible, a surgeon with specialty board credentials. While almost 95,000 doctors perform operations, only about 52,000 have board certification. Also select, if possible, a surgeon who is a Fellow of the American College of Surgeons. While these credentials do not guarantee competence, they do mean that the doctor is (or was) a qualified specialist. The documents are usually highly visible in the consulting office, but if the only way to ascertain credentials is to ask to see them, then do so. When an operation is recommended, get a second opinion from another accredited surgeon unconnected with the first surgeon. Find out if there is a medical alternative to surgery and ask to have all the advantages and disadvantages of either choice spelled out. If surgery is decided upon, make every effort to have the operation performed by a surgeon on the staff of a teaching hospital. Find out in advance what coverage is provided by your health insurance policy, including the cost of the anesthesiologist's services and of the postoperative visits to the surgeon's office.

swelling An abnormal enlargement, inflation, or distension of any part of the body occurring either internally or externally. Swelling of the lymph nodes (mistakenly called swollen glands) accompanies such infections as mononucleosis, parasitic invasions such as filariasis, cancers such as leukemia and Hodgkin's disease, and the condition commonly called blood poisoning and technically known as septicemia. Swellings that follow a bruise are usually minor, resulting from the fact that there is bleeding into the bruised tissues. The puffy swelling that indicates edema typically occurs because of circulatory failure or because of abnormalities in the composition of blood as occurs in the nephrotic syndrome. Internal organs may swell when diseased as occurs in cirrhosis of the liver. A swelling under the skin may be a sebaceous cyst. When bacterial infection is the cause, the condition may be a boil. Allergies and abscesses of any kind result in swelling. The superficial bumps that occur after an insect bite or the hives that erupt because of an allergic response are a consequence of the liberation of histamine into the skin. Any swelling of mysterious origin that persists, especially if it is accompanied by pain, should be diagnosed by a doctor without too much delay.

syndrome A group of signs and symptoms that occur together and characterize a particular disease or abnormal condition.

tampon A plug of absorbent cotton or similar material placed within a body cavity in order to soak up secretions and hemorrhagic blood, and especially to contain the menstrual flow. Tampons for this latter purpose are designed for easy insertion into the vaginal opening and for removal by an attached string. Where the hymen is still unruptured, tampons may be difficult and occasionally impossible to insert. Menstrual tampons are less likely than sanitary pads to carry infections from the anus to the vagina; however, if they prove to be the source of vaginitis, their use should be discontinued in favor of pads.

Tay-Sachs disease An incurable and usually fatal genetic disease of fat metabolism found almost exclusively among Jews of central and eastern Europe. There is a statistical probability that in 1 of 900 marriages of these Ashkenazic Jews, both partners will be carriers of the gene. Genetic counseling in advance of a pregnancy is considered advisable for those who might be carriers. When the pregnancy already exists, amniocentesis can determine whether the fetus has the disease. Should this be the case, a therapeutic abortion usually is possible.

TB *See* TUBERCULOSIS.

tear glands *See* LACRIMAL DUCTS.

teeth *See* DENTAL CARE, ORTHODONTIA.

telemetry The long-distance transmission by electronic signals of measurement data and other information. Telemetric devices, originally developed for rocketry and space science, have been adapted for attachment to telephones so that, for example, a doctor in a rural hospital can transmit a patient's electrocardiogram or electroencephalogram to medical specialists thousands of miles away for further evaluation. The technique is also widely used for testing artificial pacemaker competence by telephone.

temperature *See* FEVER.

tension Physical and emotional response to stress.

Terramycin Brand name of oxytetracycline, one of the broad spectrum antibiotics. *See* TETRACYCLINE.

testicles The principal male organs of reproduction; the sex organs; also called testes. The testicles are located within the scrotum and produce the hormone testosterone which determines the secondary sex characteristics of the male at puberty: deep voice, hair distribution, body build, and sexual drive. They also produce sperm cells. Each testis contains about 250 lobules in which tiny tubes produce the spermatozoa which leave the testicles at maturity by way of the convoluted passage called the epididymis. Removal of the testes (castration) before puberty causes male sterility and prevents the development of male sex characteristics. Castration following puberty also causes sterility, but the diminishment of male sexuality can be compensated for by testosterone injections. Castration is done occasionally to treat metastatic cancer of the prostate because the progress of this type of cancer is slowed by the absence of testosterone which is secreted by the testes.

tetanus An acute infectious disease caused by the entrance into the body through a break in the skin of the microorganism *Clostridium tetani.* A tetanus-prone wound is one which is deep, has much tissue damage and necrosis (destruction), is uncleaned for four or more hours, and is contaminated by soil or street dirt. The exotoxin produced by the *C. tetani* bacteria affects the nervous system in such a way as to cause paralyzing muscle spasms, hence the term lockjaw to describe one of the early symptoms. The tetanus bacilli grow in the intestines of all mammals and are found in soil and dust contaminated by the feces of the carriers. Once a widespread and fatal disease, particularly in rural areas and in wars, it affects fewer than 500 people a year in this country, thanks to routine immunization of infants and booster shots for children and adults. Any injury which might be a tetanus-prone wound is sufficient reason for consulting the closest doctor within 24 hours about the proper immunization and other protective measures. All wounds should be cleaned promptly and thoroughly.

tetracycline A broad spectrum antibiotic prepared synthetically or derived from several species of the genus of funguslike bacteria (Streptomyces) found in soil. The tetracyclines have no effect on viruses; they are usually prescribed, especially for patients with penicillin sensitivity for such bacterial infections as gonorrhea, pneumonia, bronchitis, meningitis and for the rickettsial diseases. Among their undesirable side effects are skin rashes and gastrointestinal irritation. They may discolor teeth and interfere with the bone development of a child whose mother took tetracycline in the last half of pregnancy, so they are contraindicated after the fourth month of pregnancy. For similar reasons the American Medical Association recommends that other antibiotics be prescribed for children under 8 years of age. Two of the brand names under which tetracyclines are sold are Aureomycin and Achromycin.

thermography A technique for recording variations in skin temperature by the use of photographic film sensitive to the infrared radiation given off by the surface of the body. The result of the test is called a thermogram. Because tumor cells produce somewhat more heat than normal ones, this procedure can be helpful in the detection of incipient breast cancer. Thermography is noninvasive, but for purposes of diagnostic accuracy it is not as definitive as mammography.

thiamin One of the B complex vitamins; also known as vitamin B_1. A deficiency of vitamin B_1 leads to neurological disorders, especially to the psychosis known as Korsakoff's syndrome, characterized by memory impairment and time and place disorientation, to paralysis of the extremities (beriberi), and to heart failure. People who eat substandard diets and those whose food is overcooked (thiamin is destroyed by heat) may not be getting enough B_1 in their food. Signs of deficiency can be detected by a doctor and corrected with a prescribed regimen of thiamin.

Thorazine Brand name of chlorpromazine.

throat disorders Any disease or malfunction affecting the pharynx or the larynx. *See* STREP THROAT, TONSILS, GLOBUS HYSTERICUS, etc.

thrombosis The formation of a clot, technically called a thrombus, in a blood vessel, most commonly in a varicose vein in the leg or in any artery in which the interior walls are roughened by atherosclerosis. The blockage of a narrow blood vessel by a thrombus may have grave consequences: when the obstruction occurs in one of the coronary arteries (coronary thrombosis), the result may be a major heart attack; obstructive thrombosis in the brain is a cause of stroke. A complication of thrombosis is thromboembolism in which a part of the clot breaks off to form what is called an embolism, circulates to other parts of the body, and causes obstruction, as in pulmonary thromboembolism. The risks of thrombosis increase not only with age, but with the use of the contraceptive pill, particularly among cigarette smokers. Two drugs used specifically to treat or prevent thrombosis are heparin, which is given intravenously or subcutaneously, and coumarin, which is taken orally. These drugs are called anticoagulants. There are also a number of drugs which have an anticoagulant effect especially when combined with coumarin. Included among these are steroids, salicylates (aspirin), and sulfonamides.

thyroid disorders *See* GOITER, HYPERTHYROIDISM.

tic Involuntary and repeated spasmodic contractions of a muscle or group of muscles; also called habit spasms or nervous tics. Such movements usually develop in childhood in response to emotional stress, and while they may subside from time to time during adulthood, they almost inevitably return during periods of fatigue or tension. Among the more common tics are blinking, clearing the throat, jerking the head, twitching the lips. Psychotherapy and tranquilizers can sometimes eliminate a tic, but the former treatment may be too time-consuming and too expensive and the latter may lead to problems more unpleasant than the tic itself. The specific instance in which involuntary spasms of facial muscles originate in a physical disorder is the symptom known as tic douloureux discussed under trigeminal neuralgia.

ticks Blood-sucking parasites. Some ticks are comparatively harmless, but others transmit disease. *See* RICKETTSIAL DISEASES, ROCKY MOUNTAIN SPOTTED FEVER, TYPHUS.

tinnitus The sensation of hearing sounds—humming, buzzing, ringing—that originate within the ear rather than as a result of an outside stimulus. Tinnitus should not be confused with the auditory hallucinations of some mental illnesses. The buzzing and ringing may be the temporary result of a blocked eustachian tube such as occurs during an upper respiratory infection or an allergic response. It may also occur after a head injury, following exposure to an extraordinarily loud noise, or as a side effect of certain medications, especially streptomycin. The diseases with which it is associated are Menière's disease, otosclerosis, and brain tumor, but most cases are of mysterious origin. If the noises can be ignored, so much the better. When they are disturbingly intrusive at bedtime, they can be masked by soft music from a nearby radio. In recent years, ultrasonic irradiation of the inner ear has achieved some success. Where a hearing problem is also present, an electronic device that produces a sound that masks the noise of tinnitus can be fitted inside the casing of the ordinary hearing aid.

Tolinase Brand name of one of the oral diabetic drugs that stimulate the pancreas to produce insulin. Because of their implication in the deaths of diabetics from cardiovascular causes, these drugs are considered to be a less desirable means of controlling the disease than proper diet and weight management alone or, when necessary, combined with insulin.

tonsils Two clumps of spongy lymphoid tissue lying one on each side of the throat, visible behind the back of the tongue between the folded membranes that lead to the soft palate. Together with the adenoids, which are located behind the nose at the opening of the eustachian tube, the tonsils function somewhat like filters, guarding the respiratory tract against foreign invasion. When they become infected, inflamed, or enlarged, they are the source of complications leading to difficulties in swallowing and to the spread of the infectious agent to surrounding tissues. When the infection is streptococcal (strep throat), antibiotic treatment must be prompt to prevent the further complication of kidney infection or heart involvement. When enlarged tonsils are a chronic cause of respiratory difficulties over several years or when the adenoids constantly transmit infection to the sinuses or the middle ear, removal by surgery should be considered. However, a tonsillectomy or adenoidectomy should not be undertaken without substantial indication that the operation is justifiable as a health measure.

toxemia The presence in the bloodstream of poisonous compounds (toxins), especially those produced by various pathogenic microorganisms; popularly called blood poisoning, also called septicemia. The toxemia of pregnancy is different and is discussed under eclampsia.

toxoplasmosis A parasitic infection transmitted to humans usually in the fecal droppings of cats and occasionally by eating infected meat. It usually produces symptoms so mild as to escape detection or to be mistaken for a cold. However, congenital toxoplasmosis, in which the infectious organisms are transmitted by the recently infected and thus previously nonimmune mother to the fetus, may be the cause of miscarriage, stillbirth, or irreversible birth defects. Animals which harbor the parasite usually show no symptoms. However, laboratory analysis of their stools will indicate whether or not this parasite is present. Pregnant women should avoid handling cat feces.

tranquilizers A category of drugs that suppress anxiety symptoms or modify disturbed behavior without effecting a cure. Tranquilizers (also called relaxants) are designated as minor if they have only the effect of allaying stress and as major if they alter such psychotic manifestations as hysteria, hallucinations, extreme aggressiveness, or suicidal tendencies. The minor tranquilizers are the most commonly prescribed drugs in the United States, especially those that are members of the benzodiazepine group (Valium, Librium). The major tranquilizers (Stelazine, Thorazine) can be numbing and, in large doses, fatal. All tranquilizers have the potential of producing mild to extremely adverse side effects. When combined with alcohol, barbiturates, antihypertensive medicines, diuretics, and antihistamines, they can result in death. Tranquilizers of any kind should be avoided especially during the early months of pregnancy, since they can cause irreversible damage to the fetus.

transcendental meditation *See* MEDITATION.

transfusion The transfer of blood or any of its components—plasma, serum, platelets—from a specific donor or from a blood bank to a recipient. When the transfusion involves whole blood, correct matching of the blood type, including the Rh factor, is a vital consideration. Plasma, serum, and platelets are compatible among all donors and recipients. Transfusions are common practice not only in lifesaving circumstances, but in any situation when replenishment of the blood supply is routine therapy. Among the more frequent causes of varying amounts of blood loss are burns, other injuries, delivery, and surgical complications. In most cases the transfusion is indirect, that is, the blood comes from a blood bank and is not transferred directly from one person to another. The technique of exchange transfusion, in which blood is simultaneously taken from the donor to replace the blood as it is removed from the recipient, is used rarely.

transplant The transfer of an organ or of tissue from one individual to another; the term is also used for the organ itself and for the grafting of skin from one part of the body to the other. Corneal transplants have the fewest complications. Following these, the most frequently and successfully transplanted organs are kidneys. Since the first successful transfer of a human heart in 1967 in South Africa, hundreds of similar operations have been performed throughout the world with varying length of survival. Liver and pancreas transplants are attempted occasionally, usually unsuccessfully. In 1976 the first successful transplant of bone marrow was accomplished. The biggest problem still to be solved in practically all such operations is the rejection by the recipient's immune system of the donor organ as a foreign invasion. This rejection, known as graft-versus-host disease (GVH), can eventually produce fatal liver damage and bone marrow disease. Until the recognition of blood types, transfusions, actually a type of tissue transfer, frequently resulted in the death of the recipient for this reason. Thus, in the case of kidney transplants, whether the organ comes from a close relative or a complete stranger, the recipient must take medicine over a lifetime to prevent rejection. The medicine, which includes various chemicals that suppress the body's immune responses, has to be adjusted in careful amounts: if there is too little immune suppression, the transplanted organ will be destroyed by the recipient's antibodies; if there is too much immune suppression, the recipient becomes vulnerable to fatal bacterial invasion.

If more lives are to be saved by organ transplants, the general public must become aware of the importance of donating organs to transplant banks. Forty states now permit residents to register their organs for donation when they renew their driver's license. Community efforts of this kind have as their goal the routine, legally binding donation at the time of brain-death of hearts, kidneys, livers, eyes, and other potentially useful body tissues.

tremor Involuntary shaking or quivering, usually of the hands, but also of the head or other parts of the body. Tremors may be coarse or fine, depending on the amplitude of the oscillation. They may occur when the body is at rest, ceasing when intentional movement occurs, or they may occur only during acts of volition. They may be slow or rapid, intermittent or continuous, and symptomatic of organic diseases that affect the central nervous system or of an emotional disturbance. They may accompany a chill or fever or may be one of the symptoms of withdrawal from alcohol, cocaine, barbiturates, and other drugs. Among the diseases with which tremor is associated are cerebral palsy, multiple sclerosis, parkinsonism, hyperthyroidism, arteriosclerosis of the brain, and late syphilis. The trembling that accompanies an anxiety attack or the onset of hysteria may be controlled by sedatives. When an organic disorder is the cause, the tremor usually diminishes with proper treatment of the disease.

trench mouth *See* GUMS.

trichomonas vaginalis A species of parasite that can cause vaginal inflammation in females and urethral inflammation in males; also called trichomoniasis.

trigeminal neuralgia Intermittent and acute sensitivity of the fifth cranial nerve (the sensory nerve of the face); also known as tic douloureux. The condition is characterized by the sudden and unpredictable onset of paroxysms of extreme pain seemingly unaccompanied by any change in the nerve itself. The disorder is of unknown origin. It is more common among women than men and rarely occurs before middle age. The spasms of pain may be triggered by such random circumstances as a draft of cold air, blowing the nose, or an anxiety attack. Spontaneous remission may occur after a month of attacks, with recurrence months or years later. Drug therapy provides some pain relief; in some cases the most effective treatment is injecting the nerve with alcohol. When these measures fail to produce results and the recurrent attacks become so frequent and so painful that they interfere with eating and interrupt sleep, neurosurgery may be recommended.

triglycerides A group of fats, also called lipids, derived from the fatty content of ingested food. Together with cholesterol, triglycerides are among the essential cell nutrients. In excessive amounts they may accumulate within the walls of the blood vessels and cause atherosclerosis. Triglyceride blood levels are measurable in laboratory tests, and when the levels are considered a threat to health, attempts to lower them are usually recommended. Countermeasures may include weight loss, change in eating habits, and, if hormonal imbalance is thought to be involved, a contraceptive other than the pill.

tubal ligation A method of sterilization in which the fallopian tubes are tied in such a way that the ovum becomes inaccessible for fertilization.

tuberculosis A major infectious disease caused by the tubercle bacillus which usually attacks the lungs and less frequently the bones, joints, kidneys, or other parts of the body; once called phthisis and consumption, now commonly referred to as TB. The disease continues to flourish wherever poverty, poor diet, and crowded substandard living conditions prevail. The infectious organisms are spread through the air from person to person on the coughs and sneezes of anyone with the disease in an active stage. Public health authorities know that in the United States and especially in urban areas, many millions have been infected with the bacillus and are carrying it in their bodies in latent form without knowing it. If resistance is high, the bacilli may be killed by white blood cells, or they may be walled up temporarily and immobilized in small masses called tubercles. Many people have gone through an active TB episode, mistaking the symptoms, if any, for those of a heavy cold: a cough, chest pains, and feelings of fatigue. Such an occurrence usually leaves a small area of scar tissue in the affected part of the lungs. It is not at all uncommon for a woman between the ages of 20 and 40 to take a tuberculin skin test as part of a thorough physical checkup and to be told that the results are positive. Under these circumstances a chest X ray is suggested to find out if the lungs show any active disease. If the patient does not have active disease, prophylactic medication is often prescribed to suppress the possibility of later activation of the dormant disease. Antituberculosis drugs almost always are completely effective in treating the active disease. Witness to their effectiveness is the closing down of practically all TB sanitariums. Treatment for active cases may begin in a hospital, but the patient is sent home as soon as the noninfectious stage is reached to resume all normal activities while continuing to take the prescribed medications. The most important of these for prophylactic purposes is isoniazid. Several drugs exist for treating the disease. Anyone suffering from a chronic cough, chest pains, breathing difficulties, chronic feelings of fatigue, weight loss, heavy sweating at night, and irregularity in the menstrual cycle is advised to have these symptoms checked to rule out the possibility of TB.

tumor A swelling in or on a particular area of the body, usually created by the development of a mass of new tissue cells having no function. Tumors may be benign or malignant; benign tumors may, but usually do not, become malignant. The presence of a tumor within the body may be unsuspected until it grows large enough to produce symptoms of pain or to interfere with the normal function of an adjacent organ or nerve. Diagnosis by biopsy determines whether the growth is cancerous or not. A malignant tumor may be treated surgically or with radiotherapy and chemotherapy. A benign growth may or may not be removed surgically, depending on its location and its potential for becoming cancerous. *See also* SWELLING.

Tylenol Brand name of an analgesic containing no aspirin; the active chemical compound is acetaminophen. It is a useful over-the-counter medication for the reduction of fever and relief of pain for individuals who are hypersensitive to aspirin in any form.

typhoid fever An acute and highly contagious disease caused by the bacterial bacillus *Salmonella typhosa* (related to the bacteria that cause food poisoning); also called enteric fever. Typhoid and paratyphoid infections are endemic wherever the laxity of public health measures results in the contamination of the food and water supplies by urine and feces containing the disease-bearing organisms. Flies may transmit the disease; restaurant workers or food handlers who have had the disease may be carriers who spread the disease unless they are scrupulous in matters of personal hygiene. The infection may also be transmitted by shellfish from contaminated waters. In a case of typhoid fever, the bacteria attack the mucous membranes of the small intestine, producing stools and occasionally urine containing the typhoid bacteria. Symptoms begin after an incubation period of about two weeks and include fever, headache, vomiting, stomach cramps, fatigue and mental disorientation. A rash of a few days' duration may erupt on the chest and abdomen. Milder cases subside spontaneously within a week or so. However, in a severe case the patient may go into delirium as the fever rises. Perforation of the bowel may occur at this stage. Fortunately, antibiotics with or without corticosteroids will effect a complete cure when administered before major complications occur. Immunization against typhoid fever in adulthood is considerably less trouble than the infection and is at least moderately effective. Travelers to those parts of the world where the disease is endemic are therefore advised to get the necessary shots against it. Since three successive inoculations are necessary over a three-week period, the immunization or the booster shots should be planned well in advance of departure.

typhus An infectious rickettsial disease transmitted by the body louse. The disease is endemic in parts of Asia, Africa, and on the shores of the Mediterranean. In another form known as flea typhus it is common in the Far East and the Southwest Pacific. Typhus is not related to typhoid fever in any way. The onset of the disease begins with a headache, acute pains in the legs and back, and sieges of uncontrollable shivering. Within a few days a rash spreads from the torso to the arms and legs, and high fever may cause delirium. Antibiotic treatment is usually effective. Untreated typhus has a death rate of one case in five. The literature of the Western world contains many accounts of typhus epidemics, especially those that occurred during the major wars. While the use of DDT effectively halted the pandemics of typhus following World War II, outbreaks still occur where primitive and overcrowded living conditions prevail. Travelers to places where the disease is prevalent should have an antityphus vaccination which provides immunity for about one year.

ulcer A chronic lesion in the epithelial tissue either on the visible surface of the body or on the lining of an interior cavity such that the tissues below the skin or mucous membrane may be exposed. Ulcers may occur for many reasons: poor circulation (bedsores, ulcerated varicose veins), infections by microorganisms (ulcerated gums, syphilitic sores), and damage caused by extremes of heat, cold, malignant growths, or chemicals.

Peptic ulcers include gastric ulcers, which occur in the stomach itself, and duodenal ulcers, which occur in the upper portion of the small intestines and are ten times more common than gastric ulcers. The immediate cause of peptic ulcers is the secretion of hydrochloric acid when there is no food in the alimentary canal to neutralize its corrosive effects. The disorder cuts across age, sex, and class. Men used to be the chief victims by far, but now half the patients are women. Children can also suffer from peptic ulcers. Peptic ulcers have long been considered one of the most typical of the psychosomatic illnesses, and there is no doubt that emotional stress is a major contributing cause. Evidence has accumulated to indicate that blood relatives of people with ulcers are likelier to develop them than other people, especially if they share blood type O. When the potential vulnerability exists, there is no doubt that it is exacerbated by tension, alcohol, spicy food, nicotine, and the caffeine in coffee, tea, cola drinks, even in decaffeinated coffee. An ulcer that is diagnosed and treated when the symptoms first appear is more likely to heal quickly and less likely to recur than if it is ignored or treated with home remedies for indigestion. The first indication is a burning pain that recurs a few hours after eating. When the condition worsens to the point where the acid that has been burning a hole in the mucous membrane eventually eats into a blood vessel and causes a hemorrhage, the condition (bleeding ulcer) requires hospitalization and emergency treatment. The presence of an ulcer is visible in an X-ray picture after the patient has swallowed barium. Conventional treatment consists in certain dietary prohibitions and recommendations combined with supervised medication. A comparatively new antihistamine drug that inhibits gastric secretions with no apparent undesirable side effects is the chemical compound known generically as cimetidine and sold under the brand name Tagamet.

umbilical cord The structure that connects the fetus to the placenta of the mother, functioning as a lifeline through which maternal blood is transmitted to the fetus and fetal blood is returned to the mother. At the time of birth the umbilical cord, which is approximately 2 feet long and is attached at what is to become the infant's navel, is tied at two points close to each other and cut in between them. The vestige dries out and falls off naturally within less than a week.

undulant fever A disease caused by drinking unpasteurized milk taken from cows (also from sheep or goats) infected with Brucella microorganisms; also called brucellosis or Malta fever. In rare cases improperly cooked meat contaminated with these microorganisms also can be a source of the disease. Characteristic symptoms are pains in the joints, fatigue, chills, and a fever that may rise and fall at various times of the day or be low in the morning and rise slowly to 104°F by evening. These fluctuations in temperature account for the name of the disorder. If the disease goes untreated, the liver, spleen, and lymph nodes become swollen and sore. Since the symptoms may be confused with those of mononucleosis or rheumatic fever, a blood test should be made so that the nature of the infectious agent can be identified. The disease is curable with antibiotics. It is inadvisable to drink unpasteurized milk (unless instructed to do so by a doctor for some particular condition), even from a herd that has been government-inspected.

uremia *See* KIDNEY DISORDERS.

ureter One of two tubes, each about 12 inches in length, connecting the kidney to the bladder. The urine produced in the kidney is transmitted by the muscular contractions of the ureters into the bladder, where it is stored until it passes through the urethra in the act of urination. Inflammation of the ureter (ureteritis) may result from the presence of a stone or cysts as well as from infection.

urethra The muscular tube, approximately 1½ inches long in women, that carries urine from the bladder to the exterior. Both sexes are vulnerable to urethritis (inflammation of the urethra) caused by gonorrhea infection. Contamination by other infectious organisms during catheterization or as a result of bladder infection is also common. Symptoms of urethritis include painful urination, swelling of the vulva, and a yellowish puslike discharge from the urethra. When untreated, the condition may develop into cystitis. When inflammation over a considerable period causes scar tissue to develop, the urethra may become so constricted that surgical correction is indicated.

urination The excretion through the urethra of liquid wastes stored in the bladder. The fluid secreted by the kidneys travels through the ureters into the bladder where it accumulates. The urine accumulated within the bladder is prevented from flowing into the urethra by the internal sphincter of the urethra (a sphincter is a circular muscle in a state of involuntary contraction). When the stimulus from a full bladder is transformed into a conscious effort to urinate, the bladder muscles are contracted and the sphincter is relaxed. The external sphincter of the urethra is also relaxed. These motor reflexes result in the deliberate discharge of accumulated urine through the urethra to the exterior. The act of passing urine is technically called micturition. Conscious sphincter control may be reduced temporarily in adults by acute fear or some other emotionally charged reaction. It may also be a sign of a neurological disease such as epilepsy or the result of a stroke. Loss or impairment of bladder control, technically called incontinence, may be a consequence of infection of the bladder or other part of the urinary tract, displaced pelvic organs, and, especially in aging men, disease of the prostate gland.

About 1 quart of urine is eliminated each day, somewhat more during cold weather and less during hot weather, since in warmer weather larger amounts of fluid wastes are eliminated through the skin in the form of sweat. On the average women urinate about four times daily, with frequency depending on the amount and type of liquid consumed, state of health, age, and other variables. For example, the consumption of large amounts of tea or coffee may increase frequency of urination not only because of the extra fluid, but also because caffeine is a mild diuretic. Frequency increases during pregnancy not only because the uterus presses on the bladder, but also because nutritional demands require a greater intake of liquids, especially of milk. The need to urinate more frequently occurs in older women as a consequence of a natural loss of muscle tone.

Any persistent abnormal sensations during the act of urination or any sudden changes in frequency or color should be reported to a doctor. Painful urination accompanied by a burning sensation is symptomatic of infections that affect the bladder or urethra. The sudden onset of abnormally frequent urination may be caused by cystitis, diabetes, or incipient kidney failure. An inability to empty the bladder completely is usually related to interference by a stone, a tumor, or partial blockage by pressure from a prolapsed uterus or to neurological disease.

urine tests The examination of a urine specimen by various laboratory procedures; also called urinalysis. Since normal urine is of constant composition within definite limits, changes in the color, consistency, clarity, or specific gravity are usually, but not always, a sign of disorder. Thus, every complete physical checkup, whether during health or illness and especially at frequent intervals during pregnancy, should always include a urine test as well as questions about urination. Any visible changes in the color of urine, which is normally a pale amber, might suggest disease. Laboratory tests check for the following abnormalities. Albuminuria (proteinuria) is the presence in the urine of certain proteins (albumins) indicating the possibility of kidney disease, inflammations such as cystitis or urethritis, or, during pregnancy, pre-eclampsia. Albuminuria may also be a response to certain drugs, and it may exist from time to time without pathological significance in the condition known as postural or orthostatic albuminuria. Glucosuria is the consistent presence in the urine of glucose (not the occasional presence of one of the other sugars) and is usually the indication of diabetes. Hematuria, or blood in the urine, warrants further examination by instruments (cystoscopy) or X-ray if the hematuria persists in order to discover what part of the urinary tract is the source of the bleeding. Among the more common causes are the presence of a kidney stone, a tumor, or some degree of kidney failure. Pyuria, or white blood cells in the urine, is an indication of an infection of the urinary tract, in most cases cystitis or urethritis. Urine can be cultured to ascertain whether and what bacteria are present.

urologist *See* DOCTOR.

uterus The hollow, pear-shaped, muscular organ situated in the pelvis above the bladder; also called the womb. When a woman is not pregnant, the uterus is about 3 inches long, 2 inches wide, and 1 inch thick; it weighs about 2 ounces. As the cradle containing the fully developed fetus, it will weigh as much as 30 ounces and expand greatly in size. The uterus is suspended within the pelvis by the uterine ligaments which are extended like wings. The fallopian tubes enter the upper part at each side. The broad and flat portion of the uterus is called the body; the lower part which opens downward into the vagina is the neck or narrow tubular cervix. During a gynecological examination the insertion of the speculum as far as the cervix enables the doctor to see many of the abnormal conditions that might affect the uterine area. Any cell changes that might be indicative of malignancy are detected microscopically during a pap test. The muscular walls of the uterus are lined with mucous membrane called endometrium that goes through the monthly changes as part of the menstrual cycle. This cycle is interrupted by pregnancy during which the lining of the uterus in its secretory stage anchors the placenta through which the fertilized egg is nourished. Among the more common disorders of the uterus are benign growths called fibroid tumors, prolapse (the dropping of the uterus from its normal position), and displacement (the forward or backward tilt of the body of the uterus from the cervix). Surgical removal of the uterus is called a hysterectomy.

vaccination Inoculation with a preparation of dead or attenuated live germs for purposes of immunization against a specific disease. The word itself, which derives from the Latin word for cow, was created at the time that Jenner developed vaccine from cowpox as a method of immunizing humans against smallpox. Until very recently, vaccination has been used almost exclusively to mean smallpox vaccination. The word is now used synonymously with inoculation and immunization.

vaccine A preparation of dead or weakened live microorganisms or of other effective agents injected into the body of humans or animals for the purpose of stimulating the production of antibodies against a particular disease without producing disease symptoms.

vacuum curettage *See* DILATATION AND EVACUATION.

vagina The passageway that slopes upward and backward from the external genitals, the vulva, to the cervix; the female organ of sexual intercourse. Within the pelvic cavity the bladder is in front of the vagina and the rectum is behind it. In the normal adult woman the empty vagina is about 3 inches long. It receives the male spermatozoa; it is also the conduit for the menstrual discharge and the final passage through which the fetus travels at birth. The vaginal opening is partially closed by the hymen, until the hymen is stretched or ruptured by intercourse, use of tampons, or physical activity. The mucous membranes that line the vaginal walls normally secrete a fluid that is acidified by normal bacteria, thus creating a chemical environment that protects the tissues from invasion by various harmful microorganisms. This environment is likely to be destroyed by douching with strong chemicals, by the use of vaginal sprays, and by certain antibiotic medicines. Under normal circumstances and especially during sexual excitation, the vaginal discharge is thin and practically odorless. During a pelvic examination, the vagina is inspected for cysts or tumors and the possible development of a fistula. Another standard procedure is the insertion of the doctor's rubber-gloved fingers into the vagina at the same time that the other hand presses down on the outside of the abdomen. In this way the uterus and ovaries are palpated (diagnosed by touch) for any signs of cysts, tumors, or other abnormalities. Aside from the changes in the vaginal walls during pregnancy when hormonal activities affect the muscles, membranes, and discharges, any unusual symptoms should be discussed with the doctor. Symptoms that require professional diagnosis include itching, burning, the onset of pain during intercourse, the formation of ulcers, and the discharge of pus.

vaginal care Since the vagina of a healthy woman is a self-cleansing organ, daily washing of the outer genital area with soap and water normally provides sufficient care. Many doctors feel that habitual douching, for hygiene, contraception, or medical treatment, may be harmful rather than beneficial. Douching and the many vaginal sprays on the market are likely to inhibit the natural secretions of the vaginal tissues, causing dryness and consequent irritation to the membranes. They also destroy the healthy bacterial environment of the area, upsetting the normal acidity that discourages the proliferation of damaging microorganisms. The genitalia of the healthy woman have a characteristic odor which is not unpleasant and which is sexually stimulating. Not only do sprays mask this odor, but they may also mask a malodorous discharge that should be diagnosed, not deodorized. As a method of birth control, douching alone is ineffective since it takes only about 90 seconds for sperm to reach the cervix after they have been ejaculated. When a mild infection does exist, a douche consisting of 2 tablespoons of distilled white vinegar in 1 quart of warm water will increase the acidity of the vaginal environment and discourage the spread of the infection. In cases of infertility where postcoital tests indicate the necessity for doing so, douching with bicarbonate of soda will alkalize the cervical environment, thus improving the chances of preserving the viability of sperm cells. With increasing age, the mucous secretions of the vagina tend to dry up, and the tissues are therefore more easily irritated. At this time, a mild nonprescription lubricating jelly or cream similar to the one used by the doctor during a pelvic examination should be applied before sexual intercourse.

vaginal discharge Any emission from the vagina, including the menstrual flow, the secretion of a clear, slippery lubricating fluid during sexual intercourse, and between periods a mucoid secretion from the cervix. A vaginal discharge is abnormal if it has a bad odor, is thick and cheesy in consistency, is yellowish or greenish in color, or is tinged with blood between periods or after the menopause. A burning or itching sensation is another indication of abnormal discharge. When the disorder exists, it may be caused by mechanical irritation (IUD), chemical irritation (sprays and douches), or infection by fungi, bacteria, or other microorganisms. Blood-streaked discharge may be a symptom of fibroids, other tumors, or cysts or of some other cervical or uterine disorder. While any abnormal discharge should be diagnosed and treated if it persists, prompt attention is especially indicated if there is any change in vaginal secretions during pregnancy, after an abortion, or during a regimen of estrogen replacement therapy.

vaginal smear A sample of vaginal secretions taken by the doctor during an internal examination for purposes of diagnosing any condition that produces such symptoms as a malodorous discharge, itching, pain during urination, or discomfort during sexual intercourse. The smear is usually transferred to a glass slide and examined under a microscope. It may also be processed in order to begin a laboratory culture that may yield information about the particular microorganisms responsible for the symptoms.

vaginitis Any disorder characterized by inflammation of the vulvo-vaginal membranes accompanied by leukorrhea or burning and itching aggravated by urination. Vaginitis may be classified as specific in cases where the infectious agent is identifiable and as nonspecific in cases where the symptoms are not traceable to a particular cause. Nonspecific vaginitis is usually treated with medicated suppositories, creams, or douches. Since the vaginal membranes are as delicate as those in the mouth, they may be irritated not only by germs, but by the chemicals in deodorant sprays, by tampons, and by contraceptive devices. Mechanical irritation is likely to increase the possibility of infection.

Valium Brand name of a tranquilizing drug in the chemical category benzodiazepine. In the United States it is a frequently prescribed drug which recently has provoked a controversy regarding its undesirable side effects such as impaired intellectual functions and its addictive qualities.

varicose veins Veins that are swollen and enlarged; also called varicosities. Varicosities include hemorrhoids (swollen anal veins), but the superficial veins of the legs, especially those located in the back and inner side of the calf, are the ones most frequently affected. Varicosities of smaller veins are visible through the skin as a bluish-red network of delicate lines going off in different directions from a particular source. A larger varicose vein is likely to have the appearance of a bumpy, purplish rope. Varicose veins are more common among women than among men, among people who spend a great deal of time standing in one place, and among the obese; they are a frequent development during pregnancy; most women over 40 develop some varicosities; and there seems to be an inherited predisposition to the condition.

Varicosities result from heavy pressure of the blood against the walls of the veins. The blood that returns to the heart from the legs must do so against gravitational force. The muscles that surround deeply buried veins support the veins and promote the antigravitational movement of the blood, and these veins are therefore less likely to become distended. All veins contain valves set into the walls in pairs. These flaplike projections are open when the blood is flowing correctly toward the heart; the valves close to prevent any reverse movement away from the heart. However, when prolonged standing in one spot or the pressure of pregnancy or excessive weight puts an abnormally heavy strain on the veins with no accompanying support from surrounding muscles, the column of blood constantly bearing down on the closed valves causes the valves to weaken and the walls to dilate. The valves may become incapable of closing. This disability in turn causes the downward flowing blood to collect in the veins, further swelling and weakening the walls. When the condition becomes increasingly serious, the knotty protrusions become vulnerable to ulceration and possible hemorrhage.

Prevention, decreasing the likelihood of occurrence, and therapy for mild cases all involve relieving the pressure on the veins. Feet should be raised whenever possible. Constriction by crossing the legs or wearing tight girdles or garters should be eliminated. Tasks that involve being in one place for a long time should be done sitting instead of standing if possible. If prolonged standing is unavoidable, moving from one spot to another and occasional walking about will provide some relief.

Symptoms such as muscle cramps in the middle of the night, swollen ankles, and a general feeling of soreness in the legs indicate that additional therapeutic measures are necessary to prevent further deterioration of the condition. Individually fitted support stockings are preferable to elasticized partial bandages and should be worn during the waking hours. Swimming, bicycling, and hiking as well as special leg exercises are effective therapy. Somewhat more drastic treatment consists of injections with medications that cause the swollen veins to harden and eventually wither so that the circulation is rerouted to healthier vessels. A more effective and permanent treatment for seriously distended veins is an operation that ties them or removes them completely. The spider-like varicosities that develop during pregnancy are likely to disappear if proper weight is maintained and beneficial exercise is routine.

vasectomy A surgical procedure which effectively sterilizes the male without impairing his hormone levels or his sexual performance.

vegetarianism A dietary regimen which, at its strictest, includes no food of animal, bird, or fish origin and derives essential proteins from plant sources. Less rigid vegetarians may or may not eat eggs, but include all other dairy products. Nutritionists do not believe that irrefutable evidence has yet been presented equating longevity with vegetarianism as such. However, every nutrient necessary for normal growth and continuing health can be obtained from meals based on plant foods plus eggs and dairy products. When eggs and dairy products are also eliminated, there is an inevitable deficiency of the essential nutrient vitamin B_{12} which comes entirely (for all practical purposes) from animal sources. Ongoing studies of the vegetarian discipline indicate the following: adherents in a particular group of young people had lower blood pressure, lower cholesterol, and lower weight than a group comparable in age on a regular meat diet. A religious sect that includes eggs and dairy products in its meals, but eliminates all meat, poultry, and fish is known to have a significantly lower incidence of heart disease and the breast and colon cancers that appear to be traceable to heavy intake of animal fats than the standard rate for Americans on a nonvegetarian diet.

vein A blood vessel through which blood is transported back to the heart. Unlike arterial blood which is bright red as a result of being freshly oxygenated, venous blood is dark, the only exception being the blood in the pulmonary veins which is being transported directly from the lungs to the heart. Because veins are less elastic and weaker than arteries they are more vulnerable to such disorders as varicosities and phlebitis.

vertebra Any of the bones of the spine. The spinal column, which supports the body's weight and which provides the bony corridor through which the spinal cord passes, is comprised of 33 vertebrae, some of which are fused together. Depending on their location, they differ somewhat in structure and size: 7 cervical vertebrae are at the back of the neck; 12 thoracic vertebrae support the upper back; 5 lumbar vertebrae are in the lower back; 5 fused vertebrae make up the sacrum near the base of the spine, and 4 fused vertebrae form the coccyx. The vertebrae are separated from each other by fibrous tissue and cartilage discs which act as shock absorbers. When the displacement of one of these discs causes pressure on a nerve, the result may be acute pain. Osteoarthritis of the vertebral bones is one of the chronic diseases of aging responsible for backaches. Back discomfort may also originate in poor posture that affects vertebral position in relation to surrounding musculature. Osteoporosis of the vertebrae causes their collapse and the consequent loss of height seen in many older people. Tuberculosis of the spine is also a cause of vertebral collapse and deformity.

vertigo A sensation of irregular or whirling motion, either of oneself or of nearby objects; also called dizziness, although this latter term often is used incorrectly to describe a sensation of light-headedness or feeling faint. There are many possible causes of vertigo. It can be brought on by rapid, continuous, whirling motion, such as riding a merry-go-round, or by watching objects in apparent rapid motion, such as telephone poles observed from a fast-moving car. It can be caused by various diseases that affect, directly or indirectly, the labyrinthine canals in the middle ear. Included among these diseases are inflammation or infection of the labyrinthine canal, tumors or vascular disorders of the brain, and gastritis.

Vincent's angina *See* GUMS.

virus A submicroscopic disease-causing agent capable of reproducing only in the living cells of plants, animals, and humans. Among humans, viruses are responsible for a long list of otherwise unrelated communicable infections ranging from the common cold to a very rare and fatal brain disease (Creutzfeld-Jakob). When a viral strain responsible for a particular disease can be isolated and transformed into an effective immunizing vaccine, the disease itself can eventually be controlled. This has been the case with smallpox and may eventually be the case with such virus-caused infections as polio, measles, and rubella. Antibiotics are ineffective, and usually inappropriate, therapy for virus diseases except in cases where the patient might be critically vulnerable to secondary bacterial infection. *See* HEPATITIS, INFLUENZA, etc.

vitamins A number of unrelated organic substances essential in minute quantities as catalysts in metabolic processes.

vitiligo A harmless, but disfiguring skin condition, especially conspicuous when it occurs among blacks, in which an abnormal loss of melanin pigment results in irregular patches of pale skin. The patches usually appear symmetrically on the face, neck, hands, and torso. The condition, which appears to be hereditary, can be successfully masked to some extent by cosmetics individually blended to match the normal skin color.

vocal cords The two ligaments within the larynx which vibrate to create the extraordinary range of human sounds. Each reedlike cord is attached at one end to the front wall of the larynx (voice box) with the ends placed closely together. The other ends are connected to small rotating cartilage rings near the back wall of the larynx. These rotations cause the cords to separate or to close, thus controlling the amount of air that passes through the larynx. When the cords are open, the air passes through the larynx without producing sounds. When the cords are close together, the air that is forced through them causes them to vibrate like the reeds in a musical instrument. These vibrations create sound waves in the form of a voice, and when the sound waves are articulated and controlled in a particular way, they produce speech and song. The pitch of the voice depends on the tension in the cords, and its depth depends on their length. Men's voices are deeper than women's because their vocal cords are longer. A common occurrence among singers and public speakers is the development of nodes on the vocal cords. These growths are usually removed by surgery. Sometimes they are malignant. *See* LARYNX.

vomiting The mechanism whereby the sudden contraction of the muscles of the stomach and the small intestines forces the partially digested contents of these organs upward and out of the mouth; technically called emesis. Vomiting and the feeling of nausea that characteristically precedes it may occur as a reflex response to tickling the inside of the throat, to an overfull stomach, to ingesting an emetic such as mustard or a poison, or to the presence of bacterial toxins acting as an irritant on the gastric membrane. It may also occur because of stimulation of the vomiting center of the brain. Motion sickness, overdoses of certain drugs and anesthetics, and emotional stress, such as strong feelings of revulsion or anxiety, can cause a reaction of vomiting. Medicines such as Dramamine and antiemetics prevent vomiting by depressing the response of this part of the nervous system. Vomiting may also occur because of obstructions in the intestines, uncontrolled paroxysms of coughing, the hormonal changes associated with pregnancy, and migraine headaches. Other less obvious causes are associated with brain injuries and disorders affecting the brain such as tumors, abscesses, or meningitis. Certain forms of mental illness or severe emotional disturbances are characterized by vomiting spells.

Any recurrent or uncontrollable attacks of vomiting should be diagnosed by a doctor. In coming to the aid of someone who is vomiting following an accident, precautionary measures should be taken so that the patient does not inhale the vomitus and fatally obstruct breathing.

vulva The term for the external genital organs of the female. The vulva surround the vaginal opening. Proceeding from front to back, they consist of the mons veneris, the labia majora and minora, the clitoris which is partially covered by the clitoral hood, the urethra, the vaginal opening, Bartholin's glands on either side of the vaginal entrance (just inside of which is the hymen if it has not been ruptured), the perineum, and the anus.

wart An abnormal growth on the skin caused by a virus; technically called a verruca. Warts may occur at any age. Since the virus can spread to lesions in the skin caused by scratching, shaving, or other factors, warts may appear in groups or in succession. Because some other skin disorder may be mistaken for a wart or because the wart itself may become infected with bacteria, a doctor should be consulted about the nature of the growth and the advisability of having it removed. Techniques include cauterization with chemicals or an electric needle or surgical incision. *See also* PLANTAR WART.

water retention *See* EDEMA, DIURETICS.

withdrawal method *See* COITUS INTERRUPTUS.

womb *See* UTERUS.

worms Parasites that invade the body and multiply within one or another part of it. They are usually transmitted by an intermediate host, and in the United States by far the largest number enter the body through food or water contaminated by the excreta of an already infected person. When intestinal infestation is heavy, symptoms include abdominal pain, diarrhea, weight loss, and anemia.

The parasite known as the pinworm is not uncommon among children and is sufficiently contagious to spread through the family if it is not diagnosed and treated promptly. The chief symptom is anal itching, especially at night. The pinworms enter the system through the mouth or nose by way of contamination on the hands.

Two other varieties common in the United States are *Trichinella spiralis,* the cause of trichinosis, and hookworms. The larvae of the trichinae, which are embedded in the muscle tissue of infected pork or other meat, are destroyed when the meat is thoroughly cooked. However, if the infected meat is undercooked ("pink pork") and the larvae survive, the digestive enzymes free the larvae in the intestines where they come to maturity. The females burrow into the intestinal walls, where they lay their eggs before they die. The larvae are then carried throughout the body, causing inflammation wherever they settle. In most places in the body they are eventually destroyed by the body's defense system, but once they penetrate muscle tissue, they coil into spirals and become encapsulated in cysts. Symptoms of infestation during the early phases include diarrhea and abdominal cramps, followed by edema, fever, chills, and profuse sweating. By the time the larvae become encapsulated in the muscles, these symptoms may have abated and additional symptoms of general fatigue and muscle discomfort appear. Muscle biopsy and serologic testing are helpful in establishing the diagnosis. While there is no specific cure for trichinosis, the disease is more discomfiting than dangerous. Although most pork is inspected for the presence of trichinae, the only foolproof method of avoiding trichinosis is to see that it is always properly cooked, gray in color rather than pink or white. An additional warning: never nibble on raw or uncooked pork products such as link sausages or frankfurters.

Hookworms enter the body primarily through the skin. Thus, anyone who goes barefoot in the country (especially children) is vulnerable to infestation, since hookworm larvae develop in soil that has been fertilized with or otherwise contaminated by human feces carrying the infection. When the larvae enter the body, the bloodstream carries them to the lungs and then to the intestines where they mature into adult worms and lay their eggs in the intestinal walls. A serious infestation causes anemia, with its attendant disabilities, as well as persistent nausea and cramps. Diagnosis is made on the basis of examination of a stool sample, and treatment is simple, safe, and almost always effective. Reinfection can be prevented by wearing shoes especially in those areas where public sanitation and general habits of personal hygiene are minimal.

For the less common forms of worm infestation, and there are many, the most practical measures for prevention include the following. Be careful about personal hygiene, especially when traveling in countries where public health measures are inadequate. Avoid eating raw fish, raw meat, and undercooked pork, no matter where it is served. Avoid swimming in any waters known to be contaminated by dangerous parasites. In countries where human excrement is commonly used for fertilizer, all fruit should be peeled, all vegetables cooked, and those that are to be eaten raw, such as salad greens, should be washed thoroughly to get rid of any worm eggs that might be harbored in the leaves.

wound A body injury, ranging from superficial to severe, in which the skin or interior tissues may be cut, pierced, or otherwise damaged. Wounds are classified as abrasions (scrapes that remove part of the skin and bleed only slightly), incisions (cuts that may be slight or deep and are caused by a sharp object such as a knife, razor, or broken glass), punctures (deep injuries caused by thin pointed objects such as nails or needles), and lacerations (jagged tears in the skin and underlying tissues). The most important aspects of emergency treatment for wounds are the control of bleeding and the prevention of infection. An abrasion may bleed very little, but since the skin is broken, the danger of infection is always present. Scrapes should therefore be washed thoroughly with soap and running water and covered with a sterile gauze. Until the doctor determines whether a more extensive wound should be stitched (sutured), firm continuous pressure should be applied for about ten minutes with the fingers over a gauze pad, a clean handkerchief, or a piece of brown wrapping paper. The pressure must not be interrupted for wiping and for inspection since interruptions delay the clotting. While a puncture wound may not appear to be serious, its potential for tetanus infection makes it one of the most dangerous types of wound. A laceration in which the skin has been torn may be superficial enough to be treated like an abrasion, or it may be so extensive as to require prompt additional care.

wrinkles The lines and furrows that mark the skin as it ages and loses elasticity. Heredity, hormonal interplay, emotional and physical health, and exposure to sun and wind are the chief factors that determine the age at which skin begins to wrinkle. Also, the skin of women who smoke seems to wrinkle earlier and more than of those who do not. Wrinkles cannot be removed or permanently delayed by creams or lotions; cosmetics can mask them, but those that claim to contain "magic" ingredients may do more harm than good. The technique of dermabrasion can temporarily erase the more superficial lines, but they will inevitably reappear as the sagging skin continues to move away from the supporting structures beneath. Cosmetic surgery can eliminate wrinkles for several years, but the decision to undergo such a procedure should be carefully considered.

xerography A mammography technique (also called xeroradiography or xeromammography) in which the images of breast tissue produced by radiation exposure are made on a Xerox plate instead of on film. The result of this technique is a blue-toned image on opaque Xerox paper rather than a film negative.

X ray Radiation of extremely short electromagnetic waves capable of penetrating certain matter opaque to ordinary light and producing images on photosensitive surfaces; also the image produced. X rays have become indispensable in medical study, diagnosis, and treatment. The radiation is created by an electrical apparatus that produces a beam of the desired intensity and scope by bombarding a tungsten target with high-speed electrons in a vacuum tube. X rays are also called Roentgen rays after their discoverer. The area of specialization dealing with X ray technology is radiology or roentgenology. Under ordinary circumstances, X rays are more easily absorbed by bone than by flesh. By placing a fluorescent screen behind the body, the bones are delineated as shadows. This technique is called fluoroscopy. When permanent records are wanted, photographic plates that are sensitive to X rays are used to produce images that can be dated and preserved as part of a patient's medical history. From its original application to injuries or disorders of the skeletal system, X ray technology has been broadened by the technique of introducing radiopaque substances into the patient's body to provide information about nonskeletal disorders such as in the gastrointestinal tract. More recently, computerized scanners have been developed that can take layered pictures of parts of the brain previously inaccessible by ordinary radiological methods.

Whether for diagnostic purposes or, more likely, as treatment (*see* RADIOTHERAPY), the danger of overexposure to X rays has become a widespread problem. Among the consequences of overexposure are destruction of skin, loss of hair and nails, development of certain cancers, and damage to the genes, the reproductive organs, and fetuses. Pregnant women should avoid exposure to X rays except in the greatest emergency. Under any circumstances a patient should always ask that a lead sheet cover those parts of her body not intended to show on the film. Because of the serious disabilities created by exposure, experts on radiation hazard advise patients to ask the following types of questions before X rays are taken. Before having a complete set of 16 to 18 pictures as part of a routine dental checkup, ask the dentist what special problem exists that can be dealt with only in this way and why a whole series has to be taken if trouble is suspected in a particular area of the mouth. When a medical doctor suggests X rays, ask what their purpose is, whether other tests do the same thing, whether the lowest possible radiation is being used to achieve the necessary result, and when the equipment was last inspected. Many states have no laws requiring that X ray equipment be checked every year to make sure that it does in fact deliver intended doses rather than perilously higher ones and that it in no way exposes the patient to unnecessary hazards because it is incorrectly operated or outmoded. If X-ray pictures must be taken, it is advisable to have them done by a radiologist. While specialists are more expensive than general practitioners, they are more likely to have the most up-to-date equipment and the best-trained technicians operating it. Anyone who has undergone a series of X rays and is moving to another city should ask the doctor or dentist for the films so that they can be turned over to whoever will be in charge of medical care in the new location. Unnecessary duplication with its attendant hazards, not to mention expense, is therefore avoided.

yoga exercises An ancient Hindu discipline, increasingly popular in the West, for the achievement of physical and mental relaxation. The exercises combine control of consciousness with various specific body positions coordinated with breathing patterns. While self-instruction is possible, beginners are likely to achieve greater proficiency in a group under the tutelage of an experienced teacher. The exercises can then be done at home or even at work at times convenient to one's own schedule.

38

Questions and Answers

Accidents

Q. Are falls a major cause of death among children?

A. No, less than five percent of falls that result in death involve children 14 or under. Fatal falls are a much more serious problem for old and middle-aged people.

Acetaminophen

See ASPIRIN.

Acne

See SKIN CARE.

Adams-Stokes disease

Q. Does the heart ever really skip a beat?

A. Although the expression is used figuratively about anyone who is excited, "skipping a beat" is something that normal, healthy hearts do not do. The skipping of a beat—the failure of the heart to contract and pump blood on schedule—is a symptom of *Adams-Stokes disease* and is marked by temporary loss of consciousness. Anyone suffering from this symptom should seek medical advice promptly.

Aging

Q. Why is the sense of taste lost in old age?

A. One reason is that taste buds diminish as one gets older until elderly persons have only 20 percent as many taste buds on the tongue as youngsters. Some brain cells also are involved, causing older persons to make more mistakes in identifying specific tastes.

Air travel

Q. Does flying in a jet airplane affect digestion or other body processes?

A. Modern jet aircraft cabins are pressurized to produce a simulated altitude of about 7,500 feet. While normal pressure is maintained, there is no health threat from a lack of oxygen or gaseous expansion in the digestive tract. *See also* EAR DISCOMFORT.

Albumin (in urine)

See TESTS AND DIAGNOSTIC PROCEDURES/URINE.

Allergy

Q. What is an allergy?

A. An allergy is a sensitivity in an individual to a substance that is harmless to others. The sensitivity may be marked by sneezing, a skin rash, digestive disturbance, or some other reaction. Eczema, hives, and asthma may be allergic reactions.

Q. What is an antibody?

A. An antibody is a substance produced by the body to combat an allergen or foreign substance that has invaded the body tissues; the antibody may combine with the foreign substance, neutralize its toxin, or otherwise render it inactive.

Q. What causes allergic symptoms?

A. In a typical allergic reaction, an allergen such as pollen or dander combines with an antibody and triggers the release of histamines. This in turn results in itching, swelling, redness, nasal discharge, watery eyes, or other physical effects.

Q. What are histamines?

A. Histamines are chemicals naturally present in human body tissues; they dilate blood vessels and render them more permeable, stimulate certain muscles and glandular secretions, and are actively involved in allergic reactions.

Q. Why do allergic symptoms resemble cold symptoms?

A. The eyes, nose, and throat are "shock organs" for several diseases transmitted by the atmosphere, including the rhino-virus responsible for the common cold. As in some allergic reactions, histamines are released by antibody reaction to the invading virus, causing nasal congestion, nasal discharge, etc.

Q. How can you find out what you are allergic to?

A. Very dilute solutions of suspected allergens can be applied to eye or nose membranes or into the skin of the patient. A sensitive person will react with typical allergic symptoms; some allergic individuals may react to a number of possible allergens in skin tests.

Q. What is "hay fever"?

A. Hay fever is a common name for allergic rhinitis, an allergic reaction to wind-borne pollens or fungi marked by nasal discharge, swollen nasal membranes, coughing, sneezing, and conjunctivitis. It usually is seasonal and affects about ten percent of the population.

Q. Some people seem to develop asthma during the Christmas season. Could they be allergic to Christmas trees?

A. Allergic reaction to spruce, fir, or pine trees is not unusual. The cause may be sensitivity of the person to the odors of evergreen or to molds commonly found on the trees. A simple way of avoiding the problem is to use artificial trees instead of evergreens.

Q. Is it possible to develop a rash from using perfume or cologne on the skin?

A. Yes. Some individuals are sensitive to oil of bergamot, a plant product used in colognes and perfumes. The effect is intensified by exposure of the perfumed skin to sunlight.

Q. Some people develop a skin rash after drinking even a small amount of alcohol. Could this be due to an allergy?

A. Some individuals experience allergic reactions similar to asthma and eczema after ingesting alcohol. They may be sensitive to alcohol itself or the alcohol may increase sensitivity to other allergens, such as ragweed or certain foods.

Q. Can allergy-caused sinus trouble be cured by moving to an area with a dry climate, like the desert southwest?

A. Many people who have moved to other regions found that a change in climate did not help their sinusitis, possibly because their sinuses were irritated by the dust in the desert atmosphere.

Ambulation

See HOSPITALIZATION/AMBULATION.

Angina

See HEART DISEASE.

Apoplexy

Q. What is apoplexy?

A. Apoplexy is a rather old-fashioned term for stroke or brain-tissue damage caused by a hemorrhage in the region of the brain.

Arthritis

Q. How common is rheumatoid arthritis?

A. It has been estimated that between two to four percent of the population have this disorder.

Q. At what age do arthritis symptoms first become apparent?

A. In most cases, at about the age of 40.

Q. Is arthritis a disease of old people?

A. Although the disease usually occurs in people 40 or over, it can occur at any age. About five percent of arthritis sufferers are young children.

Q. Are women more often afflicted with this disease than men?

A. Yes, three times as many women have arthritis as men. A common time for the onset of the disease in women is at or shortly after the menopause.

Q. Can arthritis cause a low-grade fever?

A. Some forms of arthritis are associated with a mild fever. But the cause may be an inflammation related to the pain of arthritis and should be checked by a physician.

Q. Are mud baths or mineral baths helpful in treating osteoarthritis?

A. Most of the benefit from so-called "spa" therapy probably is due to rest, relaxation, a change of environment, and diet rather than the baths themselves.

Aspirin

Q. Aspirin can irritate the stomach. Is there a nonprescription painkiller that can be used instead?

A. Acetaminophen drugs frequently are used to relieve pain in persons sensitive to aspirin. Special aspirin formulations designed to reduce stomach irritation also are available.

Q. Can a patient substitute acetaminophen for aspirin in treating rheumatoid arthritis?

A. No. Acetaminophen has not been found to relieve the inflammation symptoms of rheumatoid arthritis.

Q. Is it safe to pack aspirin around a tooth that aches?

A. The apsirin would do more good if you swallowed it with a glass of water, because aspirin must get into the bloodstream through the digestive tract to be effective.

Q. Is it true that aspirin prevents blood from clotting?

A. Experiments show that it takes several minutes longer for blood to clot in a wound of a person using aspirin. But the effect is not a serious problem except for hemophiliac patients or for those who take large quantities of aspirin over an extended period of time.

Q. Why is it necessary to drink a glass of water every time aspirin is taken?

A. Because aspirin must be dissolved in a watery solution to get into the bloodstream, and a generous amount of water is needed to dissolve the drug properly. Otherwise, the aspirin may irritate the stomach lining while slowly dissolving in whatever fluid is in the stomach.

Asthma

See ALLERGY.

Atherosclerosis

See HEART DISEASE.

Backache

Q. Are men or women more likely to have backache?

A. Backache is common among both men and women.

Q. Are tall, thin people more subject to backache than short people?

A. Generally speaking, taller people, especially if they have long backs, are more likely to develop back trouble than shorter people. Erect posture is more of a strain for them because they lack the stability of shorter people.

Bags under the eyes

See SKIN CARE.

Bilirubin

See TESTS AND DIAGNOSTIC PROCEDURES/BLOOD.

Biopsy

See TESTS AND DIAGNOSTIC PROCEDURES/BIOPSY.

Blood

See TESTS AND DIAGNOSTIC PROCEDURES/BLOOD.

Blood circulation

Q. Are there any exercises that help improve poor blood circulation in the legs?

A. One simple exercise is to lie on your back with your legs raised at a 45 degree angle for a few minutes, draining the blood from your feet. Then sit on the edge of a bed or chair until the blood returns to the feet. Repeat this several times a day.

Blood pressure

Q. Is low blood pressure dangerous?

A. Disorders due to low blood pressure are rare; your blood pressure must be very low before it can be considered a cause for concern.

Q. Sometimes a doctor will check the blood pressure of your right arm and then of your left arm. Isn't the blood pressure the same on both sides?

A. Not always. There are certain disorders in the body that can be detected by comparing the two blood pressure readings. *See also* TESTS AND DIAGNOSTIC PROCEDURES.

Blood sugar

See TESTS AND DIAGNOSTIC PROCEDURES/BLOOD.

Body odor

See PERSPIRATION.

Body temperature

Q. Is it possible for an otherwise normal person to have a "fever"?

A. Yes. Some people lack the ability to sweat properly and thus are unable to lower their body temperature in a hot, humid environment.

Q. Is a high body temperature serious?

A. Yes. It is a sign that body cells are working faster and breaking down, leading to dehydration. Each degree of fever also increases the work load of the heart and threatens the nervous system. A critical point is 103° F.

Q. Do body temperatures change during the day?

A. Yes, temperatures generally are slightly higher in the afternoon and evening, and lower in the morning. Also, the temperature in women varies with different stages of the menstrual cycle.

Boils

See SKIN CARE.

Brain/speech

Q. Is speech controlled by one hemisphere of the brain? If so, which one?

A. Among right-handed people, who probably make up about 93 percent of the population, speech is almost always controlled by the left hemisphere—the same one that controls their right-handedness. Among left-handed people, about 60 percent also have speech controlled by the left hemisphere in spite of having their dominant hand controlled by the other.

BUN

See TESTS AND DIAGNOSTIC PROCEDURES/BLOOD.

Cancer

Q. What is the leading cause of

death from cancer among men?

A. Lung cancer.

Q. Does cigarette smoking increase the chances of getting lung cancer?

A. Men who smoke are ten times more likely to die of lung cancer than men who don't.

Carbuncles

See SKIN CARE.

Cats

See TOXOPLASMOSIS.

Chest

See FUNNEL CHEST; PIGEON BREAST.

Children

Q. Some say that soap solutions sold for children's bubble blowing can be harmful to a child. Is this true?

A. Several of the special "soap" bubble preparations have been found to acquire disease organisms when exposed to the environment. Parents should supply freshly prepared solutions made from liquid laundry detergents or "no-tear" shampoos for use in blowing bubbles.

Cholesterol

A. What level of cholesterol is dangerous?

Q. In the U.S., the *average* blood cholesterol level is 245 milligrams (per 100 milliliters—the standard index). Heart disease linked to atherosclerosis (hardening of the arteries) is very high in the U.S. In some other countries, where the average blood cholesterol level is probably about 100–170 milligrams, this type of heart disease is rare. There is no one danger point for every individual, but statistically anyone with a blood cholesterol level over 250 milligrams has a much greater chance—perhaps as much as five times greater—of developing atherosclerotic heart disease than someone with a lower cholesterol level.

Q. Can blood cholesterol levels be reduced through a change in diet?

A. There is evidence that by cutting down on consumption of saturated fats (fatty meats and dairy products) and by increasing the consumption of polyunsaturated fats (vegetable oils, fish, etc.), serum cholesterol levels can be moderately reduced. In any case, it seems wise to take steps along the lines indicated simply to keep your cholesterol level from getting any higher. Adding polyunsaturated fats to the diet, without decreasing the intake of saturated fats, will not lower your serum cholesterol level. *See also* TESTS AND DIAGNOSTIC PROCEDURES/BLOOD.

Colds

Q. Are the symptoms of the common cold caused by a single virus?

A. No. About 150 different viruses have been identified as causing common cold symptoms. The fact that so many different viral strains cause the infection precludes the possibility of creating an effective immunizing vaccine.

Q. Is it all right to blow your nose when it's blocked by a cold?

A. If the nose is completely blocked by swollen membranes during a cold, blowing will not open it. Forceful blowing may only spread the infection into the sinuses and Eustachian tubes.

Q. Will nose drops help open a "stuffed" nose?

A. Nose drops should be used cautiously; they give temporary relief which may be followed by greater congestion. Continued congestion may lead to continuous use of nose drops in a vicious cycle.

Contagious diseases

See INFECTIOUS AND CONTAGIOUS DISEASES.

Corneal transplant

See EYE DISEASE.

Cough plate

See TESTS AND DIAGNOSTIC PROCEDURES.

Crohn's disease

Q. What is Crohn's disease?

A. Crohn's disease, another name for regional enteritis, is an inflammation of the part of the small intestine where the small and large intestines are joined. *See also* ENTERITIS, REGIONAL.

Dandruff

Q. What causes dandruff?

A. Unfortunately, the cause is so far unknown. Theories abound, but no one has been able to prove that bacteria, for example—represented as the cause in one theory—exist in scalps affected by dandruff.

Q. Do any dandruff shampoos or other treatments sold over the counter really help?

A. Yes, some are reasonably effective in controlling dandruff. Certainly, if you have a problem with dandruff, it would pay to experiment with various brands until you find one that works for you. If nothing seems to help, see your physician or ask him to recommend a more effective medication.

Delirium tremens

Q. Is it possible to develop delirium tremens from overuse of tranquilizers?

A. Convulsions, tremors, and other characteristic symptoms of delirium tremens can occur as side effects of certain tranquilizing drugs.

Q. What is the cause of delirium tremens?

A. This is a psychotic disorder marked by delirium, tremors, and vivid hallucinations. It occurs in people who have been chronic alcoholics for several years.

Devil's pinches

Q. What are "devil's pinches"?

A. "Devil's pinches" is a common term for a hereditary disorder marked by the mysterious appearance of bruises on the body. The bruises are essentially harmless and there is no permanent cure for them.

Diabetes

See EYE DISEASE/DIABETIC RETINOPATHY; TESTS AND DIAGNOSTIC PROCEDURES/BLOOD/URINE.

Diagnostic tests

Q. What can a doctor tell about your health by examining spinal fluid?

A. There are at least two dozen physical conditions that can be revealed by study of the spinal fluid, including meningitis, poliomyelitis, brain tumor, lead poisoning, and rabies.

Doctors and patients

The following series of questions and answers relating to doctors and patients is an edited transcription of an interview with Dr. Richard J. Wagman, editor of *The New Complete Medical and Health Encyclopedia.* The interviewer was Sidney I. Landau, managing editor of the Ferguson staff.

Q. Why don't doctors tell the patient more than they do? Why do they often seem so reluctant to tell him what underlies his condition?

A. I think this situation has changed significantly, especially as more and more people are becoming more sophisticated about illness and health. It is extremely foolish for a doctor not to discuss what is going on with his patients. It is far more frightening to the patient to be kept in the dark about his real condition.

Q. Do you think that younger doctors are prone to tell more than older doctors?

A. I think it depends on the individual. I have seen a lot of younger doctors who behave like they are 80, and a lot of older doctors who behave like young people.

Q. What about doctors who do not explain the full reason for performing an operation, for example delivering a baby by Caesarian section?

A. This is the kind of thing that would make me very upset with my doctor, because he would be talking down to me. I am speaking not only as a doctor but as a person who is involved with using doctors. I have a family of my own, after all. I don't like being talked down to. Speaking as a physician, I don't like talking down to people.

Q. Would you tell the truth to someone who was suffering from a terminal illness?

A. I like to tell the truth, and I like to tell the patient as much as I think he can tolerate, if I think the patient wants to know. This is not a yes or no sort of phenomenon; this is picked up by hints, by clues, by innuendos, by the whole approach of the patient to me in terms of the questions he or she asks about his or her illness. I prefer to answer the question honestly.

If a patient with cancer asks me point-blank, "Do I have cancer?" I will answer yes. I won't necessarily say more. I answer the specific question. If the patient asks more I will go on and answer each specific question and no more.

If you lie to the patient you wind up isolating him, often from his own family, which has to know. At least some responsible member of the family has to know. They may find it difficult to talk to the patient since they are hiding the truth. All of a sudden the patient winds up in an untenable position: he or she has no one to talk to honestly.

This is also predicated on the belief that most patients who are seriously ill know what's going on. They sense the concern of their family and friends. Most people close to the patient are poor liars. I am against isolating the patient like this.

On the other hand, there are some patients who cannot tolerate the truth in this kind of situation, and again I think it is the role of the physician to be sensitive to the clues that the patient gives him.

Q. How should a layman act when visiting someone in the hospital who is gravely ill? Should he pretend he's going to get well? Can you make any blanket rule about this?

A. Two very simple rules. One, the visitor should be himself, and should be friendly and cheerful. Two, he should stay only a short period of time.

House calls and telephone calls

Q. To what extent can the telephone replace office calls and house calls?

A. I am very accessible, and most of my patients do not abuse the privilege of calling. That is, they generally call—not always, but generally—during office hours. A high percentage of the calls can be screened by my nurse, and most of the calls involve problems of anxiety and fear rather than medical emergencies—concerns which are quite legitimate. They often make office visits unnecessary, if it's simply a matter of a patient asking a question about something that has been bothering him.

Q. Why don't doctors make house calls any more?

A. I speak for myself only. I make almost no house calls, and there are a variety of reasons. I say this as a big-city practitioner. There are simply not enough hours in the day. It becomes impossible in terms of getting around. Ninety-nine percent of the house calls are not really and truly necessary. If a patient is seriously ill—for example, someone is having chest pains—he should be seen by a physician, but he also needs to have an electrocardiogram done, for example, and the best place to do this is either in the office or in the hospital. I am very limited in terms of what I can do at a patient's home. I don't carry an electrocardiograph machine in my car. If someone really needs a house call, for instance, in a city like New York, I can arrange for someone to see one of my patients at home and call me and let me know what he has found.

Q. What if a person is too sick to come out?

A. This is nonsense. The question is, must you be seen? And if you have to be seen, then the best place for an X ray or a blood test is the hospital or the office. The trouble is, in order for me to do the greatest good for the greatest number under my care, I have to put the responsibility on the patient to come to the office or, in emergencies, to the hospital.

Q. What if a child has a fever of 105° or something like that?

A. There are emergency measures that can be dealt with on the phone, in terms of the *immediate* care that can be given. In general, pediatric emergencies present another spectrum of disease. The question is, if you have a child who has a high fever or has had a convulsion, must you come out? The answer is, something has to be done immediately—before you can either physically get dressed, get into the car, or what have you. Advice can be given on the phone. That sums up what to do until either you come or one of your delegates comes. I think the patient has to be seen.

Q. What about a bleeding ulcer in an older person?

A. Hospital.

Q. What about heart attacks?

A. The only thing you can do in the case of a heart-attack patient in terms of coming to the house is to give relief of pain. Again, in a big city so much time is lost getting from one end of the city to the other. It is much more sensible to make all the arrangements to get the patient to the hospital. This means that the person is going to be in discomfort or distress no matter what you do, but you are going to get the patient to a place where something can be done as quickly as possible.

Answering services

Q. How should one deal with an answering service that won't give you your doctor's home phone number?

A. My own attitude with answering services—which leave a great deal to be desired as a general rule—is that you must explain to them that this is an emergency and what you hope for is that they will get either your doctor or whoever is covering for your doctor in his absence. You are not calling directly, but theoretically the answering service should relay the message to the doctor or his substitute, who will then call you back.

I tell my patients that if there is something urgent and they have problems with the answering service, that it is their obligation to badger the answering service to impress upon them the urgency of the call. You have to call back if you do not hear from the doctor within a given period of time, depending upon the actual degree of urgency or your anxiety or both.

Psychosomatic complaints

Q. In a recent poll of doctors, over 90 percent said their patients suffered from hypochondria and psychosomatic ailments. Have you found this to be true?

A. I can't say 90 percent, but a high percentage of patients who call are troubled with problems in terms of anxiety about their health, including patients who have serious, real illnesses. Usually the reason for the call is something involving fear, fright, worry, or whatever word you want to use.

Q. What about those who come to see you?

A. Also a high percentage.

Q. More pronounced in women than in men? In old people than in young?

A. I can't quote statistics. But higher in women. Women come more freely to doctors than men do anyway.

Q. Older women?

A. Most patients who come to an internist are in the older age group.

Specialists and GPs

Q. How does an internist differ from a general practitioner?

A. The internist is someone who practices only adult medicine. He deals with medical diseases involving, for example, heart, lungs, GI tract, kidneys, blood, the entire gamut of illnesses in adults. He does not practice pediatrics, and he does not deal with surgery, does not deal with obstetrics or gynecology.

The internist as a specialist has really come of age only relatively recently. The internist is rather like the medical counterpart to the surgeon as a specialist.

Q. In what way is the internist a specialist?

A. Internal medicine is considered, at least in most Western countries, as a specific specialty—with special requirements in terms of training. For example, my own training involved a year of internship specifically in medicine. I didn't spend time going through a pediatric service, ob-gyn [obstetrics-gynecology], or surgery. Internists deal entirely with medical problems as an intern, then two or three years of residency, and generally a subspecialty—in my case, cardiology. A general practitioner usually has one to two years of training in postmedical school with a little bit of everything—a little pediatrics, a litte bit of surgery, a little bit of ob-gyn, dermatology, etc.

Q. An internist does not have that?

A. That is right.

Q. Is there any need for a general practitioner today?

A. A good GP is worth his weight in gold. He is, in many communities, the family physician—the number one contact. for the patient. He may take care of all the individual's health needs or be the one to refer him to the proper specialist. In the big cities, frequently the internist has taken over the role of the family physician.

Q. But isn't it true that often you go to your family doctor, who is an internist, and its seems that he is sort of an agent for leading you on to other doctors who are more specialized in various things? From the point of view of the patient, in purely practical terms, you are paying twice. The temptation is to think twice about going to the doctor at all.

A. There is a lot of truth to that, and I agree with you. This involves, in my opinion, a great deal of responsibility on the part of your—what I call your primary—physician, in this case, the internist. Before he refers you to someone else, he will have to sit back and say, can I handle this myself? Does it need handling by someone else? And this means also he has to realize that this is going to cost the patient money, and consider whether it's really necessary. Unfortunately, I am not sure that everybody does think this way. I think one should.

Q. If your regular doctor is an internist and you want medical advice about digestive troubles, should you go to him or to a GI specialist?

A. I think that is jumping the gun. I think that your internist should be able to handle this very easily. If you have an internist or a GP, one of the things you have to do is have enough faith in him. He is the one who is going to decide when you need a specialist in any field. But don't be afraid to ask him if he thinks a consultation is necessary.

Q. If a doctor you know and respect recommends surgery, is it still advisable to get a second opinion?

A. It depends on how much anxiety you have, how clearcut the situation is, and how much faith and trust you have in the doctor and the doctor's advice. For example, if you have a hernia the treatment is surgical. If you have gallstones, and you had an attack from your gallstones, the treatment is surgical. There are other areas, of course, where the treatment is less clear, such as duodenal ulcer. It all boils down to the old business of whether or not you trust the person who is taking care of you. If you don't, then I think you are in trouble to begin with. You must be able to say to your doctor: I am not sure; let's talk about it.

Q. What is an osteopath?

A. An osteopath is a physician who has graduated from a school of osteopathy. The training is similar to an MD's training but slightly different. There is a bit more orientation toward bones, joints, etc.

Q. Are MD's overqualified? Don't they spend a great deal of time learning more than they have to know in order to do the job they do?

A. If you are asking me is our training too long, yes, because so much of what we learn could probably be taught in shorter form. There are several experiments going on in medical education now—for example, taking people in their final year of medical school and making them interns. At least in my personal experience with people in this program, it is quite successful. So far as medical school goes, I do think it could probably be shortened.

Changing doctors

Q. What is the best way of finding a doctor if you do not have one?

A. There are many ways: one is by referral from someone in the community who has a doctor he is satisfied with; by calling the county medical society; or by calling the local hospital, if it is a small town, and having them recommend one of several doctors who are near you. This is a very reasonable approach.

Q. How can a patient tell if his doctor is unsatisfactory?

A. I think this is better asked of patients. One way the patient can tell, apart from not getting well, is that the patient can't talk to the doctor. If he is unhappy, he can ask his doctor for a consultation. If the doctor is unwilling, I would raise an eyebrow.

Q. If you do switch doctors, how

would you go about obtaining your medical records from your former doctor and making them available to your new doctor?

A. Easily. All you have to do is sign a request slip authorizing your former doctor to release information to your new doctor.

Q. Does he have to release that?

A. It is the customary procedure.

Q. With whom do you sign the release—the old or the new doctor?

A. The new doctor. This is very common; it happens all the time.

Personal attention

Q. Do doctors nowadays have too many patients to be able to give them enough personal attention? This seems to be one of the major complaints of patients: that doctors just don't spend enough time with them.

A. This is partially true. This depends again on the doctor. One of the reasons that many patients wind up coming to see me is because the previous doctor has not given them enough time. I think that patients have to be able to talk honestly to the doctor and ask questions when they want to. When they arrange for their appointment they can let the secretary or nurse know that they would like a little bit of extra time. This is not unreasonable. At the same time many patient's demands are insatiable in this regard.

Q. In other words, a doctor like any other busy person has to learn to turn people off in a way?

A. Right.

Q. What do you think of doctors calling patients they've just met by their first names?

A. Terrible. This is not a social situation, and I prefer that patients be treated with a certain sense of respect and formality, and feel that this is much better for everybody. I don't like calling patients by their first names.

Fees

Q. Can you give any guidelines on "reasonable" medical fees?

A. No. This is an impossible question. There are guidelines, there are very real guidelines. In fact, most fees are set as a matter of custom, form, and what is "fair" in the area. And this is the kind of thing I cannot dicsuss in absolute terms and won't, but merely suggest that the patient has to discuss this with the doctor or his delegate, meaning his nurse or secretary.

Q. It's often said that doctors don't mind discussing fees before the examination. But many people have difficulty doing so. How do *you* respond to those who ask about fees?

A. My secretary informs all prospective patients exactly what the charges will be—if the patient asks.

Q. How many of your patients discuss fees with you before being treated? Is this commonplace or an exception?

A. It is common. This raises a very good question, because any time anything that is expensive has to be done I think the patient has to be informed not just that something has to be done, but that it is going to cost money. I also think that many patients have to understand that if something has to be done and is important for their health, even if they can't pay for it now, it has to be done. If they are reasonable people they will accept the necessity of a debt. This can be arranged in terms of any convenient method of payment, even to the extent of $1 to $2 a week. This is not the problem. The point is, I think, that the patient should be informed why something that costs a lot of money is important to him. If this has to be done and the patient can't afford it and you have been taking care of him, then I think it is your obligation to see that he gets into the hands of some facility that can give him either a reduced cost or no cost.

Q. Do doctors have difficulty collecting their fees? If so, who gives them the most trouble—the relatively poor, the middle-class, or the well-to-do?

A. I really don't think that there is any basis for predicting who will not pay. Frequently the very wealthy as well as the very poor don't pay.

Q. Don't pay at all?

A. Right. There is no way to get it. You can sue, but it is hardly worth the effort or the trouble. There are a small percentage of people who will not meet their obligations, and I think you just have to write it off as an experience.

Q. When one physician refers a patient to a specialist, does he ever get a cut of the consultant's fee? Is fee-splitting of this sort common?

A. It exists. I have never done it. It is not illegal. It is considered unethical by the profession. My experience with this is zero.

Q. When you as an internist refer someone to a surgeon, do you take into consideration or indicate to the patient how expensive the surgeon is likely to be?

A. I usually mention to a patient that a procedure—especially, for example, open heart surgery—is going to be expensive. At this point, I advise him to discuss the specific fee with the surgeon. If there is a hardship situation I will discuss this with the surgeon myself, quietly and privately.

(This concludes the interview with Dr. Wagman.)

Drug abuse

Q. Why do some addicts give up their habit in their mid-30s?

A. No one knows why, but if addicts manage to survive to their thirties, their need for drugs often moderates or disappears entirely, and they become good subjects for detoxification programs. Some spontaneously give up their addiction at this age without treatment.

Q. Is this true of alcoholics, too?

A. A common pattern of alcoholism is one in which the drug is spontaneously given up for periods of up to several months, but the alcoholic then resumes his former drinking habits with the same compulsion he had before. An alcoholic who "gives up" drinking is by no means cured. Such a period is comparable to a remission in a chronic disease, not a cure.

Ear discomfort

Q. After disembarking from an airplane after flight, some people experience a stuffy feeling in the ears and a temporary loss of hearing. What causes this?

A. Although modern commercial airplanes have pressurized interiors that compensate for changes in atmospheric pressure as the plane lands, some individuals are still sensitive enough to experience the sensations described. The air in the Eustachian tube is forced into the middle ear by the increased external pressure, and is replaced by body fluids. Similar symptoms can be caused by allergy, infection, or enlarged adenoids.

Enteritis, regional

Q. What are the symptoms of regional enteritis?

A. Regional enteritis—inflammation of the intestine—is a chronic disease characterized by abdominal cramps, diarrhea, loss of appetite, fever, lethargy, and sometimes a drop in weight. However, in some cases none of these symptoms appears until the disease has progressed considerably, and most patients experience periods of remission at various times during the course of the illness.

Epilepsy

Q. Is epilepsy ever cured?

A. Drugs can effectively control or reduce the frequency of seizures of the great majority of people with this disease. For unknown reasons, some epileptics eventually become and remain free of seizures while requiring no further medication; these people can be called cured.

Q. In addition to trying to create new medicines for the treatment of epilepsy, what are some of the other areas of epilepsy research?

A. Investigations are under way concerning the surgical removal of the particular brain cells responsible for triggering the convulsive seizures, and the implantation of a brain pacemaker that could act as a circuit breaker in preventing the electrical discharges that precipitate the seizures.

Eye disease/corneal transplant

Q. What is a corneal transplant?

A. A corneal transplant is the procedure in which a clear, healthy cornea provided by an eye bank replaces a cloudy or otherwise damaged one. Approximately 90 percent of such operations are successful in restoring vision.

Q. Does a corneal transplant correct all types of blindness?

A. No. A corneal transplant can correct only those disorders of vision that result from corneal defects caused by injury or disease.

Eye disease/diabetic retinopathy

Q. What is diabetic retinopathy?

A. Diabetic retinopathy, which is one of the leading causes of blindness in the U.S., is a disease of diabetics marked by the formation of new, abnormal blood vessels on the surface of the retina, sometimes protruding into the interior of the eye. They may also bleed.

Q. What causes diabetic retinopathy? Can it be treated successfully?

A. The precise cause of diabetic retinopathy is unknown, but the chance of its occurrence increases with the duration of a patient's diabetes. Current treatment is by a process called *photocoagulation,* in which beams of intense light are flashed into the eye to cause minute burns on the retina. This procedure has reduced the risk of blindness in some diabetics by preventing the proliferation of retinal blood vessels.

Foot care

Q. What is the difference between trench foot and chilblain?

A. Both are caused by prolonged exposure of the feet to cold, short of freezing. But trench foot is more serious, with possible neuromuscular damage. Chilblain is marked by a burning, itching sensation of the skin.

Q. Is it safe to remove corns or calluses with a sharp knife or razor blade?

A. No. The best home remedies are foot baths and corn plasters which soften these horny skin formations on the feet.

Frozen section

See TESTS AND DIAGNOSTIC PROCEDURES/FROZEN SECTION.

Funnel chest

Q. Can someone with "funnel chest" engage in normal physical activities? Is surgery recommended?

A. "Funnel chest," known technically as *pectus excavatum,* is a congenital deformity in which the sternum (the bone to which the ribs are attached, forming the chest wall) is depressed, so that the chest looks hollowed out. It is the opposite of "pigeon breast," in which the chest protrudes. So long as funnel chest does not impair the functioning of the lungs, there is no need to curtail normal physical activity, and no need for surgery. The main problem is usually psychological and social, especially for young people.

Gallstones

Q. Can some gallstones be dissolved medically?

A. Yes. The result of many years of research at the Mayo Clinic and elsewhere is an oral medicine containing a bile acid that dissolves cholesterol gallstones. This new therapy eliminates the need for surgical removal in a large number of cases.

Another alternative to surgery is CDCA (chenodeoxycholic acid) an oral medicine that effectively reduces cholesterol gallstones so that the need for surgery is eliminated in many cases.

Gout

Q. Is there a relationship between gout sufferers and intelligence?

A. Legend has it that gout afflicts the famous more often than ordinary folk. Certainly many gout sufferers have been famous—for example, Benjamin Franklin—but gout can strike anybody, and there does not seem to be any scientific basis for the popular association of gout and fame. Some research suggests, however, a connection between IQ and uric acid, the level of which is elevated in most patients.

Q. Are men or women more subject to attacks of gout?

A. Men, by an almost ten to one ratio.

Q. Is gout hereditary?

A. Primary gout—that is, gout that is not caused by another disease—is hereditary.

Q. Are attacks of acute gout, as of the big toe, likely to go away without treatment?

A. Yes, usually in one or two weeks, but without treatment you are likely to have recurrences which will eventually cause degeneration of cartilage and deformity. This form of gout, incidentally, is called *acute gouty arthritis.*

Q. Are any other diseases often associated with gout?

A. Kidney stones are a frequent complication of gout. The excess of uric acid that causes gout can also result in uric acid stones occurring in the kidneys.

Growth, stunted

Q. Do stunted children show an abnormal growth pattern in their early years?

A. Yes. Stunted children can usually be identified even at an early age because instead of growing a normal two or three inches a year, their stature increases by only about one inch.

Q. When a stunted growth pattern becomes apparent, is there any possible treatment for it?

A. Yes. If the cause of the child's stunted stature is determined to be a deficiency of growth hormone, the child may be given injections of pituitary hormone. This treatment is called pituitary replacement therapy.

Guthrie test

See TESTS AND DIAGNOSTIC PROCEDURES/GUTHRIE TEST.

Hair

See UNWANTED HAIR.

Handedness

Q. What percentage of people are left-handed?

A. An estimated seven percent are left-handed. *See also* BRAIN/SPEECH.

Hansen's disease

Q. What is Hansen's disease?

A. Hansen's disease is the preferred designation for leprosy. G. H. A. Hansen was a Norwegian physician and scientist who was the first to identify the bacterial organism that causes the disease.

Hardening of the arteries (atherosclerosis)

See HEART DISEASE.

Headache

Q. Can emotional tension lead to a migraine headache?

A. In those subject to migraine headaches, emotional stress may precipitate a migraine episode.

Q. Should migraine sufferers avoid certain foods, such as chocolate?

A. Chocolate is a common offender in migraine headaches. Some individuals also suffer headaches due to allergies to milk, eggs, corn, legumes, cinnamon, and cola drinks.

Q. Does reading under a dim light cause headaches?

A. You are more likely to get a headache from reading under a light that is too bright and glaring than under one that is not bright enough. Of course, if you are tired to be begin with, reading under a dim light may cause headache from general fatigue. The eyes, however, operate like a camera, and are not strained or otherwise damaged by use under a dim light.

Q. Can air or noise pollution cause headaches?

A. Some people apparently are sensitive to air pollutants and develop headaches after traveling from rural to industrialized urban areas. Loud noises can be painful; they also can aggravate headaches caused by stress.

Q. What is a "caffeine-withdrawal" headache?

A. Caffeine causes a constriction of the blood vessels in the head, an effect that inhibits headaches. When a person who drinks large amounts of coffee or other caffeine beverages suddenly stops using the beverage, the arteries become dilated. This stretches nerve endings in the arteries, causing a headache.

Heart attack

Q. Are heart attacks the leading cause of death?

A. In western society, among the 30-to-65-year-old group, yes. They are more common among men than women, and are by far the commonest cause of sudden death; about 90 percent of sudden deaths are caused by heart attack.

Q. Are both left and right halves of the heart equally vulnerable to heart attack?

A. Myocardial infarction, the medical term for the death of heart tissue, usually strikes the left ventricle, the most muscular portion of the heart, which pumps the blood through the arteries to blood vessels throughout the body. Infarction of the right ventricle or atrium is much less common.

Heartburn

Q. What happens to cause heartburn?

A. Heartburn is a burning sensation in the lower esophagus—the tube that conducts swallowed food from mouth to stomach. It is caused by a flow of gastric juices from the stomach back into the esophagus. It can be caused from eating or drinking too much; it is also common in the aftermath of gastric surgery and in the later stages of pregnancy. It has nothing to do with the heart, but the burning sensation may be felt in the region of the heart.

Q. What can be done to relieve heartburn at night?

A. Avoid spicy or other foods that may irritate the digestive system, especially during the evening meal, and learn to sleep with the upper part of the body elevated.

Heart disease

Q. Can emotional stress trigger an attack of angina?

A. Yes, angina is often precipitated by extreme emotional excitement. Physical exertion and cold weather are also common precipitating factors, especially in combination.

Q. What causes angina?

A. The most common cause is atherosclerosis, a narrowing and hardening of the blood vessels that supply blood and oxygen to the heart. Thus, when the supply is inadequate to meet stepped-up needs, such as after a heavy meal or during strenuous activity, an angina attack may result.

Q. What is the relationship between atherosclerosis and heart disease?

A. Atherosclerosis describes a condition in which the interior of the blood vessel walls hardens and in which a deposit of various substances builds up, thus narrowing the opening in the vessel. Blood flow is therefore slowed. If it is slowed too much, angina may develop. If the flow of blood is blocked entirely, a clot may break off and be carried by the bloodstream to the heart, where a blockage could trigger a heart attack. *See also* CHOLESTEROL.

Q. How common is congenital heart disease?

A. About two to five percent of all heart disease after infancy is congenital—that is, it existed at birth.

Q. What do heart valves do and what can go wrong with them?

A. The purpose of heart valves is to permit a free flow of blood in one direction only, either from the atria (or auricles) to the ventricles during diastole, or from the ventricles to the great vessels during systole. Essentially two problems can develop:

(1) The valve can narrow, a condition known as *stenosis,* thus permitting an insufficient flow of blood; or

(2) The valve can close imperfectly or too slowly—i.e., it leaks—thus permitting a backward flow of blood, called valvular *regurgitation, insufficiency,* or *incompetence.*

Q. Can both stenosis and regurgitation exist in the same valve at the same level?

A. Yes, they can and frequently do.

Q. What is mitral stenosis?

A. A narrowing and hardening of the mitral heart valve, which regulates the flow of blood from the left atrium to the left ventricle.

Q. Does mitral stenosis occur equally often in men and women?

A. No, it is much more common in women. The reasons for this are obscure.

See also ADAMS-STOKES DISEASE.

Heart pacemaker

Q. How many people use pacemakers to control the rate of heartbeat?

A. In 1986, there were about 45,000 persons in North America wearing permanently implanted heart pacemakers.

Q. What is the purpose of a heart

pacemaker that is implanted in the body?

A. The artificial pacemaker replaces or supplements a natural pacemaker in the heart that normally generates electric signals to make the heart muscles contract. In some diseases, the natural pacemaker fails to produce a proper series of signals needed to make the heart pump blood at a normal pace. Unless corrected, as with an artificial pacemaker, the patient faces disability or death.

Q. Where is a permanent pacemaker implanted in a patient's body?

A. A pacemaker generally is implanted under the skin in an area below the collarbone. It is connected to the heart tissue by a wire running through a vein from the heart to the shoulder area.

Q. Is an operation for implanting a heart pacemaker dangerous?

A. Permanent pacemaker implantation is a very safe operation, even in elderly patients, and generally results in relieving symptoms of heart distress.

Q. Is a general anesthetic used during implanting of a heart pacemaker?

A. A general anesthetic is required if the wires for a pacemaker are connected directly to the heart muscle. However, pacemaker wires sometimes can be inserted via a catheter in a vein, in which case a local anesthetic may be used.

Q. Is a heart pacemaker heavy?

A. The average heart pacemaker, including power source, transistors, and other components, weighs about six ounces.

Q. Can the pacemaker generator malfunction after it is implanted?

A. Failure of pacemaker components, except for batteries, is rare. But some electrical equipment such as electric razors, microwave ovens, and even automobile ignitions can interfere with pacemaker activity.

Q. How long do batteries for heart pacemakers last?

A. Pacemaker batteries usually last from three to five years before they must be replaced.

Q. How can a doctor check up on a heart pacemaker after it is implanted in the body?

A. By studying X-ray pictures which will show if wires are in place, if the batteries are still good, etc. Newer model pacemakers have special markings designed to reveal important information on X-ray pictures. Wires have a special coating to make them show up better on X-ray film.

Q. Can pacemakers be powered by nuclear energy without harm to the patient?

A. Since 1970, more than 1,600 nuclear-powered pacemakers have been implanted. They have an expected life of 20 years but are still being studied for possible complications before wider use is approved.

Hernia, hiatus

Q. What is hiatus hernia?

A. It is hernia, or "rupture" of the muscle barrier between the stomach and esophagus that permits a backflow of the stomach's gastric acid into the esophagus.

Q. What is the treatment for hiatus hernia?

A. The best results can be achieved by following a careful diet, wearing loose-fitting clothing around the abdominal area, and sleeping with the upper part of the body elevated. Surgery may be recommended if conservative measures fail to improve the condition.

Herpes

Q. Is the herpes virus that causes "cold sores" responsible for any other disorders?

A. Yes. The most serious disorder caused by the herpes simplex virus is an infection of the cornea that may result in scar tissue and impairment of sight. The infection is called *herpes simplex keratitis.*

Hirschsprung's disease

Q. What is Hirschsprung's disease?

A. Hirschsprung's disease is a congenital disorder of childhood in which the colon becomes enlarged as a result of a defect in part of the nervous system that controls bowel movement. In this disorder, the colon never completely evacuates its contents into the rectum. Cases that do not respond to medical treatment may require surgical correction.

Hirsutism

See UNWANTED HAIR.

Hospitalization/ambulation

Q. Why do hospitals have people out of bed and walking about so soon after an operation?

A. Primarily to prevent the development of blood clots that might spread to the lungs. This therapy actually began by necessity during World War II when an acute doctor-and-hospital-bed shortage made it necessary to get patients physically out of the hospital earlier. The results convinced doctors that early ambulation was more effective than traditional confinement to bed. It presented fewer complications.

Hypertension

Q. What is meant by "essential hypertension"?

A. "Essential" means without a known cause. Essential hypertension refers to a group of symptoms including elevated blood pressure and progressive damage to the blood vessels.

Immunization

Q. Are there some parts of the U.S. where immunization requirements must be complied with before a child can enter a public school?

A. Yes. In many parts of the United States, local city and county departments of health require immunization against diphtheria, polio, measles, and rubella (German measles) before a child is permitted to attend school.

Immunology/SCID

Q. What is the meaning of SCID?

A. SCID stands for Severe Combined Immune Deficiency. It is a congenital disease in which a child is born with an inability to fight off infectious organisms and other foreign cells or substances that enter the body.

Q. What happens to a child diagnosed as having SCID?

A. Until recently, the condition has been fatal if untreated unless the child was kept in an isolation room which is germfree. Such rooms do exist in some hospitals.

Q. Is there any possible treatment for SCID?

A. The ideal treatment for SCID is transplantation of bone marrow from a sibling whose tissues are compatible with those of the patient. Such a donor is available in only about 15 percent of all cases.

Q. Is any progress being made in treating SCID?

A. Recent research indicates that the disorder in some patients is due to a lack of a crucial enzyme called adenosine deaminase which is found in normal red blood cells and is essential for the manufacture of antibodies. Periodic transfusions of small amounts of washed and irradiated red blood cells have corrected the SCID syndrome in a few cases.

Indigestion

Q. Is it all right to take a laxative to get rid of a stomach pain?

A. No. In fact, if the pain continues for more than an hour or so, and if it is severe, it would be wise to call your doctor. The cause could be appendicitis or another serious condition.

Q. What is the cause of stomach gas following a meal?

A. Most of the "gas" in the stomach is caused by swallowing air during a meal.

Q. Can indigestion be caused by a lack of gastric acid in the stomach?

A. Yes. There is a wide range of acid levels in normal individuals, and while some people are troubled by too much gastric acid, others can suffer from too little stomach acid.

Infectious and contagious diseases

Q. What is the difference between "infectious" and "contagious" disease?

A. Contagious in general means "spread by contact from one person to another person." An infectious disease involves an invading organism, whether it be bacteria or virus. In general, there is more of a tendency to think of infection in an isolated setting within the individual himself as opposed to someone else.

Q. But are most infectious diseases also contagious?

A. Not necessarily. Cystitis is a bacterial infection of the bladder. This is infectious within the given individual but not contagious, meaning that others are not going to catch it because they are in the same room.

Ingrown toenails

Q. How can you avoid ingrown toenails?

A. By wearing shoes that provide enough room for toes and nails, and by trimming the nails carefully—not too short—and by rounding them only slightly at the corners. *See also* NAILS.

Injury

Q. Why do some persons experience a severe chill after an injury?

A. Some people react to a painful injury or cramp with a brief chill of several minutes. The effect seems to be a reaction to pain.

Jet lag

Q. Is jet lag a serious health problem?

A. Jet lag is a popular term used to describe a disturbance in a person's normal day-night cycle caused by rapidly moving into a different time zone. It is not serious, but the human body usually needs two to four days to adjust to a new schedule for eating and sleeping. *See also* AIR TRAVEL.

Lipids

Q. What are lipids?

A. Lipids are fatty substances that are essential to living cells. An excess of some lipids, especially cholesterol, is believed to be a factor in contributing to heart disease. Other lipids which are the products of normal metabolism accumulate in the bodies of people who are the victims of rare hereditary disorders grouped together as "lipid storage diseases."

Q. What are the lipid storage diseases?

A. Among the lipid storage diseases are Tay-Sachs disease, Gaucher's disease, fucosidosis, and metachromatic leukodystrophy. All are at present incurable.

Q. Is the cause of lipid storage diseases known?

A. In each case, the particular

lipid storage disease is caused by the lack of a single enzyme among the many thousands of enzymes produced by the body for the normal chemical processes of metabolism.

Q. Do all lipids storage diseases have the same symptoms?

A. No. Symptoms vary from disease to disease. Some cause mental retardation, one causes blindness, another results in kidney failure. Practically all of the inherited lipid storage diseases result in early death.

Q. Is there any way of finding out whether an unborn child may inherit one of the lipid storage diseases?

A. Yes. Through genetic counseling, it is possible to identify carriers of the faulty genes that transmit some of these diseases.

Liver spots

See SKIN CARE.

Medical insurance

Q. Does medical insurance ever provide coverage for a second or third expert opinion on whether to have elective surgery?

A. Yes. In an attempt to curb some unnecessary nonemergency surgery, some health insurance plans provide compensation for charges incurred for a second and sometimes a third consultation.

Mg.%

See TESTS AND DIAGNOSTIC PROCEDURES.

Migraine

See HEADACHE.

MLNS

Q. What do the initials MLNS stand for?

A. A children's disease known as mucocutaneous lymph node syndrome in which the symptoms of fever, rash, swollen hands and feet, and bright "strawberry" tongue are self-limiting. However, in about two percent of all cases, a heart involvement occurs that is fatal.

Moles

See SKIN CARE.

Munchausen's syndrome

Q. What kind of disease is Munchausen's syndrome?

A. This is not a real disease but an assortment of make-believe complaints used by some people, otherwise normal, who want to obtain medical care or hospitalization.

Nails

Q. What causes a fingernail to loosen or fall off?

A. A number of things, among them fungus infections, bacterial or yeast infections, psoriasis, or hemorrhage such as that caused by hitting a finger with a hammer.

Q. Does nail polish injure the nail?

A. Nail polish protects the nails except in rare cases of allergic reaction. Nail polish remover can injure the nails if too much is applied, because the drying effect of polish remover can split the nails.

Narcolepsy

Q. What is narcolepsy?

A. Narcolepsy is a neurological syndrome in which an abnormality of the brain results in the disorganization of sleep and the components of sleep. It is estimated that this chronic and disabling sleep disorder affects about 250,000 Americans of all ages.

Q. What are the symptoms of narcolepsy?

A. There are four main symptoms of narcolepsy; a narcoleptic can have one of the symptoms, all four of them, or any combination. The first symptom is known as sleep attacks—falling asleep at unsuitable times and having an exhausted feeling most of the time. The second symptom is catalepsy—a total collapse of muscle tone usually triggered by some strong emotion, particularly surprise, anger, or great pleasure. The third is hallucinating immediately before sleep, and the fourth is a feeling of paralysis or immobility immediately after waking up or just as one falls asleep.

Q. How is true narcolepsy diagnosed?

A. Narcolepsy is diagnosed by observation of the symptoms described and by measurements of the patient's sleep patterns.

Neuropharmacology

Q. What is neuropharmacology?

A. Neuropharmacology is the study of the effects of drugs such as amphetamines, barbiturates and the like on the chemistry of the brain. Compare PSYCHOPHARMACOLOGY.

Nevus, junction

See SKIN CARE.

Newborns

Q. Is there a kind of doctor who specializes in the care of newborn babies?

A. Yes, a perinatologist is a pediatrician who specializes in providing intensive care before, during, and after birth to the newborn baby, especially to one born prematurely or with congenital defects requiring surgery.

Nurse-midwife

Q. Why aren't nurse-midwives

considered as respectable in the United States nowadays as they are in Europe?

A. They are. In 1971, the American College of Obstetricians and Gynecologists officially stated that "in medically directed teams, qualified nurse-midwives may assume responsibility for the complete care and management of uncomplicated maternity patients."

Q. How do nurse-midwives qualify for their profession?

A. A nurse-midwife begins her training by attending a three- or four-year nursing school and becoming a registered nurse. She then affiliates with a hospital in order to get one year of experience in obstetrical nursing. Student nurse-midwives must also observe and assist at about 50 labors and deliveries, and under supervision they are required to manage a minimum of 20 deliveries on their own.

Osgood-Schlatter disease

Q. What is Osgood-Schlatter disease?

A. Degeneration of the protuberant upper end of the tibia just below the knee joint. It usually occurs in adolescents during periods of rapid growth. In most cases the affected bone tissue eventually regenerates.

Osteoarthritis

See ARTHRITIS.

Pacemaker, artificial

See HEART PACEMAKER.

Perspiration

Q. Is there really such a thing as breaking out in a "cold sweat"?

A. Yes. Normally, the eccrine glands that secrete sweat respond only to exercise or heat—except for those on the palms and soles and under the arm, which also respond to emotional excitement, such as fear, sexual stimulation, etc. But under extreme conditions, emotional stimulation can make the eccrine glands over the whole body respond, even when the body has not been warmed from physical effort. The evaporation of this sweat results in a chill, or "cold sweat."

Q. What causes body odor?

A. The apocrine glands, much less numerous than the eccrine glands which secrete sweat, respond to emotional stimulation by secreting a fluid that acts on the sweat, especially under the arms, where perspiration cannot easily evaporate, to multiply bacteria already present on the skin; the proliferation of such bacteria produces body odor.

Q. What is the purpose of the apocrine glands?

A. They have no known purpose. One theory suggests that, since these glands develop only with sexual maturity and decline with age—which is why children and the elderly do not have the characteristic body odor—the odor once served as a sexual attraction to the opposite sex. Many other animals utilize body scents in this way.

Q. What's the difference between a deodorant and an antiperspirant?

A. A deodorant is designed to suppress or mask body odor. Many deodorants therefore contain antibacterial ingredients and are also pleasantly scented. An antiperspirant is designed to reduce perspiration, although many antiperspirants also have antibacterial properties.

Q. Isn't stopping sweating unhealthy?

A. No antiperspirant can suppress all perspiration; at most it is reduced by about half. Sweating is not, as commonly believed, a way to dispose of body waste. The purpose of sweating is to help regulate body temperature.

Q. Won't one build up an immunity to deodorants or antiperspirants and have to switch?

A. No, this is a misconception. You do not build up an immunity to deodorants or antiperspirants. On some occasions they may not seem to work well enough, but they have not lost their effectiveness; you have just lost your confidence in them.

Q. Why do men need a stronger deodorant than women do? Do they sweat more?

A. Men don't need a stronger deodorant than women do. The secretion from the body-odor-causing apocrine glands is about the same for both sexes. However, the fact that most women shave under their arms probably gives them an advantage, since hair serves to encourage bacteria growth.

Q. Are allergic responses to underarm deodorants very common?

A. You certainly may be allergic to a deodorant, but you should also suspect other causes, such as irritation from clothing or, in the case of women, from shaving. When drying under the arms, you should pat the area gently; hard rubbing can cause irritation to the sensitive skin there.

Physical fitness

Q. Can someone who has had a heart attack ever engage in strenuous physical activity, such as tennis?

A. Every case is different. There are many former heart patients who have, under a doctor's care, resumed their physical activities in sports such as tennis. However, it is imperative to resume such activities only after consulting your physician, and then in gradual stages of increased participation.

Pigeon breast

Q. Can pigeon-breasted people engage in normal physical activities?

A. "Pigeon breast," known technically as *pectus carinatum,* is a congenital deformity in which the sternum (the bone to which the ribs are attached, forming the chest wall) protrudes. It is the opposite of "funnel chest," in which the chest is depressed. There is usually no need to curtail normal physical activity. The chief problem is usually a cosmetic one, i.e., the psychological effect on one's social life and self-image, which can be very severe, especially for young people. Corrective surgery, however, would be extensive and complicated, and is not usually recommended in the absence of physical problems.

Prader-Willi syndrome

Q. What is Prader-Willi syndrome?

A. Prader-Willi syndrome refers to a bizarre eating disturbance whose victims, chiefly children between the ages of two and five, are afflicted with an insatiable desire for food. The disorder, which is named for the two doctors who first described it in 1956, is not inherited, nor does it appear to be related to emotional stress. Present studies indicate that it is the result of a neurological disturbance caused by malfunction of the hypothalamus of the brain.

Psoriasis

Q. How common is psoriasis?

A. About two percent of people in the United States have psoriasis.

Q. Does it affect one sex more than the other?

A. No, it affects men and women equally.

Q. At what age does it first appear?

A. Usually between the ages of 15 and 30.

Q. Is psoriasis contagious?

A. No, not at all. It is probably an inherited disorder.

Pscyhological counseling

Q. How does group therapy work?

A. Group therapy is the general term for a wide variety of therapeutic situations in which the participants try to find more satisfactory ways of living their lives through honest self-examination and the expression of their authentic feelings. Mutual respect, support, and trust are the principles on which the effectiveness of group therapy is based. The group may be led by a professional psychiatrist, a lay analyst, or a psychiatric social worker, or the leadership of each session may rotate among the participants.

Q. What are encounter groups?

A. An encounter group is a form of group therapy in which people are encouraged by each other and by a trained counselor to get in touch with their suppressed feelings of fear, rage, anger, shame, etc., by means of unrestrained verbalization and physical contact.

Psychopharmacology

Q. What kind of research is done by psychopharmacologists?

A. Psychopharmacologists are scientific specialists who study the actions of drugs such as LSD or tranquilizers on the mind. Compare NEUROPHARMACOLOGY.

Puberty

Q. Are middle-class American girls reaching sexual maturity at a younger age with each succeeding decade?

A. No. The average age at which girls begin to menstruate is 12.8 years, and this figure has remained the same over the last 30 years.

Raynaud's disease

Q. What is Raynaud's disease?

A. Raynaud's disease is a condition in which the arteries in the fingers and toes experience spasms, usually after exposure to cold. The tips of fingers and toes become bluish (cyanotic) or ashen, then sometimes red.

Q. What causes this condition?

A. It can be a complication of rheumatoid arthritis, a connective tissue disease, neurological disease, etc. It can also result from piano playing or other occupations in which the fingertips are struck or jarred repeatedly. (In such cases, the condition is usually known as *Raynaud's phenomenon.*) But Raynaud's disease is frequently not secondary to any known underlying condition. Its cause in such cases is unknown. It is known that emotional states can trigger an attack of finger and/or toe spasms, but this certainly does not preculde physiological causes.

Q. Who is most likely to get Raynaud's disease?

A. Women, by a five to one ratio, are more commonly afflicted than men.

Q. How is it treated?

A. In most cases, the condition will stay the same or improve with age (usually at about age 40). Patients subject to Raynaud's disease should definitely not smoke and should take care to avoid exposure to cold. Mild sedatives may be prescribed by a physician if spasm episodes are frequent or severe.

Reye's syndrome

Q. What is Reye's syndrome?

A. Reye's syndrome is a complication that may follow a number of different kinds of viral infections, including influenza and chicken pox. The disorder, which is extremely rare, affects mainly children and involves primarily the liver, interfering with that organ's ability to help remove poisonous substances from the bloodstream. The resulting buildup of toxic wastes in the blood results in damage to the liver, the brain, and the kidneys. Symptoms include mental confusion, severe nausea and vomiting, hyperactivity and excitability, followed by convulsions and finally coma. Because the disorder frequently is fatal if not treated at an early stage, immediate medical attention is required.

Q. How is it treated?

A. The patient is closely watched on an around-the-clock basis so that any serious complication, such as a buildup of pressure on the brain, can be immediately counteracted with drugs or by other means. Treatment may include transfusions of fresh blood to replace the patient's blood containing the toxic agent.

Q. Is there a cure for Reye's syndrome?

A. No, but the disease is believed to be self-limiting. Treatment is directed at enabling the patient to survive during the critical period in which the disease is running its course.

Rickettsial diseases

Q. What causus typhus and is there a "shot" you can get as protection against typhus?

A. Typhus is a debilitating, frequently fatal disease caused by a tiny organism called a rickettsia. The rickettsia usually is transmitted to humans through the bite of a body louse. A vaccine is available and is recommended for travelers to some underdeveloped countries of the world.

Q. Is Rocky Mountain spotted fever a disease you can get only in the Rocky Mountains?

A. No, this rickettsial disease was discovered in the Rocky Mountains but occurs in other areas as well, particularly in the eastern U.S. It is transmitted by wood ticks.

SCID

See IMMUNOLOGY.

Serum sickness

Q. What is serum sickness?

A. Serum sickness is an immunological reaction to the introduction of serum (the clear fluid portion of the blood), as an animal serum used as an antitoxin, into the body. The reaction may be acute and severe. It is a form of allergic shock or anaphylaxis, and can be avoided by always having a skin test to check for reaction before a serum is introduced into the body.

SGOT

See TESTS AND DIAGNOSTIC PROCEDURES/BLOOD.

Shaving

See UNWANTED HAIR.

Skin cancer

Q. Is skin cancer more common in the South than in the North?

A. Yes, skin cancer is about ten times more common in the South than the North because of increased exposure to sunlight in the South.

Q. Are dark-skinned people less likely to develop skin cancer than fair-skinned people?

A. Yes, blonds and redheads are more subject to skin cancer than dark-skinned people.

Skin care

Q. What is the cause of "liver spots" on the skin?

A. The brownish areas of discoloration that may appear on the skin in later life have nothing to do with the liver but sometimes indicate a minor systemic disorder. A general physical examination usually is needed to pinpoint the exact cause.

Q. Please explain why dark circles sometimes appear under the eyes.

A. Because the skin of eyelids is thin, blood in veins beneath the skin may make the area seem darker and bluer than surrounding skin. During menstruation or illness, this discoloration may become more obvious.

Q. What causes "bags" under the eyes?

A. As a person ages, tissues that normally hold the skin of the eyelids firmly become weak, and subcutaneous fat pushes the skin outward. Plastic surgery is the only cure for this effect. Puffiness of the eyelids may be a sign of fluid accumulation due to kidney or heart disease.

Q. What is a junction nevus?

A. A junction nevus is a darkly pigmented tumor, resembling a common mole, that develops at the junction of the two layers of the skin, the dermis and epidermis.

Q. Can a mole or junction nevus become a skin cancer?

A. While unusual, a mole or junction nevus can darken and enlarge into a precancerous tumor. It is wise to have a physician remove the growth before the change can occur.

Q. What is the difference between a boil and a carbuncle?

A. The main difference is that a carbuncle is bigger than a boil and involves two or more hair follicles.

Q. What is dermabrasion and will it remove acne scars?

A. Dermabrasion is a technique of rubbing away the outer layer of skin to get rid of scars. The skin is covered with bandages to control bleeding and infection and a new skin layer replaces the old in about a month.

Q. Are warts contagious?

A. Yes. They are caused by a virus and are likely to develop on moist areas of the skin or areas that have been injured.

Q. What are the medical treatments for warts?

A. Some warts can be removed by freezing them with supercooled liquids. Warts are also treated with X rays, medicines applied to the skin, and by surgical excision.

Q. Can warts be "charmed" away by suggestion?

A. There is no scientific basis for this notion; when warts disappear after hexing, the wart is regressing because of other factors and the apparent "charm" effect is coincidental.

Q. What is the cause of skin wrinkling?

A. It is not completely known why skin wrinkles, although heredity apparently is one factor. Others are loss of weight, exposure to wind and sun, and loss of supporting tissue beneath the skin as a part of aging.

Sleep

Q. During the onset of sleep, one occasionally has the sensation of falling or floating. Is this effect a symptom of a serious disorder?

A. No. The sensation of falling or floating while drifting off to sleep is a not unusual hypnagogic illusion, or hallucination. It occurs in a semidreamlike state but is not a true dream. Some people experience visual illusions—faces, landscapes, or geometric shapes—while falling asleep.

Q. Sometimes while sleeping the entire body may jerk for no apparent reason. Is this normal?

A. The sudden incoordinate jerking of a part of the whole body, called nocturnal jerking, is a natural occurrence during light sleep. The phenomenon is believed to result from a sudden release of muscle tension by a nervous system impulse in the cerebral cortex of the brain. Usually no harm is done and the event is quickly forgotten. Pet owners are well aware that this phenomenon is not restricted to humans. Dogs and cats also jerk reflexively during light sleep.

Q. What is REM sleep?

A. REM sleep is a phase of sleep during which there are bursts of rapid eye movements—abbreviated REM. This phenomenon, originally reported in 1953, coincides with a state of intense physiological activity. In addition to the rapid eye movements, the heartbeat quickens, blood pressure rises, and the rate of electrical impulses in the brain increases. The rapid eye movements are also associated with dreaming.

Q. What is NREM sleep?

A. NREM sleep (non-REM sleep) is qualitatively different from REM sleep. It seems to be a restful and recuperative state. Approximately 75 percent of all sleep time is spent in NREM sleep.

Q. Does the sleeper first experience one kind of sleep and then the other, and then wake up?

A. No. Sleep occurs in cycles: a period of about 90 minutes of NREM sleep precedes the onset of the first REM period, which lasts from 5 to 15 minutes. This alternation occurs throughout the night, with the REM phases getting somewhat longer toward waking. The NREM-REM alternation is sometimes called the *sleep-dream cycle* because dreams occur more often and more dramatically in REM sleep than they do in NREM sleep.

Speech

See BRAIN/SPEECH.

Stimulant drugs

Q. Can stimulant drugs affect the growth of children?

A. It has been found that two types of drugs (Dexedrine and Ritalin) used to treat hyperactive children seem to retard the normal gains in height and weight when administered in large doses over long periods of time.

Stitch

Q. What causes a stitch in the side?

A. A stitch—or sudden ache in the upper left or right part of the abdomen—is associated with vigorous activity, often occurs after eating, and is aggravated by cold weather. Its cause is not known, but it is believed to be linked to a decreased supply of oxygen in the blood circulating to the diaphragm.

Suicide

Q. What are the two main causes of death among young people in the United States?

A. Accidents are the leading cause of death among young people in the United States. The second leading cause is suicide.

Q. Are young people in the highest risk age group for suicide?

A. No. The highest risk age group is the elderly, who account for one-fourth of all suicides in the United States.

Sweat

See PERSPIRATION.

Tests and diagnostic procedures

Q. On some laboratory reports, test results are written as numbers followed by mg.%. Please explain.

A. Mg.% is a scientific notation that means the number of milligrams of a substance found in 100 milliliters of blood. See below under BLOOD.

Q. On your physical exam sheet, you may see something like "BP 130/74." What does this mean?

A. It means your blood pressure (BP) was 130 (systolic) over 74 (diastolic) as measured in millimeters of mercury. *See also* BLOOD PRESSURE.

Biopsy

Q. What is a biopsy?

A. A microscopic examination of the tissue cells from a lump, nodule, ulcer, or hard mass. The procedure is commonly used to determine if an abnormal growth may be cancer.

Q. What is meant by needle biopsy?

A. A sample of tissue cells from an organ is taken through a long needle inserted into the body—an alternative to using surgery to examine tissue from the liver, kidney, or other organs.

Blood

Q. What does BUN on a laboratory report mean?

A. BUN is an abbreviation for blood urea nitrogen; it is a measure of the health of the kidneys. The normal range is 10–20 mg.%.

Q. Why is cholesterol measured in blood tests?

A. The cholesterol level of the blood indicates possible premature hardening of the arteries. A normal level is 150–300 mg.%.

Q. On a copy of a blood test from the laboratory there may be a reference to SGOT. What does this mean?

A. This is medical shorthand for serum glutamic oxaloacetic transaminase; sometimes it is called simply transaminase. It is an enzyme which in abnormal quantities could indicate liver disease or coronary heart disease.

Q. Is there a blood test for diabetes?

A. Yes. An abnormally high level of sugar in the blood suggests diabetes.

Q. What is bilirubin and what does its presence in the blood tell a doctor?

A. Bilirubin is a pigment that colors the bile. An abnormally high level in the blood could mean the patient has liver or gall bladder disease.

Q. What does it mean if one's blood sugar is below normal?

A. It could indicate a tumor of the pancreas or an overactive production of insulin.

Cough plate

Q. What is a cough plate?

A. It is a sterile plate used to collect bacteria from a patient for study. The patient coughs onto the plate. The test may be used, for example, in the diagnosis of whooping cough.

Frozen section

Q. What is a frozen section?

A. A suspicious lump of tissue is frozen quickly with carbon dioxide gas, and a thin slice cut from the tissue is stained with a dye for study under a microscope. The test usually is done during surgery in order to determine quickly if the tissue should be removed or if it is relatively harmless.

Guthrie test

Q. What is a Guthrie test?

A. This is a special method of examining a urine sample in order to determine if a patient may have phenylketonuria (PKU), an inherited metabolic disease.

Urine

Q. Does sugar in the urine mean one has diabetes?

A. Generally, yes. It is one test for diabetes. However, it is possible to have the disease without a significant level of sugar in the urine.

Q. Why is a urine sample tested for albumin?

A. The presence of albumin in urine would suggest an abnormal functioning of the kidneys, perhaps due to a disease such as nephritis.

Q. Why does the lab technician check the color of a urine sample?

A. Normal urine is clear or amber in color. If it is tinged with red, the cause could be bleeding in the urethra, bladder, kidneys, prostate (in men), or elsewhere in the urinary tract. A brown coloration could indicate liver disease.

Tetanus

Q. How often should you get a tetanus booster?

A. Every ten years, assuming that you haven't sustained a wound, especially a puncture-type wound, that might be infected with tetanus germs. In that event, you should have a booster if you haven't had one in a year's time.

Q. What should someone who is not immunized do when he sustains a wound that may be infected with tetanus germs?

A. He should seek medical assistance immediately. He will be given tetanus toxoid and may also be given an antitoxin—either a human antitoxin or one from a horse or cow.

Tic douloureux

Q. Can a young person have "tic douloureux," or trigeminal neuralgia?

A. These severe facial pains can occur at any age after puberty, but usually do not begin to appear before the age of 50.

Tourette's disease

Q. What is Tourette's disease?

A. Named for the French neurologist, Gilles de la Tourette, this disease is marked by violent muscular jerking of the head and shoulders, as well as of the extremities, along with grunting, explosive obscenities uttered by the victim.

Toxoplasmosis/cats

Q. Can people catch diseases from cats?

A. Yes. Cats are the chief source of a disease called toxoplasmosis, which is caused by a parasite to which cats as well as other animals are the host.

Q. Is toxoplasmosis a serious disease?

A. Not in most cases. Animals themselves may harbor the infectious organism without showing symptoms, and probably half the adult population has been infected by the "toxo" parasite at one time or other without knowing it. In some people, the infection runs a course similar to mononucleosis; in others, it may cause inflammation of the retina. However, the disease is very dangerous if contracted by a pregnant woman. While symptoms usually bypass the mother, prenatal infection of the fetus can cause irreversible brain damage, blindness, or death.

Typhus

See RICKETTSIAL DISEASES.

Ulcers

Q. Are peptic ulcers caused by too much stomach acid?

A. Not necessarily; some individuals have high levels of stomach acid but never develop ulcers. However, oversecretion of stomach acid can aggravate an existing ulcer.

Q. What are some of the signs of a bleeding ulcer?

A. The patient may vomit blood or, more commonly, the blood will travel through the intestine and cause the patient's stools to be colored black.

Q. Will a stomach ulcer eventually become a stomach cancer?

A. A stomach ulcer may occasionally develop into a cancerous growth. A person with a peptic ulcer should be examined regularly by a doctor who can watch for possible precancerous changes.

Unwanted hair

Q. Is excessive hair in women caused by too much male hormone production?

A. Women with excessive facial hair are entirely feminine, and tests usually do not indicate an elevated production of the male hormone. It is normal for those of each sex to produce both male and female hormones; women normally produce about two-thirds as much of the male hormone as do men.

Q. Does shaving make hair grow faster than before?

A. No. Shaving has no effect on the rate of growth of hair. However, since short hair is thicker and less flexible than long hair, a trimmed beard may give a denser appearance than untrimmed facial hair.

Q. Why is it better to shave hair when it is wet?

A. Hair can absorb a great deal of water, making it softer and much easier to cut. The best time to shave body hair is after a bath or shower.

Urine & urinalysis

See TESTS AND DIAGNOSTIC PROCEDURES/URINE.

Warts

See SKIN CARE.

Weight problems

Q. Is exercising a good way to lose weight?

A. No. Exercising is beneficial for other reasons, such as maintaining good muscle tone, but it is not an efficient way to lose weight. The only way to lose weight is to diet so that your body is taking in fewer calories than it is consuming.

Wrinkling

See SKIN CARE.

X Rays

Q. How often should a dentist take a full set of X rays?

A. Unless there is some special problem, a full set of X rays—16 to 18 pictures of an adult patient's teeth—need not be conducted more often than every three to five years. Some authorities feel that a full set of dental X rays need not be made more than every six to ten years.

Index

A

B

C

D

E

F

G

H

I

J

K

L

M

N

O

P

Q

R

S

T

U

V

W

X

Y

Z